MW00526649

I Married a Soldier

One Family's Cold War Adventures

Shirley Condit Starkey

Seco Mundo Press   Tucson, Arizona

This edition was prepared for printing by
Ghost River Images
5350 East Fourth Street
Tucson, Arizona 85711
www.ghostriverimages.com

Readers may contact the author at
SJEAN007@aol.com

ISBN 978-0-9770195-2-6

Library of Congress Control Number: 2018911964

Printed in the United States of America

October, 2018

Dedication

To my very strong, resilent children, Jim, Jr., Patrick, Peggy and Rick, who are raising my grandchildren, Jesse, Rachel, Gina, Zack, Sarah, John and Ryan to be as strong and resilent as they are.

I love you all.

Praise for *The Scorpion Stings*

The Scorpion Stings by Shirley Starkey is a delightful tale of life in pre-revolutionary Iran as seen through the eyes of an army officer's wife. The trail from initial culture shock through frustration, fear and eventually delight is told with graphic expertise.

Shirley deftly sprinkles humorous incidents in a tale that enables the reader to see and almost taste and smell the musky environment that is Tehran. All of this triggers memories for those of us who have "been there" and will generate amazement in the uninitiated.

A young wife whose husband has to hit the deck running in his assigned duties, is required to do virtually every thing else including homemaking, food purchase and preparation, child care, transportation, scheduling and the hiring of help from a thin and questionable reservoir. Add to this cauldron advanced pregnancy and one begins to appreciate what Shirley Starkey accomplished. Military wives, in my humble opinion, are the un-sung champions of the Department of Defense! Read this book and appreciate what military families face during foreign assignments. It is all here, in charming detail.

Hoyt Vandenberg [signature]

Hoyt S. Vandenberg, Jr.
Major General, USAF Retired
Chief of ARMISH-MAAG, 1975-1976
Tehran, Iran

This is a true story, only some of the names have been changed.

This book combines the stories from the author's previous books, *The Scorpion Stings* and *The Monkey Drowns* and adds several additional chapters to complete the saga of the author's life as a military wife.

Map of Iran

1962

Chapter 1

Lt. Col. John Glenn is the first American to orbit the earth. Jackie Kennedy guides TV White House tour, Robert Kennedy says U.S. will stay in Viet Nam until the Viet Cong are beaten, JFK orders total ban on Cuba imports, Conservatives hold rally for Goldwater.

March 1962

The late afternoon sun streamed through the window, giving the living room a golden glow. The smell of spicy taco meat cooking on the stove drifted through the house. I sat on the floor going though some old magazines, ignoring the nausea I felt from my early pregnancy and thinking I should wake Jimbo from his nap. That little two-year old slept as hard as he played. It was the end of March and my husband Jim was attending the Army's Advanced Officers Course at Ft. Eustis, Virginia. The school would be over in May, and everyone in the class except Jim had received orders. Both of us were getting edgy.

The front door opened and Jim walked in, captain bars and aviation wings gleaming on his green uniform. I noticed a concerned frown on his face. But before I could say anything, he said, "What would you think of going to Iran?"

I jumped up. "You got your orders? Can Jimbo and I go with you?"

"Yes, yes to both questions," he answered. I was delighted and gave him a big hug. Then I stopped, frowned, a dull feeling growing in the pit of my stomach. It was 1962. I looked up and said, "Where is Iran?"

And so begin the most exciting, frustrating, and interesting two years of my life: two years spent in Iran, where long before the birth of Christ gifted men built an underground water system that is still used today. Iran, the ancient land of Persia, where, until the past sixty years life continued much as it had for thousands of years.

Jim was a Regular Army Officer who was just completing the nine-month course that warm spring day when he burst in with the news. We had been anticipating orders for Germany, and I was very unhappy at the prospect of saying goodbye to Jim while he flew off to Germany, leaving our son, Jim, Jr. and pregnant me. At that time, as the result of Russia building the Berlin Wall the previous August, no dependents were allowed to accompany men going to Germany. So the news of the orders to Iran caused mixed feelings: relief at being able to be with Jim, curiosity and nervous anticipation at the thought of venturing to a strange and alien land.

The next two months went by fast, and it was amazing how much we were able to accomplish. We received a letter from Capt. Don Hudson, our designated sponsor, who wrote that we needed to bring, in addition to our furniture, a butane cooking stove, a refrigerator, a freezer, a wringer-type washing machine and as many canned goods and non-perishable food and dry-goods as our budget allowed. Budget, ha! He assured us that when we left Iran we would be able to sell anything American-made to Iranians for at least twice what we paid.

Our days began early with Jim shaving and me throwing up. As soon as I finished, Jim would calmly and wordlessly hand me a glass of water to drink. After that I was able to fix breakfast and get on with my day. He went to class and I shopped. As I walked up and down the aisle at the commissary in my nauseated state nothing appealed to me except applesauce. I did manage to buy cases of canned corn, spinach, green beans, peas, peanut butter and loads of toilet paper and other paper products, but when all these goods were unloaded in Tehran, I discovered I had gone overboard on applesauce. At the end of our two-year tour we still had applesauce left over.

It seemed that by day we did nothing but spend money and by night the farewell parties were endless, as 87 officers prepared to leave for all parts of the world. I was pleased that we were going to such an interesting country and was sure Jim had the plum of orders. This was a MAAG assignment (Military Assistance Advisory Group) and Jim would be the maintenance officer for the airplanes as well as a pilot in support of the advisors.

In between all this activity I tried to get some information on Iran and found it was practically nonexistent. I finally found an old National Geographic Magazine dated January, 1961, with thirty-eight pages of text and pictures. His Imperial Majesty Mohammad Reza Shah Pahlavi, resplendent in his gold-braided and bemedaled military uniform, was shown receiving dignitaries in Tehran's Gulistan Palace. The Pahlavi dynasty was begun by Reza Shah, the then current Shah's father, in 1925 with the overthrow of the Qajar dynasty. One of his first acts was to change the country's name from Persia to Iran. In 1941 the Allies, concerned that Reza Shah was a German collaborator, forced his abdication and put the 21-year-old playboy son on the throne. Mohammad Reza, (referred to as Shahenshah), I discovered was currently married to his third wife, the gorgeous Farah Diba. The couple had a son the same age as Jimbo.

I poured over the pictures of dark bazaars filled with barrels of spices, shepherds tending their flocks, Caspian fishermen pulling in nets of sturgeon, turquoise-tiled domes, turbaned men with worry beads, women at looms tying the knots on half-finished carpets, soldiers patrolling the desert on camels, *chador*-clad women choosing vegetables, a village devastated by an earthquake, tribes living in tents on desolate deserts, a new dam to control melting snow, new bridges, fancy apartment buildings, and vast oil refineries. The last picture showed the Shah with the beautiful Empress Farah Diba, who was then pregnant with their first child. The whole kingdom was praying for a male heir. The text explained how the Shah was working hard, trying to drag Iran into the twentieth century. What a land of contrasts! This was going to be an exciting and daunting experience for our family.

June 1962

The plane droned on monotonously on the last leg of our journey and I tried to sleep but it was impossible. My back ached and with my growing belly it was hard to find a comfortable position. In the dim light I could see Jim. He had Jimbo on his lap and both were breathing deeply and exhaling in a soft snore. 'Those two are so lucky,' I thought, 'They can sleep anywhere.' I shifted around, stretching my legs and moving my feet in a circular motion. The baby within me responded with a healthy kick. I love that sensation; it lets me know that all is well within even though things may not be so good on the outside.

My thoughts drifted to the last few days. After the graduation ceremony at Ft. Eustis, we headed for our hometown, Tucson, Arizona. When we had arrived our families greeted us with open arms. At a party at my folk's house, attended by my brother and two sisters plus spouses and ten nieces and nephews, my siblings couldn't help giving me advice. "Be careful, Scoot," was my brother Bill's advice. My sister Toddy's comment was, "Have fun." My oldest sister Alice had always kept a close eye on me for I was the impetuous one, and she was always afraid I would embarrass the family. She said, in her best Big Sister voice, "Shirley, I've looked at the map. Do you realize Iran is right next to Russia? For heavens sake, don't cause an International Incident!" Little did I know how close I would come to that.

As the plane began to lose altitude, I returned to reality. I touched Jim's arm, "We're almost there."

He opened his eyes and shifted Jimbo on his lap. Jimbo awoke with a slight whimper and Jim talked quietly to him as he adjusted his seatback and fastened his seatbelt. I strained to look out the window and at a distance could make out the lights of Tehran. 'Well, baby,' I thought, 'welcome to your birthplace.'

We landed hard, bumping along too fast for my liking. The

plane's engine reversed and we came to an abrupt, screeching halt. Warm, dry June air infused with gasoline fumes hit us as we left the airplane and walked down the steps to the tarmac and into the terminal. It was past midnight and the airport was deserted except for the Iranian military guards in blue uniforms with gold trimmings, rifles slung over their shoulders, casually lounging at every entrance. Only three other passengers disembarked, so the wait at customs was minimal. As we entered the baggage claim area, two Americans in Army flight suits with captain insignias on their collars approached us. "Captain Starkey, welcome to Iran. I'm Jack Blake and this is Don Hudson, your sponsor." After shaking hands, Jim turned to introduce Jimbo and me. Both men solemnly shook Jimbo's hand. "We'd better collect your bags," said Don, "and don't forget to count them. Things have a way of disappearing around here." All nine suitcases were accounted for and we left the terminal. Outside, Mohammed, Captain Hudson's driver, greeted us with a big grin. He was dressed in the brown woolen uniform of the Iranian army, with sergeant's chevrons on his left arm. He wore his hat with the bill at a rakish angle, and his long, thick, black moustache would have seemed menacing if not for the pleasant expression on his face. He made a fuss over Jimbo until Hudson curtly told him to get our luggage. We piled into the aging Chevy, Jimbo on my lap with Jim and Jack squeezed on either side of me. Don sat in the front seat next to Mohammed. Most of our luggage was in the car's trunk with that remaining strapped onto the roof. I wasn't sure the car, so heavily laden, would make it, but Mohammed eased it carefully over the speed bumps and onto the highway. We were on our way to our hotel.

Deserted streets unfolded around us as we drove into the city. The lights along the avenue gave off a spooky yellow glow, and all I could see were high walls, lots of trees and very clean streets. There were few vehicles on the road; none of them used their headlights, apparently relying on the overhead lamps. As we entered the main part of the city the traffic increased. The road went around a circle that contained a large statue of a turbaned man dressed in a long coat that almost covered his ballooning pantaloons. He had slippers with turned-up toes on his feet and his right arm was extended, his hand pointing south. "This is the statue of Ferdowsi, the Iranians favorite poet," Jack offered. "This is Ferdowsi Street and all these shops sell carpets." Wide corrugated steel shutters covered the shops and were secured at the bottom with large padlocks. Further on the city began to look more modern. We came to automobile dealerships, plus furniture and appliance stores with wide glass windows revealing very little merchandise.

In about twenty minutes we reached our hotel, a narrow, dilapidated four-story building. It was directly across the street from the American Embassy on Takte-Jamshed Avenue. Inside, the hotel's small lobby was dimly lit, with no elevator, only a dark, narrow, circular staircase. Our room on the third floor was crowded with three single beds pushed together, an overstuffed chair and a small, paint-chipped vanity. The tiny bathroom had shelves and hooks for hanging clothes. Everything was red: the chair, the bedspreads, the drapes, and the Persian carpet on the floor. A lone light bulb suspended from the ceiling gave the room an eerie, pinkish luminosity. Mohammed and the three men struggled up the stairs with our luggage, which they stacked up to the ceiling in the only available corner.

Don turned to me and said, "My wife Colleen will be by in the morning to take you to breakfast. And by the way, don't drink the water in the hotel. I'm not sure it's safe."

"But how can we brush our teeth?" I asked.

"It's all right to brush your teeth. Just don't swallow any water."

Jack's parting words in a crisp, military tone were, "Jim, we'll be by to get you at 0600 hours." Jim slowly closed the door and I asked, bewildered, "Did he say six o'clock?" Jim looked at his watch. "It's after 1:30 now. We'd better get to bed." After quick showers we fell into an exhausted sleep, only to find ourselves wide awake again at 4:00, like a pair of owls. Jet lag. We continued sleeping fitfully, and finally were rudely awakened when the alarm screamed at 5:30. Jim was dressed and on his way a short time later.

I looked down at his namesake, still sound asleep. Jimbo was the image of his father, except that he had my green eyes. The little guy had taken the turmoil surrounding our trip very well...had even basked in the attention strangers show a precocious youngster. En route we had been delayed in Istanbul and spent an hour in the austere air terminal. Jimbo had been dressed in long pants with a navy blue blazer and red necktie, his hair combed carefully to one side.

12

He looked and acted much older than his two and one-half years. He noticed a group of travelers, dressed in drab but neat clothing, sitting bunched together on the benches at the far end of the waiting room. Smiling, Jimbo approached them with a hand extended for a handshake, a ritual he had discovered pleased grownups everywhere. At first these grim people recoiled, but suddenly one very old man took Jimbo's hand, pumped it vigorously and grinned, revealing a yellow, snaggle-toothed smile. This impulsive gesture brought forth the hands of everyone, and Jimbo walked around like a minister greeting his congregation. The women would grin and pat his cheek. The sullen group was transformed into a cooing, smiling band of travelers all conversing at once in a strange tongue. Responding to the attention, Jimbo started back to the beginning of the line. Jim walked over to retrieve his charge and the sight of the uniform coming toward them had an amazing effect on the people. They became sullen statues again, staring straight ahead and not speaking. It was an astonishing change. Soon an announcement came over the loudspeaker and the entourage left to board the Aeroflot plane bound for Moscow.

• • •

Jimbo awakened and my reverie came to an end. Our first day in Iran was about to begin. I gave Jimbo a bath and we both got dressed. I read several books to him to keep his mind off wanting a drink of water. Finally, at nine, the phone rang and a male voice said in broken English, "Messus Ess-tarkee, Madame here for you."

Holding tightly to the banister with my right hand and Jimbo with my left, we started down the stairs. Looking down I saw two very slender, attractive women with almost identical Jackie Kennedy beehive hairdos. Both women wore simple, high-waisted cotton dresses. They were the picture of chic. Suddenly I felt fat, clumsy and frumpy.

The dark-haired one put out her hand and in a very Southern drawl said, "Ah'm Colleen and this is Kathy. You must be Shirley."

Nodding and smiling, I said I was delighted to meet them. Kathy said, in a midwestern accent, "And who is this young man?" I introduced Jimbo and he performed his solemn shaking-hands routine. They were enchanted.

"What would you like to do first, Shirley?" Colleen asked.

"Drink a big glass of water. I've never been so thirsty. I'm sure it's because Don told us not to drink the water here."

"We'll go to the Embassy restaurant. It's just across the street. There's also a co-op for food, a bookstore and a bank where you can exchange dollahs for *rials*. You get 76 *rials* for every American dollah. Oh, yes, the Embassy has its own watah purification plant. In fact, that's where yall will get all your watah for drinkin' and cookin' while yu'all are here in Iran," Colleen said in her soft Louisiana drawl.

Outside, the grinning Mohammed promptly opened the door for us. "Allo , Monsieur Jeembo," he said.

We had barely seated ourselves when Mohammed started the car and we jolted into the midst of heavy traffic. He immediately executed a U-turn, causing the traffic behind us to come to a screeching halt, horns blaring from every direction. He headed back in the opposite direction for half a block then veered right into a narrow, tree-lined street that led to the side entrance of the American Embassy compound. He stopped dead, leaped out of the car, and opened the door with a flourish. Colleen and Kathy casually slipped out of the car, totally unconcerned about the line of cars behind us whose drivers were angrily punching their horns, creating a symphony of off-key sounds.

Shaken and breathing hard, I managed to slide across the seat, clutching Jimbo's hand, and literally crawled out of the car. As Mohammed jumped back into the car and sped away, I asked, "Has he gone mad, or does he always drive like that? I must have been too tired to notice last night."

"Oh, he's one of the best drivers. Everyone would like to get him. The General even asked for him, but Mohammed didn't want to leave us," Colleen stated, a superior tone creeping into her voice.

The day was already very hot. The vendors were congregated across the street from the Embassy entrance under the thick shade of the trees. I scanned the displays, noting a man with a fruit and vegetable cart; another man with a cart laden with pots, pans, ropes, clothespins and various other utensils; and even a portable barbershop whose owner was shaving a man with a straight razor. I later learned that the price for a shave without soap and water cost ten *rial* (7 cents). With soap and water the price was twenty *rial* (14 cents). The customer or, better still the victim, sat on a wooden stool and stared into a small chipped mirror hanging from a broken tree branch while the barber performed his torture.

The air conditioning in the restaurant embraced us in cool relief. We found an empty table and a waiter immediately brought us the longed-for ice water. Colleen and Kathy gossiped together while Jimbo and I attacked the bacon, eggs and biscuits I ordered for our breakfast. The conversation was very negative, and soon they turned to assure me I had nothing but misery to look forward to for the next two years. They seemed to be trying to outdo each other with grim stories of life in Iran. The more they talked the more depressed I became.

"Well, surely it can't be that bad," I commented, trying hard to be upbeat. "After all, you do have a driver and a maid."

"It's perfectly awful having to depend on them. They lie and steal all the time," Colleen answered primly, but remembering her earlier comment, she added, "All except Mohammed, of course. He's definitely an exception. Zara, my *badjii,* is not so bad either, but then ah know how to handle servants. We always had nigras to do our work at home."

When she left to go to the bathroom, I turned to Kathy and asked, "What's a *badjii?*"

"That's what the maids are called here. It means 'little sister' in Turkish. Shirley, don't let Colleen get you down. It really is not so bad here. My husband, Stan, and I have had a lot of fun. It's different, but if you keep a sense of humor you'll do all right." I liked Kathy immediately and felt we could be friends.

I sighed. "Thank you for the words of encouragement. I really needed that."

After Colleen returned we went to the bank, the bookstore and then the co-op. Colleen explained that we would have to pay a deposit to join the co-op in order to shop there. I was surprised at how bare the shelves were. There were a few gallon cans of milk, canned vegetables, some bacon and pork chops from Denmark, Old Spice after shave lotion and what appeared to be white American bread, which I was soon to learn, would fall apart when butter was spread on it. The co-op was arranged like a stateside supermarket except that there was very little to buy.

"Are the shelves always this empty?" I asked.

"Not usually," Kathy responded, "but the Iranian who used to manage the co-op absconded with all the funds and opened his own store down the street."

"Can't the American government prosecute him?"

"Oh, are you kidding?" Colleen jumped in with a disgusted tone. "Don't you realize we are here as guests of the Iranian government? We can't do anythin' about it and the Iranian government won't. It will take about five months to get the Co-op stocked again. In addition to leaving with the money, the manager diverted most of the goods to his new store. If you want American goods, they're available right down the street, but you won't believe the prices. The only reason there is anything here is because Muslims don't eat pork, their kids are weaned at two years onto tea and this bread is terrible. Don't buy it. It has no flavor. The Iranian bread is delicious."

'Wow,' I thought, 'something positive at last.'

"We'll go out to my house now. I would have taken you there for breakfast, but the sink is broken and our badjii has not returned from visiting her son. Ah have to rely on her to find the plumber and bring him to the house."

Outside the Embassy gates a group of Iranians were squatting in the shade talking. As we approached, one of them stood up with a grin on his face. It was Mohammed. I noticed that he was taller than most Iranians.

"Machine here, Madame," he said to Colleen, and led the way to the car. We got in and again Mohammed was off to the races, swerving in and out of traffic, narrowly missing a donkey laden with large, white water jugs, passing cars on the wrong side of the road, slamming on brakes, accelerating to be the first away from the traffic light. Soon we had left the heavy traffic behind and were on a narrow, tree-lined street, heading north toward the mountains.

I finally relaxed my grip on Jimbo and began to look outside at the landscape. Kathy, sensing my uneasiness, kept her conversation light and humorous.

"Do you see these ditches with water running in them? They're called *jubes*. That's the water supply for the southern part of Tehran. In the northern suburbs, where we live, there is well water. These ditches were constructed years ago. They were built to divert the water from the melting snow in the mountain ahead of us. As you can see, everything goes on in the *jube*."

She laughed as she made her point, gesturing at a shepard who was urinating in the middle of the water as his flock drank from it. Right next to him a man was rinsing a teacup. Further on, a woman in a white garment was bathing her baby. Disgusted, I looked away just in time to see Mohammed pass a car as a truck was bearing down on us. I grabbed Jimbo and whispered a prayer. Mohammed swerved in front of the car he had just passed, barely allowing a split second for the truck to whistle by in the opposite direction.

Colleen, noticing my blanched face, said, "Mohammed, *yavash, yavash, yavash!*" That was a mistake. Mohammed now turned around to look directly at us, ignoring the traffic. He shrugged his shoulders.

"But Madame," he said, "He deed not heet us." Beaming with pleasure, he turned back to his task. Colleen turned to me and said, "When we first arrived we were told that *yavash* means slow down, but I think it might mean go faster."

Large areas of vacant land began to appear around us, broken by isolated, walled villas. We passed an Army encampment located on Abassabad, the first road planned to connect the two major north-south roads leading to the cooler foothills of the Alborz Mountains. The road was under construction, although there was little activity. Ditches appeared without warning, so the driving was slow and tedious. We bumped along creating clouds of chalky dust that rushed through the windows, enveloping us. We rolled up the windows, but the dust managed to filter in from the floor of the car. The heat was oppressive and the stench from the unwashed Mohammed was suffocating. We endured this for two miles, then with a final thud, the car sprang onto the clean, smooth, asphalt Shemiran Road.

We rolled down the windows, gratefully drinking in the cool air as Mohammed accelerated the car. Trees appeared in great abundance; the temperature dropped noticeably and ahead of us the mighty Alborz Mountains rose like a giant wave commanding our attention. It was a hopeful sight. Looking over to the east, Jimbo cried, "Oh, Mama, look at the ice cream cone!" Following his gaze I beheld the spectacular Mt. Damavand, an 18,934-foot dormant volcano that even in the hottest part of summer is covered with snow.

The dark slate gray mountain looked like a cone filled with vanilla ice cream. "You're right, Jimbo, it is a giant vanilla ice cream cone." In different times of the day the mountain would have strawberry or lemon-colored snow, and during storms the color would turn to mocha.

The aroma of roasting kebab wafted in as we passed vendors peddling their lunchtime specialties. Stands filled with pomegranates, melons, tomatoes, apricots, peaches and cucumbers crowded the sidewalks. White clay water jugs, vases with red, pink and white carnations, roses of every hue and purple lilacs, along with tall rubber plants with large lazy green leaves, stood in rows guarding the deserted shops. It was past noon and time for nourishment and napping until the heat of the day had spent itself.

Mohammed turned into a narrow, winding alley edged by high walls. Wrought-iron gates allowed an occasional glimpse into the verdant gardens beyond. He stopped in front of one of these and honked the horn. A pleasant-faced woman opened the gate. Mohammed drove the car into a large compound overgrown with uncontrolled bushes, vines and trees. At the far end was a crudely built swimming pool. As Colleen got out of the car the women said, "Madame, sink bad."

"Yes, Zara, go get man to fix."

Zara disappeared into a side door and emerged a moment later wrapped in a white cotton *chador,* the large half-circle of cloth that devout Moslems wear to cover themselves from their hair to their feet. Only her eyes and nose were visible; the rest of her body was enwrapped in the soft folds of this enormous cape. The ends brushed the earth as she walked and occasionally one could glimpse her sandals. She scurried through the gate intent on her mission.

We were minutely inspected by Prince, the Hudson's German shepard, and pronounced "Friends" by the wag of his tail. For Jimbo, it was love at first sight, and the two of them discovered a mutual fascination for playing ball, Jimbo throwing and Prince retrieving. Colleen and I said goodbye to Kathy, and Mohammed drove her home. I turned to Colleen and said, "Kathy is very nice, I hope I get to see more of her."

"Unfortunately, you won't be able to. Her husband has orders for the Pentagon and they leave in two weeks." More disappointing news, I thought.

Through heavy, metal-framed glass doors we entered the Hudson's house, stepping into a large hall that contained several rubber plants. The sunlight streamed through the mottled-glass, casting a rainbow assortment of muted blues, greens and pinks onto the white marble floor. We proceeded to the living room, where early American furniture and braided rugs seemed ludicrous combined with the white floor, numerous glass doors and a huge, kerosene-heating stove. The single story house meandered aimlessly with no thought of design.

It was a relief to stand on terra firma once more, and I gratefully accepted the invitation for Jimbo and me to wash the grit from our hands and face while Colleen prepared lemonade to soothe our parched throats. We briefly met the Hudsons' son and daughter. Kyle was ten and Mary Ann was twelve; obviously neither wanted anything to do with a two-year-old. They asked Colleen's permission to go to a friend's house and left. Jimbo asked if he could go outside to play with Prince and I agreed after warning him to avoid the swimming pool. I settled myself in a chair where I could see the action in the garden while Colleen told me that she taught fourth grade at the American School, which was on summer vacation. Good, I thought, she's also a teacher, so maybe we do have something in common. She sat opposite me on the sofa and I noticed for the first time Colleen's beauty. A petite brunette, about a size 8, I judged… the Magnolia and Moonlight type, charming and fragile in appearance, but obviously possessing an iron will. She was the Southern Belle one expects to see in front of the ante-bellum mansion, and was somehow out of synch with the twentieth century.

She was the college sweetheart of tall, handsome, football hero Don. Marrying him in his senior year in a spectacular wedding, she watched proudly and 'pregnantly' while he accepted his Distinguished Military Graduate award, a commission in the Regular Army and the rank of 2nd Lt.

She said goodbye to the small Louisiana town and valiantly, at first, tried to carry on in remote Army posts. However, she never felt comfortable in Army life with its frequent moves, Don's long absences, giving birth to two babies in strange hospitals, attended by strange doctors and without the moral support of her doting

Southern family and her husband, who was absent for one reason or another on Army duty. She hated the Army, and if she had ever possessed a sense of humor she had lost it long before I met her. For her, Iran was a disaster.

She related to me in gory detail the accident that occurred on the previous 14th of February. It was the cause of Jim's orders to Iran. Jim's predecessor, Captain Pierce, had been flying a colonel from the Pentagon over the treacherous Zagros Mountains near Isfahan to demonstrate the capabilities of a particular airplane. Pierce took the plane too high without oxygen, became disoriented and crashed on the side of the mountain. Heavy snow and gusting winds prevented the rescuers from reaching the plane for two days. Unfortunately, the crew left the plane following the crash, thinking it was about to blow up. They became mired in deep snow and couldn't make it back to the plane site for protection. The colonel and one sergeant survived the ordeal only by periodically flailing their arms and legs to keep awake until they were rescued.

Pierce had given his wife, Brenda, a radio the previous Christmas, so she could listen in on the plane frequencies whenever he was flying. As a result, she followed the rescue attempts for her husband and the other six men. She heard the rescuers report to command station that "Pierce needs whiskey." Joyously, she reported this to Colleen. It was the next day that she learned that "needs whiskey" was the code for dead.

The sergeant and the colonel were rescued at great peril to the helicopter crew, and after a month in the hospital the two men were sent back to the States for new assignments. The remaining bodies stayed on the mountainside waiting for the summer thaw and were scheduled to be brought down in July.

I sat in shocked silence when Colleen stopped talking, not knowing what to say. I was spared comment by the return of Zara, who reported that, "Man come to feex in one hour, *enshallah.*"

Colleen frowned, "*Enshallah, enshallah,* that's all you ever hear in this place."

"What does it mean?" I asked.

"It means, 'if Allah wills it', and believe me, Allah doesn't will very many things to happen fast around here. This means the plumber may get here today or maybe not until *fardah*...tomorrow, and if anyone ever says to you, '*fardah, enshallah*,' don't expect anything for at least two weeks!"

As if to disprove the last statement, the gate bell suddenly rang. Zara ran to open it, admitting a small, hairy man wearing baggy trousers, shoes with the backs broken down, a dirty white shirt, necktie, and jacket which showed signs of being mended many times, but still properly buttoned. He sported a two-day growth of beard and wore a beige felt cap with the sides folded up against his head. He was carrying a large canvas bag that must have weighed as much as the man himself.

Entering the kitchen doorway in a very important manner, he and Zara talked at the same time. From the living room we could hear them carrying on a simultaneous dialogue in Farsi during the entire repair and, miraculously, fifteen minutes later the sink was in good working order. The happy repairman was paid and left as Zara announced, "He good man, he not Iranian, he Turk like me!"

We had a light lunch of tuna salad, then Jimbo and I were shown to a bedroom where we could rest while Colleen and Zara prepared dinner. Jimbo fell asleep instantly, exhausted by the heat and running around the compound with Prince. I couldn't sleep; thoughts of the horrible crash kept playing in my mind. When Jim and Don returned, they laughed at my fears, which I couldn't hide. When Jim stated that he was going on his first orientation flight early the next day—to Mashed, in northeastern Iran bordering Afghanistan, where one of the American advisory teams was stationed, I really got upset.

Later that night, back at the hotel, I clung almost hysterically to Jim and protested that the flying in Iran was very dangerous. He coolly and logically told me that flying in Iran could not be as bad as in Korea which was reputed to have the worst flying conditions in the world.

"I did very well there for sixteen months, Babe," he said, using the nickname he had given me soon after we were married. "And besides," he added lightly, "at least here I won't be dodging bullets."

The next morning Jim left early for his flight to Mashad. I lay awake planning my day while getting kicked vigorously by Baby taking his morning constitutional. Since nothing had been said to the contrary, I assumed that Colleen felt her duty had been fulfilled and I was on my own. In spite of my broad hints, Colleen did not invite me to use her washing machine, so I decided to get some rope and clothespins from the utensil vendor next to the Embassy, and do the laundry by hand. I mentally measured the wall and decided six yards would do just fine. Then I remembered, 'Everything in this country is measured in meters. Hmmmm, better get six meters.'

As Jimbo and I came down the stairs, the deskman nodded. "Good morning, Madame and good morning, little Monsieur." With high spirits I led my charge out of the hotel.

The traffic!! I had forgotten about the traffic! Never had I seen so many cars going so fast or heard such blasting of horns. Most of the cars I saw were small, old, battered cars from Europe with an occasional black Mercedes limousine with diplomatic license plates and official flags on the front fenders. We stood at the curb waiting for some let-up in the melee. It was unceasing. If there was a pause on our side of the street, the other side was experiencing three-abreast movement. I was not about to take Jimbo out to the center without a clear chance of making it across the entire street.

Our wait seemed eternal, and I was beginning to think the situation was hopeless when I noticed a ragged man on the opposite side of the street staring at the two of us. He seemed unusually interested in us and I grew more concerned about him than the traffic. He was small, dressed in white swaddling cloth pants and a loose-fitting white shirt covered with a green vest. A faded green turban covered his head, and his legs from knobby knees down were bare except for some pink plastic sandals. His thick moustache and the way he leaned forward in an aggressive manner was menacing. Suddenly, he bolted into the traffic and came straight toward us. I pulled Jimbo behind me, bracing myself for the assault I knew was coming. My jaw was jutting only slightly less than my stomach, and I was prepared to defend my son and myself to the death.

He stopped halfway across, holding up his left hand like Moses, signaled the drivers to halt. Miraculously, with tires squealing, all movement stopped. Like the parted Red Sea, there in front of us was safe passage to the other side. He faced us squarely and with the most dramatic bow I have ever witnessed, he swept his hand out indicating that the street was ours.

"*Enjas,* Madame," he proclaimed. I waddled across that street as fast as I could, dragging Jimbo. I could have hugged that little man. As we reached the safety of the other side, the thunderous roar of the traffic started up once more behind us. I turned to convey my thanks to my benefactor, but Moses had joined the throng of pedestrians in front of our hotel and was going about his business.

After a good breakfast, we headed for the co-op to buy some water, peanut butter, crackers, canned peaches, soap and, the most needed item, a bottle of Scotch. Out of the corner of my eye, I spotted an English-Farsi dictionary and added that to my purchases, pausing outside the co-op to learn the phrases "How much is that?" and "I would like one, please."

I practiced these two sentences as we looked for the vendor with the clothespins. Finally, we found him next to his cart, sitting on his haunches drinking tea. He leaped up as we approached, and we suddenly found ourselves surrounded by the other vendors plus a myriad of male onlookers, all curious to know what I wanted. Undaunted, I pointed to the clothespins and said in newly acquired language, "How much is that?" At least I thought that's what I was saying. My question was answered with loud, obscene guffaws, interrupted by rapid *Farsi*. My face grew red and this brought further unintelligible comments and more laughter. Once again I was rescued, this time by a young man who had learned English in school. "Madame, what you wish?"

Pointing to the items, I said "Some clothespins and some of that rope." My translator spoke volumes to the vendor, who answered volumes. One of the onlookers pulled the sack of groceries from my arms. I tried to grab it back, but my translator stopped me.

"Eets okay, Madame. Hassan hold tings for you. He help." Hassan grinned at me and the other onlookers continued to discuss my request with the vendor. Finally the translator turned to me and said, "He say hokay, how many?"

"How much for the clothespins?"

More volumes of discussion ensued and finally, "He say one *rial* each." One of the few useful facts Colleen had imparted to me was that one rial was about 3/4s of a penny. 100 *rials* equaled $.76.

"How much for the rope?"

More discussion… "Five *rial* one meter."

"I'll take twenty clothespins and six meters of rope." I pointed to the items and indicated with my fingers the number I wanted. The vendor carefully counted out the twenty clothespins, wrapped them in a piece of newspaper and tied them with a string. I brought out my change purse and started looking at all the strange coins. The sunshine disappeared and I looked up to see that all the men had moved in around us and were also trying to look into my change purse. The stifling air was heavy with the odor of garlic and decayed armpits. I felt faint, and Jimbo was starting to push his way out of the trap of the onlookers dirty pants. Quickly, I walked to the other side of the cart, dumped some change into the palm of my hand and tried again to decipher the alien numbers. My translator noted my discomfort, bawled out the offenders, and very protectively said, "Madame, I help." He showed me the one, two and five rial, carefully counting out the amount needed.

The vendor was measuring out the meters; I was trying to see that he gave me the correct length of rope while I tried to watch the translator who was counting out my money. I had a feeling of uneasiness, half expecting Hassan to bolt with my groceries, the translator to run off with my change purse, and the vendor to cheat me on the length of rope I had to have for my clothes-drying. However, it seemed innocent enough. *They're like curious children trying to be helpful*, I thought.

Our transaction completed, I thanked everyone and we headed back to the hotel. The bundles were becoming heavy, the hot noonday sun was oppressive, and Jimbo was fussing. It was lunchtime and Takte-Jamshid Avenue was practically deserted as we successfully crossed it without the assistance of Moses. Exhausted, we climbed the stairs to our room and, without his usual request for a story, Jimbo crawled onto his bed and fell asleep.

I put the soiled clothes in the bathtub to soak while I set up my clothesline. I hooked it around the transom on the window and brought it over to the high brass bedstead just as I had planned. It was not long enough. *That's impossible*, I thought. I had measured very carefully. I untied the end of the line and measured it. *Five meters! That damn vendor only gave me five meters!* The full impact of what had happened hit me hard. Perhaps it was the long trip, jet lag, terrible stories, hot weather, or my pregnancy, but suddenly, I was awash with fury. I threw myself down on the awful red bedspread, pounded my fists into the pillow and had a tantrum worthy of the brattiest kid. The tears gushed; I started sobbing uncontrollably, and then began to hiccup. In between sobs and in rhythm with my fists pounding the pillow, I called the vendor every name, obscene or otherwise, that I could think of.

The outburst stopped as suddenly as it had started, and I lay totally spent in a pool of gooey tears. Slowly, I started reasoning with myself, trying to overcome the depression that was pressing into my whole being. The realization that this was only day two of a two-year sentence made the task difficult. *Look*, I said to myself, *nothing is as bad as it seems. There has to be some good in everything. Everything happens for the best. You'll look back on this later and laugh…*

Oh, crap! None of the usual bromides were working, and I started arguing with myself.

This is a lousy place, just like Colleen said. She says all Iranians lie, cheat and steal, and don't take baths. That's ridiculous. They have to take baths. Colleen exaggerates everything. She's a whiney, miserable little person and I'm not going to be like that. She's a delicate magnolia that bruises and dies if stepped on. But I'm a cholla cactus. Step on me and you'll be sorry!

All these thoughts flooded in my mind until finally I got up, went into the bathroom and looked in the mirror. Green, bloodshot eyes looked back at me; one side of my face was cherry red. I looked as if I had half a case of diphtheria. I examined my skin carefully, wiping at my left cheek. Some of the red came off on my hands. That damned red bedspread was staining me.

I can't believe this place…land of exotic Persian carpets and they can't even dye a bedspread permanently. Suddenly, it seemed so ridiculous I started laughing. I brushed my short blonde hair and carefully pin-curled the wet ends. Being too tired to do anything else, I collapsed next to my sleeping son.

The phone rang and I heard Jimbo talking. "Will you play baseball with me? I have a new glove. My Grandpa gave it to me…. okay, okay, okay. Mama, this man wants to talk to you. He's going to play baseball with me." I put the phone to my ear. "Mrs. Starkey, this is Sgt. Coleman. Ma'am, I'm the radio operator at Ghalamorghi. I just talked to your husband and he asked me to call you. He won't be back tonight, he's weathered in, in Mashed."

"What? How can he be weathered in? This is June."

"Ma'am, there are dust storms in the area, clear up to 16,000 feet. The planes can't climb above them. Capt. Starkey asked me to tell you he'll be back first thing in the morning." As soon as he hung up I remembered that I had no idea how to reach anyone. I couldn't even call Sgt. Coleman back… we were abandoned.

Chapter 2

Coming from a town of 60,000 inhabitants, Tucson's population at the time, I was ill prepared to be an Army officer's wife, or, more correctly, 'lady'. I came into this world on Christmas day at the height of the depression, 1933. At that time Tucson had a population of 20,000 souls and my father had been told that there was not enough water for an additional 5,000 people to survive. I was born at The Stork's Nest, a maternity hospital favored by the Protestant families, while the Catholic children were born at St. Mary's Hospital.

Both my parents came from educated families; my maternal grandfather, Will Votaw, was born in Iowa two weeks after the firing on Ft. Sumter, South Carolina that started the Civil War. In the 1880's he and his brother Eli homesteaded in Nebraska. After several years of drought, Grandpa had enough, sold his place to Eli and moved to Lincoln. Though he only had formal schooling through the third grade, he was determined to get an engineering degree from the University of Nebraska. After he accomplished that, he was hired as the head of the Maintenance Department at the university. Standing over six feet tall, lean and very athletic, he excelled in all sports and was a champion tennis player in Nebraska. He started organizing afternoon football games, and when the university decided to form a football team, the president approached him with the offer to be the first football coach of Nebraska. He declined, stating that it was just a kid's game with no future. He later transferred to the

University of Colorado.

My paternal grandfather was a doctor in Colorado and my dad, Ed Condit, was an engineering student at the Colorado School of Mines in Golden when his roommate, Casey, invited him to come to Boulder. Casey was dating my Aunt Olive, who with my mother, Mabel, was a student at the University of Colorado. Casey told dad that his girlfriend had a sister and they could double date. Dad took one look at my beautiful mother and he was a goner. They were married six months later and stayed married for 62 years- until my father's death in 1990. The depression and my brother Bill came along at about the same time and my dad started working in the mines in Colorado. As the depression deepened, the mines in Colorado closed, but Dad learned that the mines in Arizona were hiring. So off they moved to Globe-Miami for the next three years, where my sisters Alice and Toddy were born. Phelps-Dodge finally had to close down in 1932 and told my dad that the family could live in the company house for nothing until the mines reopened. Mom and Dad were too proud to take handouts and, since they were both determined that the children would have a college education, the decision was made to move to Tucson. In those days most people moved to Tucson for their health, I've never heard of anyone else moving there so the infant children would go to college. Mom took the three kids to Los Angeles, where her parents had just moved, and Dad headed for Tucson to look for work. It took a long time, with Dad taking any kind of temporary work he could find. One day he heard that George Morningstar was looking for a butcher at the Piggly-Wiggly market. Dad showed up at 5 a.m., waiting at the door until Morningstar arrived an hour later. Dad informed him he had come for the job. Morningstar told him he only wanted an experienced butcher and Dad answered, "If you will teach me to butcher, I will work for nothing until you decide I'm good enough to get a salary." Morningstar was impressed, Dad was hired, and two weeks later Dad was on the payroll at $5.00 a week. Mom and the kids arrived to a joyous reunion, and I suspect I was the result of the celebration. They needed another mouth to feed like they needed a hole in the head, but they never for one minute made me feel that I was anything but important.

One of my earliest memories was going with my family out east of town on unpaved dusty Grant Road. It was very hilly in those days, and I clearly remember wondering what was on the other side of the hill. I was three years old and had wanderlust even then.

One Sunday after church I was playing on the floor in the kitchen while Mom was fixing dinner. The kitchen linoleum had squares, which I imagined were the rooms in my small doll's house. Mother had the Philharmonic on the radio when suddenly a terse voice interrupted the music. I started to ask her what happened but she quickly shushed me. After the music started, she explained that the German army had invaded Holland. I can remember feeling very sorry for the little children who wore wooden shoes.

When Toddy started to school, I bugged her insistently to teach me to read and she patiently explained how to sound out the letters. Soon I got to go on Saturday mornings with Todd and Alice to the Carnegie Library downtown. We were given a dime for bus fare and we could each check out two books for a week. Alice and Todd read each other's books and I tried hard to do the same. One day I picked up an Oz book that Todd was reading and laboriously sounded out each word on the first page. It made no sense to me, but I was very proud that I had accomplished that. As I grew older I became an avid reader, losing myself in books.

When Safeway stores bought out the Piggly-Wigglys, my dad became a manager and our future brightened. Then the war came and everything changed. Once it had been hard for anyone to find a job. Now it was hard to find any men to work. Mom, like all the other women in the United States, stepped up and helped out. At first Mom went to the Red Cross several times a week to roll bandages and cut materials for uniforms. She marched off carrying her precious Weiss scissors; these scissors would cut the material for all our dresses, formals, coats, wedding dresses, upholstery, drapes and curtains. Mom was a whiz at sewing. In the afternoon she was a Scout leader. My Brownie troop learned to knit, and we knitted squares to be pieced together into blankets for Bundles for Britain. My brother Bill was full of energy, selling Saturday Evening Posts door to door, planting our vegetable garden, and raising rabbits for sale. Bill would organize excursions all around the neighborhood looking for tin foil, string, and wire—anything to help the war effort. I adored my brother, who had given me the nickname Scoot. He

29

was six years older than I was, and I was the bane of his existence. I followed him everywhere, wanting to do all the things he and his friends were doing. He built a scooter using an apple crate, a two-by-four and a roller skate that had been taken apart. I used to curl up inside the crate while he took me on wild rides. He would set me on the handlebars of his bike for more wild rides. I was always eager for his attention; usually he was patient, but when he didn't want to deal with me he could be firm. Invariably, I would continue to pester him until he became very angry. When I saw that happening, I would run. He would chase me because he was mad; I ran faster because I was scared. I headed for big sister Alice, who could magically calm Bill down.

Dad was given the honor of opening up the biggest Safeway store in the state of Arizona. It was built on Stone Avenue and his best customer was the Papago Indian Chief. The chief would arrive every Friday and buy $500.00 worth of groceries for the Tribe. This was an amazing amount in the 1940's.

Pilots were being trained at Davis-Monthan, Ryan Field and Marana. Wives and sweethearts followed the men to Tucson, and Dad hired many of them to be cashiers in the store. As the men went off to the Pacific and European theaters, many of the women stayed on to work and save money. We would periodically have dinner parties for them at our house; I loved asking them about where they lived. One of the nicest women was named Wanda, and she invited Todd and me to spend the night in her trailer, where she played country music on the radio. That was the first time I had heard country music as we only played classical or current hits on our radio. One day my sad-faced dad announced that Wanda's husband had been killed. She went back home to Arkansas and we never saw her again. When Grand Central Airplane Plant opened, many of Dad's cashiers went off to become 'Rosy the Riveters' because they could make more money. Mom started working as a cashier leaving Alice in charge at home. Our whole family pitched in, as did all families then.

My mom and dad bought a house on Second Street, so Todd and I walked to University Heights school, always passing the house that Dillinger had lived in briefly. One of the houses on First Avenue had a flag with a blue star in the window indicating that someone in that home was serving in the military. One day it changed to gold, indicating that he had been killed. Our house was a block away from our church, Trinity Presbyterian, and after church on Sunday Dad would invite a soldier or two to have dinner with us. We had a constant stream of men from all parts of the United States dining with us.

On weekdays we ate dinner together at 6:30, when Dad arrived home from the store. Mom would come home early to fix dinner with Alice's help. Todd would set the table, but I was nowhere to be found. Usually I was riding my bike, roller skating or throwing rocks at the boys down the street. I would come in for dinner dying of thirst and would gulp down my milk the first thing. Todd sat diagonally from me on Mom's left side, and I would watch as she daintily ate her food, never touching her milk. I could not have any more milk until I finished my plate and so I glared at my sister, angry that she still had milk. Periodically she would give me a sweet smile, which really ticked me off.

Dad always had something special to impart to the family as we ate. He would talk about the current news, which was all about the war. Sometimes he would tell us about a certain book or incident at the store. We would laugh at some of the strange customers he described. One night in particular he read us the entire Rubiayat by Omar Khayyam. It took forever and he denied my request to use the bathroom until he had finished the poem. The most memorable time was when he announced that an eerie light had lit up the entire sky east of us and the papers were full of speculation. Later we learned of the atomic bomb being dropped on Hiroshima and that the test for the bomb had taken place in White Sands, New Mexico, causing that strange light.

After the war Tucson started to grow. So many GI's had come through during the war and had discovered a place without snow in the winter. Tucson had always attracted people with tuberculosis and arthritis due to the dry climate. My dad's brother-in-law Paul Cook, an Annapolis graduate, had been gassed by the Germans during the First World War and ended up in the Veterans' Hospital in Tucson with tuberculosis. When my dad came to Tucson he lived with his sister Elsa and her kids. Uncle Paul was extremely sick, and one night my dad and Elsa stayed with Paul after the doctor told them Paul would not live through the night. With encouragement from dad and Elsa, Paul rallied and eventually got well. Coincidentally, after Pearl Harbor, Paul was recalled to active duty. When he reported for his physical in San Diego the doctor who examined him was the same one who had declared that he would not live through the night.

Jim is also a native of Arizona. He was born in Clarkdale and lived in Prescott until the fifth grade. Jim, his mom and dad moved to Tucson at the beginning of World War II when his dad obtained work on the Southern Pacific Railroad. I was born in Tucson, the youngest of four, and attended school there from kindergarten through earning a degree from the University of Arizona. Our paths first crossed when I was in ninth grade, in junior high school, and Jim was a junior at Tucson High School. A friend of mine, Jane, was dating Jim and talked incessantly about him. My father, an avid baseball fan, told my family at the dinner table about this incredible young pitcher who was named the best pitcher in the state of Arizona as a lowly junior, a feat never before accomplished. The sports pages of our local newspapers ran daily (or so it seemed) articles on his prowess. I had to meet this marvel. My opportunity came one day when I noticed Jane standing at the eastern gate of Roskruge Junior High. Casual conversation revealed that she was waiting for the Great One to appear. I made small talk for twenty minutes while watching in the direction she was looking.

Suddenly, he walked across the street to where we were standing, taking long strides mostly on the balls of his feet, his heels barely touching the ground. It was a very athletic, sort of bouncing, stride. Head held high, broad shoulders thrown back, he was the picture of confidence. His hands were clinched in a determined manner, and I remember thinking, *This guy knows where he wants to go and no one better get in his way!* As he approached, I saw that he was almost six feet tall, had dark brown hair and blue-green eyes. When he grinned, his eyes and the gold filling on his front tooth twinkled. I stood there smiling at him, expecting to be introduced. Jane immediately turned her back to me and moved to block my vision. She grabbed his arm. He looked back at me and I gave a pathetic wave. She pulled him down the street, leaving me dejectedly watching them disappear.

The following year I entered Tucson High as a sophomore.

One day, by chance, I saw Jim in front of his chemistry lab and from then on I took a certain path to my history class so I would see him joking with his friends. He always had a twinkly grin and a "Hi" for me. That spring, when the yearbooks came out, he wrote in mine that my smile brightened his day. I was in ecstasy!

Jim led Tucson High to the 1949 State Championship in baseball, was again named the best pitcher in the state of Arizona, and was offered a large signing bonus from the Cleveland Indian Ball Club. He turned it down on the advice of his dad who said "Get your college education first." He accepted a baseball scholarship to play for the University of Arizona.

In high school I discovered modern dance and couldn't wait for class each day. I also worked on the yearbook, newspaper and quarterly magazine, selling advertising. In my senior year I was the Advertising Manager of the yearbook and got to design all the ads. I started a club called the Sunshine Modeling Club. A customer at Dad's store was head of the Chamber of Commerce and he asked me to be in a photo advertisement for a magazine. He wanted two others so I enlisted two of my friends and thus the club was born.

After graduation from high school, I enrolled in the University of Arizona. That Christmas I was downtown shopping when I saw Jim Starkey and Dick Keefe standing in front of Steinfeld's Department Store selling mistletoe. Dick's father was a police captain, so they had received permission to park in the loading zone to sell the wild mistletoe they had harvested from the cottonwood trees that grow in the washes. I bought some while we talked and joked for several minutes, then I left. As I returned home the phone was ringing and it was Jim, asking me if I wanted to go to the movies. Thrilled, I accepted, and we had our first date at the Fox Theater. We dated on and off during the next four months, but fought a lot as I wanted to "save the world" and his goal was more physical. When he got drafted, I was pleased, saying he deserved it.

During my first semester at Arizona I was accepted into Orchesis, the national dance honorary; I joined a sorority and worked on the newspaper, once again selling advertising. I also worked part-time at the counter in the photography department. It was 1952 and my father, a passionate Republican, was thrilled that Gen. Eisenhower was running for president against Adlai Stevenson. One day it was announced that Gen. Eisenhower was making a quick airport stop in Tucson on his way to a dinner in Phoenix. One of the photographers for the campus paper told me he had a press pass to see Eisenhower. I begged him to let me carry his case of film so I could get in to see Eisenhower, too. He finally relented and off we went. We were ushered through the gate, past the hundreds of people waiting for a glimpse of the hero of the war and were motioned toward a special parking area. As we got out, a man thrust a business card into my hand, which I ignored. As we were walking toward the special seating bleachers I noticed that to my left Gen. Eisenhower was standing alone, patiently waiting for the introductory speeches to subside so he could talk. Without a word I sprinted over and breathlessly said, "Hello, Gen. Eisenhower." "Hello, yourself," he answered. Momentarily speechless I finally blurted out, "How is Mamie?" He gave me his famous grin and told me she was fine. I wanted his autograph but the only thing I had was the card someone had handed me. I looked at it and it was a colored picture of San Xavier del Bac, a mission south of Tucson built by Father Kino in the 17th century. On the other side was a picture of a young, handsome man running for the U.S. Senate by the name of Barry Goldwater, a man I had never heard of. I asked Gen. Eisenhower if he would autograph that and he did. About that time several other people arrived also asking for autographs, and the general turned to me and said, "Young lady, would you please listen for the speakers to call my name so I won't miss my cue?" I immediately answered in a too loud voice, "YES, SIR." Our future president laughed. After the speech I rejoined the photographer who was fuming, as he did not get any pictures because yours truly had the film. As soon as we returned to the photography studio I laminated my precious card and kept it in my wallet.

Years later Jim and I were returning to Ft. Riley, Kansas after spending Christmas in Tucson. We encountered a terrible blizzard in northern New Mexico, almost going over a cliff when a semi-trailer jack-knifed in front of us. While battling a raging storm we had just crossed the border into Kansas when we saw a sign for the town of Sunflower. We had hoped to make it to the Kansas Turnpike and on to Junction City before nightfall, as we had forgotten to cash a check and our funds were very low. But the storm was worsening so Jim decided we should spend the night in Sunflower. Following foggy road signs, we struggled down a narrow, snowy road and came upon an ancient hotel. Inside was a high-ceiling lobby walled in rich, dark mahogany. Behind the immense desk stood a man who looked like he had just stepped out of a 1920's movie. Hair parted in the middle, he had on tiny, wire-rimmed glasses, and wore a high, starched collar, a cravat and a vest that sported a pocket watch. Jim asked the charge for one night and he answered gruffly, "Two dollars a night, the same thing I've been charging for thirty years." Amazed, Jim said, "We'll take it." "Then, follow me, young man." And off we went, up a wide, steep flight of stairs to the second floor. He unlocked a heavy door and ushered us in. The immense, high-ceiling room had a canopied bed in the middle and an antique dresser, two chests, a rocking chair and ottoman placed around the room. Inspecting the room carefully, Jim noticed a heavy rope hanging from the ceiling next to the window. "What is that for?" he asked. "That's the fire escape, young man," he answered in a staccato voice. "If there's a fire, open the window and swing down to the ground. The bathroom is at the end of the hall. The café across the way serves breakfast at six in the morning." Without another word he was gone.

The next morning dawned bright and sunny and we made our way to the café. After eating Jim told me we could either pay for our meal or pay the toll for the Kansas Turnpike, but we didn't have funds for both. We knew the turnpike would have the snow removed.

"Babe, see if you can pay for our meal with a check." He left me and went to check out. I approached the middle-aged lady at the counter and politely asked if I could pay for the meal by check. "No, we do not accept personal checks" she replied. "We're very good for the check," I said, "My husband is an officer in the Army."

"No, can't do it," was the firm, unimpressed reply. "But I'm a kindergarten teacher and I need to get back to teach. We forgot to cash a check and we only have money for the Turnpike," I pleaded. She wouldn't budge.

As a last resort I reached in my wallet for identification and came upon the card with Eisenhower's signature. I pulled it out and showed it to the lady, hoping she was a Republican. I needn't have worried; we were definitely in Eisenhower territory. She looked surprised and asked me how I happened to have it and I told her my story. She started laughing when I said how mad the photographer

35

was. She suddenly mellowed and told me she would accept a check for the exact amount of the meal. I kept that check for many years. It was in the amount of $2.10.

When I started college I registered as a Home Economics major, but in my sophomore year I changed to Elementary Education. That fall I was having lunch at the sorority house when I got a message saying to report to the Dean of Women's office. I couldn't imagine what I had done to rate such a call. My brother had married Helen Avery and her mother was the secretary to Miss Carlson, the Dean of Women. When I arrived she greeted me in her modulated New England accent. "Shirley dear," she said softly, "This gentleman here is looking for a candidate to represent Pima County in the Miss Arizona contest. I immediately thought of you."

Confused, I looked over at a small, sweaty-faced man with piercing black eyes. He was dressed in a wrinkled, seersucker suit, stood five feet six inches tall and weighed about 130 lbs. He walked toward me, exuding cheap aftershave lotion. Mrs. Avery introduced him as Mr. Goldstein and he gave me a wet, limp handshake. "Are you a native of Arizona?" he said in the thickest Brooklyn accent I had ever heard. "Ya got to be one, ya know."

I nodded and said, "What are you talking about?"

"Honey, we got to get a goil to represent Pima County in the Miss Arizona pageant that's up in Phoenix next week."

"But I read in the paper this summer that someone has been chosen."

"Well, there's a problem. The goil that won the contest is, how shall I say it, she ain't qualified."

"Why not?"

"Weeeeelll, she's with child and she ain't married."

"Oh!" was all I could muster. In 1952 that was a scandal. It had only been a few years since the U.S. Senate had voted to censure Ingrid Bergman for having an illicit affair with Roberto Rosselini while still married to her husband.

"So," he continued, "ya got any talent?"

"Well, I'm a dancer."

"Are you any good?" And before I could say anything else he says, "So how 'bout it, honey, ya game to go to Phoenix?"

I was very skeptical about the veracity of Goldstein and said

"Mrs. Avery, do you think this is okay?"

"Yes," she said. "Miss Carlson is going to be one of the judges. I think it would be a good opportunity for you."

I turned to Goldstein and said, "I would first have to check with my dad. We could walk to his store. It's not far." Soon after the war my dad had purchased a grocery store a block away from the main entrance to the University.

Goldstein huffed, puffed and sweated as we walked to the store. "Man, its hot here," was his only comment.

As we entered the store Dad was at the meat area cutting up some pork chops. I introduced Mr. Goldstein to my dad, who eyed him suspiciously while I quickly explained the situation. My dad started interrogating Goldstein. Dad would look at him over his glasses, with squinted eyes, ask a very pointed question and then raise the meat cleaver above his head slamming it through the meat, releasing a pork chop.

"Who is going to chaperone this pageant?" Dad asked. Goldstein, with a look like a deer caught in headlights, was sweating profusely and began to stutter, "I I I I ththink Miss Carlson is." He answered.

I chirped in with "Yes, Daddy, that's what Mrs. Avery told me."

"And what is your job in this pageant?" Dad stopped cutting meat and looked Goldstein straight in the eye.

"Oh, Sir, my job is over if you will let your daughter be the contestant. I leave tonight for New York."

This seemed to satisfy Dad but he continued the query, enjoying Goldstein's discomfort. He was playing 'bad cop' to the hilt and after torturing Goldstein for fifteen minutes, he turned to me and said, "Scoot, do you want to do this?"

"Oh, yes, Daddy, I do!" I answered enthusiastically.

"All right, then you can go to Phoenix."

Excitedly I danced out of the store with Goldstein right behind me. Outside he started mopping his face with his handkerchief. "Whew, I thought your dad was going to use that cleaver on me!"

Mrs. Avery's role in this was not over. She assured me that in addition to Miss Carlson, the Dean of Women from Arizona State College at Tempe and Arizona Teacher's College in Flagstaff would be judges. Her other son-in-law, Buzz, was the manager of the local

NBC radio affiliate, and she talked him into getting the station to sponsor me. The station paid for my formal gown, my swimsuit and my roundtrip airfare from Tucson to Phoenix. I went over to the dance room and worked out a routine. There was not much time; I only had ten days to prepare. Buzz drove me to the airport and I got on a small three-wheeled Piper Cub plane. It was my first airplane ride and I was so excited I could barely contain myself.

When I arrived in Phoenix I was met by an official of the pageant and driven to the motel across the street from the State Mental Hospital. There I met the other candidates from the other thirteen counties, as well as the young women from Tempe, Chandler, Phoenix and Scottsdale. Only Maricopa County had extra candidates from the major cities. We were an excited, giggling mass of femininity, all talking at once. We went to a fancy restaurant in a cavalcade of Cadillac convertibles, with two to a car, sitting on back of the seats, waving like movie stars to anyone who happened to look our way.

For three days we drove clear across Phoenix to the Fair Grounds in this manner. The judging was to be on the same outdoor stage used for judging livestock, and I guess we were not too far removed from that! We went through the usual routines of strutting around in our bathing suits to the catcalls of all the guys hanging onto the rail in front of the stage. We were interviewed and asked the usual question, "How do you plan on changing the world?" We all had amazing answers.

The second night the talent competition commenced and I was the third one on. My routine was done in a leotard and barefoot.... Bad mistake. The wooden floor of the outdoor stage was a mass of splinters, most of which ended up in my feet. I did a series of wild leaps, only I couldn't leap. My leaps didn't leap. The floor sagged and it was impossible to get any elevation. My grand finale consisted of a giant leap ending back stage. Unfortunately, I failed to take into consideration that "back stage" was only two feet wide, ending in three steps going down. As I flew through the air, my feet missed the stage and down I went, landing on my back on a pile of hay. When I opened my eyes, I was looking into the huge, kindly brown eyes of an Angus cow.

That evening rumors were flying that one of the judges had departed; it turned out it was Miss Carlson. Later I found out that all the judges had been told that the three top winners would be from Maricopa County. Miss Carlson refused to be programmed and left. Sure enough, the next night Miss Maricopa County was crowned Miss Arizona and her two alternates were Miss Scottsdale and Miss Tempe. The experience had been good; I had made many new friends and, having been treated to my first airplane ride, I was determined to become an airline stewardess.

After getting my degree in January, I taught second grade for one semester, and then fulfilled my ambition to go into the airlines. I survived the interviews, where the conversations went like this:

Female interviewer: "You bleach your hair."

Me: "No I don't."

F.I. "Your hair is lighter on top than underneath. You must bleach it."

Me: "I've lived in Arizona all my life. The sun bleaches everything there."

F.I. "I don't believe you."

I left the interview knowing full-well I had failed. Much to my surprise, I received an acceptance and ticket to fly to Cheyenne, Wyoming to the United Airlines School two weeks later. The school was very hard especially the chapters on Emergencies. Failing this you were out. I studied as I had never studied before being a consummate coward. If I couldn't save the world at least I could prepare to save myself in the event of a crash. The Emergencies tests lasted two days, and at the end I was amazed to be singled out as the first person in five years to ace all of the tests.

After graduation I was assigned to Chicago. I had three roommates, Nancy from San Diego, Melissa from a small town in Missouri, and Grace from an even smaller town in Indiana. Talk about Babes in the Woods! We found an apartment at 10 North Delaware, between State Street and Rush Street, in a building that was ten stories high. After moving in, we heard from the elevator operator that Al Capone's former mistress occupied the penthouse and we were the only girls in the building who were paying our own rent. He said this in a voice that indicated something was definitely wrong with us. One day I was in the cleaners next door leaving my uniform, when an old man (he must have been at least 40 years old) asked me for a date. I declined and after the man left the counter man asked me if I knew who that man was. I said I didn't and he informed me that I had missed my chance, as the man was one of the wealthiest men in Chicago.

Our only uniform was a sky blue tailored jacket and skirt. We were required to wear a girdle, three inch heels and hose and a saucy cap worn ½" above the left eye. Our nails had to have red polish so dirt would not show. Every so often a supervisor would get on board to check on our appearance. They would pinch your fanny to make sure you had on your girdle. The pilots invariably offered to be the tester.

As a new hireling I was assigned to fly the Convair airplanes. The Convairs carried 32 passengers and I was the lone stewardess on board. After greeting passengers I hung their coats in a closet, gave them chewing gum and collected their tickets. After giving the usual safety spiel, checking to be sure seat belts were fastened, I sat in a jump seat until we were safely airborne. Then I would serve a meal, pour coffee, collect trays and clean up the galley. It sounds simple enough, except that the Convair only flew at 8000 feet and most of my flights were over the Great Lakes. With the changing autumn weather the ride frequently imitated a roller coaster, and my sensitive stomach reacted accordingly. I would get so nauseated I'm sure my green face clashed with my blue uniform. I was completely miserable until my feet returned to terra firma. I had joined the airlines to see the world and soon discovered the only world I saw was the cab ride from the airport to a hotel and back.

I had some interesting experiences while flying . One day a tall, beautiful blonde came on board wearing a full-length mink coat. I offered to hang it up for her but she declined. During the flight as I walked down the aisle I noticed the blonde had fallen asleep. Her coat had slid open and she was bare-naked! I got a blanket and covered her up. When she left the plane she gave me a funny grin and said, "Thank you, very much." Boy, did I want to hear her story!

Another time four men wearing identical plaid vests, beige pants and straw hats got on the plane. "Your mother likes to dress you alike?" I inquired.

The first man said, "We're a barber shop quartet on our way to Omaha for a contest."

"In that case," I replied, "You'll get no lunch until you sing for your supper."

"That's a deal" so after the plane took off we were entertained by *We were sailing along,* and *Goodby my honey.* It was a fun flight.

The Conair's food storage bins were located in the back of the plane facing forward. In preparation for landing all the doors to the bins had to be securely locked. One day I failed to do that and as the plane came in for a landing I heard a crash as casseroles came sliding down the aisle, spewing scrambled eggs, hash-brown potatoes, toast and sausages. A very large lady sitting in the first row looked down at the mess and said, "Well, if I had known you were going to throw this food a way I would have asked for seconds."

One night two men got on my flight, one of them was very drunk. After we took off, the pilot announced that there was a lot of turbulence ahead and to please keep seated. The drunk got up and started walking around. I went up to him and sternly told him he had to keep seated. "I will if you will bring me a drink", he said, slurring his words.

"I'm sorry, sir, I cannot do that while there is turbulence. However, I will bring you a cup of coffee."

His companion said, "That would be much appreciated."

Turning to the drunk, I firmly said, "You must sit down right now." He did but by the time I came back with the coffee, he was up again. "Down, now." I commanded.

Sheepishly he sat down and took the coffee and then said, "Why are you being so nice to me?"

Through clinched teeth I said, "I intend to *kill* you with kindness." Both guys started laughing but I was not amused. If the plane had hit turbulence and dropped suddenly I would have been in danger, ending up on the ceiling.

Later, one of the guys sent a letter to United Airlines stating how impressed he was with how I handled the situation. These letters are called orchard letters while the complaining ones are referred to as onion letters.

I was working a flight from San Francis and one of the passengers was a prizefighter named Bobo Olsen who was scheduled to fight for the middleweight champion in Chicago. When we arrived I was pulled out of the plane by a photographer who started putting boxing gloves on me. Then he posed me boxing Bobo. The picture was on the front page of the Chicago Tribune. Bobo gave me four tickets for the fight but I had no intention of going so I threw them away. I later learned that I could have sold them for a lot of money. How naive was I!

Coming off a flight late one night I dreaded the thought of catching a cab to go home. Bob, the flight engineer, a very handsome man with a wicked sense of humor, asked me if he could take me to my apartment. I was so relieved and grateful for his invitation. As we drove away, he didn't head out the usual way and soon I realized he was driving around to the back of the airport where the maintenance sheds were located. Then he parked the car. *Oh, crap! What am I going to do now?* I wasn't going to be a victim so I decided to hit the situation head on. In my perky, stewardess voice I said, "So, Bob, are you married?" Looking surprised, he answered, "Yes I am."

"Have any kids?"

"Yes, I have a seven year old daughter."

"What's her name?"

"Linda."

"Is Linda in second grade?"

Looking perplexed, he said "Yes she is. How did you know? School just started last month."

"Well, I'm a second grade school teacher. Does Linda like to read?"

"No, she is having a difficult time with reading," That's all I needed! For the next 20 minutes I held a parent-teacher conference with Bob, giving him all kinds of ideas on how to help Linda. Finally, he said, "Well, I guess I'd better get you home." He started the car and I heaved a sigh of relief. When we got to the apartment Bob said, "Thank you for your advice on helping Linda, Shirley. But I have some advice for you." Pausing, he quietly but emphatically said, "This is not the life for you. Go back to Tucson and teach second grade. The kids need you." I smiled and thanked him for the ride home.

When I got to the apartment I found all three of my roommate's home, which was very unusual. I told them of my experience and they were shocked, "Don't you know Bob's reputation? He's known as Don Juan and puts a notch in his belt for every conquest. So,

Shirley, was he good?" Nancy grinned maliciously.

"What?? I only talked to him about his daughter", I protested. They laughed and refused to believe me. *Why would my roommates not believe me?* I was furious. I went in my room thinking, *Bob is right, this really is not my kind of life.*

One day my roommate Nancy worked a flight from Chicago to Denver and turned the plane over to another stewardess, who was to take the flight onto Seattle. An attorney on board was headed to an important trial but needed to make a phone call. As he left the plane to make the call, he asked the stewardess not let the plane leave without him. It was against all the regulations to hold a plane for anything other than an emergency but this stewardess, ignoring the rules, held it up for ten minutes. Unbeknownst to all, a young man had planted a bomb in his mother-in-law's luggage after buying a $100,000 policy on her life. He had carefully programmed the timer to blow the plane up over the snow-covered Rocky Mountains, where it would be impossible for rescuers to reach until summer. Since the stewardess held the plane for ten minutes the bomb prematurely went off over Longmont, Colorado. Eye witnesses reported that the back of the plane was blown out. With rapid decompression the passengers and crew were sucked out and fell to their deaths. This was the first time it was known that a bomb was used on a commercial airline in the United States.

Two days later a jilted boyfriend entered a United Airlines plane and shot his former girlfriend and another stewardess. We lost a total of five stewardesses in those two days. I had nightmares of being blown up over some Iowa cornfield so I contacted Miss Erickson, who did the hiring for teachers in Tucson, to see if there was a position open for me to return to Tucson. She enthusiastically told me she had an opening in a second grade class for me. So I made the decision to return to Tucson to teach.

When Jim was drafted in the Army he was sent to California for Basic Training; and immediately after that, he was on his way to Infantry Officer's Candidate School at Ft. Benning, Georgia. After nine months of vigorous training he became (in his words) 'brainwashed' and loved the Army. The newly commissioned 2nd Lt.s in the OCS graduating class were divided into two parts. The casualties in Korea at that time in the Medical Service Corps and the Finance Corps were so great, the Army had to augment these two branches with Infantry officers. Jim was assigned to the Medical Service Corps and was sent to Ft. Sam Houston for the Basic Officer's course. There this spit and polish new Infantry-trained 2nd Lt. was put into classes with drafted doctors who had no idea even how to salute properly. In order to avoid classes he had already completed or had no interest in, he and four other Infantry graduates volunteered for flight training evaluation and physical. Jim passed, and was soon on his way to Ft. Sill, Oklahoma for helicopter school where he graduated as a medical evacuation pilot. He was assigned to a Medical Army Surgical Hospital (MASH) unit in Korea. In later years, as we watched the TV show MASH, Jim told me that the show was accurate in its depiction of the wacky doctors and pilots. Americans are great at finding fun even in the most devastating circumstances.

When he returned from Korea in April of 1956, he asked me for a date. Remembering his obnoxious ways, I refused at first. He persisted and when he mentioned that he had tickets for a prizefight Saturday night, I relented, remembering the missed opportunity of the Bobo Olsen prize fight. I was curious to see what was so special about a prizefight. I decided that I would go and give Jim such a bad time that he would never bother me again.

When Jim came for me on Saturday I was surprised to see a friend, Mike Deir and his date in the back seat. This did not deter me and I immediately started giving Jim a bad time and, to my surprise, Mike's date Mary Ellen chimed right it aiming her barbs at Mike. The guys were shocked and couldn't understand why we were being so mean. Pretty soon we started laughing and ended up having a wonderful time. We went out the next night and every night until Jim had to report for duty. Much to my surprise I found him to be funny, charming, kind and very intelligent. After our second date I knew I wanted to spend the rest of my life with him.

He asked me to come to Ft. Bragg, North Carolina after my school was out for the summer and I happily accepted. After two months of meeting and partying with his friends Jim came to my door one day and said, "Here, kid, I brought you something." He tossed me a small box which I quickly opened. Inside was a beautiful diamond ring. Impetuously, I immediately put it on my left hand ring finger and cried, "When are we getting married?" Jim laughed and said, "We can get married today if you want to!" That would never work. We both knew our folks would be devastated if we didn't get married in Tucson so I returned home the next week to make plans. We were married on the 28th day of September 1956.

We honeymooned in New Orleans while driving from Tucson to Ft. Bragg, North Carolina, where Jim was stationed. While driving on a narrow macadam road in Mississippi, listening to a ballgame on the radio, Jim suddenly accelerated the car and shouted for me to start looking for a motel. When I asked why he shushed me and yelled, "Just look for a motel." It was only eleven in the morning and I wondered what kind of a man I had married. During a radio commercial Jim explained he was looking for a television to watch the game. An unknown pitcher for the New York Yankees named Don Larsen was pitching a perfect game in the World Series. I don't know much about baseball but I have won many bets on what year Larsen pitched his perfect game. October 1956 is seared in my memory.

Before our wedding Jim had applied to change from the Medical Service Corps to the Transportation Corps. He felt that with aviation becoming so prominent in the Army, the Transportation Corps was the place to be. He assured me we would probably only be at Ft. Bragg a month before he would be sent to Fixed Wing School in Texas.

We arrived in Fayetteville and starting looking for a furnished apartment. The pickings were very lean and we finally had to settle on a duplex on Bragg Blvd. It was awful but we assured ourselves it would only be for a month. The duplex had a tiny front yard with a wooden fence, beyond that were the railroad tracks that went from Fayetteville to Ft. Bragg. Beyond that was the four lane highway and beyond that was a gigantic Budweiser sign that flashed on and off all night long. Twice a day a freight train loaded with coal thundered past our home, shaking everything. The living room had two walls painted fuchsia, the other two walls painted gray. There was a chartreuse couch, a red fabric chair, a brown plastic chair, a coffee table and two side tables. In the center of the room was a large, kerosene-burning stove sitting on the wooden floor. Not exactly my daydream of a perfect love nest, but it was only for a month, I thought. It ended up being six months, and during that time the

45

Suez Crisis and the Hungarian Revolution occurred. Jim's unit was on alert and I got my first taste of being married to a military man when I learned that Jim could not leave our apartment during the weekends in case he got called up. "What exactly does that mean?" I asked.

"It means the Army can send me anywhere at any time."

"Well, what do I do?"

"Babe, the Army doesn't care what you do," he said in a teasing voice. I must have had a devastated look on my face because he quickly added, "Don't worry. I don't think it will go that far. Besides, they have all kinds of troops in Europe that would be called up first."

On our one-month anniversary, Jim walked into the apartment carrying a wall-eyed Boston bull terrier pup with a big red ribbon tied around his neck. I was thrilled. When we married I had left my dog Spooky, a mix breed that looked like an animated dust mop, with my folks. Spooky barked constantly whenever he was in a car so he obviously didn't qualify as an Army dog.

We decided to name our new dependent Pug. It turned out to be a good name, because he was very pugnacious. He never saw a big dog he was afraid to attack and got into trouble on more than one occasion. The first time happened two days before we were ready to leave Bragg for aviation school in Texas. Pug got into it with the chow next door and ended up with a broken leg. The vet put a cast on him and off we went back to Tucson before reporting to Texas. We smuggled Pug into motels by wrapping our 'baby' in a pink receiving blanket.

After four months at Camp Gary, Texas, Jim was sent to Ft. Rucker, Alabama for the Advanced Aviation Course. We found a lovely place in the woods in Enterprise, and since it was September, I applied to teach in the local school district. I was hired as a homebound teacher and had four students that I visited in their homes. I was on half salary, but if four more homebound students could be found I would be on full salary. Not realizing how sensitive the racial question was in Alabama, I told the superintendent that I would be willing to go into a Negro family home to teach, if there was a need. After all, our schools in Tucson had been desegregated in 1946. The superintendent stared at me for a moment and then said in his thick southern drawl, "Ms. Starkey, you'all don't know what yo saying. You would not like going into a nigra's house and besides, haven't you read yo contract? It specifically says you will not promote the mixin' of races. Surprised at his reaction I went home and read my contract and that is exactly what it said.

One Saturday Jim suggested that we go to Ft. Rucker and play golf. I had only played golf once before but I was game for anything. It was a beautiful autumn day and there were few people playing. Jim took me to the driving range and gave me lessons. I tried hard and finally got the jest of it and was ready to tee off. I did pretty well at first but soon ran into problems getting more turf flying than the ball. Jim had moved down the fairway and I was hacking away when suddenly a ball came flying by, barely missing my right ear. Wow! That was close! I was furious and walked over, picked up the ball and put it in my pocket. I went back to my ball and continued harassing it. I few minutes later an aide-de-camp came running up demanding to know if I had seen General Sullivan's golf ball. Innocently I replied, "No." When I caught up with Jim I told him what I had done, he was not amused, "Butch, I can't take you anywhere, can I?" That was the last time he ever took me golfing.

After completion of fixed-wing school, Jim got orders to go to Ft. Riley, Kansas. Again we had a hard time finding a place to live. We finally had to settle on an upstairs apartment in a farmhouse. It was January and very wet and muddy. Twice I backed the car off the driveway into slushy mud and the farmer next door had to pull me out with his tractor. We lived there for two months, until we found a very nice house in Junction City. I applied for a teaching job and was hired as the kindergarten teacher. It was 1958 and the United States was shocked that Russia had put Sputnik into orbit. We would sit outside the Officer Club bar at the airfield with our friends from the aviation unit Jim was assigned to and watch Sputnik move across the darkened sky.

When school started in September, I had 35 students in the morning and 32 in the afternoon. Ft. Riley was one of two forts where the Army sent men in mixed marriages, as all of the southern states had laws against miscegenation. I soon learned that the kindergarten teacher's best friend is the janitor. Mr. Jenkins was a crusty old retired Army sergeant who had nothing but bad things to say about officers. I charmed him, as I needed his help with all those children. One time I made the mistake of giving out all of the puzzles at once, the result being a room full of puzzle pieces. Mr. J. gathered them up, took them home, put them together and brought them back the next day. He was especially invaluable when winter came and we had to get the children dressed in coats, hats, scarves, mittens, gloves and the always-too-small rubber overshoes.

One evening the news was full of a story about a school in Chicago that caught on fire. The kindergarten was located in the basement, just as my class was, and all the children and the teacher were trapped and subsequently died. That night I couldn't sleep. I kept trying to plan an escape route if our school caught on fire. The next morning I found that Mr. Jenkins was thinking the same thing. There was only one way in and out of the basement so we inspected the windows. The building was 100 years old but with great difficulty Mr. Jenkins was able to pry open two of the windows. We made a plan in case it was necessary and fortunately it never was. Mr. Jenkins made my difficult job bearable.

The principal thought that if you taught the children anything, including the alphabet, they would be bored in first grade. This was not how I had been trained, and when I surreptitiously started teaching the beginnings of phonics, she caught me and threatened to fire me. So I ended up babysitting. Then the Army decided to send a division from Ft. Riley to Germany and bring a division from Germany back to Ft. Riley. All year long there was a dizzying constant stream of youngsters coming and going; at the end of the year the total number of students assigned to me was 92. I couldn't remember most of them and I couldn't have taught them anything even if I had been given permission. The last two months of the school year I was happily pregnant but nauseated. It was a relief when school was over. With the big troop movement we became eligible for post housing and soon moved into a new three-bedroom apartment.

Army posts require a lot of space in order to have tank maneuvers and various war games. Consequently, most posts are in remote areas where there is little to do off-post. The people who live in the surrounding towns tend to be wary of military people. While they enjoy the money the Army brings to their town they cannot understand why anyone would want to have such a nomadic lifestyle and they make little effort to socialize with the military knowing they would be moving soon.

Military wives have a problem. They have left their families and childhood friends in order to follow the man they love. The soldier has his work and career to occupy him and a loving wife to come home to. What does a wife have? Wives can be put into two groups: those who adapt to new experiences and those who hate being in the Army. The Officer's Wives Club provides many activities from coffees, luncheons, running Thrift Shops, bridge, golfing, crafts etc. so there is little reason to feel neglected, (though some relish that) Many couples get together for dinner parties and other activities such as bowling and bridge. .

The Army is big on protocol and there is much to learn as a newlywed. I wasn't given a manual on how wives are supposed to act and I made many innocent mistakes which my patient husband forgave me.

One day Jim announced that we had been invited to the house of Captain Sherman and his wife for dinner and bridge. I was pleased and up for the challenge so Jim set me down and explained the fundamentals of bridge. We had a lovely dinner with lively conversation. Then we sat down to play bridge. It was okay at first but then I noticed the Sherman's' were making funny hand gestures. "When am I going to learn the secret hand signals?" I asked. The Sherman's were shocked and Jim was horrified. I thought he was going to hide under the table. He had known what the Sherman's were doing, which was against the rules, but as a Lt. he was not about to say anything to a Captain! At that point the party was pretty much over and we were never invited back.

The new battalion commander had taken over and Jim received orders that he and I would make a formal call on Col. and Mrs. Cahill. I had learned from Sally, my friend, that we would need to leave our calling card for the Cahill's when we left. Jim didn't tell me anything about what to expect but I was excited to be going. I chose my most flattering maternity dress, hoping to hide my seven month bulge. We were told to arrive at 3:30 on a Saturday. We were on time but as we approached the Col. Sherman's Quarters the parking area was at their back door. "Jim, I think we should go to their front door, shouldn't we?" He agreed and we took the sidewalk around to the front of the house. A hanging branch almost took Jim's hat off, there were weeds growing everywhere and the steps were littered with fallen leaves. Jim rang the doorbell and a startled Col. Cahill answered the door. "I didn't expect you to come this way but come right in, Lt."

"Col. Cahill, may I present my wife, Shirley."

"It's nice to meet you, Shirley and this is Mrs. Cahill." We were ushered into the living room and I was in awe. A large, red Oriental carpet covered the floor, the beige couch had throw pillows in rich, vibrant hues and there were various items of copper and brass around the room. I had never been in such an interesting room. "Mrs. Cahill, where did you get such wonderful things?"

"We just came back from a tour in Turkey," she said. I wanted to know all about Turkey, where they lived, and what it was like. At one point Col. Cahill asked me when our baby was due. I answered, "In two more months," and proceeded to ask something else about Turkey.

Suddenly, Jim looked at his watch and jumped up, "Oh, it's time for us to go, Col. Thank you for having us." He grabbed my arm and pushed me toward the back door. I saw where there was a silver tray with calling cards on it. I turned to tell Jim we needed to leave our card when he jabbed me in the back with his finger and hissed, "Keep walking." When we got out to our car he was furious. "Damn it, Shirley," he yelled. "Are you trying to get me kicked out of the Army?"

"Why, what did I do? Why did you make us leave so soon?"

"Because we are only allowed fifteen minutes for the visit and we were there for Col Cahill to learn more about me and my family and all you wanted to talk about was Turkey. I've never been so mortified in my life."

I yelled right back, "You never told me anything about what was expected of me. I don't know anything about your damn Army," I started sobbing.

Jim took several deep breaths and calmly said, "You're right, Butch. I should have explained to you. We were only supposed to be there for fifteen minutes because everyone in the battalion visits the Cahill's and each of us received the exact time we were to be there and when to leave. I'm sorry I didn't explain it to you. Let's go home and forget about it." He started the car.

A week later I was at the Officer's Club when I saw Col. Cahill walking toward me. *Oh good. I can apologize to him*, I thought. As he glanced up and saw me I greeted him with a big smile and started to say something when suddenly he wheeled around and walked rapidly into the Men's room.

Our baby's due date was Thanksgiving, and two weeks prior to that I was playing bridge at a friend's house when we heard screaming fire trucks rushing past the house. Running outside, we learned that the artillery exercises had set fire to the dry grass and the wind was whipping the blaze toward our housing. Our quarters were the last on the block where the fire trucks were headed. My friend Rita drove me down to our quarters and there I saw the fire about two blocks away headed straight toward us. I ran clumsily into the house to get Pug and hurried out with him in my arms without locking our door. Pug immediately saw our neighbor's German shepherd and Great Dane. Springing from my arms, he proceeded to start biting one dog's heels, then the other. Each dog thought the other one was doing it, as Pug was so small they hardly noticed him. The big dogs started fighting each other while Pug nipped at them. Frantic, without any thought, I plunged into the melee, grabbed Pug and got in the car. As we were driving away I noticed men, including the commanding general, manning shovels digging a trench to stop the fire. Rabbits ran past with their backs on fire. Smoke was everywhere; it was a disaster and I thought our place would be burned up. We went back to Rita's house and stayed until we saw fire trucks leaving. Miraculously, the wind had shifted just as the fire reached our clothesline, so the flames had moved away from the houses, crossed the highway and ran along behind the schoolhouse, where it was put out. I returned home and walked into our quarters to find sooty fingerprints all over our cupboards and many empty water glasses on the counter. I was pleased that the guys fighting the fire had been able to quench their thirst.

James Edward Starkey, Jr. made his entrance on 1 December 1959. He was very long, with skinny arms and legs plus big feet and hands. His hair was dark like his dads; his green eyes were like mine. He weighed 8 lbs. 6 oz. This was amazing, as the Army doctors had only allowed me to gain 20 pounds. After three days in the hospital we brought him home. Jim carried him into the house, only to discover he had dirtied his diaper. We placed him on the counter in the kitchen and tried to deal with the situation. Before we knew it there was "stuff" everywhere and Jimbo had peed in his father's face. I was getting upset and Jim ordered me to leave the room. I went into the living room and lay down on the couch. Soon Jim had everything under control and brought my sweet-smelling baby to me. He was very concerned about Jimbo's left ear, which stuck straight out from his head. He didn't believe the pediatrician's explanation that this was caused by the way Jimbo had been lying in my womb and that it would flatten out naturally. He helped it along by taping the ear to Jimbo's head with Scotch tape! He was a very caring father.

When we arrived at Ft. Riley, Jim started taking classes at night to get his Bachelor's degree. A college degree was important for an officer's promotion. He finally had enough credits for the Army to send him to Omaha on Operation Bootstrap when Jimbo was eight months old. Once more we were looking for housing. No one wanted to rent to "Bootstrapers," as they were only there for six months. Finally, we found a trailer owned by a divinity student who would rent it to us. There was a fence around the yard for Pug. It was really small, but it would work fine for six months. The owner of the trailer park posted a sign that said, "All Dogs Must Be Kept on a Leash". Everyone obeyed the rule except the owner. He let his Doberman run wild. Everyday the Doberman would come by our trailer and naturally, Pug tried to attack him through the fence. A loud barking, growling match would ensue until I brought Pug into the trailer.

One golden autumn afternoon I decided to take Jimbo out in the stroller. I put the leash on Pug so he could go with us. We had proceeded past three trailers when, from my peripheral vision, I saw a black flash. I turned in time to see the Doberman lunge at Pug. I looked up, saw a lady watching and I shoved the stroller toward her yelling, "Take care of my baby, please." I pulled the leash up behind me as high as I could to get between the Doberman and Pug. I started kicking at the Doberman. I was wearing old, sturdy saddle oxfords, and I was getting in some pretty good kicks when I noticed the park's owner watching, doing nothing. Furious, I kicked the Doberman square in the side of his head and he backed off whimpering. That was when the owner called him off. I turned to look at Pug, whom I had practically choked to death, as his feet had barely been able to touch the ground. The Doberman had cut him in his left eye and it was dangling out. I picked him up and rushed across the highway where there was a veterinarian's clinic, and left him there. I retrieved Jimbo and returned home in a state of panic. When Jim came home, he took one look at me and knew something was wrong. As he stared at me, I told him what happened. Without a word he raced over to the owner's trailer and started yelling. The owner's name was Farhart and Jim managed to mispronounce it several times during the shouting match. The owner told Jim we had to move. Jim told him he couldn't make us move, as we didn't rent from him. This shouting match went on for half an hour until Jim threatened to smash Farhart's face. Farhart finally backed down and apologized for his dog, saying he would pay the vet's bill. When Jim came home we decided Farhart might make the divinity student move his trailer, which would be a real hardship on him, so we decided to find another place to live.

We found an apartment across the street from Mutual of Omaha's headquarters, met the very pleasant owner and his wife and moved in. They hadn't asked us and we didn't mention that we had a dog. One day I came home to find a torn paper on the floor under the kitchen table. It was from our landlord. Apparently, he had come by to check on his property and Pug had barked at him. He wrote a note stating that we couldn't have a dog, slipped it under the door where Pug proceeded to play with it. What to do now?

Jim called his dad and Grandpa agreed to keep Pug until Jim was finished with school. When we went to Tucson after Jim's graduation, his dad gave us a choice…we could have Jimbo or we could have Pug, but not both. Now Spookie was my dad's dog and Pug was Jim's dad's dog.

Soon after returning to Ft. Riley, Jim received orders for the Advanced Officer's School at Ft. Eustis, Virginia. And from there we moved to Iran.

Chapter 3

Supreme Court bans official prayers in school, Rev. Martin Luther King jailed in Georgia for leading protests, South Viet Nam Communists down American helicopter, killing five soldiers, satellite sends first worldwide TV show.

June 1962

Tehran, Iran

A loud banging on the hotel door startled me out of a sound sleep. Both Jimbo and I jumped out of bed.

In my toughest voice I asked, "Who's there?"

Jim laughingly replied, "Who were you expecting? Let me in. Something is blocking the door."

Jimbo and I had pushed the big chair in front of the door for extra protection during the night, and we immediately shoved it to one side to let Jim in. We both attacked him: Jimbo grabbing his leg while I clung to his chest, hugging him as hard as I could.

"Oh, Jim, last night was horrible. I didn't know how to reach anyone. No one called to see if they could help. Jimbo and I went downstairs to the restaurant, but didn't know what to order that would be safe so we ended up with soup and hot tea…then we ate crackers and peanut butter in our room. I've never been so scared in my life." The words came gushing out.

He looked into my eyes. "Babe, it's all right. I have a Jeep and our driver is outside. We're moving today to a better hotel. Tomorrow Mohorram, an Iranian holiday starts, so I'll be off for three days. Things will get better, don't you worry. But first, get dressed and we'll go to the Embassy for breakfast."

Jim dressed Jimbo while I got ready. Downstairs we met Karim, our assigned driver. He was short and stocky with coal-black eyes and a huge, bushy moustache that wiggled when he smiled. His khaki uniform was neat, but his scruffy, unpolished shoes had the backs broken down to allow him to wear them like bedroom slippers.

Introductions were made and, as usual, Jimbo received the most attention from Kerim. It was obvious that children, especially boys, were highly prized in Iran. Jimbo and I climbed into the back of the Jeep and Jim sat in the front. Jim explained that we would be issued a sedan as soon as one became available. In the briefing Jim had attended the first day, he had been told to keep his driving to a minimum and only drive when the driver was not working on Friday and Sunday, our official days off. I would never be allowed to drive, as Iranian jails did not separate females from males and in any accident an American was automatically at fault. It was not uncommon for Americans, after an accident, to spend the night in jail until the Embassy could gain their release. The American Government had not secured from the Government of Iran a Status of Forces Agreement, which basically gave the American military a form of diplomatic immunity.

Kerim, unlike Mohammad, eased the jeep into traffic and made an orderly u-turn to get us to the side entrance of the Embassy. Inside the cafeteria, while waiting for our breakfast, I amused Jim with the account of our trials the previous day. While it hadn't been so funny at the time, I had to laugh on retelling it.

After our breakfast the world seemed a lot brighter. We looked at everything in the co-op, bought more food items and prepared to move to the Vanak Hotel. While we were having breakfast Jim had sent Karim to the water station to get a five-gallon jerry can full of potable water for us to take to the hotel. We returned to the American

Hotel to pack our suitcases. The Jeep was too small to carry all of them, but we took what we could, and Jim made arrangements to return later in the day to retrieve the rest.

We drove west on Takht-e-Jamshid Street and then north on Pahlavi Avenue. Poplar and locust trees lined the sidewalks, forming a thick canopy over the street. The sidewalks were crowded with women carrying baskets and haggling with the food vendors in preparation for the coming holiday. Men in black suits were standing in clusters, smoking and listening to a radio; a small boy was chasing a stray dog, and a shoeless man was leading a donkey with panniers filled with vegetables. The donkey was festooned with turquoise beads between his ears and around his neck. Crowds of people were wandering back and forth into the street ignoring the traffic. A man, leading a gaggle of geese, marched down the middle of the street as if he owned it. Off to one side a peasant rode a huge camel, the bells around the camel's neck adding to the hubbub. Masses of cars, our Jeep included, were weaving at a snail's pace through the hodgepodge.

A sheet of black *chadors* obscured the front of the bakery. It looked like a convention of crows as servants waited for the first ironing board-shaped loaves of *nune*, the staple of the Iranian diet. This is the delicious bread that Colleen had mentioned. The unleavened dough is shaped on elongated wooden boards with six-foot handles; the baker shoves the board into the oven and, with a jerk, flips it over dropping the dough onto red-hot pebbles, where it quickly bakes to a golden brown marked with the indention's of the pebbles. The baker announces to the waiting crowd that the bread is ready for sale by hanging a loaf on the long nail protruding from the side of his shop.

We passed a mosque draped in black bunting, huge signs in Arabic hanging across the entrance. Crowds of people in black mourning clothes milled about. A loudspeaker blared strange discordant music occasionally interrupted by a male speaking in Farsi. As we continued north for several miles, the crowds and traffic thinned out. Kerim turned west onto a dirt road. In front of us the land became a drab ochre expanse. At a distance we saw a lone white building surrounded by a high wall and large green trees.

Kerim stopped the Jeep at the guardhouse, speaking to the

uniformed guard who opened the gate. The entrance to the Vanak Hotel was elegant, with massive concrete griffins guarding the marble stairs. Lush tropical plants marched up the steps, dripping red flowers like blood over the sides. The doorman, dressed in a flashy gold and scarlet uniform opened the door with a flourish and said, "*Befarmaid*" (welcome). While Jim was negotiating the price with the desk clerk, Jimbo and I wandered around the lobby admiring the marble floors covered in Persian carpets of every hue. Huge marble urns were filled with palm trees, and Christmas tree lights were festooned around the columns holding up the roof and balconies. I spied two elevators. It was a marked change from the American Hotel we had just vacated.

Our large room on the second floor was bright and cheerful with a view to the north of the Alborz Mountains. It had a king-sized and a single bed, a chest of drawers, a dressing table and two overstuffed chairs flanking a coffee table. The soft pastels of the décor were a welcome change. Only a small amount of red appeared on the carpet. We even had a large closet complete with clothes hangers. French doors opened onto a balcony that contained a table and chairs for four people. The balcony overlooked a verdant expanse surrounding an Olympic-sized swimming pool with trees and flowers bordering the walls and walkways.

Kerim and a porter brought our belongings from the jeep and stored them in the large closet. "We'll go back to the hotel and get the rest of the things, Babe. You and Jimbo better get some rest," said Jim, giving Jimbo a pat on his head. After they left I read Jimbo several stories, until we both collapsed on the big bed and fell asleep.

When Jim returned he told me the deskman at the American Hotel wanted extra money, as he had guarded our belongings. Kerim explained to Jim that *bakhshesh* (a tip) is expected in Iran, whether earned or not. This was our first experience with baksheesh, but it would not be the last.

Jim dismissed Kerim for his holiday telling him to come at 6:30 in the morning on Saturday. While Jimbo slept on, Jim and I sat on the balcony relaxing for the first time in weeks. We watched families frolicking in the pool while the piped music played a haunting tune. There were some gardeners toiling away, some cutting the grass with push mowers and others following, cleaning the debris. These men had large, short-handled, wide-angled brooms that forced the user to bend over to sweep the cuttings into a dustpan. The scene was tranquil. "Just think, Jim," I said, breaking the silence, "here we are in exotic Persia. If we had a lamp we could rub it and a genie would get us our every wish."

"If you had a wish what would it be?"

"That our orders are suddenly changed to Europe," I answered laughing.

"Don't be silly, this is the chance of a lifetime. We can always go to Europe, but who do you know who has ever been to Iran?"

"That's true and I'm determined I'm going to enjoy living here if it kills me," I replied.

We sat in silence listening to the muted cries of the children in the pool, to the strange eastern music, smelling the freshly cut grass and thinking life was good.

Suddenly the music changed and blasting over the microphone came the sounds of Chubby Checkers and the Twist. In our thoughts, we were immediately swept back to Ft. Eustis, and dancing wildly while some of our friends had a snowball fight right in our living room!

New Year's Eve on an Army base is always fun. The ball of the season takes place at the Officer's Club with the men handsome and gallant in their dress blue uniforms and the ladies outdoing each other in glamorous gowns. The next day, New Year's Day, the required call on the commanding general takes place again at the Officer's Club. Many arrived sporting bloodshot eyes and massive headaches. Jim and I decided to host a party at our quarters for our close friends on New Year's Day evening. Our friends thought we had lost our minds.

"Are you sure you want to do this after the party last night?" our friends asked.

"Yes, we intend to do just that. You will come, won't you?" we asked. Everyone said they would, so the party was on. Jim mixed up an innocent sounding concoction called Bride's Bowl Punch. It contained pineapple juice, lemon juice, soda, rum and a liqueur. It tasted very refreshing.

The party started and Newt Cox brought the latest dance craze record, the Twist. We ate and danced. We got thirsty and drank. The more we danced, the thirstier we got and the more we chugged the punch.

Jim was in the kitchen mixing more punch when Dick Hartert came in and leaned on the refrigerator and said, "This punch is so-o-oo good and I am not even drunk." As he said those words he quietly slid down the refrigerator and passed out.

It started snowing outside and we opened the front door to cool off. The next thing we knew, snowballs were flying as Bob Edwards and Ted Benson attacked each other. It was the wildest party I've ever been to and the most fun! The next day when I was cleaning up, I found an extra shoe. The good news was that we all lived within walking distance of each other, so no one had to drive home.

Now, as Chubby Checkers continued to blare out over the swimming pool, half way around the world, Jim made the comment, "It's a small world after all."

We had a late dinner, as is the Persian custom, in the ornate dining room of the Vanak. Contrary to the popular belief that alcohol is verboten in Muslim countries, we were able to order any liqueur, mixed drink or wine we desired. Our meal started off with crème de *leemu* soup. I could have made a whole meal of the soup. This was followed by *chelo kebab*, the national dish of Iran, and broiled tomatoes. The long-grained rice grown north of the Alborz Mountains in the tropical Caspian area has a distinct nut-like flavor. Raw rice is called *berenj*. When it is cooked it is called *chelo*. The kebab is ground lamb, patted around flat kebab swords and cooked over a charcoal fire. It is served with a mound of rice that has an indention into which a raw egg yolk is placed. The rice is sprinkled with sumac, a red spice with a sour flavor. The diner immediately covers the egg with the rice causing it to cook quickly. The mixture of flavors and textures is manna from heaven. All three of us ate with great relish. "If this is an example of Iranian cooking," I said, "we're going to love it here."

After bathing Jimbo, reading him a story and putting him to bed, we again sat on our balcony enjoying the cool evening. From a distance we heard strange sounds, crying and moaning broken by the singsong call of the *muezzin*. The celebration of Moharram was beginning.

Moharram is extremely sacred to the Shi'ite branch of Islam practiced by most Iranians. It commemorates the martyrdom of Hussein, the grandson of the prophet Mohammed. In 680 A.D. after the murder of his father Ali, Hussein set out to claim the title of caliph. Cavalry led by the son of the governor of Syria massacred him and his party. The shock of this killing caused the Shi'ites to break away from the mainstream Sunnis. During the two days of mourning called Ashura, devote Shi'ite Moslems march through the streets beating themselves in self-flagellation. The shouting men whip their bare backs with a mass of dog chains attached to a wooden handle. The women follow behind beating their breasts with their fists and crying to Allah. This mass outpouring of grief and emotion lasts for hours.

As the evening wore on, the babel became louder and louder. Finally, having enough of the bedlam, we went inside, shut the doors to the balcony and fell asleep to the distant moans and cries.

The American Embassy warned Americans to avoid all streets south of the Embassy, as that is where the most fervent processions marched. So the next morning we got into the Jeep and drove north on Pahlavi Road and over to Shemiran Road to the American Officer's Club for breakfast. The streets were deserted, as the Iranians were sleeping off the excitement of the night before. I sat in the front with Jimbo on my lap, both of us gripping tightly to the bar in front of us. The Jeep lacked a door so we were completely exposed. We turned off *Shemiran* to *Kuchee Shahrzad* and came to a high wall surrounding a city block. The wrought iron gates were wide open and we drove through a tree-covered park to the two-storied mansion in the center of the compound. Several cars were parked next to the building. We entered the double doors and were faced with stairs that led up to the alcove and dining room. A skinny, young man asked in broken English for our name. Jim gave his rank and name and the young man disappeared through the doorway behind the desk. A few minutes later a huge man with a shiny baldhead and big grin greeted us in an Italian accent.

"Sir," he said, extending his hand. "I am Mike. I am the Club's director, and who is this very beautiful young lady and handsome gentleman with you?"

Jim made the introductions and said, "We just arrived in country and we're very hungry for breakfast."

Mike put out an enormous paw that completely covered my hand and shook it vigorously, then turned to Jimbo and did the same. "Come, come my little man. We will get you some delicious food."

We followed the two of them to a table by the window and soon were facing plates full of ham, eggs and fried potatoes with toast and juice on the side. We had all the coffee we could drink, and Jimbo had a cup of hot chocolate. From our window seat we could see a swimming pool, so after eating we took a tour of the compound. The pool was enormous, even larger than the one at the Vanak. Beside the pool was a snack bar and dozens of tables with umbrellas sticking out of the centers. Families were lounging around the pool. Amid the laughing and splashing we heard cries of "Marco Polo." There was a grassy area that had swingsets and other paraphernalia for the children. One portion was fenced off for little tykes, allowing them to play safely away from the pool. There were trikes, large balls, trucks, doll carriages and a playhouse. Several preschool-aged children were busy making use of all the equipment.

We walked around the pool to the other side and discovered a softball field and volleyball court. There was certainly a lot to entertain all ages. We went back to the pool and let Jimbo play in the contained area while we sat in the shade, watching the action. We were very sorry we had not brought our bathing suits. A couple arrived with two pretty little girls, one dark haired and the other with flaming red hair, both around the same age as Jimbo. The little girls got into the baby pool while the parents settled into the chairs next to us. Never missing a chance to start a conversation, I said, "Your daughters are so pretty!"

"Why, thank you", answered the mother. We promptly introduced ourselves and we learned that Norman Liebshultz was the pediatrician assigned to the dispensary. The command was not large enough to warrant a full military hospital, but the dispensary had a flight surgeon/obstetrician, a pediatrician and several general practitioners, as well as a veterinarian. Any place where the Army sends troops a veterinarian is assigned for food testing.

Norman was a compact man about 5 Ft. 8 inches tall with dark, receding hair and brown eyes. His petite wife Barbara with large, expressive brown eyes was as pretty as she was talkative.

We soon fell into an extended conversation, and I learned that they had arrived in country three weeks before us and were still househunting. After describing some of the houses they had seen, she sardonically said, "We're thinking of building."

Barbara told me about a play school that she had put the girls in so that she could concentrate on finding a place to live. Mrs. Mathews, the wife of the director of USAID, (the United States Agency for aid to Iran), ran the school. I gratefully wrote down directions to the school.

The little girls came out of the baby pool shivering. Barbara dried them off and took them over to the play area. I walked over with her and we introduced the redhead, Sherry, and the dark-haired Lisa to Jimbo. He immediately took Sherry's hand and led her to the sandbox. He was obviously smitten.

We visited with the Liebshultz for the rest of the morning, had a sandwich and then drove back to our hotel. There was a message waiting for Jim from Don Hudson inviting us to a party that night, to be attended by the men and wives of the Aviation Section.

The heat was taxing and we all took advantage of a nap. We awakened late in the afternoon, took showers and dressed for the evening.

As we were turning onto to Palavi Road, the excitement began. Jim was driving and the traffic was thick with cars coming in every direction. Where there were supposed to be two lanes of traffic there would be four cars fighting for the space. One car stuffed full of men in black suits and women in black *chadors* on our right suddenly decided to make a left-hand turn right in front of us. Fortunately the brakes worked and we narrowly missed a bad accident. Jim loved the challenge, while I was terrified. Since there was no door on the Jeep, it seemed as if all the cars would end up in my lap. I held onto Jimbo and the bar in the front of the Jeep. I was concerned that I would telegraph my fears to the little guy, but I need not have worried. He was as thrilled at the madness as his father. After thirty minutes of my heart in my throat, we made it safely to the Hudson's house.

The gardener opened the gate and showed us where to park. We entered the well-lit foyer and were greeted by Don, who promptly made introductions. Colleen came out of the kitchen and invited Jimbo to go into Kyle's room where he and Mary Ann were watching reruns of "Have Gun Will Travel" on the American Television. I followed them into the bedroom to make sure Jimbo would be okay. I did not have to worry; he settled right down, staring at the TV.

Upon meeting the other wives, I quickly got the feeling that I was an intruder. One of the wives was obviously irritated that we had already been assigned a car and driver. "We had to wait a week before we got any transportation," she stated. Joan Blake seemed friendly, but from the others I sensed resentment, almost as if it were my fault that I was there and not the very popular Brenda Pierce. Earlier Jim had stated unequivocally that Pierce was at fault. "It was pilot error. Anyone who takes a plane over a 10,000 foot mountain without oxygen is an idiot. It's one of the first lessons you learn in flight school."

Jack Blake's wife Joan didn't smile easily and had a no-nonsense look about her, which made sense after she told me she was a nurse. She and Jack had been married for ten years and had no children. At great expense, they had brought their two dogs, a Labrador retriever and a Great Dane over to Iran. From her conversation it was obvious that these canines were doted upon. She was very cordial and invited us to dinner the next night.

The rest of the men and wives of the Aviation Section became a blur to me. I felt very uncomfortable as the women, with the exception of Joan, made no attempt to include me in their conversations. I was relieved when dinner was announced.

Colleen had a bountiful buffet for us, with a combination of American and Persian food prepared with the help of Zara. We had sliced ham, rice, *khoreshe holu* (a sauce made with chicken and peaches to be put on the rice), an enormous green salad, sliced tomatoes and chocolate cake. I made a plate for Jimbo and took it into the bedroom for him. The dinner was not served until well after eight, and at nine o'clock we said our goodbyes, using our sleepy son as our excuse. Jack gave Jim the directions to his house and asked us to come at six o'clock the next evening.

The next day was Ashura, the most important day of Mohorram. The poorer sections of Tehran were immersed in parades of mourning throngs beating themselves. We again went to the Officer's Club for breakfast. Afterwards, since we had been told it was safe to do so, we took the Jeep north to see the sights. We happened on a large park where the less devout Muslims and non-Muslims were picnicking. Everywhere we saw Persian carpets casually thrown on the ground to be used as ground cloths. Men were sitting in groups, drinking tea and arguing passionately. Some of the women were covered in *chadors* and some were dressed in stylish western outfits but all were in separate groups from the men, tending to babies and chattering happily. Children of every size were kicking balls and chasing each other. Teenage boys had a rollicking soccer game going. Everyone was enjoying a relaxing holiday.

Vendors were selling slices of watermelon, cantaloupe and honeydew melons from pushcarts. A portable grill was set up for roasting kebabs and vegetables. A large metal box on wheels had dry ice in the bottom to keep the yogurt cold. Nearby a young man was selling nune from the back of his bicycle. He had draped dozens of the thin, elongated breads over the back fender; the bottom one had brown mud splattered on it.

We walked all over the park soaking in the sights and smells. Jimbo was finally getting a chance to run. "Run to that tree and back to Daddy," I told him. He obeyed gleefully, running as hard as he could, touching the tree and heading back to his dad. Jim would grab him, lift him high in the air and swing him around. His squeals of delight brought smiles from the Iranian families. We spent an hour enjoying the park and then headed back to the Vanak for naptime.

That evening we drove to Blakes' house. It was in the northern most section of Tehran, in an area called Tajrish. Jack had given Jim a map to their house. It was not the ordinary map with street names and addresses but had, instead, notations such as, "turn right at green lamp post" or "take the left road at the fork where there is large tree." Sometimes the streets were marked only in *Farsi,* sometimes not at all. With me acting as map-reader, we wended our way up a poorly constructed dirt road to a spot where four newly built houses stood. The Blakes lived in the farthest one. We stopped at a wall with double metal gates and Jim got out to ring the bell. It took several minutes for Jack to open the gate. "Bring the Jeep inside or you're libel to not have any tires left," he ordered. He opened both sides of the gate, and we drove in and parked next to Blakes' black Chevy. A beautiful black Labrador retriever and a brown Great Dane immediately surrounded us. Jimbo whooped with delight and allowed Jack to lift him from my lap so he could greet the dogs. The Lab had a ball in his mouth and dropped it at Jimbo's feet. Right away we had a ball game.

Blakes' house was located at the northern end of the compound, and had a huge garden and swimming pool in front. The freshly cut grass and multi-colored flowers were a restful change from the dusty road we had just traveled. We proceeded along the pathway to the two-dozen steps that led up to the porch. The house was faced in white marble with glassed doors all the way across the front. As we got to the porch, we turned to check on Jimbo and noticed the panoramic view of Tehran. Shades of rose, magenta, blues and purples cast a tranquil veil on the city. It was dusk and only a few lights were on, and in the distance the desert stretched south for miles. Jack called the dogs, making it easier for Jim to corral Jimbo. Joan came out to greet us and we entered their home.

The interior was spacious and Joan had done an excellent job of decorating. Their Danish modern furniture looked exactly right with the white marble floors and colorful throw rugs. The living room had large rubber plants next to a bookcase full of the current bestsellers. On the floor was a red, orange and dark blue carpet in geometric designs. Joan informed me it was a Baluchi carpet, made by the nomadic tribes that lived in southern Iran. She explained that they had not yet decided to keep the carpet, but Reza, a carpet dealer had left it for them to get used to it. "You mean they leave carpets without you paying for them?"

Jack joined in, "Yes, they'll do that for Americans, but not for any other nationality. Not for French, Danish, Germans and especially not for the English. They say that only the Americans are so honest they would never steal."

"Wow, that is nice," I exclaimed.

"You're right, it is nice. The Holbrooks have been here a year and they said during the winter they had carpets all over the floors. It really helped on these cold marble floors. The Iranians say the carpets only get more beautiful the more they are walked on."

"Would you like to see the rest of the house?" Joan asked.

"I would love to."

She led me past the dining room into the kitchen. It looked like any American kitchen. The house was new and the Iranian had tried to copy American homes as much as possible. The Blakes had their own appliances, but were pleased to find a house with built in cupboards, as well as closets, which was unusual for Iran.

There was a large room next to an American bathroom. The Blakes used this room for a storage room. At the back of the house was a very small room and a Persian bathroom. The Persian toilet was a hole in the floor surrounded by ceramic with indentions on either side. To use, one planted ones feet on either side of the hole and squatted. There was no toilet paper; instead a water jug was placed on the right. Joan explained that the user poured the water from the jug with the right hand and wiped with the left hand. This is why you never touched an Iranian's left hand. High up and attached to the wall was an oblong ceramic bowl and a hidden pipe coming down to the floor. A chain was attached to the bowl and, when pulled, water flushed into the hole.

She led me up the curved staircase to the second floor landing. Three bedrooms and a western-style bath completed the house.

"This house is so enormous. How do you keep it so clean?" I asked.

"We have a houseboy who is not too good, but I'm training him," she answered.

We joined the men in the living room, where Jack had been telling Jim about their experiences shopping for housing. They had arrived in February and spent two months in the hotel before finding this house. The landlord had asked an exorbitant price at first, but after a month of negotiation came down to a reasonable amount. "You have to be patient and persistent. Don't expect anything to be easy," were their words of caution.

Jack grilled steaks and I helped Joan put the rest of the meal on the table. We had a most enjoyable evening. Since the next day was a workday, we did not linger long after eating. On the way to the Vanak, Jim remarked, "There are so many nice things about living here and so many weird things. We're going to have to keep our sense of humor or we're going to go nuts."

Kerim arrived right on time the next morning to take Jim to

Ghalamorghi. He returned at 9:00 driving a black 1958 Chevrolet that had been assigned to Jim. Jimbo was so disappointed that we didn't have the Jeep any longer, but I was pleased. Kerim took us to the Officer's Club for breakfast. I discovered his English was not as good as I originally thought, and I constantly had to check my dictionary for the *Farsi* word that I needed. Strangely, my high school Spanish kept getting in the way. Half the time I was speaking in English to him and the other half in Spanish. I'm sure I confused him.

Mike greeted us as we entered the dining room. "Ah, my friend Jeembo! Come, come I will bring you a good breakfast." When we were seated I ordered scrambled eggs. "No, no eggs, Mama" Jimbo exclaimed.

"What" Mike said in mock horror, "you no like eggs? Then, my little man, I will bring you a special Italian breakfast!" and he disappeared into the kitchen. We drank our orange juice while waiting, and soon Mike appeared carrying a steaming plate. With a flourish, he placed it in front of Jimbo. It was spaghetti covered in freshly ground Parmesan cheese and melted butter. With a smile Jimbo attacked his breakfast, cleaning up the plate. For the next five weeks before we moved into our house Jimbo wanted Mike's Special for breakfast.

As we got into the car Kerim announced, "You see Tehran."

"Yes," I answered, absentmindedly, thinking he was merely practicing his English.

He started the car and we headed down Shemiran. Instead of cutting over to Palavi Road, Kerim continued going south. In English I cried out, "Kerim, where are we going?" He merely grinned. I pulled out the dictionary. Where, where, where, w x y z. I frantically leafed through the book...aha, *kojas*. Go, go, go, *raftan*. "Kerim, *raftan kojas?*"

Laughing, obviously pleased with my *Farsi*, he said, "You see Tehran, Madame." I leaned back and decided we didn't have anything better to do, so we would see Tehran.

We proceeded south, going past the American Embassy. The further we got the worse the traffic became. We soon came to a traffic circle and in the center was the gigantic statue of a man in a flowing coat and turban that we had seen coming in from the airport. "Ferdowsi," Kerim announced, nodding to the statue.

"Remember, Jimbo. That's the statue we saw when we came from the airport." I said. Ferdowsi Street going south from the circle was lined on both sides with carpet shops. Outside each shop two or three carpets were hanging from pegs in the wall. The street was a riot of reds, blues, saffrons, blacks, greens and beiges. Some designs were geometric, some were floral. Merchants in turbans were calling out to potential shoppers. The hurrying women wore chadors, the covering of devout Muslims. Most were in white *chadors* for the summer, but some wore the heavy black *chadors* required for mourning widows.

We proceeded further south, the traffic getting more clogged. We began to encounter many carts pulled by donkeys, a necklace of blue beads draped between their ears, panniers of brightly colored embroidery hung from their backs. A three-wheeled motorcycle went past with a cart attached to the back wheels filled with watermelons. On the side of the street near the jubes we saw scraggly looking, emaciated dogs. A merchant came out of his shop waving a rag to chase the dogs away. Children were playing with a bright pink plastic ball. We passed an outdoor teashop with men lounging around a table drinking from the small glasses. On the counter behind them sat a gleaming brass samovar. Next came a hardware store with giant tin tubs stacked against the wall. Everywhere signs and advertisements were in Farsi. It was stifling hot. Loud music blared, mixed with excited voices. Kerim had to stop frequently to let pedestrians wander across in front of our car. I didn't know what Kerim had in mind and I started to get very wary. Were we being kidnapped?

Just then he turned down a divided, tree-lined street and suddenly all was quiet and cool. We traveled for a couple of blocks and came upon several Iranian soldiers carrying rifles. They were dressed in cobalt blue uniforms trimmed in gold braid, with epaulets on their shoulders. They reminded me of the ushers in the glitzy Los Angeles movie theater I went to with my grandmother when I was twelve years old. As we approached them, one soldier raised his hand for Kerim to stop. Much Farsi ensued and the soldier looked sternly at Jimbo and me. Kerim continued to talk and all at once the soldier indicated that we could proceed. The soldier saluted; Kerim and Jimbo both returned the salute. We paused briefly at a wrought iron gate attached to two large pillars. On top of each pillar sat a golden lion bearing a crown decorated in colored stones. A golden arch soared from each pillar over the golden gate. Through the gate we could see a long road and parts of a huge mansion at the end, enormous trees blocking our view. More soldiers stood at attention. Kerim announced, "Madame, *manzalee Shah-en-Shah*" and we drove off. I fumbled through the dictionary until I came to the word *manzel*. It means house. Then I realized he was showing me the Shah's Gulistan Palace.

We drove further south past more mansions and then onto a small alley. At the end was a modest two-story house with a large garden. Kerim stopped and got out to open the door for me. "Enjas, Madame," he said, indicating I was to get out.

"What are we doing here?" I asked in Spanish.

"Come, come" he insisted. I reluctantly got out and, holding Jimbo's hand, followed him through the gate to the front door. He rang the bell and a pleasant lady answered, beaming when she saw Kerim, then gave him a hug. Kerim spoke rapidly to her and she turned; putting her hands on each side of my face, she kissed the air next to my ears. Then she turned her attentions to Jimbo, fussing and talking to him in gentle, singsong voice. She pulled us into her house, jabbering constantly to Kerim, and led the way to a red velvet couch. We sat down, not knowing what else to do. She disappeared into another room. I looked anxiously at Kerim and he beamed at me, spouting something in Farsi. He showed me a picture of the lady with Kerim and many other people, so I deduced that she was his sister. Her name was Ashra. Soon she returned with drinks filled with ice. She offered them to us, but we had been told to never drink from a glass with ice, as the water was polluted. I politely refused. She insisted and I refused again. Still she insisted, but I was adamant. She turned to Kerim and spoke harshly. He answered, shrugging his shoulders. I could tell I had offended both of them but I didn't know what else to do. I had left the dictionary in the car. After several moments of uncomfortable silence, I turned to Kerim and said, "Hotel. Jimbo asleep." I wanted to let him know that Jimbo needed his nap. He understood and we all got up. I thanked Ashra for her hospitality as graciously as I could. I felt awful. I could see in her eyes that she was both hurt and angry. I asked Kerim how to say goodbye and he told me "*Khodah fez.*" I turned to Ashra and repeated "*Khodah fez,* Ashra," and she gave me a weak smile.

As we left Jimbo said, "Mama, I wanted some soda." I explained to him that we needed to be very careful what we drank. He was not happy, Kerim was not happy and I was miserable. I had obviously insulted her hospitality. I vowed to learn Farsi as soon as I could.

The next Monday after breakfast I showed Kerim the map to the nursery school Barbara Liebshultz had mentioned. We arrived at a huge compound filled with children playing on swings, slides, teeter-totters, tricycles, playhouses, and all kinds of toys. It was a happy, noisy crowd with children speaking in English, Farsi, some French and German. I found the owner, Carol Mathews, giving instructions to one of the other teachers. She was a large-boned, very tall lady with a regal bearing, a narrow face, long slender nose and thin lips. She had limp brown hair worn pulled back in a ponytail and would have been considered unattractive except for her intelligent, electric blue eyes. When I introduced myself she gave me a sparkling smile that lit up her whole face. I liked her immediately. Her husband was the head of the US Aid office in Iran. They had lived here for fifteen years, and she had started the school soon after the family moved to Tehran so that her children would have some playmates. The school grew every year, and when her children started in the American School, Carol kept the nursery school going. Her children were in the States going to college and she laughingly said, "And I'm still here, taking care of little ones."

She showed me around the ground floor classrooms that divided the children according to age. Every classroom had several tables, each surrounded by six chairs. There were bookcases full of paper, paints, crayons, scissors, glue, and books. "Where do you get all these supplies?" I asked.

"Every summer we get Home Leave, and when we return we bring boxes of supplies. I also buy books from departing families, so we manage nicely," Carol answered. We did not go upstairs, as that was the Mathews' living quarters.

Jimbo had abandoned me as soon as I started talking to Carol, and when we came back outside I saw that he was playing with some other little boys. He obviously felt at home.

I turned to Carol and asked her how many children were enrolled and how many teachers she had. She told me she had sixty children, four teachers and five Iranian *badjiis.* "Well," I said, "if you can take one more, I would like to enroll Jimbo." She handed me some papers to fill out, told me her charges and explained that the school was in session from 9:00 am to 12:00 noon everyday except Friday and Sunday. The children were a real mixture of the United Nations. There were children from England, France, Denmark, Germany and Sweden as well as Iranians and Americans. There were Catholics, Protestants, Jews, Armenians, Muslims and Bahais. Talk abut a melting pot, this was it. I thought this would be a good experience for our little guy.

Thursday evening Jack and Joan invited us to attend a party at an Iranian's house. The host was a fellow who had invited Jack on a hunting trip up near the Caspian Sea. The Blakes assured us that it was perfectly acceptable for them to bring us to the party; it was a Persian custom that one never knew how many people would show up at a gathering. We weren't expected until 9:00, so we put Jimbo to bed and hired one of the maids at the hotel to watch him.

The home was immense, sitting in the middle of a beautiful garden lit by torches lining the driveway. Joan had a bouquet of flowers for the hostess; I mentally made a note to bring such an offering to the next party we were invited to. The salon had an enormous Persian carpet on the floor. The medallion in the center was ultramarine blue with flowers of every hue entwined around it. In the center of the medallion was a rosette of pink and red flowers and green vines. It was the most spectacular carpet we had seen. The host explained that it was from Isfahan, the famous city south of Tehran. When I told him the carpet was very beautiful, he gallantly said, "It will be yours, *fardah.*" That confused me and I looked at Jack who said, "We'll talk about it later."

More guests arrived and soon we were all sitting in a large circle. The houseboy brought around scotch, vodka and soft drinks along with some very sweet, honey-covered orange rinds. For more than an hour we were plied with drinks and sweets. At ten o'clock the houseboy opened the sliding doors to reveal a huge table groaning with platters of meats, rice, khoreshes, and various fruits. We were handed a plate and a fork, then immediately the guests surrounded the table. They would put whatever was in front of them on their plates and immediately start eating. Invariably I would get a mouth-

71

ful of food and someone would ask me why President Kennedy was doing such and such or did Kennedy only marry his wife because she is beautiful. It was as if they thought I had a direct line to the Oval Office. Trying not to talk with my mouth full of food, (an American custom, certainly not a Persian one) I would try to answer intelligently. Suddenly I was aware that the whole group was slowly moving to the left, eating whatever was in front of them as they moved. We danced around the circle until we were back where we had started and then everyone left the dining room and sat down in the salon. Between fielding questions from every side, I had not had a chance to finish what was on my plate. A houseboy came around with hot cloths for us to wipe our hands; another houseboy brought each guest an orange on a plate with a small knife. We peeled and ate the oranges; again a houseboy brought hot cloths. When we were finished everyone got up to leave. We said our good-byes, so stuffed we barely made it to the car. Once we were on our way I asked Jack about the host's comment that the carpet will be mine. "Didn't you go to Charm School?" he inquired.

"What's that?"

"That's the school in Washington DC where you learn the protocol of the country you are being sent to."

Jim interjected, "Jack, we didn't have time for that. I had to fight to get any leave to see our folks before coming here."

"Well, what you heard from our host is called *taarof*. It's a form of politeness, very flowery speech to make a person feel important. If you tell an Iranian that the carpet is beautiful, by custom he is required to say, "It is yours tomorrow." They never mean it and you noticed our host said *fardah, Enshallah*. He's off the hook because he is sure Allah will not will it to be yours. So don't compliment anything. But if you had asked him how much he paid for the carpet, he would not be offended and would tell you."

"Oh, that's why the lady in the red dress asked me how much my necklace cost. I didn't know what to say to that! I should have gone to Charm School."

That weekend Jim, Jimbo and I went exploring. It was nice to have Jim do the driving and going north on Palavi Avenue we came to a sign that read "Zoo". We turned onto a long paved road lined with sycamore trees; a cool breeze fanned our brows. Parking the car we walked to a kiosk and paid the 200 *rial* entrance fee. The zoo was quite small and most of the animals were scruffy and unkempt. As soon as Jimbo saw the lion he ran over for a closer look. Suddenly we noticed that in the cage with the lion was a tan-colored dog about the size of German shepard, very skinny and covered with mange. We couldn't believe that a dog could share the cage with a lion, especially since the lion looked like he could use a good meal. We found the manager, who spoke English, to ask him how this happened.

"Oh, Monsieur, the lion was brought to us when he was a small baby and we found this dog who fed the lion along with her babies. Now the lion thinks the dog is his mother!" He was laughing as he told this story. We shook our heads in amazement.

Iranians in general do not like dogs; some believe dogs are the lowest form of reincarnation. One of the worst insults is to say to a person "*Pedari sag*" ("Your father is a dog"). All along the jubes would be homeless dogs of every description, and it was not unusual to see them being mistreated. On one occasion a friend of ours rescued a pup that had a heavy cord tied tightly around his neck. This was a form of slow torture; if the cord were left on, the pup would slowly choke to death as it grew.

On Monday Jimbo started school and we settled into a routine. Jim would leave for Ghalamorghi at 6:00 a.m., Kerim would return to take us to the Officer's Club for breakfast and then we would go to Jimbo's school. Colleen told me about a good hairdresser and I was anxious to go to a beauty shop. The salon was downtown near Ferdowsi Circle and was owned by a German who had been the head of the Gestapo in Iran during the war. Since the Nazis had lost the war, he could not return to Germany. I called for an appointment on the Saturday before we were to go to another party. Arriving a little early for my appointment, I picked up a magazine from England. Leafing through it I came upon a Horoscope. I looked up my birthday (December 25) and read, "An event is occurring today that will affect the rest of your life." I turned to the front of the magazine to see the date. Cold chills went down my spine. The date was the 14th of February; the very day Pierce had crashed the plane into the Zagros Mountain.

Chapter 4

It was time to start to look for a house and the next Monday Jim called as soon as he got to Ghalamorghi. "Babe, Kerim tells me he has a cousin, a real estate agent, who knows of a very nice house that would be perfect for us. He's going to pick the cousin up and bring him to the hotel. After you have breakfast and take Jimbo to school go with them to see this place."

That sounded great and I excitedly got dressed.

Kerim arrived with cousin Ali, a skinnier version of Kerim complete with the handlebar moustache. Ali spoke fairly good English. After dropping Jimbo off at his school we headed down Shemeran Road almost to the British Embassy. We were in an area of older homes surrounded by nine-foot walls. We stopped at a green metal gate; Ali got out and rang the bell. A very old man dressed in black, baggy pants, a long, white overshirt, green, pointy-toed slippers and a brown felt cap opened the gate. His scrawny shoulders were bowed inward and his long beard almost reached his knees; his toothless smile welcomed us. Ali explained that this was the gardener. As we entered the huge compound, it became obvious that the little man had more than he could handle. The grounds were overgrown with twisting vines, knee-high weeds, and in the center of the garden was a cement-lined cistern full of slimy green water with strange bugs scooting over the surface. There were many fruit trees, some in bloom and others so laden with green fruit that their branches were touching the ground. We followed the gardener as he led us up the broken brick path. The front of the two-story house was bowed, with wings extending out on both sides, curving steps led to the massive wooden door. The little man rushed ahead of us to open it, bowing repeatedly. Musty odors assailed our nostrils as we entered the dark interior. I stood for a moment allowing my eyes to become accustomed to the light. A wide staircase rose from the round foyer, reminding me of the scene in Gone with the Wind where Rhett Butler carried Scarlet O'Hara up the stairs. A dramatic chandelier was draped in clouds of spider webs and mold was everywhere. We moved to the left, following the gardener into a library filled with built-in bookshelves. The hallway beyond led into a series of what seemed to be storage rooms or servants' quarters. We returned to the foyer and went into the right wing. A living room, formal dining room, and a smaller room overlooked the garden; a roach-filled kitchen completed that wing. We went upstairs and discovered six bedrooms and two bathrooms in the Persian style. In its day, this was an elegant home, but now it looked like a set for a Boris Karloff-Bela Lagosi horror movie. It was so creepy; I could hardly wait to get out of there. I thanked Ali as we dropped him at the corner, picked up Jimbo from school and returned to the Vanak Hotel.

Two days later Ali had more houses to show me. Reluctantly, I agreed to go. We visited more aging, moldy houses within extensive gardens down in the center of Tehran. I told Ali we preferred a house in the northern suburbs closer to Jimbo's school and the Officer's Club, so he started showing me brand-new homes on tiny lots in the middle of barren, treeless expanses. The houses and walls were whitewashed, the compounds bare of any growth, the oppressive heat visibly vibrating. (One thing I learned about the houses in Tehran is that the ones on the north side of the street had the compounds in the front with the houses at the back. On the south side of the street it is the opposite: the house is directly at the street line with the compound to the rear. In every case the southern walls were glass doors allowing the sun to warm the house during the cold Iranian winters. The Persians discovered solar energy a long time ago.)

After two weeks of hunting, I was sick with despair. I knew we would be living in a hotel room for the next two years. There was not a house in Tehran for us. I conveyed these feelings to Jim in my usual calm manner. Bawling uncontrollably, I vented my frustration on him. After several minutes of listening to my rantings and ravings, he quietly but firmly assured me that things had to get better.

Magically, the next day Don Hudson came to our rescue. He had heard of a home, not too far from their place, that an American family had just vacated. After work he took Jim to see it. Elated, Jim returned to the hotel to tell me all about it. The next day we went to see it. It was perfect. The home was on the south side of the street so the walls were right at the property line. We entered a small foyer. To our left was a window and a door to the servant's room, beyond that a door that led to the side of the patio. Outside was another door that led to a room with a Persian-style toilet and sink. Back in the foyer the double metal door led to the large all-purpose room that was so big there were three columns placed within the room holding up the roof. We stood there taking it all in. The southern exposure of the room had metal-framed glass, double doors. Beyond that was a porch, a swimming pool enclosed with a wrought-iron fence and a small yard with grass and trees. To our immediate left we could see an American-type bathroom and a large room with a closet taking up one wall. Stepping down the two steps into the great room, we walked toward the patio. To the left of the door to the outside we discovered more double doors into another large room with floor-to-ceiling windows looking out to the pool. Outside, we noticed two trees next to the house, one of which was growing through the overhang of the roof; the other was dead.

We went back inside up the steps into the kitchen. It was completely bare except for one wall that contained the sink on the left with a tile-covered drain board extending across the entire wall. In the middle of this work area was an indention into the wall with a chimney that served as a draw for a charcoal fire. The mottled glass windows along the north wall faced the street, letting in a lot of light. Wrought iron bars on the outside protected them. The floor sloped toward an uncovered drain in the center of the room. The rest of the room was empty…no cupboards of any kind. Jim stepped off the space and we talked about where the stove, refrigerator and freezer would go.

"What will we do about cupboards?" I asked.

"That's why we brought a Sears catalogue," he replied. "We'll put the stove over by the back door that goes into the garage. The refrigerator and freezer will go under the windows and this wall is where we'll put cupboards."

My kitchen was in place and I was ready to move in. Then I remembered that I hadn't seen the upstairs. The curving steel stairs were next to the kitchen door. The footholds were slabs of marble with no backings. While very sturdy they had a delicate look. Upstairs we inspected the three bedrooms and American bathroom. A door from the hallway led out to the roof where the tree from below rose dramatically, shading the room we had decided would be Jimbo's. The clothesline was off to the side.

"I'm sold," I announced as we descended the stairs.

"Yes, I think this will work. I'll contact the owner tomorrow. Don wants to check the water level of the well before we sign anything."

"A well? We have a well?"

"I'll show you," Jim said, leading me back into the kitchen and through the garage door. On the floor of the garage was a metal door with a handle. He lifted it and I looked down. In the darkness I could just make out water.

"This is called the *umbar*. It is where we will store our water. We'll have to pump the water from the well into this umbar and from there up to the roof." He closed the steel door and led me back into the kitchen. He pointed to a switch by the side of the sink that I had not noticed before and indicated a pipe coming down from the ceiling into the sink, which I also had not noticed before.

"On the roof over the bathroom upstairs are four fifty-five gallon drums. This switch will start the water pumping up to the drums and when they are filled the excess water will come down through this pipe into the sink. That tells us when to turn the pump off."

I was trying hard to follow all this, but I'm sure at this time my eyes glazed over. I am the most mechanically challenged person in the world. All I wanted was my own house with my own kitchen to fix wonderful meals for my family. Who cared about pumps and wells and umbars!

"But the problem," Jim continued, ignoring my distress, "is that we must be sure the well has water. If, for instance, the guy next door decides to dig his well deeper than ours, we will not have water." Looking around to make sure the realtor was not in hearing distance, he quietly said, "Tonight Don and I are going over the wall to check the depth of the water in the well."

I don't know how scientific the well checking was, but I was happy when Jim returned that night and announced that the well was full of water.

"Tomorrow I will meet the landlord and negotiate the lease", he said.

The next day Jim and the realtor met with Mr. DeHeshti, a prosperous middle-class owner of a John Deere tractor dealership. He was short, about five feet six inches tall, with a Santa Claus belly; his shiny, round head was bald except for fringes over his ears and around the nape of his neck. His cocker spaniel brown eyes, effervescent smile and hearty demeanor were evidence of a true salesman. Ushering Jim into his office, he dismissed the realtor and spoke to his secretary. She left the room and Mr. DeHeshti, who spoke excellent English, invited Jim to sit down. The secretary returned with a tray of tea in small glasses set into brass holders, a bowl of sugar cubes and some sugar cookies. After the requisite two cups of tea the negotiations commenced. When money is involved my husband is clever, careful, patient, persistent and determined. He really enjoys the give and take of bargaining. (Once we spent three weekends driving all over western Kansas looking for the best deal in furniture.) After several minutes of haggling, the price came down to an amount Jim felt we could afford. Then Jim broached the subject of the telephone. In Iran, in order to have a phone, you had to buy a phone number that could be used anywhere. The numbers were sold much like stocks; everyday the price was different, but always very expensive. Jim was required by the embassy to have a phone and he wanted Mr. DeHeshti to buy it. At first Mr. D. refused, "Capeetan Eestarkey, you must buy the telephone for it will be yours to use."

"Mr. DeHeshti, I will be here for only two years. Why would I pay over $300.00 for a phone number I cannot take back to the United States? But if you buy it, it will always be yours."

"But, Capeetan Eestarkey, you can sell the number when you leave Iran."

Jim was adamant that we would not buy a telephone number. He was unwilling to risk so much money, and after more tea and more talking Mr. DeHeshti consented to buy the phone number.

He told Jim he had never met an American who could bargain before and he obviously enjoyed the challenge. Finally they shook hands and agreed to meet at the American Embassy the following Monday at 10:00.

Jim made an appointment with the proper embassy official for Monday and arrived on time. Mr. DeHeshti did not show up. Jim phoned his shop and Mr. DeHeshti apologized and told Jim he would meet him the next day. Again Jim was there and the landlord was not. Again Jim called and with more apologies the date was set for the following day. This went on for the next three weeks. We never really knew why Mr. DeHeshti was reluctant to come to the embassy. His name was not on the list of undesirables. We speculated that perhaps he was trying to rent the house for more money and was putting us off, but we had no facts to bear this out. Finally, the lease was signed and we eagerly went to our home.

As we walked through the great room I realized our furniture would be lost in this 30 x 40-foot expanse. We would have to create areas of a living room and a dining room and leave a lot of spaces empty. The walls and ceiling were gunmetal gray, my least favorite color. Wires hung from the walls at ten-foot intervals waiting for light fixtures. In Iran tenants are expected to furnish light fixtures. When Jim went to arrange for the electricity to be turned on, he was told that the city had installed the electricity but the wrong meter. A city maintenance man had to change it, and we could not move in until we had electricity. At Mr. DeHeshti's request, Kerim and Jim went to the city electric office to make these arrangements. They were promised that a man would be there "*fardah*" to make the change. Days went by, weeks went by and no electric man arrived. Finally, after three weeks, Jim hired an electrician that worked for the embassy to change the meter. The official meter changer never arrived.

While in the Co-op one day I ran into Norma Whitney, one of the wives I had met at Colleen's house. She was the one who was very angry that Jim had been able to get a car and driver the second day we were in Iran. Much to my surprise she was extremely nice to me. We had a lengthy conversation and she invited us to dinner the next night. Norma was a pretty, slim brunette with olive skin and sparkling green eyes. She was my height, had an easy laugh and good sense of humor. We became good friends. Howard looked ten years older than Norma with his bushy eyebrows and squinty eyes that peered through the haze of his ever-present cigar. Jim promptly nicknamed him "Ole Seegar." His rough features showed that he had led a biker-type of life before finding himself in the Army. He laughed easily and was always ready with a joke. He and Norma bickered a lot, usually in jest. We always enjoyed their company.

The next day Howard took Jim on another orientation flight to Tabriz. As they were cruising along Howard asked Jim where he came from. Jim answered, "Tucson." Oh," said Howard, "I have only been there once, but I met the meanest son of a bitch named Bill Loveless. Do you know him?"

"Sure I do. He is married to Shirley's sister." Howard clamped his teeth on his unlit cigar and never said another word during the flight.

When Jim reported the conversation to me I was shocked. My brother-in-law is one of the nicest and calmest people I know. "Did you ask him what he was talking about?"

Jim replied, "No, I didn't say anything else and neither did Howard." Men! They never ask enough questions.

Jim was given the assignment to fly the American ambassador to the dedication of the dam at Karaj. They took off from Mehrabad Airport along with other planes carrying various Iranian dignitaries. Jim was determined that the ambassador would be at the head of the pack of planes. The ambassador was on his last official assignment before rotating back to the State Department in Washington, and when he realized what Jim was doing he calmly said, "Captain, slow down. We don't have to be first."

Jim replied, "But Mr. Ambassador, you should be first. After all, it's our tax dollars that paid for this dam."

The Ambassador chuckled, "Captain Starkey, I appreciate your enthusiasm, but you need to calm down. This country operates very differently than ours. I know that's our money at work, but I can't afford to have the Iranians 'lose face' by showing up before their dignitaries. The most important quality one can have while serving in this country is patience."

I ran into an embassy friend at the co-op one day and was complaining to her about my latest badjii and her lack of understanding.

"Shirley, hasn't anyone told you about the scorpion and the monkey?"

"No, why?"

"Maybe this story will help you to understand this country. A scorpion was sitting by the side of the river when a monkey walked by. "Monkey, will you take me across the river on your back?" he asked.

"Scorpion, I couldn't let you on my back. You might sting me and then I would die."

"Monkey, don't be ridiculous. I've got to get to the other side of the river so why would I sting you?"

The monkey thought about this and finally said, "Scorpion, I guess you're right. Jump on my back and I will take you to the other side." The scorpion jumped on the monkey's back and the monkey started swimming across the river. When he was halfway across, the scorpion suddenly stung the monkey.

Shocked, the monkey cried out, "Scorpion, scorpion, you fool, you have stung me and now I am going to die and you will drown. Why did you do that?"

The scorpion shrugged his shoulders and answered, "It is the Middle East."

I looked at my friend puzzled and after a minute I said, "That doesn't make any sense."

"That's the whole point. Nothing in this country makes any sense."

Pierce, the officer who had died on the mountain, had been the commanding officer of the Army Aviation Branch. Captain Blake became the temporary chief after the accident. The new commander, Major Buckheimer, arrived in the latter part of June. As he was introduced to the other officers he pointedly looked at Jim's insignia and stated flatly, "I hate Transportation Officers." Not a good beginning.

He never said why he had such a prejudiced attitude and, of course, Jim never asked. Major B. was a small, balding man with beady, unblinking blue eyes. His attitude was belligerent and uncompromising, definitely a small man's complex. He made the next two years difficult for all those under his command and, to those over him, he was constantly blaming his subordinates for his failures.

He was unpopular throughout ARMISH-MAAG. Jim commanded twenty-five men in his job as head of the maintenance section and this did not sit well with Major B., as he only had the pilots under him, as well as Jim. Never mind that Jim's men were also part of Major B's. command. He did not like the idea that Jim had direct control.

July

All this time we were still in the hotel. Every day seemed an eternity. The weather got hotter, my big, fat stomach got bigger, and I got more disgusted and disagreeable. Finally, something to look forward to: The Fourth of July, the holiday every American ex-patriot lives for. It was the chance to go to the American Embassy and listen to John Sousa's marches, eat hotdogs and mingle with other Americans. I waited for the day with great anticipation.

I carefully ironed Jimbo's navy shorts and red and white shirt. With his navy University of Arizona baseball hat with the red A, he was the all-American boy. Jim had an early flight, so Kerim drove us to the embassy and then went to Ghalamorghi to wait, as Jim was to meet us at the embassy after his flight. The co-op portion of the American Embassy was located on the far southern end of the compound, and I had been there many times, but never had I been to the official north side.

Taking Jimbo by the hand, I marched expectantly in the main gate to the Embassy. Looking around I saw only Iranians: some selling food, some acting as clowns and others just strolling around. What were they doing in MY embassy? I was furious! They had no right to be there. This was American territory and I didn't want to see any Iranians today. I walked further into the compound and began to see some Americans, but I was still unhappy. Suddenly, the air was filled with the sound of "The Star Spangled Banner" coming over a loud speaker. I stopped, told Jimbo to take off his hat and put his hand over his heart. I looked up to a sight I will never forget. There, against the cerulean blue Persian sky, our flag was gently moving in the breeze. The undulating stripes of white and red with the blue field seemed almost iridescent. The musical sounds carried on the wind, clear, forceful, emphatic, telling the world we are the best. Emotion overcame me and I had to wipe my eyes. I have never been so proud to be an American. Anyone who has ever lived in a foreign country can understand my feelings. To this day, wherever I am, when I hear our national song played, the vision of seeing Old Glory flying over the American Embassy in an alien land, returns to my mind.

As the sounds of the national anthem faded, I heard my name called. Barbara Liebshultz came over with her two curly-haired moppets, who impulsively hugged Jimbo.

"Guess what," Barbara said excitedly. "We found a house and moved in this week. We have a huge yard and the gardener's wife is our badjii. I can't believe we are finally settled."

I told her about our hoped-for house and about the reluctance of the owner to come to the embassy. Comparing notes, we discovered that we would be living within three blocks of each other. Enshallah! (If Allah wills it.) We walked with the children to the play area and while we watched them, we talked about our plans for our homes. It was so good to have an adult conversation with an American that my bad mood left me. By the time Jim showed up, we were talking and laughing with a large group of fellow ex-pats, the term American people overseas call themselves.

We took Jimbo over to where a camel driver was trying to get a camel to lie down to let children ride him. The camel was resisting, showing his immense dissatisfaction by baring his yellow teeth and uttering menacing growls. The driver got angry, started yanking on the reins, when suddenly the camel turned and spit in the driver's face. The driver went ballistic and with his crop started beating the animal, screaming obscenities. With a satisfied look on his face, the camel lay down and the driver started herding the children onto the camel's back. Jimbo excitedly got in line for a ride. When his turn came, we followed as the driver led the camel around the outside perimeter of the compound. Jimbo's grin was testament to his enjoyment and it was hard to get him to disembark when his turn was over. After a trip to the bathroom to wash our hands, we got in the food line, inhaling the pungent smell of barbeque. Long tables under the trees were piled high with breads, condiments, salads and marvelous desserts, while some of the embassy employees manned the grills. We were treated to ribs, hotdogs and hamburgers. It was a feast for a king or a shah. What a wonderful day!

• • •

Soon after the lease was signed, Mr. DeHeshti invited us to his home for dinner. We arrived at an old mansion very much like the first house I had looked at. The gardener met us at the gate, and we wended our way through an enormous, unkempt garden. Mr. De-Heshti met us and, fussing over Jimbo, led us into the living room, where Mrs. DeHeshti was receiving. She was an imposing figure, a head taller than her husband, with a Mae West physique. Her black-dyed pompadour rose high above the thin, arched spider-like eyebrows. Her long, aquiline nose slid down to very full red lips. She had a haughty manner, carrying her chin high as she looked down at the world from jet-black eyes. Coldly gracious and completely in charge, she soon made it obvious who wore the pants in that family. As I looked at her, I kept thinking of the wicked stepmother polishing the poisoned apple for Snow White. We followed her into the salon where, much to our surprise, in the room filled with Victorian-style furniture and knick-knacks, was a Norge refrigerator. We made no comment until Mr. DeHeshti proudly pointed out that they had just purchased the refrigerator from an American family. Like the true salesman he was, he proudly opened the door for our inspection. This modern convenience was a wondrous thing and we admired it. Mrs. DeHeshti excused herself and left the room. Soon a badjii entered with tea for us. Mr. DeHeshti showed Jimbo how to hold the sugar lumps between his teeth while sipping. Since the hot tea made the sugar melt Jimbo kept getting more sugar. Mr. D. laughed merrily enjoying our offspring.

Our dinner started with a cold yogurt soup that contained cucumber, raisins, green onions and fresh dill. It was followed by *morgh polo* (chicken with rice). Mrs. D. explained that the word for chicken is morgh and cooked rice is called polo. This polo had onions, cinnamon, raisins, and apricots in it. We all enjoyed it very much. Kleenex in a box sat on the table; these were used as nap-kins. Our conversation was mainly about the United States, what our home there was like and the always-asked question, "What do you think of Iran?" We never met an Iranian who didn't want our opinion of his country.

Then, turning to me, Mrs. DeHeshti asked what religion we belonged to. Surprised at the question, I quickly answered "Presbyterian".

"Ees eet part of the Catholeec releegion?" she asked. The way she said it made me wonder if I was being tested. I soon discovered I was right. I told her that it was a Protestant religion and then she said proudly, "We are Bahaiis."

Deciding it must be all right to talk religion at the dinner table in Iran I stated, "I've never heard of the Bahaii religion. Can you tell me about it?"

Eagerly she responded, pronouncing the 'w' like a 'v', "The Bahai releegion vas founded here in Eeran one hundred and feefty years ago. Ve believe vomen should be equal to men. Ve believe ve should have universal education and vorld peace. Ve believe en Jesus Christ, en Mohammad and en Moses. Ve believe en everything!" Emphatically she was shaking a fist as she proclaimed her beliefs. Jim and I looked at each other, speechless.

Mr. DeHeshti joined in by saying, "The Moslems do not like us because we do not think women should be held back. Mrs. DeHeshti never wears the chador," he said smugly. They asked many questions about President and Mrs. Kennedy, as if we knew them personally. The couple that occupied the White House captivated them, like the rest of the world. When we said goodbye, they promised to come to dinner as soon as we moved in.

After getting our electricity problems solved, we had our household goods delivered. Then we started to get settled. Jim cautioned me to be careful when using the vacuum. Since the electricity was 220 volt we had to use a transformer to convert the electricity to 110 in order to use our American appliances. If I were to plug the vacuum directly into the 220-volt jack, the insides would burn up and we would not have a vacuum. To complicate matters further, the jacks for the electricity were next to the phone jacks and looked exactly alike. Cautioning me, Jim said, "For heaven sakes, don't plug the phone into the electric jack. The innards will be fried!"

The downstairs room near the kitchen became the food *umbar* (the Farsi word for storage). Jim made shelves to hold the many canned and boxed items I had bought, but there was not enough room for all the cases of applesauce. We only opened one case; the rest were stacked in a corner. We measured the area in the kitchen and chose the cupboards we wanted to order. They would come in pieces, and Jim would have to put them together. Our kitchen table and chairs went in the center of the room. Jimbo promptly parked his baseball bat in the open drain in the floor with his baseball cap on top.

The great room windows presented a major problem. I had numerous drapes of every size from our many Army moves, but none fit these windows. They were really not windows, but rather four double doors; each door was 80 inches wide and 115 inches high. The curtain rod above these doors was a simple metal rod with tiny clothespin-like pinchers that rolled either way. I decided to order 40 yards of white fabric, thinking it would look dramatic.

Jim designed metal wall fixtures, and one of the men in his maintenance shop made them. The sides of the fixtures fit against the wall; the center was angled out so that the light would filter up as well as down the wall. Painted the same as the wall, they were invisible during the day, and by night they cast an impressive triangle of light above and below the fixture. The romance of this was marred by the sight of the huge, ugly brown kerosene stove next to the wall in the dining room. This provided the only heat for the whole house.

One of the first things Jim did was to arrange for two metal containers to be brought to the house to hold the potable water Kerim brought from the embassy purification plant. The small ten-gallon container was placed in the upstairs bathroom over the bidet. The large twenty-gallon container was placed in the kitchen to the right of the sink with a spigot hanging over it. This provided the water that was used for drinking, cooking and washing the dishes.

Since one of the trees on the patio was dead, Jim sawed it down to table height and had a top made in his maintenance shop so we had a convenient place to eat outside.

Jimbo had been pestering us for a dog, and one day Jim brought home a pup that looked much like a German Shepherd. Our offspring immediately named him Jeep-jeep, in honor of the transportation he thought we deserved. The two of them were buddies from the beginning. We took the dog to the vet to have him checked for worms or any other disease and he was pronounced perfect. We were beginning to look like a settled family.

One Sunday Kerim took us to the marble quarry south of Tehran and we bought an irregular-shaped brown and white piece of marble. Jim had his men in the maintenance shop make a stand for it and lo and behold, we had a very modern coffee table.

Three weeks later our Sears order arrived and Jim, with the dubious help from his namesake, put the cabinets together and painted them white. It was good to get our dishes and cooking utensils out of the umbar and into the kitchen. I got busy on the sewing machine making the curtains. Dealing with so much material was a challenge, but I finally got them made. It was a Saturday and Jim had half a day off. I was anxious to get the curtains hung to surprise him, and with the help of our current badjii, Mariam, and Kerim we got them hung. Kerim was very upset that I asked his help and he pleaded with me that this was not men's work. I insisted, as I was afraid to climb a ladder in my clumsy situation and Mariam was too fat and short to reach the rods to hook the material to the pincers. Grumbling all the time, Kerim attached the curtains as Mariam and I held up the weight. As soon as we finished, Kerim, his face puckered up in a pout, said he had to go to Ghalamorghi to "pick Capeetan". All the way home he complained to Jim about having to do "women's work."

I closed the curtains and went back to the kitchen to admire my handiwork from a distance. Expecting to be pleased with the drama of our great room, I was awash with disappointment. It looked like I had hung up a bunch of old white sheets instead of artistic drapes. When Jim came home he was greeted again with tears. Tears came so easily to me in those days. My gallant warrior had a solution...he always had solutions. Taking Jimbo, he went with Kerim to a store. He soon returned bearing two cans of spray paint, one a Kelly green, the other an electric blue. Ordering me to keep Jimbo with me by the kitchen door, he shook the paint cans and with one can in his left hand and the other in his right he started spraying the curtains I had labored over. I was stunned and sank down on the stoop in front of the kitchen, clutching Jimbo next to me. His arms moving rapidly, Picasso sprayed in large circles, looking like a whirling dervish. He really got into the act, dancing along the curtains, then standing back to check his work and making adjustments. Clouds of spray mist hung in the air. At times we could hardly see the artist. At first I had started to protest, but then decided if this didn't work I would have to start again and anything was better than the plain, awful white. The more he worked, the better it looked. In fact, it was terrific! All this time Jimbo was cheering his father on, as excited as I was. Finally, the paint ran out and Jim came back to admire his work. We greeted our paint-speckled hero with a standing ovation. All three of us agreed that we had the best drapes in the country of Iran, or at least the most original.

Servants were required in Iran, as we were told never to leave our home unattended. It was common for a truck to back up to the gate; an accomplice would go over the wall, open the gate and let the truck in. Household goods would be loaded onto the truck and spirited away. By the time the occupants came back, there would be no furniture. With all the homes surrounded by high walls neighbors would be unaware of what had happened. So the challenge was to find an honest badjii or houseboy who could do the required work.

We can say that during the two years we lived in Iran we had twenty-seven servants. They came and went at an alarming rate. Our first badjii, Gosee, applied for work and Kerim assured me she would be good. I hired her and she arrived the next day without any baggage, although she was to move in to the room off the entrance hall. She worked for a couple of hours in the morning and then asked to go to the shop on Dowlat Avenue to buy some cigarettes. I agreed, so Gosee went and never came back. When I asked Kerim why she had done this he only shrugged his shoulders.

My neighbor across the *kuchee* (Farsi meaning little street) from us was a German lady, who had married her Iranian husband thirty years before and had lived in Tehran ever since. Mrs. Zakarians told me about a badjii who had worked for her when her three children were small. She assured me that Mariam was a hard worker, very honest and good with babies and children saying, "Mrs. Starkey, she will be like part of your family." She brought Mariam over that afternoon and was very helpful in translating our transaction. I thought that Mariam looked big, but it was hard to tell since she had her chador on. I decided she looked strong enough to handle the heavy work of mopping the enormous floors, washing the clothes in the kitchen and carrying them up to rooftop, so I hired her. She came back later that evening with her suitcase and moved into the badjii bedroom. With her chador off, she was huge, probably over 300 pounds. After eating and cleaning up the kitchen she went to bed.

The next day Mariam slept in and I had to call her to get up when Kerim came back to take Jimbo and me to school. On the way home I shopped at the stalls for fresh fruits and vegetables, and when I arrived Mariam was mopping the floors. That was a good sign and I smiled in relief. When she had finished the floors, I showed her how to treat the fruits and vegetables. Many of the vegetable gardens used sewage for fertilizer, so we were obliged to soak all fruits and vegetables in Cholox water for fifteen minutes and rinse them many times using the potable water from the embassy purification plant. Mariam obviously knew how to treat the produce and even showed me the best way to wash romaine lettuce, the only lettuce available in Iran. Rather than pealing off each individual leaf, she cut it down the middle, allowing the treated water to get into all the crevices. She told me she always treated the vegetables at Mrs. Zakarian's house.

The first time I stopped at the green grocer stall on Dowlat to buy fruits, I picked up an apricot to examine it to make sure the skin had not been perforated. The owner was very upset and wanted to choose the fruit himself. I shook my head and indicated that I would be very careful not to bruise his produce. He frowned and stood next to me, watching intently. I made a big show of carefully examining while gently holding the fruit. After I had chosen some apricots and apples he put them in a sack. I gave him my best smile and said, "Merci, Monsieur." I received a big grin in return. From then on he always allowed me to pick the vegetables and fruits. I was discovering that treating Iranians of all social levels with courtesy and smiles while trying to speak Farsi made friends.

My next task was to show her how to use the washing machine. It had a large tub with an agitator in it, one hose that hooked onto the kitchen faucet, allowing the tub to be filled. Another hose at the bottom of the tub drained the water into the sink. After the clothes were washed and put through two rinsings, they were put them into a large cylinder that had holes in the sides. When a switch was thrown, the cylinder would spin the water out of the clothes. It was a step above a wringer-type machine. Mariam had to carry the clothes upstairs to hang them on the roof. This was easy until Jimbo decided it was fun to stand at the top of the stairs and not let her pass. With the full laundry basket and her girth she was helpless. She couldn't turn around, couldn't set the basket down and couldn't get past the impish child.

Suddenly, I would hear a plaintive, "No, Jeembo, no, Jeembo, ma-a-dam, ma-a-dam." Iranians always catered to the males and this was especially true of servants. Mariam would knock herself out trying to please Jimbo, but he still deviled her. I would sternly tell Jimbo to get out of the way and let Mariam do her job. With a smirk on his face he would leave, but the scene repeated itself every time Mariam tried to get up the stairs. One day I was upstairs and heard her shrieking. I raced down the stairs to find Mariam running around the living room, her skirts hiked up, her bloomers showing, as the Little Devil fiendishly chased her on his tricycle, laughing hysterically. By the time I finally got Jimbo to stop, all three of us were laughing. It was the first time I had seen a smile on Mariam's face.

Day by day it became increasingly difficult to get Mariam to work, but it was never a problem to get her to eat. Food was vanishing at an alarming rate. One afternoon she could not be found. I looked everywhere for her. Finally, I went outside and stood by the swimming pool and called her name. Faintly, came a soft "Ma-a-dam." I followed the sound around to the side of the house and found Mariam stuck in the badjii bathroom. She was wedged in so tightly there was no way to get her out. It was then that I realized how much of the disappearing food had disappeared into Mariam. As I was trying to figure out what to do, Jim and Kerim arrived. I met them at the front door and explained the problem. After several minutes of hilarious laughter, they went to see what could be done. They tried pulling on her arms but she shrieked in pain. The matter was settled when Jim got a screwdriver and took the door off the hinges. The released Mariam was delighted and told us everything would be fine if we kept the door off. We declined and with not much sadness paid her and thanked her for her service.

Gathering up Jim's tropical worsted uniforms, I asked Kerim to take me to the closest laundry-dry cleaner on Dowlat Avenue. The sign in English above the door said *Barf* Cleaners. I looked up the word in the Farsi dictionary and found that it meant "snow." Kerim and the owner had a lengthy conversation, after which Kerim told me about a very good badjii named Zahra that the owner recommended. That afternoon Kerim brought Zahra to our house. She was young, very pretty and spoke flawless English. She explained that she only did ironing but would help me find a live-in badjii. I arranged for her to come the next day to iron. She did an expert job on everything, and for the first time since arriving in Iran, we had a closet full of pressed clothes. She told me she would send a girl for me to interview the next day. After Jim met Zahra he made the comment, "She is too intelligent to be a badjii."

Moneer, the new badjii, arrived in the morning. She was a slight, very young girl, and when I had her carry a large can of kerosene to fill the stove in the dining room she had trouble even lifting it. After half a day she disappeared, never to return. So much for Zahra's help. The next day the jubilant Kerim announced that he had solved my problems. He introduced me to his friend Batoul, who had worked for an American major Kerim had worked for. She was built like a lady wrestler, even though she was only 4 ft. 11 in. tall. She had had a very hard life; her husband had divorced her, taken her eight-year-old son and five-year-old daughter with him, and she was not allowed to ever see them again. After a lengthy interview I hired her and soon was delighted with my decision. She worked like a dervish, washing, ironing, waxing furniture, sweeping and watering the lawn, skimming the pool, cleaning the garage, in addition to the usual bed-making and kitchen duties. I was in hog heaven, particularly since my girth was expanding and I was getting varicose veins. I had to wrap my legs in the morning before I could even get out of bed and had to elevate them throughout the day. For two weeks Batoul worked miracles on the house in such a cheerful manner that even Jimbo liked her. When she was through with her work, she would play ball with him and was teaching him some Farsi words. On Friday she left for her day off and promised to return the next day in the evening. She did not return until Monday morning just as I was getting ready to take Jimbo to school. I was relieved that I didn't have to leave the house unattended and vaguely noticed a difference in Batoul. On the way home I realized that she had makeup on, something I had never seen before. She did her work as usual but after dinner she came into the living room wrapped in her chador.

"Madam, I no spend the nights here, work day."

"Why, Batoul? We agreed that you would live in. What is the matter?"

" Father say I no stay at night. Work the day."

"But, Batoul, my baby is coming soon and I need you here to take care of Jimbo when I go to the hospital."

"Sorry, Madam, can not do. Father says no." With that she turned and walked out. I followed her outside and, lo and behold, there was a taxi in the kuchee, driven by a young, handsome Iranian. Batoul got in the front seat next to her "father."

Tuesday Kerim brought another badji. Osra was tall by Iranian standards, probably five foot nine inches, with an athletic, almost male-like build. Her coal-black hair grew out of her forehead just an inch above her bushy eyebrows. She was very self-assured, carried a bundle of papers attesting to her many abilities, among them the talent of making "terrific martinis." She wanted more money than we had been paying but since it was getting close to my due date, we agreed. She worked as hard as Batoul, but never spent extra time with Jimbo. When Jim met her he commented to me, "I don't think we have to worry about Osra having a boyfriend."

Two weeks later we got word that our good friend, Jim Hesson, who had been a classmate of Jim's in the Transportation Advanced Course at Ft. Eustis, had arrived in Tehran from Germany. He was assigned to MAAG Pakistan as the maintenance officer, in the same capacity as Jim's, and had been to Germany to pick up an airplane to fly back to Karachi. I consulted with Osra on what to fix for dinner.

"Madam, me fix *ghormah sabzi*."

"What is that, Osra?"

She described the dish, and the most I could make out was that it was made with beef, rice, tomatoes, green peppers and eggplant. I made a list of the things she requested and left for the shops. I decided to leave all this in her capable hands. When I returned

Osra was busy browning onions and ground beef. I made a peach pie before leaving to pick up Jimbo at school. After eating lunch Jimbo and I retired upstairs for our naps.

I awoke to wonderful odors drifting up from the kitchen. I dressed Jimbo in his best shirt and pants while I put on my prettiest maternity outfit. At six o'clock Jim arrived with Jim Hesson and his co-pilot Ben Nixon. Hesson, from Minnesota was tall and handsome with blonde, Nordic features and an engaging smile. He immediately grabbed Jimbo and threw him up in the air as Jimbo squealed with delight. Ben spoke reservedly in a New England accent. Jim fixed Scotch for the fellows and we sat in the living room comparing notes on living in Iran and Pakistan. Jim's wife, Joyce, and I had a lot of fun playing bridge back in Virginia, and I was anxious to hear all about her and their children. At six Osra announced that dinner was ready.

We settled into our chairs and started on the huge salad. Both Ben and Hesson ate with relish, explaining to us that in Pakistan they never ate lettuce because it was full of an amoeba that couldn't be dislodged from the lettuce or the body's system. "Our lettuce here is fine if you soak it in chlorine water. Shirl can take you to buy some tomorrow to take back to Pakistan," Jim offered.

"What about steaks? Can we get some here?"

"Yes, the Embassy Co-op has lovely steaks from Denmark," I replied. "Tomorrow we'll load up on both lettuce and steaks."

"Joyce will think she has died and gone to heaven," said Hesson with a smile.

Osra appeared with a large platter and set it in front of Jim. We all stared at it with surprise. Around the edge of the platter Osra had alternated stuffed tomatoes and bell peppers on a bed of lettuce. It was very decorative. But what caused our amazement was the eggplant in the center. Osra had stuffed the round eggplant and somehow sewed it back together, and boiled it. The natural deep purple of the eggplant had faded into a bilious gray; it looked like a cow's stomach sitting there. I thanked her and as she retreated back into the kitchen we all just looked at each other, not knowing what to say. Jim dished a tomato and bell pepper onto our plates, carefully avoiding the centerpiece. The filling was delicious, a wonderful mixture of beef, rice, onions and different spices. The freshness of the tomato and crunchiness of the pepper gave a variety of taste and texture pleasures. When we were ready for dessert I carried the platter into the kitchen. Osra was shocked that the eggplant was not touched. I told her that we were so impressed with the meal that we saved the eggplant just for her. She beamed in appreciation and I was relieved that we had not hurt her feelings.

Chapter 5

Marilyn Monroe kills herself, first man killed climbing the Berlin Wall, 20,000 killed in Iran's worst earthquake, Mississippi's governor defies federal court order to integrate Ole' Miss, JFK federalizes Mississippi Natural Guard, the Cuban Missile Crisis that scared the world for a week.

September 1962

Since the household problem seemed to be settled, I turned my attention to the lawn. It was the end of August and according to Kerim the lawn should have winter seeds planted. I asked him to buy the seeds and find a man to do the work. He came back later that day with a short, slight man who had a deformed left foot. The customary worker's beige felt cap sat on his curly head; a long shirt almost covered his ragged pants. It had been awhile since either his clothes or he had been treated to a bath. He carried a burlap bag of seeds. After we had negotiated the price of labor and I had paid Kerim for the seeds, he set to work. It was a lovely day and I sat outside watching the gardener sow the seeds. He was halfway through when I left to use the bathroom. When I returned, he was gone. I ran to the front door and looked down the street just in time to see him limping around the corner as fast as his bandy legs could carry him. The seed bag was gone and I never saw the little weasel again. I was furious, telling Jim that if I ever saw that gardener again his life was in peril. When I confronted Kerim about it he acted as though he didn't understand a word I was saying. A couple of weeks later seeds sprouted on half of the lawn.

The next day, while shopping at the green grocers, I noticed the flower shop next door had some violets for sale. My mother always had violets in our garden at home, and I was suddenly homesick. I bought several plants, picked Jimbo up from school and after lunch put him down for a nap. I took the violets to the backyard and carefully set them in the ground near the swimming pool. Wanting them to get a good start, I manipulated the water gauge to allow the water to drip slowly onto them. With great satisfaction I sat on the patio reading a book. At 3::30, I became sleepy and went upstairs to nap. Walking into the bathroom I could not believe my eyes. The whole ceiling was on the floor! I looked up and could see the sky between the steel beams that were holding up the four 55-gallon drums filled with water. The floor was a mess of mud, straw and dung. Apparently, while I had watered the violets, water was also being pumped up to the drums and had overflowed onto the roof. I called Jim to tell him what had happened. "Shirl, that's impossible. There is no way to divert the water in the garden."

"Well," I answered, "there may be no way to do it but I did it. I guess the water just overflowed and washed the ceiling away. What should I do now?"

"Don't do anything until I get home. We'll have to notify Mr. DeHeshti. Go take your nap." As I hung up I thought I could hear him laughing. The disgruntled Osra cleaned up the floor while muttering something in Farsi.

That night Jim called Mr. DeHeshti, who said he would send a man to fix the ceiling, fardah. Two weeks later the man still had not arrived.

I was beginning to have some false labor pains and one night when the moon was full I got up, went into the bathroom and threw up my dinner. Jim came in and asked me if I was all right. Before I could answer a loud, crashing noise startled us. It sounded like a train was going by. "What was that?" I cried. Just then the house began to vibrate convulsively.

"My God, it's an earthquake!" Jim yelled and, grabbing me under the arms, pulled me into the bedroom away from the damaged ceiling with the heavy water drums. He sat me in the chair by the window and ran to get Jimbo. I lowered my head on the marble sill, so queasy I didn't care if the world was ending. As the room continued to shake, I lifted my head and looked out the window and saw the shadow of our house swaying back and forth across the ground. The swimming pool in the garden across the kuchee had waves two feet tall sloshing back and forth. Suddenly, I could hear howls of fright as the residents of the area ran outside in panic. After what seemed like an eternity, the shaking subsided. We sat on the bed, the three of us hugging each other, listening to the chaotic screams emanating from the streets. Finally, too tired to be kept awake by the pandemonium, we went back to sleep, Jimbo between the two of us.

In the morning we examined our home for damage. We discovered that except for the slightly bent steel frames on the patio doors, all was well. Since it was Sunday, we spent a leisurely day dining beside the pool and occasionally taking a dip. At 6:00 we turned on the television to watch Gunsmoke on our Armed Forces Television Network. The Shah gave permission for the U.S. government to have this station, which could broadcast from six in the evening until twelve midnight, but under no circumstances was it allowed to have any newscasts. Censorship was the order of the day, as the Shah kept a tight rein on any international news coming into the country. For a couple of current event wonks like us, this was very frustrating. We did subscribe to Time Magazine, U.S. News and World Report, Life Magazine and the International Herald Tribune in order to keep up with the rest of the world, and these came to us through the APO New York address, as did all our mail. However, everything arrived several days after the fact, so we felt as if we were living in a giant bubble, looking out at the world but not understanding what was occurring. Our television programs consisted of several cowboy shows, the Dick Van Dyke Show and, of course, I Love Lucy. The Iranians, who wanted to learn English, enthusiastically viewed these broadcasts.

Monday was Labor Day and Jim didn't have to work, so we left early in the morning for the festivities at the Officer's Club. We were looking forward to a lavish buffet served by the pool and visiting with our friends. As soon as we arrived we were assailed with rumors about the earthquake. We joined Norm and Barbara Leibshultz at a poolside table while the kids alternated between swimming and playing in the gated toddlers' area. Norm had heard through the hospital that there was extensive damage in many villages north to Tehran. Norma Whitney and Colleen joined us, as Ole' Seegar and Don Hudson were in Germany attending High Altitude School. We exchanged notes on how we had reacted to the quake, and Barbara told us her badjii and gardener had been hysterical, running into the middle of the compound refusing to go back into their house.

After brunch our new ambassador, the Honorable Julius Holmes, made a speech. This was the first official news we had heard detailing the extent of the earthquake. He told us that the epicenter was in Qasvin, a town 60 miles northwest of Tehran. The area was filled with many villages built along the rugged, bare mountains. The flimsy mud and stone huts had collapsed instantly crushing the peasants sleeping inside. The estimate was 20,000 dead with an additional 25,000 homeless. President Kennedy had ordered a 100-bed Army hospital along with medical personnel to be airlifted from Germany. Mr. Holmes stated that supplies would be arriving at Mehrabad Airport and all of Armish-Maag would be mobilized to get the supplies to the stricken area. While countries from all over the world were sending help, the United States, as usual, was committed to sending more than the rest of the world put together. It was a sobering speech and, soon after, Jim was contacted to report for work at five the next morning. Everyone started to leave, calling the children out of the swimming pool and the play areas. The holiday mood suddenly turned somber as we left thinking of the devastation visited on so many people.

The next day huge transport planes started arriving at Mehrabad, and Mr. Holmes made a speech formally turning the goods over to the Shah's Prime Minister. 1,000 U.S. Army blankets were moved from the planes to waiting trucks, but by the time these reached Qazvin they numbered only 500. The next day army blankets could be purchased in the bazaar for 800 rials. Trucks full of tents, food, and medical supplies moved out of planes and onto the road to the earthquake site. The small airport outside of Qazvin was kept busy with planes and helicopters bringing in doctors, nurses and medical personnel. As the first planes landed, a peasant slit the throat of a lamb in the thousand year-old sign of welcome. The squeamish newcomers nodded respectfully, sidestepped the blood and left the aircraft as quickly as possible.

Jim was working everyday from six in the morning to six at night, supervising putting together the helicopters that had been sent in cargo planes from Germany. It was his job to test-fly the helicopters after his maintenance crew assembled them. He always made the chief mechanic go with him on a test flight, which made the chief very vigilant about his crew.

One day he was asked to fly a photojournalist to the site. He watched as a badly injured girl about ten years old was brought in on a stretcher to be airlifted to a hospital in Tehran. The photojournalist, whom Jim described as a small, ferret-like, pushy New Yorker, loudly demanded that an American nurse, a pretty one at that, be brought to have her photo taken with the child. Twenty minutes passed before a satisfactory nurse was found, meanwhile the child was in terrible pain. This picture appeared on the cover in the following issue of Life Magazine.

One of the doctors in our small hospital, Major Kazemi, was Iranian born, married to a beautiful, dainty French wife, educated in the United States, and was now serving in his native country. His knowledge of Farsi was invaluable to the other medical staff. When the saddened Shah came to survey the damage and the work being done to alleviate the suffering, he heard Major Kazemi speaking Farsi. "Where did you learn to speak our language so proficiently?" he asked. When Major Kazemi told him he was Iranian the Shah was furious. "Why are you working for the United States when you should have returned to help your own people?" he demanded.

Courteously Major Kezemi replied, "Sir, that is what I am doing right now."

Tents were brought in for temporary housing until permanent housing could be built. The peasants were shown how to erect them so their families would have protection against the coming winter, but they refused to put them up unless they were paid for their labor. The energetic Americans finally got them up while the Iranians drank tea and watched.

The rescue work went on for several weeks with the U.S. Army hospital working day and night. Finally, the work was finished, but the Shah demanded that the hospital be left in Iran. President Kennedy disagreed, and one dark night the 100-man hospital was spirited out of Iran and returned to Germany.

It took a week after the earthquake for us to receive letters from Tucson, and one day Jim brought home a letter my very emotional mother had written. I was appalled when I read her first sentence:

"Dear Shirley,

I don't know if your eyes will ever see my words. We've been told that 100,000 people are dead in Tehran." The letter went on about how important my family and I were to her and to Dad and what would they do without us. I sat down immediately and fired off a letter describing our experiences and assuring her that all was well with us. We later learned that an AP reporter had sent out a news story that started with "If this earthquake had hit Tehran, 100,000 people would be dead." Some enterprising headline writer had shortened it to "100,000 people dead in Tehran." Don Hudson's father heard this and suffered an almost fatal heart attack, not knowing Don was in Germany at the time.

Three days after the earthquake, LTC. Patterson, the veterinarian, was the Duty Officer. A phone call came in and a heavy Russian-accented voice said to the Sgt. who had answered, "Please make an announcement that at two in the morning another earthquake will hit Tehran and all Americans should leave."

The Sgt. reported this to the colonel who laughed, "Sgt., no one can forecast an earthquake. The Russkies are just making mischief. They would love for us to leave Iran. Forget about it."

Two nights later the telephone ringing downstairs awakened us from a sound sleep at a quarter after midnight. It was Norma Whitney calling. Since Ole' Seegar was away, she had stayed up to watch TV, and at the end of the broadcasting day a very agitated Pvt. had made the announcement that another earthquake was going to hit Tehran in two hours. She asked Jim what she should do. "Norma, to my knowledge there is no way to forecast an earthquake

but let me call the Embassy and see what they say. I'll call you back."
Jim called the American Embassy, the Armish-Maag Duty Officer
and the American hospital and it was confirmed at all three places
that there was no way to forecast an earthquake. In every case Jim
was told that the streets were full of hysterical Iranians. He called
Norma back and told her what he had learned. "But, what should
I do?" she asked.

"Go back to bed. That's what Shirl and I are going to do," he said.

Hesitating, she said, "Oh, I think I better get the boys up and
sleep outside, just in case".

"Do whatever makes you feel comfortable, Norma, but I'm going to bed." With that he hung up and we went upstairs. Suddenly,
we were aware of a commotion outside. People were surging out
on Dowlat Street just as they had when the real earthquake hit. We
crawled into bed and had a good night's sleep.

Arriving at Jimbo's school the next day, I discovered that we were
the only ones not covered with mosquito bites and suffering from
runny noses. Sheepishly, the teachers and arriving parents said they
slept outside just in case there was an earthquake. That evening Jim
announced that the Shah was enraged that a false announcement
had been made and he threatened to sue the American government
for one million *tomans* (one *toman* being ten rials).

"That's insane. After all the help we have given him to relieve
the quake victims? I can't believe this!" I was incredulous.

"I think he was more upset that his precious edict about no news
was broken than about the people rioting in the streets. Incidentally,
the Pvt. who made the announcement had a sudden change of orders
and left this afternoon for the States. The poor kid was just the guy
that closed up the station. He received a phone call one minute
before midnight and was told he could save thousands of lives if he
let people know of the impending earthquake, so this 19 year-old
kid decided to be a hero. Uncle Sam sent him back to save his neck."

"By the way, changing the subject, Kerim got himself assigned
somewhere else. I'll get a new driver tomorrow."

Surprised I asked, "Why did he get assigned someplace else?"

"I think it had something to do with you getting him to do what
is, as he put it, 'women's work.' He was constantly telling me that

he was a driver and was not supposed to hang curtains."

"So that is why he has been so sullen, almost rude actually. He doesn't even talk to Jimbo like he used to. Well, good riddance. We'll find someone better," I optimistically replied.

Nasser, our new driver, was young, about 25, tall and lanky with reddish hair and freckles on his olive skin. He did not speak a word of English. That first day we hired him, Jim came home early so we could go to the Meat Run.

"I'm not sure how long this Nasser will last. He drove through two red lights coming here. I had to swat him on the head with my newspaper to get him to slow down. I was yelling *Yavash, yavash* (slow down) at him and he completely ignored me. When you are in the car with him, Babe, you must be very firm and take your dictionary. He doesn't speak any English, and he has a very heavy foot, so make sure he understands to slow down. And use the dictionary on his head if you have to."

"Do you think he'll object if I make him hang curtains?" I said facetiously.

The Meat Run occurred every month when the commissary in Ankara, Turkey sent American meat to us. Since 90% of the cows in Iran were tuberculin, we were warned not to buy any local beef. Pork was nonexistent. We were allowed to order 14 pounds of meat monthly for each family member, no matter the age. For our family the amount was 42 pounds, and when the baby arrived we would add another 14 pounds. More than enough to satisfy us, assuming that what we ordered came in. In typical Army fashion, rank has its privileges; in other words, meat was doled out starting with the General, then the Colonels, Majors to the Captains etc. We arrived at four o'clock and sat until five when the list came down to Captains. We got lucky and almost all of our order was in. I had ordered 10 pounds of pork chops and got a huge slab of uncut chops that must have weighed 20 pounds. "We'll have to have a party so I'll have an excuse to cook this much meat," I said to Jim as we headed for the car.

"That sounds good to me," he answered.

Nasser and Jim loaded the meat in the trunk and we got in the car. With a skidding of tires, Nasser jolted the car forward and bolted out of the side entrance, smashing into another Armish-Maag car going down the street. In those days none of the cars had seatbelts and I was thrown to the floor. Jim helped me up, checking to make sure I was all right. Then he got out, checking on the other car. An angry Major Shahrabani got out of the car and started screaming at Nasser in Farsi. Mark Shahrabani was another native-born Iranian who had emigrated to the U.S., became a citizen, married an American and joined the army. His wife Jane, pregnant with their fourth child, emerged from their vehicle badly shaken up. After the shouting died down, Nasser, slunk back to the car. Jim learned that Shahrabani had been dissatisfied with the drivers he had been assigned, so he had pulled Nasser out of the ranks of the Iranian army, determined to teach him to be a perfect driver. It hadn't worked. Nasser had wrecked Shahrabani's car twice and Mark had fired him, which is why he was assigned to us. In fact, Mark had just gotten his car out of the shop this day from Nasser's last incident, and it obviously needed to go in again. Our bumper showed some scratches, but Mark's right fender was crushed in. After the tongue-lashing he had received from Shahrabani, and with threats from Starkey, Nasser drove home at a normal pace.

Ever since the election of John F. Kennedy, due in part to the choosing of Lyndon B. Johnson to be his running mate, LBJ had become a thorn in JFK's side. According to all the reports we read in the newsmagazines, it was not a secret that Johnson and Bobby Kennedy despised each other, making cabinet meetings difficult. JFK temporarily solved the problem by sending Johnson on a "fact-finding" mission around the world. He arrived in Tehran late in August to be wined and dined by the Shah. The Kennedy Administration demanded that the Shah institute basic political reform to blunt the growing communist threat to the stability of the region. In return the United States would provide armaments to Iran, including helicopters. Soon after that, Major B. had a new assignment for Jim. "Starkey, you're such a smart guy, having gone to the Advanced Officer's Course," he began sarcastically, "you write a staff study giving the pros and cons about the abilities of the Kaman and Huey helicopters. The U.S. is trying to decide which one to give to Iran. I need it by next Monday." Jim had eight days to complete the study, no time to write to the States for information. The only reference he had was an aviation magazine that he subscribed to, so he sat down and wrote six pages of arguments comparing the two choppers, using some facts from the aviation magazine and his own opinion. He concluded that the best helicopter for the terrain, weather and altitude in Iran was the Kaman. He turned the report in two days early; Major B. never made a comment. Later, Col. Martin, Major B's. boss, congratulated Jim on his paper. "Captain Starkey, you did a fine job on that staff study. I sent it to the Pentagon and received word that it was well received."

"Well, sir," Jim replied. "I didn't have much to go on, so I basically decided, considering everything, that the Kaman would be the best."

"You mean Major Buckheimer didn't tell you that the decision to send the Kaman had already been made and they just needed a staff study to back it up?"

"No, sir, he just told me I had eight days to write it."

Col. Martin walked away, shaking his head.

Gertrude, Major B's. overweight, overbearing spouse thought that her job as the Commanding Officer's wife was to be a Mother figure to all the pilots' wives. She came by one afternoon for tea and for two hours pumped me for details of our personal life. I deflected these as well as possible, repeatedly trying to change the subject, until she finally started talking about Heshmat, her driver's wife. Mahmood and Heshmat had eight children and needed money badly, so Gertrude had hired Heshmat to be her badjii. She was a good worker but according to Gertrude, had the worst smell about her body imaginable. It was so bad that she was sent to the bathhouse the day she was hired. For the rest of the day she was acceptable, but the next morning the odor had returned. Gertrude tried to send her back to the bathhouse but Heshmat declined. Mahmood translated, "Madam, very bad to go to bathhouse more than once a week. Koran tells us this." The next day Gertrude had a very detailed discussion with Mahmood about female hygiene and how to douche and even gave him a douche bag. When Gertrude told me this I could not believe my ears.

"You mean you described to Mahmood how to use the douche bag?"

"Of course I did. He wouldn't have known if I didn't tell him."

"Did Heshmat use it?" I asked.

"Mahmood said she did."

"Did it help?"

"No," Gertrude replied, "but at least I tried."

October 1962

On the 21st of October, rumors of a crisis abounded in our nation's capitol. President Kennedy abruptly cancelled his congressional campaigning; the biggest joint military maneuvers in memory began off the island of Vieques near Puerto Rico and the Joint Chiefs of Staff were asked not to leave the Washington area. On Monday the 22nd, President Kennedy bluntly told the country that the Soviet Union had started to build offensive missile and bomber bases in Cuba. Although the Soviets declared the bases were merely defensive, the president asserted that the missile sites were built to accommodate intermediate-range weapons that could strike most of the major cities in the Western hemisphere. He then announced that he was ordering a blockade on Cuba to stop the shipments of military equipment. He demanded the withdrawal of all offensive weapons from the island and threatened retaliation against the Soviet Union if missiles were launched from Cuba against any country in the Americas.

• • •

I was upstairs working on the baby's room when a huge commotion emanated from the kitchen. I could hear Osra's excited voice and a male's response. Hurrying downstairs to the kitchen, I saw Osra standing at the open window in a heated conversation with Ali, the man who bought empty bottles. "What's the matter?" I asked. Osra and Ali started shouting together in Farsi. I put my hands up to stop them, shook my head, indicating that I didn't understand what they were saying.

Osra and Ali both pointed their fingers in a shooting gun position and said, "Russki, boom, boom, boom. Armrikiee boom, boom, boom." They kept repeating this phrase until I ran for my dictionary. I knew they were talking about Russia and America and I looked for the word WAR. It was not in my book. Just then Jim arrived and before he could get out of the car Nasser was at the window, joining in the hysterical melee.

A worried looking Jim indicated I was to follow him upstairs. In our bedroom he turned and said, "I've just come from a briefing at the Embassy. Russia has put nuclear warheads in Cuba aimed at the United States. Kennedy has ordered a blockade of Cuba and we are on the verge of war. If the word comes, you are to pack one suitcase for you and Jimbo, take as much non-perishable food and water as you can and drive with Nasser over the Alborz Mountains until you run out of gas."

I stared at my beloved in disbelief. "You are joking, of course."

His curt reply was, "I've never been more serious in my life."

"Where will you be?"

"Wherever I'm sent."

Emphatically speaking, trying to keep from panicking, I slowly said, "You do realize this baby is due next week. I'm supposed to deliver my baby with the help of that idiot Nasser and our three-year-old son in the middle of some God-forsaken mountain. You have got to be kidding."

"No, Babe, I am not kidding, and you had better start thinking about it now."

I did start thinking about it and the whole idea was so ridiculous I couldn't believe I was hearing it, so I started giggling. Soon I was laughing so hard tears sprang to my eyes and I sank to the floor hysterical. After several minutes, I looked up at my husband. He had the shocked look on his face of someone who was witnessing a woman who had gone round the bend. And that is exactly how I felt.

He helped me up, sat me on the bed and held me tightly. I started crying copious tears while he rubbed my back and softly told me things would work out. Yeah, yeah, I really believed that!

For three days we waited breathlessly for current news from the

Embassy. Several Eastern bloc ships bound for Cuba changed course to avoid a confrontation with the United States. Then on Thursday, Khrushchev, the Soviet Premier, agreed to a United Nations proposal to stop sending missiles to Cuba if the United States ended its blockade. Kennedy allowed American representatives to talk to U Thant, the Acting Secretary General of the United Nations. On Friday, the White House made public an intelligence report showing that work had speeded up on the Cuban missile bases to make them operational. The next day the Pentagon revealed that a U-2 spy plane was missing over Cuba, several other planes had been fired on, and the Defense Department warned that the U.S. was ready to shoot back. 14,000 Air Force reservists were called to active duty. Khrushchev made an offer to end the crisis if the United States removed all U.S. weapons from Turkey. Kennedy refused. Then on the 28th of October, miraculously Khrushchev blinked and agreed to all of Kennedy's demands to take the missiles out of Cuba. The whole world let out a collective sigh. No one was more relieved than I.

It was easy to overlook the importance of our presence in Iran while concentrating on the frustrations and minutia of everyday living. Iran, since World War II, had been one of our most important allies due to her strategic location, lying directly south of the Soviet Union. Our mission there was to provide the Shah with military assistance in fighting off communism, and to resist invasion and subversion. When the Cuban Missile Crisis occurred, I was suddenly made aware that we were not in Iran just to make my life miserable but to perform an important function.

A Halloween party was planned for the children at the Officer's Club, and I asked Jim for a suggestion for a costume for Jimbo. He designed a space helmet and had it made from the nose cone of an L-23 engine. It was complete with a Plexiglas window and curly antennas sprouting in the air. We dressed our young charge in the red, long john pajamas I had ordered in preparation for the cold winter. Jim had a pair of red hunting socks, which we filled with Kleenex, and pinned on to make it look like he had four legs. His red plastic rain boots completed the outfit. All the work paid off, as he won second prize, which was a toy red fire engine complete with sirens and blinking lights. After the party he went outside to play with Jeep-jeep who kept grabbing his "second" pair of legs. We watched, laughing, as Jimbo hopped on his swing, pumping as fast as he could, while the dog frantically jumped up and down trying to capture the extra legs.

Daily Major B. had been questioning Jim about my condition. Don't kid yourself; he didn't care a rat's patootie about my pregnancy. He was anxious for me to deliver so he could send Jim to Germany for the three-week High Altitude Flying School. How kind of him to consider waiting until after I had delivered! What a guy!

My due date had been changed so many times I didn't know if I would ever deliver. The doctor in Tucson had told me to expect the baby the sixth of November. Captain Milton, the ob-gyn specialist, as well as the Flight Surgeon, had predicted the 28th of October. Both days were past with nothing happening, but every night when I got into bed the baby began his calisthenics. I swear the kid had a trampoline in there; one night while I rested my big, fat stomach against Jim's back the bambino let go with such a healthy kick Jim yelled, "Ouch!"

The night of 8 November I was exhausted and went to bed early. Strangely enough all was quiet within me. I slept the sleep of the dead until three a.m. when all hell broke loose. My contractions started in great heaving waves, and before I knew it they were four minutes apart. We called Capt. Morris and he told us to get to the hospital immediately.

Three hours later eight pound eight ounce Patrick Joseph decided to make his appearance. Through the gas-induced fog I saw that he was very long, with huge hands and feet, a skinny body and a big head. Golden blonde hair sprouted from his scalp like a dandelion gone to seed. He was beet red all over and his face was screwed up with an angry look. He was howling indignantly, furious at being disturbed and mad at the world. I had to giggle at the sight and was so relieved to see my healthy baby. Jim had a huge grin on his face; he was ecstatic to have another boy.

Patrick's head of hair was the talk of the hospital. One of the doctors who had taken his residency at the Indian Hospital in Gallup, New Mexico said he had seen that much hair before, but only on a Navajo infant, never on a Caucasian baby.

Major Arnold, a five-foot tall and almost as wide Army nurse, brought Patrick to me for his first feeding. She was old-time no-nonsense Army, in charge, confident and religious in her care of her patients. She had oiled his hair and parted it on the left side in an attempt to control it. Though the hair was neatly combed over to the right side, the back was sticking straight up. He was sound asleep and reluctantly awakened to be fed. I couldn't get over how cute he was in spite of his hair. The next feeding Major Arnold had combed his hair from the right to the left. It didn't help. The third time she had his hair parted down the middle and slicked back. He looked just like Calvin Coolidge, lacking only the stiff collar to complete the image. I was laughing when she said, very seriously, "Mrs. Starkey, I've parted this kid's hair on the left, on the right and down the middle. No matter what I try it still looks like Hell." She turned and stomped out of the room.

On the third day we were allowed to go home. Jimbo was fascinated with his little brother. "Can I teach him to play baseball?" were his first words of greeting.

"Why don't we wait until he gets a little bigger," I suggested.

We hadn't been home two hours when coming downstairs, I saw Jim and Jimbo on the floor in the living room with Patrick in his carrier between them. Jim was brandishing the electric clippers he used to cut Jimbo's hair.

Rushing over to them I demanded, "What are you doing?"

"What does it look like? I'm giving Pat a haircut."

"He's only three days old. That's too young!" I sputtered.

Ignoring me, Jim started the clippers and with one pass shaved off half of Patrick's hair. It fell in great clumps around him. Patrick was screaming but that didn't deter his father. Two more passes and the job was complete. I rushed to comfort my baby, crooning softly to him until he quieted down. I looked down at the clean-shaven head with its halo of gold and had to admit it was an improvement. Rubbing my cheek over the spiky fuzz, I said, "Jim, you really should check with me before you do things like this, don't you think?"

"Why? You said yourself it's an improvement."

Two days later Jim had to leave for Germany to attend the three-week High Altitude Flying School. I didn't want him go, but the Army doesn't give wives a choice. He told me that when Nasser returned from the airport I was to send him to the Motor Pool to get a major checkup on the car. "You'll be without a car for three days so if you need something take care of it now," he advised.

"We're fine. Jimbo can stay home from school during that time to get used to Patrick. It will be good for all of us."

While Jim was packing, we discussed what he could buy at the Frankfurt Post Exchange and I made a list. With hugs and kisses for the three of us, he was off. After Jim left, Osra started acting very strange. I was beginning to lose patience with her. If I walked into the kitchen she made me feel as if I was intruding on her turf; she became very dictatorial toward Jimbo and finally she demanded twice her salary since "Capeetan was gone." I told her I could not consider paying her more money, then I told her she could leave. Osra was shocked that I fired her. She was unprepared for my stand. Iranians are used to the "superior" male, and I could only assume that she felt I had been abandoned by my "protector." She thought I would cave to her demands for more money but we were already paying her more than I thought our budget allowed. In a huff, she packed her things and left.

When Nasser arrived, I sent him to the Motor Pool as Jim had directed. I settled in with our two boys, glad to have the house to ourselves. Osra's scowl was not missed and I decided I would worry about getting another badjii the next day.

After calling around to all our friends, requesting that they tell their servants that I was in need of a badjii, I reluctantly called Gertrude. She was very helpful saying that she would send Heshmat over to spend the night so I would not be alone.

Mahmood arrived with Heshmat an hour later. She was less than five feet tall with wide flaring hips, heavy hairy legs and a mop of curly, henna-colored hair. Iranian farmers put henna on the buttocks of female sheep, believing that it will make the sheep more fertile. Why Heshmat would rinse her hair in henna when she already had eight children baffled me. She had large, expressive brown eyes, a beautiful smile and a hearty laugh. I liked her instantly, in spite of the slight odor I detected. She brought a pallet and pillow and decreed that she would sleep on the floor at the foot of the stairs every night to protect me until I found another badjii.

The next day after lunch, I put Pat down for a nap. Coming downstairs I heard a gagging sound from the kitchen. Entering I saw Jimbo on the floor, a box of kitchen matches beside him. He was trying to spit out something.

"Did you eat some matches?" I demanded. He shook his head up and down. I rushed him to the bathroom and had him spit everything out. I called the dispensary and told the corpsman what had happened. "Ma'm, you say your son ate matches?"

"Yes, yes," I answered, expecting to be told to make sure Jimbo spit it all out. Instead, much to my surprise, he said, "You get him down here as quickly as possible."

"Oh my God, what am I going to do now? I don't have a car and driver."

"Then we'll send the ambulance. Where do you live?"

This really scared me, because I knew it was almost impossible to get the ambulance sent. I gave him directions and told him the map of our house was on record at the hospital. I hung up and waited for an hour. When the ambulance failed to show up, I called several people to see if they had a car and driver available. Fortunately, Norma's was there, so I grabbed Pat and Jimbo and waited in the kuchee for her driver. We raced to the hospital and I didn't care how fast or reckless the driver was going. Jimbo's stomach was pumped and everything turned out okay. I was told that if the matches had been Strike Anywhere matches the chemical that is put on the heads could have caused damage to the nervous system. Fortunately, these were ordinary matches; otherwise the delay in getting to the hospital might have caused big problems. The Iranian ambulance driver couldn't read the map and never did find our house. This is the reason the ambulance was sent so infrequently.

When Jim had been gone three days I called the Motor Pool to find out when I could expect the car to be ready.

"Motor Pool. Sgt Tompkins speaking."

"Sgt., this is Mrs. Starkey calling. When will our car be ready?"

"Mrs. Starkey, we don't have your car here. When was it brought in?"

"Three days ago. Nasser brought it down for a major overhaul."

"Just a minute, Ma'am. Let me check further." Sgt. Tompkins was gone for several minutes and when he returned he informed me that Nasser had never arrived with our car. Later he called back to say that our car had been found. It was in an accident up at Tajrish and was totaled. Nasser had been running drugs and had disappeared. Since the Shah had a no tolerance attitude on drugs Nasser may have met his maker, I hoped.

My husband was in Germany, I had a newborn, the badjii had left, our son had eaten matches and had to have his stomach pumped, and now the car was totaled, to say nothing of the not-to-be-missed Nasser. There was no car or driver available to me and I still had not found another badjii. I wondered why I had ever promised Jim I would follow him anywhere.

The weather suddenly turned wintry, with a brisk wind blowing down from the Alborz Mountains. The earthquake-damaged doors in the living room allowed a lot of cold air to enter the house, and the big, ugly kerosene stove did very little to warm us. Taking a big round of Army green tape I went outside and attempted to tape the cracks in all the doors where the metal was bent. In my enthusiasm I even taped the door we used to get into the house! With difficulty I removed it so I could get back inside. I was concerned about keeping Patrick warm. We had a bassinet that we put inside his crib and had a blanket draped over the bassinet and the outside of the crib to keep out any draft. Since there was no heat in the upstairs Jim had purchased a small Aladdin kerosene stove and had warned me not to leave it on in Pat's room, but rather to put it in the entrance of the room where there would be plenty of air circulation from the stairwell. Dressed in his flannel pajamas and covered with two blankets, Patrick stayed cozy. With Jim gone, Jimbo had nightmares in which he said his Daddy was crashing into some trees. He would awaken crying and tell me about it. Unnerved, I ended up allowing him to sleep in the bed with me. Every night I made sure Jimbo's baseball bat was by my side of the bed. I would defend my boys with my life if I had to.

Things looked up when Norma brought over Shala, a very tall, thin girl with a sharp, hooked nose. She did not have the humor of Heshmat, but she had no odor and she could stay at night. She wasn't very bright and I had to show her over and over how to do anything. Barbara sent her driver to pick up Jimbo for school. He was delighted to share a ride with his two little girlfriends, Sherry and Lisa. Barb also let me use her car and driver for the day to go shopping. I was anxious to get the birth announcements printed on the blank vellum note cards my mother had sent. The driver Ali knew where a print shop was located so we proceeded south past the American Embassy, down Ferdowsi Avenue into the madness of Lalazar Street. Carts, cars, buses, camels, donkeys and pedestrians flooded the street. We moved along snail-like for several blocks until we came to the printing shop. Lalazar was famous for men pinching women who were not wearing chadors, so I made sure Ali let me off in front of the shop. I leaped out of the car and rushed into the store. I had written what I thought was a clever poem that I wanted printed in Persian on the front of the card with English translation on the inside. My poem read:

From the hot and arid Persian land
Home of mosques, mullahs and burning sand
Camels, rugs and the Throne of Peacocks
Is born a boy with golden locks.

I showed the poem and cards to the shopkeeper and he agreed to do the printing. I was to pick them up the following Monday. Arriving home with the groceries, I discovered that Shala had plugged the telephone into the 220-volt electric outlet and burned up the phone. Now I had no telephone.

I put up with Shala only because I had no choice. Someone had to be in the house at nighttime or when I was out. We managed for the next week; Barbara's driver took Jimbo to school and I begged and borrowed a car and driver whenever I needed to shop.

Monday I used Joanne's vehicle and driver and returned for the birth announcements. I walked into the store, greeted the shopkeeper, who looked at me strangely and promptly walked into the back room. He was gone for several minutes only coming out when another customer entered the store. After a profusion of Farsi they concluded their business. I waited patiently until the customer left.

"I have come for my birth announcements," I said politely.

"Madam, I cannot print your announcements," the shopkeeper said.

"Why not?"

"If I print your announcements I will be arrested," he stated flatly.

"Whhhat did you say?"

"The SAVAK will arrest me!"

"The SAVAK? What is that?"

"The SAVAK is the Shah's secret police. They are everywhere, and if I were to print this bad announcement I would be arrested.

"Why would the Shah have you arrested for printing the announcement of my baby's birth?"

"Because, Madam, you say terrible things about Iran in your announcement."

"What terrible things do I say about Iran? Show me," I demanded.

"First you say, 'From the hot and arid Persian land' Persia is not so hot and arid. It is very beautiful. And then you say 'Home of Mosques and Mullahs.' The Shah will not like that."

"But you do have mosques and mullahs!"

"Madam, I know we do, but the Shah would have SAVAK arrest me if I said this. And then you say 'camels!' Why don't you say that we have automobiles? We are not such a backward country that we do not have automobiles. Just look outside and see all the automobiles," he said proudly, waving his hand toward the pandemonium in the street.

Looking outside I saw crowds of cars with horns piercing the air, all jockeying for a front position, ready to leap ahead when the light changed. He was correct, Iran did have automobiles. The man was clearly in fear of loosing face as well as his liberty, so I decided I had better compromise. I said, "Let's change the announcement to read:

"From the rich and fertile Persian lands,
Home of flowers, fruits and burning sands,
Caviar, rugs and the Throne of Peacocks,
Is born a son with golden locks."

Would that be okay?" I asked.

"Madam, what is a rug?"

"The beautiful rugs that are made in Iran."

"What is a rug?"

"A rug is what you put on the floor. You know, a Turkoman, Tabriz, Isfahan rugs." My voice was rising in frustration.

"Oh, you mean carpets. In Iran we have carpets, not rugs." The last two words were spoken in a disgusted manner as if he were speaking of dirt.

"All right, we can put in carpets in place of rugs so it will read Caviar, carpets and the Throne of Peacocks. Will that work?"

"Oh! Yes, Madam. That is good. I can have these ready by Thursday."

"Wonderful. I did not understand and please know that I don't want you to get into trouble with the Shah's police."

"Thank you, Madam. Thank you very much." Smiling broadly, he shook my hand.

I returned on Thursday to pick up the announcements. Reading the finished product I saw that the shop owner had changed the words 'burning sands' to 'shinning sun'. I was irritated but since it was too late to do anything I paid the bill. I hoped the recipients would know that I did not make the error in spelling.

Returning home, I discovered Shala had broken my beautiful crystal cake plate, a wedding gift from my favorite aunt. The evidence was in the garbage can, but still she insisted she was not to blame. I was to discover over and over again that Iranians hate to admit a mistake. With Jimbo in school it must have been ghosts who did the dastardly deed. Angrily holding my temper I gave Shala her weekly salary and told her she could leave early for her Friday holiday. She never returned. On Saturday I called Gertrude and made arrangements for Heshmat to come back. Jim was to return sometime within the next two days, and I decided to wait until after he came back before embarking on training another badjii.

While Jimbo was always put to bed in his room after his story, every night his Dad was gone he would awaken crying and crawl in bed with me. Accustomed to Jimbo sleeping next to me, that night

I awakened, immediately sensing he was taken from me. Opening my eyes I saw Jim, bathed in the light from the street, standing next to the bed, holding his son in his arms. Crying in delight, I leaped up and hugged them both. Jimbo woke up and smiled sleepily at his dad. Jim carried him into his bed, with me following closely. We checked on Patrick and returned to our room. Jim laughed when he saw the baseball bat. "Babe, what did you expect to do with that?" Primly I replied that I planned to defend us with it. "Well, it didn't work. I came in the noisiest taxi I ever heard. I'm surprised it didn't wake up the whole neighborhood. And who is that woman sleeping at the foot of the stairs? I almost stepped on her. She didn't wake up either. Some protection you have here!"

"Well, now I have my Great Protector. I don't need a baseball bat or a badjii to sleep in front of the stairs. I'm so glad you're home. Maybe life will return to normal," I replied. I was soon to learn that normal does not exist in Iran.

Chapter 6

Pope John convenes Vatican II, Eleanor Roosevelt dies, Soviet Union closes Cuban Missile base.

The next day dawned bright and sunny though very cold. After breakfast Jim called the Motor Pool and was greeted heartily with the statement, "Captain Starkey, welcome home. We have a new car and driver for you. We'll send them right out."

"How long have you had this car and driver?"

"For a couple of days, sir."

Having had his ears burned off by my descriptions of my problems Jim inquired, "Why didn't you send this car and driver for my wife's use while I was gone?"

"Sir, we have learned the hard way that when a new driver has been hired it is important for the officer to indoctrinate him before he is introduced to the wife. Remember, sir, in this country wives are not so important."

When Jim relayed this to me I exploded in a string of expletives. Shocked, Jim said, "Babe, I have never heard such language from you before!"

"Well, my vocabulary is increasing with each day we are in this bleeping country!"

While waiting for our new driver I gathered up Jim's uniforms so the new driver could take them to the Barf Dry Cleaners on Saltanabad Avenue.

Jim introduced me to Asghar, our new driver. His name sounded very much like Oscar and that was what we ended up calling him. He was very big for an Iranian, over six feet tall with broad shoulders, had skin like a Hershey bar and a full moustache that wound down his cheek and curved up at the ends. His thick eyebrows were low over his squinting eyes, which gave him a menacing look. He didn't smile when he met Jimbo and me and I could sense instantly that Jimbo was wary of him; nevertheless, I was happy to have a driver especially since he spoke reasonable English.

Jim left to go to Ghalamorghi and dropped Jimbo off at school on the way. I went into the kitchen to clean up the breakfast dishes, got Patrick up for his breakfast and bath, whistling happily all the time. Life was looking up; it just had to get better. Jim had taken the burned out phone with him. About ten o'clock I was surprised when Asghar returned not only with a good phone but also with a new badjii the man at the dry cleaner had recommended.

Rafat was beautiful, tall and slender as a model with creamy light brown skin and enormous deer-like eyes. She smiled easily showing perfect white teeth. She wore her silken, black hair tied back at the nape of her neck. She looked like a dream walking and could speak English. I was sure she couldn't work well but, I had no choice, so I hired her. I showed her the maids' room and bath and left her to get settled. When she emerged she was wearing the uniform I had purchased for Osra. It was much too big and I vowed to order a smaller one when we sent the next order to Sears. Much to my shock, she was quick, industrious and found things to do without me telling her. I kept pinching myself, thinking this couldn't be real.

Oscar and I left to get Jimbo and when we arrived back Jimbo was instantly enchanted with Rafat. He kept hanging around the kitchen talking to her. Good grief! My three-year-old son was in love! Rafat was wonderful to Patrick, was a very good cook and laughed and teased Jimbo. The whole family loved her. She patiently showed me how to cook rice and khoreshes the Persian way.

Having been born in a foreign country to American parents on official duty for the American Government, Patrick became the recipient of four certificates of birth. The most important one is from the State Department with its fancy seals and ribbons stating that Patrick is an American citizen. He also has one from the Iranian government stating that he is an Iranian citizen since he was born in Tehran. Not to be outdone, Armish-Maag gave him a certificate of membership in the "Persian Knight Tribe" and was declared a bonafide "Persian Bacheh" (bacheh is the Farsi word for 'baby' and when Pat was upset we referred to him as our bitchy bacheh). When we returned to the United States we immediately wrote to the Department of Immigration and Naturalization to get another official birth certificate. We were advised by the State Department to do this so there would never be a question of nationality. To this day whenever Patrick shows his passport with the place of birth noted to be Tehran, Iran, eyebrows are raised.

The first of December was Jimbo's third birthday and we invited the Leibshultz family and some of his friends from school for a party. We had ordered some toys from the Sears catalogue and the children played happily with them while the adults visited. One of the couples was from the Embassy and later we were invited to a party at their home. Sarah, our hostess served the most wonderful Chicken Curry with numerous condiments. I was very impressed as I listened to the Embassy people talk about the various countries they had lived in. This was the fifth assignment Sarah and her husband George had overseas, having been in Nigeria, Sudan, India and Burma prior to their assignment to Iran. But when Sarah mentioned a woman's name and said this woman was so cosmopolitan having lived in eight countries, I was floored. I thought I could qualify as being cosmopolitan since living in Iran, until I met Sarah. And now Sarah didn't consider herself to be worldly! I had a lot to learn!

The time had come for us to repay the DeHeshtis for the interesting dinner we had enjoyed at their home. Jim wanted to include two of the fellows from the Field Teams, one a Captain Miller was stationed in Mashad, a city in the northeast part of Iran; the other, a Captain Burns was stationed in Tabriz, a city in the northwest part of Iran. Both of them were married but could not bring their families to Iran, as the duty outside the capital was a hardship because of lack of housing, schooling and the other amenities families required. Their tours were only twelve months duration. Jim had brought back from Germany a Grundig tape recorder and player and Captain Burns, who had an extensive collection of music, would make tapes for us to enjoy. So we had a wonderful collection of instrumentals by Mantovani, Cole Porter, Gershwin and current Broadway hits along with various jazz selections. Since the electricity was not always constant the music would get very slow and deep and suddenly fast and high. It ebbed and flowed like the ocean but we didn't care, it was the music from home.

I consulted Rafat about the menu and she suggested we start with Ashe Torsh, a soup that is made with apricots, prunes, walnuts, chick peas, small meat balls, onions, dried mint, and cinnamon, for the first course. That would be followed by roast chicken, kukune bademjan, (a soufflé made with mashed eggplant, eggs and sharp cheese garnished with yogurt} and kateh, rice that is cooked in such a way that the bottom of the pot has a layer of golden, crunchy rice called todday. I agreed after ascertaining the eggplant would not be stuffed. Rafat made the soup the day before as she explained it was always better the second day. My contribution was Death by Chocolate Brownies for dessert.

When our guests arrived I took their coats while Jim offered them drinks. I was pleased with the way the room looked as I had filled the spaces around the pillars with tall rubber plants, and had Jimbo's old bedroom curtains, which were brightly striped denim made into poshtis, the giant pillows the Persians use to sit on. These were stacked in areas around the room. A carpet dealer had brought over several geometric tribal carpets for our approval and these were placed around the vast floor. Jimbo used the spaces in between the carpets as streets when he rode his tricycle. The fire in the fireplace, Jim's dramatic drapes, the lights on the wall and lit candles gave that enormous room a warm glow. If only I could make the ugly kerosene stove disappear! Mrs. DeHeshti was taking all of this in and I could tell she was impressed.

Mr. DeHeshti, looking around the room, stated, "Capeetan Estarkey, you have wasted no time in purchasing some carpets I see."

"No, Mr. DeHeshti, we have not purchased anything as yet. The dealer has left these here for our approval."

Surprised, his eyebrows rising in disbelief, Mr. D. slowly said, "You mean the dealer left these here without getting any money?"

"Yes, he said he would come back next month to see if we want to purchase them."

"I cannot believe this. I have never heard of such a thing! To not get some money first is unheard of. What if you take them without paying him?"

"Mr. DeHeshti, that's ridiculous. I would never dream of doing that!"

Shaking his head in amazement, Mr. D. quietly said, "You Americans are very different from Iranians."

I noticed that Mrs. DeHeshti was zeroing in on Captain Miller. "Capeetan, where en America are you from?" she asked, trilling her R's and looking the tall Captain Miller straight in the eye.

"Ah'm from Alabama, ma'am," was his soft reply.

"From Aleebama? Esn't that en the south?"

"Yes'm, it is"

"And esn't that where you leench Neegroes?"

"Oh, no ma'am!" was the shocked reply from Miller, backing away from his interrogator. Mrs. D. stepped toward Miller and Miller kept backing up as Mrs. D. peppered him with accusations.

"I read in the papers that you leench Neegros en the south." She insisted.

"Oh, no ma'm, I would never do that!" he said, backing away from the Wicked Witch.

I ran into the kitchen saying to Rafat, "We need to serve the soup now!" When I returned I saw that Mrs. D. had backed Miller clear to the fireplace and he was in danger of catching his clothes on fire.

Dramatically, and too loudly, I announced that dinner was being served. As we were seated Mrs. D. kept up her commentary about how the Iranian people knew that Southerners lynched Negroes. Jim informed her that we had lived in the South and this simply was not true of all Southerners. "Unfortunately, this has happened a few times and the news media makes a big deal of it. There are murders that take place in Tehran but that doesn't mean all Iranians are murderers, does it?"

Mrs. DeHeshti glared at Jim, not expecting him to contradict her. Mr. D. with an amused look on his face changed the subject, quickly turned to me and asked in the same trilling speech, "Mee-sus Estarkee, 'ave you ever seen a woman who was reeelly a man?" Stunned silence filled the room and my jaw dropped open. I gulped and finally croaked, "Mr. DeHesht, how would I know?"

Dead silence and then he roared with laughter, slapping his thigh very pleased with himself. The others smiled hesitantly. I got up to tell Rafat she could clear the soup bowls. I never did get over how in Iran it was perfectly OK to ask the most personal questions but it was not OK to mention that you like the carpet on their floor.

The rest of the evening we carried on a somewhat strained conversation until the electricity went out. It was not unusual to have blackouts and we always kept a large supply of candles for these times. The pilots excused themselves because they had an early morning flight and the DeHeshtis took the hint and to my great relief, left at the same time. Laughing, Jim said, "Babe, I wish I had a picture of the expression on your face when DeHeshti asked you that question!"

"I didn't know what to say!"

"You couldn't have answered it better. That answer was perfect! Don't worry; we can't be concerned about the strange DeHeshtis. We have fulfilled our obligation to them and we won't ask them here again, unless, of course, you want to!"

"Fat chance", I muttered, as I started to help Rafat clear the table.

Christmas was fast approaching and we needed to get a tree. Big problem! In Iran it is illegal to cut a tree, as they are so scarce even in the mountains. Norma came to our rescue. "We get our Christmas trees at the Russian Embassy," she told me.

"The Russian Embassy? Are you sure?"

"Oh, yes. They have them leaning against the outside walls. The trees are brought in from the Caucasus Mountains and are beautiful."

The next Friday we went to the Russian Embassy and purchased the largest, fullest evergreen tree we had ever had. It took up a whole corner of our immense living room; the clean, fresh mountain smell permeated the whole house. Living in Iran was full of contradictions. In a Moslem country we were able to buy a Christmas tree from an atheist nation in a capitalistic bartering system. Go figure!

On Sunday Jimbo was invited to a Christmas party given by

the parents of his Christian Armenian friend from school. We drove him to the home and were assured by John's mother that the party would last four hours and for us not to worry about him. As we drove downtown to look at carpets I said to Jim, "A party for three year olds lasts four hours? I don't think so. We better plan on no more than an hour and a half." When we returned two hours later we were met by the hysterical mother and crying children. The Santa Claus they had hired got too close to the fire and his beard flamed up. The father threw Santa on the ground and proceeded to beat the fire out while the children watched in shock. We arrived right after that and tried our best to calm the mother and children to no avail. We did not know any of the other children, as Jimbo was the only American child at the party. We finally left and all the way home Jimbo kept saying, "Santa won't be here this Christmas, he's in the hospital." That Santa did end up in the hospital more for the beating from the father than from the flames.

Four days before Christmas it started snowing. The snow came down for more than twenty-four hours, an unheard of amount. Usually if it snowed it was only for an hour or so and would quickly melt when the sun came out. It was a nice respite because Jim got to stay home those four days, as traffic in Tehran came to a complete standstill. Mehrabad Airport was closed for three days because there was no snow removal equipment available. The airport was finally reopened when the Iran Air pilots ran the jet planes up and down the runway to melt the snow.

Christmas Eve I got Jimbo up to go to the bathroom before I went to bed and as we returned to his room we heard bells outside. I knew they came from the wagon and horses bringing potable water from the mountains to the people in south Tehran but Jimbo, his eyes wide open exclaimed, "That's Santa Claus! Mama, do you hear him?" "Yes, Jimbo, you better get to sleep so Santa doesn't forget to stop here!" With that he jumped into bed, hugged me fiercely and plopped his head on the pillow and soon was fast asleep.

We spent a quiet Christmas day playing with Jimbo and Patrick. Pat was thriving, gaining weight and sleeping through most of the night. He was a happy baby and his smile lit up the room. We fixed a pork roast, and Rafat cooked rice for us (being a devout Moslem she wouldn't touch the pork called gusht-e-khuk). With the canned spinach and applesauce our meal was complete. Since my birthday is on Christmas Day, several days before Jim had asked Rafat to order a cake from the bakery. After dinner she told me she had to go to the store for something and would be back shortly. She returned with a single layer cake frosted with bright flowers and the Iranian flag. I never knew if that was her idea or the baker's, and maybe they thought I was lucky to be in Iran.

The Wednesday after Christmas we met our friends for dinner at the Officer's Club. Kay and Phil Rosser had a daughter in third grade at the American School. During the meal, Mike the Club Officer came to our table to tell Phil he had a phone call. When Phil returned he was annoyed. The phone call was from Sally, their eight year old daughter. She had called to report that their badjii was having a baby. "That's preposterous," Kay exclaimed. Then both of them started to describe to us their problems with Sally not telling the truth. Twice more our meal was interrupted with calls from Sally, insisting the badjii was delivering a baby. Finally, in exasperation the Rossers decided they had better go home.

The next day Kay called with an apology for cutting our meal short and then using the phrase we would hear and say many times in Iran, "You'll never believe what just happened!" The Rossers arrived home to discover their daughter sitting on the living room floor holding a brand-new baby, a look of ecstasy on her face. The badjii was in her bathroom scrubbing the blood from the toilet. Nearby was a plastic bag with the sac and umbilical cord. Questioning Sally, they learned that she had been in the bathroom with the badjii watching the entire process. She told her mother the badjii had squatted over the toilet and grabbed the baby as he emerged. Sally helped by actually cutting the umbilical cord with a pair of scissors. Kay never did figure out how Sally knew what to do, as she didn't think Sally knew a word of Farsi and the badjii didn't speak any English. Her parting words were, "I guess I won't have to explain to Sally where babies come from!"

• • •

January 1963

About the same time that we moved to Iran, my mother, who worked for the University of Arizona met an Iranian student named Mostafa Byat. Mostafa was from one of the Thousand Families of Iran, had spent the last sixteen years of his life in school either in Europe or the United States, had just graduated with a degree in Engineering and was returning to Iran to live permanently. My mother gave him our address and he had contacted us soon after arriving in Tehran. We invited him to dinner and he brought his cousin, who had also studied at the University of Arizona and the cousin's new wife, a native Tucsonian of Mexican descent. We had a wonderful time talking about the U. of A. and Tucson. It was like talking to fellow Americans. Mostafa and his cousin Ali were ready to take on the life the wealthy Iranians led; partying and traveling to Europe and the United States, giving and attending luncheons, teas and dinners within Iran and when time permitted, managing the incomes from the farms and villages owned by the family. Maria, Ali's wife, was ecstatic about living in Iran. Her mother-in-law had welcomed her with open arms and Maria even had her own servant. For her, life had never been better.

During the past year the American government had become more alarmed with the popular rising of the communist Tudah Party in Iran. One day early in January the University of Tehran became the scene of student demonstrations. The military arrived and crushed the protests, vandalizing and in some cases criminally attacking some of the female students. President Kennedy called on the Shah to institute reforms to counteract the communist threat if he was to continue to get American aid. In an effort to win support of all his subjects, the Shah announced sweeping reforms called the White Revolution, a bloodless transformation of Iranian society. Among the provisions were the privatization of certain factories and profit sharing for the workers, electoral reforms including for the first time the right of women to vote, and land redistribution. He called on women to abandon the chador and dress in western clothes. His father, Reza Shah had decreed in early

1930 that women remove the chador and even had them arrested if they appeared in public wearing them. Devout Moslem women of the wealthy class remained within the walls of the harems during the entire reign of Reza Shah, never setting foot outside their compounds. When Reza Shah was forced to abdicate in 1941 in favor of his son Mohammad Reza, women again appeared in public wearing the chador. In 1963 many women wore the chador but many did not. It was hard to tell if chador-less women were Moslem or some other religion as the Shah was lenient toward all religions.

The Shah decreed in the White Revolution that all children, male and female would get a high school education. Upon graduation they would either go into the military, the Red Lion and Sun (the Red Cross of Iran) or the Literacy Corps to serve their country for two years.

The land redistribution consisted of the government taking lands that had been held for generations by the Thousand Families and the clergy. The plan was to distribute it to the peasants who had worked the land. In this way the Shah hoped to build loyalty from the 75% of Iran's population who were landless serfs. The aristocracy (the Thousand Families) would lose their income, as would the mullahs.

This plan enraged the Thousand Families, who lived luxurious lives from the monies collected from their lands and villages. Their offspring were sent to prestigious schools in Europe and the United States; they built huge mansions in Tehran and on the Riviera, and frequented the haunts of the rich and famous. With their properties gone how would they live?

The ulama (the Shia clergy) would not only lose incomes but the Shah's decree that women abandon their chadors inflamed them. No Moslem women should ever allow a man outside her family to see her head uncovered. And the thought of sending young people to the villages to teach the children to read and write was shocking. Everyone knew the only person in the village who could read and write was the local mullah. How was he to control his village if everyone was literate?

The riots started soon after the Shah made his announcement. The American Embassy told all Americans to stay in their compounds until further notice. We didn't see Oscar for three days but Rafat stayed with us and even managed to find us the English language Kayhan newspaper. A small article on the front page told of a mullah in Tabriz, who had told his followers to cut off the breasts of any woman seen without a chador. The mullah's name was Ruhollah Khomeini.

The Shah's forces put down the revolt after three days and we heard that hundreds of people had been killed in clashes all over Iran. After the fourth day work resumed, Jimbo returned to school and I had Oscar take me to the Embassy Co-op for needed supplies. After shopping there Oscar stopped at my favorite greengrocer not far from the Embassy. I was busy choosing vegetables when urgent shouts came from down the street. Oscar, pale and frightened ran into the store to tell me to get into the car immediately as rioting was starting again. All the storekeepers along the street pulled down the corrugated metal shutters that protected the shops, fastened them with large padlocks and left. The street was filled with the sounds of the metal crashing, people shouting, cars screeching and horns honking. I jumped into the back seat and Oscar yelled for me to lie down so that no one would see that he was driving an American. I did as I was told, holding on for dear life as the car careened around corners. Oscar had never driven so fast and when we came to Abbasabad Avenue, where the Iranian army had a huge base, I carefully raised my head expecting to see government troops on the move. Much to my surprise the compound was deserted with the exception of one lone soldier squatting in the dirt urinating.

I felt it was safe for me to sit up and I ordered Oscar to go to Jimbo's school to pick him up. I only wanted to gather my kids in my arms in the comfort of our home and warn Jim of the danger. I noticed that the back of Oscar's neck and tunic was wet as drops of sweat careened down from his head. He was visibly frightened.

"Oscar, why did you want me to hide?" I inquired.

"Oh, madam, it is very dangerous to drive Americans."

"Dangerous? What are you saying?"

"Madam there are many people in Iran who do not like Americans."

"Who are these people?" I demanded.

"I do not know, Madam."

"Why don't they like Americans?"

"I do not know, Madam." In spite of my insistent questioning he refused to say anything else.

Reaching home I called Ghalamorghi and learned that Jim was on a flight to Isfahan. I told 'ole Seegar of my experience and he made a joke about taking out the rag heads. I was not amused. I asked him to have Jim call me when he returned. By five o'clock whatever trouble there was had been taken care of and Jim returned home safe and sound. Things quieted down and life returned to normal, if anything in Iran can be termed 'normal'.

Our days off were Friday, for the Moslem holy day and Sunday, for the Christian holy day. During the winter there was not very much to do so we decided to educate ourselves about Persian carpets. On Friday we would visit the carpet shops on Saltanabad owned by Jews and on Sunday we would go to Ferdowsi Street and the Bazaar to the Iranian-owned shops. The ritual was always the same. We would arrive to be greeted profusely by the shopkeeper who would clap his hands demanding that tea be brought to "his very good customers". We would sit on poshtis drinking tea while the shop-keeper would fuss over Jimbo. Having finished the required two cups of tea, we would stand while the assistants would drag carpet after carpet from a huge pile and place it in front of us, always watching for our reaction. Jim always had his stern face on but it was hard for me not to show any emotion. Most of the carpets were wild with color; so many of them had a bilious green together with the red, saffron, and blue. Some of them were pale pinks, greens and blues; too feminine for our tastes. As the pile in front of us became taller and taller the dust became thicker and thicker. If a carpet caught our eye we would signal with our hands so we could look closer, turning over the corner to see how closely the knots were tied. We would ask questions about where the carpet had been made, what the pattern was, thus learning more every time we went to a carpet shop. If we found one that was especially appealing the dealer would bring it to our house, lay it on the floor and leave it for several weeks to let it 'grow' on us. The Persians believe that the more the carpet is walked on the prettier it becomes.

• • •

Bargaining is a way of life in many countries in the world but Iranians are particularly adept at it. After the tea ceremony the shopkeeper shows his goods, always watching the customer's face. It behooves the customer to maintain a casual, even bored expression so as not to give a clue as to one's thoughts. If something is interesting to the customer, he asks the price; when told the amount, frowns and shakes his head indicating the price is much too high. Sensing an imminent sale the shopkeeper asks the customer to name his price. The customer names a very low price at which time the shopkeeper might give what we Americans referred to as The Camel Kiss. Camels are dirty, rude, obnoxious, and haughty animals; they carry their heads very high and appear to look down their nose, their thick-lashed eyes half closed. They frequently give a disdainful snort when they do not approve of what is going on around them. When a shopkeeper does not approve of a price the customer suggests, he emulates the camel by quickly raising his head at the same time flaring his nostrils, curling his lips and clicking his tongue against the roof of his mouth. Then he lowers his head as he blows air through pursed lips, making a chewwww sound.

The first time I witnessed the Camel Kiss I was insulted and left the shop. Discussing this with other Americans I learned that this was a common way to bargain. Deciding 'when in Rome, do as the Romans do', I practiced the Camel Kiss in front of the mirror until I got it down pat. I was delighted the first time I tried it on a shopkeeper and saw the shocked look on his face!

Trial and error taught me when to discern the shopkeeper had reached the end of his bargaining. To try to get him to give a lower price would cause him to 'lose face'. On the other hand, I didn't want to 'lose face' either. I learned to satisfy both needs by saying, "I will pay your price if you will include that jug." For instance, if I were trying to buy a copper tray I would find some small copper object to add to the purchase. This almost always worked and both of us were pleased with the outcome. I ended up with so many 'objects d'art' that my friends and family became the recipients of Iranian art.

I loved the bargaining and after returning to the States found shopping at Safeway to be very boring. (No one would argue over the price of carrots.) I also enjoyed playing a little game with whoever was my current badjii. Tomatoes, onions, green beans, cucumbers and fruits were cheap and plentiful and were a mainstay of the Iranian diet along with eggs, panir (goat cheese) rice and bread. I never cared how much the badjii ate of those items so when the badjii invariably asked me the price I had paid, I would exaggerate and tell her a lower price than what I had actually paid. She would be very impressed and exclaim, "OOO madam, khali khoob!" (Very good) But if I happened to find some bananas, which were scarce and dear and I didn't want her to eat them, I would say, "Oh, I paid too much but Monsieur and little Monsieur like these so much, what can I do? I must buy them!" and I would quote an enormous price to her. She wouldn't touch anything that was special for Monsieur if her life depended on it, which in an Iranian household might be the case.

When it came to bargaining I was a rank amateur compared to Jim. He would sit on the floor opposite the shopkeeper, drink tea and argue about the price of a carpet. He would dramatically point to the veins on his arm and exclaim, "How can you charge so much? You are trying to take the blood from my arm! You are trying to take the milk out of my babies' mouths!" The shopkeeper would start laughing and ask, "Capeetan, are you sure you are not Persian? Or if the carpet dealer were Jewish, he would say, "Capeetan, you are more of a Jew than I am!" To watch Jim in action is better than going to the movies.

I had just walked into the kitchen to tell Rafat that I was leaving to pick up Jimbo when the phone interrupted our conversation. An excited man was speaking rapidly in Farsi. I motioned for Rafat to take the phone and listening I could tell she was upset. When she hung up she told me her five-year-old daughter had been hit by a taxi and she had to go to the hospital immediately. I told her to call a taxi and I gave her some money. She gathered her things, promised to let me know how her daughter was and left.

I did not hear from her for three days until she suddenly appeared at the door. She was visibly changed, looking wan and drawn as if she had not had any sleep. She told me her daughter had run out into the street to chase a ball, had been hit by a taxi going too fast and had a broken leg. I was not aware she had any children. "Oh, yes, madam, my daughter live with husband."

"I didn't know you have a husband, Rafat."

"Well, he no husband now. He divorced me, he keeps daughter. Madam, the doctor say I buy gold nail to mend daughter's leg. I must have $100.00."

"Rafat, that is a lot of money. Why doesn't your husband pay this since he has your daughter?"

"I not know, madam. He say me ask you for money."

"Rafat, I don't have that kind of money. I would like to help you but I don't have a lot of money. I can give you the money I owe you for your work but I don't have any more than that."

She seemed to understand, told me she would return as soon as she could and she left. Jim felt as I did, that the story was strange. We had never heard of using a gold nail to mend a leg but how were we to know what kind of medicine was practiced in Iran, if indeed the nail would even be used on the leg. We wondered if we were being conned by divorced husband, the doctor or even Rafat. I couldn't believe that Rafat would do something like that.

We waited for four days and heard nothing from Rafat so I asked Oscar to see if he could find another badjii for us. He brought Delshot to us. There was nothing significant about Delshot except that she was dumb as a rock. She was very good to the boys and demon Jimbo took full advantage of out-smarting her. We decided we could put up with her until Rafat returned. Unfortunately, we never heard from Rafat again.

The ten pound sack of sugar I bought at the co-op was one solid cube due to the fact that it had come by ship to the Persian Gulf and trucked up to Tehran. It was explained that the humidity of the voyage caused the sugar to solidify. Whenever we had to use some sugar we pounded it with a mallet. I had neglected to show Delshot how to do this. One day Norma came by and I asked Delshot to bring us some tea. We were sitting in the living room talking and suddenly became aware of a pounding noise coming from the kitchen. Walking in to investigate I found Delshot sitting on the floor, her full skirt spread out. On the skirt was a large lump of sugar, which she was beating with Jimbo's baseball bat that had been standing in the drain in the middle of the kitchen floor. I don't know when the skirt had been washed and the drain was where the mop water went.

I had been asked to tutor a seventh grader from the American School in math, history and English. Scott was the son of an Embassy official and had lived all over the world. He had had a lot of advantages as far as culture was concerned but his schooling had been sporadic at best. Scott would arrive after school and I would work with him for an hour, mostly helping him with his homework. Delshot had instructions to entertain Jimbo while Scott and I worked on the kitchen table. Jim came home early one afternoon and after meeting Scott he went to greet Jimbo. From the living room he observed Delshot and Jimbo at play in the backyard. That is, it was play for Jimbo but a lot of work for Delshot. Jimbo would throw his volleyball into the empty swimming pool and demand that Delshot retrieve it. "*Buro*, (go) Delshot." he proclaimed pointing to the ball that was rolling to the deep end of the pool. Delshot always did what Jimbo told her to, and never seemed to catch on to his impish ways. She obediently climbed over the wrought iron fence, her skirt flying, showing her bloomers and would retrieve the ball. Invariably, she would hand the ball to Jimbo so she could hoist her leg and get over the fence. Jimbo waited until she was out and with a fiendish laugh would throw the ball back into the pool and the scenario would be repeated. I tried my best to stop Jimbo when he was deviling her but was not always around to do it. She appeared to adore the little monster no matter what he did. Oscar barely tolerated Jimbo especially after Jimbo learned the Farsi word for garbage was 'ashgal' and would purposely mispronounce our driver's name.

One day Jim came home and laughingly told me how an Iranian officer gets the point across to his minions. As Jim was returning to his office he saw an Iranian captain shouting at six men for not policing up the ditch that runs in front of Jim's office. The Captain was short and squat with a baldhead and huge moustache; he was pacing back and forth in front of the men with his hands clasped behind his back, shouting in Farsi. Every few minutes he would stop directly in front of one of the men and, without slowing down his monologue, would whip his right hand around and soundly slap the man right in the mouth. After he tired of that he had each man grab his right ear with his left hand, put his right finger on the ground and pivot around the finger as fast as he could. As each man became dizzy, the Captain would give him a kick in the seat of his pants that sent the poor guy sprawling. After completing this, the Captain put his hands in his pockets, smiled as he walked away quite pleased with himself. The ditch has been spotless ever since this incident.

The following Friday we were invited to a party at Mostafa's family home. It was an all-day affair with food and drinks in abundance. Mostafa had invited his cousin and many other relatives around our age. The talk soon became political with much criticism of the Shah. Mostafa complained that, unlike the United States, in Iran there were no large corporations like General Motors where he could apply his Engineering Degree. There was nothing for him to do and now the Shah was taking away all the family's property. He was very worried and didn't know how this White Revolution would affect their family. All of his male relatives concurred with him but I detected from the females that they were pleased that the Shah was giving them the right to vote. They complained bitterly about the Shah's twin sister, Ashraf, building extravagant palaces. Jim and I just listened not wanting to give our opinion on their country's problems but it was obvious that these young people were very upset with the turn of events following the Shah's White Revolution. Mostafa and his cousin had changed a lot since they had returned to Iran.

Chapter 7

February 1963

Jim arrived home in the middle of the day, stating that an airplane had gone down in the desert southeast of Tehran and it needed a new engine. He was taking some mechanics and drivers to trek through the *Dashti Khavir* (Desert of Death) to reach the downed airplane. He estimated that it would take several days just to reach the plane. The Topographic Team was in Iran specifically to map the whole country and Jim had been given the current maps the TOPO pilots had made. He assured me that he would be in radio contact with Ghalamorghi, and someone there would keep me informed about the mission.

Jim had no sooner left than Delshot became ill. I sent her home and called the ironing badjii, Zahra, to help out until Delshot could come back. Oscar was sitting outside in the car when Zahra arrived in a taxi. When he escorted her in it was clear that he was smitten by her good looks, and she was flirting with him outrageously. I had never seen Oscar so animated. Zahra, on the other hand, was swishing her chador around as she twisted her shoulders and hips in a seductive manner, all the while smiling and blinking her eyes. It was laughable.

Trying to get things back to business, I said, "Zahra, I need to have you clean the house, as Delshot is sick."

"Oh, no, Madam, I do not ever clean houses. I only iron. I have a cousin who has just come from Hamadan who will clean your house," she confirmed in perfect English.

That sounded good to me, especially if she was better than Delshot. "Good, can she come today?"

"Oh, yes, Madam. I will go get her. Can your driver take me?"

I was a little hesitant about that, as I wasn't sure I would ever see Oscar again. But I needed a badjii, especially at night, so I reluctantly told Oscar to take Zahra to pick up her cousin. Oscar's face lit up at this opportunity and they left.

Much to my surprise, Oscar arrived with Minou within an hour. I showed her around and then left to get Jimbo from school. Arriving back home I noticed that Minou had cleaned up the kitchen and mopped the floor. It looked better than it had since Rafat left.

I fixed our lunch, fed Patrick and put both boys down for a nap. I read a book for a while and then dozed off. The doorbell awakened me, and I got up and went in the bathroom to wash my face. I heard voices that were not familiar. Coming downstairs I saw my Danish neighbor, Benita, standing on the landing in front of the kitchen. I had paid a call on her the previous week and she was returning the call. I could sense something was wrong; the air was thick with uneasiness. Minou had a strange look on her face, Oscar was concerned and Benita looked hesitant. I greeted Benita and showed her into the living room. I told Oscar I didn't need him the rest of the day and he could go home, then I asked Minou to bring us tea. I couldn't shake the feeling that something was very wrong.

While waiting for our tea, Benita and I made small talk. As Minou came in with the tea, her head was bowed but she kept looking at my guest. *What is going on?* I wondered. Minou left, glancing over her shoulder at my guest. A few minutes later she was in the backyard sweeping the fallen leaves. She kept close to the glass doors, her head bent down but eyes sneaking a look at us.

Benita appeared nervous as she regarded Minou. Suddenly she said, "Shirley, may I be frank?"

"Please do. What is going on here?"

"May I ask where you got your badjii?"

When I told her about Zahra, she nodded knowingly and said, "I'm not sure how I should say this. You may not want to hear what I know about Zahra and Minou."

"If there is something wrong with them I need to know. Please tell me." Benita, encouraged by my statement, proceeded to say the following: the European community had ostracized Zahra because it was discovered that she and her lawyer husband were head of a large robbery ring. She had a reputation among the Europeans of coming into a household to iron and then proceeding to cause dissention among the other servants. The Europeans were either embassy personnel or oil consortium employees living in Iran for many years. They employed cooks, houseboys, nannies and maids to manage their huge mansions. Zahra would cause so much trouble that some of the servants would leave or get fired. Then she conveniently would bring in a relative, who had just arrived from some remote village to work. Later on, items began to disappear. This had gone on for a long time. At first Zahra was not suspected, but after awhile some began to wonder, as Jim had, why such an intelligent women would be a badjii. Investigations proved that Zahra and her husband were involved in these robberies, but the Iranian officials would do nothing, either because they were being paid off or because they felt the wealthy Europeans deserved what they got.

Benita told me that Minou had been hired by her best friend Sasha to help take care of three children. Sasha thought the world of Minou and taught her everything about caring for the house and children. When Sasha's father became ill, she left Minou in charge of the household while she went to Denmark to care for her father. She was gone three months and when she returned she noticed a vast change in Minou. Suddenly, Minou was wearing heavy makeup, and for several evenings in a row the family heard a car honk in the kuchee and Minou would leave and be gone for half an hour. That was when they discovered that Minou was subsidizing her salary by prostituting herself and she was fired.

Shocked, I sat in silence until Benita said, "Shirley, I don't want to tell you what to do, but I thought you would want to know this."

Gaining my voice, I said, "Of course, I want to know this. Minou could be infected and I have a three-month old infant. Fortunately, she hasn't even touched Patrick since she just started work today. I'm going to get rid of her right now!"

I got up, took 50 rial out of my purse and called to Minou, "Minou, *buro.* (go)" I said and handed her the money. She never said a word, but left quickly.

After Benita left, I scrubbed with Clorox every place Minou had been. Then I remembered I had recommended Zahra to Debbie, the wife of the flight surgeon/ob-gyn doctor, who had delivered Patrick. Since I felt responsible for recommending Zahra to Debbie, I wanted her to be aware of what I had learned. I called Debbie and after I had relayed everything Benita had told me there was silence on the other end of the line. Finally, Debbie said, "What do you think I should do? Zahra comes here every Tuesday to iron."

Now that surprised me and I said, "Debbie, I just fired the badjii Zahra brought here and Zahra is never welcome in my house again. If I were you I'd fire her."

"How could I fire her? She is my friend!"

"What? She's a servant, for gosh sake, and she heads a robbery ring!"

"Well, I just don't know what to do. She's a good friend and my kids love her. I don't want to be an Ugly American!"

"Debbie, do what you want to do, but I will never allow her in this house again." I hung up the phone, wondering about Debbie's attitude. Over and over again I was to witness Americans' seemingly desperate desire to be liked.

In 1958 two men, American Foreign Officers, who had intimate knowledge of Americans overseas wrote a book called *The Ugly American*. It told fictionalized stories, though based on fact, about Americans living abroad as businessmen, military advisors, diplomats, ambassadors and Foreign Service officers. It basically made the argument that people were being sent overseas with no knowledge of the host country. These persons made no effort to learn the language and customs and spent most of their time having cocktail parties within the American "expat" community. I certainly agreed with that. It was a best seller and seemed to impress on the collective mind of Americans that we should try harder to be liked. It was not uncommon for an American to be called "ugly," and many people were defensive on the subject. One such "author" arrived in Tehran right after we had moved into our house. Jim was given the assignment of flying her all over Iran to interview Americans. Her plan was to write a rebuttal to *The Ugly American* and show that Americans were doing a good job of being ambassadors without portfolio. Apparently she

137

had the backing of someone in high places, because she was given the royal treatment in every country she visited. The woman was able to get anywhere she wanted to go, stayed in the best hotels and spent her time interviewing Americans when she wasn't sight-seeing. She never paid for anything. She stayed in Iran for a week and then moved on to Turkey. To my knowledge her book never got written.

The next morning I called Gertrude and asked her to have Mahmood bring Heshmat over to our house. Heshmat did not like to spend the night, as she had eight children at home, but she would temporarily if her mother-in-law looked after the children. She helped out at our home the times in between the many live-in badjiis I hired. When she arrived smelling like a goat, I sent her to the bathhouse and gave her some stick deodorant, explaining how she was to use it. She nodded knowingly as I demonstrated by raising my arm and pretending to rub the stick in my armpit. The next day the odor had returned. I asked Heshmat if she had used the deodorant and she looked surprised. "Oh, no, Madam. I give to Mahmood for face."
"For his face? Why did you do that?"
"Mahmood say it for after shave for face."
When Mahmood came to pick her up his face was chalk-white and he could barely move his lips.

The items we Americans take for granted frequently befuddled Iranians. Norma called one day to announce that a new shipment of goods had finally arrived at the Co-op. This was the first big shipment to come from the States since the old manager had absconded with the funds and diverted the goods to his new Iran Super market. Excitedly she told me that hairspray was available, though it was rationed two cans per customer. The next day she called again furious that her badjii had used an entire can getting rid of mosquitoes. I had to laugh at her predicament. "Well, Norma, you can be happy. At least your mosquitoes have curly hair!"
When I thought Osra would last a long time, I ordered two blue and white uniforms and a pair of flannel pajamas for her. She only had one pair of bloomers, one skirt, and one blouse that she wore daily. There was never an opportunity for her to wash her clothes.

With Patrick on the way, I wanted to be sure she was wearing a clean uniform. It had the added advantage that her "civilian" clothes would be clean when she had her days off. With the weather turning colder, I knew the warm pajamas would be welcome. In spite of my insistence, Osra kept all her clothes on but added the pajamas over the bloomers and the uniform on top. I gave up trying to get her to leave her clothing off and became satisfied that the outer layer was clean. Maybe she was afraid someone would steal her clothes; that seemed to be the only logical explanation. When she left our employ the uniforms stayed, but the flannel pajamas were gone. Those two uniforms lasted through all the many badjiis I hired.

The day after Jim left, Gertrude came over to check on Heshmat (and probably me) and to tell me that Major B. had decided that one of the pilots would fly over Jim's desert convoy every day because the radio transmissions were not working properly. Jim's orders were to have the convoy circle once when the plane appeared, to indicate that all was well. If they didn't circle that would tell the pilot that there was trouble of some kind. She announced that today everything was fine and I was not to worry. My only worry at this time was getting Delshot back.

While Jim was gone I received a phone call from Jan Howard, an old friend from Tucson. Jan was in Tehran for some much needed R and R (rest and relaxation) and shopping. I invited her for dinner and we had a wonderful time just talking. Her husband was with the United States AID Mission to Iran, and they were living in Rasht, a city on the southern shore of the Caspian Sea. The Alborz Mountains north of Tehran were shale and treeless on the southern exposure, but at the summit the landscape changed dramatically. On the northern side of the mountain the climate became similar to that of Southeast Asia, with enormous trees entwined in vines, waterfalls and rushing streams snaking through ravines and air heavy with humidity. The homes were built on stilts so that rushing water caused by the monsoons could pass under them, and on the hillsides the farmers grew tea and rice.

Jan told me that living in Rasht was very difficult, due to the wetness, which bred all kinds of disease. It was estimated the 90%

of the cows were tubercular and many of the people were either carriers or had active cases of tuberculosis. Jan's husband Bill was a veterinarian working for U.S. Aid to eliminate the problem. Due to the humidity, cholera and typhoid were common. She did have good news, announcing that the Shah had just signed an agreement with Foremost Dairies to build a milk plant in Tehran. Dried milk would be imported from Denmark and reconstituted. Until that happened, Iran babies would still be breast-fed until the age of two and then weaned onto tea. By the time our tour was up we were able to buy milk in cartons that tasted just like fresh milk from home. This was a great improvement over the canned whole milk sold in the co-op, which usually had clumps of butterfat floating in it.

After Jan left I told myself that life was not too bad; it could be worse. In retrospect, I realize I had been suffering from post-partum depression, prolonged undoubtedly by the adverse conditions of living in Iran. I was crying at the slightest provocation and having trouble sleeping, so Captain Morris had given me some sleeping pills. On the fifth day of Jim's departure, I took Jimbo to school and than told Oscar to take me to Joan's house. Feeling very hopeless, I thought that talking to no-nonsense Joan, who was a nurse, would help me. I rang the bell and after a long period of time she opened the gate. She was wearing a pair of yellow rubber gloves and a frown on her face. Smiling, I said, "Hi, Joan. I thought I'd drop in for some conversation. How are you?"

She seemed very surprised and then said, "Well, I can't visit with you now. I'm very busy cleaning. Goodbye." And she closed the gate. I was shocked, and I could feel my face get very red. I fought to keep the tears from rolling down my cheeks. She couldn't have hurt me more if she had slapped me in the face. I got back in the car and told Oscar to take me home. I rushed into the house, not saying a word to Heshmat, ran up the stairs and threw myself on the bed, crying. I fell asleep for two hours and awoke still depressed. I went into the bathroom, took out the sleeping pills and, not trusting myself, flushed them down the toilet.

I was getting daily reports on the desert trek and was glad to hear that Jim had reached the downed plane. They camped there for three days and then started back toward civilization. When he came home he told me how irritated he was at having to stop progress everyday to drive around in circles. "Babe, this was a real adventure. We started out fine, with four trucks and a Jeep being driven by the Iranian drivers. We were given the best drivers from the Iranian Army, according to Col. Assimi. He had assured me that these drivers knew all about driving in the desert. We had two three/quarter ton trucks; one of them pulled a water trailer, a wrecker and a two and one/half ton truck with the airplane engine on it. I took four of my maintenance men, one each to ride with the drivers. We were going along at a good clip until we had to leave the asphalt highway and start across the desert. That's when we found out that the drivers didn't have the slightest idea how to drive in sand, didn't know what four-wheel drive was and were utterly useless. My guys and I took over the driving with the Iranians sitting there sightseeing."

"We came to several *wadis*, the surface streams of water that look like wet sand on the beach, but act almost like quicksand because there is more water underneath than on top. Our wonderful desert drivers had no idea how to cross them. The first one we came to we crossed without any problem. The next one we had to drive back and forth until we found a place to cross. On the third one we came to, I was leading in the Jeep and all of the sudden the front wheels of the Jeep fell in. We got that pulled out okay and found a better way to cross. Everything was going well. We got the Jeep, the truck with the water trailer, the other three/quarter truck and the truck with the engine on it over the *wadi,* but the wrecker started sinking. At one point the sand was up to the running boards. We started tying the wrecker to all the other vehicles in order to pull it out when I noticed we were short-handed. I looked around and saw that our drivers were building a fire and starting to boil water for their tea. I screamed at them to get to work. They were very belligerent, telling me this was their teatime. I yelled even louder and they finally abandoned their tea party and came to help us."

"I can imagine what you told them," I said. "Go on, what else happened?"

"Well, when we got to the plane we changed the engine and Major B. flew in with Ole' Seegar and then flew the plane out to Ghalimorghi. The funniest thing was when we stopped to eat and I passed out the C-rations. We had a choice of steak and gravy, ham and lima beans, hamburger patties or pork and beans. I very carefully explained to the drivers the c-rations that had *gushte khuk* (pork) in them and to a man they said they could eat it and they liked it. No problem at all. They ate it with relish as we were going out to the wreck but as soon as we were returning and the drivers could see the lights of Tehran in a distance, they picked up the pork and threw it as far as they could, crying, *"Khub neest"* (no good). They went crazy, accusing us of trying to poison them by giving them the bad pig meat and we just about had a riot."

"At one point we came across a man fully dressed in a coat and tie just walking in the middle of the desert. We don't know where he came from or where he was going, but he was dressed for something. Our drivers had a long conversation with him, but when we asked what he was doing the drivers just shrugged their shoulders and said, *"Namidanam"* (I don't know). This has been a very interesting experience, to say the least."

I then told him of my experience hiring the prostitute and finding out that Zahra was the head of a robbery ring. "I knew there was something fishy about her. Her English was too good," Jim replied, and we both forgot the incident.

We were at the Liebshultz's house for dinner when Norman relayed to us his experience of running into the new chief of Operations Section, Colonel Murray. The Operations Section included everything concerned with the Hospital, the Aviation Branch, the Motor Pool, the Legal, Postal, Pay and Personal and anything that wasn't directly under the Advisory Group. Colonel Murray was the Big Cheese over all of this. Norman, being a doctor, never went through the spit and polish course that all other officers did. He was given a direct commission out of medical school. Consequently, Norman was not too concerned about the length of his hair. But Colonel Murray was. He saw Norman at the Officer's Club at lunchtime and in front of two dozen men read Norman the Riot Act about his shoddy military appearance, unpressed uniform and hair length. Norman was still shaking over this encounter. He said that Colonel Murray is huge, probably six feet four inches tall with massive shoulders. "He towered over me, I've never felt so insignificant in my life and he has piercing blue eyes that just drilled into me. I never want to encounter him again!" was Norm's reaction. Within the next few days' rumors were flying about Colonel Arthur Murray. The rumors were that he was the fifth generation to graduate from West Point; his father and grandfather had both risen to the rank of Major General. The first Murray to go to West Point had been in the Revolutionary War, as a drummer, and General Washington himself had signed the orders sending Murray 1 to West Point after the War. As the rumors made their rounds they became more exaggerated.

A few weeks after Jim returned from his desert excursion he had an early morning flight so I was up at five a.m. to prepare his breakfast. After he left I relaxed, reading a book until the boys awakened. This was a fairly common way to start our day. I didn't expect Jim home until five p.m. but was very surprised when he arrived at one. He burst into the room, his eyes flashing in anger. Before I could say anything he bellowed, "What in the Hell are you doing threatening a badjii?"

I was stunned, "What are you talking about?" Jim started up the stairs and I followed asking again "What are you talking about?"

"That badjii Zahra is suing you for one million rial. She says you are telling lies about her."

"Jim, I'm not telling lies about her. I told you what happened when you were out in the desert. I've never said anything to anyone other than Debbie Morris, and the only reason I did that was because I originally recommended Zahra to her and thought it was fair to warn her."

Jim was taking off his flight suit, getting ready to jump in the shower. "What are you doing home at this hour?" I asked.

"When I came in from my flight, Major B. gleefully told me you were in deep trouble and I had to go see Colonel Murray and explain everything to him."

Oh, m'gosh. Jim is going to meet The Colonel Murray for the first time and I'm to blame, I thought. I reviewed for Jim exactly what had happened when Zahra brought over the badjii Minou. Then I told Jim the strange reaction Debbie had when I told her what our neighbor had said. I wondered what Debbie did about firing her. As Jim started to shower I went downstairs to call her.

"Debbie, you remember when I told you what my Danish

neighbor had said about the badjii Zahra? What did you decide to do about that? Did you fire her?"

"Oh no, I didn't fire her. I told you she is my friend. So I told her what you had said and asked her if she really was a thief and she said she wasn't so I've kept her."

My mouth dropped open and I croaked, "Debbie, that is the stupidest thing I have ever heard." I slammed down the phone.

I went upstairs to tell Jim what Debbie had done. He was still angry with me, so I said, "I'm going to Benita's house to get more information."

I ran outside and around the corner, down the block and turned into Benita's kuchee. I rang the bell and tried to catch my breath. Her houseboy opened the gate and I saw Benita kneeling in front of a bed of peonies, digging in the dirt. I told her what had transpired and she became very excited. "What is the matter with you Americans? You can never stick together. When are you going to realize these Iranians are not your friends, they are your servants. I can not believe your friend Debbie. She must be out of her mind!"

"Benita, my husband has to go to Colonel Murray's office and explain everything to him. What else can you tell me about Zahra?"

"Well, for one thing, you are not the first person she has tried to sue. My friend Karen fired her after it became known that she headed this robbery ring. Zahra showed up at Karen's door with a paper demanding money, and Karen simply tore it up and threw it in her face. And that was the end of that. You tell your husband that I will come with him to talk to this Colonel and tell him exactly what bad people Zahra and her husband are."

"Oh, thank you very much, Benita. I'll tell Jim that, but I'm sure he will want to take care of this himself."

I quickly returned to the house and relayed our conversation to Jim. As I thought, he declined Benita's offer, but I could tell he felt better about my actions. He was dressed in his green uniform and was finishing polishing his brass and shoes. He quickly went down the stairs and I heard him say, "I hope to Hell I don't get drummed out of the Army because of this!"

The next few hours were an eternity. I couldn't concentrate on anything. I finally got the boys up from their naps and took them outside to play. Essa, our current badjii, came out and put Pat in his stroller and walked him around the pool while I pitched the ball for Jimbo to hit. At least that took my mind off what Jim was going through.

He arrived home at 4:30 in a very good mood. I couldn't wait to hear what happened. He told me he walked into Colonel Murray's office, saluted and Colonel Murray told him to sit down. "Norm is right, he is an enormous man. He handed me a paper to read that this badjii had tried to deliver directly to the Ambassador. Fortunately, Colonel Yerby waylaid it and gave it to Colonel Murray. We would have had a real international incident if Colonel Yerby hadn't stepped in. The paper claimed that you have been spreading rumors and she wants you and the government to pay one million rials. Here's a copy of it. He handed me the paper and I read:

It is about seven years that I am working as a maid, in the houses of American, English, Dutch and German Advisors in Iran. My services have been so satisfactory that I have got plenty of written certificates of my dismissal because of change to their duty stations.

It is about five months that the wife of Captain Starkey is making troubles for me. Namely, wherever I start to work she gets in touch with the people, by telephone or visiting them, and introduces me as a thief. Thus, not only she defames me and spoils my prestige but also has caused me a damage of about 30000 Rials.

In view of the fact that any accusation should be confirmed by logical reasons, I hereby request you kindly to summon her for reasonable proof against accusing me a thief, which I consider an insult to my good service and good fame so far I have tried to gain, and plead for the damage I am suffering from.

Thanks for your consideration at earliest convenience.

With best compliments and regards.

Yours truly,

Zahra Kalatchi

"This is ridiculous," I exploded. "This only happened three weeks ago and I only told Debbie. This woman is a blatant liar. Where does it say she wants one million rials from me or the government?"

"Apparently this was on a separate paper and I didn't see that."

Jim went on with the tale of his meeting with Colonel Murray. "After I read the paper I told Colonel Murray exactly what had happened, what Debbie had done and what Benita said and, before he could say anything, I added, 'Colonel Murray, sir, I think my wife did exactly the right thing.'

"All of the sudden Colonel Murray rose up out of his chair with his right fist high in the air. He is so massive it was real scary. He shouted, 'God damn it, Captain Starkey!' He suddenly banged his fist on the desk, spewing papers everywhere. His eyes were blazing and at this point I thought he was going to hit me, and then he calmly added, 'I think so too. We need more people with guts like your wife!'

"I was completely speechless and then Colonel Murray added, 'I'll get this answered right away. Don't worry about this any more, I'll take care of it.' Then he proceeded to interview me about my whole life and Army career, and when I got up to leave he said, 'Captain Starkey, you tell your wife she did exactly what I would have done.' So, Babe, you and I are off the hook." Smiling, he gave me a big hug.

It must be explained that the Army expects its officers to not only be upright citizens but to control the behavior of all dependents. Once, when we were living at Ft. Riley, Kansas, our Boston bulldog got out and was picked up by the Military Police. Jim got a letter of reprimand for not controlling his dependent, Pug Starkey. The paper the MP's filled out had a statement to check that said, "Was the dependent under the influence of alcohol?" This paper came down through the chain of command and Jim was kidded about it unmercifully.

Two days later Jim received a copy of Colonel Murray's answer to Zahra:

Re: Allegations Against Mrs. Starkey

The allegations against Mrs. Starkey, made by you, have been checked and do not appear to be founded on fact.

If you will secure proper security clearances from the Embassy you have no problem in identifying yourself to a new employer, or in proving your honesty.

The procedure quoted below outlines the steps you must take yourself.

"Reference Chapter VI, 20.1, Organizational, Function & Procedure Manuals."

Get a Form Letter from US Embassy to the Police Department requesting Police Identification.

Go to the second floor, Police Department, Sabt Avenue, with three (3) passport size photographs and your identity papers (Sejil).

After police processing, one picture and a copy of your Sejil, and police department report on finger printing should be sent to the Security Office, US Embassy. Room 104, with a request for clearance. (Forms for this are available at the US Embassy.)

Zahra never did follow up on getting a clearance from the American Embassy, and I never heard from her again. Fortunately, my sister's prediction that I might cause an International Incident was avoided.

Two weeks later a large reception was held for all of the units under Colonel Murray's command. As Jim and I walked into the room, this giant with a balding head and piercing eyes approached us. In a booming voice, he said, "So this is the young lady who tried to start an International Incident!"

I quickly looked at Jim for help and saw that he was laughing, "Babe, I'd like to introduce you to Colonel Murray. Colonel Murray, this is Shirley, the troublemaker I live with."

Colonel Murray grabbed my hand in both of his enormous paws and shook it vigorously, giving me a big grin. "It's a pleasure to meet a gutsy little gal like you." He turned and put his arm around a petite, gray-haired lady and pulled her toward him, "I'd like you both to meet my wife Jane."

We visited for a few minutes until some other people arrived and the Murrays went to greet them. I was glowing under his compliment and later that evening Jane Murray asked me if Jim and I could come to their house for dinner the following week. I was delighted and accepted without checking with Jim. Imagine, a lowly Captain getting an invitation to a Colonel's home!

When we arrived at the Murray's home, it was clear that Jane had a marvelous touch in decorating. They already had some brilliantly colored carpets on the floor, the couches were beige with brightly striped pillows and many plants filled the room. She had taken strands of donkey beads and displayed them with what looked like very old pottery. The donkey beads are called that because whenever you saw donkeys you saw turquoise beads festooned between their ears or around their necks. These beads are of unbaked clay and are painted in various shades of blue-green. The superstitious Iranians claimed this gave the donkeys protection from the Evil Eye. I asked her where she got the beads and the old pots.

"Shirley, I found this marvelous shop downtown where the shopkeeper is selling pots that have been dug up north of Tehran. If you would like I will take you there. The donkey beads are easy to buy in the Bazaar."

I accepted her invitation with relish and we made a date to shop the following Wednesday.

Our dinner was roasted wild boar that Colonel Murray had shot on an expedition on the north side of the Alborz Mountains. Since a Moslem doesn't eat pork, the wild pigs were free to roam and eat from the rice fields of the Caspian region. The meat was sweet and tender. Both being hunters, Jim and Colonel Murray had a lot to talk about. It was a special evening spent with two special people.

The following Wednesday Jane Murray and I went to downtown Tehran. Their driver could speak English exceptionally well and had been the one to tell Jane of the place where the pots were sold. We were further south in Tehran than I had ever been. We entered a dark, dank, musty shop where Mrs. Murray was greeted effusively. The shopkeeper showed us many old pots of every size, some mended and some in pristine condition. I fell in love with an enormous pot that looked like a giant measuring cup with a pouring spout and handle. It was way beyond our means, so I settled on four small pots in excellent condition. The shopkeeper told me these pots were from the Amblesh period circa 200 BC. I treasure these pots to this day, though I have never had the validity of their age verified. Our house has always contained many donkey beads so we can avoid the Evil Eye.

I hired and fired three more badjiis while waiting for Delshot to return. When she came back she seemed more distracted or stupid than before. I finally let her go and decided I would have to get along without a badjii, when much to my surprise a badjii in a gray chador appeared at our door one day asking for work. She was of medium height and weight with a round face, clear smooth skin and caramel-colored eyes that crinkled when she smiled. Her name was Maluke and she had papers written by her previous employer. I recognized the name on the papers as that of an American Embassy officer whom we had met briefly. Maluke told me the family had gone back to the United States. She was available to live-in and with no hesitation I hired her. She was quiet, industrious and learned quickly. She fit right in with our family; all of us liked her, especially because she had a good rapport with Jimbo and Patrick. When Jimbo tried his devilish ways with her she laughed heartily, didn't let him get away with anything, and he loved it.

Throughout the winter there had been rumblings of trouble for the Shah. The American Embassy sent out word that it was unsafe for Americans to travel by car outside Tehran. In the south, the Bakhtiari tribe was angry that the Shah wanted to take their weapons away. Muhammad Reza Shah's second wife, Soraya Esfandiari, was a princess in the Bakhtiari tribe, and when the Shah divorced her after seven years of trying to conceive an heir, he incurred the enmity of the tribe. When he demanded their weapons, the tribe went on a rampage. The Shah sent his air force in to quell the uprising. The vision of jet planes flying through the steep mountain passes chasing men on camels was bewildering/stunning!

One hundred forty one kilometers south of Tehran is the city of Qom, the second most sacred place in Iran. It is here that the sister of the 8th Imam, Fatima, is buried. The Shiis branch of Islam believes that there were twelve Imams who succeeded as leaders following the death of Mohammed. It is believed that the twelfth Imam disappeared in the year 940 and will reappear in due time. Qom is famous for the *madreseh* (school) for mullahs. Here a teaching mullah named Ruhollah Khomeini was gaining notice by preaching against the Shah.

When the news of more trouble came out, our good and faithful Oscar grew more nervous about his dangerous mission of driving for an American family. He complained constantly and became a real nuisance. Whenever he was parked waiting for us, whether it was downtown or right in front of our house, he would lock himself in. We would have to knock on the door to wake him up and the odor from the man was overwhelming. Flies loved him. Grumbling, he would wait for orders, never saying a thing. Suddenly, one day he appeared with a huge grin on his face. He hadn't smiled like that since Zahra was flirting with him. He announced, "Capeetan Estarkey, I go work for very big Iranee General." Jim paid him the wages due to him and wished him well. I said, "Good Riddance," when Jim reported Oscar's departure. "I guess he thinks he'll be safe from the hordes that are against the Shah."

Jim arrived with our new driver the day after Oscar left. Gholum was a small, spare man with a huge handlebar moustache, twinkly dark eyes and a ready smile. He was very likable, was married, had three small sons and loved children. He lived near us and would ride his bicycle to our house, so Jim allowed him to park the bike in our entrance hall. Both our boys liked Gholum immediately. As Patrick got older and was able to sit up he would ride in a carseat that fit over the back of the front seat next to Gholum. When Gholum wasn't philosophizing with Jim or me he would sing or talk to the boys. The carseat had a steering wheel with a horn and Gholum taught Pat to honk the horn. When Pat did this, the two of them would laugh. Jimbo loved Gholum and would run to him to be picked up and thrown into the air, squealing with delight.

I had learned the hard way that if I gave something to a current badjii, other items would start disappearing, but if I sold an item to them at a very cheap price, they didn't steal from me. The scorpion stings again! Gholum was the first servant we had who had small children and so I would set up a rack of the children's out-grown clothes to sell to him. I charged very little: a pair of pants would be 3 rial (2 cents), a warm jacket 10 rial (7 cents). By paying for the item Gholum saved "face" and his boys had good American-made clothes. If he was waiting for me during mealtime, I would instruct Maluke to feed him, and the two of them would sit in the kitchen chatting in Farsi. When crazy drivers in the right lane would make a left-hand turn in front of us, Gholum would state philosophically, "Eeran good place, eeranees bad people. Beeg bomb come all eeranees gone, Eeran good place." Then he would laugh good-naturedly.

We didn't know it at the time, but our servant problems were over. Gholum and Maluke were with us until we left.

March 1963

Maluke informed me that Mr. Zakarian's 94 year-old mother had died. The Zakarians lived across the kuchee from us and Mrs. Zakarian had recommended our first badjii, the very fat Mariam. Visitors started arriving toward the late afternoon, and by the time Jim came home from work there were expensive cars everywhere, blocking the entrance to our house. Gholum had to park in the next block. There was much discussion in the front of our building among the drivers, and soon the breathless Gholum came in to inform us that the Empress Farah was to pay a condolence visit to the Zakarians. "Gholum, you mean the Shah's wife will be here in our kuchee?" I excitedly asked him.

"Madam, drivers say lady who died was important person to Shahenshah."

"Holy cow, I'm going upstairs to watch for the Empress," I yelled to Jim as I took the stairs two at a time. "I wouldn't miss this for the world!"

I pulled up a chair next to the window where I had a good view of the people going through the gate and milling around the compound across the street. Special lanterns had been placed two feet apart within the garden, giving an ethereal glow to the scene. People kept arriving in droves— the men dressed in black suits, the women in black chadors. I had never seen chadors like these; they were of transparent silk. The ladies who wore them were beautifully made up, and wearing opulent jewelry, their hair piled high. It appeared they were trying to outdo one another. The chatter was subdued as everyone kept a watchful eye on the gate. I sat glued to the scene for twenty minutes before the sirens started. Eight soldiers in dress uniforms marched into our kuchee, forcing the drivers to move the cars so a limousine could enter. It stopped and out stepped the Empress Farah Diba, a gorgeous lady dressed in a diaphanous lace chador with a mantilla fastening it to her head. Holding her head high, the Empress slowly strolled into the hushed compound as everyone bowed to her in great deference. Graciously she floated from group to group, making small talk, paying equal attention to all. After she had made the rounds, she moved toward the front door with the rest of the people following her inside. I was breathless with awe and sat there for several minutes in quiet contemplation. I could not believe I had just seen the Empress of Iran. Jim broke my reverie as he came into the room saying, "Shirley, when are we going to eat?"

"How can you ask about food when the Empress just arrived in our kuchee?" I cried, not believing my ears. "I can't wait to call Colleen and tell her. Boy, will she be green with envy! I'm sure she'll tell everyone!"

After dinner I called Colleen to describe my impressions. I purposely did not call anyone else; I was curious to find out how many people would hear about it. I went back upstairs, but the limousine was gone and only ordinary people were still standing about the compound. The wake was still going on long after we went to bed.

The next day I sent Maluke over with a note of condolences for the Zakarian family. All day long I fielded calls from astonished Americans wanting to check for themselves what had really happened. Colleen really was a good conduit of gossip.

Chapter 8

JFK makes Winston Churchill a U.S. citizen, in Britain 70,000 march in A bomb protest, Alabama governor defies federal integration orders.

No Ruz, the Iranian New Year, is celebrated on the first day of spring, or the vernal equinox. This generally falls on the 21st or 22nd of March. The preparations for the celebration begin many weeks before the event. It is the only really happy holiday Iranians enjoy, and many of the traditions reminded us of our Christmas, Thanksgiving, Halloween and Easter. Preparations begin weeks before with a complete cleaning of the home. Curiously, the carpets are placed in the road, wrong side up for cars to drive over them and knock out the dirt. (When we first witnessed this and tried to drive around the carpets, the minders yelled and shook their fist at us.) The carpets are then taken to Rey, a town south of Tehran that is blessed with hot springs. Men, their pant legs rolled up, stand in the middle of the springs dunking the carpets and scrubbing them with Tide. After numerous rinsings, they are laid on the side of the hills that surround the springs. The hills are alive, not with the sound of music, but with the colorful Persian carpets. Meanwhile, the house is polished from top to bottom.

Housewives gather together weeks before to make baklava, *nune shekari* (sugar cookies) and *badam choragi* (almond cookies). There must be ample food of every variety to feed the family, friends and neighbors who visit each other during the thirteen days of festivities. Two weeks prior to *No Ruz*, seeds of lentils are planted in a water-filled shallow bowl. The seeds sprout and form a green cake.

Several nights before the New Year, children wearing masks and veils go to the doors of friends and relatives, beating a large bowl with a spoon, making as much noise as they can. They are invited in, where candy, money and other gifts are put into their bowls. Beggars take advantage of the holiday by dressing in outlandish costumes, painting their faces and playing out-of-tune instruments. (They seem to prey mostly on American homes, as we are the soft touches.) The doorbell would ring and the ghastly "music" would start, while the men, their faces blackened, did their obscene version of a belly dance. One of the men would come forward with a bowl, asking for baksheesh. We would pay, just to get rid of them.

It was important that everyone has a new outfit and employers are expected to double the month's salary to allow for this expenditure. The children decorate eggs as we do at Easter time.

It is traditional to return to the family home, and the roads are filled with cars going to all the villages throughout Iran. Relatives begin arriving bearing bouquets of yellow daffodils and red tulips. Food is cooked in great abundance, enough to feed a battalion for a month. Whole lambs are grilled over charcoal fires, cauldrons of rice are prepared and the tables are laden with different dishes made with chicken, fruits and vegetables.

The evening before the vernal equinox, bonfires are set and everyone who can, jumps over the fire chanting to the sun, "May your red radiance come to me. May my yellow tiredness go to you." The tradition of No Ruz began with the reign of Cyrus the Great in the fifth century B.C., when the Persians followed the teachings of the prophet Zoroaster and his sun worshippers, and it has survived for 2500 years.

A special No Ruz table is set with *haft sin* (seven offerings) filled with items that begin with the letter S in Farsi; apple (*sib*), garlic (*sir*), vinegar (*serke*), greens (*sabzi*), wild rue (*sangin*), grain (*samanoo*) and sumac. Also on the table is a mirror to deflect evil; painted eggs to symbolize fertility; two candles to represent light and dark; a bowl of goldfish to portray life. (I asked Gholum what he fed his goldfish and he replied that the fish didn't need food, as they ate water!) The radio announces the precise time of the vernal equinox and everyone gathers around the table watching the goldfish. The goldfish is supposed to turn completely around and face the opposite direction from where he had been at the exact moment of the beginning of spring.

The celebrations go on for two weeks and on *Sizdah* (the thirteenth day) everyone is supposed to leave the house at sunup and have a picnic, preferably near a running stream. The green cakes of the sprouted lentil seeds are thrown into the water, and with it are supposed to go all the anger and bad feelings family members had felt toward each other during the past year. It is considered bad luck for anyone to return home before sunset.

This year it snowed the night before, and during the day too, but that didn't faze anyone; the next day the newspaper carried a picture of the Shah and the rest of the Palavi family enjoying an outing while the flakes were falling.

Our part in No Ruz consisted of providing Maluke and Gholum with extra money and fending off the offending beggars, again with money. While Gholum and Maluke were with their respective families, we enjoyed having the house to ourselves. As much as we liked our servants, it was wonderful to be alone.

In 1963 No Ruz coincided with the lunar month of *Ramazan*. The rest of the Muslim world calls this month *Ramadan*, but in Iran it is *Ramazan*. It is a holy month of fasting from dawn to dusk when no food, drink or smoking is allowed. It commemorates the death of Ali, the Prophet Mohammed's son-in-law and the first convert to Islam. When *Ramazan* occurs in the winter months it is not so bad, but when it falls during the hot summer, when the sun rises early and sets late, the extremely hot weather makes it almost intolerable. Tempers are short, as people have to get up early enough to eat breakfast before dawn and then later stuff themselves after the sun goes down.

In the early years of the reign of Muhammad Reza Shah, the *ulama*, the Shia clergy, had no interest in confronting the shah as long as they were allowed to have control of offensive secular entertainment and could have religious instruction in schools. This was a holdover from the days of Reza Shah. But as the old *ayatollahs* died off, younger more militant *mullahs* emerged. The leader of these was Ruhollah Khomeini. In 1960 he wrote a book titled *Towzihih-e Masail (Explication of Problems)*. It contained rulings on everything from the correct way to face while defecating to the relationship of religion to state. Its publication gave Khomeini the status of *ayatollah*, a sort of honorary title. In other words, he became an *ayatollah* because his students called him that. He used the drama and emotion of *Ramazan* to incite the passion of his followers against the Shah's White Revolution. During a ceremony commemorating the death of the sixth Imam, the Shah sent men undercover to interrupt the proceedings. A riot ensued and the mullahs lost but were humiliated that security forces had entered their sacred sanctuary. Khomeini sent messages to the Shah, who ignored them. Khomeini continued to harshly oppose the Shah. The Shah sent an emissary who tried to get Khomeini to move to Najaf, a holy city in Iraq. He refused. Then the Shah ordered the conscription of seminarians, which until then had been exempt from military service. This backfired, as now the soldier-seminarians, based in Tehran, received messages from Khomeini that their wives secreted within their clothing. The new conscripts began to congregate for prayer and to encourage the other soldiers to join them and listen to Khomeini's instructions. Khomeini accused the Jews of being behind the Shah's edicts and appealed to other Arab states, saying that the clergy of Iran were opposed to relations with Israel. The Shah was lenient toward all religions, including Christians, Bahaiis, Armenian Coptic Christians and Jews. Knomeini was a thorn in the Shah's side and the unrest continued.

In the springtime the camel caravans come into the city with fertilizer for the gardens. The camel drivers learned that Americans would pay to allow their children to ride these filthy animals. We were eating dinner on Sunday when Maluke came in to announce, "Monsieur, many camels here." Jimbo leaped from the table and ran to the front door. Before we got outside, we could hear the distinctive sound of camel bells, the graduated chain of brass bells that hang around each camel's neck. The gigantic dromedaries glided down the kuchee, their jumbo hoofs stirring clouds of dirt. They are strange animals; at first glance they seem haughty and aloof but then you notice the sad brown eyes veiled in thick, long lashes.

A tall, dark-skinned man with a hooked nose led them to the front of our house. He was dressed in baggy, white trousers that were hiked up to his knees, pink plastic slippers and a long, navy blue tunic. He had on a white turban with fringed edges. His smile revealed snow-white teeth and he asked, in Farsi, if Jimbo could ride. Jimbo was jumping up and down in anticipation, begging his father. Jim gave his permission and the driver had the lead camel kneel down. Jimbo climbed onto the saddle that was covered in a colorful blanket with huge tassels dangling from the hems. The camel immediately rose when he felt Jimbo on his back. I held my breath while Jim called to Jimbo to hang on tightly. The camel, led by the driver, loped off down our street and around the corner, Jim following close behind. Maluke brought Patrick out and put him close to the other camel's face. Pat stared in wonder, and when the camel snorted his disapproval, Patrick, his face covered in camel spit, howled indignantly. I rescued him, took him into the house, washed his face and tried to calm him down. We returned outside, staying away from the second camel until the rider returned. The grin on Jimbo's face attested to the thrill of the ride. He begged his dad to go again, but we convinced him that he would get another chance another day. Jim paid the driver and we went inside to finish our dinner.

It was time for the annual festival at the Officer's Club and the Operations Section was given the job of coming up with a program. Col. Murray decided which skits were to be performed by the Motor Pool, Aviation, Hospital and Personal Sections. Aviation Section received the assignment to do a skit on the Meat Run. Of course, Major B. told Jim this was his job. Jim called me with the news and requested that I come up with something, as he was to meet Col. Murray in the afternoon.

"You just found out this morning that you have to have a skit this afternoon? Wow! We can always count on Major B. to try to get you in trouble, can't we?"

"Babe, don't worry about it. This is just the first meeting, but I would like to have something to show Col. Murray," he said as he hung up. A skit on the Meat Run! Boy, was I excited! Even after eight years of being married to the Army, it still rankled me that R.H.I.P. (Rank hath its privilege). Nowhere was it more evident than the Meat Run. No matter how early I arrived at the monthly Meat Run I had to wait until the brass had picked over the goods. I sat down at my typewriter and the words flowed. I worked on this for the whole morning, only stopping long enough to pick Jimbo up from school and feed him. I sent Gholum back to Ghalimorghi to get Jim so he could change his uniform before the three o'clock meeting with Col. Murray. By the time Jim arrived, I had a finished skit. I excitedly said, "Let me read this to you."

"I don't have time now. I want to shower and shave. I'll read it on the way down to Murray's office.

Disappointed, I handed Jim the paper as he left. As Gholum maneuvered the car through the afternoon traffic to Armish-MAAG headquarters Jim read what I had written. When he had finished, he thought, "Oh, my God, Shirl has done it again. I can't show this to Col. Murray. He'll really be angry." Trying to decide what to do, he walked into the meeting. Col. Murray was sitting at the head of the conference table and Jim was the first to arrive. Seeing the sheaf of papers Jim was carrying, he took them as Jim reluctantly told him that I had written the skit. With a guarded look on his face and holding his breath, Jim watched carefully for Col. Murray's reaction. As Col. Murray came to the punch line he roared his approval.

"Captain Starkey, that little wife of yours has hit the nail right on the head. This is terrific!" Jim started breathing again. The rest of the committee arrived and Col. Murray proceeded to read the paper to them. They all laughed when he had finished and started working on the rest of the program.

I won't bore you, dear reader, with whole program, just the part I wrote:

Scene opens with a scruffy man standing behind the table as a newly arrived Lt. walks in.
Lt.:" I'm here for my meat."
Attendant: "Yeah, you and everybody else."
Lt.: "I'd like a 12 lb. turkey."
Attendant: "Sorry, no turkeys this time."

Lt.: "How about ten pounds of tenderloin?"

Attendant: "No tenderloin this time."

Lt.: "Well, I'll take ten pounds of the beef over there", pointing to a pile of meat.

Attendant: "No can do."

Lt.: "Why not? There must be 300 pounds of it."

Attendant: "I'm saving it for the makeup."

Lt.: "For the makeup! What is that?"

Attendant: "That's for people who stay afterwards and need more meat."

Lt.: "You mean I have to stay until the end of the meat run to see if there is anything left over that I can get?"

Attendant: "You got it."

Lt. (shaking his head): "I'll take five pounds of butter."

Attendant: "We don't have any butter today."

Lt.: "What is in those small, rectangular boxes over there?"

Attendant: "Oh, that's margarine."

Lt.: "Ok, I'll take some margarine."

Attendant: "You can't have any margarine. You didn't order it, you ordered butter."

Lt.: "That's because there is only butter listed on the order form."

Attendant: "I can't help that. I can only give you what you order."

Lt.: "Well, at least you have shrimp and I ordered ten pounds of it."

Attendant: "You ordered breaded shrimp and this is plain shrimp."

Lt.: (getting more frustrated, between clinched teeth his voice rising) "All right, already. Give me the fresh shrimp and a loaf of bread."

Attendant: "Calm down, Lt., we do have some chicken for you."

Lt.: (with a sigh of relief) "How about that! Give me 15 pounds of chicken."

(Attendant leaves, comes back with a large carving knife and a very small, scrawny chicken. He places the chicken on the table and proceeds to cut it.)

Lt.: "Hey, is THAT my chicken? What are you doing to it?"

Attendant: (holding up half a chicken) "That's all I can give you."

Lt.: (Screaming hysterically) What do you mean, that's all you can give me. I ordered 32 pounds of meat and all I end up with is half a skinny chicken. At least you could give me the whole chicken!"

Attendant:"Around here, Lt., in order to get a full bird, you have to be one!"

The crowd gave a standing ovation as the actor said those lines. In all modesty, I must admit my portion was really the only funny part in the whole program. Afterward Col. Murray came up to me and announced, "Little lady, next year you're going to be in charge of the whole program. That was damn good!" To this day I adore that man!

• • •

A week later we extended a dinner invitation to Col. and Mrs. Murray and, feeling that I had a special rapport with the Col., I decided to tell him my West Point story. Ignoring my husband's squinty, warning eyes I proceeded:

When Jim and I first married, we were sent to three different posts so that Jim could become proficient in flying fixed wing aircraft. Prior to that, he had been with a MASH unit in Korea flying helicopters. As we bounced from post to post I gradually came to learn some of the Army nomenclature, including the fact that the Army has 'posts' while the Navy and Air Force have 'bases'. I felt like a character in a popular soap opera of the time called Stella Dallas: namely, "Can a naive young lady from a small, desert town find happiness married to rising, talented Army officer?"

When Jim completed Fixed Wing training, he received orders to report for duty to the Aviation Section at Ft. Riley, Kansas. After much trouble we found a place to rent in Junction City, where I taught kindergarten for a year until finding myself pregnant. After the school year was over, we moved on post to the officer's quarters (in the Army one lives in quarters, never houses) at Ft. Riley. It was the first time we had not lived surrounded by civilians. I explained all this to Col. Murray and went on with my story: One day I was hanging out laundry when I noticed that the quarters next door had new occupants. The backdoor opened and the distaff member (that means the wife of the officer) of the household came out to put something in the garbage can. Waddling over to her, I called out

I Married A Soldier

as she was turning to go back inside. In my most friendly manner I introduced myself and welcomed her, saying it was nice to have a neighbor. She was standing on the top of the three-step stoop and, turning slowly around, she swept her eyes from my hair to my toes. Grandly, not telling me her name, she asked, "Where was your last post?"

What a strange way to start a conversation, I thought. "We have been here a year but prior to that we were in Ft. Rucker, Alabama" I answered with a smile. With an arrogant tone to her voice she asked, "Tell me, were there many Pointers at the fort?"

This was really getting weird, and I wondered why she would care about dogs. Slowly I answered, "Well, I don't remember seeing any," and then, trying to be helpful, I added, "but most Army people seem to prefer boxers."

She flung her head back as if I had slapped her. Raising her nose in the air, flaring her nostrils so that the nasal hairs were visible, she whirled into the house and slammed the door.

I stood there speechless, wondering what had just happened. Slowly I made my way back to the clotheslines, trying to figure out what I had said to get her so upset.

When Jim arrived for lunch a half an hour later, I told him what happened. I was unprepared for the hysterical laughter that was his reaction. After finally calming down, he explained that the woman was referring to West Point, that graduates were called "Pointers."

The good Col. Murray reacted with the same spontaneous laughter. I must admit he was the only West Pointer who ever thought that story was funny. He was a remarkable, unassuming man.

Anyone who graduates from West Point should be proud, as West Point is harder to get into than any Ivy League school and tougher to finish. I had a bridge buddy who was married to a "Pointer" who made the sarcastic comment that, "They get told they are special and some of them believe it." Unfortunately, some of the wives think that makes them special, too. It turned out that my neighbor was married to a third generation West Pointer whose father was a two-star general, and HER father was a third generation Annapolis man who had three stars. Whenever I saw my neighbor, I would smile and say "Hi" while watching her retreating back. So much for neighborliness.

Norma called and started her conversation with the common beginning, "Shirley, you will never guess what just happened to me." She went on to tell me that she had gone down into the bowels of old Tehran to pay their rent. It was important to dress very conservatively when going to the Bazaar *Bazorg* (the big bazaar), as Shiite fundamentalists peopled it. When Norma first arrived, she had gone to the Bazaar dressed in a sleeveless blouse and short skirt and had been pinched several times. Since then she had refused to visit the Bazaar without Ole' Seegar, but he was in Germany on training, so she sent her driver inside to pay the landlord. She waited in the back seat, keeping her face hidden but observing the scene around her. The car was parked next to a *jube,* and sitting beside it was an old crone tending to a little boy who was about two years old. The woman, wrapped in a dark chador, was holding the boy close to her. He was naked except for a too-small shirt. The toothless old hag was intent on playing with the boy's penis until it started to swell. When it was fully erect, she would slap it vigorously. The little guy would shriek with pain and try to pull away. The women would hold him tightly, her long, bony fingers clutching his side while laughing hysterically. The boy's maddened screaming would finally die down and the ritual began again. "That was the worst thing I have experienced in our two years here," Norma declared. "Why do suppose the woman was doing that? She must be a real man-hater!"

Once more I was speechless. Norma went on, "When our driver returned, the old lady looked scared and left quickly with the little boy. I don't know if Ali saw what she was doing and said something to her, or what. I was just glad to leave. I can't wait to get out of this crazy country."

My voice returned and I said, "Jim says that what is wrong with this country is that men squat to pee. Maybe there is something wrong with the women, too."

I hung up the phone, shaking my head.

Two days later I was asked to substitute at the American School for a second grade teacher named Elaine, an American married to an Iranian. She had failed to report to school for two days; and the superintendent could not get any information from her family, so

I was called in to take over the class. I taught for two weeks before the true story came to light. The third grade teacher, Deborah, was also married to an Iranian. She confided to me that Elaine had had a very bad marriage in which she had wanted to leave. Her husband had on occasion beaten her and shamed her in front of his family. When she first arrived in Iran her mother-in-law made her clean the latrines, the most degrading job of housekeeping. Soon she became pregnant and when she delivered a boy her status rose slightly, but when she next had a daughter it fell again. Her husband finally allowed her to teach at the American School if she gave him the money. She would give him only half of what she really earned and hid the other half. She had told the third grade teacher that her husband passed her around for sexual favors among his brothers, cousins and even his father. Deborah kept urging her to leave, but it is the law in Iran that the husband can keep a wife's passport, and her husband had refused to give it to her. After eight years of marriage and many negotiations, the husband agreed to let her leave but their children had to stay with the family. This was not an option for her; she was determined to get her children and herself out of Iran. Conspiring with Deborah, and through contacts, she met and befriended one of the TOPO pilots, a Lt. O'Rielly-a redhead, freckled Irishman. Lt. O'Rielly felt sorry for her and they made a plan in which O'Rielly would fly Elaine and her two boys over the border to Turkey.

Deborah said, "O'Rielly fell in love with Elaine and wants to marry her eventually when he gets out of the Army." When she did not return to school the principal contacted the family again and was told that Elaine would not be working anymore nor would the children return to school. We were all concerned that she might be being held a prisoner. No one could find out a thing about Elaine or the children. I said to Deborah, "You're married to an Iranian. Does he treat you this way?"

"Heavens, no. Not all Iranians are animals. My husband is a doctor and was trained at John Hopkins University. He is a wonderful man and has even given me my passport. I feel like I am married to an American. In fact, we are thinking of going back to the States, as my husband is not very happy working here. It isn't easy living here, and this is the reason I work here where Americans surround me. The first few years were a difficult adjustment for both my husband

and myself, and working here keeps me happy, although I would like to return home." And in an afterthought she said, "Shirley, do not mention to anyone what I told you about Elaine."

Of course, I asked Jim about it, and he answered, "That is ridiculous. Don't believe a word of it." Happily, four months later Elaine wrote a letter to another teacher who had APO privileges saying that she and her kids were safe in Michigan with her family.

Not long after that, I got into a conversation with Maluke about her marriage. In a combination of Farci, English and pantomime she told me she was married at fourteen after she had undergone female circumcision. Not knowing what she was referring to, I shook my head to indicate I didn't understand. She then, to my great amazement, went into graphic descriptions of the operation. I shook my head in disbelief at what I thought I understood. I was learning more about the conduct in this part of the world than I wanted to know. My naiveté was fast disappearing.

One day as Maluke was leaving for her day off wearing her chador I asked her, "Maluke, why do you still wear the chador? The Shah has said you may take off the chador."

"Madam, chador good. Everyone same. Some have good clothes, some have bad, no one know." In her broken English Maluke was saying that if you wore the chador no one could tell if you were rich or poor. It was the great equalizer. I'm sure the real reason was that it kept her from being hassled by the fundamentalists.

I said goodbye as Maluke walked out the door. I messed around in the kitchen preparing dinner, but felt uneasy due to the quietness of the house. My mother's intuition kicked in, and I walked out of the kitchen in search of my oldest. That's when I heard a strange sound upstairs. As I started up the stairs Jimbo came down pointing to his throat, his face beginning to turn blue. He was clutching a marble in his hand, and I knew immediately he had a marble stuck in his throat. I set him down on a step and, without thinking, I put my index finger in his mouth being careful to push my finger hard to the left side of his throat. I hooked my finger around the round object and pulled it out. I felt a rush of relief and looked down at the large shooter I held in my hand. Jimbo gasped for breath and started crying. I joined him, hugging him hard, and the two of us cried for several minutes, clinging to each other. We embraced for several minutes and finally I released him. I then took his head in both of my hands and, looking intently into his wet green eyes, dramatically emphasizing every word, said, "Jimbo, promise me one thing…Never, never put anything strange into your mouth. Remember what it is like to have your stomach pumped? You didn't like that, did you? And if I hadn't come out of the kitchen just now, you could have choked to death, and then we wouldn't have a Jimbo anymore. You're too important to us, so you must promise me you will never put strange objects in your mouth!"

With a stricken look on his face he nodded in agreement. We went upstairs and I gathered up the marbles, deciding these toys would only be played with under supervision.

Jim came home early that afternoon bearing a large cardboard box. It was full of wiggling desert tortoises, five in all. He had been on a flight to the western deserts and, upon landing, noticed a little boy playing with a tortoise. He offered to buy the animal and the offer was quickly accepted. From nowhere several other boys appeared wanting to sell tortoises. Apparently this part of Iran had many of the reptiles, and Jim soon found himself paying for four more.

He released the tortoises in our backyard, and they all started eating the grass. There were three very large ones, one medium size and one very small one, about the size of a softball. Two months before we had to get rid of Jeep-jeep, as he had become uncontrollable. He did not allow anyone, including us, into the backyard. While the tortoises were not exactly watchdogs, they fit our backyard very well.

One of Jimbo's favorite toys was an H-shaped wooden bench that had colored pegs in the center. This came with a wooden mallet that allowed the child to pound each peg until it was flush with the bench, then turn the bench over so he could pound the pegs again. Jimbo loved the pounding action.

One day I noticed him pounding on something in the garden. Walking outside, I was stunned to see him beating on the smallest tortoise. I yelled as loud as I could for him to stop. He looked at me with enormous eyes as I grabbed him and shoved him hard onto a chair.

"Stay right there, do not move", I growled. Turning to the tortoise, I saw that his shell was cracked. I ran to our medicine cabinet and retrieved a can of BFI, a powder used to stem the flow of blood. Returning outside, I quickly hosed the back of the turtle, letting the water flush the blood so I could see the damage. The poor animal had two large cracks in his shell, and I could see flesh between the cracks. I poured half a can of the BFI on him watching until the blood began to clot. It was only then that I turned to my charge, who sat wide-eyed and ashen-faced. Seeing him so disturbed, I calmly talked to him about being good to animals. He started sobbing and telling me how sorry he was to hurt his favorite tortoise and promising that he would never hurt him again. *Good grief*, I thought. *Is this what it is like to raise boys? And I have to go through this with a second one?* When Jim learned what happened, he told me not to expect the tortoise to live, as he would probably get worms in his body. Miraculously, this did not happen and our little tortoise, which came to be known as Scarface, survived.

One evening Jim made the comment, "I made a big mistake today. I accidentally flew into Iraq."

"Did you damage the plane?"

"Why would you ask that?"

"Well, you said you flew into a rock. I just want to know if the plane was damaged?"

"I meant I flew over the boundary between Iran and Iraq, which if I had been caught would have been big trouble."

We both started laughing at our George Burns-Gracie Allen routine.

It was time for the Hudson's to leave Iran and they were in the throes of selling a lot of their goods and having the rest packed up. Jim was designated to be the sponsor of Hudson's replacement, a Lt. Tricinella. He arrived with his very pretty wife, Denise, and two gorgeous blond daughters, ages four and six. Nick was a dark-haired, handsome man of Greek ancestry, six ft. 4 inches tall and built like the linebacker he was in college. With the Hudsons and the Triinellas in a hotel, we gave the welcome and farewell party. Colleen came to the party complaining that the packers had stolen their new, yellow Grundig portable radio their son had planned to carry on the airplane. I tried my best to keep her away from innocent Denise, not wanting Denise to be as discouraged as I had been. I introduced her to Gertrude, who was delighted to find someone to mother and immediately took Denise under her wing. Several weeks after our party, when the Hudsons had returned to the States, their very honest and faithful badjii, Zara arrived at our door asking for work. When I told her we were very happy with Maluke, she produced a brand-new, yellow, portable Grundig radio from her chador and asked me to buy it. "Where did you get the radio?" I asked.

"Madame Hudson gave it to me," she replied.

June 1963

Jim had left early for a flight to Abadan, and it was midmorning when Gertrude called saying that the Embassy had ordered all Americans to go home and stay in their compounds because rioting was breaking out all over Iran. I phoned Ghalamorghi and was assured by Ole' Seegar that the pilots were waiting for Jim's return and planned to convoy through Tehran. He told me not to send Gholum back for Jim, as it might be too dangerous; he would give Jim a ride home. Gholum took me to school to get Jimbo, and there I found parents and kids in an uproar to get home. After lunch I waited impatiently for word from the airfield. Finally at two o'clock Ole' Seegar called to say Jim was landing and that they would be on their way in a five car convoy within minutes. Time dragged on; the boys awakened from their naps and I played with them in the living room, trying not to convey my worries to them. I was so relieved when a little before six o'clock Jim arrived.

As we ate dinner, he told me that they avoided south Tehran where the big bazaar was, as that was a hotbed of Shah resistance. They had taken a back road which eventually came to the major highway west of Tehran that skirted to the north. There they came upon the Coca-Cola factory, where the rioters were breaking windows. The road wended its way up into the foothills of the Alborz Mountains, and finally they ended up in Tajrish and then made their way home.

While the riots continued for three days we enjoyed the vacation, taking full advantage of the swimming pool. Again we were without current news until Jim returned to work on the fourth day and brought home the three-day-old New York Herald Tribune. The June 6th paper headlined, *Army Rules Tehran After 20 Die in Rioting*, with the sub-heading *As Shiites Fight Reform*. The Associated Press story continued:

The Iranian government clamped martial law on Tehran tonight after troops and thousands of religious demonstrators fought throughout the day. Most of the demonstrators were protesting Shah Mohamed Reza Pahlavi's land reform and women's rights programs on religious grounds. Under the land reform, some Moslem shrine properties are being handed over to landless peasants. The rioting in various parts of the city followed the arrest of religious leader Ruhollah Khomeini, leader of Iran's Shiite Moslem majority.

The story went on the say that the security forces had at first fired warning shots into the air, but aimed at the mobs when the shots were ignored.

The bazaar and many shops and offices were set on fire. Street battles, explosions and anti-Shah demonstrations spread from the bazaar area throughout the capital. Cars were overturned and set on fire. Soldiers guarded government buildings with machine guns, tear gas and bayonets. Three unveiled women were massacred by one mob. General Hassan Pakravan, assistant premier and security chief, said the movement to disrupt order was financed from outside Iran. He hinted that the culprit was the United Arab Republic President Gamal Nasser.

The next day the paper said there were 93 dead and that the troops were ordered to shoot to kill. Troops sealed off 24 blocks of the capital after crowds from the bazaar district stormed the nearby government radio station. Riots broke out in the cities of Qom, Kashan, Rey, Isfahan, Shiraz and Varamin. The troops dispersed the mobs in the Tehran bazaar and occupied it. The Shah and his family took refuge in the summer palace in Saadabad.

The riot had started because the Shah had ordered the arrest of Khomeini after he had delivered an incendiary speech against the Shah. The charismatic Khomeini was a true believer in the absolute law first set down by the Prophet. From the beginning of Islam, according to him, religious truth and political power were one and the same. He wanted Iran to return to *sharia,* the body of Islamic law composed in the Koran. Since the beginning of the Moslem conversion, Iran had been under the law of *sharia* until Reza Shah visited Turkey in 1934. There he learned of the progress Ataturk had made in bringing Turkey into the 20th century by turning that country into a secular state. The Shah had returned to Iran and plunged into an accelerated program of social and economic modernization. New criminal codes were based on French law and the new Ministry of Justice set up its own secular law school. The *ulama* were weak against the despotic Reza Shah, and for thirty years acquiesced to the monarchy, until Khomeini came on the scene.

Khomeini's speech was a bitter attack on the Shah, on Israel and on the United States. He was trying to topple the Shah due to the land reform and new rights for women. He called the Shah a "wretched, miserable man." This was the last straw and he was arrested, along with some other ayatollahs.

With so much unrest in Tehran, the American Embassy ordered Americans to avoid traveling south of the Embassy unless on official business. Daily I was concerned for Jim's welfare, as the only way to get to Ghalamorghi was through the southern part of Tehran. This curtailed our visits to the Bazaar in search of Persian carpets on the weekends, so we confined our shopping to the Jewish merchants along Saltanabad Street. We hadn't bought any as yet but were learning more and more about the difference between tribal and village rugs.

In April the American School seniors were planning their Senior Trip to Moscow, Russia. I was envious, comparing my Senior Trip from Tucson High. (We went by bus to a park in Safford, Arizona, where the temperature was over 100 degrees. We ate beans and hotdogs and on the way home, winding through the mountains, I got sick. At Superior, Arizona, I threw up everything causing the class comic to rename the town Inferior.) I received a phone call from the principal of the high school telling me that one of the teachers could not go to Russia and would I consider going as a chaperone? I immediately called Jim at Ghalamorghi and he answered, "Babe, do it. It's a chance of a lifetime." I filled out all the paperwork the Russian Embassy required and turned it in. I waited for a week before getting the disappointing news that my visa had been denied. It seems the paperwork was turned in one day too late. When the seniors returned they were full of tales of strange men following them and hidden microphones in their rooms, which the brats promptly stuffed with chewing gum. By the time the tour returned to Tehran, the chaperones were practically basket cases saying the kids were lucky to get out of Russia. On the other hand, the Russkies probably thought we deserved them.

In May, with the end of school, military and embassy orders arrived and many families were leaving Tehran, with many more arriving. The whole atmosphere of the American community changed and became more sociable. We found ourselves involved in bridge, square dancing, and bowling, as well as the softball games between the various units. Our boys loved to watch their dad compete in softball. Jimbo would cheer lustily and Patrick would laugh and clap his hands in the excitement.

The Liebshultz' decided to have a party to celebrate both Barbara and Norman's birthday, but they only wanted to invite their close friends. However, protocol demanded that certain people be invited, so the clever Barbara solved the problem: she sent out invitations stating that the party was to begin at one minute after midnight. As she suspected, only the people who always managed to have fun accepted the invitation. Maluke's expression when I told her we would be going out at midnight showed that she thought we were nuts! It was a huge success and the most fun we had enjoyed since leaving Ft. Eustis.

We passed our first year anniversary, pleased with our situation; Maluke and Gholum were the main reason we were able to enjoy our tour. Maluke was so good to the boys, and they both responded to her easy good nature. She talked constantly in Farci to both boys and Jimbo became bilingual. Gholum also loved to talk to the boys, especially to Patrick, who sat next to him in his car seat. Soon Jimbo was demanding to sit up front so he could join in the conversations. Gholum was very entertaining and became our official Persian philosopher. His comments about his fellow countrymen's driving habits were amusing.

Patrick was trying to crawl, and I would frequently find Maluke squatting on the floor, encouraging him. She would motion for him to come to her and say, "*Bota beetah, Kucheeloo*" (('come here, little one'). He would laugh and try hard, sometimes falling flat on his face.

Finally, after a long first year, we were able to enjoy ourselves. I said to Jim, "Isn't it nice that things have quieted down?" I should have bitten my tongue because the very next day Jim received a phone call from our landlord, Mr. DeHeshti.

"Capeetan Estarkee, I am having a problem because of the Shah. He is giving land away to peasants and no one is buying my tractors. I cannot pay the rent on this big house, so I must ask you to leave my house so I can move in."

"Mr. DeHeshti, you signed a two-year lease with me, so I do not have to leave."

"Yes, yes, I know, but it is important to my wife that you leave. I will give you $350.00 if you promise to leave."

That was a lot of money to us, so Jim agreed that we would move. I was not happy, as I felt the Wicked Witch only wanted to live here because she had seen how nice the house looked. But Jim convinced me that $350.00 was a lot of money, money we could use to buy a carpet. I was sold on that idea, so I started on a two-week house-hunting period. Again I saw a lot of huge, ugly, and mostly old mansions. Many of our friends were living in a new American-style housing area near Tajrish that was a gated community offering round-the-clock security. The rent was almost double our current rate, but Jim finally relented, saying the generous offer from our landlord would help make up the difference. "But you'll have to give up the carpet, Babe." We found an available house and Jim called Mr. DeHeshti. He said he would be over that evening. To our surprise, he arrived with Mrs. DeHeshti, who immediately started inspecting our home. I followed her all around answering a million questions. We returned to the living room in time to hear Jim say, "Mr. DeHeshti, we will be able to move by the end of the month, as soon as you give me the $350.00 you promised me."

Mrs. D. let out a yelp and commenced hammering DeHeshti in rapid Farci. DeHeshti turned beet-red and stammered to Jim, "I I I did not tell you I would give you money to move."

"You certainly did, Mr. DeHeshti. I do not lie. Remember, you and I signed a two-year contract, so I do not have to leave."

Much rapid Farci ensued and suddenly they left without a word to us. We looked at each other, bewildered. The next day Mr. De-Heshti called and in a voice like melting butterscotch assured Jim that since we were such good tenants they had decided to let us stay.

Chapter 9

Kennedy speaks at the Berlin Wall, "Ich bin ein Berliner", Soviet Union puts first woman into space, John XXIII dies, Pope Paul VI crowned, Civil rights leader Medgar Evers is murdered, Buddhist holds fiery protest in Saigon, Martin Luther King speaks at the Lincoln Memorial, I Have a Dream.

Armish-Maag maintained several cabins outside of Chalus, on the Caspian Sea. Jim became eligible for one of them in July, so we made arrangements to drive there. Major B. would only give Jim four days leave but that didn't matter. I was so excited to be leaving Tehran that I had us packed in about three hours. Our Ford had a big trunk, so we were able to bring Pat's stroller and playpen. In the crevices we put various balls and toys for the boys. Gholum arrived at five a.m. the morning of our departure as excited as we were. He had not been to the Caspian area in several years and was happy to be our guide and driver. We waved goodbye to Maluke, telling her to take good care of our home while we were gone.

The sun was just beginning to come up as we left the city. The low clouds looked like cotton candy in many shades of coral, pink, orange and yellow. Mt. Damavand was bathed in a rosy glow emphasized by the surrounding turquoise blue sky. As we entered the main highway going north, I looked all around at the surrounding ochre hills. My eyes felt as if I were exercising them as I gazed at miles and miles of endless earth. I realized I had been looking at walls for a year. Even downtown, the shops and buildings were right at the sidewalk edge. In the residential areas I saw nothing but high enclosures with green trees folding over the edges on either side of the street. For a year I had been moving around in tunnels of mud walls. How wonderful it was to be able to see for miles and miles.

Ahead of us were the commanding Alborz Mountains, slick, gray and forbidding, bare of any trace of greenery. It seemed strange to those of us who were used to the mountains of southern Arizona, so full of color with purple sagebrush, green mesquite and palo verde trees, saguaro, ocotillo and other cactus with blossoms of every hue.

We entered a narrow valley where the ramparts rose sharply on both sides of the highway. We traveled for several minutes on wide asphalt paving; just as the road became steep, it also became very narrow. The Ford chugged along as Gholum shifted gears, and the switchbacks seemed endless as we progressed our way up the mountain. From dizzy heights we could see down into desolate ravines. A lone car going downhill too fast met us on a curve. Quickly, Gholum hugged the side of the cliff and averted a collision by inches. In unison we all exhaled in a loud, "Whewwww".

Fortunately that was the only vehicle we met during the hour and a half it took to climb to the summit. The last few miles the road was extremely steep, and as Gholum shifted into first gear the Ford shuttered in a loud groan. We held our breath, willing the car forward, and were elated as we reached the pinnacle. Our hair-raising experience was quickly forgotten as we beheld the view on the other side of the mountain. To our great amazement, we looked down on a lush green forest. Gholum had stopped the car and turned to watch our expressions, a huge grin lighting up his face. "Capeetan, Eeran very beautiful, no?"

Jim nodded silently and then said, "I could see from the air that the Caspian side of the Alborz was green, but I never expected this."

Gholum started the car, keeping it in first gear, then slowly we descended into the valley, noticing immediately the drastic change from hot, dry air to a cool, humid atmosphere. On either side of the road vines twisted up the tropical trees; flowers appeared- red, fuchsia, white and violet. The air was perfumed with a combination of honeysuckle and orange blossoms. Water cascaded down the scraggy cliffs, meandering over rocks and collecting in swirling pools. Never had we witnessed such a diametric change in climate.

The landscape became less dense as we entered a wide valley. Houses emerged, held up by stone stilts allowing rain run-off to pass underneath. With the thatched roofs, these dwellings could have been in Cambodia. This side of the mountain gets up to five feet of rain per year. Rice paddies appeared in the low areas and tea was growing on the sides of the rolling hills. With Patrick loudly signaling lunchtime, we stopped by the side of the road for a quick picnic. Gholum eyed the sandwich with suspicion until I explained that the Iranian nun was spread with peanut butter and jelly, not the "unclean" *gushte khuk* (pork). He took a tentative bite, chewed a moment, raised his eyebrows and smiled broadly. We had a peanut butter/jelly convert!

We continued our journey with Patrick lying down between Jim and me for a nap. Going over a small rise we entered another valley. Sweeping his arm to the west Gholum exclaimed, "This Alamut, Assassins." Following his gestering we saw that high craggy cliffs dominated the skyline and indeed seemed to disappear into the clouds. Puzzled, we tried to find out what he was talking about.

He tried hard to tell us but his English was very limited though not as limited as our Farci. After awhile he gave up. Later, we learned from Major Shahrabani, who had made a study of Iranian history, that Gholum had been referring to the so-called Old Man of the Mountain, Hasan-e-Sabbah. He was the first Lord of Alamut who in 1162 founded a cult of young recruits whom he would send out to murder his enemies. The cult was part of an offshoot of the Shiite Moslems, the Isma'ilis, who in 760 A.D. broke away from the main branch over a succession dispute. By the early eleventh century the Isma'ilis had scattered throughout the Middle East. Hasan-e-Sabbah, claiming divinity for himself, broke away from all Moslem tradition, built an impenetrable fortress high up in the Alborz Mountains, and peopled it with young men, controlling them by providing them with hashish. They were known as "hashishiyyin," the term that evolved into the English word "assassins." They were one of the most effective terrorist groups in history. Anyone who paid a huge price to the Old Man of the Mountain could get a recruit to assassinate an enemy. In 1256, under Hulagu Khan, Mongol armies came from the east, marching across the Siberian plains toward Persia. When they came across Alamut, they destroyed the castle and its fabled library.

We discovered Chalus to be a very small village of single story, dreary, mud huts. A sandy park was the center of activity, where peasants laid out their wares on colorful blankets. We stopped and the ever faithful, protective Gholum followed me out to buy some fruits and vegetables. A Turkoman woman, dressed in a full skirt and over-blouse, had set out a vivid display of produce. She was as color-ful as her goods, with a red and orange scarf on her head and many layers of gold necklaces cascaded from her neck. Her voluminous skirt was a riot of color; her blouse embroidered in flowers. It had been a long time since her face and hands had seen soap and water, and I hesitated before buying anything. I carefully inspected some apples and tomatoes to make sure the skins had not been damaged. She started to protest my handling of the goods, but Gholum as-sured her that I would be careful. At least that is what I thought he said. For all the Farci I knew, he could have told her I was the Shah's sister, because her attitude changed to one of great deference. Several women sat around her, and I noticed that none of them had on a chador. They were all dressed in the same full skirts, over-blouses in many bright colors belted at the waist. Huge earrings dangled from their ears and jangling bracelets encompassed their wrists. A baby suckled at the breast of one of the women and many small children played nearby. I paid for my purchases and thanked the woman in Farci. She smiled, showing bright, white teeth. We walked back to the car, passing a stall with fly-covered lamb carcasses hanging from hooks. Nearby was a fire pit where a hawk-nosed man, with a patch over one eye, tended to a spit of aromatic, roasting meat.

We drove beyond the village to a row of cabins situated on the gray sandy beach. To the north, we could see the dark, cold waters of the Caspian Sea and our enemy, Russia. Our cabin was sparse but adequate and we quickly unpacked. Jim gave Gholum some money for his dinner and lodging and told him to come by in the morn-ing. Jimbo was so excited to play in the sea, he could hardly stand still long enough for me to put on his swimsuit. Unfortunately, the sand was not really sand but tiny pieces of gravel, very hard on our feet. The water was so cold Jimbo only stayed a few minutes. I put Pat in his stroller, but found the wheels sank deeply, not allowing me to push him. He protested loudly while trying to crawl on the stones. We ended up sitting on a blanket and feeling the millions of bumps underneath us. Jim grilled hamburgers and we ate outside watching the sunset. The clouds changed from white to brilliant reds and orange with an undertone of purple. The sea became golden, and we watched the whole sky change in a chorus of every color in a painter's pallet. For several minutes we were in awe of the grandeur of the scene. Suddenly, it all turned gray, and with a disappointed sigh, we returned to our cabin.

During the night the rain awakened us. The staccato sounds of raindrops on the tin roof soon lulled us back to sleep. The morning dawned bright and clear with the fragrant smell that accompanies the freshly washed earth. Gholum arrived after breakfast. He informed us that the Turkoman tribesmen were in town to barter for horses, utensils, jewelry and carpets.

"Capeetan, you must come. Many fine carpets here." He didn't have to say it twice; we immediately prepared to go to town.

The Turkoman are a non-Persian, nomadic tribe which for centuries has roamed through northern Iran, Turkey, Afghanistan and southern Russia. They ignore country boundaries and even the Russians leave them alone. They are a handsome race, tall and regal, carrying themselves with great pride. Their high cheekbones and slant eyes reminded us of the native tribes of Arizona. The men wear a traditional black sheepskin hat that adds six inches to their formidable height, a formal long, black, dress coat over ballooning black pants held in by high boots. Their skin is burnished brown and leathery; their squinty eyes view the world with caution, and they sport wispy beards on the lower part of their chins. They carry the *tesbih*, or string of beads, sometime referred to as "worry beads" because they move them through their fingers nervously. We were told that the Crusaders saw the beads that the Moslem men carried and adopted them to become the rosary.

In contrast to the darkness of the male's dress, the women's was a riot of color. From their headgear to their pantaloons red predominated, interspersed with green, dark blue and black. Their jewelry was mostly gold, inlaid with coral, onyx, amber and shells. I found a pleasant-faced young woman and after some bargaining came away with two unusual necklaces. I was carrying our very blond Patrick, and the ladies all gathered around to run their hands over his crew cut. Patrick was not amused. In fact, he howled indignantly, which produced much laughter from the women. Jimbo was with his dad, who had gravitated to an open-sided tent where there was a large display of carpets. I found the two of them seated on *poshtis*, drinking tea and discussing various subjects. Gholum cautioned me not to join the men, as in Turkoman society that is frowned upon. Patrick and I wandered about with our protector while Jim and Jimbo stayed in the tent. I bought some cucumbers, onions and peaches for us. Then I spied a five-foot chain of garlic and bought it for Maluke. She was very fond of making pickled garlic to eat with bread and yogurt. After thirty minutes, Jim and Jimbo emerged from the tent, triumphantly carrying two five-by-three carpets. Both were of the traditional elephant-foot design, one in red, white and black and the other in red, green and black. Gholum took our purchases to the car while we walked over to watch the males haggling over sheep, horses and other livestock. Even though we couldn't understand the spoken language, we could follow the body language. It was a fascinating study in human interaction.

While we were watching the goings-on, an Englishman approached Jim and started a conversation. It turned out that he was an expert in fisheries and was in country to help the Iranians reach their full potential in marketing caviar. The finest caviar in the world comes from Persia, thanks to the sturgeon that swims in the southern shores of the Caspian Sea. Caviar is the roe or eggs from the sturgeon and is an expensive delicacy, prized by gourmands around the world. For years, from 1893 to 1928, Russians held a concession from the Iranians for the fishing stations, refrigerating and processing plants that prepared the caviar. Then it was shipped to Russia and sold as Russian caviar. In 1928 the Russian monopoly was broken with the granting of a 25-year concession to a joint Irano-Soviet fishing company. When the concession ended, the Shah decreed that an Iranian government company would solely control the caviar production. The northern Caspian Sea is too cold for the sturgeon to survive, so Russia buys most of the Iranian annual caviar production.

There are five varieties of sturgeons: the most valuable is the

Beluga, which can weigh up to 220 pounds and can yield between 37 and 44 pounds of caviar. Small grain caviar is black; the larger grains are either grey or yellowish in color. The latter is called "golden caviar" and is reserved for the use of the Shah and his guests. Our newfound English friend, Mr. Cooper, was explaining all this to us. He told us he lived in Tehran and invited us to his home for the following Friday. He promised that we would get a chance to taste some very good caviar. We accepted the invitation, looking forward to the experience.

We spent the rest of our time in Chalus walking the beach with our shoes on looking for shells. We found very few of them but did find two glass floats, which we imagined, came from some Russian fishing vessel.

Our trip back to Tehran was even scarier, coming down the bleak side of the mountain, for we could see the sheer drops that commenced a foot from the edge of the road. We were very relieved to leave the mountain and enter the mayhem of Tehran traffic.

We arrived home to discover we had new American neighbors across the kuchee. Maluke had become good friends with their badjii and was anxious for us to meet the newcomers. After getting settled into our routine, I made some cookies and took them over. Mary Smith was a warm-hearted, gracious lady. She and her husband John had been living in the Middle East for eight years. They had two grown daughters who had families of their own back in Florida. With the daughters out of the house, and after selling his insurance business, the Smiths decided they needed some adventure, so had volunteered to join U.S.Aid. The U.S.Aid people were delighted to get someone of John's business background and after some schooling in Washington DC, he was posted overseas. His first assignment was to Turkey, where they stayed five years, until their assignment to Iran. They had been in the country for three years. Mary was a petite brunette with a soft southern drawl, and I liked her immediately. John was a big surprise: he was over six feet five inches tall, bald as a cue ball, was loud, very funny, with a definite Eastern accent. He regaled us with problems he had run up against dealing with the Turks and Iranians until we were laughing so hard tears rolled down our cheeks. They were wonderful neighbors.

Two weeks after our trip to Chalus, Jim called from Ghalamorghi to tell me to start cooking one of our 14-pound pork roasts, as he had invited twelve pilots for dinner. "Where in the world did you find twelve pilots?" I asked.

"Babe, these guys are from Germany flying helicopters on their way to Viet Nam." We had been reading in Time Magazine that President Kennedy was sending more advisors to Viet Nam to shore up the presidency of Diem. That evening we heard all the latest scuttlebutt about the growing problems in Southeast Asia. It was obvious that this would be the next major problem in combating communism. Concerned, I later asked Jim if he might be sent to Viet Nam after our tour in Iran was up.

"I don't think so, Babe. This tour is considered an accompanied hardship tour." That was the first time I had heard that description, but I agreed with it!

During the summer and early fall of 1963, galvanizing events were occurring throughout the world. President Kennedy sent troops into Alabama, where violence had erupted after Negroes led by Martin Luther King and Malcolm X demonstrated against the state's segregation policies. Pope John XXIII died and Pope Paul VI was enstalled; JFK went to Berlin and made his "Ich bin ein Berliner" speech; Buddhists were setting themselves on fire in Viet Nam; and at a civil rights rally at the Lincoln Memorial, Martin Luther King gave his "I Have a Dream" speech. We continued to live in our little bubble, learning of these earth-shaking events days after they occurred. Life in Iran was quiet with Khomeini in jail and out of the picture.

October 1963

With the Shah in total control and Khomeini under House Arrest, it became possible to travel south again. Jim was going to lose leave time if he didn't take some before the end of October. He wanted me to see Isfahan and Shiraz, places he flew to constantly.

"You'll love both cities, Shirl. They are very beautiful. Persepolis is near Shiraz, so we'll be able to see that, too." Since we would be driving the full length of Iran, he thought the trip would be too hard on the boys, and they wouldn't get much out of it anyway. We had sponsored the Whitfields in mid-July and had become good friends. When Sharon and Rod offered to care for the boys, we took them up on it. They had two girls the ages of Jimbo and Patrick, so it sounded like it would work out okay. Maluke would stay on at our house and again Gholum would drive us.

We deposited our sons early in the morning, headed south past Ghalamorghi, past Rey with the carpets drying on the hills and onward through a bleak desert. The desolate, beige landscape was mostly sand and rocks, with only occasionally some scrubby bushes, and even those were a dusty olive color. There were no other cars on the single lane highway, but from time to time we passed lone figures on donkeys. Off to the left we noticed a large, single, squared, dun-colored building. Gholum informed us that it was a deserted caravanserai, one of the dwellings built centuries ago as refuge. These were built about 20 miles apart, a day's march for the camel caravans that followed the Silk Route from China to Europe eons ago. The caravanserai was a mud-walled sanctuary built around a central open space that provided shelter and protection, as well as water, for the traveler and his animals. A solitary gate guarded the entrance, and there were a few windows and some small holes used as rifle slots evident in the gaunt structure. We saw a central court with arcaded sides that contained small rooms providing privacy and cooking facilities for travelers. Animals were stabled in the passages between these rooms, while baggage and merchandise were stacked in the central courtyard. Gholum explained that it was an ironclad rule that anyone entering a caravanserai was safe from any enemies, even if the enemy was also spending the night there. Violence was verboten.

I laughed, "It's like the kids game Kings X."

We were coming to the city of Qom, where Khomeini had started his crusade against the Shah. Gholum told me that since I did not have a chador, I must stay in the car and keep myself hidden as he and Jim went to visit the Gold Mosque, the shrine of Fatimah.

Irritated, I did as I was told. While they were gone, I noticed that there were no women around, only a small number of *mullahs* in black robes and white turbans (with neatly combed beards). Also shuffling aimlessly around the area were scruffy looking, unkempt men with hairy faces, playing with worry beads. Not my kind of town anyway, I consoled myself. The guys returned and Jim regaled me with descriptions of the beauty of the Mosque.

In a snit I ignored his remarks and said, "Well, we need to find a bathroom."

"No we don't," Jim teased, "Gholum and I already used one." Reading my expression he told Gholum that "Madam needs to find a toilet." We proceeded out of the main part of Qom and came to a park on the outskirts of town. Gholum pointed to an uninviting, broken-down shack. Having no choice, I rushed to use it. I entered the dismal, smelly interior and tried to lock the door, but there was no lock. Turning around I saw that there was only a hole in the ground. Just as I lifted my skirt and squatted, I saw between the huge cracks in the door that a man holding a jug was coming right toward me. I was panicked but couldn't stop the stream. Just then I saw Jim waylay the intruder and, after a conversation, the man handed the jug to Jim and Jim gave him some coins.

Jim knocked on the door, "Babe, this man brought a water jug for you to use in place of toilet paper." He slipped it through the door and added, "I'll stand watch here." I was relieved in more ways than one!

We picnicked in the park and then proceeded on to Isfahan. Jim, pointing to the east, said, "This is where we left the road on our route to the airplane." The *Dasht-e-Kavir*, known as the desert of death, stretched for miles of white, salt-permeated sand undulating in the heat of the day. "This is where we turned off the highway and discovered the drivers had no idea how to drive," he said.

"Who lives in such a desolate place?" I wondered.

"Well, while we were driving, the third day, we met a man who was just walking. He had a coat and tie on and looked like he was just going for a stroll. My "driver" talked to him and found out he was on his way to Isfahan. He didn't appear to even have any water with him. This country and its people are truly amazing!"

The road wound up some hills, and we came to a village built on the side of the crest. Faces, young and old, looked out at us from the open doors and curtainless windows of the mean, adobe hovels. Chickens raced across the road to avoid our tires; children ran next to the car calling out, their hands outstretched. "The children want baksheesh, Capeetan." Gholum stated.

"They learn early, don't they?" was Jim's remark.

Coming off the hills we could see men in the fields of the low-lands plowing. It was a scene right out of Biblical times. Walking behind a plow being drawn by a donkey, the farmer was carefully making rows for planting. Even with the earth turned up, the soil did not look very fertile. "What grows here, Gholum?" I asked. He shrugged his shoulders. I tried again, "Where do they get the water?"

"*Qanats*", he answered, curtly. Turning to Jim I said, "What's he talking about?"

Jim pointed to a giant molehill in the distance and explained, "Qanats are the subterranean canals that bring the water from the melting snow in the mountains through the desert to the different villages. These were built thousands of years ago, and the men who take care of the qanats pass the job from father to son. It is a very dangerous job because of cave-ins, so the men who do this work are highly respected and are paid very well."

"How do they take care of the qanats? Exactly what do they do?" I asked.

"You know when you go to the ocean and see the holes made in the sand by crabs as the tide goes out?" Jim asked. As I nodded he went on, "From the air, that is exactly what the qanat system looks like. These are holes dug in the earth every so many meters. There is a ladder that goes inside each of these holes, down to the underground river. The qanat men's job is to make sure the flow is unimpeded. They clean the sand, bushes or other debris that have clogged the river. Because the river flows underground, there is not much evaporation. It is a remarkable system that has kept this country alive for centuries."

Noticing that Gholum was unresponsive, especially for him, Jim said, "Gholum, stop the car. Let's get out and take a break."

Gholum grinned, "Break ees good, Capeetan." We stretched our legs and Jim reached into the cooler and handed Gholum a bottled orange drink Iranians love. Happily, he chugged it down and his mood improved instantly.

Jim pointed to the west toward the saw-toothed Zagros Mountains. "See that tallest peak over there? That's where Pierce crashed the plane." I looked up at the summit of the overbearing mountain and, shivering, thought, 'How amazing that one misstep could change our lives completely, to say nothing of the lives of the relatives of the dead men.'

Gholum indicated that we were approaching Isfahan. Ahead we could see an inviting green oasis. The tall trees that lined the road into the city were a welcome change from the monotonous, khaki-colored landscape. We pulled up to the hotel on the main street and checked in, anxious to clean up from our journey. Jim gave Gholum some money for his lodging and food, telling him to meet us at the hotel in the morning. We showered, changed clothes and walked around the hotel while waiting for the dinner hour. The Abassi Hotel was an early 18th Century caravanserai built to finance the *madresseh* (school) next door. It had been converted into a hotel just seven years before. The décor was lush, with fabulous tapestries hanging from the walls, burgundy velvet upholstered couches, and crystal chandeliers that illuminated tables inlaid with lapis, coral and amber stones. After finding the dining room on the ground floor, we went outside. The wide avenues were lined with magnificent trees ablaze in the fall colors of rust, red, gold and yellow. We wandered the streets taking in the sights. Trees were glowing in various shades of green, orange, and yellow, with early fall foliage giving the city a golden cast. Beautiful fountains filled with goldfish were in abundance, and in many cases children were trying their best to catch the fish with their hands. The streets were filled with chador-clad mothers tending babies, men standing, agitating the ever present worry beads, vendors selling bread, fruit juices and kabobs; there was an unexplained air of happiness and excitement.

Isfahan is one of the most beautiful cities in the world. The avenues are wide and tree-lined, the jubes ran clean and clear, the buildings impressive. Flowers bloomed in every hue imaginable.

We continued our walk south toward the Zaindeh Rud, the river that is the lifeblood of Isfahan. We came to the Allahverdi Khan Bridge that was built in the early 1600's. It has thirty-three arches on the lower level, plus many more arcades on the upper level, where pedestrians can stroll or picnic in the niches that overlook the river. It is just one of the myriad architectural wonders of Persia. We wandered and watched until the setting sun sent waves of crimson washing over the deep blue sky, telling us it was time for our meal. As we returned to the hotel the air was filled with the haunting song of the muezzin, in a minaret, calling the faithful to prayer. We dined on chelo kabob and Shiraz wine and gratefully fell into bed.

We were at breakfast when a short, broad-shouldered Asian man approached us. Jim jumped to his feet, a big smile on his face, and said, "Richard, how are you? Join us! Shirl, this is Lt. Woo, our resident expert on all things Persian."

Lt. Woo sat down, his moon face wreathed in a grin the size of a slice of watermelon. I extended my hand and he grasped it with a grip that brought tears to my eyes. Jim later told me that he had been a wrestler in college and continued to wrestle at the local *zur-khanehs*, the gymnasiums where the Iranian men stayed in shape by whirling 80 pound Indian clubs to the rhythmic beat of drums.

"Captain Starkey, Sir, I am at your service," he intoned seriously. "As soon as you are ready we can start our tour."

I looked at Jim with raised eyebrows. "What are we doing?"

"Richard has kindly consented to giving us a tour of Isfahan. He has become an authority on the history of Iran."

"I don't know how much of an authority I am," he modestly said, "but there isn't too much to do here except read when we're not working. This country is fascinating, and I like it more all the time."

We finished our breakfast and, walking outside ,met Gholum. "Do what you want to the rest of the day, Gholum. We won't need you today," Jim told him.

Lt. Woo led us to his Jeep and, climbing in, I remembered our first days of terror in Tehran. Happily Isfahan's traffic was calm and orderly. Woo drove several blocks, parked the Jeep and led us down a short alley. We emerged and, with a gasp, I beheld an enormous rectangle. The center held a huge fountain with flowers and grass surrounding it. Wide avenues encircled the center, and on the south end stood a beautiful mosque tiled in turquoise. Lt. Woo explained that we were standing in the Maiden Shah, a square planned and built by Shah Abbas I in 1612. "It is 1,680 feet long and 520 ft. wide and is one of the biggest in the world, three times larger than St. Mark's Square in Venice." He pointed out the wide avenue that enclosed the garden area. Buildings along the avenue contained shops stuffed with copper, brass, carpets, jewelry and other souvenirs. Shopkeepers stood in the doorways inviting customers inside. Horse and buggies were available for rides around the square, men in dark blue cotton shirts and pants patrolled the grounds picking up garbage, children frolicked in the grass, men argued in the teahouses and chador-clad women haggled at the vegetable stands.

"At the far end is the bazaar. We'll go there later, but right now I want to take you to the Ali Qapu Palace." Woo pointed to an unimpressive wooden building on the western side of the square. "From there we can get a good view of the whole square," he explained.

As we walked through the gardens toward the Ali Qapu Palace, Woo explained that Persia has for centuries been overrun with invading armies. Genghis Khan and his army swarmed over Persia in 1219, murdering the inhabitants of whole cities. Thirty years later Genghis Khan's grandson, Hulagu, repeated the devastation, destroying qanats, salting the earth, causing death by starvation for thousands. Then one hundred years later Tamerlane, the Tatar, invaded all of Persia. In Isfahan the Tatar soldiers slaughtered 70,000 souls, stacking their heads in a tower. Then they entertained Tamerlane by playing polo with the severed heads of the city's leaders.

As he finished his grisly account, we entered the Ali Qapu Palace, climbed narrow, steep stairs six stories high and emerged onto a wide veranda overlooking the Maiden Shah. From our high vantage point, looking south we could see the grand blue and turquoise Royal Mosque; facing it on the northern end were the archways to the Bazaar; and across from us was the Sheikh Lotfollah Mosque, built by Shah Abbas I for the women of his harem. Woo continued with his history lesson, telling us that the capital of Persia had been Qazvin, (the city mostly destroyed in the year before's earthquake), until Shah Abbas I ascended the throne at the age of 16. This charismatic leader inherited a nation torn apart by internal squabbling, occupied in the northeast by the Uzbeks and in the northwest by the Ottomans. After uniting Persia and purging all foreign invaders, he moved the capital to Isfahan in 1598. Here he employed artists and architects to build a magnificent city with wide avenues, dramatic bridges, and the crowning glory, the Maiden Shah.

We went into the Music Room, where the triple ceiling was constructed from a series of cutouts in the form of vases. The room was said to be acoustically perfect. The walls of the whole building were covered in a boring, beige stucco-like substance. Woo informed us that the Empress Farah had commissioned the restoration of the building. They had already uncovered incredible miniature paintings on some of the walls. These were painted by Persia's most famous calligrapher, Ali Abbasi.

"Oh, I guess that is who our hotel is named for!" I exclaimed.

We retraced our steps to the Royal Mosque and climbing more stairs walked along an arcade that overlooked the center court. We were admiring the intricate tile work, when I noticed two women at the far end of the walkway. Something about them looked familiar, and I watched as they walked toward us. Suddenly, I was stunned to recognize them. There in front of me stood Anne Meyers and Stephanie Harris! I knew Anne and Stephanie from the University of Arizona, where we were in the same education classes. We frequently walked together going to our respective sororities for lunch; they left me at the Pi Phi House and I went on to the Chi Omega House. Talk about a small world! I introduced them to Jim and Lt. Woo, who looked very excited. They told me they had been teaching third grade at an Air Force Base in Libya and decided to take the year off to see the world. Woo was falling all over himself trying to make small talk and invited them to join us.

We finished touring the part of the mosque we, as infidels, were allowed to see and left to have lunch. After our repast, Woo took us away from the city to see the famous "shaking minarets." He climbed up one of the minarets, placed his hands on opposite walls of the narrow structure and shook back and forth. The rest of us had our hands on the other minaret and could feel it moving back and forth in unison with Woo's movements. He told us that this structure had been standing and entertaining tourists for several hundred years.

He took us to see the pigeon towers, which from a distance looked like a fortress. These were built before the 13th century to collect guano for the melon fields that surround Isfahan. They stand several stories high with a multitude of openings where the pigeons roost. There is one small door that is opened once a year to collect the manure; no other openings are at ground level, to prevent snakes from infiltrating. The towers have intricate carvings, no two alike. On the tops of two of the towers were stork's nests.

From there we crossed the Allahverdi Bridge to the town of New Julfa, the Armenian community. After a successful campaign in Armenia in the early years of the 17th century, Shah Abbas I forcibly transported thousands of Armenians to Isfahan and settled them on the southern bank of the Zaindeh Rud. Armenians were famous for their skill, industry and thrift, and the Shah needed their talent to develop the commercial life of his new capital. He allowed them to build their own churches and schools and to keep their own language. We visited the All Saviors' Cathedral, plain on the outside but lavishly decorated on the inside. After spending a half-hour inspecting the church, Jim called a halt saying, "I've had enough of mosques and cathedrals for today. Let's go back to the hotel."

Throughout the entire afternoon Woo had directed all his comments to Anne and Stephanie, who in turn joked and flirted outrageously with him. As we returned to the hotel, Jim and I were not surprised when Lt. Woo invited them to have dinner with him at the Team House while pointedly ignoring us. As they drove off I cattily said, "Well, THAT wasn't very nice!"

"Babe, you've got to understand, these guys at the Team House can't fraternize with the local Moslems. It's a real treat for them to be around American women." Three weeks after our vacation Jim flew down to Isfahan and reported to me that Anne and Stephanie were still living at the Team House. Now I knew how they could afford their world travels.

The next morning a pouting Gholum arrived. He was hurt that his job of Tour Guide had been usurped by Woo. Jim greeted him enthusiastically and laid out our plans for the day. Gholum responded with a grin, happy to be needed again. On previous trips Jim had been taken to the shop of Mahmood, the premier coppersmith of Iran, and he gave Gholum directions to the shop. "Babe, we want to go there first to order some trays for Christmas presents. Mahmood is the man the Shah chose to do all the copper work for the World's Fair. He is a real artist." We spent a good part of the morning buying copper and brass trays for Christmas gifts.

As we left, Gholum took a wrong turn and we ended up in the

courtyard of a madresseh just as the students, all male of high school age, were changing classes. As Gholum stopped the car and attempted to put it in reverse, we were surrounded by a pack of boys pushing and shoving. They fought for a space at the windows and soon the interior of the car was dark as the gawking faces obliterated every bit of sunlight. They were all staring at me, their scowls just inches away. I gasped as panic washed over me. It was a frightening moment, but fortunately our windows were rolled up. Gholum could not drive off without running over someone, so he bravely opened his door and in Farci demanded that the boys let us leave. One of the boys said something, which Gholum answered, and then they calmly backed away. Relieved as we drove off, Gholum said, "Capeetan, this is Koran *madresseh*. Boy say Madam should wear chador."

I took a deep breath, and narrowing my eyes, I stared at the back of our faithful driver's head and thought, *How many times am I going to be chastised by this guy for not wearing a chador?* I wondered how he had answered the boys, deciding to myself, *I bet he told them he would make sure I wore a chador from now on!*

We went back to the Maiden Shah to go to the Bazaar- another work of art commissioned by the brilliant Shah Abbas I. It seems that everything Shah Abbas touched was artistically special. It was during his reign that the statement "Isfahan is half the world" was coined.

We were told the Bazaar was a labyrinth of narrow passages winding for almost seven miles. The dirt floor had hardened to the consistency of concrete from centuries of feet pounding it down. The walls were grimy with the soot from the many kerosene stoves and lamps. The vaulted ceilings were high with holes at the top that let in some natural light, but still the overall effect was shadowy. It was not gloomy because of the constant, ant-like activity. People in all manner of dress scurried to and fro intent on business. A herd of sheep plunged through the crowds, followed by their keeper wielding his staff and shouting orders. We jumped to one side to avoid getting run over. The bazaar was crammed with craftsmen of various skills, each occupying an open site on either side of the corridor. One section was devoted to carpets; another to goldsmiths selling jewelry and still another to the coppersmiths hammering out the intricate designs on bowls and pitchers. In the tinsmith section we saw limitless samovars displayed, all stacked on top of each other.

We came to the cloth section, attracted by the colorful bed-spreads, tablecloths and bolts of material. One man was carving designs in a block of wood while another man rolled red dye over a completed woodblock. He looked up at us, gave us a yellow, tooth-less grin, and dramatically began to stamp the design on the cloth by carefully laying it on the fabric and then pounding it with his right hand. He looked up at us to see if we were impressed. Pleased at the attention, he took a different block, rolled blue dye on it and repeated the process. The air was filled with the sounds of pound-ing fists as ten men worked diligently. Our man used four different blocks with different colors and the result was an intricate pattern that was truly beautiful. I bought two bolts in two different patterns to make into tablecloths.

As we came to the food section, a strong smell of spices perme-ated the air. Myriad tones of reds, purples, gold, rust and brown spices were piled in pyramids on copper trays. Next to them were the barrels of salt and various peppercorns.

"Madam," Gholum said, "you can find anything in the Bazaar." He didn't have to convince me of that, for next we came to huge, artistic displays of fruits and vegetables, followed by the smelly meat section. Behind the displays sat men talking, drinking tea, playing with their worry beads and reading newspapers. Young boys ran carrying trays of tea glasses encased in silver filigree holders to serve potential customers. One small boy accosted us, wanting to show us something. We didn't understand what he was saying until Gholum translated. "Boy want you to see blind camel."

"Why?" was Jim's response.

"Camel never leave Bazaar. Camel work here," Gholum ex-plained. "Come with me."

We followed, not wanting to be left to our own devices. The boy led us through a narrow hallway to a dark open area; the only light came from a small hole in the ceiling forty feet above us. As our eyes adjusted to the dim interior, we saw in the center an enormous dromedary walking in circles. His halter was attached to a crossbeam that allowed a great stone wheel to turn in a caldron containing su-mac. The camel's eyes were milky-white, evidence of his blindness. The boy talked at length to Gholum, who then interpreted to us that the camel was brought here when only a year old and had never left this room. In fact there was not a door large enough for the camel to go through. The wretched animal spent his entire life walking in circles, grinding spices in this dark cavern.

Happily we left that dismal scene, passing through a door into a sunshine-filled courtyard crisscrossed with racks of brilliantly dyed wools. Women manned the large vats filled with steaming dyes, pushing the wool around with long paddles. They would pick the yarn out of the dye bath with giant tweezers and hang it dripping, over the frames. We entered a gymnasium-sized room filled with looms of unfinished carpets. Little girls, the youngest five years old, sat in rows at the looms with their laps full of yarn of many colors. They held a straight razor between their middle and ring finger of their right hand. With their left hands the children would grab a single yarn and put it around the vertical strands while their right index finger looped it into a knot. Quickly they would move the razor down to cut the strand, dropping the rest onto floor beneath the loom. Their hands moved so fast it was hard to follow the action. Each had a picture of the design they were working on above the loom, but we never saw one look at it. Instead they were chattering and giggling happily to each other. Beneath the loom, toddlers of three and four gathered up the discarded strands, returning them to baskets. The teacher, a girl of twelve, supervised the workers. It was impossible to see the carpet design, as the threads were two inches long. Periodically a woman would approach with shears and trim the yarn: suddenly the intricate pattern would appear. A man approached us and after polite greetings, we asked if we could take some pictures.

"No, monsieur, please do not. Unfortunately, there are people in your country who get very upset that small children are working. You can see that our girls are very happy. Listen to their chatter. We will stop shortly and give them a very good meal of *ab gusht* (soup), bread, apples and tea."

We had to agree with him that the little girls all looked very happy, but when I asked him, "When do the girls go to school?" his mood changed. He retorted, "The girls do not need schooling when they have a good job." We learned later that several years ago the Shah had sent a beautiful Isfahan carpet to Eleanor Roosevelt. When Mrs. Roosevelt was informed that it was made by small children, she returned it with a very cold note stating that Americans did not believe in child labor. This was a real slap in the face and the Shah never forgave her.

We left the Bazaar and walked to the area where the miniature artists worked. Persia has always been famous for miniatures, whether in paintings or on tiles, but the most desirable are the inlaid boxes with the intricate designs formed with camel bone, copper, turquoise and various other semi-precious stones. We were amazed to observe the countless Iranian talented artists who worked in every media.

Hunger pains announced that lunch was long overdue, so we returned to the hotel, and gave Gholum the rest of the day off.

We left Isfahan early the next morning for Shiraz, 495 kilometers south. As soon as we left the lush city, the bleak desert took over. We sat in the back seat and talked about what amazing things we had seen in Isfahan and how pleased we were with our purchases.

Going over a small hill, we came into a bowl-shaped valley. About a mile off the road we saw many black tents, women at cooking pots, small children chasing goats and a lone man guarding some sheep. "Qashqai", Gholum explained. The Qashqai are one of the southern nomadic tribes of Persia. These tough people spend the winter in the warm lowlands and the summer in the high mountain valleys of the Zagros Mountains. The twice-yearly migration from one place to the other must be a sight to behold. The whole community is on the move; sheep and goats are herded by boys, followed by camels and donkeys burdened with the tents, cooking utensils, baggage, and women and children. All around strut the tribesmen on horseback, shouted orders competing with the bleats and bells of the animals. Slowly the massive migrations move toward their goal of either the warm lowlands or the cool Zagros. Just as the Alborz Mountains cut across the top of Iran from west to east, from the southern end of the Caspian Sea to the Afghan frontier, the Zagros moves from north to south down Iran's western flank, from the Turkish border to the Persian Gulf. It was into the heights of the Zagros that Captain Pierce flew his plane.

"Gholum, could we go over to meet some of the people and maybe take some pictures?" Jim asked.

"Baleh, Capeetan" (yes). Taking a bag of hard candy and our camera, we walked over toward the people. Immediately, all movement stopped as the women and children stared at us. Looking around I saw that everyone had the same chalky coloring on skin and clothes, and then I realized it was dirt. I wondered how often they had water for washing. An old man marched defiantly toward us and Gholum started talking to him. He eyed us suspiciously while listening to Gholum, and after much discussion nodded in agreement. We proceeded toward the waiting women and I noticed a wrinkled-up old crone, the matriarch of the tribe, sitting high on some blankets. I held out some candy and in pantomime indicated that is was good to eat. With a disapproving frown, she unwrapped a piece and popped it in her mouth. Sucking loudly, she had a sudden look of pleasure cross her face. She nodded in agreement when I indicated I wanted to give some to the children. I started handing it out and was suddenly surrounded in a crush of waiting hands. Fortunately I had enough candy to give some to everybody, the women and old man included. Suddenly, a ferocious looking man with heavy brows knitted in a frown galloped toward us on a spirited brown horse. As he skidded to a stop in front of us in a cloud of dust, the women and children scattered. Barking to the old man and pointing an accusing finger at us, he demanded to know what we were doing there. The old man answered in a pleading voice. Getting off his horse, he moved close to Jim, looking him straight in the eye. Jim, unflinching, returned his gaze. The tough warrior lost the stare-down and turned to Gholum, questioning in rapid Farci. Gholum answered and then turned to Jim and said, "Capeetan, man tinks you from government. He no want you here. He tinks you Shah man."

"That's okay, Gholum. Tell him we are not from the Shah, that we are Americans on vacation and would like his permission to take some pictures." Gholum translated and it was clear from the horseman's demeanor that he was not pleased with what he heard. He motioned for us to leave, ranting in a loud voice. We turned and moved toward our car. As we drove away Gholum explained that the Shah was trying to get the tribesmen to stay in one place, cultivate the land and give up their weapons. It was all part of the White Revolution, but was being defied. After all, the Qashqais had been living independently and unhindered through generations of Shahs, for thousands of years.

We continued southward through more desert, then some villages surrounded by cultivated fields. Finally, to the east in the distance, the spires of Persepolis rose against the sapphire sky.

"Are we going to Persepolis now?" I asked as we came to the turnoff for Persepolis.

"No, we'll check into the hotel in Shiraz and come back out here early tomorrow morning," Jim replied.

Shiraz was a disappointment for me, since I expecting it to be as spectacular as Isfahan. It didn't look much different from Qom or some of the other smaller cities we had seen. After checking into the hotel, we went on a short sightseeing tour. The bazaar was small but colorful, as it was full of Qashqai, Lurs and Bakhtiari tribesman dressed in tribal clothing. It was market day and crowded, so we did not linger.

Shiraz is referred to as the City of Poets, roses and wine and we set out to see why. While the West is familiar with the poet Omar Khayyam from Edward Fitzgerald's translation of the *Rubiayat*, the Persians say their greatest poet is Hafez. Born in 1324, he is said to have memorized the entire Koran. He lived his whole life in Shiraz and is buried there in a grand rose garden and mausoleum. Also buried nearby is Sa'di, another native of Shiraz. He wrote in verse and prose of his views on life. He is referred to as the Persian Shakespeare. His tomb has a turquoise dome and reflecting pool full of fish. Both tombs are close by one another in tranquil, lovely settings of rose gardens and bougainvillea-covered arches.

We set out early the next morning to visit Persepolis, the magnificent complex started by the founder of the Achaemenian dynasty, Cyrus the Great, sometime between 520 and 515 BC. His successor, Darius, continued to add to the various structures, as did his descendents for the next 150 years. Alexander the Great destroyed it in 331 BC in retaliation for the destruction of the Acropolis by King Xerxes, Darius' son and successor. In this part of the world, memories are long, people do not forget and revenge is not only sweet but mandatory—even centuries later. We learned of the conquests of Alexander the Great in our high school history classes, but never knew that the Persians had been the first to conquer so much of the known world. First Cyrus and then Darius led their armies to conquer and rule lands from the east as far as the Indus River, north as far as the Danube River and west to Egypt. Darius even had plans to cut a canal between the Red Sea and the Nile River, a forerunner of the Suez Canal. He died before he could accomplish this project. The Achaemenians introduced weights and measurements, coinage that stimulated foreign commerce, encouraged the propagation of new plant species to all parts of their conquered territory and dug the *qanats* that allowed for agriculture to flourish. It was an enlightened time in Persian history.

As we arrived at the entrance to Persepolis, an eager guide welcomed us. Hassan, speaking good English, assured us that he knew all there was to know about Persepolis, as he had been guiding Americans for five years. After several minutes of negotiations, Jim hired him. Hassan proved to be an excellent guide and we soon learned that he had been schooled in England, that his family belonged to the elite 1000 families of landowners who were having their lands distributed to the serfs. Since he could no longer count on being a rich landlord, he was trying to find work. He was hoping to get a position at the University of Shiraz, but in the meantime he was guiding tourists at Persepolis.

We set off to climb the doublewide flight of stone steps that Hassan explained were built to accommodate groups of horses. The top landing led to the Gate of Xerxes, which is referred to as The "Gate of All Nations". Protecting the gate is a pair of statues of a bull and a winged man. At the entrance to the destroyed Winter Palace is a bas-relief showing the king stabbing a winged, horse-like monster in the head. The eastern staircase to the audience hall or Apadana is decorated in bas-reliefs depicting Persian nobles and officials chatting as they make their way to the king's New Year reception. In the *No Ruz* tradition, they are each carrying gifts to the king. Hassan pointed out that their costumes and gifts showed their nationalities: Persians with the tall hats, Median with low round hats, Babylonians bringing gold, silver, cloth and horses. Elsewhere Ethiopians, Libyans, Egyptians and Indians are depicted, demonstrating the diversity of all the subject races. The staircase was buried under sand and rubble for 2,000 years, which kept the carvings in pristine condition.

We came to a large piece of black marble with much graffiti on it. Hassan pointed out one signature. "This is Stanley's writing, the man who was looking for Livingston. You remember that his newspaper sent him to Africa to find Livingston. He came through here on his way." He pointed to the writing and next to it was the date 1871.

"Why would he come through Iran on his way to Africa?" I asked.

Hassan laughed and said, "Everyone wonders that. We think he was just taking advantage of his editor and decided to see as much of the world as he could."

We spent four hours walking around the 33 acres while Hassan gave us a truncated version of the history of the Achaemenian society. He pointed to the cliffs overlooking Persepolis where the tombs of Darius the Great, Xerxes l, Artaxerxes l and Darius II were carved. I was getting cross-eyed with so much information to assimilate and thought he would talk forever. When he suggested we go to Pasargadae, the palace of Cyrus the Great, 25 miles away, we declined.

"But you must see Pasargadae," he insisted. "There is an English archeologist working there. You will see how we excavate our past."

"Thank you, Hassan, but we must get back to Tehran to our children." Jim said as he handed Hassan his pay. "You are a wonderful teacher. I hope you get your chance to teach at the University."

We returned to the hotel, had lunch and took a nap. The next morning we rose early and, as we were leaving, Jim directed Gholum to drive to Pasargadae to see the excavations. As we approached we could see a lone column rising in the sky and capped with a monstrous stork's nest. Several workmen in the traditional brown felt hat were bent over the earth gently brushing the dirt aside. A tall, straw-hatted Englishman in white shirt and pants was walking among the men, watching their labor. Gholum parked the car and Jim got out to ask permission to see the excavation.

The archeologist, Richard Campbell, was pleased to see us. "Let me show you what we are doing here. We are trying to learn what life was like 500 years before the birth of Christ." We watched as one of the workmen unearthed a shard of pottery. "We keep all of these pieces and catalogue them. This is the way we can tell what part of the palace we are excavating. It's a giant puzzle and requires great patience to persevere," Campbell said in his distinctly upper-class English accent. We watched the work for fifteen minutes and Campbell was right. It was like watching paint dry. We bade farewell to Campbell, thanking him for showing us around.

We arrived in Isfahan and made our way to Mahmood's to claim the trays we had ordered. Mahmood was delighted to see us and said, "Would you like to come with me to have tea with Yah-yah Bakhtiari? He is the head of the Bakhtiari tribe and the cousin of Soraya, the Shah's ex-wife. But do not mention the Shah to him. Yah-yah hates him for divorcing Soraya."

We eagerly accepted the invitation and Gholum drove us to Yah-yah's residence. A servant showed us into a large reception hall and after several minutes a very tall, handsome man with a huge handlebar moustache entered. He was wearing a beige cashmere, v-necked sweater over black silk pants that were held at the waist by an ornate silver belt. The legs of the trousers were wide, so that it looked like he was wearing a long skirt. Leather sandals encased his large feet. In his right hand he carried a pink, long-stemmed rose, which he smelled from time to time as he paced the room. Mahmood introduced us and he smiled, showing perfect white teeth. He bent over and kissed my hand. I nearly swooned as visions of Valentino danced in my head, and I could have sworn I heard the Sheik of Araby music!

I was startled back to reality as he clapped his hands and ordered his servant to bring us tea. After drinking two cups of tea and charming us with his conversation he suddenly turned into a used car salesman, had the servant bring in a huge carpet for our inspection, and started his sales pitch. That is when we figured out why we had been chosen for this great honor. Mahmood thought these rich Americans would want to buy a carpet and he would get a nice commission for introducing us to Bakhtiari. Unfortunately, these rich Americans had spent more than they should have on Christmas presents. Jim explained that the carpet was lovely and we would be honored to have it but, unfortunately, we could not afford it. The mood changed drastically. Bakhtiari wished us "Good day," whirled and left the room. Mahmood was upset, as our refusal to buy the carpet had caused him to lose face with Bakhtiari. In somber silence we drove Mahmood back to his shop.

Anxious to get home to our boys, we headed out for Tehran. We arrived in Qom as the sun was setting. The Mosque of Fatima glowed in golden splendor in the late evening light. The surrounding desert was colored with soft lavenders, corals and magenta reflecting the multicolored clouds that marched across the heavens. We looked in awe as the glorious display disappeared in minutes. Soon the ink-blue Persian sky took over.

We had traveled alone on the ribbon of road for half an hour when ahead of us we saw the headlights of an oncoming car. As we watched, the headlights disappeared only to appear again. Gholum reacted the same way—turning off our headlights and then turning them back on. Surprised, we saw that the other driver repeated the action. "What are you doing?" yelled Jim.

"Capeetan, I am telling the other driver that I am not asleep."

"Telling him you're not asleep! For God's sake, we'll run into each other!" Jim bellowed at the back of Gholum's head.

"But, Capeetan, how do I let him know I am not asleep?"

"Use the dimmer switch."

"The what?"

"The switch that dims the lights!"

"I have never heard of this switch! Where is it?"

"It's the button on the floor next to the accelerator. Just touch it with your foot and the lights will dim but not go out."

Gholum did as he was told just as the other car whizzed past us. We let out a collective sigh of relief as Gholum said enthusiastically, "Oh, Capeetan Estarkey, Americans are so smart. Who knew what that button was for! I will have to tell all the other drivers about it!"

"My God, how long has he been driving a car and didn't know there was a dimmer switch," Jim muttered to me.

It was late when we arrived to pick up the boys, who were not unhappy to be awakened. I smothered them with kisses as I held the little guys in my arms. I was so glad to be home. The next day Jimbo talked non-stop about how Patrick had been very unhappy and cried a lot. Pat refused to smile at me, making me feel very guilty for leaving him. I cuddled him, gave him treats and tried my hardest to get him to smile. It took him three days to finally come around and reward me with his infectious grin.

Jim was working long hours and didn't have time to cut the boys' hair, so I took them to the barbershop. Jimbo got his haircut first as Pat sat on my lap watching. When it was Pat's turn, I put him in the chair; as soon as the barber put the cloth around him he started bawling. Patrick did not like strange Iranians, mainly because every time we took him downtown strangers would try to rub his blonde head, superstitiously believing it would bring good luck. The barber tried to calm him, I tried to calm him, but nothing would get him to stop.

Suddenly, Jimbo started attacking the barber, shouting, "Stop hurting my brudder." He kicked the barber in the shins, the barber screamed, I grabbed Pat, threw some money on the table and, yanking Jimbo away with my other hand, left the shop.

"I don't care if the boys have curls down to their waists, I will never take them into a barbershop again!" I declared that night to my husband, who was doubled over laughing.

A few days later, I took the boys to a photographer to have pictures made for grandparents. The boys were sitting on a cloth-covered table, smiling, when the photographer turned off all the lights. It was pitch-dark and suddenly the photographer flashed a brillant light at the boys. Shocked, Patrick howled, his face beet-red, while Jimbo looked disgusted at his little brother. So much for portraits for Christmas!

Two weeks after we returned from our trip, we were at a party when Jim introduced me to Capt. Lopez. "Babe, you remember the British archeologist we met in Pasargadae? Capt. Lopez has been helping him on the weekends."

"Yes, Mrs. Starkey, when I get out of the service I want to get a degree in archeology. By the way, Jim, did you hear about the great find last week?"

Jim answered no, and Lopez proceeded to tell him that Campbell had decided to dig next to the tall column with the stork's nest on top. At the base of the column, they unearthed a clay vase with two pairs of earrings, a bracelet and a comb all in gold with diamonds.

"The rule for excavating in this country is that if you find anything it must be turned over immediately to the Antiquities Museum. Campbell's contract says he is to have unobstructed access to any find in order to document it. His career depends on his past finds. Campbell came by our house first to show me what he had found, which is against the rules. He could really get in trouble if the government finds out. But, Jim, you should have seen the earrings. They were so delicate. There was a large diamond at the earlobe and three thin strips of gold curled down to hold three small diamonds. When you held them, the slightest movement caused the thin springs to bounce, making the diamonds shimmer and sparkle. It was amazing. But, unfortunately, when Campbell brought his photographer to the Museum the next day to take additional pictures, the officials there would not allow him to see the pieces. He has appealed to the Director of the Museum, who refuses to let him document the find. Campbell is livid and swears that if he finds anything else of value he'll head for the airport and smuggle it out of the country. You can't take these Iranians at their word. Their word means absolutely nothing."

Chapter 10

John F. Kennedy shot in Dallas, Lee Harvey Oswald killed, JFK buried in Arlington, Lyndon Baines Johnson our President.

Jim had an early morning flight to Ahwaz, the town on the southwestern area of Iran near the Iraqi border. The temperatures even in November were so hot that he had to leave Ahwaz before 10:00 a.m. in order for the plane to get over the Zagros Mountains. We got up at 4:00 a.m. and I was not too happy. We had been out late the night before, and I groggily made my way downstairs to make coffee and breakfast for Jim. I heard Gholum approach down the kuchee on his bike. As was our ritual, I poured a mug of coffee, picked up the car keys and opened the door.

"Good morning, Gholum" I said, opening the door wide so he could bring his bike into the entrance hall.

"Oh, Madam, I not good, I very bad. I very sorry."

Yeah, you and me both, I thought. *I don't want to hear your problems.* Silently I handed him the keys and the mug, turned and walked back into the kitchen. I heard him close the front door and start the engine of the car.

Jim always manages to look alert, no matter the time of day, and he cheerfully ate his breakfast while I scowled over my coffee.

Since I could never get back to sleep, whenever we had to get up early, I took the opportunity to sit in the big chair in the living room and read a book before the boys awoke. Twenty minutes after Jim left the phone rang. It was Denise. "Shirley, our driver just said that President Kennedy has been shot!"

"Whaaat, that's ridiculous. No one would shoot our president. Don't believe it, Denise. Last year the Russians tried to panic everybody about an earthquake. It's probably them playing another trick. We're used to that around here."

I said goodbye and went back to my book. Thirty minutes later Jim called from Ghalamorghi confirming that indeed our President had been shot.

"Gholum told me that when I got in the car. I didn't believe him but one of the Iranian majors heard it broadcast on the Iranian station. See what you can get on the short-wave radio. My flight to Ahwaz has been cancelled, so call me if you learn anything."

I turned on the radio and started dialing from the left. There was a lot of static, and I kept getting programs in various foreign languages. As I frantically dialed, I kept thinking this could not be true. Who would want to kill the President? Finally, I got the Voice of America. The announcer spoke extremely slowly so foreigners could follow and it seemed an eternity as he said, "Thiiissss issss thhhhe voiceeee of Ammmeriicca reporting from Tangiers. Theee neeeext programmmm you willll heaaar willlll beee in Hungarian!" More frantic dialing until I heard some English. The announcer was saying the president had been riding in an open car in Dallas. I was listening carefully to the rest of the sentence when Jimbo walked into the kitchen. The phone rang, and as I turned to answer it, Jimbo twisted the radio dial.

"Don't do that!" I yelled as I answered the phone.

Jim said, "Babe, it is true. Someone shot Kennedy while he was riding in an open car in Dallas, Texas. We just learned that he has died."

"Oh, my God, what do we do now?"

"Good question. We've been told to go home so I'll see you soon." I hung up the phone, walked back to the kitchen, shaking my head in disbelief. It had to be a big mistake; no one would shoot our president. I mechanically started fixing breakfast for the boys, my mind in a state of numbness. What was the country going to do now?

When Jim came home he said everyone was gathering at the Officer's Club to await further news. We assembled in the dining room with many of our friends, exchanging speculation on who had done this horrible deed. We stayed a couple of hours, but no one had any real news and the local radio wasn't any help, so we went home.

The next morning Jim called the Duty Officer to see if he should report for work. He was told that the Shah had proclaimed a five-day mourning period for the entire nation in honor of President Kennedy's death, and all non-essential work was stopped. We decided to go to the corner store on Dowlat Street to get a copy of the Kayhan International newspaper, which was printed in English. Their copies were all sold out. Gholum drove us toward town as we looked for shops that might have the Kayhan. As we went past several embassies, we noticed the flags were at half-staff. We were out of luck until we got to the big bookstore on Ferdowsi Street. Gholum found a place to park about a block away. As we walked toward the store, crying Iranians stopped us to say how sorry they were that our president was dead. The bookstore was crowded with people of every nationality trying to buy a paper. People formed in groups reading the paper and discussing the events in many languages. When they noticed we were Americans they rushed to extend their condolences. We thanked them graciously, feeling as if we really were Ambassadors at Large, though we had not realized how popular our young president had been with the rest of the world.

We were able to buy copies of both the Kayhan International and the Tehran Journal, and pushing our way through the crowd, we tried to return to our car. We were stunned by the emotion of the Iranians, who kept approaching us, grabbing our hands and in broken English insisting they shared our sadness. One man said, "President Kennedy was ours as much as yours!" As Gholum drove us home, he turned on the radio so we could hear the funeral dirges being played on the local station in honor of JFK. I shuddered as Jim commanded Gholum to turn it off.

It was an eternal wait until the Paris edition of the Herald Tribune reached us via APO. We didn't want to rely on the Persian version of events; we wanted news directly from the United States. But, by the time we received the paper, the news was three days old.

Gholum heard on the radio that the accused assassin, Lee Harvey Oswald had been shot to death, and to this I said, "Good," not realizing that with his death the world would never be 100% sure of who was behind the assassination and why it had occurred.

When Jim returned to work, an Iranian major asked him, "What will become of your country?"

"What do you mean, Major Moftakhar?"

"Capeetan, your president has been assassinated. Will you not have a civil war? In Iran if the Shah were to be assassinated (may Allah forbid it) we would surely have a civil war."

"No, Major, there is no danger of that. The United States has a very strong Constitution that states that the vice president will take over immediately. That is why our new president is Lyndon Johnson." Jim then proceeded to give an abbreviated explanation of American Civics. Major Moftakhar was astonished and, shaking his head, said, "You Americans are hard to understand. If such a thing happened in my country the streets would be red with blood."

Headlines in the Kayhan International paper said in bold type "A PANG IN THE HEART OF TEHRAN." It went on to state: "The sudden murder of President John F. Kennedy yesterday rang a piercing cry into the heart of Tehran. A heavy mourning spirit enveloped the city as everyone heard of the shocking personal loss. People broke out in tears. Work was practically brought to a standstill as all classes stared in confounded silence, hardly able to believe the nightmare."

On December first I went to Mr. DeHeshti's office to pay the rent. He grabbed my hands and tearfully said, trilling his R's, "Meesus Estarkee, I am so sad for your loss. Thees is a tragic loss to the world, Meester Kennedy belonged to us all." He moved closer to me and his voice changed suddenly into a conspiratorial whisper, "You know who really killed him, don't you? It is the wealthy manufacturers in your country who do not want peace, because then they will not make so much money. It was they, along with the Southern segregationists, that did this terrible thing. They also do not like the idea that Jackie Kennedy is so beautiful."

What kind of crazy reasoning was this, I thought. I tried my best to dissuade him of his conclusions, to no avail. Suddenly, he changed the subject and started asking me questions about whether I thought Barry Goldwater or Richard Nixon would be the Republican candidate for the 1964 election. Knowing we were from Arizona, he asked about Goldwater's stand on segregation, foreign aid and whether his wife was pretty and seemed very surprised that we were not personal friends of the Senator. He peppered me with questions, opinions and declarations of doom for the future of the United States and the world ad nauseum until I excused myself, saying I had to get Jimbo from school. I wondered what Mr. D. read that gave him all these opinions.

The next few days the Kayhan International carried pages of articles on Lyndon Baines Johnson, his biography and speculations on how he would govern. There were many comparisons on the difference between the sophisticated Kennedy and the informal Johnson. The underlying suggestions were that the United States had inherited a bumpkin instead of a statesman. When President Johnson announced his decision not to make any immediate changes in the cabinet, it soothed the fears of the international leaders who had been afraid of drastic changes in American policy. One of LBJ's first phone calls was to Premier Nikita S. Khrushcev saying that he intended to continue John F. Kennedy's efforts to improve relations with the Soviet Union. Slowly, the news reports became more optimistic and hopeful; life began to return to normal.

We had a birthday party for Jimbo on the first of December and were now looking forward to Christmas. We had mailed our purchases as soon as we returned from Isfahan and had received confirmation that all had arrived in good shape. Packages from home and from Sears and other mail-order stores were well hidden (we thought) from our curious four year-old old. We came home early from a bridge party one night to find Jimbo crying hysterically. He had found one of the hidden toys, a Crashmobile, had sent it into the wall where it fell apart, just like it was supposed to do. He was quite convinced Santa Claus was punishing him for getting into his gifts!

• • •

Jim called at noon and through the static on the phone line I could tell from his voice that the call was very important. "Where would you like to go when we leave Iran?" he said.

"You got your orders?"

Gruffly he said, "Just answer the question."

"Jim, did you get your orders?" I demanded.

"Yes, now answer the question."

I thought for a minute and said, "Ft. Leavenworth for Command and Staff College."

"No, it's even better than that. Guess again."

Better than that? I thought, "That's the next step up the career ladder! Jim, nothing is better than that!"

He laughed, "You're beginning to sound just like an Army wife. No, I have been selected to go for my Master's Degree at a civilian university. Where would you like to go?"

"Anyplace where we can drink the water and I can drive a car."

"What would you think of the University of Arizona?"

I was stunned into silence for a moment, and then squeaked, "Home? You mean we're going home? Right back to Tucson?"

"That's exactly what the orders say. 'To report not later than 4 June 1964 to the University of Arizona, Tucson for 18 months for the purpose of obtaining a Master's Degree'."

"That's incredible! I can't believe it... That's fantastic! No one deserves it more than you do! Starkey, there really is a Santa Claus!" I babbled on, barely able to contain myself. I was dancing around, the long telephone cable wrapping and unwrapping around me. "Our folks are going to be beside themselves. Oh, Jim, who says nice guys finish last!"

With a laugh, he hung up. I closed my eyes, taking myself back to Arizona and home, home to that magnificent desert with the incredibly vivid colors. The place where the rosy earth is overladen with every color from the artist's palette. The palo verde trees are a dusty green until May when they explode into bright yellow blossoms. And then, there is the majestic saguaro cactus...writers tend to describe it as a 'gentle giant looking for a place in the sun,' or some other insipid description. The saguaro survives hellish-hot summers, freezing winter nights, constant wind and occasional heavy downpours of rain. They are not gentle giants; they are phallic symbols, defiant giants making obscene gestures to the world. When you look at a hill covered with spiky saguaros it looks as if someone forgot to shave.

Laughter from the kitchen brought back my wandering thoughts.

"No, no, Monsieur Pater-ick," Maluke was chiding my younger son in her soothing voice. She looked up as I walked through the doorway.

"Madam, Pater-ick *dust naderee espinoch.*" It was obvious that Pat did not like spinach. He sat in his high chair trying to knock Maluke's hand away. Maluke persisted, dodging the tiny fists, deftly putting the spoon in his mouth. He pushed it out with his tongue, wrinkling up his nose in distaste. Maluke scooped the strained goop from his chin and with a flick of her wrist had his mouth full again. Thoroughly disgusted, Pat gave a Bronx cheer, peppering Maluke's face, giving her what looked like green measles. We both whooped with laughter, and Pat banged his fists on the tray delighted that he had amused us so. The gunk flew in every direction, covering the walls, the cupboards, my blouse and drenching Maluke.

"Madam, me no feed Pater-ick espinoch." Laughing, she put the bowl in the sink, quickly cleaned the tray, and released Pat from his prison.

"I'll take him, Maluke, I think its bath time… for all of us!" Hugging him close, I bounced up the stairs sing-songing, "We're going to Tucson, we're going to Tucson!"

Christmas was especially festive with the knowledge that we would soon be going back to Tucson. As was our custom of inviting two other families to share our Christmas dinner, we chose the Liebshultzs and the Whitfields. We were a cross-section of America with the Protestant, Catholic and Jewish faiths being represented. I asked Barbara and Sharon to bring two dishes traditional to their respective families for holiday feasting. Sharon had been telling me of this wonderful salad her family always served at Christmas. It had many ingredients, including bell pepper. We started the meal with her wonderful salad, excited to try it after her enthusiastic description. After saying grace, we attacked the salad and everyone started to choke. Our mouths were filled with fiery pepper, the vapors racing up our nostrils. I looked around and all of the adults were various shades of red. Sharon was so upset she started to cry, saying through her tears, "The salad is not supposed to be hot!" As we pulled ourselves together we realized that what looked like the innocent green bell pepper we had in the States was actually the hottest pepper we had ever encountered. The scorpion stings again!

Our Christmas present to ourselves was beautiful 8x11 Kashan carpet. The beige background was entwined with tendrils of green leaves. The medallion in the center was a profusion of red and blue flowers plus more green leaves. We also bought an antique bronze Russian samovar with stamps on the front indicating the year 1882. We were told that samovars were practically non-existent in Russia except in museums because during the Russian Revolution samovars were melted down for ammunition.

Soon after New Years, Jim received word that we were eligible for an R and R to Athens, Greece. The children were too young to go, and I was reluctant to have Pat stay with strangers, since he got upset so easily. Mary Smith, our wonderful neighbor across the kuchee, insisted that we allow the children to stay with Maluke, and Mary would supervise everything. Barbara said she would pick up Jimbo for school. Since the R and R was only for four days, we decided that is what we would do.

We left Tehran in an Air Force C-130, used for large cargo items. It was not pressurized and had metal benches that fold down from the sides for passengers. Not exactly first class, it wouldn't even qualify as tourist class, but it's what was transporting our military. Immediately after takeoff we encountered thunderstorms. Bouncing around, I felt as if I were back in the old Convairs getting nauseated. I was coming down with a cold, so the trip was especially uncomfortable. With great relief we landed at the Athens airport. We shared a cab to our hotel with Joe and Laura Hogan; Captain Hogan was the dentist at the infirmary. The rain had stopped and the clouds were billowing up to the stratosphere in a mass of purples, pinks and deep grays. We entered the city driving up a steep hill and, as the road curved to the left, we could see high up on a hill the magnificent Acropolis. Surrounded by dark clouds, the late afternoon sunrays shone down directly on this amazing, white-marbled, ancient structure. The columned citadel had a halo around it and looked like a picture out of our children's Bible. We gasped in awe. I had expected the Acropolis to be as far from Athens as Persepolis is from any large city.

But there it was, within walking distance from the heart of the city.

At the entrance to the hotel we were approached by a Greek named Demitrie offering to guide us around the city. Jim started bargaining with him and Joe quickly entered the negotiations. Soon it was agreed that for two cartons of cigarettes Demitrie would be our guide for three days. "Are you sure that is all it is going to cost us?" Laura asked in a skeptical tone.

Joe put his arm around her and proudly said, "Honey, you have just witnessed the two best bargainers in all of the Middle East. Stick with me, kiddo and you'll go places!"

In a disgusted tone she muttered, "Yeah, I noticed."

We spent the next three days touring the city with Demitrie giving us a lecture on all things Greek. He told us so many stories about various Greek gods and goddesses our heads were swimming. He took us to the palace to watch the Changing of the Guard. The soldiers were dressed in short blue skirts and white blouses with large, puffy sleeves. They wore white tights and black shoes with colorful tassels; as they marched they lifted their knees waist high. The blue-skirted soldiers were soon replaced by an all-white clad group. Demitrie explained that King Paul was gravely ill and Queen Fredericka had commanded Crown Prince Constantine to pay a call on his ailing father, so the Guards had changed into their dress uniforms in honor of the visit. As we watched, a limousine drove into the parade ground and trumpets announced arrival of the Crown Prince.

The last day after checking out of our hotel we visited an outdoor market and couldn't resist buying a dozen of the enormous artichokes and as many bananas. As we were paying for our purchases, a loud speaker started playing funeral dirges, and an announcement was made that King Paul was dead. The reaction was immediate: all the stores closed and the farmers put their produce in wagons and left. It created a huge traffic jam but Demitrie managed to get us to the airport. Jim and Joe gave him the agreed upon two cartons of cigarettes, but then Demitrie demanded an additional fifty dollars for his services.

"But we agreed we would pay you in cigarettes," Jim protested.

"Oh, no, Capeetan, the cigarettes were for me giving you excellent lessons in history: the fifty dollars was for me to drive you around!"

Laura and I started laughing while Jim and Joe dug into their wallets. I turned to Laura and asked, "What is the saying about Beware of Greeks?"

When we returned to Tehran, we found our offspring contented and the house immaculate. We gave the artichokes to the Smiths and you would have thought we had given them gold coins! We found out that was their favorite vegetable and they hadn't seen one in three years. Our boys were more impressed with the bananas than the gifts we had purchased at the PX. Patrick had never seen a real banana and Jimbo hardly remembered them. We brought back many gifts for Maluke and Gholum, as well. It was a happy homecoming.

Chapter 11

President Diem of South Viet Nam dead, suicide reported, Chief Justice Earl Warren to head JFK death inquiry, Jack Ruby given death penalty, 23 year old Constantine new king of Greece, Gen. Douglas MacArthur dies.

The time had arrived for us to sell our household goods, and I was very excited at the prospect. We felt we had perfected the art of Persian haggling, but we needed information on what prices to expect. Determined to have the upper hand on any negotiation, Jim sent me with Gholum to investigate what was available in the shops and what the prices were. There were very few shops that carried furniture and electrical appliances. The merchandise was shabby; the furniture was wrought iron or very cheap plastic. Wood was non-existent, and the electrical appliances were imported from Germany. The store models were not for sale; the customer would choose from the displayed models, pay the full amount at the time the order was placed, and wait anywhere from three to six months for the shipment to arrive. If the shipment was lost or stolen en route, there were no refunds. The prices were astronomical; an apartment-size refrigerator sold for three times its cost in the States, and then the customer was required to pay import tax, which could be as much as the original cost of the item.

At every shop Gholum would tell the salesman that our goods would be for sale on a certain date and give directions to our house. These salesmen promised they would bring their own customers to our house to buy from us, explaining that they knew "American furniture very good, Iranian furniture very bad." The salesman would expect the buyer to pay him baksheesh for this information and for translating.

After checking on prices, we made a list of all the items in each room that we wanted to sell. We had two columns of prices, our asking price and the lowest price for which we were willing to sell the item. When we were ready for the "grand sale," Maluke and Gholum passed the word along through the Farci grapevine. The carriers of the word were the bottle man, garbage man, bread man, Irangas man, the shoe repair man who set up his shop on the corner under an oak tree, the badjiis, houseboys, drivers and kuchee cop. It seemed everyone had someone in the family who was "very rich."

They descended in hordes the first few days, but these were mostly self-styled brokers looking for a bargain. They would ask the price and when told they would respond with a "camel kiss," stating that the item was not worth the price. I refused to budge on the price when they were so rude. I would say, "I really don't want to sell this. I will take it back to the United States." It came as a surprise to them that the U.S. government paid for our shipping. Eventually they would leave, after buying a small item we had never thought of selling. One man bought my *Joy of Cooking* cookbook, though it was doubtful that he could even read Farci. After a week of this I became discouraged, as we had only sold our refrigerator.

The following weekend, a Mr. Shamsi came and, fortunately, Jim was home. I had become weary of showing our bazaar, listening to derogatory remarks and the constant haggling, so I quickly used the excuse that Patrick needed me, leaving Jim to negotiate.

He and Mr. Shamsi got along very well and by the time I returned, Jim had sold all of our living room furniture, including the marble-topped wrought iron coffee table we had purchased in Tehran. After Mr. Shamsi left, Jim handed me a check and a piece of paper.

"I told Mr. Shamsi we would call him when we are ready to move. That's the phone number where he can be reached, and this is his check for the full amount. His bank is at Dowlat and Zhaleh Road; have Gholum take you there tomorrow."

"Do you think the check is any good?" I asked, remembering all the times in the past eighteen months when I had been tricked.

"Well, if it isn't, we still have the furniture and we can resell it. I don't think he would have agreed to let us keep the furniture until we leave if the check is not good. You have to trust these people sometimes."

The next day Gholum drove me to the bank. It was a small white building, not very imposing at all. The lobby was not as large as our living room. I walked to the counter and said to the young man, "Salaam, alekam. Mr. Shamsi has given me a check."

The young man stared at me and then at the check. He muttered in Farci and walked to the adjoining room. Soon he emerged with a stocky, bald, middle-aged man with a huge handlebar moustache.

"Good morning, Madam, may I help you?" he inquired in impeccable English.

"I have come to cash this check." I said as I handed it to him.

He looked at it and smiled, "Yes, yes, Madam, will you be so good as to wait a moment?" and he left.

I glanced around at the two dozen men in the bank who were staring at me with curious, unblinking expressions on their faces. I was used to it by then, and was no longer unnerved, but I still didn't like it. *Perhaps I should have worn a chador,* I thought.

Avoiding the stares, I looked up at the bulletin board, where a notice in English caught my attention. It listed the rates the bank paid to depositors.

DEPOSITORS INTEREST

1 to 10,000 Rials	5%
10,001 to 50,000 Rials	4%
50,001 to 100,000 Rials	3%
100,001 to 500,000 Rials	2%
Over 500,000 Rials	1%

The banker returned with a fistful of money. Carefully, he counted it out to me, the full amount. "Will there be anything else,

Madam?" he asked as I stuffed the bills into my purse.

"Yes, there is. I was noticing your sign here and I don't understand why your bank pays less interest for more money." I pointed to the last line on the notice, and the banker's eyes followed.

"Well, Madam, it is simple." He smiled as if he were explaining something to a child. "If one has so much money, one does not need the interest, no?"

For the next three weeks brokers "representing important people" came to the house to view our goods. Invariably, I would be treated to insistent bargaining with the inevitable "camel kiss" and the parting comment, "You are charging too much." And since I refused to bargain with them, they would leave. I became very annoyed, discouraged and disgusted with our tag sale. Slowly, ordinary buyers who wanted our things for their own homes would come by, and if they were courteous, I would lower the price. I managed to sell most of our goods.

About a week before the packers were expected, a young man came to the door asking about the furniture. He said his name was Assad and that he worked for the Americans at Gulf District. He was getting married soon and needed furniture. Almost everything had been sold with the exception of Jimbo's Early American bedroom suite and our bedroom suite, which was Danish Modern with a lovely warm fruitwood finish. We were anxious to get rid of Jimbo's but not ours. We had decided to only sell our bedroom suite if someone were willing to pay replacement cost. I showed him Jimbo's room but Assad did not like Early American furniture. When we moved to our room he exclaimed excitedly when he saw our furniture. "Madam, this is perfect. How much?" When I told him the price he frowned and in a shocked voice said, "That is too much. I will not pay that much!"

Calmly, I answered, "That is the price."

Assad started screaming, "How can you charge so much?"

Trying to contain myself, I replied, "That is my final price. I really do not want to sell this." I started down the stairs, but Assad did not follow. Calling me back he offered a little more, this time in a conciliatory tone. I repeated my price and pointing to Jimbo's room said, "You can buy the other furniture for much less." He returned to his anger and yelled, "I do not want the other furniture!"

Witnessing his drastic change of moods, and knowing only Maluke and I were in the house, I was anxious to get rid of him. I started down the stairs and again he upped his price, but I refused to answer him. I walked into the kitchen and told Maluke to show Assad out. He started arguing with Maluke and I got angry, opened the front door and told him to leave.

An hour later he was back, this time with a shy, pale wisp of a girl, his fiancée, who looked to be 15 years old. Assad was all charm.

"Madam, may we see the bedroom set?"

"Certainly, come this way, please." I purposefully led them into Jimbo's room.

"No, no, Madam, not this one, the other one."

"Assad, I do not believe you can pay for that one, but I will show you again." When we walked into our bedroom the girl clapped her hands in delight when she saw the furniture. They talked excitedly in Farci as she bounced the mattress with her hands. She stopped suddenly, blushing when he told her they could make many babies on this bed. She glanced at me to see if I understood and I pretended I didn't.

Now Assad starting bargaining in earnest, but this time he managed to keep his temper. I shook my head, repeated the price and motioned with my hands that it was a final price. Assad persisted but I held my ground. For fifteen minutes longer he argued and finally, irritated, I said in Farci, "The bedroom suite is not for sale. Leave this house!" The girl started down the stairs but Assad angrily persisted. Again I ignored him and walked downstairs. The girl was talking rapidly to Maluke, who was nodding sympathetically. Maluke turned to me and pleaded the case for me to sell the furniture to the couple.

Thoroughly aggravated, I stated emphatically that the furniture was not for sale. The girl looked very sad and Assad was rabid but they left.

In early April the new Iranian Prime Minister Hassan Ali Mansur felt that the clergy had been successfully defeated and convinced the Shah that Khomeini should be released from House Arrest and returned to Qom. Late at night Khomeini was quietly driven to his home. Much to the Shah's consternation, Khomeini's return was treated as a major festival. For three days the celebrations took on the mood of a special holiday. The charismatic mullah sat calmly and dispassionate as thousands of pilgrims came from all over Iran to pay him homage. Prime Minister Mansur sent his Minister of the Interior to convey his best wishes. If the Prime Minister thought this would mollify Khomeini, he was sadly mistaken. Khomeini treated this as a victory and continued his fight against the Shah. After many confrontations, eight months later the Shah again had Khomeini arrested. Some of the Shah's advisors recommended that Khomeini be tried for treason and either executed or imprisoned, but the Shah feared this would make him a martyr. Instead, Khomeini was quickly driven to Mehrabad Airport put on an Iranian Air Force plane and deported to Turkey. It would prove to be the Shah's biggest mistake.

Two weeks prior to our departure date we were to move into a hotel. This would allow ample time for our goods to be packed and for Jim to clear up the paperwork necessary for leaving the country.

It would take two days for us to be packed. On the first day only two men arrived to pack the cartons. One, the driver, was big, with a massive stomach that barely allowed him to get behind the wheel of the truck. Though he was in his late thirties, his round head was bald, heavy eyebrows formed a straight line over his dark eyes and a thick mustache covered his mouth. He had the enormous arms and shoulders of a zurkhaneh athlete. (These are the men who frequented the gymnastic clubs where they exercise with heavy Indian clubs, steel bows and chains to the rhythm of drums and bells. They follow a ritual accompanied by a Director who chants verses from Ferdowsi's 10th Century Persian epic called Shah Nameh.) The second man was just the opposite: tiny, ancient, scrawny, missing his front teeth and wearing a light green turban. He looked like a puff of wind would blow him away. He was barefoot, wearing black pajama pants and a dingy gray shirt. He marched importantly into the living room, settling himself on the floor cross-legged fashion. His name was Reza and the younger one was Ali. Reza shouted an order to Ali, who promptly brought in stacks of old newspapers and then carried our Rosenthal china to the old man, setting each piece carefully on the floor. Quickly Reza started wrapping the china. Each piece was wrapped in seven or eight sheets of newspaper with the speed and dexterity of the rug weavers.

Our china was brand new, a Christmas gift from Jim and I was concerned something would happen to it. Politely, I told Reza to be very careful so as not to get anything broken. His answer to me was to pitch a newly wrapped plate clear across the marbled-floor room. I let out a gasp, putting my hand to my chest and staring in horror at Reza. He roared with laughter, his pinched face full of glee, looking like a picture of Rumpelstilskin. Then he leaped up, agile as a mountain goat, grabbed my arm and led me to where the piece had landed. Swiftly he unwrapped it to show me it was not broken.

"Madam," he cooed in broken English, "I not hurt pretty dishes."

Shaking, I hurried into the kitchen to tell Maluke to make sure Hassan had plenty of tea and sugar while he was working. I also told her to make some rice and vegetables for the men's lunch. Keeping them happy would ensure our goods were safely packed.

The rest of the day I concentrated on watching Ali pack the items in the bedrooms, while Maluke kept an eye on Reza. Every time I came downstairs he would pitch another dish and laugh, very pleased with himself. It took him all day and part of the next day to wrap and pack our china and crystal, but we didn't suffer even a tiny chip.

Jim stayed home the second day to supervise the move. It was a madhouse, starting at eight in the morning when five packers arrived. Reza started working in the kitchen, wrapping our everyday dishes. Buyers sent their servants to pick up the furniture and appliances they had bought. Potential buyers came for last minute bargains and we sold Jimbo's bedroom set.

About ten o'clock Assad showed up, again wanting to see our bedroom suite. I had told Jim about Assad's previous visit and his erratic emotions, so, as I led Assad upstairs, Jim followed.

Looking at Jim, Assad said, "Capeetan, what is the price?" Jim quoted the same price I had told him.

"But, Capeetan, you can not want so much today. This is the last day you can sell."

"That's okay, Assad, we really do not want to sell this furniture."

He frowned and started to say something, thought better of it and then replied, "I will pay your price, Capeetan. I will return later with the money." He left and Jim turned to me, "That was easy. Why did you have such a hard time with him?"

I was steamed, "Did it ever occur to you that he behaved himself because he was dealing with a man? Besides that, he won't be back. He only said that to save face."

Much to my surprise Assad, and his fiancée and another couple returned after lunch. He handed me a full sack and said, "Here is the money you want, but it is still too much to pay for your awful furniture."

I took the sack and Jim said, "Babe, go into the study and count it." I went to the room off of the living room, which was the only place in the house where there were no packers. Sitting on the floor, I opened the sack and a musty smell filled my nostrils. The bills were in 50 and 100 Rial notes, all very worn, dirty and reeking of wet earth. I wondered if this was the girl's dowry that had been buried.

It took the better part of an hour to sort and count the bills, but the exact amount of rials was there. I found Jim and Assad arguing. Assad and his fiancée were unhappy to discover all the bedding and pillows were gone from the bed had, in fact, already been packed in cartons ready for the trip back to the States.

Assad, showing his temper, belligerently demanded the blankets and pillows. Jim was very patient in explaining that the bedding was not part of the furniture.

"In Iran bedclothes always go with the bed. You have charged us too much and now you try to cheat us!"

Calmly, Jim shrugged his shoulders, "Assad, we do not want to cheat you. Here is your money." He took the sack from me and pushed it toward Assad. The fiancée started protesting and pleading in Farci. Assad, realizing his bluff had been called, handed the money back to Jim and ordered his friends to move the furniture. After several trips, all of our bedroom furniture was lined up in the kuchee and the two girls left to find a truck for hire.

"Isn't Assad delightful?" I asked Jim.

"Not really. He's an obnoxious little bastard!"

Jim and I were standing in the bedroom observing the action out in the kuchee when I noticed my dresser was a shade lighter than Jim's chest of drawers.

I commented to Jim, "Why is the finish different?" He explained that my dresser had been close to the bedroom windows and probably got slightly faded due to the reflection from the white walls of the compounds across the kuchee.

Almost simultaneously, Assad noticed the difference. With a whoop and shouts in Farci he burst through the front door, past the startled packers, Maluke and Gholum. He bounded up the stairs into our bedroom, the observers following in his wake.

"Capeetan Esstarkey, you cheat me," he screamed, his face contorted in rage. He lunged toward Jim, "You are an Ugly American!"

That did it. Jim's patience snapped and the Irish temper took over as he grabbed Assad by the necktie, jerked him up so their noses were almost touching. Assad's toes barely brushed the floor, and his face started turning purple. He tried to say something, but only a garbled croak came out. I knew Jim's next move was to throw Assad down the marble stairs. If he did that, he would end up decaying in a Persian jail.

Touching Jim's back I pleaded, "Let him go." Suddenly, from the corner of my eye, I saw Assad's friend bounding through the door, bent on attacking Jim. My reflexes were swift and on target. I whirled as the friend passed me to reach Jim and let him have it with a powerhouse punch to the chin that sent the unsuspecting friend flying across the room and into the closet.

The room around me froze like a scene from Sleeping Beauty. I started toward the crumpled heap, intending to jump on him, for I had tasted the sweet fruit of revenge and I wanted more.

Jim released Assad and grabbed me, holding me high while my feet pounded helplessly in the air. The shocked audience slowly came to their senses. The first to react was Assad who shouted, "Call the Gendarme!"

Jim quickly responded, "Yes, call the Gendarme, Gholum. I want the Gendarme here to see this."

The 'crumpled heap' slowly righted himself, rubbing his chin, muttering. Gholum spoke in Farci to Assad, motioning dramatically to the wretched man in the closet. The packers all started talking at once. Only Maluke was silent, but her round, brown eyes looked at me with admiration.

Jim turned to me and commanded, "Take the boys and the sack of money and leave at once. Get John Smith over here, quickly!"

I grabbed the money, ran down the stairs to get Jimbo and Pat from the backyard; Maluke followed, her face beaming. With her right fist punching into her left palm, she kept saying over and over, "Madam, pow-ee, madam, pow-ee," and she would squeal with laughter. Apparently in her eyes I had struck a blow for Women's Liberation, which I was glad to do.

I swept Pat up, still holding onto the sack of money. "Maluke, get Jimbo!" I called as I raced out the front door. Maluke, dragging Jimbo, was right behind me. I could hear all the arguing coming from the open window of our bedroom as I frantically rang the Smiths' bell. Miraculously, John himself answered the gate. My throat was dry, my heart was pounding and I could barely speak. I pointed up at our bedroom window and whispered breathlessly, "John, help Jim!"

John's six foot six inch frame sprang into action and without another word from me he bounded across the kuchee, his bald head gleaming in the sunlight. Maluke quickly closed the gate and the four of us were safe in the Smiths' compound. We ran past the swimming pool just as Mary came out the front door.

"Shirley, what's wrong, what's the matter?" she cried. All I could whisper was, "water!" She ran back into the house, returning with a glass of water. Maluke took Pat from me and led the children back to the kitchen to relate the happenings to the badjii Mariam. I sat down and drank the water: still shaking uncontrollably, I tried to explain the crazy situation to Mary.

We were sitting on the porch, and from there we could see the windows of our bedroom. Suddenly, Jim and John were looking down at the kuchee, laughing. We could hear shouting from beyond the wall and the sound of a motor. After several minutes all was quiet. I was still trembling when Mariam and Maluke brought out some tea. Both badjiis had satisfied, even smug, smiles on their faces.

"Drink this, and then I'm going to give you an aspirin, and I want you to lie down!" Mary sounded like a big sister and I obeyed her.

Soon Jim and John returned to check on me. Jim's face was flushed with pride, "Babe, are you all right?"

"Oh, I'm fine. What happened when the Gendarme came?"

"The Gendarme never came. Gholum convinced them that it would look very bad for your victim if the Gendarme were told that a woman had punched him out."

"Damn it, Shirl," John said, "that's not fair. You had all the fun!

Why didn't you call me sooner, so I could have punched one of them! I've wanted to do that for eight years!"

Feeling better, I returned with Jim to help supervise the last of the packing while Maluke stayed at the Smiths' with our boys. As I entered the house, I saw that the packers had their heads bowed, appearing to be concentrating on their tasks, but their eyes followed me, watching my every move. The old man didn't throw any more dishes; he set them to one side almost reverently. There was no chatter or laughter and as I went from room to room, even the subdued conversation ceased.

Gholum appeared crushed. He had taken his job of driving seriously and took a great deal of pride in protecting me as well as the boys. Whenever we had to go downtown, he walked directly behind me to make sure I was not pinched. Now he was shocked to find I was not as helpless as he had thought.

By decking Assad's friend I had punctured the Iranian male ego.

Later that night, after a wonderful meal at the Smiths' house, replete with good wine and warm friendship, we checked into the newly completed Tehran Hilton Hotel. The management, in an effort to start filling the hotel rooms, had offered American personnel a ridiculously low price— a bargain we could not refuse.

The two rooms were beautifully decorated, and from our 17th floor suite, we could see the lights of Tehran. The coffee-table held a massive basket of fruit and an ice cold liter of Russian vodka. We put the boys to bed and sat together viewing the lights, drinking the vodka and talking about the events of the past forty-eight hours. Our laughter combined with the vodka and we felt total relief. A complete catharsis of all the pent-up frustrations of the past two years, liberated with one swift blow! We finished the vodka and I couldn't stop giggling.

We could not leave Iran until Jim had cleared with the military section, motor pool, hospital, the co-op, the Embassy, the phone company and the electric company. It seemed he needed clearance from half of Tehran. This was quite time consuming, but not impossible. The one hitch came in trying to pay the electricity bill on the house.

Since the man came to read the meter only every three months, a trip to the main office in Tajrish was necessary. Gholum went inside with me to translate if necessary. The clerk explained that we would have to wait until July to pay the bill because our meter was not scheduled to be read until the last part of June. I tried to tell her we were leaving Iran on May 16. She was polite but firm, "It is impossible." Exasperated, I turned and walked back to the car while Gholum carried on a conversation with the clerk. He ran after me and said, "Madam, it is no problem. I go to man's house, get him and take him to read electricity. But you must pay baksheesh to man and girl clerk."

"How much baksheesh?"

"Only 20 or 50 rial. Maybe 20 to girl and 50 to man."

"Why does the man get more baksheesh?"

"Man has too many babies."

"Do you know this man?"

"No."

"Then how do you know he has too many babies?"

"All Iranian men have too many babies. Man have one baby, that baby hungry." He shrugged his shoulders. "Man have no money for food…man have too many babies." He shook his head sadly.

I never could argue with Gholum's logic. "Okay, Gholum, let's go find the man. Give the girl this 20 rial so she will tell you where to find him." Smiling, Gholum returned to the office and obtained the necessary information.

We found the man easily. He was sleeping under a tree next to the electric company, the remains of his lunch in his lap. We drove him to our house while Gholum and the meter man chatted amiably. The meter was read, we returned to the office, paid the bill and collected the necessary receipt. Gholum paid the meter man the 50 rials and he sauntered back to the tree to resume his nap. As we drove off I asked, "Gholum, how many babies does the man have?"

"Oh," answered Gholum innocently, "no babies. He not married."

• • •

It was still dark when we loaded the suitcases into the car for the ride to Mehrabad Airport. Jimbo, still half asleep, sat in the front seat with Gholum. The trip through the deserted city was very swift, much like our entrance almost two years before. We were silent, each caught up in our own thoughts. For me it was hard to imagine we were actually leaving.

We checked our baggage and walked to customs. Jim reached into his pocket, pulling out the last of our rials, and handed them to Gholum. With tears in his eyes, Gholum solemnly shook hands with Jimbo, and lightly pinched Patrick's cheek.

It was as difficult to say goodbye to Gholum as it had been hard to take our leave of Maluke the day before. They were part of the good we found in Iran and will always be remembered with affection.

We walked through customs, past the baggage area and out to the tarmac, where the the beautiful words, PAN AMERICAN, leaped out at us from the side of the shining jetliner. A baggage man came running after us and tugged at Jim's sleeve. "Baksheesh, Monsieur," he demanded, his palms outstretched.

"Go to Hell," Jim answered curtly, turning to grin at me.

At the top of the steps, we turned to wave to the lone figure on the upstairs balcony. Gholum was waving with both of his arms.

As the plane soared into the air, the first rays of the morning sun bathed Mt. Damavand in a pink glow.

"Look, Mama," cried Jimbo, "there's our giant strawberry ice cream cone!"

Tehran faded from view, watched over by the Alborz Mountain range. The endless desert in shades of lavender, coral and beige stretched away forever. Across the terra cotta land, the ancient *qanats* burped in perfect cadence on their way to Isfahan. I gasped for breath as suddenly I was awash in a wave of nostalgia.

'Iran, you sonofabitch, I'm going to miss you!'

Chapter 12

The United States is suffering from race riots, anti Viet Nam protesters, the murder of Dr. Martin Luther King and Bobby Kennedy. The war in Viet Nam rages on.

Kansas 1969

To be assigned to attend Command and General Staff College is a big step up the ladder of promotions so when Jim's orders came in January, I, as an impartial observer, screamed with excitement. "It's about time the Army started appreciating you!"

Jim laughed. "Babe, I can always depend upon you to be my biggest supporter. Let's go to dinner to celebrate." And so in June the packers came once again to get us ready for a major move from Ft. Eustis, Virginia across the country to Ft. Leavenworth, Kansas. Within a week our household goods were on the way, we had cleared quarters and said farewell to our many friends, knowing full well that we would probably meet them all again in another time and place. That was life in the Army.

We loaded up our big Ford station wagon with our pug, Bandit, three window air conditioners, a huge aquarium with two alligators and two turtles, five suitcases, a box of toys, and an ice chest full of sandwiches and snacks. I would drive the station wagon with four year-old Peggy and either Patrick, our six year-old, or Jimbo, our nine year-old, with me. The two boys would take turns riding in Jim's pumpkin-colored Fiat Sport Spyder (when Peggy first saw the little car she exclaimed, "Oh, look at the Funbuggy!" and that became its name). Jimbo, being the oldest, was the first to accompany Jim. Our first leg was to Thomas Jefferson's home, Monticello. We took a tour and marveled at all the inventions of our third president. We were especially impressed with the elevator and dumb waiter and intrigued with the duel writing pen that allowed Jefferson to make an instant copy of anything he wrote. After the tour, we picnicked in a grove with a view of the whole estate.

As we started toward West Virginia with all its hills and valleys, Jim took off like Andy Granitelle, the race car driver. Driving the big station wagon, it was hard to keep up with the bobbing orange car in front of me. It reminded me of sitting in a movie theatre as a kid, following the bouncing ball as we all sang along. After two hours of this, a massive headache struck me and I needed to stop. I signaled with the headlights for Jim to stop, but he ignored me. Up and down, in and out went the roads, Jim passing trucks with abandon. I was getting more and more upset with Jim ignoring my signal to stop. Finally I saw a rest stop and pulled in, deciding to stay there until Jim realized I was not behind him. Peggy, Pat and I got a drink of water, put the dog on a leash, and went to the bathroom. I had been resting in the car with my eyes closed for about fifteen minutes when Jim drove up, anxious at first, then angry that we had stopped. "Why did you stop? Now I have to pass all those trucks again. Why didn't you signal me?" he yelled.

"I had to stop. I have a screaming headache and you ignored my signal to stop." I complained, angrily.

"I did not see any signal."Jim was raising his voice even more.

"Well, I kept hitting the headlights back and forth and you completely ignored me." My raised voice matched his.

"Don't you know it takes some time for the shutters on the headlights to come up? If you keep hitting them, they never come up. How was I to know you wanted to stop? Now, damn it, I have to pass all those trucks again."

"Can you please not drive so fast? I can't keep up with this big car."

At this point, we were yelling at each other, other families at the rest stop were staring at us and the children were off in the woods, pretending they didn't belong to us. Jim calmed down and said, "Let's look for a place to have lunch." I agreed and after some coffee, my headache disappeared. We made one other major stop at Mammouth Cave, Kentucky to view the blind fish, and two days later we were at our new home- Ft. Leavenworth, Kansas.

Kansas was, as we remembered, very hot and muggy. Jim checked in and was told where our quarters were. "You mean we don't have to wait for a place to live?" I said in amazement. "Do you realize this is the first time in our married life that we have not waited for housing? Maybe the Army is finally appreciating you."

Following a map, we found ourselves in Burnham Circle, one of the many housing circles, and drove up to number 6, our home for the next year. We piled out in great excitement and rushed up the steps. Jim unlocked the door and we found ourselves in a 12 by 18 foot room. The doorway to the left led to a tiny, Pullman-sized kitchen with a door to the outside. Going back through the main room we found four very tiny bedrooms and two bathrooms. Jim and I stared at each other in amazement. We had been promised a four bedroom house, but this house could not have totaled more than 850 square feet. Finally Jim spoke, "There must be some mistake. Get in the car, kids. We're going back to the Personnel Office."

Unfortunately, it was not a mistake. Jim was told that this was our house, and we would have the use of a large warehouse for any furniture that would not fit. I figured that would be at least half of our goods. "I guess we're lucky we were not scheduled to live in a tent." I muttered, furious that, after all Jim had done for the Army, we were being treated so shabbily.

Like a good little Army wife, I vowed to make the best of the situation - I knew Jim's hands were tied. We went back to number 6 Burnham Court to figure out what furniture we would be able to use. We decided to give the largest bedroom to the boys for their bunk beds and their dressers, which held the big tank for the alligators, or, rather, caimans. We would take the next biggest one, then came Peg's and finally, the smallest would hold Jim's desk and chair (and nothing else) but at least he would have a place to study. The main room served as living room and dining room, as the kitchen was only big enough for one person at a time. The movers brought our furniture, and we sent all non-essential furniture to the warehouse. The house was filled with unpacked boxes for me to sort through. Jim quickly put the air conditioners in the windows of the dining room, our bedroom and the boys room to our great relief. The air-flow was constant and kept the whole house, with the exception of the kitchen, comfortable.

Jim's classes started almost immediately, and the children found new playmates, leaving me free to unpack boxes, put up curtains and make our humble abode livable. I was angrily unpacking, sorting and trying to decide what we had room for and what would have to go into storage when an older man, wearing a faded blue jumpsuit and baseball hat, appeared at the door. Politely he said, "Ma'am, I have come to replace this old mailbox."

I hadn't noticed the box before and was surprised to find that it was an old-fashioned, one-inch thick glass mailbox, one corner broken off, that had probably been there since the Indian Wars. I was in a bitchy mood, incensed with the Army for putting us in a house fit only for the Munchkins.

As the man removed from the carton an ordinary black tin mailbox, I said spitefully, "I don't like that color. I would like to see something else." Startled, the man looked at me wide-eyed. "Ma'am, this is the only kind we have."

Mustering a snotty attitude, I said, "I don't care. I would like one in blue."

Appalled, he answered, "Oh, Ma'am, you couldn't have that. That would be against Regulations."

Damn, Regulations! I thought. *I'm so sick of Army Regulations. I'm going to paint my mailbox any color I want.*

I immediately left the house, went to the PX and chose the brightest orange paint I could find. Finally in a happy mood, I was singing as I covered the ugly black mailbox with three coats of sunshine orange. I hung it up daring the MP's to arrest me for failing to follow Regulations!

As I returned to the sorting and unpacking, a special report came on the television. Excitedly, the announcer said that Neil Armstrong had just set foot on the moon and proclaimed, "That is one small step for man, one giant step for mankind." From New Zealand to Denmark, from Tokyo to Chicago, the whole world gasped in awe and, from all corners of the globe congratulations poured in to the United States. The TV audience was estimated at 600 million, one-fifth of the earth's population. That same day the news leaked out that the junior senator from Massachusetts, Ted Kennedy, had driven his car off the Chappaquiddick Bridge the day before and left Mary Jo Kopechne to die inside the sinking car. Wasn't it ironic that President John F. Kennedy had challenged the United States to put a man on the moon ten years before and the very day his dream was fulfilled, his little brother's stupid mistake became known? Talk about a good-news/ bad-news day; July 20, 1969 certainly was that!

"Mom, look at what I found!" Jimbo came crashing through the front door closely followed by Patrick. I saw that he was holding up a worn, dirty chamois cloth.

"Where did you get that?"

"I found it down by the creek. Pat and I are going to make harnesses for our gators. Where are the scissors?" I handed him a pair of scissors, and they both headed for their bedroom. The fall before, we had been in a pet store buying seeds for our now deceased cockatiel when we saw a tank full of baby caimans. The boys were fascinated by them, and Jim and I decided to get them for the boys' birthdays. Pat's birthday is 9 November, and Jimbo's is 1 December. Pat named his Supercalifragilistic, (after the song Dick Van Dike sang in the movie *Mary Poppins*) and Jimbo named his Hardy-har-har. Each was only six inches long and we could hold them in the palm of a hand. They loved to be on their backs and have their tummy's rubbed and would open their mouths wide in a big smile. Not wanting Peggy to feel left out, we got her two water turtles. We invested in a super-sized tank, which was filled with about three inches of water and put in large flat stones to give the reptiles a place to bask in the artificial light. It was fun to watch the alligators swim with the turtles hanging onto their backs. At first we purchased minnows for food, but that became too expensive and made the tank dirty. Jim's solution was to take the kids fishing. When they brought their catch home, Jim would cut it into small pieces and put them in the freezer. Once a week, the kids would throw frozen fish pieces into the tank - because the alligators were so hungry- they instantly gulped down the morsels and had a very startled look when the fish ice cubes hit their stomachs! The tank was kept clean because the little turtles, acting like miniature vacuum cleaners, scrambled after the leftovers the alligators had missed.

The caimans were now nine inches long and I was not sure how long we could keep them, as we had been told they grow as much as 14 inches in a year. The boys discovered a creek that ran though Ft. Leavenworth not far from our quarters. It was full of small, bass-like fish, so they now had easy access to 'gator food.

Burnham Court was a cul-de-sac with five houses. We had wonderful neighbors: all the men were students like Jim and all the wives were dealing with the same things I was, so we had a lot in common. Our next-door neighbor to the west was a first-generation Greek couple. The Daolus family had three huge teenage boys that the high school football coach immediately contacted. Next to them were the Campbells, who had one very pretty sixteen year-old daughter named Linda. Frequently, we asked Linda to babysit for us. On the east were the McGuires, a newly married couple possessing a beautiful Irish Setter named Barney. Cathy McGuire, a petite red head (the same shade as Barney's coat), possessed a wicked sense of humor. (We joked that Barney was bigger than our dining room.) On the other side of them were the Hamptons, Bob and Heidi. Heidi was from Germany and was a very talented artist. One afternoon I invited all the wives to our place for coffee and suggested that we form an international gourmet club. This was met with great enthusiasm, and it was decided we would meet once a month. The hostess would choose the country and cook the main course and provide wine for that course; the rest of the group would either be responsible for the canapés and drinks, the salad course and wine, the dessert course and wine and finally the after-dinner coffee and brandy. Time-Life had published a series called *Foods of the World*, which I had purchased, and we used these books for our dinners. We called it a traveling dinner party, as it made sense to have each course at a different house, allowing each hostess to get things ready ahead of time. It was especially good for us, as we could check on our kids as we walked from house to house and didn't have to get a babysitter. By the end of the dinner evenings, stuffed to the gills, we would stagger home, barely making it into bed. One month the theme would be Russian, the next, Chinese and so forth. Athena Daolus was an amazing cook! She had to be, with those big, strong kids, who were always hungry. The boys would come home from school and 'snack' on a handful of homemade *spanakopita*, the Greek spinach-cheese pie. It made Jim's mouth water to see that! All of us looked forward to Athena's moussaka when she chose the Middle East for a theme. We were not disappointed. Heidi chose German food for her main course and we were treated to weiner schnitzel. While we wives vied to be the most original in each of our undertakings, it was the husbands who really got into the act. They became the experts in wine and after-dinner drinks and would run into each other at the local liquor store.

The 1200 students were organized into to various groups and sections and, as with everything in the Army, rank rules. Jim was assigned to Group D. The ranking officer was a surgeon, LTC. Joseph Robinson, and the next four ranking officers were in charge of Sections 1 through 4. Jim was the head of Section 2. The four section heads and wives were invited to the Robinsons' quarters for cocktails one afternoon, to discuss ways to socialize in order to keep morale high. From the beginning of our country, Army posts have been built in isolated areas, so by necessity military jobs and social events were intertwined. It is true that civilian towns spring up around Army posts to support the troops, but civilians tend to look suspiciously upon the nomadic military families and, in most cases, are not very welcoming.

When it was time for Jim and me to go to the Robinsons' quarters, it was raining hard, and I was huddled under an umbrella trying to keep my hair dry, when Mrs. Robinson answered our knock. I smiled and said, "Here's Mary Poppins!" imitating Johnny Carson in an effort to be funny. Mrs. R. stared at me as Jim hit me in the ribs. "Mrs. Robinson, I am Jim Starkey, and this is my wife, Shirley," he said.

Looking at Jim with a tight smile, she primly replied, "Do come in".

She was very thin, only five feet tall with dark brown hair curled tightly to her scalp in an old-fashioned style. She had large brown eyes that had a deer-in-the-headlights expression, and her humorless, thin mouth was turned down at the corners. She was wearing a full skirt in a patchwork design and a peasant blouse. Her shoes were bright red pumps with four inch heels. The outfit seemed out of place, not fitting in with her demeanor.

We entered just as a tall, balding man rose from a chair, extending his hand. "I'm Dr. Robinson and this is my wife, Rose," he told us.

Jim introduced us to him just as the doorbell rang again and two other couples entered, followed by another couple. Introductions were made and we settled down to get acquainted. Conversation was lively as we sipped wine and munched on cheese and crackers. Jim was the only aviator there, so we did not have friends in common with the other couples.

Suddenly, Dr. Robinson stood up and, taking charge, announced that he wanted everyone to tell the others a little bit about themselves.

Dr. R. had a hooked nose, intelligent close-together eyes, a protruding, bobbing Adam's apple and a wisp of sandy hair that he combed across his forehead, in vain effort to hide his baldness. He spoke in a clipped, authoritative style and proceeded to tell us that he was a surgeon at Johns Hopkins University when, as an Army reservist, had been recalled to active duty and had just returned from Viet Nam. Rather than having his civilian career interrupted again, he had decided to stay in the military. He was hoping to get an assignment to Walter Reed Army Hospital in Washington, where his surgical skills could be put to use.

Mrs. Robinson sat in a wing-back chair with her hands clinched in her lap, not uttering a word. Her husband did not ask her to speak about herself. The first couple to speak was Walt and Mary Dodson, then Sharon and George Staples, then Jim and me, and, finally, Susan and Bill Bradley. Dr. Robinson asked what activities we would like to plan and the first to speak was George Staples, who suggested a bowling tournament among the four sections. That was greeted with approval and then Sharon Staples announced that she would be happy to plan a coffee for all the ladies. Other ideas flew about the room, most of them from the Staples, who seemed determined to be the social leaders. George said he would organize the bowling tournament and Sharon, looking at a calendar suggested a day for a coffee, announcing she would make the arrangements at the Officers

Club. Mrs. Robinson nodded in agreement, seeming to be happy to have someone take responsibility. Dr. Robinson thanked everyone for their cooperation and said how pleased he and Mrs. Robinson were to meet us all. We said our goodbyes and noticed the rain had stopped as we walked to the car. As we drove away I said, "Wow, the Staples are good at taking over, aren't they?"

"That's okay with me. It will be fun to have a bowling league. I'm looking forward to that," Jim commented.

School for the children started the first week of September; Jimbo in fourth grade, Patrick in first and Peggy in pre-kindergarten. Since the children were out of the house most of the day, I was able to join an oil painting class. Jim and I joined the mixed doubles bowling league that met on Tuesday nights. We soon discovered why the Staples wanted the bowling league; they had been the champions of the bowling league in Ft. Benning, Georgia, their last assignment. George arranged for twenty teams, with two couples in each team, and each bowler put ten dollars into the kitty to be given to the three top winning teams at the end of the tournament. Jim was a good bowler, averaging 185, and our team was among the top scorers when the time came for us to play the Staples team. That night Sharon Staples sidled up to Jim and coyly said, "Jim, which foot do you start on when you bowl?" Jim started thinking about it and when he got up to bowl, he was completely confounded and kept starting on the wrong foot. I don't believe he scored 110 that evening. That score knocked us out of the running for a prize and, at the end of the tournament, the very competitive Staple team shared the $400 first prize.

Every Wednesday morning I took a class in oil painting taught by a strange fellow whom the class nicknamed Casper, the Friendly Ghost, because he claimed to be a warlock. He was a very good art instructor, but even better at regaling us with stories about witchcraft, the occult, extra-sensory perceptions and all things mystical. He stated that he was clairvoyant and able to forecast events just by looking at a person or at an object belonging to someone. Of course the class challenged him to prove his claim. He insisted that it was possible to foretell the future and that the Russians had a lot of people working on exploring that possibility. We started bringing various objects from family members, and he would tell us something about the person to whom the objects originally belonged. He was amazingly accurate. My friend Beverly Wilcox brought in a picture of her son. When Casper looked at it he became agitated and reluctant to say anything. Beverly insisted and finally he said, "I hate to say anything but…. just tell your son, do not go to Iowa." Beverly shook her head in disbelief and said, "I doubt if he would, since he lives in Kansas City."

That night I received a phone call from her. "Shirley, you'll never believe this, but my son John called me a while ago and said he had been in a car accident, but wanted me to know he wasn't hurt, although the car was totaled. I told him what Casper had said, and after a pause, he quietly told me that the accident happened on Iowa Street! Boy, did I get goose bumps hearing that!"

Christmas was soon upon us and with the school closed for two weeks we decided to head to Tucson. We packed the car with wrapped presents and suitcases, loaded up the kids and dog and were on our way. The northern winds had brought cold weather to Kansas, and we were happy to get to the warmth of Arizona. We stayed with my folks, as Jim's mom had no room for us. To help with expenses after Dad Starkey died in October of 1968, she shared her home with another widow friend, Mrs. Powder. After spending time with various family members and friends, we headed back to Ft. Leavenworth in time for New Years. We were told to expect orders for Jim's next assignment after the first of the year, and we were anxious to find out where we would be going following graduation.

"Guess what I heard today?" Jim said as he walked in the door one evening.

"You got your orders?"

"No, nothing like that. I heard an interesting thing today. The government has said the meat packers can no longer use wooden chopping blocks and will have to start cutting meat on a type of plastic. So, they are selling the wooden chopping blocks…some people are buying them to use as firewood."

"What a waste that would be!" I exclaimed.

"Well, I thought we'd go to Kansas City and buy one for our kitchen. Not for this kitchen, but for a normal sized kitchen. We can take it to the warehouse for storage until we leave," Jim replied.

Saturday we headed for Kansas City in our big Ford station wagon. Walking into a meat packing plant, we were led to an enormous room containing the unused chopping blocks. We were amazed at how many there were. I was particularly taken with an oblong-shaped block with intricately carved legs, but it was too big and heavy for us to get into our station wagon. We settled on a square one of solid wood with straight legs and paid $35.00 for it. Four men were needed to load it into the back of our vehicle. We were told it weighed almost three hundred pounds, and it barely fit. Jim slowly drove back to Ft. Leavenworth, and on the way we had to cross some railroad tracks. Gingerly, Jim eased the wagon over the tracks and we all sighed with relief when we were on the other side.

At the warehouse the man in charge looked in disgust at our block. "Oh, crap!" he muttered, "Another one of these. Hey, Harry," he yelled, "get the crane. We have another damn chopping block to store."

A heavy snowstorm engulfed Kansas late in January, forcing the schools to close for two days. I made a big pot of chili, baked some cornbread and the family gathered around the dining room table, eating and later playing a raucous game of Monopoly. After two days of cabin fever, attempting to keep the kids from killing each other, we heaved a sigh of relief when the sun came out and the schools reopened. No one was happier than I was to wave goodbye as the boys left for school. The roads were cleared but icy as I gingerly drove Peg to her pre-kindergarten. She was chattering happily all the way to the school. As soon as I stopped, she gave me a big hug and kiss then bounced out of the car, calling to her friends. I felt liberated as I drove to the rec center to join my painting class. My friend Beverly set up her easel next to me and was concentrating on a landscape when Casper, the instructor, came walking by. He looked first at my painting of some sunflowers, made a helpful comment then moved on to Beverly's painting. He was in the middle of critiquing her work when he suddenly stopped and turned to her, saying, "I see you in Persia."

"You see me where?" she asked.

"I see you in Persia," he repeated and walked away.

She turned to me. "Persia? Where's that?"

"That's the old name for Iran. We were sent there ten years ago," I answered. Beverly shook her head in disbelief and returned to her painting. That evening she called me. "Shirley, it's happened again. Old Casper was right. I told George what Casper said today, and George got the funniest look on his face and said, 'Bev, I got orders today to go to Iran!'"

"You're kidding, right?"

"No, George's orders are to report to Tehran by the first of June. You're going to have to tell me what it's like over there."

I laughed. "I can tell you plenty!"

It was March before orders started coming in and the anticipation was high. Every night I waited for Jim, hoping he would news of where we would be living. I was watching the news and setting the table when Jim walked in the door announcing, "I got my orders today. We'll be going to San Salvador."

"That's terrific. That's in Central America, isn't it? What will you be doing?"

"I'm to be the military attaché in El Salvador, and we'll live in the capital, San Salvador."

"That's great. We'll be able to use our high school Spanish… El burro es un animal." I laughed, then paused. "Seriously, this is good. All of us will become fluent in Spanish." (I'm always trying to find new ways for our family to learn something.) The next morning, after dropping Peggy off at school, I went to the bookstore to get some Spanish language books. The bookstore was unusually crowded and I was standing in a long checkout line when our neighbor Kathy McGuire walked up. "Well, we got the bad news yesterday," she moaned. "Jeff is going back to Viet Nam. Have you received orders yet?"

"Yes, Jim was told yesterday that he'll be the military attaché in El Salvador and we will be living in San Salvador, which is why I'm buying all these Spanish language books." As soon as I said that, the woman standing in front of me whirled around and looked directly at me with a shocked look on her face. She put down the books she had been waiting in line to pay for and dashed out of the bookstore. Karen and I looked at each other and I said, "What was that all about? Do you know that woman?"

"No, I don't. That was very strange." After I paid for my books, Kathy and I went to the coffee shop, forgetting the incident.

Two days later Jim called to say the orders to go to El Salvador had been rescinded and we were returning to Iran.

"WHAT?? Are you kidding?" I yelled. "What happened to El Salvador?"

"It was decided to send a spook instead, and I am to be the advisor to the Shah in Transportation and Aviation. It's a very good job, Babe, and besides that, we know what to expect in Iran." He hung up the phone and I sat there dazed at this turn of events.

Yeah, I know what to expect when living in Iran, I thought. *Well, at least this time I won't be pregnant! This time I will really be able to enjoy Iran.*

Glancing at the clock, I was jarred back to reality and realized it was time to pick up Peggy from her pre-kindergarten class. I did not dare be late because the week before she had scared us when she walked home from school. I was running late that morning when I dropped her off in front of the school and continued on to the Thrift Shop to take in some clothes the kids had outgrown. Peggy had walked into her classroom, only to find it empty. She checked the office, and no one was there. She had been absent the day before with a sore throat when it had been announced that the whole school would have a picnic in the park behind the school to welcome the much-anticipated springtime. Not knowing what else to do, she started for home. For a four-year-old, this was very daring. She had to walk three blocks to go past the commissary, where prisoners from the Leavenworth Penitentiary worked sacking and loading groceries. From there she had to cross the four-lane highway that cuts through the center of Ft. Leavenworth and then walk on to the housing area where there were dozens of look-alike cracker box houses that were assigned to the students. Fortunately, Jim was at home studying for a test when Peggy walked in and tearfully told her Dad how scared she was.

Holding her tightly, Jim asked, "Peg, how did you manage to find our house?"

"Daddy, I looked for our orange mailbox," she replied, sniffling. He comforted her, and by the time I arrived twenty minutes later she was calmly coloring. Jim told me what had happened. Alarmed at what could have been a tragedy, I returned with Peggy to the school, ready to demand an explanation from her teacher. The secretary was in the office and explained that she had been assisting the teachers with the refreshments at the park. "I'm so sorry this happened, Mrs. Starkey, I must have been down at the park when Peggy arrived and couldn't find anyone. Come with me, Peggy, and I'll take you to the picnic." Satisfied with the explanation and apology, I watched as Peggy happily left with the secretary to join her friends.

So this day, I vowed, I would not be late. The road to the school was lined with trees sprouting new-green foliage. The crab apple trees were in bloom, and the ground was dark with moisture from the melting snow. The sky was cobalt blue, a perfect background for the fluffy white clouds. Birds were announcing that spring was here. *What a beautiful day,* I thought, as I parked the car and merged with the other waiting mothers.

The doors burst open and the kids piled out, running, laughing and rushing to their mothers. Peg arrived breathless - with a huge grin on her face, her blond pigtails flying. Hugging me hard, she said, "Look at the picture I painted." (Possessing a sunny outlook Peggy has been a delight from the moment of her birth. She questions everything, her electric blue eyes watching intently.) She excitedly told me about her day in class and how she and her friend Mary Ann had won the jacks tournament during recess. We talked about her picture, and then Peggy announced that she was very hungry for a tuna fish sandwich. She chattered all the way home about her school day and was still talking while she set the table and poured the milk. I did not mention our new orders; I would leave it up to Jim to make the announcement at dinner.

Peggy awoke from her nap just as Patrick arrived home from school. His bright blue eyes were shining behind his glasses as he proudly showed me his paperwork for the week. As usual, each paper had a happy face and "Good Work" comments from his first grade teacher. (Patrick is a perfectionist in everything he does. He can be very serious and quiet but when something amuses him his laughter is infectious.) Hungry as usual, Pat went in the kitchen for some milk and cookies.

Jimbo arrived home and joined his brother in dunking cookies into the milk. He finished quickly and changed into his blue-and-yellow Pirates baseball uniform. (He is very athletic and excels in any sport he tries. I only wish he approached schoolwork with the same gusto.)

"Come on, kids. We've got to get Jimbo to the game," I yelled.

The children piled into the station wagon, and we left for the baseball field. This was the final game of the season, and Jimbo was scheduled to be the pitcher, so we couldn't be late. The game was in the second inning when Jim joined us in the bleachers. It was so exciting, and we cheered until we were hoarse. The Pirates won 12-to-9 and Jimbo was grinning from ear to ear as he received the accolades from his coach and teammates.

That evening, as we set down to eat, Jim informed the children of our change in orders. "We will be going back to Iran. That's where Pat was born," he announced.

The three children looked intently at their dad, and in a very serious tone Patrick dryly stated, "I don't remember that!"

We all laughed, and then Jim asked, "Jimbo, you remember living in Iran, don't you?"

"Oh, yes, that's where I had my stomach pumped. And," he added, his green eyes accusing me, "I hadn't eaten the aspirin and I told you that!"

The things kids remember! "Well, Jimbo, I couldn't take a chance." Turning to Pat and Peggy, I explained, "In Iran, we had to have a maid and she was called a *badjii*. One time, when your Dad was away and our *badjii* was off, I went upstairs to check on Jimbo. He was only four at the time and was supposed to be taking a nap. I discovered that he was chewing an aspirin with the almost empty bottle of aspirin next to him. The bottle had been full just a few days before, so I thought Jimbo had eaten many of them. Fortunately, our driver was in front of our house, so we rushed Jimbo to the hospital, where his stomach was pumped. It turned out that he had only eaten one aspirin, just as he had said, but I couldn't take a chance. We found out later that the *badjii* had stolen the rest of the aspirin."

Jimbo was pleased that he had been vindicated and asked, "Mom, do you think Maluke and Gholum will work for us again? Turning to his siblings, he said, "You'll like Maluke. She always irons your underwear!"

"Who's Maluke and Gholum?" Patrick demanded.

With an important air Jimbo answered, "Maluke was our badjii and Gholum was our driver."

"Why did we have a driver?" Pat asked.

"We had to because I was not allowed to drive a car in Iran." I quickly replied, expecting the usual 'why' from Pat. Fortunately, Peggy quickly asked, "Can we take Bandit with us?"

Before Jim could answer, Jimbo interrupted, asking if they could take their alligators to Iran.

"We'll take Bandit but we cannot take the alligators. Maybe we can donate them to the Kansas City Zoo." Jim replied.

"What will we do with my turtles?" Peggy asked.

"Maybe the zoo will take those, also." Jim answered. The children continued to ask questions about Iran and Jim got the Atlas to show them where the country was. They were so excited to learn we would have to fly half-way around the world to get there. The conversation lasted more than an hour until Jim decreed that it was time for showers and bed.

The spring of 1970 was filled with turmoil. University students were rioting against the Viet Nam war on every campus from Berkley to Boston. The papers were filled with stories demanding troop withdrawals and the military was upset at the one-sided reporting of the media. A vice-president of CBS was invited to speak to the 1200 officers attending the Command and Staff College. When Jim came home from the lecture he was livid. "Babe, you won't believe what that arrogant S.O.B said. When he asked for questions from the audience, one of the majors raised his hand. 'Sir,' he said, 'I was the leader of a platoon in Viet Nam when a reporter urged a young eighteen year old private to cut off the ears of a dead Viet Cong so he could take his picture. At first the private resisted but the reporter told him it would be a nice souvenir to send his folks. So this young kid cut off the ears and the reporter took his picture, promising to send a copy to the private. Instead, that picture ended up on television and in all the newspapers in the States and all over the world. As you remember, it caused an uproar and more demands for us to get out of Viet Nam. And, Sir, I believe it was wrong of that reporter to urge the private to do that and for the news media to take advantage of it and publish that picture.'

When he sat down, the CBS man glared at him and the rest of us and said in slow, menacing voice, "I want every one of you to know that I could make or break any one of you at anytime I choose."

"Babe, you should have heard the boos from all of us."

When Jim arrived home one Monday evening at the end of April, he was carrying a large manila envelope from our sponsor in Iran, LTC Delahanty. Along with a letter welcoming us, there was a notebook-sized booklet that answered almost every question we had. The most important revelation was that we could bring our own car and I could drive! No more difficult drivers to hire. At the back of the booklet were some common Farsi words, so I started renewing my limited kitchen Farsi. It was decided that Jim would leave Friday afternoon and drive our Ford station wagon to New Orleans for shipment to Iran. The booklet stated that it usually took two to three months for the car to arrive in Tehran, so we had to get it on the way.

My mood rose with the news that I would be able to drive, and I started thinking about the advantages of returning to Iran. For one, we would not have the culture shock that we had experienced before. Two, and the most important to me, was that I was not pregnant. On our first tour, being five months pregnant with all the emotional baggage that accompanies that condition, it seemed I did nothing but cry for the first year.

I started making lists of all the things we needed to do before we left the States. We all went down to apply for diplomatic passports and to get the necessary shots. Jim and I got International Drivers Licenses. Buying a standing freezer, a refrigerator and a butane stove with oven put a dent in our budget, but Jim insisted on including a portable filter for a swimming pool. These were non-existent in Iran at the time of our first experience and we frequently had to drain the swimming pool to keep it clean. Peggy and I spent a lot of time at the commissary buying canned goods, peanut butter, and paper products to take to Iran, as I knew how hard it was to get the supplies Americans are used to. At the PX we loaded up on cosmetics, toothpaste, tooth brushes, lotions, deodorants and other personal hygiene products. We made sure we had every available catalogue to take with us.

With the papers full of stories of the Mylai Massacre trial, the bombs exploding in New York City, and the constant marches against the war, it seemed as if the whole world was falling apart. This only encouraged the college students at universities all over the country to add to the upheaval. In the springtime, a young man's fancy wasn't turning to thoughts of love, but rather to thoughts of rioting. And then it happened. At traditionally apathetic Kent State in Ohio, the news that the Americans had gone into Cambodia sent the students into frenzy. Expecting trouble, the university officials requested the National Guard be called in to assist in crowd control. This infuriated the students, and they started throwing rocks at the troops. The Guardsmen, acting on previous orders to shoot if attacked, fired into the protesters, killing four and wounding eight. The whole country was outraged, and when a horde of angry citizens stormed toward Ft. Leavenworth, the Commanding General ordered the gates to be closed. We were on lock-down, much as it must have been during the Indian Raids of a century before. After several days, everything quieted down, as university students were forced to return to class for finals if they hoped to keep their student deferments.

It was the end of school, not only for Jim, but also for the children. We had parent-teacher conferences, the report cards came out and Patrick had all "A's", while Jimbo's Little League baseball team won the trophy for the most wins, thanks to Jimbo's pitching ability. He had an amazing arm for such a young athlete. Peggy's teacher wrote a glowing report on how well 'she played with others.' There were farewell parties for us all. At last the time came for the moving of 1200 students and families to all parts of the world. The moving vans came from as far south as Corpus Christi, Texas and as far north as Chicago. We were given one day for the packing and loading. If you weren't around, you would be packed anyway. The Johnsons were on orders for Alaska, and their time for packing happened to be the same time as graduation. While they were gone to the celebration, the packers came in and packed everything - including a full garbage can. Their household goods were well on the way to Alaska when their orders were changed to the Pentagon. It took four months for them to receive their belongings, along with the very fragrant garbage can.

Our station wagon was on its way to Iran and our only mode of transportation was Jim's little Fiat Sport Spyder. While the kids could fit into the back seat, it was very crowded, so it was decided that Peggy and I would fly to Tucson while Jim, Jimbo, Pat and Bandit would come in the car.

While perusing the *Foods of the World* cookbook in preparation for our Italian gluttonous walkabout, I came across a story about a wine called *Est! Est! Est!* from Montefiascone, a town near Rome. Eight hundred years ago, in the twelfth century, a German Cardinal Johann Fugger, a famous wine lover, was coming to Rome from Augsburg, Germany. He sent his steward ahead to taste the wines at each village with the instructions to write the word *Est* on the doors of the taverns when the wine was good. When the Cardinal reached Montefiascone, he found the door of the inn marked, *Est! Est! Est!* Inside, his steward was on the floor, happily drunk! The Cardinal started drinking the wine, consumed much more than his steward, and immediately died. He is buried in the town; the inn and wine is still called *Est! Est! Est!*

I was intrigued by the story, and when Jim decided we should break up our flight to Tehran, I came up with a brilliant idea. I told him the story of the wine of Montefiascone, and suggested we go to Rome, rent a car and drive down to taste the wine that was reputed to be the best. He agreed, and we made our plans.

We took the alligators and the turtles to the Kansas City Zoo. The Manager presented the boys and Peggy each with a special certificate praising them for their contribution. They were especially pleased with one of Peggy's turtles, saying it was a species not found in the zoo. Graduation arrived, the packers came and went, a cleaning team came in to clean our quarters, Jim signed the necessary papers to vacate post, and we moved into a motel. That night we went with several other families to an outdoors Cajun all-you-can-eat shrimp place and, after stuffing ourselves, danced to a crazy band. The next day Peggy and I boarded a plane for Tucson, while Jim, Jimbo, Pat and Bandit started driving west.

We spent two weeks visiting with my folks, Jim's mom and our friends plus doing lots of shopping for shoes and clothes. We were allowed two suitcases each, plus carry-ons that contained the clothes and personal items we would use in Italy. We bought small cases for each of the children to carry books, games, art supplies and toys to amuse them on the long plane trip. We made it clear that it was their responsibility to take care of their property. Jim stored the Fiat in a secluded corner of his mom's yard, taking out the battery and covering the car with canvas. We visited Jim's mom and her renter, Mrs. Powder, said our goodbyes, then my dad drove us to the airport. Bandit rode in the luggage area in a locked cage as we flew from Tucson to Chicago to board a Northwest-Orient Airlines flight to JFK.

Arriving in Chicago, we discovered that the Northwest-Orient Airline crew had decided to strike that day, and we were put on the last flight deadheading to New York City. Bandit and our ten suitcases did not make that flight and when we got to JFK, we discovered that he and the luggage were at LaGuardia Airport. Jim went into action while the kids and I waited in a lounge. Eventually he came back and announced that our dog and suitcases were being flown by helicopter to JFK. We had some dinner while we waited. When Jim inquired about Bandit the agent asked, "What breed of a dog are you looking for?" Jim replied, "A pug." The agent quietly said, "Somebody probably took him. Those small breeds have a way of disappearing around here. But you can go downstairs to the baggage area and ask for Mr. Rossini. He can help you." Jim raced downstairs and into Mr. Rossini's office and there was Bandit, lying with his head on Mr. Rossini's foot. Mr. Rossini apologized, "I broke the lock so I could take your dog for a walk, and I gave him some water." Relieved that he didn't have to give our children the news that their beloved pet was gone, Jim shook Mr. Rossini's hand and thanked him profusely. As an afterthought, he asked about our suitcases and was told they were being sent to our next flight.

Checking in with Pan-Am, we were told we could not use the cage for Bandit and instead were given a cardboard box for him. "Your dog can stay in the cabin with you. Just put the box on the floor beneath your feet," we were told. Happy to have Bandit with us, we boarded the plane. Immediately, our noses were assailed with the stench of body odor; the whole plane was full of Italians returning home from vacation. We had forgotten that most of the world does not bathe daily, nor use deodorant as fastidious Americans do! The good news was the air conditioning worked just fine.

I carried Bandit while Patrick carried the box. When the stewardess saw the box, she said in an annoyed voice, "Why do they keep giving out those boxes? They don't fit between the seats! Just keep your dog at your feet." She grabbed the box from Pat and threw it into one of the storage units. For the nine-hour flight Bandit slept with his head on my foot. Pugs are the easiest traveling dogs.

We had to awaken the kids when we arrived in Rome at 5:00 a.m. As we got off the plane, Bandit headed for the closest pillar, and we thought Rome would be flooded. After collecting our luggage and placing it on carts, we looked for a place to store things while we were gone. A young boy about 12 years old asked, in broken English, if he could help us. Jim told him we needed to store our suitcases for four days. He led us to a sleepy-looking man sitting at a desk in the middle of the concourse. Jim asked the man where the lockers were for storing suitcases. "We have none, but we can help you. Bring them here," he said, "and we'll stack them against this pillar. They will be safe." Jim and I looked at each other, thinking the same thing. Jim said to the man, "Someone will be able to steal them." "No, no, have no fear. I will lock them," he assured us. He immediately started stacking the suitcases. When he finished, he took a ball of twine and strung the handles together. Satisfied, he smiled, "Now they are safe." "When in Rome," Jim muttered as we left for the car rental place. Herding the sleepy kids and Bandit into a small Fiat, we drove out of the airport and onto highway going south along the coast. The kids immediately fell fast asleep, leaning against each other in the back seat.

Dawn was breaking and the mare's tail clouds shown in shades of pink, orange and gold. In the distance, beyond the pastel-colored beach bungalows, the waves lapped upon the sand. For an hour, Jim and I enjoyed the scenery while the children slept. As the sun rose in the sky, the temperature did also. The oppressive heat soon caused the children to awaken and demand water. They had slept through the breakfast served on the plane, and they were very hungry. We looked for a hotel and restaurant. That is when it hit us: we had forgotten to change dollars into lire! "Look for a bank, Babe." Jim commanded. We drove through several villages looking for someplace to change money. After many miles, we came to a crossroad where there was a building with the sign 'Pension' hanging from the roof. A man was setting up chairs around the tables in the patio, getting ready to serve breakfast. Jim got out of the car and asked, "Do you speak English?" The man frowned; his mouth turned down and shook his head. Jim tried Spanish; "May we get some breakfast?" The man looked at us with a sour face and started to leave. Jim followed him, "Well, can I buy some water with dollars?" The man violently shook his head, turned away, walked into the building and slammed the door. Jim returned to the car and we drove to the next village where we found a man sweeping outside another pension. On the bar at the entrance were several bottles of water. Jim held out an Kennedy fifty cent coin. Trying Spanish, he said, *"Litre aqua, por favor."* It was close enough that the man understood and he looked suspiciously at the coin. Jim repeated the phrase, adding *"por ninos,"* pointing to our children and thrusting the coin toward the man's hand. The man took the coin, put it between his teeth and bit down. Satisfied that it was a solid coin, he nodded and handed Jim a bottle of water. Jim returned to the car and as the children took turns drinking the water he said, "Babe, I think this is a bad idea. We're not going to get much help in these villages without lire. Maybe we should return to Rome."

You're probably right," I answered. "I'm not feeling too good about the way our suitcases were left in the airport either." So it was decided to abandon our *Est* quest and I got out the map. Since we had meandered through several villages, we couldn't figure out where we were and how to get back to Fumichini airport. Jim turned the car around and started in the general direction of Rome. After an hour, we came to a major highway and read the word Roma 16 k. on a sign. The traffic became heavier and crazier, with horns blaring and fists shaking at anyone who was going too slow. This was Jim's kind of driving, and we raced along with the rest of the pack. As we entered the city and came to traffic lights, Jim would tell me to ask a pedestrian the way to the airport. Nobody spoke English - or at least pretended not to. At one point we ended up in a dead end behind the Tivoli Fountain. How this happened is beyond me, but suddenly we were surrounded by gendarmes, all yelling at us. They frantically motioned for us to leave, ignoring our pleas for directions to the airport. Setting off into the manic traffic, Jim said to me, "Shirl, ask for Fumichini Airport with an Italian accent!" So at the next stoplight, leaning out the window, I yelled at a man waiting to cross the street, trilling my 'r's like my Czech grandmother did, "Fumichini Airrraporrto"! It worked like magic, the man dramatically pointed down the road and hollered, "Vavavavoom," and off we were to the races. To our amazement, we saw a sign directing us to the airport. It was noon by the time we turned in the rental car, entered the building and found the pillar with all our suitcases. The sleepy man did not seem surprised to see us. Jim asked him how we could find a hotel, and he led us to a desk where a pretty brunette was filing her fingernails. Jim explained that we needed a hotel room for four days. She spoke excellent English and after two phone calls she announced that we had two rooms in a hotel in the heart of Rome. After getting dollars changed to lire, we piled the suitcases in a taxi station wagon. Our cab driver spoke English and explained that he drove "a beeg car because Americans always brought too much luggeege."

To our surprise, the Hotel Miami was on a quiet street just two blocks from the Via Veneto. We were given two spacious bedrooms. The smiling concierge showed us our rooms, emphasizing the comfortable bed by bouncing it with her hands. She grabbed Bandit, enveloping him in a giant hug. Next, our three *bambinos* got her attention. In broken English, she commented on Peggy and Pat's blonde hair and Jimbo's dark hair. She recommended the *trattoria* next door, and she said she would take care of Bandit while we were gone. After spending a relaxing two hours eating spaghetti, salad, bread and red wine for us and milk for the children, we returned to our rooms. We fell into bed and slept the sleep of the dead until morning.

The children awakened us and clamored for breakfast. We went downstairs to the reception room, where we were served coffee with milk, hot chocolate, jam and tubs of butter for the warm rolls that were crunchy on the outside and soft on the inside. "Where is the peanut butter?" Patrick demanded. "We might see if we can find some in a store," Jim replied. That was not to be, Italians had never heard of peanut butter.

We asked directions to the Vatican from the concierge, and then she added, "I take care of Bandeet, you go Vatican." Happy to have a dog sitter, we set out for the streetcar. It was almost eleven in the morning when we arrived, and the sun was beating down on us. We were very thirsty and spotted a kiosk filled with bottles of beverages of every kind. Jim took our orders: Pat and Jimbo ordered cokes and I asked for a Fanta, an orange soda common in Europe and the Mideast. Peggy, pointing to a bottle filled with pink liquid, said, "Daddy, may I have the pink soda?" Jim complied with her request and gave the vendor our orders. All of us were eagerly gulping our sodas when Peggy wailed, "Daddy, this tastes awful!" Jim, taking a sip of her soda, cried out, "Good grief, this is an aperitif!" He promptly gave Peggy his coke and he drank her pretty pink soda!

We spent three hours walking all over the Vatican, taking pictures of the children with the Swiss guards, gawking at the Michaelango paintings on the ceiling of the Sistine Chapel and admiring the view of Rome from the topmost balconies of the Vatican. Heights make me uneasy, so I stayed back as Jim, Pat and Peggy leaned over the edge to look down on the ant-like people milling around several stories below. Jimbo shares my dislike for heights and stayed with me.

Finding a small bistro, we ate some pizza and salad and finally headed back to our hotel. The concierge had adopted Bandit; taking him for a walk and letting him sleep at her feet. She was a great pug sitter! We returned to our room exhausted, and all fell into bed for lovely nap.

It was after five o'clock when we awoke and time to decide on dinner. The concierge introduced us to a young man who was very helpful. He told us about a restaurant that had wonderful food and even signaled a cab to take us there. It turned out to be huge outdoor establishment filled with foreigners, mostly loud Americans shouting '*Garcon*' to the waiters. Our waiter told us that this was the place for the famous fettuccini Alfredo and urged us to try it. After our antipasti salad the waiter brought a huge platter, set it before us and, with a flourish, dished huge amounts onto our plates. Eagerly, we took our first bite and in unison looked at each other in dismay. The noodles were undercooked and covered in a pale, glutinous sauce that tasted like flour paste. It was awful! None of us wanted to eat it and with that Jim motioned to the waiter to bring us our check. We did not leave hungry, as we had all enjoyed the wonderful bread that was served with our salad. Upon returning to the hotel, we met an American who frequently came to Rome on business. We regaled him with our experience, and he laughed saying he, too, had been conned by a young man into going to this restaurant. He later learned that it is a notorious tourist trap catering to unsuspecting Americans. He suggested that we try the real Alfredo Restaurant the next day.

The next morning, we took a bus tour of Rome to see the Coliseum, the Pantheon, the Spanish steps and many other landmarks. We were able to get off at each destination and spend time looking around. That night, we decided to try the real Alfredo's. We were ushered into a large room while waiting for a table. The walls were filled with pictures of Alfredo with various celebrities from Hollywood and politicians from every country. In every case, both Alfredo's and the celebrity's mouth was wide open, preparing to accept a huge amount of pasta. We were growing tired of looking at tonsils when the maître d' showed us to our table. It was in the garden next to the picket fence that separated the restaurant from the sidewalk. Honeysuckle vines meandered around the pickets, and crocus and iris bloomed along the walk. It was a beautiful night, and colorful Chinese lanterns above us bathed the diners in an iridescent glow. The waiter approached and said, "You wish some fettuccini Alfredo?"

"Good heavens, no," replied Jim. "We had some last night. Please bring us a menu."

"Very well, sir" said the waiter as he disappeared. We patiently waited for five minutes and Jim signaled to the waiter. He again asked us, "You wish some fettuccini Alfredo?"

""No," said Jim firmly. "We would like to see a menu."

"Very well" he answered and left. About that time, an elderly lady carrying a basket of roses approached us from the sidewalk. It was obvious she was selling her flowers. Jim asked me if I would like a rose. Being conscious of our funds my economical side declined. Then he asked Peggy, and she delightedly accepted a pink rose. Looking at me, she smiled. Did I detect from my daughter a female "he likes me better than you" look? Hmmmm.

Several minutes later, Jim once again signaled the waiter and the scenario was repeated. Peggy announced that she needed to go to the bathroom. As she and I wended our way through the crowd, two large customers conversing with a waiter blocked us. Politely I said, "Excuse me." Nothing happened. I loudly repeated, "Excuse me," to no avail. Finally in a super-loud, school teacher voice I said, "*Movimente*" and they promptly moved. I don't know if there is such a word in Italian, but it worked! When we returned to our table, Jim said, "I believe, if we want to eat, that we will have to order the fettuccini Alfredo." I agreed and Jim called the waiter over. "We've decided we would like some fettuccini Alfredo." The waiter beamed and enthusiastically said, "Right away, sir". Within fifteen minutes he returned with a platter of fettuccini enveloped in a light cheese-infused sauce. He stood next to us to watch our reaction as we tasted it. It was, as they say, *magnifico*. It was wonderful; it was manna from heaven and the best thing we had tasted in forever. We exclaimed our approval and the waiter beamed. We told him of our experience the night before and he assured us that this was a frequent complaint against that restaurant, but there was nothing to be done about it.

The next morning we boarded a local bus to go to the Catacombs on the outskirts of Rome. The bus stopped at every street corner, allowing us to observe the common people and the districts in which they lived. It was off the beaten path from the usual tourist haunts. By the time we arrived at our destination, it was noon and the Catacombs were closed until 3:00. We spotted a large billboard advertising a *trattoria* 400 meters away. We trudged up the hill to the entrance, only to discover another 50 steps up to the restaurant. By the time we arrived, panting, we were ready for some refreshment. The children had lemonade while we had a light wine. We sat under a grape arbor enjoying the view of the rolling hills while we ate our lunch of spaghetti Bolognese. The hills were filled with olive trees growing in corduroy-like rows. Some were planted north and south and while some were east and west, forming the pattern of a crazy patch-work quilt. We were the only American family among the many Italians. After lunch, Jimbo and Pat took out the marbles from their pockets and started a game. Soon some of the Italian children came to watch, and Jimbo asked them to play. Without speaking the language, the children started playing marbles, and everyone got along fine. I was amazed and pleased. When we were ready to leave, all the Italians came and shook our hands, smiling generously at us. It was a real people-to-people exchange!

We were at the door of the Catacombs when it reopened and spent the next hour walking up and down stairs in dimly lit corridors, viewing the subterranean burial chambers of the early Christians. Peggy was frightened of the many skulls peering out from between rocks. Jimbo and Pat thought it was a spooky place, but seemed to enjoy it. We caught a cab back to our hotel in time for a short rest before thinking about dinner. The American businessman at our hotel had also recommended a restaurant situated in an old castle, and the kids were excited to eat there.

We had to walk across a moat to enter the restaurant, and the maître d' looked askance at the children. He promptly ushered us into a small room as far from the entrance as possible. The other diners rolled their eyes at the sight of us. After we had ordered, we quietly talked with the children about the suits of armor, the lances, the ball & chains, and various other medieval armaments and weapons that decorated the walls. Toward the end of the meal, Peggy announced that she needed to go to the bathroom. Jim said that he was finished and would take her. When the busboy came to take our dishes, he asked if the boys would like to see the dungeon. He was about 20 years old, and for some reason I didn't trust him, but when Jimbo and Pat begged to go, I said we would all go. We entered a darkened, winding stairwell that only went up. I thought the busboy had said a dungeon, which I thought was like a basement. The boys scampered up and out of sight when the busboy in front of me suddenly turned, and, getting close to my face, made smooching, kissing sounds. I was highly offended and angry. I instinctively drew back my hands in a clawing position, made a horrible face and growled as loudly as I could in an imitation of a lion. The kid had a shocked look on his face at first, then he shrugged his shoulders as if to say 'nice try.' He turned away and left us. I called to the boys, and we immediately returned to our table. Jim and Peggy had come back, and Jim informed us that it was a good thing he had taken Peg, as the bathrooms were co-ed. I told him about my experience with the busboy, and we all had a good laugh. When we left, the maître d' complimented us on how well our children behaved, unlike other American children. Walking outside, I heard Jimbo say to Pat and Peggy, "We have to behave. We know what will happen if we don't!"

The next morning, we packed up and headed for the airport on our way to the next adventure - Tehran, Iran.

Chapter 13

Tucson, Arizona, 1964 - Korea, 1965

As we left Iran in 1964, we were ecstatic to be going back to Tucson for eighteen months. When Jim was at Ft. Eustis in the Advanced Officer's Course-1961-2, he was singled out to apply for the Army's Master's Degree Program. He returned the form stating his preference for the University of Florida, Arizona State University or the University of Arizona, all three chosen for their mild climate. He never mentioned it to me and promptly forgot about it himself. He was shocked when the news from the Pentagon arrived in Iran, ordering him to go to the University of Arizona for a Master's Degree in Industrial Management. We could not believe our good fortune, after dealing with the frustrations of the past two years in Iran, to be returning to our hometown.

Our first stop after leaving Iran was Rome, where we planned to spend two days. After checking into the hotel recommended by Pan-American Airlines, I told Jim that I wanted to introduce Patrick to ice cream, an unknown commodity in Tehran. The concierge was very helpful, giving us directions to the nearest gelato parlor. It was a bright sunshiny day as we walked the three blocks to the parlor. While there was a lot of traffic and noise, it was very organized and calm compared to what we had been used to in Tehran. The drivers stayed in their own lanes and, although they honked and waved fists at each other, they didn't seem to be angry. The gelato parlor turned out to be a wagon with one side open revealing the tubs of various flavors and a man standing behind them, ready to serve us. Jimbo and I ordered chocolate, while Jim ordered vanilla for himself and Patrick. Since there was no proper place to sit down, the boys and I sat on the curb, slurping up the marvelous flavors. Jim was embarrassed by this scene and hovered in the background, but always kept an eye on his injudicious family.

Near our hotel was a shop that specialized in Venetian glass and I spied an especially pretty pink-and-white stripped candy bowl. "Jim, I'd like to get this for my sister Alice. I think she would like it," I said. Jim thought it was a good idea, since we were planning to spend several days with Alice's family in New Jersey while we bought a car. The helpful shopkeeper asked me if I would like her to pack it in a special box. I agreed so she went in the back room, returning with a box tied with a sturdy cord. We walked across the street to a restaurant and after eating returned to our hotel to pack for our flight the next day.

After Rome, we stopped at Barcelona where the highlight of the visit was taking the boys to a bullfight. At first I was against taking a four-year-old and an eighteen-month-old to such a gory spectacle, but Jim was adamant about wanting to see a Spanish bullfight. Rather than trust an unknown babysitter with our boys I consented to take them with us. The bullfight started at nine p.m., so we all took a long nap in preparation. We arose, took showers and got dressed in great anticipation. Taking a cab to a restaurant close to the bullfight ring, we enjoyed our meal of *paella*, the Spanish dish of rice, pork, chicken and seafood in a saffron-flavored tomato sauce. The food was wonderful, and even little Patrick relished the exotic flavors. When we left the restaurant, the cashier gave the boys each a sucker, and we walked the short distance to the bullring. The crowds were thick, so Jim lifted Pat on his shoulders while he purchased the tickets. We entered the circular arena as the band was playing martial music, the vendors were crying enticements to the spectators, and the milling crowds were talking and laughing in an exciting carnival atmosphere. The colors were overwhelming, as it seemed that everyone wore their brightest outfits for the occasion. No sooner had we found our seats then a cheer went up and the parade began. Two majestic horsemen entered the ring, one going to the left and the other going right.

The horses were decked out in vibrant-colored quilts that covered their flanks while the men were dressed in fuchsia-and-black tight pants with a short-waisted fuchsia jacket. They wore big felt hats with the brims rolled upward. In their right fists they held a long, wooden pole with a lethal four-inch spike on the end.

"Those are the *picadors*," Jim whispered to us. "Their job is to puncture the neck muscles of the bull, causing him to lower his head."

"Why?" whispered Jimbo.

"So the bull fighter can kill the bull." Jim answered.

I was thinking it was a bad idea to bring the boys, but when I looked at them they were both wide-eyed with excitement. Behind the *picadors*, the *matador*, wearing a gold and mocha-colored suit of lights, made his appearance, walking with his head held high, his cape slung over one shoulder. A cheer went up from the audience but, when the fierce-looking, immense bull came charging into the ring, the crowd went wild. The *matador* waved his cape enticingly, leading the bull toward the *picadors* and the dance began. It was a dance as dramatic as any I had ever seen and as graceful as a ballet. The bull raced toward the cape, and the *matador* moved the cape away; again the bull headed toward the cape, and again the *matador* stepped to one side and the bull ran past. This happened several times, until the bull showed signs of fatigue. Then the bull saw the *picadors* and charged toward one of them. The *picador* deftly maneuvered his horses as the bull roared by. Whirling, he came back, his head lowered as he tried to gore the other *picador's* horse. That was what the *picador* was looking for, and he plunged his pic into the bull's shoulder. The dance continued until the last of the pics were in the bull's neck muscles. Blood was oozing, the bull was livid and turned his fury on the *matador*, who teased him with the red cape. After minutes of playing with the bull, the *matador* made a clean kill. The enthusiasm of the crowd was infectious, and we were cheering as hard as the Spanish were. During the next fight, the crowd booed the matador for his clumsy kill. The last fight, the bull was able to gore the *matador*, who was carried off the field on a stretcher to the groans from the crowd.

"Oh, Jim, this was a mistake to bring the boys here." I wailed. Jim started to answer me when a loud hurrah went up from the fans. Looking up, we saw that the *matador* had returned from the ring to finish the fight. In spite of his bleeding wounds, he continued until he had achieved a clean kill. The crowd exploded, the band struck up a march and the *matador* moved all around the arena, accepting the adulation of his zealous followers, as a great profusion flowers rained upon him.

Jim turned to our boys saying, "Did you see that? He didn't give up. Just remember, you never give up!" For his bravery, the *matador* was given the bull's two ears. It was almost midnight when we maneuvered our way out of the arena, following the mass of screaming humanity. As we walked along the boulevard past the backend of the bullring, the massive doors suddenly opened and the last bull fighter came out. The crowd surged toward him and lifted him up because he had shown such courage, then carried him on shoulders for several blocks while shouting joyously. The boys were pumped up and full of questions about the *matadors*, *picadors* and all things related to bullfighting. As we talked we looked for a cab, all the while walking toward our hotel through darkened streets. As we came to a major intersection, we realized our hotel was only three blocks away so we continued our walk. Afterwards, looking at the map, we learned that our hotel was sixteen blocks from the bullfight ring and, most amazingly, our little ones had walked the whole way without a whimper; their adrenaline and the enthusiasm of the crowd kept them going strong.

Our flight to New York was interrupted by a stop at Lisbon, for a larger transcontinental plane. As we entered the terminal, we were each (including the boys) handed a sample bottle of Lancer's wine by two beautiful young ladies dressed in colorful costumes. We found a bench in the waiting room and, while Jim and I were having a conversation, Jimbo took his little brother for a walk. They kept returning to us and then leaving again. Being engrossed in our talk about how the kids would like the United States, it took awhile before we realized that the seat next to us was filled with samples of Lancer's wine. Our two charges had been getting in line over and over to receive the free samples, and the two pretty girls, laughing, kept giving them more. We tried to return the extras, but they declined to accept them saying they got paid according to how many samples they handed out.

Arriving at the New Jersey home of my sister Alice and her

husband, Bill Loveless, we happily shared the wine. As we were talking and laughing about our adventures I retrieved the box with the candy dish from Italy. Handing it to Alice, I was eager to see her expression when she opened the gift. It was my expression that changed when I saw what was in the box. It was not the dish I had paid for, but was instead a stripped pink-and-white dish with a huge chip out of it. Since there was no piece of glass from the chip, it was obvious the dish I bought had been switched to the broken dish. I was livid and embarrassed and wanted to fly back to Rome to croak that shopkeeper. That discovery ruined the whole evening for me.

Bill, an engineer with Shell Oil, was posted to the main office in New York City. We had wonderful days with their children, Susan, Donald and Virginia-plus Bill's niece, Bonnie and nephew, Eddie. Pat and Jimbo were impressed with their big cousins and followed them everywhere, asking a myriad of questions. We bought a car, spent a day at the World's Fair and five days later headed for Arizona. After two years of confinement behind walls, the wide-open spaces of our remarkable country were heaven to us. We headed toward Arizona planning to stop at my sister Toddy's home in Midland, Texas, where brother-in-law Joe Caid was an engineer at Johns Manville. Before we left Iran, I had impressed upon Jimbo the fact that in the United States one could drink water directly from any faucet. As we walked into the Caid house Todd's first words were, "The water here is bad, so don't drink any water other than the bottled water we have in the kitchen."

With great relief we arrived in Tucson and found that both sets of grandparents were excited to meet Patrick and get reacquainted with Jimbo. We found a house to rent on Calle Betelgeaux, replaced the furniture we had sold in Iran, then settled into civilian life for the first time in our marriage. Jim started summer school at the University of Arizona and treated it as if he were in the Army. He was up early and either went to class or to study in the library and was home by five. By July, we had the happy news that I was pregnant. Life was good.

Before we left Iran, we had noticed that Patrick's left eye would turn in whenever he was tired. By the time we arrived in Tucson, the eye was turned in all the time. I took him to the ophthalmologist I had used before we were married. His solution was to tell me to bring Pat back when he was old enough to recognize the big E on the chart. I complained to my mom, who told me about a nursing service that provided the name of doctors who specialized in various fields. I called the number and reached a very accommodating lady who gave me the name of several ophthalmologists. "Which one would you recommend?" I queried.

"I'm sorry, ma'am, I cannot recommend a name."

I tried a different tack, "If you had an eighteen month old child whose eye was turning in, who would you take your child to?"

"I would take him to Dr. Patterson."

I thanked her profusely and immediately phoned Dr. Patterson's office. I explained the problem to the secretary and got an appointment the following Friday. Dr. Patterson turned out to be wonderful with Pat but very short with me and my detailed questions. At one time he said, exasperated, "Mrs. Starkey, I don't have time to give you a college course in ophthalmology." He had a child's merry-go-round on a shelf twenty feet away from the chair Pat was in. He would say, "Now, Patrick, do you see that little boy riding on the white horse? Watch carefully and you will see him pouring Coke in the horse's ear." Pat would stare intently while Dr. Patterson examined his eyes with a strong beam of light. He gave me a prescription for glasses and told me to make sure Pat wore the glasses and, if necessary, recommended ties that could be put on the frames to prevent him from taking the glasses off. "These glasses will not straighten Pat's eye out but it will help him see. He'll probably have to have an eye operation when he's older," he explained.

When the glasses were ready, Pat put them on and suddenly got an amazed look on his face. He kept walking around, picking up leaves or rocks and intently examining them. He never once refused to wear his glasses and would put them on the first thing in the morning. His whole personality changed, and we realized that the child hadn't been able to see before.

From the time we married, Jim and I had only been in Tucson for a couple of weeks at a time while on leave. Now that we were living there, we made the unpleasant discovery that Margaret, Jim's mom, was an alcoholic. We tried hard to help Grandpa deal with this, to no avail. It certainly added additional drama to our life.

Jim had promised the boys that when we were in Tucson they could have a dog. We bought a darling Beagle puppy that Jimbo named Barney, after his favorite storybook character. At first Barney was a delight, and Pat and Jimbo loved him. Then he started chewing on anything he could find: books, toys, towels, shoes and his favorite, socks. Nothing was safe from his jaws, so he was soon relegated to the back yard. In short order our lawn furniture and our garden hose started disappearing, only to emerge later in huge Technicolor piles all over the yard. One day he decided to eat an ornamental pepper plant. His face swelled up, his eyes watered and he couldn't get enough to drink. For two days he was a perfect dog and we thought he was cured, but it was not to be. On the third day, he started chewing on the bricks of the house. That did it! We put an ad in the paper; a young man answered it and immediately wanted Barney. We were happy to see him go! Three weeks later, under the Humane Society section of the paper, was a picture of Barney with the caption, "I'm looking for a new home. Will you adopt me?" Poor Barney, I hope he found a good home.

A few weeks later I was playing bridge with the other Army wives when one of the women asked if we knew anyone who wanted a dog. She told me she had a pug that she didn't want because he shed too much. I didn't know what a pug was, but I told her I would like to see the dog. When I saw that little blonde dog with the black mask, pushed-in nose and curly tail, I was enchanted. The dog's name was Pug, just like our old Boston terrier that Grandpa Starkey had. Pug fit into our family as if he had always been there. He was the right size and playfulness for the boys and, best of all, he didn't chew on things. One day Grandpa Starkey brought his Pug over to play with our Pug. What a mistake! The Boston terrier attacked our pug and promptly broke his leg. The vet set his leg in a cast and Pug would gallop around the house making clickity-clack noises on the tile floor. We had him for four months when one day the boys went out the back gate to play with their friends and didn't close the gate. Pug got out, ran into the street and got run over. We were all traumatized by losing our beloved pet. Jim and I decided we could do without a dog for awhile.

The boys were very unhappy at not having a pet, so one day I took them to the pet shop and purchased a baby cockatiel. At least a bird wouldn't get run over. The owner assured us that we had purchased a male who would grow colorful plumage and be a talker. The boys named him Charlie Brown. As the bird grew older, the coloring did not change from the original grey. I talked to him constantly, trying to teach him some words, but Charlie was silent. Charlie Brown never uttered a word - but did start laying eggs! That's when it dawned on us that we had a female. Oh, well!

In the fall we went to the football games and cheered our Arizona wildcats; I joined the student military wives group for luncheons and bridge; we enjoyed being around our families and friends. One night at Christmastime I was making cookies late and was very tired with an aching back. Jim finished studying and came into the kitchen, asking if he could help. I readily agreed and sat on a chair while Jim got busy rolling dough and cutting cookies. When he started chuckling, I looked over his shoulder and was shocked to see that the side view of Santa Claus had an extra long appendage not meant for children's eyes! Jim continued with his creative cookies until we were both laughing hysterically.

The headlines in the Arizona Daily Star blared the news of the death of Bruce Kelly in Viet Nam. It was like a punch in the stomach to me, as my family and the Kelly family went back many years from the time when my mother and Mrs. Kelly ran the Brownie troop at Miles School. Ann Kelly and my sister Toddy were best friends in first grade there, while I, a mere kindergartner, was the bane of their existence, always pestering them for attention. Mother and Mrs. Kelly had worked at the Red Cross every week sewing uniforms during World War II. Ann and Todd remained good friends throughout school: Dr. Kelly was a professor at the University of Arizona, and Todd and I each took classes from him. Bruce was several years older than Ann, and we didn't know him very well, but it still felt as if we had lost a member of our own family.

Our baby was due the middle of March, and my ballooning stomach made dealing with two active boys wearing. The fifteenth of March came and went and still no baby. At my checkup Dr. Lacock informed me that my baby was breech, and he would try to turn him before the delivery. On the 25th, Dr. Lacock tried to turn the baby, who refused to budge. "Mrs. Starkey, I'm afraid you have a very stubborn kid in there. I won't try to turn him again, as I have learned the hard way not to insist."

"What do you mean, you learned the hard way?"

With a pained expression Dr. L said, "When I was a young doctor, I tried to force a breech around. The umbilical cord wrapped around his neck, and he was stillborn."

I sucked in my breath and whispered, "What happens when a baby is breech?"

"The baby is born feet first instead of head first. Don't worry about it. It will be fine. I've handled these births many times, and all the children turned out fine," he assured me.

Two days later my good friend Mary Ellen called and demanded, "Shirley, you and Jim come for dinner tonight. Mike said that if you have to go to the hospital, he'll drive you in the ambulance and you can ring the siren." I readily accepted, looking forward to the diversion.

When I told Jim's mom about Mary Ellen's offer, she said the boys could spend the night with them, so we were free to enjoy a rare night out. Upon arrival Mike fixed a huge martini for me and I had the first alcoholic drink that I'd had since I learned I was pregnant. Boy, did that taste good! We had a wonderful meal with lots of laughs. Mike kept saying, "Shirl, isn't something happening? Today is my birthday. You should have that kid tonight in my honor. Besides, I've got the funeral home ambulance parked in front, and you can ring the siren!" How I wanted to be able to do that!

We left at 11:00 and were in bed by midnight. I was so uncomfortable I couldn't get to sleep. At four o'clock, my labor started, and I started counting the time between pains. At six, the pains were four minutes apart, and Jim called Dr. Lacock. "Get your wife to the hospital right now. I'll meet you there," he commanded.

Alarmed at the seriousness of his tone, Jim, who understands direct orders, told me to get dressed right now. We were out the door in fifteen minutes. There was no traffic that Sunday morning so we arrived at Tucson Medical Center before the doctor. Four hours later, with a final push, my baby arrived. "You've got a beautiful girl," Dr. Lacock announced.

I've got a girl? What do I do with a girl? was my first thought. I raised my head just as the doctor placed our daughter on my stomach to cut the cord and saw that this tiny thing was navy blue. I was scared to death, and all I could do was pray. I have never prayed so hard in my life. In an instant, my baby was whisked away to a table and surrounded by Dr. L and eight or ten assistants. All I could hear were suction sounds; no one spoke a word while I continued my non-stop prayers.

Oh dear God, make sure my baby is okay was my mantra. After what seemed like eternity, my baby was taken away, and Dr. Lacock came to me.

"Will the baby be alright?" I asked.

"She'll be fine. I'm having her put in an incubator as a precaution" he assured me.

"Why was she so blue?"

"When a baby is born," he explained, "as soon as the chest comes out there is an automatic reaction that forces the baby to take her first breath of air. This works fine when it is a normal birth with the head coming out first. But because this was a breech birth with the feet coming out first, the head is still inside the womb - so the baby inhales the embryonic fluid. That's why I wanted you here as fast as you could get here. I knew this would be a problem, and I had to have a lot of help to suction her lungs. She'll be fine. We got all the gunk out of her lungs."

"You didn't explain that to me when you told me she was breech." I said frowning.

"You're right, I never do. Why should I worry you? I'll see you later." With that he whirled around and left me to the nurses.

I was wheeled out, put to bed and promptly fell asleep, only to be awakened by Jim. He was so excited, "Babe, we've got a beautiful little girl. She is so tiny and has all her fingers and toes and is so cute," he gushed. "What should we name her?"

"I don't care, I don't care," I said, then went back to sleep.

Soon he awakened me again. "What should we name her?"

Groggy from the whole ordeal, I muttered, "Jim, I don't care. Just let me sleep."

"What about the name Peggy? I've always liked that name."

"Okay, I like it too, but don't you mean Margaret?"

Emphatically he said, "No, I mean Peggy. Make it Peggy Ann."

"That's fine with me, hon. Now can I go to sleep?"

When I awakened several hours later, Jim was there. He had been at his folks' house to tell the boys about their little sister. "See, Dad, I told we were having a girl this time," Jimbo announced. Two-year-old Patrick couldn't understand what was going on. He kept asking Jim, "Where is Mama?"

Jim told me all these things, and then he said, "I'll be back in a minute." He was gone quite awhile, and when he returned I asked, "When are the nurses going to bring Peggy to me?'

"I don't know. I'll go check." And he ran off.

Perplexed at his actions, I demanded to know what the problem was when he finally came back He confessed that he had not been able to see Peggy and was still trying to find out why. Just then a nurse came in with my evening meal and we both pounced. "Why can't we see our baby?"

The nurse looked at her watch and said, "Your pediatrician, Dr. Zee, is making rounds now and should be in to see you soon."

As she left Jim and I looked at each other, puzzled. "Dr. Lacock told me Peggy was all right. What is going on?"

With clenched teeth, Jim said, "I don't know but I'm going to find Dr. Zee right now." Quickly he was out the door, leaving me terrified.

Ten minutes later Jim, looking relieved, arrived with Dr. Zee. Dr. Zee explained, "As Peggy lay within your womb, her face was pressed against your pelvic bone, so that when she was born, her left eye was open, causing temporary paralysis. She wasn't able to blink. To prevent blindness, she was placed in a humid incubator. This is not unusual, and I expect by morning you can have your baby in the room with you."

Early the next morning, a nurse brought in this tiny, perfect little girl. She had wispy blonde hair, deep blue eyes and a rosebud mouth. Both our boys had been over eight-and-half pounds, 23 inches long, with skinny bodies, big heads, hands and feet. So to me Peggy seemed so small. She only weighed six pounds compacted into a chubby eighteen inches. While I was changing her diaper, a volunteer came in to get the information for registering her birth. She was surprised that we intended to name our baby Peggy instead of Margaret, but I insisted. I learned later that Jim was unaware that

Peggy is a nickname for Margaret, his mother's name.

While we were living in our little domestic bubble, the rest of the world was in turmoil. Lyndon Baines Johnson was elected president; in Russia, Krushchev was deposed by Brezhnev; Martin Luther King was arrested along with 770 others for leading the Selma, Alabama march against segregation. Race riots in Watts, a Negro section of Los Angeles, raged for five days. LBJ reported to Congress that the North Vietnamese patrol boats had made unprovoked attacks on American ships in the Gulf of Tonkin. Congress replied by voting almost unanimously to give President Johnson greater authority to strike back against the communists of North Viet Nam. All across the United States, students start protesting America's involvement in Viet Nam. The military students at the University of Arizona were told not to wear their uniforms on Armed Forces Day.

Problems were cropping up in Tucson also. Our house on Calle Betelgeaux was the first street south of Palo Verde High School. The school was on a split shift, and at noontime we were subjected to students driving their cars wildly, playing 'chicken' down Betelgeaux. On several occasions, one of the cars ended up driving across our lawn. We tolerated this, but grew alarmed when female students at Palo Verde High School kept turning up missing. I started taking karate lessons for self-protection. Rumors abounded about drug and sex clubs at the high school.

Then the police arrested Charles Howard Schmidt, Jr. Known as the Pied Piper of Tucson, he was able to fascinate teenage girls, get them to give him money and anything else he wanted. His well-to-do parents had adopted him as a baby, managing to spoil him rotten. He barely made it out of high school and stayed in a small house on his parent's property, living on the $300.00 a month they gave him. He was a real creepy character, standing five feet four inches tall in his bare feet. To make himself look taller, he wore custom-made cowboy boots with stacked heels and stuffed the boots with crushed cans wrapped in rags. He dyed his hair jet black, used heavy pancake makeup and whitened his lips. He would parade around the school grounds with his ungainly gait attracting girls and male misfits. When the police had enough evidence to arrest Schmidt, he led the officers to a remote area of the desert where the dead girls' bodies were found. His arrest for murder caused nationwide attention, and suddenly, Tucson was on the map as journalists from *Life*, *Time*, the *New York Times* and magazines and papers from all over the world poured into town. Since Schmidt's hangouts were mainly on Speedway Boulevard, *Life* Magazine did a story on The Ugliest Street in America. Schmidt was out on bond awaiting his trial when Jim graduated in January 1966 with his Master's degree. Since Jim's orders were to go to Korea for a year's tour, he wanted us away from Palo Verde High School. We moved to a home five miles away. Months later, the trial of Schmidt lasted only a few weeks; he was convicted of killing the two Fritz sisters, receiving the death penalty. But before he could be executed, he had to stand trial for a third murder. He was convicted of that, sent to the Florence, Arizona penitentiary and, while awaiting his appeal, was stabbed to death, saving the state of Arizona a lot of money.

Jim was not happy with the Korea orders, and he called the Pentagon to ask for his orders to be changed to Viet Nam. "Why would you do that?" I demanded. "There is a war going on there and you might be killed!"

"Babe, that's my job. That's what I get paid for…to defend this country, no matter where the war is. Besides that, this Viet Nam war is not going away for awhile. If I go to Korea for a year, I'll be sent to Viet Nam for another year. I don't want to be away from you and the kids for two years. It's bad enough to be gone one year."

I heaved a sigh of relief when his request was denied and he was scheduled to leave for Korea in February. I hoped the Viet Nam thing would be over before he would have to go.

His parting gift to the children was a tan-and-white basset hound puppy we named Ringo Starkey. Ringo's ears almost touched the ground, and with his huge feet and very sad yellow eyes, he was both cute and comical.

The children and I went to the airport with Jim and tearfully said goodbye. Jim hugged each of the children, gave me a big kiss and was gone. We returned home to a very empty house, and I squared my shoulders thinking, *He'll be home in 365 days.*

Six weeks after Jim left, I decided to organize a monthly coffee for the Army officer's wives who stayed in Tucson while their husbands were deployed overseas. I sent out 30 invitations, spent several days cleaning and cooking. My mother-in-law, Margaret, was horrified that I was inviting people that I did not know into my home. She didn't understand the comaraderie that is inborn among military families. To my surprise, all 30 ladies descended on my house at ten o'clock on the given day, all talking at once. I soon discovered that I was the only wife whose husband was not in Viet Nam. As I passed coffee, small sandwiches and cakes, I overheard comments from the women who were telling each other all the bad news their husbands were writing about from the front lines. Nobody asked me where my husband was, and I wasn't about to mention that Jim was safely in Korea. Noon came and went and my guests stayed, gossiping until two o'clock, when their children were due home from school. The wives were so hungry for the companionship of their peers that I passed a tablet around for addresses and phone numbers and promised to send each of them copies. It was decided to make the coffee a monthly event and my friend June offered to host the next coffee exactly one month from that day. After everyone left, I went to the mailbox and retrieved a letter from Jim. Much to my amazement, I read that he would be home the following Thursday! His letter said, "The Army has taken a giant vacuum and sucked out all the helicopter pilots from Korea to send back to the States to join units to be deployed to Viet Nam."

"Wow, Jim will be home Thursday!"

I ran around the house, wringing my hands, going from room to room of my immaculate home. I had cleaned like a dervish in preparation for the coffee, so there was really nothing for me to do until Jim's folks brought the children home. As I was dancing with excitement, the phone rang and my sister Toddy said to me, "Shirley, what's wrong? I just knew I had to call you!"

Todd and I had always had a close relationship and had on occasion displayed the ability to know when something was wrong with the other. I guess it was a form of telepathy. "Nothing is wrong, everything is right!" I exclaimed. "Jim is returning to Tucson Thursday. We'll be moving to Ft. Mammoth, New Jersey, as soon as we can contact the movers." We chatted for awhile and as soon as I hung up I called my Mom at the University of Arizona's Park Avenue Bookstore where she was the manager.

Jim arrived home in April just after Peggy's first birthday. We immediately began the preparations for the packers. We had a Pontiac sedan and Jim built a platform to go over the backseat to the back of the front seat. He covered the plywood with an old mattress pad. The children would ride on that while Ringo would ride underneath on one side and our desert tortoise Samson would be in his cardboard box on the other side. Charlie Brown, the cockatiel, would be in her cage at my feet. As we were supervising the packers Jim received a phone call from the Pentagon telling him his orders had been changed from Fort Mammoth, New Jersey to Ft. Benning, Georgia. Being a flexible military family we adjusted. "At least it is in same general direction," was Jim's comment. I was excited because we could go through New Mexico where my sister Alice and family were living and onto Houston where Toddy and family were living. Both families had been moved since we had been at their homes two years before. After our good-byes to friends and family we were on our way. We left Tucson before sunrise and the kids, snuggled in their blankets and pillows, slept another three hours. We stopped in St. Johns, Arizona for gas and breakfast. As soon as we stopped my job was to get Ringo out from under the platform, then let the boys and Peg out to use the bathroom. After breakfast we went to a park to let the kids get rid of some pent-up energy. Driving east on Interstate 40 the hills of Arizona and western New Mexico looked like waves of the ocean; brown sands, sparsely covered in creosote rolled on endlessly with purple mountains dotting the background. At Gallup, New Mexico the ground suddenly became red with high bluffs interspersed with veins of yellow and deep charcoal brown.

Ciniza is a small refinery plant for Shell Oil twenty miles east of Gallup. Our brother-in-law, Bill had been sent there from the New York City office. There were seven homes for the management team just off the highway. The houses were in front of the giant circular tanks and refinery buildings; beyond that were blood-red bluffs rising into the cerulean sky. The whole Loveless family came out to greet us. Their neighbor's German shepherd came over growling at Ringo. Patrick got between the two dogs and the German shepherd rose up and bit Pat on his left cheek. First aid was applied promptly and Bill talked to his neighbor, who assured him that the dog had the required rabies shots. We spent the night and in the morning continued our journey.

When we arrived in Houston late that night we told Toddy about the dog bite. Toddy informed us that even with the rabies shots it was not possible to be sure the dog did not carry a rabies germ. Jim called a vet and was told the same thing. "You need to make sure that dog is quarantined." Jim called Bill, who went next door to inform his neighbor of the need to quarantine. He called back with the unfortunate news that the neighbor was so disgusted with his dog's third attack on a child that he shot the dog in the head and buried him in the desert. When he and Bill went to dig up the dog they discovered that the coyotes had beaten them to it. Only a carcass was left.

Jim immediately took Patrick to the emergency room of the nearest Army hospital. There he received the news that Pat would have to undergo rabies shots in the flat muscle of his stomach once a day for the next two weeks. These shots had to be administrated every 24 hours and could not deviate one hour either way. It was eleven in the morning when Pat received his first shot. I was frantic for our son and rushed to hug him when they returned from the hospital. Pat seemed strangely unmoved by the ordeal. Jim told me Pat was stoic, not uttering a whimper when he received his shot. We sat down with the atlas to plan our next stop in order for the shots to be given within the time frame necessary, always figuring time changes. Our next stop was at an Army hospital with the shots given in the stomach. Our third stop was at an Air Force hospital where Jim was informed that the shots did not have to be given in the stomach but could be given in the large muscle of the thigh. This was very good news. When we arrived at Rucker Army Hospital in Alabama the doctor refused to give Pat the shot in the thigh, stating that it must be given in the stomach. Jim was adamant, insisting that the doctor check with a higher authority. The doctor returned and said, "Major Starkey, you are right. The shot can now be given in the thigh."

While Jim and Pat were in the hospital the rest of the family sat in our car, which was parked in the shade of a magnolia tree. All the doors were open; the dog was sniffing the world while Jimbo walked around with him; I had put Charlie Brown's cage on the hood and he was happily listening to the wild birds; I was reading a story to Pat and Peggy. To our surprise Kay Benson came walking up. Kay had been our neighbor in Ft. Eustis and while we corresponded at Christmas we hadn't seen each other in five years. We chatted until Jim and Pat arrived and after a few minutes of conversation Jim said we had to leave in order to get to Fort Benning in time for Pat's shot the next day. We started loading up the kids in the back, the dog underneath, the bird at my feet and ourselves. I turned to say goodbye and noticed a startled look on Kay's face. She laughed and said," I've never seen anyone travel the way you do!"

Upon our arrival at Ft. Benning we learned we would be housed in a large two-story duplex, circa 1920, with an attic and a basement. The houses were built around a huge parade ground with the commanding general's quarters across from us. There was a screened-in back porch that faced the parade ground. Under the carved staircase was a storage room perfect for kids to hide in. The ceilings were high with fancy moldings, all the wood was dark and rich and everything smelled of history. It didn't take much for my imagination to think of all the soldiers and their families, with their triumphs and tragedies that had lived there during the last forty years. If only the walls could talk!

We had barely started to move in when Jimbo disappeared only to return with a couple of boys his age. He introduced us as if he were our official greeter.

Jim was assigned to the 213th Black Cat Company, with the additional duties as commander of the 329th Maintenance Detachment. The 213th pilots flew the Chinook helicopters and it was Jim's job to make sure the choppers were in good flying condition. The company was training to go to Viet Nam the following December, when the kids and I would return to Tucson. Soon after our arrival Jim announced that he had to go to Ft. Eustis for one month for further maintenance training. Not willing to have the family separated even for one month we packed the car again and left for Virginia.

We were able to rent a furnished apartment and during the week the kids and I spent a lot of our time swimming and socializing at the Sand Pool at Ft. Eustis. On the weekends I decreed that one day would be spent at the beach and the other day would be for education. Being a consummate history buff I was determined to take advantage of the rich heritage of Virginia and to my mind, three and six year olds were not too young for indoctrination. That following Saturday we left Peggy in the careful care of Miss Mary, the no-nonsense but kindly, Director of the post nursery and we headed for Chowning's Tavern in Williamsburg. We were the first customers of the day and were ushered into a vacant dining room. As we settled in, I started on the History lesson, "Do you realize that George Washington, Thomas Jefferson and Patrick Henry used to eat in this very tavern?" I asked.

"Who? Who's that?" queried Patrick. I patiently explained the pedigree of each man, emphasizing his contribution to the founding of our country.

Jimbo said, "Did George Washington sit here?" pointing to our table.

"Probably" I replied.

"Where did Patrick Henry sit?" Jimbo persisted. I pointed to the table across the room, "Maybe over there."

Patrick was listening to this in his usual laser-like concentration and suddenly blurted out, "I don't see Patrick Henry."

"That's because he's dead." Jim chimed in.

"Well, where's George Washington?"

"He's dead, too."

"Why is George Washington dead?"

Impatiently Jim replied, "Because he was an old man. Now, let's order the Bruinswick stew that this place is famous for."

The waiter brought us brown bread and stew and we eagerly started to eat. Patrick continued to look around the room as if expecting someone important to walk in but he said nothing.

Jim had bought us tickets for a play to be given outside in a park. It was dusk as we found our seats in the theater in the round. The play was about the start of the Revolutionary War and took place in a colonial home. As the play opened the couple who lived there was discussing the impending clash between England and the Colonists. I thought it was way above the boy's head and didn't think they were paying much attention. Suddenly, the lady of the house looked out the window and dramatically announced, "Here comes George Washington." Patrick whirled to me and in the loudest voice bellowed, "YOU TOLD ME GEORGE WAS DEAD!"

It brought the house down and even the actors had a hard time keeping straight faces!

The next weekend we headed for Norfolk and toured an atomic submarine. As we were climbing the outside stairs a gust of wind whipped the scarf off my head and into the ocean. Peggy and the boys were very upset about that. Later we toured the memorial of General Arthur MacArthur, walking around the displays that were on the walls surrounding the black marble mausoleum. "What is in that big black box over there?" Jimbo asked.

"That's where General MacArthur is buried." I replied.

"So, he's dead?"

"Yes, he's dead." Not wanting to get into another 'dead' discussion I quickly changed the subject. That night the kids talked of nothing except that Mom's scarf is in the ocean and there's a man buried in a big black box. That's when Jim and I decided that from then on we would spend the weekends at the beach. So much for history lessons!

We returned to Ft. Benning to discover that Samson, our desert tortoise had caused an uproar during our absence. Jim had built a small tortoise-proof fence in the backyard where Samson was content to eat the grass and other vegetables the children gave him. He became a neighborhood pet with all the kids vying to make sure he had fresh water, spinach, apples and various greens. All our neighbors promised to take care of him while we were gone to Virginia. One day he disappeared even though the fence was intact. Panic ensued and the neighborhood grapevine went into action. The older kids organized groups to spread out all over the parade ground searching for the itinerant tortoise. When that failed they were sent to check all the houses, in the shrubs and bushes in both the front and back yards. Seven year old Jason Dawson triumphantly came forth with the prize. Claudia, my neighbor, described the excitement when Samson was returned.

"Shirley, that was the most fun we've had all summer. This kept the whole neighborhood occupied for more than four hours. I was especially proud of Matt, my twelve-year-old for organizing the search. He maintained a command post in your backyard, kept track in a notebook of where he sent which kid so he knew what areas had been searched. Later when I told my husband Jack about it, he asked Matt if he could see the notebook. Matt explained his strategy and Jack was impressed. He teaches Tactics to new recruits so he took the notebook and made a whole class lecture on organizing searches!"

I was amazed and thanked Matt profusely. "Matt, will you tell everyone who helped find Samson to come to our house tomorrow at three o'clock for lemonade and cookies?"

"Yes, Ma'am Ms Starkey, we'll all be there."

"What a neat kid," I thought, "I wonder where Matt will be twenty years from now? A Wall Street titan, a U.S. Senator or an Astronaut…anything is possible."

One Saturday Jim was involved in training exercises, Jimbo was at a friend's house, Peggy was napping and Patrick and his friend Buddy, who lived in the other side of our duplex, were playing in the backyard. I had checked on them earlier and then got involved in fixing dinner. The doorbell rang and, to my surprise, Pat and Buddy were standing on the porch flanked by two military police.

"Ma'am, these two decided to crash the Commanding General's party," the tall blonde M.P. said, with a twinkle in his eye. "General Simpson asked me to return the boys to you."

"Thank you very much, Sgt. I appreciate it." I said laughing.

Escorting the boys inside I asked, "Pat, why did you go to the General's house?"

With a very serious look Pat answered, "Mama, there were a lot of people going over there and we wanted to see what was happening."

"Well, honey, we don't go to someone's party unless we are invited. Just remember that, OK?" He nodded and went back out to play.

The 213th Helicopter Company, known as the Black Cats, had an artist come up with a logo of a black cat with an arching back and this was painted on all the choppers. As commander of the 329th Maintenance Detachment Jim had two Warrant Officers, as well as 100 enlisted men, under his command. At both Benning and Eustis he was undergoing intensive training in flying and maintaining the new CH-47 Chinook helicopters. The Chinook is a multi-mission, heavy-lift transport helicopter. Its primary mission in the Army is to move troops, artillery, ammunition, fuel, water, barrier materials, supplies and equipment on the battlefield as well as aircraft recovery. In addition to the training involving the CH-47, the company received intensive indoctrination in avoiding being captured and what to do if captured. Three teams were formed headed by the team leaders; Jim, Major Adams, and Major Bennett. One Friday Jim announced that he would be gone all weekend as the company was going on an Escape and Evasion course. A unit from Benning would try to capture the men of the 213th and of course, the 213th would try to evade them. At 11:00 Saturday night the doorbell ringing wakened me. When I opened the door there was my hero: dirty, hungry, thirsty and exhausted but very pleased to have tricked the 'enemy'. After a shower and some bacon and eggs Jim fell into bed and was instantly asleep.

The eight months of preparation before going to Viet Nam were arduous. Jim spent long hours training his men in the maintenance of the Chinook as well as test flying the choppers. As always, Jim made sure the head mechanic was in the cockpit with him when he did the test flying.

In August Patrick was invited to his friend Buddy's third birthday party. He was so excited to be going that I was shocked when he came home afterwards with a disgusted look on his face. "What's the matter, honey? Didn't you have a good time at the party?"

With a frown on his face he firmly said, "Mom, do you know Buddy had a choo-choo train on his birthday cake and it was not even a real train? When I have my birthday party I'm going to have a cake with a *real* train on it." *"Oh, boy, how am I going to handle this,"* I thought, rolling my eyes. "Well, Pat, your birthday is not until November but I'll see what we can do about it." This seemed to placate him but not for long. Every few days he reminded me that he intended to have a real train on his birthday cake.

September came and Jimbo started first grade. The school was two blocks away and, on that first beautiful fall day, Pat, Peggy and I escorted Jimbo to the schoolyard. Jimbo wasn't real sure he wanted to do this, "Mama, why don't I stay home with you guys," he asked. I assured him that this was an important step and that he was a big boy now but it was obvious that he didn't buy it. His teacher, Mrs. Harris had a big class that was ever changing depending on military orders. By the time the 213th was ready to deploy to Viet Nam in December I'm not sure she even knew all her student's names.

November arrived with the dreaded birthday party looming. Obviously, I couldn't put a real train on Pat's cake; I would have to make a train. How would I do that? Patrick informed me who was to be invited so we got the invitations out. He also reminded me that he had to have a real train on the cake. I had to face the challenge. Kraft Foods came to my rescue when they brought out a new item: soft caramel candy. Prior to that, their caramels were so hard that you were in danger of pulling out your teeth if you bit into one. The day before the party I made a large sheet cake of rich chocolate interior and white frosting. The next morning, Saturday, while Jim and the kids blew up the balloons, filled the goody bags for each guest and got the hotdogs, condiments and rolls out, I started on the cake.

I rolled the soft caramels between my hands to form the railroad tracks that circled the cake. Then I made four individual cars with M and M's for wheels; the engine had a chimney of licorice. It looked too bare so I added frosted green trees and little red houses and a train station. It was a work of art and I was completely caught up in my masterpiece. Jim broke my creative mood by announcing that the kids were beginning to arrive. "Jim, what do you think of the cake?" I asked.

"It's fantastic but you have got to stop right now."

"Would you tell Pat to come in here to see the cake? I can't wait to see the expression on his face when he sees the 'real' train!"

A few minutes later Pat walked in like a general reviewing the troops, and stared at my creation.

"Well, Pat what do you think?," I said, anticipating a big compliment.

After awhile, with a frown, he announced, "The train is going the wrong direction!"

Eager to please, I said, "Oh, I can fix that." And I picked up the train and set it down on the opposite direction.

Pat nodded his head once and marched out of the room. I was

stunned as the full import of what just happened hit me hard. Then I became furious and I wanted to strangle the little brat!

The 213th was due to deploy to Viet Nam in January but Jim had to get to Stockton, California in December to supervise the preparation of the Chinooks for travel on an aircraft carrier. He and his pilots were to be posted at the Stockton Army Depot. Jim took leave, we cleared post and left for Tucson while the pilots of the 213th ferried the helicopters to Stockton.

Our return trip was similar to the trip to Georgia except that Ringo had grown to full size, about three feet from nose to tail. The children still rode on the platform with Ringo underneath. He no longer fit on one side of the driveshaft and much to his distress had to lay the full width of the car with his stomach over the driveshaft. Every time we hit a bump we could hear him groan. We had a gas stop in Mississippi and, as usual, Jim got out filling the gas tank while I took Ringo out for a walk. The only way to get him out of the car was to grab his tail and pull. We were watched carefully by two elderly black men sitting on a bench in front of the station. As I pulled Ringo out, an inch at a time, the men's eyes got larger and larger the more I pulled. Jim was watching the men's reaction and when this huge Basset hound finally appeared the men started grinning. They looked at Jim, started laughing uproariously while slapping their knees.

We arrived back in Tucson before Thanksgiving, rented a house on Malvern Place and settled in. Jim left for California to supervise the preparation of his Chinooks for the sea voyage and I got Jimbo enrolled in school. Jim was able to come home for four days during Christmas. The war in Viet Nam was escalating and so were the anti-war protests and Jim was concerned about our safety.

"Babe, be very careful who you talk to and never tell strangers that I am in Viet Nam. There have been many incidences of families of soldiers in Viet Nam being harassed and threatened."

Jim was due to leave before the New Year but that got delayed. Every day he called with reports of when he would be leaving. One night in early January he called and said, "We are definitely leaving Monday afternoon. Could you get a babysitter and fly out for the weekend? I'll call you tomorrow and I hope the news is good."

Excitedly I called my mother, "Mom, do you think you could take care of the kids so I can go to California?"

"No, honey", she said, "we're in the middle of inventory at the bookstore and I can't take time off. Why don't you take the children with you? I know Jim would want that."

"What a great idea! I'm going to make the reservations right now!"

The next night Jim called. "What's the good news?" he asked.

"The bad news is, I cannot get a babysitter. The good news is I'm bringing the kids with me. We'll arrive at the Oakland airport at 6:30 tomorrow night."

Mom was right…Jim was thrilled!

The next day, Thursday, I sent a note to Jimbo's teacher explaining that Jimbo would not be in school on Friday. I left Pat and Peg with Mrs. O'Reilly, the lady that babysat with Pat's friend Joe, and I shopped for new clothes for all of us. The boys were excited to be going on a plane again and told Peggy all about flying. She too, got excited. My niece Marilyn took Ringo and Charlie Brown to her house. Dad drove us to the airport and when it was time to board the plane the boys sprinted across the tarmac and clamored up the steps. Peggy was pulling on my hand so hard I had to run to keep up with her.

It was fun to watch the children's excitement about flying but soon after we ate they quieted down and snoozed. It was dark when we arrived in Oakland and when the kids saw their dad they bolted toward him and almost knocked him down with their enthusiastic hugs. Their elation increased when they saw the apple red Thunderbird convertible Jim had rented. We drove to a restaurant for hamburgers and then to our motel room. After putting the kids to bed we sat on the balcony drinking wine and talking about the upcoming long year. Jim reiterated what I was to do about money, insurance, our stock portfolio and taking over all the things he usually did. Our washing machine was giving me trouble because it wouldn't automatically start to spin out when the washing cycle was through. It worked fine if I manually pushed the knob but Jim told me to buy a new bigger machine. I agreed with that and promised to go to Sears when we returned to Tucson.

The dawn broke bright and clear. After breakfast Jim took us to the aircraft carrier Kula Gulf, where Jim's helicopters were being loaded. The helicopters were wrapped like mummies for protection from the salt air. That evening we had dinner at a restaurant that was located on the pier and was reputed to be the hangout of the late writer John Steinbeck. This area was the setting of his book, *East of Eden*. I neglected to mention this fact to the children not wanting to get into another 'dead' conversation.

The next morning we drove to San Francisco to spend the day at the zoo and in Chinatown. Monday, after packing our suitcases and checking out, we went to Jim's office while he cleared up some last minute details before the Kula Gulf sailed in the afternoon. It was a cool, beautiful northern California afternoon with puffy, white clouds on the horizon. We parked the car and walked to the gangplank for one last farewell. With hugs and kisses we said goodbye and Jim joined the rest of the crew on the deck. The kids and I waved madly as we watched the Kula Gulf leave the pier. As it moved out into the Pacific the setting sun caused the clouds in the sky to become flaming orange. The four of us continued to wave at the silhouette even though we could no longer see Jim. As we returned to the car tears were streaming down my face. Jimbo, feeling as if he were the man of the family, insisted I let him drive. "Jimbo, you're only six years old. You don't know how to drive." I exclaimed, laughing.

"I bet I could if you'd let me. My dad told me to take care of you," he replied vehemently. With that I wiped my tears and hugged my protector. I pulled out the map and showed him where the airport was. "You can help me best if you tell me how to get to the airport so we can turn this car in and go back to Tucson." He was satisfied with this assignment and I was touched at his concern. As we left the dock the radio was playing "I left my heart in San Francisco". To this day whenever I hear that song the vision of the Kula Gulf moving across the water into the sunset comes to mind.

Chapter 14

Tucson - Viet Nam 1967

The children and I returned to Tucson and settled in to a long, long year of waiting. Whenever we were apart, I would write a letter to Jim every night, telling him everything that had happened during the day, just as if he were with me. He told me it would take fourteen days for the Kula Gulf to get to Viet Nam, so each night when I wrote him I would put a number on the outside of the envelope. By the time he got to Viet Nam, Jim had sixteen letters to read.

After two weeks, I eagerly looked for letters from him, and soon I was flooded with a dozen letters he had written while on the Kula Gulf. He told me about one of his men, Captain Dawson, whom Jim was worried about. All the way over to Viet Nam, the captain spent most of the day sharpening his large hunting knife and talking about how he was going "to get me some gooks." When they arrived in Vung Tau on the southern coast of Viet Nam, Captain Dawson could not fly a helicopter to the base in Phu Loi because he had diarrhea. This went on for weeks and he was losing weight rapidly, and for all his tough talk, being in Viet Nam literally scared the shit out of him. Jim had to transfer him to a non-flying unit, and soon he was medically discharged.

Jimbo was so impressed with the aircraft carrier Kula Gulf, he started drawing pictures of it. There were some scraps of lumber left over from our move and he asked me for some nails so he could build a 'real' Kula Gulf. Patrick chimed in, wanting to also build an aircraft carrier, so a trip to Ace Hardware was in order. We purchased another good hammer and some nails, but I declined the request for paint. At home the boys spent hours hammering, making very creative aircraft carriers. The next Saturday, after stopping by Der Wienerschnitzel for our picnic of hotdogs and milk shakes we headed for Reid Park to sail the aircraft carriers. Much to my surprise, they floated.

I bought a new, larger washing machine at Sears and, when it was delivered and hooked up, the Sears man kindly put the old machine in the carport so I could sell it. I put an ad in the paper and three nights later two men appeared at my door wanting to look at the machine. I showed it to them and carefully explained that it worked very well except that the knob had to be turned manually in order for the rinse cycle to begin. "Oh, that's no problem," one of the men said and agreed to buy it at the price of $35.00. He gave me the money and said he would pick it up the next day. When I came home that next afternoon, the machine was gone. Three nights later at 9:30 the doorbell rang. It was the buyer, who said, "What is your name?"

"What do you want to know for?" I asked suspiciously.

Angrily, he replied, "That washing machine doesn't work right, and I want my money back."

I patiently reminded him that I had explained what the matter was and that he had agreed to buy the machine anyway. He got very angry and shouted, "I don't want your damn machine. Give me my money back! By the way, what is your name?" he repeated.

I was frightened, but didn't want him to know that, so I growled through clinched teeth, "That's none of your business!" I slammed the door in his face and locked it. He pounded on the door, shouting, and through the door, I yelled, "I'm calling the police!" Swearing loudly, he left.

Three afternoons later a man appeared at the door holding a piece of paper. "Did you sell a washing machine to a Mr. Harris?"

"I sold a washing machine to a man, but I didn't know his name. Why do you want to know?" I asked.

The man looked down at the paper and said, "Boy, you should

see what he says about you!" Without thinking, I fell for the trap, grabbing the paper. "Thank you, Ma'am, you've been served." And he departed, leaving me with a subpoena to appear in Small Claims Court. The jerk was suing me for a total of $42.50, the amount of the sale plus the filing fee. He also called me Jane Doe as, fortunately, he did not know my real name.

Our next door neighbor, Gordon Alley, was an attorney. He and his wife Reenie had welcomed us to the neighborhood the very first day we moved in. They had a little girl Peggy's age and a new baby boy. Jimbo frequently went next door and asked Reenie, "Can your Daddy play ball with me?" They got a kick out of the request and, if Gordon was home, he usually complied, coming outside to throw the baseball with Jimbo. He was very good to our kids. When I saw Gordon's car in the driveway, I took the subpoena over to him. I told him the whole story and then I asked, "What should I do with this?"

"You're supposed to appear in Small Claims Court. This guy sounds like a real head case, so you better let me handle this. With Jim in Viet Nam, this guy might give you big problems."

"Thank you, Gordon, I owe you one."

In my nightly letter to Jim I conveniently left out any mention of this problem, not wanting him to worry about us.

Gordon called a few days later and said he would appear in Small Claims Court on my behalf. "What time will you be there? Can I come down and watch?"

"Absolutely not. I don't want this guy to ever see your face again. I'll take care of it."

I couldn't wait for the appointed date to find out what happened. Gordon was laughing when he described the scene. "This guy, Mr. Harris, started acting like Perry Mason presenting a case. The judge told him, 'You can't make a motion like that.' So Harris says, 'Well, how can I do it?' Then the judge said, 'Mr. Harris, I am not your lawyer.' So this guy says, 'Well, Judge, should I get a lawyer?' And then the Judge said, 'That is up to you.' He pounded the gavel and dismissed the case."

"So is it over?" I asked.

"It is for now."

But it wasn't. Three days later, when I came home, the old washing machine was dumped in the middle of the front yard. I went to

Gordon. "What should I do now?" I asked him.

Gleefully Gordon said, "Don't touch it. This is a great opportunity. We'll charge Mr. Harris $2.00 a day for storage." He filed the necessary paperwork and we waited. Jim's mother was mortified that our house looked like poor white trash lived there and refused to come over as long as the washing machine was there. Jim's dad, whom the kids called Grampa Starkey, frequently came by to check up on us and play with the children. My mom and dad, used to my impetuous ways, just shrugged their shoulders as if to say, "It's another of Shirley's crazy deals."

Mowing the lawn became a problem of avoiding the machine. I didn't care if the mower nicked it, but I did want the grass around it to be gone, so I had to hand trim it. Then I considered planting geraniums in the machine, so I could act as if it were a New Age art display.

A month had dragged on with Mr. Harris owing us over $60.00 for storage when Gordon received a call from an attorney for Mr. Harris. "What is going on here?" he demanded. "Why is there so much secrecy about this women's name? Is there a lot of money involved?"

Gordon laughed, "No, there is not a lot of money involved. Let's make a deal. If you will drop this lawsuit, we will stop charging storage fees."

"Who is this woman?"

"If we can make this go away, I will tell you the whole story - but believe me there is no 'big money' involved."

Somehow these two attorneys agreed to settle the matter and after the paperwork was finished the other lawyer said, "Why is the woman's name a big secret?"

"She is my neighbor. Her husband is in Viet Nam, and I didn't know what your client might do if he knew that. So I told her I would take care of it."

The other lawyer agreed. "Oh, man, Harris made it sound so mysterious, and he thought there must be a lot of money involved. He's a real piece of work. I don't blame you a bit for being cautious."

When Gordon told me this, I said, "Oh, good. Now I can get rid of the washing machine."

"No, you can't. We have to serve notice on Mr. Harris that he has 30 days to pick up the machine or we will resell it."

"You mean I can't move it?"

"No, it has to stay exactly where it is."

Thirty days later, Gordon informed me that I could resell the machine. "Heck, no, I'm calling the Salvation Army." Gordon refused to bill me for all his work, claiming this was the most fun he had ever had practicing law. I hoped the attorney for Harris charged him plenty!

In late January, three astronauts, Roger Chaffee, Edward White, and Virgil (Gus) Grissom were killed in a flash fire that engulfed their Apollo 1 spacecraft. The United States went into mourning for the men and everyone was saddened by the delay in the space program. The military funerals were televised on a Saturday while Jim's dad was at our house. Grandpa Starkey was very impressed with the pomp and circumstances surrounding all military funerals, and he turned to me in awe. "If Jim is killed in Viet Nam, is that the kind of funeral he will have?" My blood ran cold.

"Bite your tongue, Grandpa, it's not going to happen," was my sharp reply.

Realizing how those words sounded, he apologized.

Six o'clock Easter morning dawned bright and sunny. I put Ringo outside and went into the kitchen to make coffee. A strange car pulled up in front, and a man started to get out. I had heard that telegrams from the government were delivered on weekends by civilians, and I gasped in horror, thinking something had happened to Jim. I raced back to our bedroom, flung myself into the bed and covered my head with the bedspread.

Please, dear God, don't let Jim be killed.

The doorbell rang, and I heard Jimbo answer it. There were muffled voices, and then Jimbo came running into the bedroom, shouting, "Mama, look what Daddy sent us."

Drying my eyes, I sat up and saw a beautiful arrangement of Hawaiian bird of paradise flowers sent as an Easter present.

In one of Jim's letters he described another trouble-making captain that he had to replace. Captain Carmona, a self-described

Ladies Man, managed in the short time at Stockton to get one of the secretaries pregnant, in spite of the fact that he was married. While on the Kula Gulf he had reported for duty drunk. Jim forced him to get all the booze from his footlocker and pour it down the sink. Carmona was furious. When the unit arrived in Phu Loi, Jim reported the incident to his superior officer, who promptly, permanently transferred Carmona to Vung Tau. Several months later, a very drunk Carmona was on the third floor balcony of a hotel with a Vietnamese whore. They were leaning against the rail, locked in passionate action, when the railing broke and they fell to the ground. Both sustained broken backs as well as other injuries; Carmona was given a dishonorable discharge and sent back to the States.

One Saturday morning, the kids were playing in the front yard while I was working in the kitchen. The kitchen faced the front of the house, and I kept a close eye on them. Jimbo, as usual, was organizing their play. This time he decided to use Peggy's jump rope to tie Ringo to the big red wagon and, with Pat and Peg in the wagon, he was walking Ringo around the yard. This was a good plan until Ringo spotted an elderly couple across the street, walking their cocker spaniel. Suddenly, with a loud bark, Ringo sprinted down the driveway with Jimbo fast behind and Pat and Peggy holding on for dear life. I was out the door in a second giving chase. As Ringo lunged across the street, I saw a truck bearing down on the wagon. Fortunately, the driver stopped in time, just as the cocker spaniel, with terror in his eyes, wrapped his leash around the couple's legs in an attempt to avoid Ringo. I rushed up and grabbed Ringo, pulling him back. The couple was able to control their dog while avoiding falling down. Jimbo was alarmed, but Pat and Peg were grinning. I looked up at the truck driver, and he was hysterically laughing. It must have been a sight to see: a basset hound pulling a wagon full of kids, another kid chasing, a wild-eyed woman chasing everybody and an elderly couple trying hard to keep their balance. Thank goodness no one was hurt.

The war in Viet Nam was escalating and so were the protests. Cassius Clay, the heavyweight boxing champion who preferred to go by the name of Muhammad Ali, his Moslem name, was stripped of his boxing title for refusing to be drafted. 2500 members of Women Strike for Peace organization stormed the Pentagon, demanding to speak to the Secretary of Defense, Robert McNamara. Hippies from San Francisco to New York held 'Love Ins' with signs reading "Make Love Not War". Late one night I was getting ready to turn in when the phone rang. It was a female voice on the other end of the line, "Mrs. Starkey, are you any relation to Major James E. Starkey?"

Chills ran up my spine, and I gasped for air. Getting control of myself, I asked in a steely voice, "Who wants to know?"

"Oh, ma'am, Major Starkey is okay" was the apologetic answer. "He's being recommended for a medal for bravery. I spoke to him today, and he told me he was from Tucson. I'm writing an article about his exploits, and I wanted to mention you and your family in it."

"Please, do not mention us or his parents in the article. There are crazies here causing problems for military dependents, and I don't need that."

She promised she would not use our names and, since she sounded very nice, we chatted for a few minutes with her filling me in on her conversation with Jim. Two days later a small article appeared in the paper with the headline,

Tucsonans Saves War 'Copters.

SAIGON (AP)-Army Maj. James E. Starkey, Tucson, Ariz. is credited with piloting his big Chinook helicopter into combat areas to recover two disabled smaller helicopters. "We scrambled out there in a hurry and scooted in and picked up the Huey so fast that the Charlies didn't have a chance to take aim," he reported. The crew later maneuvered their Chinook back in to the combat zone and picked up another downed Huey helicopter in a sling-load device and hauled it away.

The article went on the say that Jim was a graduate of Tucson High and received his Master's Degree from the University of Arizona. Nowhere were the children and I mentioned, much to my relief. This was not the case with Jim's folks. Both were very unhappy that they were not referred to in the story. They were remembering the Second World War, when everyone was in favor of the military and families took pride in having their loved one's exploits written up in the local paper. I tried to explain why I had requested that our names be left out, but they did not understand.

With their Dad being gone for such a long time, I worried about the children forgetting him. I made sure we talked about Jim everyday, and at night the children always included him in their prayers and kissed his picture goodnight. They wrote letters and drew pictures to send to him. One day a package arrived that contained a small tape recorder and tapes. Jim had the other recorder with him, so we could 'talk' to each other. The first time we used it, Patrick had a problem understanding the concept. His conversation went like this:

"Hi, Dad….Dad?…… Dad? …..DAD?…..MOM, Dad's not answering me!"

That was Jim's favorite taped conversation.

One evening, as we were eating dinner, the children were in a fractious mood, arguing incessantly about some inconsequential subject. In an effort to cheer them up, I told them I would make a bibbity-bobbity-boop treat. "What is that?" they demanded.

"It is a surprise, so close your eyes." They did. I took out the box of food coloring and dropped in a lot of different hues of color into each glass of milk. After stirring the liquid, I said, "Bibbity-bobbity-boop-ZOT. Open your eyes!" The kids were surprised and thrilled with the purple, orange and green milk and, happily, their mood changed for the better.

"Let's do it again, Mama" they cried. So I complied, and we experimented with different colors of milk, which the kids quickly drank.

The next day I was in the kitchen when I heard, "MOM, COME QUICK!" I rushed into the bathroom to find Jimbo pointing to the toilet. Looking down into the bowl, I saw the most beautiful, tri-colored turd ever seen.

In June, Jim had been in Viet Nam for six months and was due for an R & R to Hawaii. My sainted sister Alice called and offered to take care of the children while I joined Jim. This was an amazing offer, as she and Bill lived in a very small four-bedroom house with five pre-teenage children in Ciniza, New Mexico. My niece Marilyn offered to care for Ringo and Charlie Brown while we were gone. We took a plane to Albuquerque, where Alice met us then drove us to Ciniza. The Loveless charges welcomed our little ones with enthusiasm, and our kids were in awe of their big, junior high-aged cousins. The family had two horses, and Jimbo and Patrick could not wait to learn to ride them. With the wide open spaces of New Mexico, there was loads of room to roam, and the warm weather kept the children happily playing outside. I stayed two days to see that the children got acclimated to the new situation. The boys had no problem taking directions from either Aunt Alice or Uncle Bill, but with Peggy, it was different. The children were expected to ask permission from Uncle Bill to be excused from the table when they were through eating and all complied, with the exception of two-year-old Peggy. The last night I was there, I purposely did not eat dinner with the family, instead choosing to stay in the other room, observing to see how my children behaved. Dinner was over and the seven older children politely asked to be excused, carried their plates to the kitchen and disappeared outside.

Peggy said to Uncle Bill, "I want to get down."

Calmly Bill answered, "You must ask to please be excused."

Peggy looked at Bill and pursed her lips together, defiantly. A few minutes later she said, "I want to get down."

Again Bill told her what she needed to say. Again he got the same stubborn response. Alice was still sitting at the table to show her support. Trying another tact, Bill smiled and pleasantly said, "Peggy, how should you ask to be excused?"

Peggy would have none of his charm and just glared at her uncle.

She tried again to get her way and Bill, with great patience, refused. This went on for fifteen minutes; it was a contest of wills between two tough, stubborn Titans. Finally, Peggy said, "I go potty." With that, Bill threw up his hands in total defeat. He looked at Alice and, with a resigned tone in his voice, said, "I give up!" He pushed his chair back and left the room. Peggy turned to Aunt Alice and with the most angelic smile and voice said, "Aunt Alice, may I please be excused?"

"Yes, you may, but don't you have to go potty?"

With a half-smile, my blond, blue-eyed cherub sweetly said, "No."

After that episode, I had no problem leaving my angels with Bill and Alice and, with a giggle, I flew to Honolulu. I arrived there the day before Jim and filled our hotel room with exotic flowers. As Jim got off the airplane, I put a lei around his neck and gave him a big kiss. He had lost a lot of weight and was sporting a moustache, but it was heaven to be with him. Jim was hungry for Mexican food, and we found the one Mexican restaurant in Honolulu. It was in a grubby part of the city, in a shabby, rundown, paint-peeled, ugly building. We ordinarily wouldn't have stepped inside such a mean hovel, but Jim was determined to get a Mexican fix. We had dinner and the meal was in the same shape as the building; ugly and terrible! What a disappointment!

It was hot and humid and, due to our northern European skin, we could not spend much time on the beach, but we soon discovered the Monkey Bar in Pearl Harbor. The drink of choice was a Blue Hawaiian, and we sat watching the monkeys cavorting behind the bar in a glass enclosure. It was such a pleasure to be able to have an adult conversation...to be able to ask a question and get an answer. I told Jim about getting the call late at night from the reporter and how scared I was.

"Jim, why was that reporter interviewing you?"

"It was no big deal. I happened to be coming in from picking up a couple of Huey's that had been shot down, and she was there asking questions."

"What do you mean, it was no big deal? The article sounded like it was a very dangerous mission."

"Babe, this is my job. I do this type of thing all the time. A chopper goes down, I go out, pick it up and bring it back for my maintenance team to repair. The very first assignment I got when we arrived in Phu Loi was to help evacuate a firebase. The division had a big move on, a fire broke out at one of the bases, so we went in, picked up the troops and then returned to get the 105 Howitzers and the ammo. By that time the fire was very close to all the ammunition, so it was a real hairy situation. We managed to retrieve all the ammo, as we flew off, we could see that the fire had engulfed the whole region."

"Are you ever fired on when you are on these rescue missions?"

"Sometimes. We had a close call once when one of our Chinooks went down in a rice paddy. I took a Chinook with my maintenance guys and a new engine, another pilot brought another Chinook in to take the crew of the downed copter and the guns back to our base. We worked like crazy to get the repairs done, but couldn't finish before dark. I had talked to the commander of the Special Forces camp that was about a quarter of a mile away from our downed aircraft, and he had assured me that during the daytime there was no problem with the Viet Cong. So when it became dark, I requested that the commander assist us in securing the area during the night. These 'brave' Special Forces guys refused, saying they never left their compound at night. We had ten guys, with Warrant Officer Hill, my assistant maintenance officer, myself and eight enlisted men. We staked out a perimeter about 100 yards from the chopper and kept watch at four-hour shifts. We took the guns off the chopper and had our personal weapons to protect us. The good news was that we were not attacked.

"Another time, we received incoming rocket mortars in the middle of the night. Wally Adams and I were sharing quarters, and we rolled out of our beds and dove underneath them. Outside our tent we had stacked sandbags three feet high for protection. I was between my bed and the refrigerator, so I was shielded on two sides. Some shrapnel came through our tent, but didn't do much damage. The Viet Cong got our supply trailer with all our records. The Air Cav was on the other side of the airbase, and they lost two Hueys and had several people wounded. One of our civilian mechanics had a leg wound. By the way, I saved a rocket motor as a souvenir. I'm using it as a bookend.

"But my real good news is that I am now the commanding officer of the 534th Transportation Aircraft Maintenance Company with the Aircraft Operational Detachment. I took it over last month, and I'm making some big changes."

"Jim, that's great. It sounds like you are enjoying this. How many men do you have?"

"I have 300 men, four officers and two warrant officers. I found a bit of a mess when I took it over, and you are right, I am having a good time making changes. The company had deep trenches dug all around the outside area in an effort to drain the excess rain away from the tents, but it only succeeded in filling up with putrid, mosquito-laden water. I've had them drained and filled up with dirt, making the ground slope away from the field. The men were working two eight-hour shifts and I've changed it to two twelve-hour shifts. The morale has improved because there is not so much idle time to grouse about their lot in life. On their time off, I've had them build some air raid shelters. We got some steel culverts, placed them over three foot trenches and put sandbags on top. We have five of them located around the compound, so that if we get a mortar attack everyone runs into those and stays safe."

Jim continued, "I have this interesting kid in the unit, PFC Hoffmann, from Pennsylvania. He's an artist, and one day I saw him drawing Hex signs, the kind the Pennsylvanian Dutch put on their doors to keep out the evil spirits. I've asked him to make enough to put on every door in the compound to keep the VC away. There's another kid named Shapiro, a skinny, little guy from someplace in the Northeast, a fast talker and a great negotiator. I've sent him to Saigon to trade with the Engineers. He's getting cement, plywood, screens, 2"x4"s and roofing, so the guys can build permanent barracks in their spare time. He's told the Engineers that he'll trade trips down to Vung Tau for some R&R if we can have the needed materials. So we fly the Chinooks to Saigon, pick up the Engineers, fly them down to the beach in Vung Tau, take them back to Saigon, pick up the supplies and go back to Phu Loi. We've completed two barracks, and the troops are so happy to be out of tents. It's amazing how hard those kids work when they have a goal to make their lives more comfortable. After we get everyone out of tents, we'll build a mess hall and orderly room."

"Who did the plans for all this building?"

"One of my Lt.'s has an engineering degree, and he has drawn the plans and is supervising the work. Also, we now have a shower. We got four tanks, bolted them together, sealed it and put it on a wooden stand to form a water tower. The height was limited due to the capacity of the pump. But now we have a shower. Everyone is getting enthusiastic about our building projects, and we never lack for volunteers. My first sergeant built a mailbox out of plywood that is an exact replica of the mailboxes back home. He's painted it blue with the official post office seal on it, so the kids have a place to mail their letters to their families." Jim had been talking nonstop for almost an hour, telling me all about his new job. It was obvious that, as always, Jim was making the best of any situation he finds himself in.

The week went by too fast, and once again I tearfully watched as Jim flew off, back to Viet Nam. I took a cab to the United Airlines terminal and flew back to Albuquerque.

As I expected, my kids had a wonderful time. The cousins, on the other hand, were getting a little tired of being bugged by the little ones. Alice informed me that Bill had just received orders to move back to the headquarters of Shell Oil in Houston, so they were getting ready to move and buy a house in time to get their children in school. I decided to take the kids to Boulder City, Nevada to visit my Aunt Lil and Uncle Bill before heading back to Tucson. I made arrangements to take the train to Kingman, Arizona, where Aunt Lil would pick us up. We were up at four o'clock in the morning in order to catch the six o'clock train in Albuquerque. Alice drove us to the station, and the children were so excited to be going on a train, especially since Aunt Alice had packed all kinds of goodies for them to snack on. We read, played games, drew pictures and ate snacks all the way across northern Arizona. Our porter was a tall, lean black man with a contagious laugh who spent a lot of time entertaining the children with card tricks. In the afternoon, the excitement, the early awakening and the monotonous scenery took its toll and all three of the kids fell sound asleep. I sat there, watching my angels and thinking about how much Aunt Lil and Uncle Bill meant to me.

Aunt Lil is my mother's oldest sister. She and Uncle Bill never had children but had always treated my siblings and me as her own. She was the vice-principal and dean of girls at the Boulder City High School; a tough but fair disciplinarian. Uncle Bill was from Arkansas with only a high school education, but he was a shrewd, calculating business man. He came to Nevada to work on the building of the Hoover Dam in the 30's, when that was the only job available during the Great Depression. He met Aunt Lil at a dance in Kingman, where she was teaching, and soon after that they were married. He realized that the workers on the dam had learned to like the dry, desert climate of Nevada and talked about staying permanently. He quickly figured out that more housing was needed, and he started building small frame homes which sold quickly. His business grew like Topsy and he prospered.

I first met Uncle Bill when Aunt Lil took Toddy and me to Boulder City after we had been in Los Angeles celebrating my grandparent's 50th wedding anniversary. We arrived a little after eleven and were met by Uncle Bill. I was twelve years old and wary of this stern-looking uncle. There was no air conditioning in those days, and the temperature was over 100 degrees. In spite of the heat, Aunt Lil promptly made a big dinner complete with the biscuits Uncle demanded. Todd and I were perspiring heavily as we helped her in the kitchen. When dinner was ready, Aunt Lil told me to sit to the left of Uncle. I wanted to butter my biscuit and saw that the butter was on his right. Very pleasantly, I said, "Uncle Bill, may I please have the butter?"

He looked at me with a frown on his face, then reached for the butter. I put my hand out to receive it and, as he passed to me, he suddenly flipped his hand so that my thumb went deep into the butter. With a shock I held up my thumb and, unlike little Jack Horner, I did not have a plum, but a blob of gummy butter on it. I looked at Uncle, expecting to see him angry. Instead his blue eyes twinkled merrily, and he laughed uproariously. The rest of us did too. From then on I was not afraid of Uncle Bill.

When I graduated from high school, Mom asked me to go to Boulder City to help Aunt Lil drive her mother-in-law back to Arkansas. I was thrilled to have the opportunity to see more of the country and excited to go to Boulder City. On the way up, I decided I would get even with Uncle Bill. When I saw him again, I was very subdued, almost rude, in acknowledging him. I made sure I was sitting next to him at dinnertime, and I purposely placed the butter away from him. He asked me for the butter and, as he reached for it, I flipped my hand so that his thumb plowed into the soft butter. I loved the shocked look on his face as I crowed, "I've been waiting five years to do this!" He laughed, and from then on we were buddies.

We were in Boulder City for a couple of days getting ready for the trip and then, early one morning, Aunt Lil, Grandma Honeycutt and I headed out on our way to Arkansas. We stopped at the

Grand Canyon and had a picnic the first day. Grandma Honeycutt couldn't sit in the car for a long time, so it took us three days to get to Bastrop, Louisiana, where one of Uncle Bill's sisters lived on a farm. This trip became a real eye-opener for me. When we stopped at a gas station in Texas, I discovered that a Negro was not allowed to drink from the same drinking fountain as I was.

"Are they kidding?" I asked Aunt Lil.

"I'm afraid not," she answered.

When we arrived at Aunt Bessie's farm, I discovered that I had to use an outhouse, as there was no indoor plumbing and, in place of toilet paper, there was Sears Roebuck catalogue. In spite of the heat, Aunt Lil would not let me go barefoot, because she was afraid I would contact worms. Two days later, we drove to El Dorado, Arkansas where I met a niece of Uncle Bill's. Her name was Janet, and we hit it off immediately. She took me to an outdoor skating rink, where her friends kept coming up to me asking me to say something. "You'all shure do tawlk funny. Ah just louuve yo accent," they would say. I couldn't believe that I had an accent. After visiting several relatives, Aunt Lil and I said goodbye. We headed toward New Orleans, stopping in Vicksburg and Natchez on the way. I was soaking up the scenery and history, especially about the 'Wah of Nauthern Aggression', as the natives called it. The anti-bellum homes were magnificent. In New Orleans we took a bus tour of the city and, as we left the bus ,the driver asked if we wanted to go on a night-time tour. "Oh, Aunt Lil, I would love to," I said.

"I'm not sure you should go to such places," she answered.

"Well, it is better that I go with you, isn't it?"

"I guess so," she answered and bought the tickets. That night I dressed in my big-skirted, apple green toile dress with the puffy sleeves and big sash. As I combed my hair, I thought I looked very sophisticated. We got the front seats in the bus as the tour started. We drove out to a large restaurant that advertised a stage show, and I figured it must be like the ones we had seen in Las Vegas. We were the first off the bus, and when we entered the restaurant, the maître'd showed us to a table in front of the stage. After dinner, the lights dimmed and a spotlight was pointed at the stage band as they started playing a rousing number. They played several pieces so loud we could not carry on a conversation and then, with a drum roll, a girl in an orange-and-chartreuse long dress made her entrance. She moved around the stage flipping a long faux fur stole, not dancing, but sort of marching, to the music. She flipped the stole over her shoulder and, in an instant, her skirt came off, revealing long, black, mesh-clad legs and an orange Bikini bottom. She continued her march, her high heels clicking in unison to the tune, the stole draped flirtatiously across her face so that only her eyes showed. With great drama, she threw the stole away and suddenly, she had no top, one nipple had an orange tassel attached and the other nipple had a chartreuse tassel. The music became a steady drum, drum, drum and the performer started moving her breasts so the tassels started twirling. First the tassels twirled the same way, then they twirled the opposite direction, going to the outside, and then they twirled inward so the tassels hit each other. I couldn't believe what I was seeing; I was staring in amazement at the talent, and I'm sure my mouth dropped open. Later, I learned that while Aunt Lil couldn't see my face, she was amused at the reaction of the band members. Instead of being bored, as was the usual case, the band members were in hysterics watching my shocked reaction to the performance. After I returned home, I took the tassels from the high school graduation mortarboards that Toddy and I had saved and taped them on my nipples. I tried to replicate the action I had seen in New Orleans – to no avail. And, boy, did it hurt to take them off!

The porter interrupted my reverie when he announced that we were arriving in Kingman. I shook the children awake and started gathering up our belongings. Aunt Lil met us at the depot and, as we got to the car, I saw Uncle Bill sitting in the front seat. My mother had told me that Uncle Bill had suffered a stroke, but I was not prepared for the change in him. One side of his face was inert, and he had trouble speaking. Aunt Lil kept a handkerchief nearby to frequently wipe the saliva dripping down his chin. As sad as that spectacle was, he still had a twinkle in his cobalt blue eyes.

We drove north to the Hoover Dam and stopped long enough for the kids to lean over the wall to see the vast expanse of the dam and, on the other side, the blue and beautiful Lake Mead. It was dinnertime when we arrived in Boulder City and, after eating, I bathed the kids and tucked them into bed.

The next day we took the children to the swimming pool, and after lunch Peggy took a nap while the boys went outside to play. Aunt Lil and I were having a good time visiting when, after a while, I realized I had not heard nor seen the boys. I went outside and called them…no answer. I told Aunt Lil I was going up to the pool to see if they were there. They were not. I started walking up to the park when I heard a car honk. Aunt Lil and Peggy were in her car, wanting to help with the search. The three of us drove all over the city looking for Jimbo and Patrick. As we returned to the house, I was beginning to panic. Then we saw a jeep with the boys inside. I leaped out of the car before Aunt Lil could stop. I thought some maniac had them, and I was ready to do battle when Aunt Lil called out, "George, what are you doing with my nephews?"

"Oh, Mrs. Honeycutt, do these boys belong to you?"

"Yes, they do, and this is their frantic mother. How did you happen to have them?" She turned to me and said, "Shirley, this is George Simmons, a former student of mine and now our deputy sheriff. George, why don't you have your uniform on?"

"I'm off-duty now, but I saw your nephews walking in front of my house. Since I didn't know them, I asked where they lived. My conversation with your oldest here sounded like Bud Abbott and Lou Costello!" He proceeded to describe his conversation with Jimbo, which went like this:

"What is your name?"

"Jimstark." (from the time he could talk, he always called himself that)

"Where do you live?"

"Tucson."

"Where is your Dad?"

"Viet Nam."

"What are you doing here?"

"Visiting Aunt Lil."

"Where is your mother?"

"At Aunt Lil's."

"Where does Aunt Lil live?"

"I don't know."

"At this point I said to your nephew, 'Why don't we drive around? Do you think you will recognize the house'?"

So they drove around, and Jimbo was able to recognize Aunt Lil's house. They had rung the doorbell, but Uncle Bill was taking a nap and didn't hear them.

The next day, Uncle Bill asked Aunt Lil to take him in the wheelchair to the backyard. There he ordered Jimbo to take the heavy clippers, climb the tall ash tree and trim the branches. Uncle was shouting directions, and Jimbo was following them. Jimbo was fifteen feet from the ground, and I was frightened that he would fall. I watched in amazement as our six-year-old wrapped his legs around the tree trunk while he trimmed the branches. He did a very good job, and Uncle paid him a silver dollar. Jimbo was so proud of himself! That night Uncle Bill said he wanted the children to see Las Vegas at night, so we piled into the car and toured the city. The children's favorite was the big, neon sign of the cowboy beckoning the gamblers with his hitch-hiking thumb waving back and forth.

We returned to Tucson and celebrated the fact that we had passed the half-year mark when Jim would be coming home from Viet Nam. In our absence, a new family had moved into a house three doors from us. They had a boy named Edgar, who was Jimbo's age. Jimbo and Edgar became inseparable; Edgar would show up at our house right after breakfast, and I usually had to send him home at dinnertime. His mother didn't seem to care where he was, but I always wanted to know what Jimbo was doing.

Patrick had an eye problem that our ophthalmologist said would probably require surgery but, before we went to that extreme, he wanted Pat to be seen by a Doctor England in Phoenix. He arranged for an appointment, and the kids and I drove north the one hundred miles to the Arizona capital. Dr. England turned out to be a six foot tall blonde, gorgeous gal to whom Pat took an immediate liking. Patrick was usually suspicious of strangers, but he really liked Dr. England and complied with any of her requests. Once a month, we would leave Ringo in the backyard and leave very early for our eleven o'clock appointment. After the checkup, we would stop for hotdogs and milkshakes, and then start back to Tucson.

After one of those trips, we arrived at our street to see several police cars and an ambulance blocking our way. A policeman walked toward our car, and I rolled down the window. "Why are you here?" he asked.

"We live in that house down there," I said, indicating our home. "What's wrong?"

"There has been an accident. Please keep going," He said in an officious manner.

When we got home, we saw several neighbors standing around, and we learned the awful truth. Edgar's fourteen year-old brother Mark had been playing with his dad's pistol that he had found in the nightstand. It was unloaded, but Mark knew his dad kept bullets in a box on the top shelf of the closet. The box contained several types of shells, and Mark tried them until he found a shell that fit. He was loading the shell when the gun accidently went off. Edgar was in the bathroom across the hall, combing his hair, when the bullet entered his temple. He died instantly. I was horrified to think that if we had not gone to Phoenix, Edgar would have been at our house and would still be alive. I had to explain something to the children, and then I reiterated to them what I had heard Jim say -- every gun is loaded and if you saw a gun you were not to touch it but to report to an adult immediately. What a tragic way to learn a lesson.

On the world front, Israel smashed the Arab coalition in the Six Day War, recapturing Jerusalem from Jordan; General Westmoreland called for more troops in Viet Nam; a 'peaceful' anti-war rally in Washington DC stormed the Pentagon, where participants burned draft cards; the Shah of Iran was crowned King of Kings in Tehran; black power advocates called for a revolution as vicious race riots ravaged major US cities and the first Negro, Thurgood Marshall, was confirmed as a Supreme Court justice.

Jim wrote, with great pride, that his company had completed the two buildings; one for the Orderly Room and Jim's office and the other one for the Mess Hall. Jim had a young kid from New Orleans who really knew how to cook. The word got around, and suddenly Jim's Mess Hall was becoming a meeting place for the top brass who wanted to get out of Saigon to see "what the war looked like." He reported that Hoffman, the kid he sent out to get materials for all the building projects, came back with a Jeep for Jim. Jim was stunned to learn that the Jeep was scheduled for a three-star general. He sent Hoffman back to where he had picked up the vehicle after yelling at him, "Do you want to get me kicked out of the Army?" "Oh, no sir, Major Starkey, I was only trying to do something nice for you since you have been so nice to me." Jim's comment in his letter was, "That would be a good example of killing me with kindness!"

One day we were driving on a dirt road on our way to Sabino Canyon. Jimbo suddenly yelled, "Mom, stop!" I slammed on the brakes, and saw that Jimbo was already leaving the car, running toward a fence. A Jack Russell dog was hanging from a fence-pole. The dog had been barking at our car, jumping up and down as if on a pogo stick, when the fence pole got caught between his collar and his neck, choking him. Jimbo quickly grabbed the dog and lifted him up so that the dog to could breathe. I unhooked the dog from the fence pole and, after a cough, the dog was fine. We drove up to the house to let the owner know what had happened. The lady was very grateful and very impressed with the quick thinking of Jimbo. He literally saved the dog's life.

September came, and it was time for Jimbo to start school. As the days grew cooler, the time seemed to go faster. Soon it was Halloween, with all the fun of that holiday. I was working on the kid's costumes when I received a phone call from Jim. He was on R & R in Hong Kong. We talked for several minutes, exchanging information, and then he said he had seen a red Turkoman carpet and did I want it? Is the Pope Catholic? Of course I wanted it. "I'll go buy it right now," he said with a laugh.

"Do you know where we will be sent when your tour of Viet Nan is over?" I asked. He still had not received any word on his next assignment, but was hoping to be home by Christmas. I wanted the phone call to go on forever; just hearing his voice sustained me for days.

Tucson was growing rapidly, and most of the schools were on split shift. My niece, Marilyn, attended Palo Verde High School on 22nd Street, in the morning shift. One night Ringo, our comical basset hound, escaped from the yard and disappeared. The children and I toured the neighborhood calling and whistling for him, to no avail. At six o'clock the next morning, I was awakened by the ringing of the phone. It was Marilyn, calling to say that Ringo was at the school. I leapt out of bed, threw on some clothes and leaving the sleeping children, drove like mad to Palo Verde High School to collect our pet. Every day Marilyn got a ride with her English teacher, who always came to school early. As her teacher pulled up in his usual parking place, Ringo was just sitting there. Marilyn frequently came to our house after school and had taken care of Ringo on several occasions, so Ringo knew her well. We could only surmise that Ringo had become lost and, being a hound, smelled Marilyn at that parking place and decided to wait for her. The amazing thing is that Palo Verde High School is three miles from our house.

Ringo was a great dog in many ways. He would lie on the floor and allow the kids to put Charlie Brown, our cockatiel, on his back. Charlie would walk up and down, and Ringo never flinched. If the kids were taking a bubble bath, frequently Ringo would join them, much to their delight. They would make bubble hats on the top of his head and laugh uproariously. When playing on their swing set, Ringo would go down the slide with them. He was a good pal. But something strange was starting to happen. Sometimes Ringo would growl at the children when they were playing. I couldn't understand it until the lady who lived behind us told me that, when we left Ringo outside while on our long trips to Phoenix for Pat's eye appointments, the boys next door would throw rocks at him. The boys, brothers nine and ten-years old, were the scourge of the neighborhood, always causing trouble, swearing and starting fights. We had experienced a couple of run-ins when the boys were teasing Jimbo and Pat. I talked to their mother, who turned out to be as bad as her kids, so from then on I told Jimbo to avoid them. I started leaving Ringo in the house when we left. One morning Peggy petted Ringo while he was snoozing, and Ringo turned and growled at her. That night I was preparing to cook a round steak for dinner when the kids called me into the living room to see Batman on TV. I watched with them for a few minutes, then went back to the kitchen. The steak had disappeared. I looked around and under the dining room table was our happy Ringo with the steak in his mouth. I grabbed him with one hand and the steak with the other, trying to get it away from him. He growled fiercely, and I commanded him to let go. He growled even harder, and I started pulling on the steak. Suddenly, he let go, only to grab my wrist. He was biting hard, and I knew I had a no choice; if I wanted my hand I had to give him the steak. I did so and also decided I had to get rid of him. He hurt me badly, and I knew if he ever bit one of the children he would break bones, plus cause some major psychological trauma.

Margaret, my mother-in-law, worked with a lady whose husband had a basset hound and wanted another. The children and I took Ringo to her house and met the husband George, a big, burly fireman. He immediately accepted Ringo and then told us that his basset hound was always pulling the laundry off the clotheslines. He thought if he had two they would only play each other. On the way home, we laughed, knowing that there would now probably be two basset hounds tearing the clothes off the lines!

The children immediately started a campaign for another dog. I remembered how the pug named Pug had been such a good dog and decided that was the breed to get. The next week we acquired a blond male pug. Jimbo wanted to name him Bandit after the dog on the TV show *Johnny Quest*. When Pat and Peg agreed, the decision was made.

Christmas was rapidly approaching, and Jim wrote that we would be going to Ft. Eustis - and that there was a chance he would be home for Christmas. I tried not to get my hopes up, but worked hard getting everything ready, just in case. I really splurged and paid $20.00 for a perfect tree. The kids and I decorated everything in sight. Three days before Christmas, I got a letter from Jim saying he wouldn't get home until after the New Year. I was so disappointed, but decided the tree would stay up so Jim could see it. I tried to keep it looking nice, but it started shedding, just like my hopes. In the end, fearing a fire hazard, I pitched it.

Another letter came with the news that 'maybe' Jim would be home for New Years and not to plan on meeting him at the airport. He would take a cab home. I only confided this news to my parents, not wanting the children or Jim's folks to get their hopes up. New Years Eve the house was spotless, the children and I watched the ball drop on Times Square ushering in 1968, after which I put them to bed. I changed into a sexy negligee I had purchased and waited and watched old movies until I fell asleep on the couch. At three a.m. I awoke and went to bed.

New Year's Day, Jim was still in Viet Nam. His roommate announced that he was giving up smoking for his New Year's resolution. Jim decided to do the same and made a bet of $1.00 that he would not be the first to break the resolution. Jim has not touched a cigarette since that time, as he doesn't want to lose the $1.00! After a frantic two days, I heard from Jim that he was on his way home and at six in the morning of January 4th he called from the Los Angeles airport, angry at the plane delays. He said he was scheduled to be on the next flight and should be in Tucson by 9 a.m. barring any other delays. I flew around getting the kids up, dressed and breakfasted and just made it into the terminal in time to see Jim coming down the ramp, smiling broadly. The kids raced at him, almost knocking him down, each clamoring to hug him. He wore the biggest smile I have ever seen and, to me, it was such a relief to have him home safely. As we walked in our front door the phone was ringing and Grampa Starkey was demanding to know when Jim was coming home. "He just arrived!" I shouted, "Come over right now!"

My hero came back with a bunch of medals: the Legion of Merit, two Bronze Stars for valor, a dozen Air Medals with V's for valor and a myriad of Vietnamese medals. But more important than that, he came home.

Chapter 15

Ft. Eustis, Virginia 1968-1969

Once again we were mired in organizing for a move. Jim decided we needed to get a new car and settled on the biggest station wagon Ford built. The kids were happy to have plenty of room for themselves, Bandit and Charlie Brown. The movers came, packed us; we cleaned the house; cleared with the real estate lady; said goodbye to family and friends and started across country to Ft. Eustis, Virginia. In the previous year Shell Oil had relocated the Alice's family to Houston, and Toddy's family had left Houston and been relocated to Atlanta, Georgia due to Uncle Joe being transferred by Johns Manville Company. My mom and dad were constantly changing listings in their address book, trying to keep up with their nomadic daughters!

We headed out on Interstate 10 toward Houston. For Christmas, Alice had sent Peggy a tiny turquoise cross. I bought a white short-sleeved sweater and pink pleated skirt for her, and as we got close to the Loveless home, Peggy insisted I let her change into that outfit, so Aunt Alice would be impressed. I clamored over the two seats, in order to reach the suitcases in the back of the station wagon. I was bent over the seat, frantically searching through the luggage for the requested items, all the while Jim was yelling at me for directions on what streets to take. This was the ultimate in multi-tasking that we modern women are famous for! I found the map and gave the directions to Jim while I changed Peggy's clothes. As we drove up the tree-lined street, Jimbo spotted Alice in front of the house, talking to a neighbor. As soon as the car stopped, the boys rushed out to ask Alice where Donald and Eddie were. I helped Peggy out of the car and grabbed Bandit's leash. As I turned to greet my sister, I noticed Peggy, her nose in the air, regally walking past Alice, not saying a word. Alice looked startled, and I whispered, "Peggy insisted on changing into that outfit for your benefit."

Immediately Alice gushed, "Oh, Peggy, don't you look pretty!"

Peggy grinned, very pleased and sweetly said, "Hello, Aunt Alice," and followed her brothers into the house.

My kids were so excited to see their big cousins again, and the boys went outside to start a basketball game while Peggy was invited into Virginia and Bonnie's room. Susan and I helped Alice in the kitchen, where we prepared dinner. We ate barbeque that night while we caught up on family gossip.

The next day we continued our journey, stopping at Todd's house in Atlanta. Todd's twins, Karen and John, were born three months after Peggy's birth. It was fun to watch the almost three year-old 'triplets' interact. At first Karen was excited to have a new girl friend but, when she noticed John following Peggy, her attitude changed. She started physically dragging John away from Peg. Poor Johnny... caught between two aggressive females at such a young age! Todd's husband, Joe Caid, was a remarkable cook when it came to Mexican food. That night Jim and Joe drank Scotch as they worked in the kitchen, Jim being the *sous chef,* following Joe's directions.

Jim and Joe had been friends since both were active in football and baseball at Catalina Junior High and later at Tucson High. While Jim was on a baseball scholarship at the University of Arizona, Joe was in the Marines in Korea and, after Joe got out of the Marine Corps and was getting his Engineering Degree at the University of Arizona on the G.I. bill, Jim was in Korea. After Joe came back from Korea, he married Toddy, and after Jim came home from Korea, he married me. They constantly gave each other a bad time about their respective military assignments. Joe would make snide remarks about pilots not getting their fingernails dirty, and Jim would tell Joe the Marines are still looking for a few good men. It was all in good fun, and they respected each other. Those two guys had a connection on several levels and were really good friends.

While all the food we ate that night was amazing, the very best was Joe's signature dish, *chili relleanos*. I've never tasted better *chili relleanos*, although I try that dish in every Mexican restaurant we visit. Joe suggested we come back in the summer so we could camp at a beautiful national park in the mountains of northern Georgia. We made plans to invite the Loveless family to join us. We left the next morning for our final push to Virginia.

When we arrived at Ft. Eustis, we got the bad news that there was a two month wait for post housing. We had discovered long ago that it was preferable to live on post rather than among civilians, who generally took a jaundiced view of the life of the vagabond military, which they considered only a step away from being gypsies. This was especially true in the South where, if you couldn't prove that your great-grandfather had served honorably in the 'Great Cause of the Wah Between the States,' you were not worth knowing. We didn't want to sign the required one-year lease on an expensive civilian house, so this meant a furnished apartment in the Stoneybrook area just south of the post. We settled in as best we could, registered Jimbo in school, and Jim bought a dark green Morris Minor car for his transportation to and from post.

This is where it gets to be fun being an Army wife. Not every woman is cut out for unexpected surprises, but I love challenges - and this certainly turned out to be one. For two months I would have to make do in a small two-bedroom furnished apartment with the minimum kitchen utensils. Did I say 'minimum'? How about a beat-up, one-quart pan with lid, one very small frying pan with a broken handle, a two-piece toaster, four place settings of bent aluminum silverware, four plastic plates, cups and saucers? Obviously, a trip to the PX was in order. After dropping Jimbo off at school, Patrick, Peggy and I went shopping. Good food and the preparation of it is very important in our family; we always ate together, usually around five-thirty, when Jim would come home. I cannot cook without the proper equipment, which is why my kitchen has ended up with duplicates and sometime triplicates of just about every utensil, gadget and gismo that I think I cannot live without.

The news was full of the Tet Offensive, the shocking attack by the Vietnamese communists that started on the last day of January. Tet is the Vietnamese New Year, occurring during the first seven days of the lunar year. A Tet truce had been negotiated between South Vietnam and the communists, as it had been in past years, but the Viet Cong General Giap ignored it, launching a broad surprise offensive that spread from the cities of the Mekong Delta to Saigon and up to the Highlands. Even the American Embassy was breached for a period of six hours before the attack was repulsed. The Americans and South Vietnamese counter-attacked and crushed the Viet Cong. It stunned our nation, as well as the world, as this was the first time the Viet Cong had moved out of the jungles into the cities. This was seen on the television sets all over the world and, though the offensive was a failure for the Viet Cong from a military viewpoint, it rallied the antiwar protesters and caused Senator Robert Kennedy to declare that the United States could not win the Vietnam War. Years later, General Giap wrote in his autobiography that the Viet Cong were ready to give up after suffering such a horrendous defeat during the Tet offensive but hung on after viewing the televised antiwar riots from America.

At the same time, the North Koreans captured the *Pueblo,* a U.S. surveillance ship captained by Commander Lloyd Bucher, saying the ship had "intruded into the territorial waters of the republic and was carrying out hostile activities." A tense confrontation ensued between the United States and North Korea with American forces in South Korea being placed on military alert. It was an election year, and Minnesota Democratic Senator Eugene McCarthy announced he was running for the presidency against Lyndon B. Johnson. He was an anti-war candidate with the slogan, "Come clean for Gene." He won 40% of the vote in the New Hampshire Democratic primary. The next day, New York Senator Robert Kennedy announced his candidacy. Two weeks later, bowing to the public's 26% approval rating on his running of the Viet Nam war, President Johnson stunned the nation by declaring that he would not seek a second term. Five days later, Martin Luther King was assassinated and riots broke out between the blacks and police in major cities across the nation. Chicago, Washington DC, Baltimore and Cincinnati were hit the hardest, but civil disorder occurred in smaller locations, even in Newport News south of Ft. Eustis. During all this time the military was on full alert, going into a riot prevention mode, and we saw very little of Jim.

After a tense two months, calm was restored, and Jim received word that we could move on post. I heaved a sigh of relief. We moved into a three-bedroom duplex on Summerville Circle. Our backyard extended forty yards to the dense woods and, beyond that, was a bluff that ended in a stream that fed a small lake. Someone had tied a thick rope over a large branch. The knots in the rope made a perfect swing. The neighborhood kids introduced Jimbo to grabbing onto the rope and swinging out over the bluff. Of course, Pat, and even little Peggy, wanted to try it. The things kids do to give a mother a heart attack!

Military life tends to be either good or bad as far as living conditions are concerned, but life within the military is a warm nest where, as an officer's wife, you always have a place, depending upon your husband's rank and position. You are immediately welcomed with invitations to dinner parties, luncheons, teas, and bridge games. This tradition goes back to the time of the winning of the west where army posts were isolated and social life, by necessity, revolved within the military community. It is still true today, because you are far away from your hometown, parents, siblings and school friends. You make friends easily and bond quickly with special confidants. The people you meet all have the same life experiences. The children, referred to as 'Army Brats,' adjust quickly as long as they have plenty of other brats to play, laugh and fight with. They tend to grow up to be accomplished, successful adults, able to take in stride whatever life throws at them. We always told our children that while we didn't live in the same house forever, our roots were within the family. To this end, we had special rituals that were constant, no matter where we were living. One of them was to sit down together to share our evening meal, and after Grace we would toast each other with the boys saying, "To us," and the girls saying, 'Forever.' As everyone launched into enthusiastic eating, one person would start Purple Pig. He or she would put a finger on the side of his/her nose, and the last person to emulate the action was declared the Purple Pig. That person would be responsible for starting the game at the next meal. It kept everyone conscious of their surroundings and their head out of their plate.

The movers arrived and got us unpacked. Jim, being a Transportation officer, insisted the movers unpack everything to make sure there was no damage or missing items. I hated that, because it became an uncontrollable chaos with opened boxes everywhere and kids grabbing out special toys they had missed. My first chore was to find the bedding as soon as the movers set up the beds so the family could get a good night's sleep. Next order was the kitchen so the family could eat. It generally took a good week before we were really settled, and when the paintings were on the wall, it felt like home at last. That's when the sewing machine came out, and I started making or redoing curtains and drapes. I had a foot locker full of curtains that never seemed to match the windows of our newest abode.

In June, Robert Kennedy won the California Democratic primary and was shot by Sirhan Sirhan, a Jerusalem-born Jordanian. Prayer vigils were held, but the senator from New York died twenty hours later. Within four years the two Kennedy brothers and Martin Luther King were assassinated, campuses were being overrun with student demonstrations and Negros were holding sit-ins all over the South. It seemed as if our country was falling apart.

Summer time arrived, and after conference calls between Alice, Toddy and me, it was decided that the families would go to a campsite at Noon Tootla in northern Georgia after first converging at Todd's home to get organized. My sisters and I went to the supermarket for the supplies. Alice immediately whipped into the manager's office to tell him that we were planning a huge family reunion and to ask if we could have a deal on the prices. Toddy was chagrined, especially when Alice made it sound as if the reunion was for hundreds. The manager complied and gave us a ten percent discount. On the way home, Toddy grumbled that she would not be able to face the manager from then on. "Oh, Todd, don't worry about it. Managers do that all the time. You just have to ask them," Alice assured her. Soon after Jim met Alice at our wedding, he recognized that Alice was always taking charge - and from then he referred to her as 'Big Al.' That day she definitely proved that she was Big Al!

We started off early the next morning, going north almost to the

South Carolina border. We passed miles of fields of crops with pine and oak forests entwined in kudzu until the road started moving into the foothills of the Great Smoky Mountains. We were pulling a pop-up trailer so getting it up the steep inclines to the top of the mountain was challenging. Soon we set up camp, Joe and Jim dug a hole for a latrine, we took turns cooking and cleaning up, the fathers and the big kids went hiking and fishing while the three mothers watched the 'triplets.' The weather was perfect, no one got hurt and it was a memorable three days.

As we were driving back to Ft. Eustis, we heard on the radio that Russian tanks had moved into Prague, Czechoslovakia in a crackdown on the more liberal government of Alexander Dubcek. There were thousands rioting in the streets, with angry Czechs fighting back with guns, Molotov cocktails, sticks and even bare hands. Chicago also witnessed rioting as the Democratic convention was underway. Anti-war protestors were bludgeoned by the Chicago police during a demonstration, and over one hundred were hurt, including some children. The crowds were unhappy that the Democrats had nominated Hubert Humphrey for president, over the anti-war candidates Eugene McCarthy and George McGovern. In Miami, the Republicans nominated Richard Nixon, who proclaimed that his first priority was to bring an honorable end to the war in Viet Nam. At the Olympics in Mexico City, Tommy Smith and John Carlos were ousted for raising their fists in a black power salute while getting their medals; Arthur Ashe was the first black male to win a major tennis title, the U.S. Open; and finally, the Princess of Camelot, Jacqueline Kennedy, stunned the world by marrying Aristotle Onassis.

School started, and Jimbo entered second grade while Patrick started kindergarten. I took Pat to school the first day, but after that he was to catch the bus in front of our quarters. I was nervous that he would be scared, so when the bus arrived, Pat got on - and immediately Peggy and I got in our car and followed the bus. I thought we were being sneaky, but after school Pat said to me, "Mom, how come you and Peggy were following the bus?"

Feeling guilty at being found out I answered, "Well, I just wanted to make sure you got to school okay." Frowning, Patrick confidently answered, "Don't worry about me, Mom. I can take care of myself."

Jim bought bikes for himself and me. On his bike he attached a seat over the back fender for Peggy to ride in, and the family took frequent trips along the many bike trails around Ft. Eustis. Jim was the leader, then came Pat, then Jimbo and finally I brought up the rear. One glorious October day we were riding the trail that paralleled the Potomac River. The cloudless sky was manganese blue, the trees glowed in various shades of red, orange and yellow and there was slight breeze blowing. I was in a happy mood and thought to myself, *This is a perfect day.* And just as suddenly, coldness came over me. *It's too perfect, something is going to happen.* This thought shook me up and a few moments later I saw Peggy fall off Jim's bike. I rushed over to her and found that she was fine, just a little shaken. I was relieved that my premonition of disaster was unfounded, and we went on with our bike ride.

The next afternoon I received a phone call from my mother-in-law, Margaret. "Dad is dead," she said.

"What are you saying? Who is dead?"

"Dad is dead. He died a little while ago while sitting on the couch. The medics just took him away," She answered in a trembling voice.

I slowly sank to the floor, not wanting to understand what she had just told me. How could this be? Grandpa was only 59 years old; he was planning on retiring in three more years.

"Grandma, I'll call Jim, and he will call you as soon as he can," I told her. It was Monday and I knew he had an important meeting that day. I called his office and told the sergeant to get Jim on the phone immediately. When he answered the phone there was a shocked silence as I related the news to him and in a broken voice he said, "I'll be home as soon as I can clean up some things here. Call the airlines and get me a reservation. And you better pack my civilian suit."

I called the airlines and made reservations for all of us for early the next morning. I called my dad and asked him to meet us at the airport at noon. My neighbor said she would take care of Bandit and Charlie Brown. By the time Jim got home, I had all of us packed. He was surprised that I had decided that all of us should go to Tucson but was very pleased. Early the next morning we drove to Newport News and flew back to Tucson.

Upon arriving, we learned that Grandpa had suffered a heart attack and that he had been in the Southern Pacific Hospital in San Francisco for the month of September. Margaret had failed to tell us, that not wanting to upset her precious son. Considering that Grandpa smoked two to three packs of Camels every day, was worried about his son being in Viet Nam and upset with Margaret's drinking, it is not surprising his heart gave out. He was one of the kindest men I have ever known, and the saddest part was that my children would not have him in their lives.

As soon as I heard Margaret say she wanted an open casket at the funeral, I immediately made arrangements for the children to stay with Mrs. O'Reilly, a neighbor from our Malvern house, while the funeral was going on. Margaret was furious with me that the children would not be attending. I tried to explain that I wanted the children to remember their Grandpa as laughing and tickling them not as a cold corpse. She did not understand, but Jim backed me on the decision.

The day after the funeral, the children and I flew back to Virginia while Jim stayed behind to deal with the financial and legal matters. One afternoon, I looked out the back door and saw an enormous turtle walking out of the woods, heading toward our house. I ran out, calling to Peggy and Patrick. I grabbed a metal chair and large box the kids had been playing with, held it over the turtle and captured the monster. I wanted to hold onto him until Jimbo came home from school, so he could see it. We kept piling things on top of the box to secure it as the turtle struggled to get away. Jimbo arrived fifteen minutes later, and we somehow got the turtle into our wagon. By this time, we had eight or ten other children with us. I pulled the wagon while Jimbo and some of the older boys held the box, the other kids trailed behind. We looked like the Pied Piper leading the rats as we started down to the creek to turn the turtle loose. The ground was steep as we approached the water, and suddenly the wagon tipped over. I jumped out of the way as the turtle made a mad dash down the hill and into the creek and disappeared into the muddy waters. I called Jim that evening and told him of our experience and was chastised vigorously. "Are you crazy? Don't you know those snapping turtles can take your arm off? Babe, quit taking chances like that. Let the kids read about such animals or see them in the zoo."

I shrugged, "I thought it would be an interesting story Jimbo could share at Show and Tell. I guess once a teacher always a teacher."

After two weeks, Jim called and said that it would take six weeks to get Margaret's Social Security and Railroad Retirement benefits coming in, so he was bringing her back with him to live with us. He rented one of the rooms in Margaret's home to an old neighbor, Mrs. Powder, so the house would be occupied. He told me to lock up all the liquor in the cedar chest in our bedroom. Post engineers brought us a single bed for Peggy to use in the boy's room. I fixed up Peg's room for Grandma Margaret so she would have some privacy. She did not appreciate my efforts and turned out to be a very difficult house guest. At first I tried to entertain her, including her in invitations I received. We went to a luncheon at the Officers Club, and we were standing at the head of the staircase when Mrs. Evans, the commanding general's wife, arrived. I whispered to Margaret, "That lady in the black dress is the commanding general's wife," knowing this would impress her. Margaret, leaning over the banister and squinting her eyes said, in very loud voice, "She's not very attractive, is she?"

I grabbed her and quickly pulled her into the dining room and hissed, "You can't say things like that. Do you want to ruin Jim's career?"

She looked at me blankly, not saying a word, but behaved herself the rest of the day. She had almost nothing to do with the children. To my disappointment, there were no card games or conversations between Grandma and the kids. She did question Pat about where the key to the cedar chest was, apparently suspecting that we kept the liquor there. She refused to make her own bed when I requested that she do so and, with an imperious tone said, "You are not treating me like a guest at all."

"What do you mean?' I yelled. "I have a husband, three kids, a house to take care of, meals to prepare, laundry to do, the only thing I ask of you is to keep your room in good order." She put her nose in the air, walked in her room and slammed the door. "Now I know what it is like to have a teenager in the house," I reported to Jim when he came home that night.

Margaret spent most of the day moaning and groaning that "Herman (Grandpa) had no right to leave me. What am I supposed to do?" In my kindest voice I would try to reason with her to no avail...she would end up saying she was going to kill herself. After listening to this threat several times, I lost my temper and snapped, "Stop talking about it and do it."

With a shocked look on her face, Margaret retorted, "I would never do that...that would be a sin." But it worked – she never again threatened to kill herself.

I became a Top Sergeant, forcing her to take a bath, standing in the doorway while she bathed. I tried to talk to Jim about it, but he thought I was exaggerating. Years before, Grandpa had told me that when Jim told Margaret that he was going to marry me she was so dispirited she called her sister, Agnes, and the two of them cried for three days. I thought he was exaggerating, but now I know it was true. I now know I did not marry the son, I married 'The Sun.'

Margaret was a fairly good cook, but her specialty was macaroni and cheese. The soft, cheese-infused pasta was delicious, and while it was a favorite of everyone, Jimbo was especially fond of it. "Mom, do you think Grandma will make macaroni and cheese while we are at the scout meeting?" he asked one morning. I was the leader of Jimbo's Cub Scout troupe, and we met at the home of Yolanda Peterson, my assistant. Lt. Col. Peterson was an instructor at the school, and was scheduled to stay in Ft. Eustis until his retirement - so unbeknownst to the post engineers he had enclosed the back porch of his quarters, making it into a large family room. It was a great place for our meetings, especially in inclement weather. Since I wouldn't be home until six o'clock, I thought Jimbo's request would solve the problem of what we should have for dinner.

"Margaret, would you make your wonderful macaroni and cheese dish for dinner tonight? I asked in my sweetest voice.

Margaret looked at me blankly and said, "I don't know how to make macaroni and cheese."

"What are you talking about? You always make it for us. It's

Jimbo's favorite meal," I said with a quizzical look on my face.

In a very determined voice, she answered, "I have never made macaroni and cheese in my life!" She stuck her nose in the air and walked into her room. She left me with my mouth hanging open.

Our routine, when Jim walked in the door at a little after five, was the same; the kids would hug him and he would play and talk with them a few minutes, then they would leave to go outside or to their room. Then he and I would sit and visit for about fifteen minutes before I put dinner on the table. Margaret was a devious witch and would do nothing all day until she saw Jim driving up – then suddenly she would be very busy unloading the dishwasher. She thought we were in a contest for Jim's approval. One time Jim said to me, "Are you letting my mother do everything around this house?"

"Don't kid yourself," I sarcastically said, "this is the first work she has done all day." I did not mention to Jim all the problems Margaret and I had, as I knew it would do no good. He worked hard all day and didn't need problems at home. Besides that, I thought I could handle everything myself. One evening Jim and I had a disagreement about something, and he laid the law down in no uncertain terms. When I glanced at Margaret, she had a satisfied smirk on her face as if to say 'Ha Ha, you lost.' I got so mad that when we went to bed later, I couldn't sleep. It was after eleven when I heard a noise in the hallway and the door to the big closet being opened. I crept to the door and saw Margaret reach in the extra refrigerator for a gallon bottle of red wine we kept there. I woke Jim, and as he went into the hallway he caught Margaret red-handed, chugging the wine. A big yelling match ensued, and she fled back to her room, slamming the door.

"I thought she was only interested in the hard stuff," he remarked, coming back to bed. "We'll have to get rid of the wine tomorrow." He promptly went back to sleep as I lay there thinking how lucky we had been that Jim made a career of the Army. I knew that if we had stayed in Tucson, she would have broken us up. I was so innocent and all-trusting when we married, she would have rolled over me like a Sherman tank. But not now, not after I had survived living in Iran.

Pat and Jim's birthdays arrived with each of them receiving baby alligators (or caimans). Margaret told us we had lost our minds getting the boys such pets and she refused to even touch them. However, she did approve of the two water turtles we bought for Peggy.

A big storm blew in the day before Christmas, and the temperature plunged. I had placed Charlie Brown's cage by the Christmas tree next to the big windows so she could enjoy the lights. Unfortunately, it was so cold that night a draft came in from the windows freezing Charlie. There was a wail of shock when, in the morning, the children discovered their beloved pet dead. The presents from Santa Claus got ignored for just a moment while I tried to comfort them, but soon they were excited about their presents. Later in the day, Jimbo got a shoebox, while Pat and Peggy found clean rags to place in the home-made casket for Charlie. They reverently buried their pet in the flower bed next to the front door.

The first of January, Margaret's pensions came through and it was time for Margaret to return to Tucson, an event I had looked forward to. It hit me hard how dumb I had been to keep Jim in the dark about my problems with Margaret when he announced to me, "Having my Mom live with us is working out so well, why don't we buy a house in Stoneybrook so she can live with us permanently?"

Shocked and without thinking, I snapped, "You do that and I'll divorce you!"

Jim's eyes flew open wide in surprise, and I broke down crying and dashed into his arms. He said quietly, "It's been that bad, huh?"

"Yes," I answered, "it's been that bad." Two days later, he put Margaret on the plane for Tucson. Knowing her proclivity for alcohol, Jim maintained total control of Margaret's finances, depositing an allowance in her checking account every month. He had the bank statements sent to our address so he could monitor her spending. It was a relief to have the house to ourselves again.

Jim was very enthusiastic about his job. He was given the task of designing and heading the computer department for the Transportation School, the first Army school to have such a department. He was sent up to Rome, New York to contract with IBM for timesharing. He came back to describe this fancy new machine, the

311

size of our duplex that was able to store all kinds of information. As usual, he did an outstanding job and was promoted to Lt. Colonel and received orders to attend Command and Staff College in Ft. Leavenworth in June.

In November the Republican ticket of Richard Nixon/Spiro Agnew had won the presidency. In December the three man Apollo eight team were the first astronauts to circle the moon. This was a proud moment for us because the captain of the mission was Frank Borman, who graduated from Tucson High, the class of 1948.

Just before Christmas, my Mom called to tell us Uncle Bill had died. We sent a single rose in a vase to Aunt Lil with a note that said, "Chin up, Auntie, we love you." She wrote the nicest letter saying that rose really cheered her up and she wanted to come see us. We looked forward to it. Aunt Lil was five feet two inches tall and almost as wide, with thick glasses that magnified her eyes - and with a hearty laugh, she was great fun. She was due to arrive in April, and we were looking forward to it.

In addition to the alligators and turtles, the kids started collecting other critters. The Siamese cat next door kept bringing baby rabbits home, dropping them on our back porch and the kids insisted I save them. Try as I might, the bunnies always died. We also had baby blue jays to try to nurse back to health, but I was a total failure as a vet. Jimbo found a little green snake which he kept in a terrarium in his room, and it survived for many months. Two days before Aunt Lil arrived, the snake disappeared. We looked everywhere, to no avail. I told the kids not to mention the lost snake to Aunt Lil. We picked her up at the airport, and her smile was a welcome sight. She loved being with the kids, and she taught them to play King's Corner, a card game, and loved to read to them. Peggy would sit on her lap and hit the skin that hung down from her arms, making the fat swing back and forth. Aunt Lil would laugh at that. On the weekend, we took her all over Williamsburg, Yorktown and Jamestown. She always wanted to pay for everything but Jim would never let her.

Monday Jim went to work and Jimbo went to school, so Pat, Peggy, Aunt Lil and I set out for Ft Monroe to see where the Marimac and Monitor had their famous sea battle during the Civil War. Pat wanted to take Bandit, and I allowed it. We found a parking place close to the ramp that led up to the fort. We got to the top and looked all around the Chesapeake Bay, reading the information about the naval battle that helped change the course of the Civil War. Bandit kept tugging at the leash, wanting to sniff every tree and bush and, seeing that there were not many people around, I released him. There was a two foot wall all around the area. Suddenly, Bandit leaped up on it and to my shock, disappeared. I ran to the wall and looked down. There, twenty feet below, Bandit was lying on the cement, not moving. Horrified, I started running toward the ramp calling to Aunt Lil, "Bandit just fell off the wall." Aunt Lil held Peggy's hand and tried to grab Pat, but he bolted after me. We reached Bandit, who was still alive. His eyes were open, his tongue was hanging out in a strange way and he was hyperventilating. I was frozen and didn't know what to do. Miraculously, just then a garbage truck came around the corner. Two men got out and came over to see what had happened. I told them that Bandit had just fallen, and one of the men went to the truck and pulled out a large piece of cardboard. The two of them scooted Bandit onto the cardboard and gently carried him to the back of our station wagon. "Ma'am, there is a vet clinic right outside the main gate of the fort on the right." I thanked them profusely while Aunt Lil and Peggy climbed in the front seat. Patrick was in the back seat, his hand on Bandit's head, keeping him quiet. I drove as quickly as I could, just daring the MP"s to stop me for speeding. Bandit started howling and scooting around, dragging his feet. Aunt Lil kept telling Pat not to touch Bandit as he might get bitten; Pat ignored her and continued to try to calm Bandit. As we left the fort, there was a large sign with the words, 'Veterinary Clinic' in large letters. I heaved a sigh of relief as I parked the car and dashed into the building, loudly stating my problem. The receptionist immediately got the vet, who followed me out to the car. He reached in to where Bandit was, grabbed his rump and scruff of his neck, quickly picked him up and went into the office. I followed, amazed at the ease with which the vet acted. He went into the back room, closed the door and I waited. Soon he returned and said, "Your dog is in shock and I gave him a shot. I will examine him as soon as he comes out it. You'll have to leave him here overnight. Call me in the morning."

"Doctor, do you think he will live?"

"I can't tell yet, but I will tell you that I have several cases like this every year - and most of them live."

"You mean you get dogs that fall off that wall a lot?"

"Yes, I do. I don't know why there is not a sign up there to keep dogs on a leash. But you go home, try not to worry and call me tomorrow."

We drove home in silence with me chastising myself for bringing the dog in the first place and then letting him off the leash.

That night, after dinner, Aunt Lil went into convulsions and vomited. We were scared to death and thought she was going to die. We started to call the ambulance when she came around, explaining that she had a hiatal hernia that was caused by stress. She took her medicine and appeared to be all right. At 6:00 a.m. the next morning the vet called and reported that Bandit had no broken bones, just a slight concussion and he was ready to come home. Bandit lived another seven happy years, but for a long time he could not lift his leg to urinate without falling over, and when Jim whistled for him, he would go the opposite way.

One day Jim came home and announced, "Shirl, I've reached the age where I either have to have a mistress or a sports car." Without blinking, I immediately said, "We'll go shopping tomorrow."

Jim had already decided what he wanted, so he placed an order for a Fiat Spyder either in white or blue. A month later, he received a call from the dealer in Williamsburg. He told Jim that the car had arrived from Italy but that it was not in the color he had ordered. "What color is it?' he asked. "It's orange" was the reply. Nonplussed, Jim said we would come down to look at it. On the way to Williamsburg, Jim said, "I'm not sure I should get an orange car. It might be too flashy." We arrived and were led to a tangerine-colored sports car. It was very bright. Jim and I were both wondering if it was too colorful for an up-and-coming Army officer when Peggy clapped her hands in glee and announced, "Look at the Fun-buggy!" Indecision went out the window and we had our Funbuggy. The kids loved it, and Jim was ecstatic.

School was over, summer was here and it was time for the movers again, as we prepared to go to Ft. Leavenworth, Kansas so Jim could attend Command and General Staff College. We had invested in three window air conditioners, which Jim had installed using the tough green Army tape. He and Jimbo started taking the air conditioners down when lo and behold, there was the little green snake that had been missing since before Aunt Lil's visit. Actually, it was the remnants of the snake as only the skin was there; all the rest of it had evaporated.

Chapter 16

It's 1970 and We're Back in Tehran

The Pan-American flight from Rome carried us over the cerulean blue Mediterranean Sea and, as the plane banked for landing, we had a perfect view of the snow-white buildings with sienna-tiled roofs of Beirut, Lebanon. The hills surrounding the city were a luscious green. We had a forty-minute layover and it felt good to get out and stretch our legs. The children were fascinated by the other traveler's costumes. There were Arab men in flowing robes with head-dresses, their wives covered in *burqas*; Indian women in *saris*, and Europeans wearing the latest fashions. It was the ultimate people-watching experience.

We returned to the plane and were on our way to Tehran. The trip was long but the food and service was good. The children amused themselves with coloring books and watching movies. After a filling meal of chicken *cordon blue* we all fell asleep. When I felt the plane starting to descend, I woke the children so they could see the lights of Tehran.

Arriving at 11:00 at night, we discovered that Mehrabad Airport had become a major, modern terminal, with airlines from all over the world represented. A warm breeze was blowing as we deplaned and walked past a column of military men in blue uniforms with gold trim. A helpful porter assisted us in collecting our ten suitcases. Emerging into the waiting room, we spied a sign with our name emblazoned in red paint held by our sponsor, Lt. Col. Delahanty. He was dressed in Levi's and a colorful Hawaiian shirt emphasizing his rotund shape. He was the height of Jim but a good bit heavier. He had a white-blond crew-cut, a pleasant, ruddy face, and a chubby, broad smile that forced the half-closure of his blue eyes. Looking at our family, the dog and the ten suitcases he laughed, "Maybe I should have brought a tank!" We managed to squeeze everything and everybody into the station wagon, and we were on our way. The kids were wide-awake, anxious to see the city. The drive into Tehran was another surprise. The many bright streetlights showed off the high-end shops full of clothing, cars and appliances. Driving down Ferdowsi Street, the huge statue of the poet Ferdowsi welcomed us with his outstretched arm. We turned on Takht-e-Jamshid Avenue and stopped at the Tehran International Hotel, where a suite of three rooms had been reserved for us. To my relief, we had a refrigerator, a small table with four chairs, a sofa and overstuffed chair in living area and two bedrooms with king-sized beds. Before saying good night to Delahanty, we made sure it was true that the tap water was good. He assured us that the water was very good to drink. "I'll pick you up at 8:00 tomorrow morning," he said to Jim, and with that he left. Our sleepy children happily crawled into bed. Jim and I took our showers and, after the long trip, it was a relief to collapse into dreamland.

The next morning we were having breakfast in the hotel when Delahanty arrived to take Jim to the office. After they left, the kids and I returned to our rooms to play King's Corner, now the children's favorite card game. Around noon Jim returned with a car, and we left to go to the Officers Club for lunch. The familiar musky smell of Tehran: the diesel exhaust, the kerosene, the kebabs being barbequed on the sidewalk, the baking bread, - all these odors rushed at us as we walked to the car. Women in white summer chadors were doing the morning shopping, a scowling mullah in a white turban was walking briskly with his black robes flowing around his sandaled feet, a hooked-nose merchant was lounging in front of his shop languidly smoking a cigarette while observing the street scene. We threaded our way between the pedestrians, stepped over the *jube* and into the black Chevrolet sedan with the ARMISH-MAAG license plates that Jim was assigned to until our own car arrived. "What is that ditch for, Mom?" Patrick asked.

"That is called a *jube,* and it was built many years ago to bring the water from the melting snow from the mountain up there," I said, pointing north to the Elburz Mountains. "Those mountains are so high, you can see snow up there even though it is summer."

Jim started the car and, as we edged into traffic, the blaring horns, people calling in Farsi, squealing brakes and the *muezzin* calling the faithful to prayer added to the familiarity. *Now I know I am back in Tehran*, I thought. Our chattering children were wiggling in excitement over a new adventure in a new city. The traffic was more manic then we remembered, plus it included many, many more cars. Jim had learned from Delahanty that Iran was now manufacturing a hundred cars a day. These cars are named *Peykan,* and, unfortunately, 99 of each 100 were staying in Tehran. There were five lines of cars trying to merge into the two traffic lanes; the drivers were honking their horns while screaming in Farsi, and gestures were flying. For twenty minutes, we endured screeching brakes and burning rubber. Through all this, Jim was very calm and even seemed to be enjoying the chaos. As we crawled along Old Shemiran Road toward Saltanatabad Road, the congestion petered out. We started north toward the cool foothills of Shemiran with the towering Elburz Mountains looming in front of us, its highest peaks still covered in snow.

"Hey, kids, wait until you see Mt. Damavand. You remember the snow cone mountain, don't you, Jimbo?" I eagerly said, pointing to the east.

"Where is it? I don't see it." The children said in unison. I kept looking toward where the mountain used to be, but saw nothing but a thick, brown haze. Turning in all directions, I realized that Tehran was engulfed in an impermeable, solid layer of grime. Even the foothills of the Elburz Mountains were shrouded in a dusky mist. The pollution was so bad that off on the horizon the 18,600 ft Mt. Damavand was obscured.

Jim turned the car into Kuche Yakchal that led to the American Officers Club. As the ten foot walls of the club came into view, Jimbo exclaimed, "I remember this place. This is where Mike lives."

"Who's Mike" Pat demanded.

"He's the nice, fat guy who used to give me spaghetti for breakfast," Jimbo replied.

"He gave you spaghetti for breakfast? Yuk! who ever heard of that," Pat said in a disgusted voice.

I quickly chimed in, "We'll just have to see if Mike is still the club manager. Wouldn't that be great?"

We drove through the big gates, parked the car and walked up the stairs to the foyer. We were met by a pleasant-faced Iranian in a red uniform with a grey *karakul* hat on his head. "Good afternoon, sir. What is your name, please?" he asked.

"I am Col. Starkey. We just arrived in country last night."

"Welcome, welcome, Col. Estarkey. Please come this way." As he started to guide us to a table, Jimbo said, "Is Mike still here?"

Looking surprised, he said, "Oh, you know Mike? No, Mike is no longer here. He has gone back to Italy to take care of his sick mama." He led us to a table next to the big picture window and handed us menus. As he left Patrick, a curious frown on his face, whispered, "Hey, Dad, why does he call you Estarkey?"

"Well, Pat, apparently it is difficult for Iranians to pronounce an English word beginning with the two letters 'S' and 'T'. You'll hear them say, 'estart' and 'estop' instead of start and stop. You'll get used to it. I'm sure we do not pronounce Farsi words correctly either."

I looked around the familiar room and outside at the Olympic-sized swimming pool and felt comfortable, as if I had come home. The interior of the club had not changed at all. It was still decorated in red and black in a Spanish motif complete with phony coats of armor on the walls in the style of the 1950's. We ordered hamburgers and milk shakes while watching the kids play Marco Polo in the swimming pool. "Dad, can we go swimming?" Peggy asked. From the time Peggy was able to walk, she has loved to be at the beach or at a swimming pool. "Not now, Peg. I've got to get back to work. But after work, we'll first go to the Embassy co-op for some groceries, and then we'll come here to swim and have dinner. Is that okay?" That got a big cheer from our offspring.

"By the way, one of the fellows at work told me about a real estate agent who he felt was pretty good. Do you think you would like to go out with him tomorrow?" Jim asked.

"Sure," I replied. "We might as well get started, because we know from past experience that it will take a long time. Kids, do you want to go house hunting tomorrow?"

In a chorus they replied, "Yes!"

Jim dropped us off at the hotel and returned to work while I read some stories to the children before we all fell asleep. By the time Jim arrived at 5:00 o'clock, we were ready to go shopping. We bought milk, bread, peanut butter and lunch meat for sandwiches and snacks to keep the kids happy. After returning to the hotel to put the food away, we were on our way with our bathing suits, towels and flip-flops in a canvas bag, looking forward to a cool dip. There were several families at the pool, and Jim introduced me to Major Ebert saying, "Major Ebert is the one who recommended the real estate guy you'll be going out with tomorrow." Major Ebert extended his hand, "Please call me Bob - and this is my wife, Carol." He introduced their four children: an older boy Pat's age, a girl Peggy's age and two younger boys.

Right after breakfast, Mohammad, the real estate agent, arrived dressed in a well-worn suit, white shirt, blue necktie and wearing shoes with the backs turned down. Devout Muslims wear shoes like that so they can slip out of them easily before praying. He had a nice smile and asked me what kind of a house we wanted. I answered that we wanted a house with a big yard and a swimming pool. "That is what I will show you," he confidently said. We drove down a modern, limited-access highway. Mohammad proudly pointed out the new, high-rise apartments being built, saying, "*Shahenshah* make new homes for poor people and big roads to drive on." He continued to talk about how the Shah was doing so much for everyone. "My daughter is going to school just like my sons," he proudly stated.

He drove us to a residential area, passing a man whipping the donkey that was pulling a load of bricks in a two-wheeled cart. The kids were fascinated by the sight. "Why does the donkey have blue beads between his ears?" Pat asked.

"They believe the blue beads bring good luck. These are the same blue beads that we have in our house. I think they are pretty, don't you? And maybe they do bring good luck," I answered.

We came to a walled compound with a rusty green gate. Mohammad got out and rang the bell, and soon an ancient man with a weathered, leather-like face appeared. On his head he had a close-fitting cap of beige felt. His thick grey eyebrows were knitted in a suspicious frown, and his mouth was turned down. After some conversation, he opened the gate, and we all entered the overgrown, jungle-like compound. We moved past an algae-filled swimming pool and entered a mansion that had once been elegant. I had the strangest feeling of *déjà vu,* and my mind went back to ten years before. I immediately said, "Mohammad, this will not work. Let's look someplace else." We continued to view several similar houses until the kids were hungry and started misbehaving. We returned to the hotel and Mohammad assured me that *fardah* (tomorrow) he would have more houses to look at. He left, and we went to our rooms and I made sandwiches. The next day we went to a different area of brand-new houses where the grounds were nothing but sand. There was not one tree or blade of grass to soften the glare that vibrated from the chalk-white houses. Mohammad said he had nothing else to show us, so we finally gave up. "Jim, I don't think Mohammad has anything we would be interested in. Maybe we need to find another agent," I complained.

We now had Thursday and Friday off, as opposed to the Friday-Sunday days off that we had before. The powers that be had decided that church would be on Thursday, and that way we would have two days off in a row. On Thursday, Jim decided we should forget about looking for a house. I was in complete agreement with that. We spent the weekend at the Officers Club, swimming and meeting other people. We learned a lot about how the Shah had improved Iran in the ten years since we had been here. The electricity was stable all over the country; there were no more black-outs at inconvenient times. The water was good to drink right out of the tap in all the major cities; in the factory south of Tehran, Foremost Dairy was providing reconstituted milk from the powdered milk brought in from Denmark. One of the first things General Saleh, the head of the Transportation Command, told Jim proudly was that his son Mahmood was almost six feet tall because he had loved to drink milk. Jim said that when Saleh told him this, he had puffed up like a bandy rooster stretching his five foot frame to the maximum. "The Shah is making Iran into a modern country," he exclaimed.

We decided that from then on, after eating lunch in the hotel room, Jim would take us to the Officers Club so the kids could swim in the afternoons. I met a lot of the ladies, and we usually ended up playing Bridge while keeping an eye on the children. That Saturday

Jim mentioned that he had run into Captain Mostafa Badiee, who had been a student at Command and Staff College. "Next Friday he has invited all of us to his home for lunch. We'll have to remember to buy flowers for his wife. Tonight we've been invited for dinner with the Delahantys. I guess we had better take flowers for them, too."

We went back to the hotel and while Jim left for work, the children and I took a nap. That evening Jim mentioned that he had met Lt. Col. Herb Canfield, who had just arrived in country. His family was not coming until he had rented a house. Jim and Herb found another real estate agent and decided that Herb, the kids and I should go out looking for houses in the morning. "If he doesn't mind the kids going along, that sounds like a good idea to me. Maybe this guy will have something worthwhile. The sooner we get into a house, the better." I replied.

The Delahantys lived in an apartment, as their only child, a girl, was back in the States in college. Rose Delahanty had fragile-looking antique furniture and seemed very nervous around our children, as if expecting them to ruin something. Our kids behaved very well, as usual, and when we left Rose told us we had a lovely family. For dinner Rose served us fried chicken, mashed potatoes with cream gravy, peas, salad and ice cream. Having a meal of regular American food was a treat. The Delahantys had bought several Persian carpets and when Jim admired them, Delahanty gave him a card with the name of the dealer whom he bought the carpets from. When we left Tehran ten years before we had purchased one room-sized and three area carpets. We were disappointed that we had not bought more carpets and were determined to add many more this time.

Herb arrived right after breakfast the next morning. He was six feet three inches tall with a very thin build, had sandy hair, funny eyebrows and a big grin. He had a great sense of humor and liked the kids. He said he had a boy, sixteen, a girl, twelve and another one, seven. His mother-in-law lived with them. The family had stayed in Georgia waiting for Herb to get a house. Herb sat in the front seat with the driver, a real estate agent. To the amusement of the kids, he kept turning around to tell Knock-knock jokes as we started off to look at houses. Everything turned out to be the huge, old homes with the big compounds and a swimming pool - usually green with algae- that the kids and I had already seen. To make matters worse, Tehran was in the midst of a heat wave. It was very hot, the roads were dusty, endless, and the air was stifling. Just when I had despaired of finding a house, the agent took us on a rocky road near the Niaveran Palace, the Shah's summer retreat. The area was new, with a few palatial homes interspersed with vacant lots. The house he wanted to show us was a white-marbled mansion on the south side of the *kuchee*. (small street)

We rang the doorbell and a bent-over, ancient man came to the gate, looking sternly at all of us. He had grey hair, a hooked nose, crinkled brown skin and raisin-black eyes. His snow-white baggy pants were well-worn. He had on a white long-sleeved shirt that was buttoned to the neck and over that was an open green vest. His brown shoes were broken at the back. The agent spoke to him, and he nodded in agreement, opening the gate wide so we could enter. He shuffled in front of us, bent over at a ninety degree angle, and almost stumbled while leading us toward the front door. I looked around the very small front compound, noticing the cement floor on the left, a small tree and grass on the right next to the main walkway. The house was an upside-down L-shape with the tail of the L extending to the street. This part contained three rooms; the one next to the street was probably for the man who was showing us around. Back of that was the bathroom containing a sink and Persian toilet, and behind that was a room with hookups for a washer and dryer. There was a fourth doorway that was the outside entrance to the kitchen. To my surprise, the kitchen had cupboards. I noticed there was plenty of space for a refrigerator and freezer. I walked back outside and entered the two front doors into a very large entrance hall. To the immediate right was the doorway to the kitchen, and between the kitchen door and the double-wide glass doors to the dining room was an immense, ugly oil stove meant to heat the whole house. There was a window pass-through from the kitchen to the dining room. Across the entrance room on the left was another room, and next to it was a bathroom. A curved staircase made of steel rods and slabs of marble rose dramatically to the second floor. To the right of the stairs was a hallway that led to the back compound. In front of us was another room, and to the right of that was the entrance to the L-shaped living room and dining room. The south wall of the living room had four double-wide glass doors that opened out onto the patio. All the rooms were over-sized. We walked out to the back yard. The back porch's roof was held up with four dramatic columns that rose beyond the second story to the roof. There was a long, narrow swimming pool on the right with a weeping willow tree at the end. The grass-filled yard was enclosed by a six-foot wall lined in dark green shrubbery. On the porch were three huge palm trees in pottery tubs. We came back in and mounted the stairs that led into another entrance room as large as the one downstairs. There were four bedrooms and two bathrooms that led off from the entrance room. It was perfect. I went back downstairs to talk to the agent. Jim had told me our housing allowance was $350.00 per month, a good deal more than we would get in the States. I asked the agent the price and was crestfallen when he told me the rent was $500.00 a month. Well, so much for my Dream House.

When we got back to the hotel, I told Jim about this wonderful house and how disappointed I was that it was out of our price range.

The next Friday, the heat-wave continued - with temperatures in the 100's and a dusty wind blowing. We arrived at the Badiee home and were greeted by Mostafa in the entrance hall. We removed our shoes and were led into a large room covered with carpets and giant pillows to sit on. We were served luke-warm Coke and pistachio nuts while Mostafa introduced us to his father, mother, and wife. Only Mostafa spoke English, so the conversation was limited. Jim and I tried what scarce Farsi we remembered, and the family seemed pleased at our dismal attempts. His mother made a big fuss over our children, while Fatima, his mousy wife, headscarf shadowing her face, remained silent. Mostafa explained that he had a baby son. I suggested he bring the little boy in so our children could see him. After much Farsi between Mostafa and his mother, his mother finally agreed. Fatima had no voice in the decision; mother-in-law ruled the roost. Our kids had been sitting in wide-eyed wonder, watching with interest but not knowing what to do, until the toddler came in. Instantly, they started talking to him and playing peek-a-boo, while little Ali laughed. Pretty soon we were all laughing, enjoying the infectious giggle of the infant. A *badjii* came in and said something to Mrs. Badiee, who motioned us into the dining room to eat. The first course with cold yogurt soup, followed by a crisp green salad, *berenj* (rice) and *khoreshe fesenjan*, a chicken dish made with pome-

324

granates and walnuts. The meal was delicious, and I silently prayed the fresh salad ingredients had been cleaned well. The dining room was crowded and stifling hot. Mrs. Badiee kept pushing us to eat more. Suddenly, I became dizzy and nauseated. I drank some hot tea, which seemed to settle my stomach. We returned to the living room, where we were served oranges on a plate with a knife. I peeled oranges for the children and, after an appropriate length of time, we said our thanks and made our exit.

All the way back to the hotel, my stomach was churning and I barely made it to the bathroom before I threw up the meal. Jim handed me some water and helped me into bed, where I promptly fell asleep. At midnight I awoke suddenly and barely made it into the bathroom to throw up again. Jim gave me some Pepto-Bismal and I tried to sleep some more. All through the night, I was up throwing up; Jim was forcing me to drink Pepto-Bismal and water, but an hour later everything was repeated. By morning I was having the dry heaves and could barely keep my head up. Jim got the children dressed and announced that he was taking me to the hospital. As he practically carried me down the hall, I heard Jimbo whisper to Pat and Peg, "Mom's pregnant."

Oh, my God, bite your tongue, I thought. I don't remember the trip to the hospital, the nurse preparing me for bed or the tubes being put into me. I slept all that day and the next night. The following morning, I awoke feeling weak but a lot better. Mrs. Delahanty came to see me, demanding to know why I hadn't told her I was in the hospital. I couldn't think of an answer to such a stupid question. Jim and the kids arrived after lunch to inform me that we had a house. "We have a house? Where is it?" Before Jim could say anything, the kids were jumping up and down and Jimbo cried out, "Mom, we're going to live in the big white marble house that we looked at!"

I looked at Jim. "What is he talking about?" Looking very pleased, Jim said, "With you in the hospital, I had to take time off to care for the kids - so we went house hunting. When I saw that white house, I decided to see the owner. It turns out that the house is owned by Colonel Atlassi, who is the commandant of the Shah's Palace Guards. He told me that the Shah gave him money interest-free to build this house to rent to Americans. He agreed to rent it to me for $350.00 if I would leave the pool filter for him when we leave. I met with Col. Atlassi this morning at the Embassy to sign the lease, so we can move in as soon as our household goods are here. I've been told they are in Bandar Abbas, the major port on the Persian Gulf right now, and should be up here in a week. Also, our car is here and being processed right now. We should have it in four days."

I could not believe what I was hearing. "You mean we don't have to spend two months in the hotel waiting for the landlord to come to the Embassy like before?" Boy, this time I could really begin to enjoy Iran! Suddenly, I felt terrific and demanded to be released from the hospital.

On the way out to the house Jim said, "Oh, by the way, the old man you saw at the house is named Negadar. He goes with the house. That was part of the agreement that we pay Negadar and keep him as our guard and gardener. He has a wife and boy in south Tehran but only goes to see them once or twice a month. Otherwise he is there to watch the house. And, another plus, he likes Bandit, which is unusual for an Iranian. He speaks a little English, but you'll have to brush up on your Farsi."

Negadar met us at the gate with a big, toothless smile, eagerly showing us around. He seemed different and walked better. I think that at that moment he adopted us. As he pointed to the cement area on the left he proudly announced, *"Machine enjas."*

"What did he say?" Pat demanded.

"He means that this is where we'll park the car," Jim answered. As we entered the foyer, the temperature dropped significantly. "With these marble floors and high ceilings, I don't think we will need the air conditioners. They won't fit the windows anyway, so we'll sell them," Jim remarked. We decided that the big room to the left of the hallway would be the *umbar*, the storage area for all the food-stuffs we had brought over. The other room to the left of the living room would be my artist studio. I noticed that in the living room, dining room and entrance hall as well as the bedrooms there were only hanging wires from the ceiling where light fixtures should be.

"Jim, are we supposed to furnish the light fixtures like we did the last time?"

"I'm not sure. It's not in the contract." Jim answered. We moved to the upstairs and decided that Peggy would have the room to the north that overlooked the front compound and was next to the second bathroom; Pat would have the opposite room that faced south; Jimbo's room also faced north and opened up to the flat roof that was over the kitchen, laundry room and Negadar's room. We could walk out there for an unobstructed view of the whole neighborhood and the Elburz Mountains. Our bedroom was opposite Jimbo's and faced south. Our bathroom was bigger than our bedroom had been at Ft. Leavenworth. I was continually amazed at the size of all the rooms.

After another week in the hotel, it was finally moving day. The first thing we noticed when we came in the house was that all the light fixtures were in place. We wondered if our house was bugged, but then we laughed, thinking that the only thing a listener would hear would be the kids fighting! The Iranian Transportation Officer, Mr. Naderi, arrived to supervise the movers. He brought five men and soon the house was a beehive of activity. I stood at the front door directing traffic with an *enjas* (here) or *bala* (upstairs). One spindly little man came in carrying our 150 kilo chopping block on his back. With pained look he whispered, "*bala?*" I laughed and said, "No, *enjas*" and pointed to the kitchen. He smiled with relief.

The boys were thrilled to each have their own room and happily made the decision on where the furniture would be placed and, at Jim's orders, unpacked their clothes and toys. Peggy was just as adamant about deciding where to place her furniture. The gas dryer needed a special hookup that had to be ordered, so in the meantime I had to hang the clothes outside. I stretched a line between the pillars on the back porch to dry the clothes and thought about Dolly Madison doing the same thing at the White House. A Major in Jim's office was leaving and sold Jim his dish washer. It fit right in our kitchen and eliminated our need to hand wash dishes. It was hard to believe we were settled in this beautiful house with our up-to-date American appliances. Army life is certainly Feast or Famine - but never dull.

As soon as we got settled, we enrolled both boys in baseball. We always had the boys involved in either football, basketball, baseball or swimming depending, on the season. They had no time to get into trouble with physical activities, homework and Scouting taking up their time and energy. The first time we went to Jimbo's baseball game, we were surprised to see that the bleachers for the spectators were beyond right field. You practically needed binoculars to see the batter. Someone at the game explained to us that the year before the parents had been so involved in yelling nasty things to the rival players that the Commanding General had decreed that the parents would have to sit far away. Sometimes a benevolent dictatorship works! The only kid who could get heckled by some jerk was the one in right field.

Another Lt. Col arrived in country to work in the same office with Jim and Herb. Ken Stover (known as Smokey) and his wife Donna had one son, Bill, who was a few years older than Jimbo. Jim, Herb and Smoke all shared a car and one driver named Hussein. Hussein would come to our house to pick up Jim, then go to Herb's house and finally to Smoke's home, which was located at the end of a cul-de-sac. He would get out, ring the bell, and then turn the car around. Brigadier General Sullivan, the head of the Air Force section, lived across the street from Stover. Every morning the General's driver would come for the general and his aide-de-camp. As Hussein started down the street, the driver for Gen. Sullivan would pull out in front and the two cars, both black Chevrolet's with ARMISH-MAAG license plates, would head down to Headquarters. It was the same every morning; like clockwork, the two cars would convoy together.

The new head of the Army section arrived the last week in July. Brigadier General Oliver Patton and his beautiful wife named Ann, who had been a professional singer until she married an Army officer, moved to a home near us. They had five children, all grown and living in the States except the youngest girl, who was a senior in high school.

Soon after we moved in, a vendor appeared at the gate one Thursday afternoon. Negadar came in to tell us that a dealer named Mansur was at the gate with some carpets. He had four Baluchi tribal carpets to sell. The Baluchis are a tribe of more than a million nomads who live in southeastern Iran near the Pakistan border. The Baluchi carpets are in geometric designs in deep shades of blue and crimson. The largest of the four was one meter by two meters with the other three one meter by one and one-half meters. They were exactly what our vacant marble floors needed. Jim wasted no time in opening up our *umbar* where the three window air conditioners were sitting in the middle of the floor. The vendor's eyes nearly popped out of his head when Jim told him that these were for sale. "*Sarhang*," (Colonel), he said enthusiastically, "I will trade you the carpet of your choice for the three air conditioners."

Jim laughed, "Mansur, I have been to Bandar Abbas, Ahwaz and Abadan in the summer. I know the temperatures reach 120 degrees by nine in the morning. You can take these air conditions down to the Persian Gulf and name your price. I will trade you these three air conditioners for these four carpets."

"Oh, no, *Sarhang*, you are mistaken. I will not be able to get much money for these old air conditioners. How do I know they will even work?"

"We can plug these in right now and show you that they work."

Rubbing his chin thoughtfully and looking at Jim out of the corner of his eye, he finally asked, "*Sarhang*," will you take two carpets for the air conditioners?"

Shaking his head, Jim emphatically answered, "No, I will take four carpets for the air conditioners."

Mansur frowned and stared at Jim. Jim returned his stare, neither one of them would blink. Finally, Mansur looked around at the goods on the *umbar* floor. His eyes lit up when he saw the pressed glass punchbowl and the twelve matching cups. "*Sarhang*, I will agree to this if you will give me the big bowl and cups," he said with a smile.

Jim nodded, "It's a deal, Mansur." They shook hands. Nagadar and Mansur carried the air conditioners to the vendor's car. Mansur returned and carefully packed the punchbowl and cups in a cardboard box. He shook his head. "*Sarhang*, you are a difficult man. You will do well in Iran."

I danced with glee after he left. The children had been watching the bargaining with great interest. "Dad," Pat said, "do you think he will be able to sell the air conditioners?"

"Don't worry about that, Pat. He will be able to get a lot of money for each air conditioner, enough to buy ten carpets. Also, although we only paid $20.00 for the punch bowl and cups, he will be able to sell that to a wealthy Iranian family for four times that amount. Iranians will buy almost anything American. He did very well by Iranian standards, and we did extremely well by American standards. Everyone won on this deal."

Nagadar was beaming. *"Sarhang, khali khub, khali khub!"* (very good, very good). He looked at Jim with admiration. I started placing our new purchases in the living room. The Kashan carpet we had bought our first tour was in the dining room and the red Turkoman that Jim had bought in Hong Kong while on R & R from Viet Nam (with the tag on the back indicating it came from a dealer on Ferdowsi Street in Tehran, Iran), one that covered a whole room in an American home, didn't cover half of our Iranian living room. Our new purchases were placed strategically in the remaining area and made the room come to life.

Jim ran into Gholum, our old driver, down at the Motor Pool. He had been promoted to Master Sergeant and was driving for an Iranian general. He asked Jim if he would talk to General Saleh, the head of the Transportation Division in the Iranian Army, about Gholum being Jim's driver. Since Jim was the Transportation Advisor to General Saleh he declined, saying, "Gholum, I'm sorry, but I've just met Gen. Saleh, and it wouldn't be proper for me to request a favor." Gholum said he understood. The next Saturday Gholum came by our house with Maluke, our old badjii. Gholum looked the same - lithe and trim, with his bushy handlebar moustache and big smile. Maluke had aged a lot, gained weight and had colored her hair bright red. She was working for a German family, and she wanted to work for us again. "I'm sorry, Maluke but I am looking for a badjii to come in just one day a week to mop, dust and clean bathrooms," I told her.

Since we had all our convenient appliances I didn't need anyone else. I was glad not to have another woman in the kitchen wrinkling her nose if I cooked pork. Maluke said she had a friend she would send to me. The next day, Maluke's friend, Ashraf arrived at nine and I showed her what I wanted. As she started cleaning the downstairs bathroom, Negadar came in and started mopping the floor. "Madame, I do work. No *badjii enjas.*" This was the first indication I had that Negadar expected to be more than a guard and gardener. He had been waiting for me to tell him what to do. I paid Ashraf for a full day's work and, as she left, I heard her yelling at Negadar. Negadar never said a word; he just grinned and showed her to the gate.

This did not last very long. Soon Negadar had more pressing duties: watching the gate to prevent strangers from coming in, watering the lawn or gossiping with the neighboring gardeners. I talked to our neighbors, the Shoemakers, who had a *badjii*, Ishmat, who only worked three days a week for them. We decided to hire her for the other two days, much to the relief and approval of Negadar. However, Negadar turned out to be worth his weight in gold. Not only was he the gardener and guard, but he was relentless in keeping track of the children playing in the *kuchee*. During the summer, the boys were out in the street playing soccer with the kids of various nationalities from the neighborhood. Negadar protected our three as if they were his own. Jim and Pat would go roaming with their BB guns and one time they shot a neighbor's pet pigeon. Caddy-corner from us were two houses each owned by the two daughters of the Shah's Court Minister, Mr. Alam. The daughter in the first house was married to an Iranian who collected rare pigeons. It was one of these that Jimbo shot. Jim and I did not hear about this till many years later but, according to Jimbo, Negadar and the neighbor's gardener covered up the dastardly deed so that owner (or we) never heard a word about the incident.

Peggy learned to roller-skate at Ft. Leavenworth, after holding on to her dad just one time. From then on she lived to roller-skate. There was a sidewalk in front of our house and the house next door, and she would leave the front compound, carefully place a rock to keep the gate from locking, then would skate to the corner. When she returned, she would find the gate closed. She rang the bell and Negadar opened the gate. Peggy would enter the compound and pretend to go in the house. As soon as Negadar returned to his room, she would go out the gate, replace the rock and skate to the end of the block. Again Negadar would remove the rock and close the gate. Returning, Peggy would ring the bell and when Negadar answered she would say, "*Neest, neest* (no, no,) Nagadar". Shaking his head, Negadar would reply, "*Kuchek khanum* (little lady), gate be locked." He was determined to protect us from intruders, even if the intruder was our daughter.

Twice a month when the weather was good Negadar's friend, Ali Baba, would set up his portable cobbler shop in front of our house. Servants from all over the neighborhood would bring shoes, belts and purses to be repaired and shined. It became a party atmosphere with kids playing in the street, a radio blaring Persian music, Negadar and

Ali Baba gossiping and laughing while Ali Baba worked. Negadar would make some tea and, if I was home, I would send out cookies.

Our house in the foothills of the Elburz Mountains was on the southern-most road of a housing development built near the Shah's summer palace. The four paved east-west roads from the palace going south were named *Golestan Chahar* (four), *Golestan Sey* (three), *Golestan Do* (two) and *Golestan Yek* (one). Our street was unpaved and unnamed so we referred to it as *Golestan Neem* (zero). (*Golestan* means 'rose garden.') The empty desert sloped south from our house for miles. Half a block from our home was a landfill used by everyone in the *Golestan* area. Early in the morning, the goat herder brought his flock to feast on the discards left by the servants. We would be awakened by the sounds of bleating and clanging from the bells around the goat's necks. The goats were not the only ones to enjoy this banquet; huge flocks of fat pigeons would fly directly over our house and glide onto the ground in order to gorge themselves. While we were swimming, Jim noticed the flyby and decided to shoot the pigeons. He had his shotgun resting on the porch until he saw the birds overhead. He shot several of them and the noise brought Negadar running to see what the commotion was all about. When he realized what Jim had done, Negadar brought out a gunny sack. Jim sent the boys off to pick up the dead birds and give them to Negadar to clean. When the birds were cleaned, I decided to cook them for dinner. I basted them with olive oil and herbs and roasted them in the oven. When we started to eat them, it was a major task to find the meat amongst all the many bones. Negadar had used the pigeon's innards to make himself an aromatic stew. I sent Jimbo out with some rice, lettuce and tomatoes to add to Negadar's dinner.

"Babe, from now on we'll give Negadar all the birds I shoot. There is plenty of room in the freezer to keep them so he will have them when he needs them. It's a good idea for you to supplement his diet. He looks pretty frail and we want to keep him healthy. I know we pay him a salary, but let's make sure he gets more protein." I completely agreed with Jim and every time I went shopping at the little store on Saltanatabad Road I would buy him a half kilo of the *panir*, (goat cheese) as well as eggs and rice. When Jim told Negadar he could have all the pigeons he shot, the arrangement pleased Negadar so much that while we were swimming he would stand at the front gate watching north for the pigeons. When he spotted them coming he would run to the back door shouting, "*Sarhang, Sarhang,* maybe a million!" Jim would get his shotgun ready and fire as the birds flew over. The kids ran around the corner to gather the bounty and hand them to the grinning Negadar. This had the added advantage of us being the only Americans who were never robbed during our two-year tour. The word got around on the Farsi grapevine not to mess with the *Sarhang devoneh ba tofang* (the crazy Colonel with a gun).

Jim discovered the carpet shop of the two Jewish brothers that Delahanty had mentioned. The older and apparent boss was Solomon, a taciturn, shrewd-looking man with a suspicious expression on his face that I found off-putting. The younger, Elias, was the direct opposite. He had a friendly, smiling, open manner, and he was the one who dealt with the customers. Elias was tall and slender with the agility of a born athlete. One day he brought a dark blue, rust and beige Ardibil tribal carpet to our house. I loved it immediately. Jim asked the price and then announced that it was too much money. "Col. Estarkey, I will leave this beautiful carpet here for you to enjoy, and we will talk about the price later," Elias said. He did and every month for the next eighteen months he would bring other carpets for us. Some, we would want to keep and others we sent back. Every time, Elias and Jim would bargain over the Ardibil. "You are taking the milk from my children's mouth!" Jim would declare. "Oh, Col. Estarkey, you have more money than God has!" Elias would answer. This would go on for an hour while the two of them would drink many cups of tea.

It was the first of September and time to get the children registered in school. While in Tucson we learned that Doctor Robert Morrow, the retired Superintendent of Tucson Schools, had accepted a two year position at the American School in Tehran. The year before he had replaced Mr. O'Reilly, the principal of the high school, who moved up to take over the Superintendent Langforth's office while Langforth went back to the States for a sabbatical. This year Dr. Morrow would stay on as the high school principal while O'Rielly goes back to the States for further schooling.

I clearly remember the first time I met Dr. Morrow - when I was five years old. Church was over, and my Mom and Dad were standing under the chinaberry trees that shaded the walkway in front of Trinity Presbyterian Church. They were visiting with some other adults when my Sunday school class was over, and I came running to meet them. Just as I arrived, I saw a tall, sandy-haired smiling man approach them. He was dressed in a white linen suit, wearing a cobalt blue necktie that matched his eyes, white shoes and a white Panama hat. He was so elegant I thought he must be a movie star and the handsomest man I had ever seen. He shook hands with my folks as they carried on a conversation. Suddenly, he looked down at me and asked, "And who is this young lady?"

"This is my youngest daughter, Shirley," my mom replied. My mother always had the habit of introducing someone to me but never telling me who the person was, to my great annoyance. As my sisters and brother showed up, my folks said their goodbyes and we started walking home. "Who was that man, Momma?" I demanded.

"That was Dr. Morrow," she answered. "He is the principal of the School for the Deaf and Blind." That really confused my five year-old mind and I thought, *How could he be the principal for the School of the Deaf and Blind when he wasn't deaf or blind?* Soon after that, Dr. Morrow was hired to be the Superintendent of Tucson School District.

During the Second World War, thousands of men were stationed for a short period of time at Davis-Monthan Air Base. Many discovered that they liked the warm, dry weather of the Southwest. After the war, they started returning in droves with their families, so that by the time I was teaching school, Tucson was building four new elementary schools a year - and most of the older schools were on split-shifts. Dr. Morrow deftly negotiated all the problems this brought on, and in addition, he decided that when President Harry Truman desegregated the Armed Forces in July of 1948, he would follow suit and desegregate our schools. He was courageous and fair in all his dealings, and the Tucson populous thought he walked on water. Tragedy struck the Morrow family when I was in junior high when their only son, Bobby, was asphyxiated in the middle of the night due to a faulty gas heater.

When I started teaching Bonillas school, Dr. Morrow never

failed to step into my classroom at least once a month. He religiously visited every classroom in the school district. He was a marvelous superintendent, and Tucson School District still has never had a superintendent to come up to the standards set by Dr. Morrow.

That day in Iran I was excited to renew our acquaintance and, as I walked into his office, he greeted me effusively. "Shirley, can I count on you to substitute when we need you?"

"I'll be happy to help in any way, Dr. Morrow."

"For Heaven's sake, call me Bob. We've known each other too long for formalities. Now tell me about your family." We visited for quite awhile and then I left to register the boys. I was delighted to learn that Jimbo would have two male teachers. His fifth grade teacher, Mr. Carson, and I spent considerable time talking about Jimbo's lack of interest in things academic and his over-interest in sports. I left feeling that Mr. Carson would take an interest in our oldest. Pat was entering second grade and since he was so focused in first grade, I didn't think he would have a problem. For Peggy, I discovered a private international kindergarten and grade school just one block from our house. The principal spoke excellent English, and the classes were taught in English. Most of the students were from wealthy Iranian families with a sprinkling of English, French, and Danish children added in. It turned out that Peggy was the only non-Iranian child in her kindergarten class.

The second week in September I was walking Peggy to school. As she was skipping along the sidewalk, chattering away, she exclaimed, "Momma, do you know they have the best cookies and fruit juice at school?" I tried to be as enthusiastic as my charge, but my whole being was exhausted. I couldn't understand what was wrong; I was nauseated, tired and my feet felt like lead. I just knew I had contacted some kind of weird disease. I called the hospital and made an appointment for the next day to see the head of the hospital, Col. (Dr.) Reed. After an examination, he ordered blood and urine tests. Two days later I returned to Dr. Reed's office. "Well, I know what your problem is, Mrs. Starkey. You are pregnant."

"I'm WHAT?" I cried incredulously

"You're pregnant."

"I can't be! Are you sure?"

"Yes, I am positive."

"I can't be pregnant, I'm too old. I'm thirty-seven. No one has a baby at thirty-seven." I sat there in shocked silence, trying to comprehend what Dr. Reed just told me. "I don't know what to do. I've been having horrible pains in my abdomen. Maybe I have a bad pregnancy and I should have a D and C."

"You mean an abortion?"

"No, I just meant a D and C. I had a bad pregnancy right after my first child was born, and I carried the fetus for five months even though the fetus had died at three months. I feel the same way now that I did then." I was talking fast, trying to convince myself that I was only asking for a minor procedure to take care of my 'problem.'

"Well, I can make an appointment for you with Dr. Kazemi, our OB-GYN doctor. You would have to have the abortion at his hospital, Tehran General. But before I do, you should talk this over with your husband. You're lucky. An abortion is legal here in Iran, but not in the States."

"Thank you very much, Col. Reed. I'll let you know."

Why does he keep calling it abortion? It's just a D. and C., I thought as I left. *This makes me angry, calling it an abortion.*

Jim was as surprised as I was at the news that I was pregnant. I told him about the conversation I had with Col. Reed and that I could go to Tehran General for the procedure. Jim looked very thoughtful and after a bit, quietly said, "What do you want to do?"

"Well, I don't think I want to be pregnant. I'm just too old. You remember Mrs. Turner, the lady who lived down the street from you in Tucson? You played ball with her son Jack, and when Jack was in the Marine Corps, Mrs. Turner had two more babies - and they were hellions, completely undisciplined and just ran wild. She was just too old to deal with young kids. I don't want to be like that."

"Okay," Jim replied. "If that is what you want to do." I called Dr. Reed and asked him to arrange everything with Dr. Kazemi, and two days later Jim drove me to Tehran General Hospital. Peggy was with us, as we didn't ever leave her alone with Negadar. Two nurses came for me and whisked me away to be prepped. As I removed my clothes to put on a hospital gown, the two nurses started remarking on how beautiful my nipples were. "They are so pink and lovely" they squealed. I was taken aback, *What kind of women are these,* I thought, quickly and nervously putting on the hospital gown. Finally, they let me return to the room where Jim and Peggy were waiting. I started talking about how awful the Turner kids were, trying to reinforce my decision. Jim was strangely silent, watching Peggy coloring. As the two nurses came to get me, I hugged Jim hard, looked into his eyes and asked, "I'm doing the right thing, aren't I?" Jim answered, "Yes, I think so." But his eyes had the saddest look I had ever seen; they were not agreeing with his words. I climbed onto the gurney and suddenly I was being whisked down the hall. As I stared at the bright florescent lights flashing by, I thought about my darling Peggy.

What if I am getting rid of another pretty little blonde? I can't do this. I'm not like Mrs. Turner; we wouldn't raise hooligans like she did. She acted old even when she was young, I can't do this, I thought, panic enveloping me.

We entered the operating room; only the two nurses and a technician were there. The technician came at me with a needle. I started crying and shouting in Farsi, *"Bas dashtan, bas dashtan"* (stop, stop). The nurses and the technician froze, staring at me. Suddenly another door opened and a very large, muscular Iranian man burst into the room, holding his dripping hands away from his body. "Mrs. Starkey, what is it?"

"Who are you?" I demanded.

"I am Dr. Kazemi. What is the problem?"

Urgently I answered, "Doctor, can you examine me and see if this is a good pregnancy?"

"Certainly, Mrs. Starkey, let me finish scrubbing up." He went to the sink, rinsed his hands and when one of the nurses had helped him put on gloves, he returned to me. After his examination, he took his gloves off and came to my side. "Everything looks perfectly healthy. You have a normal pregnancy."

"Oh, Dr. Kazemi," I pleaded through buckets of tears, "I want to keep my baby!" With that, the doctor grabbed me in a big bear hug and cried, "I'm so glad." Both of us were weeping copiously. I pulled away, staring at him in shock as he quickly released me. Bringing himself under control, he said, "Mrs. Starkey, what I was prepared to do for you is the hardest thing a doctor can do. Children are the most precious things we have. You will not be sorry for your decision."

He left the room and soon the nurse was wheeling me back to where I had left Jim and Peggy. They were not there. I put my clothes on and sat in a chair, waiting for them. As they entered Jim said, "That was quick. Is it all over?"

"I changed my mind."

"What?"

"I changed my mind. I couldn't go through with it. We're going to have another baby. I hope that's all right with you."

Jim was grinning broadly as I got my second bear hug. "Oh, Babe, I'm so glad. I can't think of anything I want more. Thank you for not going through with that."

"What are you talking about?" Peggy demanded. I looked over at our daughter. She had her hands on her hips, a questioning look on her face, with blue eyes squinting. How could she know that her presence in the room helped make me realize what a mistake I was making? I gathered her into my arms and lifted her so her dad could hug her too. Jim smiled at her and said, "Your mother is going to have a baby. You're going to have a little brother or sister."

"Well, it better be a sister. We have too many boys already," she said with an impish grin at her dad.

Chapter 17

That evening, we told the boys about the new baby. This started an argument over what the baby's sex should be. Jim called a halt to that when he announced that we would be happy with either a boy or a girl. "We should start thinking of names for either, so we will be prepared," he said. This brought on another round of suggestions, and when Jimbo came up with the name 'Caboose,' we were all laughing. That night I went to bed very pleased with myself.

When I went to the hospital for my first OB appointment I met Jane, a no-nonsense red-headed nurse who was married to Dr. Kazem Kazemi. Along with all her regular duties, she taught Lamaze classes. "What is Lamaze?" I asked. She explained, "It is a series of exercises and breathing that helps you to deliver babies easier."

"Well, sign me up. I'm for anything that will make labor easier." Jane met Dr. Kazemi when both were in training in the United States. Dr. K. was from a wealthy Iranian family, who had sent him to the States for schooling from high school on, which is why he spoke English with no accent. I told Jane about our drama in the operating room and she smiled. "Yes, he told me all about it. The reason he was so emotional is because we have been trying for years to have a baby."

Every day I would walk to Peggy's school to pick her up, we'd have lunch and then we would retire to her bedroom for a story and nap. I could barely keep my eyes open long enough to finish reading to her. I would fall asleep and when I awakened, Peggy would be quietly sitting on the bed playing with her toys or looking at a book. She always let me sleep as long as I needed, to even though she was through with naps. One day she was very upset when I met her in front of the school. "What's the matter, honey," I asked.

"Momma, I don't want to go to that school anymore."

"Why not? I thought you liked it. Don't you have any friends?"

"No, I don't. All the kids just stare at me, and no one will play with me."

I talked to the principal relating Peggy's concerns. "Meesus Estarkey, I'm afraid we have a problem. Peggy is the only child in the kindergarten who is not Iranian, and the only one in the school with blonde hair and blue eyes. I'm sorry to say this, but the children think she is strange and don't want to associate with her."

I was stunned and then angry. It was the first time we had faced prejudice. Furious, I snapped, "We will not be back. I'll find another school for Peggy." I marched out of the school dragging Peggy behind me. That afternoon, I called Carol Ebert, who had a daughter Peggy's age. "Carol, what kindergarten does your daughter go to?"

"Janie goes to the British Kindergarten over on Saltanatabad Road". She answered. "She has a wonderful teacher, Mrs. Fahti. Janie thinks she is Mary Poppins." The next day I took Peggy to the British School and met Mrs. Fahti. She was short and a little on the rotund side with a kind, loving face framed by gray hair pulled into a bun. She wore a dark blue, long-sleeved dress with a crisp white collar and had tied a clean white apron under her ample bosom. She was very much in charge and spoke with a brisk but kindly British accent. I liked her immediately and sensed that Peggy did, too. The school was run by three British ladies, with Mrs. Fahti being in charge. There were ten children in each three year-old class, four year-old class and, with Peggy, there would be ten in kindergarten. Mrs. Fathi was delighted that Peggy would be in her class and asked if Peggy could stay that morning. Peggy grinned at me, waiting for my approval. I nodded my agreement and Peggy ran off to play hop-scotch with Janie. Within weeks, she was talking with a British accent, referring to tea-time, when they ate biscuits, (rather than cookies) and was looking forward to

Father Christmas. Peg was also learning to read, do numbers and was excited to go to school every day.

The east side of our house was attached to the adjoining house owned by another officer in the Shah's palace guard and rented to the Shoemakers, a family from Texas. Bob Shoemaker was an oil executive whose job was to oversee his company's Iranian employees. They had a girl several years older than Peggy and a six year-old boy with muscular dystrophy. The little guy could only get around by dragging himself with his arms and was totally homebound. Patricia Shoemaker was a sweet and patient saint, in my estimation. We were at their home having drinks one night when Bob was regaling us with his latest problem. He had hired former goat herders to live as guards at the site of the remote oil rigs. The men, in order to keep from being too lonely, had each brought a female goat to the job. When one of the guards discovered another guard being too friendly with his goat, he became jealous and, in a fit of anger, killed the offender. Bob's dilemma was how to explain to the company brass in Houston, Texas the sexual mores of Iranian goat herders.

Dogs have a difficult time in Iran as most Moslems believe dogs are unclean and are the lowest form of reincarnation. However, landowners are not averse to keeping dogs as guards for their property. Many of the lots in our area were vacant and most of them were walled-in to prevent squatters from moving in. Once the property had squatters on it, it became very difficult for the owner to evict them. Many of the owners whose main home was in downtown Tehran, used their walled property as private picnic spots. Gardeners were hired to live there with their families and to tend to the fruit trees, vegetables and flower beds, while keeping squatters out. In one of the walled gardens across the street, a gardener and his family lived in a small house built in the corner of the yard. The owner had brought over a big, black dog to guard the property, but the gardener hated the dog and frequently beat him. Nagadar could hear the dog crying out in pain during these beatings, and he would complain to me. There was nothing we could to about it; we were not about to get involved - especially after Col. Atlassi told us the property was owned by the Shah's attorney general. While driving in Tehran, we would see dogs living around the *jubes*. The shopkeepers hated them, as customers would avoid going into the shop. It was not unusual to see shopkeepers throwing rocks at the dogs to get them to leave the area. Another cute trick, usually performed by teenage boys, was to tie a cord tightly around a puppy's neck, so that as the pup grew he would be strangled to death.

The property on the west side of our house was vacant and part of the wall had been knocked down. When we moved in, the kids discovered three dogs living there, one a sturdy, red chow-German Sheppard-mix male that Negadar had named Cheemie; one, a black, long-haired male the kids named Blackie; the third, was a blonde Labrador retriever female named Lady, who was pregnant. All three were in good shape, as they had first choice of the groaning board that was the garbage dump. Negadar, unlike most Muslims, liked dogs and especially the dogs next door, because they were the first to alert him to any strangers approaching. Cheemie, the chow, was very good at climbing, and at night we would see him parading on top of the walls that surrounded our back patio. He took it upon himself to protect us just like a sentry. Since Bandit's dog food was disappearing more than it had in the States and Bandit was not gaining any weight, I thought perhaps the squatter dogs next door were getting their just rewards for their diligence. After Lady had her pups, it was impossible to keep the children from checking on them every day. After the pups were weaned Nagadar found good homes for them in the neighborhood.

It was an exhilarating thought to know that our big station wagon was in the compound - and that I could drive it. During our entire tour, I made sure I never drove further south than the American Embassy due to the mad, kamikaze traffic. I would drive Peg to school, the boys to football practice either at Gulf District or over on Pahlavi Road, go to the greengrocer and the shop that sold eggs, cheese and rice on Saltanatabad Avenue and then down Dowlat to the *Barf* (snow) dry cleaner. Even in this comparatively quiet area, I had to deal with exuberant Persian drivers, who appeared to have a death wish. Iranians have a saying that loosely translates into, "The road is mine." They all drive as if they believe it, so it was important to constantly keep alert and conscious of my peripheral vision. It was not unusual for a driver to enter a major road without bothering to stop or to check for other traffic. Frequently, they would pass on the right to make a left turn in front of the car they had just passed, or pass on the left and then turn right in front of the other driver. This was not the only hazard of driving in Tehran. One day while driving down Dowlat, a dusty, broken half-paved road, I was stopped by a herd of sixty or more goats. The ragged goat herder made no attempt to guide the goats off the road, and so I was stuck there for several minutes. Having nothing better to do, I was looking at the goats and marveling at how many different colors they represented. Then I noticed an overly large billy goat with intense yellow eyes. His eyes hypnotized me, and I couldn't look away. We stared at each other until, suddenly, Mr. Billy Goat lowered his head, raced through the herd and butted the car on the driver's side door with an enormous thud. It scared me to death, and I sat frozen in place until the herd passed by. Thoroughly shaken, I cautiously drove to the dry cleaners. When I got out, I saw a huge dent made by Billy's horns. I told Hassan, the dry cleaner (whom I had known from our last tour), about my experience. He laughed and said, "Meesuss Estarkey, never look in the eyes of a goat - or he will butt you."

When Jim came home, I related the incident to him and showed him the dent. He shook his head in disbelief and sarcastically remarked, "You don't really expect me to buy that story. A goat did it! Yeh, and, did he eat your homework, too?"

The fourteenth of October, the Shah's birthday was to be celebrated by a display of the Armed Forces of Iran at Qom, the site of the *madreseh* (school), where the Ayatollah Ruhollah Khomeini preached against the Shah in the 60's. During our first tour, the Shah had issued an edict referred to as the 'White Revolution,' which forced the wealthy landowners and mullahs to give up their lands to the peasants; gave the women the right to vote and to remove their chadors; decreed that girls would, after high school graduation, enter either the Armed Forces, the Red Lion and Sun (the Iranian Red Cross) or the Literacy Corps. Members of the Literacy Corps were sent out to the villages to teach the children to read and write. Prior to that, in each village there was only one person who could read and write - and therefore controlled everything in the village, and that was the local mullah. The girls of the Literacy Corps were subjected to all manner of abuse from the clergy and other males. Khomeini, wishing an end to the secular law imposed on Iran in the 1930's and the return to Sharia law in order to control all women, led the revolt against the Shah's edict. Much rioting ensued, and the Coca-cola plant was burned and cars were overturned. Then Khomeini called on men to cut off the breasts of any women not wearing a chador. He continued to foment riots by preaching sedition from his class-rooms and mosques in Qom and other cities during most of our first tour. After months of Khomeini's subversion, the exasperated Shah finally sent him into exile. We speculated that the choice of Qom was to show the Shah's strength to the members of the *ulama*, the Shia clerical hierarchy.

In spite of suffering from the usual early pregnancy morning sickness, I told Jim I would like to go to the Shah's birthday event with him. Jim and I were flown to Qom in a military plane full of generals from the Pentagon. The seats were placed parallel to the length of the airplane. The flight was not smooth, and the up and down movement of the plane did not help my unsettled stomach. I sat there staring at the shiny, just-polished shoes of a two-star general from Washington and silently prayed that I wouldn't throw-up on them. We landed, to my great relief, before I could disgrace myself, and walked to an arena facing a huge, imposing field. Jim led me to seats at the top of the stands, and we settled in just as the ceremonies began. The band began playing the Iranian National Anthem, and an Honor Guard escorted the Shah, the Empress and their entourage to their seats. For twenty minutes, scores of gleaming uniformed men marched by in perfect formation carrying rifles in an upright position. As they left the field, transport planes flew high in the sky and suddenly, the air was full of parachutists. What was astonishing to me was that all the parachutists were women! (I bet they didn't wear chadors when they were off duty.) Next we were treated to a fly-by reminiscent of our navy's Blue Angels. The planes did acrobatics high up in the sky and, at the conclusion, two fighter planes roared past the stands at a lower level than where we were sitting. They were mere feet above the ground. One false move and we all would have been obliterated. It was an amazing display of scary, brazen confidence. When the show was over and we were walking to the plane, I remarked to Jim, "I hope we are not creating a Frankenstein."

A sergeant in his office knew of a man who could guide Jim, Smokey and Herb on a bird hunting trip in the Elburz Mountains on the up-coming long weekend. Jim got out his hunting and camping gear, the bird vest and his shotgun and eagerly prepared for the adventure. They left work early Wednesday afternoon and expected to return Saturday afternoon. Jim walked in Friday morning looking exhausted and very angry. "We got arrested," he told me.

"You what?"

"We got arrested for hunting on the Shah's private hunting preserve. We were hiking along a path when we were suddenly surrounded by uniformed men who had guns trained on us. The first thing they did, after making us lie on the ground, was to take our shotguns. No one spoke English and our guide, Habib mysteriously disappeared. We tried to tell our captors that we were American officers working for the Shah, but they only shouted at us. We were finally brought to an outpost where we talked to an English-speaking officer. We told him that we had hired Habib to guide us, and we had no idea we were in the Shah's hunting preserve. He took our driver's licenses and ARMISH-MAAG cards and went into his private office to make a phone call. It was a long time before he came out and gave us back our identifications. He told us we were free to go but he refused to give us back our shotguns."

"Who is this Habib? Do you think he did this on purpose? Why did he disappear?"

"Babe, your guess is as good as mine. I'm going to call General Patton and see if he can help us." Gen. Patton was not helpful at all. He was an Easterner, reared in Washington DC, and had never been hunting. Smokey and Herb were from the South and, like Jim, hunting was a rite of passage. Jim appealed to Col. Atlassi, thinking that since he was with the Shah's Palace Guard, maybe he could help. That didn't work. Next he talked to Mr. Malek, the Armenian attorney who worked for the legal officer at Gulf District. When nothing was happening, Jim finally told Gen. Saleh about the incident and how anxious he was to get his shotgun back, as it had belonged to Grandpa Starkey. That seemed to do the trick, and the shotgun was returned.

Fall was upon us, and the nights grew cooler. One afternoon I came downstairs from my nap and was surprised to find the three huge pots with the palm trees that had been outside, were now indoors, aligned against the glass doors of the living room. Col. Atlassi had sent some soldiers over to move the plants indoors before winter arrived. I got the feeling I was not in charge of this house. The following week, winter hit, with cold, blowing winds coming down from the snow-covered Elburz Mountains. That evening, Negadar came into the house and said to Jim, "*Sarhang*, many bad robbers around. Me stay in house by big stove tonight, guard you."

"That's a good idea, Negadar. Thank you for thinking about it." Jim came back into the room, chuckling, "It's really getting cold outside. Negadar wants to sleep inside next to the stove to guard us from robbers. I told him it was fine. Let's go to bed so he can get settled in." I started upstairs where the children were watching TV in the entry hall. I had placed an old nine-by-twelve rug up there and had the heavy cotton panniers, which were made to go over the backs of donkeys and used to carry vegetables, cement or manure, made into cushions. These were sturdy enough to withstand anything the kids could do to them. The cushions became forts and were thrown around in all sorts of games and pillow fights. That area was always comfortable in any kind of weather - and especially in the winter when the heat from the downstairs stove rose. It was the kid's favorite place to play. Jim went to the front door and called, "Goodnight, Negadar," and joined us upstairs. Several minutes later we heard the front door open and Negadar shuffle in. Later that night I remembered that I had forgotten to take my pregnancy medication. I went downstairs and saw that Negadar had brought in his bedroll and placed it next to the stove. He was snoring loudly, as was Bandit, who was asleep next to Negadar. I walked right past them going into the kitchen and neither stirred. So much for protection against robbers! In the morning, around six o'clock, we heard the front door open and close. At seven I came down to start breakfast when the front door opened. Negadar, bent at the waist, hobbled in carrying a large can filled with kerosene for the stove. Bandit attacked him, growling fiercely while grabbing at his pant-leg. Pugs don't have much of a bite, so no damage was done. Negadar shook his head and grunted,

346

"Bandeet *devoneh sag.*" (Bandit is a crazy dog). All winter, every night at nine o'clock, Jim would go to the front door, call "Good night, Negadar," and we would go upstairs. Negadar would come in with his bedroll, and he and Bandit would settle down to sleep together. The next morning, repeating the comedy, Bandit would attack him, and Negadar and I would laugh. When spring arrived, suddenly there were no more robbers for Negadar to guard against, and he went back to sleeping in his room.

I went to the hospital to learn the Lamaze method of birthing, which was started by a Swiss nurse by the same name. Jane Kazemi turned out to be an excellent instructor. Lying on mats on the floor, I learned to hold my right leg up in the air for several minutes while forcing the rest of my body to completely relax. Then we'd try the other leg, then the right arm and then the left arm. From there we progressed to breathing exercises. We chose a song to sing while enduring labor pains. Jane suggested *Jingle Bells* or *Mairzee Doats*. I chose *Mairzee Doats*. Once a week we practiced various exercises, relaxing, puffing through our mouths and singing *Mairzee Doats*. The words were sung so fast it sounded like a foreign language but words sung separately made sense:
"Mares eat oats and does eat oats and little lambs eat ivy
A kid will eat ivy too, wouldn't you?"
Jane had a series of black-and-white posters that showed the steps from conception through birthing. I asked her if I could borrow them to show the kids so they would know what to expect and why my shape was changing. After homework was finished, I gathered the children in the living room and started my lecture. First came the picture of the penis and the vagina, and with a pointer, I clinically explained how the seed got into the vagina. When I glanced at the children, their mouths were wide open and their eyes looked like they were dropping out of their sockets. I quickly went on to show the pictures of the different stages of the baby growing, and finally the birth itself. "Are there any questions?" I asked.
Numbly, the three shook their heads. Finally Jimbo asked, "Can we go out and play now?" I nodded, and off they scampered.
That went pretty well, I mused.
That night after dinner the kids were eating ice cream in the

kitchen, and Jim and I were sitting at the dining room table reading the mail Jim had brought home. Through the pass-through window I heard Peggy say, "See, this is where I keep my eggs." I peeked through the window and saw that Peggy had lifted her blouse and was pointing to her belly button!

Jimbo's baseball team was playing a game at the Noncommissioned Officer's Club over on a side street near Pahlavi Avenue. It was my turn for the carpool, so Jimbo, Pat, Peggy and two of Jimbo's teammates piled into the station wagon and off we went. As we were driving down Pahlavi Avenue, suddenly a black Peykan car came careening out from a side street. I slammed on the brakes, but could not avoid hitting the back side of the sedan. I leaped out of the station wagon and waddled over toward the other driver as he ran up to me. He started screaming that I owed him money for wrecking his car. I started arguing with him just as a well-dressed Iranian man came over and, in perfect English, asked me if he could help. I told him what had happened and he said, "Do not worry, Madam. I will take care of it." He turned to the man and in rapid Farsi the two carried on, for the longest time, an extensive conversation as crowds of onlookers watched. Ten minutes later, the aggrieved party walked to his car, opened the trunk and balling up his fist, he pounded the inside of the car, popping out the huge dent our station wagon had put in the side. Giving me a dirty look, he climbed in the car and, with tires squealing, he drove away. I looked at amazement at my benefactor who smiled and said, "I convinced him that he would lose if he tried to take you to court, as I would testify that he was at fault. I also let him know that I am an attorney. Also, these Peykan cars are like driving a tin can. You could see how the dents can be easily knocked out. Madam, now you and your children can safely go on your way." I smiled at his description of the car and thanked him profusely.

We invited the Shoemakers, the Delahantys and Dr. and Mrs. Morrow to join us for Thanksgiving, which was fast approaching. The Morrows were the only ones to decline, opting instead to go to Egypt for the holiday. We asked the two families to each bring two of their favorite traditional foods. Patricia Shoemaker brought her special homemade pecan pies and cornbread while Elizabeth Delahanty brought a Jello salad and Brussels sprouts, a dish I cannot abide but that Jim relishes. We never could get celery stalks in Iran, but celery root was available. Iranians had never heard of yams, but the canned variety was available in the embassy co-op. The co-op got in a supply of turkeys; we had brought cranberry sauce and other canned vegetables in our shipment, so we had a very lovely dinner.

The first of December we received word that we were to sponsor a LTC Johnson Hubble, who was due to arrive in March. Determined to give him all the information he needed as soon as possible, I sat down at the typewriter as Jim dictated to me. We wrote everything we could think of to help Hubble prepare for this assignment, and also included the latest booklet from ARMISH-MAAG and the one that the American Women's Club had printed. Ten days later we received a very nice letter that told us that Hubble was bringing his wife, Sarah, and sixteen year-old daughter Carolyn. They had a son, Duncan, who was a West Point cadet, and another son, Richard, who had just graduated from college. He added that they had been on a Military Advisory assignment to Burma many years before and knew how hard it was to get certain items. Was there anything we needed? I sat right down and wrote a letter asking them that if they had room in their shipment of household goods would they please buy us a crib, high chair and playpen. I added that my condition was a big surprise, which was why we were unprepared. I told them we would send them a check immediately if they could perform this task for us. Johnny and Sarah Hubble were several years older than we were and they later told us how much fun it was to see the looks from people when they shopped for baby furniture. Johnny claimed that he got admiring glances from the salesman.

The American School was built on three sides around a large concrete patio. When the physical education classes played baseball or football, the children would march up a hill two blocks to reach the playing field. Patrick came home one day and excitedly told us that his class was walking up the hill for P.E. when they passed a mansion where the cook was in the yard cutting off the head of a goose. The headless goose took off and ran toward the children, spraying blood all over. The kids scattered in all directions until the goose fell over. Jim laughed and said to Pat, "You're lucky, Pat. Not many kids get this kind of an education! Think of the stories you can tell your friends in the States."

After Thanksgiving, we had to order our Christmas presents from the States if we hoped to get them in time. I got out all the catalogues we had brought from home and gave the kids paper and pencils so they could make out their list to send to Santa Claus or, as Peggy said, Father Christmas. Pat and Jimbo marked every male-oriented item they found, while Peggy was more discriminating in her choices. She wasn't very interested in dolls but really wanted a Winnie the Pooh. She also marked the Susie Cook-off Oven; the description said that it really baked cookies. I told Peggy that I did not think Santa would bring that as he would think it was too dangerous to use with the 220 volts electricity we had in Iran. "Honey, anytime you want to bake cookies let me know, and you can use the real oven." I said.

"Can we make cookies right now?' she asked.

"Let's do it after school tomorrow and surprise the boys." Peg thought that was a good idea.

"Father Christmas is very smart, isn't he? He knows this electricity is too dangerous," Peggy solemnly intoned.

I never could understand adults who thought children should only be told straight facts. Fairy tales, the Easter Bunny, Tooth Fairy and Santa Claus help children develop their imaginations. To answer questioning older kids, I would only say, "If you don't believe in Santa Claus, he won't come to see you". One time I heard Jimbo say to Patrick, "Pat, don't say anything to Mom. She still believes in Santa Claus!"

When we were in Iran before, the only place to buy a Christmas tree was at the Russian Embassy. It always amused us that in a Moslem country we capitalists bought our Christmas trees from an atheist communist country. This time we discovered that an enterprising ex-pat who was married to an Iranian woman had planted fir trees in a vacant compound owned by the wife's family and was doing a brisk business. Everyone piled into the car and off we went to buy a Christmas tree. After extensive discussions, with all five of us voicing our opinions, we chose the tree - the biggest and best tree in the lot and watched while it was being cut down. Jim brought out a long rope and with the help of several laborers tied it to the roof of the station wagon. In the spirit of the season, I tried to start a Christmas carol as we drove home. Almost in unison the kids cried out, "Mom, puleeeze don't sing."

Negadar helped us bring it into the house smiling and saying, "*Khali khub, Sarhang.*" (very good, colonel) We placed it next to the fireplace and decorated it with balls and tinsel, as well as popcorn strings. Jim had picked up all the packages arriving from our family and Sears and Roebuck and hid them in the *umbar.*(storage rom) While the children were in school, I wrapped packages, placed them under the tree, leaving the presents from Santa in the *umbar.*

Several days before Christmas, Col. Atlassi surprised us with a present. It was a large wooden bowl with inlaid mother-of-pearl designs, and it sat on a stand of three carved elephants. Jim and the boys had made a bar that sat in the foyer between the living room and dining room doors. They had covered the front in a green leather-like plastic and nailed a brass shield in the center with brass figures of kings like the ones at Persepolis on either side. The top was a slab of marble we bought in Rey, the city south of Tehran. It was the perfect place for the bowl, and I kept it filled with the delicious, famous Iranian pistachios - everyone's favorite snack.

Christmas Eve we went to a party for the children at the Officers Club. There were all kinds of games, hot chocolate for the kids and hot mulled wine for the adults, and a buffet of traditional Christmas fare and then Santa Claus appeared, with a huge sack full of toys. Miraculously, Santa called out each child's name and mentioned something special about the child. Jimbo got a football, Pat got a fire engine and Peggy got a Winnie the Pooh stuffed animal. On the way home Peggy said enthusiastically, "Santa got me exactly what I asked for. AND, I got to see the *real* Santa Claus!"

We got the kids into bed and, after the big excitement of the evening, they were pretty tired. "Hurry up and get to sleep so Santa can come here with the rest of your presents."

"Why can't we stay up and say hello to him again?" Pat wondered.

"No, you get to bed. Santa will be in a hurry, as he has lots of places to go." Jim answered.

Jim and I went into our bedroom, and ten minutes later the kids were sound asleep. We took the Santa presents into the living room. One of the items we chose for each of the kids was a Punch 'em clown - a tall plastic balloon of a clown with a sand bottom. Jim and I blew them up and set them in front of the tree. The object was to hit the clown in the face as hard as possible: the clown would fall back and immediately come forward ready to be hit again. The three clowns were different sizes and had different faces. Both of us were tired from all the excitement of the day and, after taking Bandit out back to go to the bathroom, Jim called out to Negadar, "Goodnight, Negadar." Then we went upstairs and fell asleep the minute our heads hit the pillows.

Suddenly, Jim rose out of bed, waking me up. Glancing at the alarm clock I saw that it was 2:00 am. Hearing a commotion coming from below, we both dashed downstairs. Looking like Lazarus arising from the dead, Negadar, his back straight, was slowly sitting up and plaintively pleading, "No, Jeembo, no." Jimbo had awakened Pat and Peggy, dragging them down to see what Santa had brought. The boys were busy punching the clowns while Peggy stood off to one side with an unhappy frown on her prune-like face. She never wanted her sleep interrupted. Jim ordered the kids to get to bed and Peggy complied immediately, while the boys tried to linger to inspect the rest of the loot.

Christmas morning we awoke to snow on the ground. It was only a few inches, just enough that the neighborhood was full of kids of all ages throwing snowballs. I roasted a pork roast, made Persian rice and served it with green beans and apple sauce. The kids and Jim disappeared for awhile and came back with a birthday cake for me. It had white frosting with 'Happy Birthday' written under the Iranian flag. It started snowing again, and the rest of the day we enjoyed playing games with the children.

One thing that hadn't changed from our first tour was the fact that we were allowed only a five minute news broadcast at noon. The Shah's reasoning was that he had invited Americans to Iran to help him, and if Iranians (who listened to everything American and watched our television shows every night) heard all the negative things, especially about the Viet Nam war that our news media broadcast, they would not think so highly of America. We listened to the broadcast religiously, and were shocked to hear that the news of that day in December, was that the twelve-storied Pioneer Hotel in Tucson, Arizona had burned. That was all that was said. Later, Dr. Morrow came by with newspaper clippings about the fire. We learned that Harold Steinfeld, who had built the hotel in 1929, had perished along with his wife Peggy and twenty-six other people. A young man, Louis C. Taylor, a four-time parolee from the State Industrial School for Boys, was arrested.

On the second of January, Jim was sitting at his desk when he felt a strong pain in his lower back. He had been in the hospital for a back problem when we lived in Ft. Eustis, and this pain was similar, so he immediately went to the hospital for a checkup. After an examination, he was admitted and was placed in what is called the William's position; the bed is fixed so that the feet and head are high and the rump is low. The ligaments of his lower back were not doing the job of keeping his bones off a disk, so being in this position took the pressure off the disk and allowed the swelling to go down. The doctor expected him to be bed-bound for at least three weeks. Jim called me and gave me a list of items to bring to the hospital. The first week he read seven books and by the second week he was getting antsy, and giving the nurses a bad time. Patrick's Cub Scout group was having a competition among the members to make something that worked, out of such items as a paper plates, rubber bands, tooth picks, straws, paper clips, empty spools of thread, string and pins. The Scouts were to get help from their fathers, so Patrick brought everything to the hospital. This was just the thing to keep Jim occupied. He spent hours planning the project and ended up with a cannon that moved on wheels made of paper plates and shot darts from a straw. He gleefully terrorized the nurses, who I'm sure were looking forward to getting rid of him. Jim was finally released from the hospital with the orders to wear a special back brace for the next month.

Soon after I became pregnant, I started having problems with the veins in my legs, and Dr. Kazemi ordered me to get a special girdle and heavy hose to help the problem. When I awoke in the morning, I was told to stay bed and keep my legs high in the air while I wrestled the heavy stockings on and hooked them to the girdle. It became a comedy act every morning with Jim donning a back brace and me fighting to get my girdle on without attaching half the bedding to it, then putting on the hose while reaching for the roof with my toes.

Patrick had been having a lot of problems with heavy colds, strep throat and some hearing loss, so the pediatrician told us Pat would have to have his tonsils and adenoids out. Since the small hospital didn't have the facilities for this, it would have to be done at the Army hospital in Landstuhl, West Germany in the summer.

One night as Peggy was watching me put on my nightgown she patted my stomach and said, "Momma, you're getting awfully fat."

"Oh, you think this is fat?" I answered. "Just wait until your birthday in March. My stomach will be out to here," I said, extending my hands out a foot from my stomach.

Looking thoughtful, my little darling said, "Well, you can bring out my cake, but then you had better hide in the closet!"

When we had been in Iran before and attempted to buy something, I found myself highly offended by the Persian habit of what we came to call the 'Camel Kiss.' Throughout most of the underdeveloped world and, especially in the Middle East, it is traditional to never pay the first price the seller demands. It is part of the process for the seller and buyer to 'discuss' the ultimate fare by the seller telling the buyer his price and the buyer, in turn, saying, "That is too much. I will pay this much." This goes on with the seller coming down a little and the buyer coming up a little until there is agreement. The first time I witnessed the Camel Kiss I was in the midst of a discussion I was having over a brass samovar. I purposely came in with a very low price and, upon hearing this, the shop keeper sneered at me. He flared his nostrils, flipped his head back while clicking his tongue on the roof of his mouth and breathing out through his lips with a loud chuuuuu sound. I was so insulted I left the shop and never returned. When I complained to some friends, they laughed and told me this happened all the time and referred to it as the Camel Kiss.

I decided to "when in Rome, act like a Roman," so I practiced the Camel Kiss in front of the mirror until I had perfected it. The first time I used it in a negotiation I was satisfied to see the shocked look on the shopkeeper's face. Later, I found it worked just as well when negotiating in Mexico. I never consciously taught the Kiss to our children but I discovered that they picked it up by watching when I shopped. Jim had decreed that he would pay for good grades in a desperate attempt to get Jimbo to work harder in school. When the report cards came out, Patrick had all A's and B's. That afternoon he waited impatiently for Jim to get home. As Jim entered the front door Patrick yelled, "Dad, this is going to cost you." Jim happily paid up, and Pat pestered me to take him shopping. We entered the brass shop at the corner of Saltanatabad and Dowlat. Pat meandered all around, looking and feeling various objects and asking the price. Then he would shake his head and mutter, "That's too much." He finally picked up a brass lion and asked the price. "It is 150 rial." Mimicking the Camel Kiss, Pat responded, "That's way too much. I will give you 50 rial."

"Oh, no, no, no, I will lose money. You can have it for 120 rial."

"I will give you 70 rial," Pat persisted.

"My last price is 100 rial," the shopkeeper said, with a smile. With that, Pat pulled 70 rial out of his pocket and placed it on the counter. The shopkeeper looked at the money and shook his head. "I will lose money on this," he said as he started wrapping it up. As we left, the man said to me, "Madam, you have a very good bargainer in that little man." Pat grinned all the way home.

Ever since the Christmas conversation about making cookies, Peggy had started helping in the kitchen. In the evening, she would set the table and make the salad. We got some very interesting combinations - as I encouraged her creativity. After dinner, Pat would clear the dishes and Jimbo would scrape, rinse, and put them in the dishwasher. Jim and I have always been an advocate of cheap child labor.

Peg's kindergarten was only in the morning, so frequently when I picked Peggy up at school we would drive to the bakery shop on Dowlat just as the bread was coming out of the ovens. The bread, called *nune,* was unleavened. Peggy and I would patiently wait for the crowd to leave and buy a piping-hot loaf that the baker had just removed from the oven. He would wrap it in newspaper and, with a big smile, hand it to Peggy. She would hand him two rial while smiling sweetly. The baker would look at me and say, "*Khaili qashang dukhtar.* (very beautiful girl)". "*Savid mu qashang (*white hair beautiful).*" Pat and Peg had very blonde hair and blue eyes, which intrigued all Iranians. Peggy and I would take the warm bread home and give half of it to Nagadar. The rest we would spread with butter, peanut butter and add syrup as we would for waffles. It was so delicious when fresh, but after a day it was like chewing on dried shoe leather.

In February the Shah hosted a meeting of oil consortium executives from the Persian Gulf OPEC members that included Iran, Iraq, Abu Dhabi, Kuwait, Qatar and Saudi Arabia. The Persian Gulf OPEC members wanted to raise the price of a barrel of oil from $2.28 a barrel to $2.34 a barrel and would guarantee that price for the next five years. The oil executives would agree only if this price included all OPEC members. They capitulated only after the American ambassador, with the backing of the Nixon administration, sided with the Shah, and an agreement was reached between Gulf OPEC members and the oil consortium. Three months later, Libya raised the price per barrel of oil from $2.55 to $3.45.

The Hubble family arrived on the late night Pan American flight. Jim and I took them to the hotel room where we had stocked snacks and drinks for them knowing how long distance flights mess up sleep and eating patterns. We knew instantly that we would be friends. Johnny Hubble had an infectious laugh and a playful sense of humor; Sarah was friendly and fun from the very beginning. Their pretty, teen-aged daughter, Carolyn, was very excited to be in a different culture. We spent many days showing them around and helping them find a house.

Once a week I went to the hospital for Jane Kazemi's Lamaze classes. In the early 1970's, Lamaze classes had just begun to spread across the United States and had yet to include expectant fathers in the movement. Birthing was still just between the woman and her doctor, no fathers allowed. In addition to the breathing and relaxing exercises, the class talked about nutrition for both the mother and new-born; how to keep a positive attitude while becoming a big, fat, clumsy shadow of your former self; how to prevent varicose veins and all the other changes one has while pregnant. Jane took us through, step by step, what to expect when our time of delivery came. I wished I had had this class way back when Jimbo was born, as I am sure I would not have spent forty-eight hours in labor if I had known what to expect.

One day as I was leaving the Lamaze classes, a high school student asked me for a ride to the Officer's Club where he was a forward on the basketball team. His name was Mike O'Brien; he had lived in Tehran for seven years, as his father was a senior Embassy official. I knew of his father, so I told him I would be glad to take him to the club. He was a very bright kid, and we were having an interesting conversation as I started the car. "Mrs. Starkey, do you know the shortcut to the Officers Club?" he asked.

"No," I answered. "Show me the way. I always like to take short cuts." He pointed to a side street, and I turned into it. The macadam road soon turned to dirt and became very narrow. The mean adobe huts lining the road looked like the ones in the villages south of Tehran, even though they were only a block away from the sprawling metropolis. I slowed as we came down a hill and noticed on my right, two donkeys in front of a decrepit hovel. As the car came up next to the donkeys, suddenly a small boy raced out from between the parked donkeys, chasing an errant ball that was rolling across the street. I slammed on the brakes and heard the child screaming.

Mike looked out the window and said, "Pull up quick, you're on his foot!" I moved the car forward to release the boy when a mob of men and one chador-clad woman rushed toward us. The woman in the black chador was keening shrilly, saying something in Farsi that sounded like, "Whymeee, Whymeee". Suddenly, the car doors opened and the station wagon was full of men and the woman, who had the child on her lap. The child was crying and clinging to his mother. I saw that he was wearing pink plastic boots. Everyone was yelling at once. I looked at Mike, who said, "Mrs. Starkey, don't say anything." Then he turned to the mob, (there were seven men plus the mother and child in our station wagon) and started speaking in fluent Farsi. Several men answered, and I heard the word *Gendarme*.

"Yes," I said. "Let's go to the *Gendarme*!"

When Mike translated what I had said, they agreed, and we started for the nearest *Gendarme* station. The mother stopped her keening and told the men that the child needed to go to the hospital. So I was told to go to the nearest Iranian clinic. Off we went while the hysteria in the back seat continued. When we arrived, I asked Mike to talk to the receptionist while I called the Legal Office at Gulf District. We waited while the paperwork was being typed, and finally the child was taken in to have an x-ray of his foot. Mr. Malek, the Armenian who was the local attorney who worked for the U.S. Government, arrived and introduced himself to me. "Mrs. Estarkey, what can I do for you?"

I explained what had happened, and Mike verified my statement. Mr. Malek said, "Stay right here. I will be back." And he left to talk to the other parties. He was gone quite awhile, and when he returned he was carrying the pink plastic boots the child had been wearing. He was smiling broadly as he showed me the boots. There was a distinct tire mark over the toe of one of the boots. He was laughing when he said, "This boy is only three years old, and he was wearing his big sister's boots, which were way too big for him. You ran over the boot, but you never touched his toes. The x-rays showed that the foot was unharmed. You may leave now, and I will take care of this for you. You are not to blame, and the doctor already told the family that."

With a sigh of relief Mike and I left to get him to his game on time. "Mike, I don't know what I would have done if you had not been with me. Thank goodness you speak such good Farsi!"

"Mrs. Starkey, it was my pleasure. This certainly was an interesting day!"

"You're right. I'm not sure I can take many more of these 'interesting days'!" I replied.

Chapter 18

January 1, 1971 the United States began its second decade of involvement in Viet Nam. In Cape Kennedy Apollo 14 is launched on another moon mission. Senator George McGovern of South Dakota opened his campaign for the Democratic presidential nomination pledging to remove all U.S. troops from Viet Nam if elected. OPEC decided to set oil prices without consulting buyers, causing much fear among the western nations. In February the threat of an oil production stoppage was removed in a meeting in Iran with an agreement between 23 oil companies and six Persian Gulf states. The settlement increases the payments of oil companies by $10 billion to Iran, Iraq, Saudi Arabia, Kuwait, Abu Dhabi and Qatar. In Lichtenstein, the male electorate refused to give women the right to vote.

In Tehran the days were crisp and cold with several snow days. Jim came home one Wednesday and said, "Let's take the kids skiing tomorrow at Abe Ali, where the Shah has built a ski resort. We can rent the equipment, and the kids can take ski lessons." I had never been skiing, and being pregnant I would not try to, but that sounded like just what all of us needed to get rid of the winter blues. The kids were so excited to have the opportunity to learn to ski, especially Jimbo and Pat, who had been hearing about skiing from their friends. It didn't take us long to get ready.

The next morning, the cloudless sky was a deep shade of ultra-marine. It was very cold, but we were all bundled up. We packed extra clothes for the children, and, waving goodbye to Negadar, we were on our way toward the mountains. The newly-paved road was clear, and we made good time, arriving in less than two hours. The ski area at Abe Ali was impressive, with mountains for expert skiers, as well as hills for beginners. We found the shop, where Jim started the negotiations for equipment, and soon the kids were fixed up with goggles, boots, skis and poles. Jim then hired an individual instructor for each child. We watched as they were being taught. All three of them were fearless and soon were going up on the tow rope with the instructors. Each instructor held his grinning charge around the waist as they glided down the hill. This was repeated a couple of times, and soon we lost track of where each child was. We were standing at the bottom of the hill, stamping our feet, trying to keep warm and looking around for them. Suddenly, I spotted Patrick on the rope tow without his instructor. "Jim, there's Pat on the lift without the instructor!" We saw Ali, Pat's instructor, sitting with some other men drinking tea. By then Pat was at the top of the slope, poised with skis and looking down the mountain. He waited a few minutes and then swiftly pushed off and down he came. My heart was in my throat as I saw my son tucking his ski poles under his arms, bending over and going like a bat out of Hell. I heard Jim shout, "What form, he's a natural, another John Paul Killy," Then he hollered, "Oh my God! He doesn't know how to stop!" About that time, Pat was thinking the same thing as he careened down to the bottom. He stopped all right! Right on his face, his glasses flying off as he tumbled over and over. I was sure he had broken every bone in his body. We dashed for him, with Jim getting there first. He lifted him up, and Pat had the biggest grin I had ever seen. "Oh, Dad!" he shouted to the sky. "That was so much fun!" After determining that Pat was not hurt, Jim angrily took off to find the instructor - who by then had mysteriously disappeared.

"Patrick, why did you try to go down by yourself?" I breath-lessly demanded.

"Well, Mom, that guy was too slow. I wanted to go fast, and

he wouldn't! So I decided to go myself, but when I got to the top of the hill, it really looked steep, but I decided to go down anyway. That was so much fun! I want to go up again!"

We located Jimbo and Peggy and, while Pat described his thrilling actions to his envious siblings, we went into the café for some hot tea and lunch. The rest of the afternoon the kids practiced using the rope tow on a smaller hill. Their first experience on skis was positive, and today all three are confident, excellent skiers.

We had not seen my adventurous Aunt Lil since her visit to us in Ft. Eustis, so when she wrote that she would like to visit us in Tehran, the whole family was thrilled. After she had retired from teaching and Uncle Bill had died, she started traveling all over the United States. It was only in the previous year that she had ventured overseas, taking a tour to Europe. Coming by herself all the way to Iran was a big deal. I wrote to her saying that the best time to come would be during *No Ruz*, the Iranian New Year that was celebrated the first day of Spring.

Aunt Lil's letter said she would arrive at 1:00 am 12 March on KLM Royal Dutch Airline, so we started making preparations. We moved my art junk into the *umbar* and turned the downstairs room into a bedroom - after borrowing a bed and dresser from our friends, the Stanfords. I wrote Aunt Lil how excited we were that she was coming, and that Peggy had announced the fact to her class. Then I facetiously added, "Don't forget to bring a pantsuit so you can ride a camel."

Leaving the kids asleep in their beds, Jim and I drove to Mehrabad Airport in record time through the darkened streets of Tehran, parked the car and anxiously awaited the arrival of our beloved Aunt Lil. The plane made a perfect landing, taxied to the terminal and stopped as the steps were wheeled to the doorway. Suddenly, the plane started up again. "My God, Jim, Aunt Lil is being high-jacked!" I cried in panic. We watched in horror as the plane circled the airport, and we let out a sigh of releaf when it returned to a gate closer than the first one. Our aunt hurried down the stairs, breezed through customs and strode with great authority toward us, all five foot two inches of her rotund body belying her 73 years. Her sparkling hazel eyes were huge behind her thick glasses, and an infectious laughter rang out as she hugged us both. Jim placed a necklace of blue donkey beads around her neck as I presented her with a bouquet of flowers. We collected her luggage and led her to our station wagon. "Aunt Lil, you seem very rested after such a long trip."

"I had the whole row of seats to myself. The steward took out the armrests and gave me three pillows to lie on, so I got to sleep the whole way from Athens," she bubbled.

"You're turning out to be quite the world traveler. How would you like to go to Russia?" I asked.

"Where do I sign up?" was her quick reply. She was always quick to make decisions, but this had to be a record. Betty Morrow had called to see if I wanted to go to Moscow and Leningrad with the American Women's Club tour. I wanted to, but Dr. Kezimi said I could not, as it was too dangerous with my being seven months pregnant.

"There is a tour leaving in eight days sponsored by the Women's Club, and I have already signed you up. Do I know my Aunt Lil or do I?" I said, laughing. Aunt Lil was my mother's older sister, and the two of them were always game for anything. The middle sister, my Aunt Olive, was completely different, never wanting to travel anywhere, even though her husband traveled the world for an international mining company.

Negadar greeted us with a smile and helped carry in the suitcases. Since it was so late, Jim went immediately to bed, while I helped Aunt Lil settle in. The next morning, I had hoped to make the children be quiet to let our guest sleep, but it didn't work. Peg and the boys beat me downstairs and dashed into Lil's room for hugs and kisses.

"You kids get back upstairs and get ready for school and let Aunt Lil rest," I demanded.

"But I want to show Aunt Lil my room," Peggy wailed.

Before I could reply, Aunt Lil said, "Shirley, I have no intention of resting. I did not come all the way to Iran to rest. I'll put my robe on and go see the children's rooms." And so she did, in charge as always.

We ate breakfast, the boys caught the school bus, and it was time to take Peggy to her kindergarten. Peggy climbed into the back seat with Aunt Lil in front. As I started the car, I saw Negadar approach on Lil's side. Thinking he wanted to say something, I lowered the window just as Negadar raised the garden hose to wash the window. Aunt Lil got sprayed! Negadar was so upset, I thought he was going to cry - but Lil was laughing. I leapt out of the car and ran to the laundry room to get a towel to dry her off. Negadar was genuflecting and moaning, "Madam, I sorry, I sorry."

Drying off her face, Aunt Lil assured him, "Negadar, it's okay."

Negadar looked very surprised at Madam's attitude. As we drove away, Aunt Lil said, "I think your gardener thought he was going to get caned for getting me wet."

"If he had been working for an Iranian, that would have happened." I commented.

We were driving down single-laned Dowlat Street when suddenly, a car sped out from a side street. "Look out!" Aunt Lil shouted.

Patiently, I said, "Aunt Lil, the traffic here is insane. Your job is to sit quietly and pray." She didn't say another word, but I'm sure she was praying.

After dropping Peggy off at her school, we stopped at the green grocer, and Aunt Lil took pictures as I was bargaining for our produce. We next went to the market to get eggs, rice and *panir*, the goat cheese that Negadar liked. We returned home and gave Negadar his cheese. He was all smiles when he looked at Aunt Lil, grateful that she was not mad at him for the water episode, and from then on he was always trying to help her in any way he could. When the flowers we had given her at the airport faded, he picked some of the flowers in the garden for her, presenting them with a great flourish.

Aunt Lil watched as I soaked the fruits and vegetables in a Chlorox solution for fifteen minutes, rinsed them four times in clear water, dried and wrapped them in towels and put them in the refrigerator. I wiped the eggs with a Chlorox-soaked towel while carefully examining them for any cracks, rinsed them and put them in the refrigerator. "You're awfully careful with the food," Aunt Lil observed.

"We have to be, because some of the fruits and vegetables are fertilized with human waste. We've been very careful and never got sick the last time we were here and, knock wood, we haven't been sick this time. The only time I got sick was when we ate at an Iranian home and I ended up in the hospital with IV's, and I don't want any member of my family to have that experience."

We left for Peggy's school, as it was close to lunchtime. We parked in the usual place and Peggy came out, grabbed Aunt Lil's arm and insisted that Aunt Lil come in to meet her teacher. As we entered the school compound, a four-year old boy cried out, "Here she comes!" and led the way into the schoolhouse. Peggy had been telling everyone about her great-aunt, and Lil was greeted like royalty.

Before I could make the introductions, Mrs Fahti came forward, her hand outstreached. "So glad to meet you, Aunt Lil". she said in her cultured English accent. Aunt Lil laughed and I made the introductions. Looking at the two of them, I was struck by their similarities - the same heighth and shape but also the same 'I'm in charge' attitude.

"Mrs. Honeycutt, Peggy has told the whole class about you. It is a real pleasure to have Peggy in my class. She is a very observant child. Do you know the other day she asked me if my shoes would float. I said, 'Whatever in the world made you think of that,' and she answered, 'because the heels are cork.' 'And how do you know that cork will float,' I asked and she said she liked to float the cork from her Daddy's wine bottle!"

The next day, I took Aunt Lil shopping for warm boots to wear in Russia, and she was successful in finding some fur-lined, low-heeled ones. We met Jim at the Embassy for lunch, and then we went shopping in the co-op. As we entered, we heard a lot of commotion and discovered that the Shah's brothers and their military bodyguards were buying out the liquor store. One of the clerks said, "If you want any Scotch, you're out of luck. Everytime these guys come in, they clean us out."

"How come the Shah's people get to come in here?" I asked.

"That's part of the agreement our government has made with the Shah. We were told to help them in any way we can, and so we do."

Aunt Lil looked confused, "I thought Moslems don't drink alcohol."

"That's what they say, but we know different."

The following Thursday, Jim and I took Aunt Lil down to the Grand Bazaar in south Tehran. We picked up, as a guide, an Iranian soldier, Mahmood, who worked in Jim's office. When Tehran was founded, one of the first things to be built was the bazaar, and over the ensuing years it was added to and came to meander over many acres. The main entrance had imposing arches soaring three stories high and the floors were of dirt made hard from centuries of feet walking over them. On either side of criss-crossed lanes, shops and stalls offer goods and crafts from all over the Middle East. Skylights allow light to come in, and most of the shops have Christmas lights festooned over their wares. There are distinct 'shops' within the baazar, which are rented from the *bazaaris,* the wealthy, religious men who control the activities of the bazaar. The bazaar is more than just a place to shop; it is the heart of the city, of commerce and industry. Politics and religion depend on its prosperity. The taxes the rich merchants pay funds the mullahs and politicians, keeping both in business.

The first area we came to was the brass and copper section full of *samovars, hookah* pipes, platters, plates, pots, vases - anything you could think of in carved or filagreed metal, and all were polished to a bright sheen. The hammering sounds of the artisans pounding designs into the metal mingled with the shopkeepers hawking their wares and the arguments of the purchasers. Stacks of tin *samovars* reached the ceiling and, as we walked by, the dealer called out to us that his prices were the best.

We walked down the narrow, dark aisle toward the gold section, where all the items are displayed in well-lit cases. We paused there, watching a couple looking at wedding rings. The young man was arguing vehemently with the shopkeeper while the embarrassed young girl bent over, trying to hide within her chador. We moved on, ignoring a begger who was trying to block our way. Mahmood growled menacingly at the begger, who quickly left. As we came to the carpet area, Aunt Lil spied a carpet that she wanted to look at, and immediately the merchant called out, "*Khanoum,* welcome to my humble shop. Please come in." He clapped his hands and motioned to a small boy who ran off. "*Khanoum,* isn't this beautiful and look at this masterpiece," he said as he pointed out several carpets. He ushered Aunt Lil in as one of his helpers brought a chair for her to sit in. Two other helpers started picking carpets off a stack and holding them up for Aunt Lil to look at. Aunt Lil was smiling at all the attention from the smooth-talking merchant, who was intently discribing in great detail all the attributes of the carpets. Soon the small boy returned with a tray of glasses of tea encased in brass filigree holders and a bowl of rough-cut sugar cubes. Jim explained to Aunt Lil that she was to hold a cube of sugar between her teeth while she sipped the tea, Persian style. Always game for anything new, Aunt Lil complied. The merchant continued to spend time explaining the origin of each carpet, and we saw hundreds of the amazing hand-woven works of art. Finally, Aunt Lil said, "Jim, let's leave. I can't think anymore. This is too much information for me to digest."

We thanked the merchant for his time and told him we would be back. As we left, Jim said, "Aunt Lil, I'll get Elias to bring some carpets to our house, if you are interested in buying one."

We walked passed the myriad stalls of fabric for clothing and upholstery making our way toward the loud pounding sounds coming from the men making the hand-stamped cloth. We stopped to watch the men the men at work. Aunt Lil bought three bridge-table sized cloths to impress her bridge buddies back in Boulder City.

The pungent smell of spices assailed our nostrils as we passed gunny sacks filled with saffron, cloves, turmeric, chili powder, sumac, coriander, ginger, cuman, cinnamon, nutmeg and allspice all displayed in towering pyramids. Next came displays of candy and beyond that the green grocers displays for vegetables and fruits. The lanes meandered for miles, intersecting each other, and if we hadn't had Mahmood with us, we never could have found our way out of the Bazaar.

"*Sarhang, Sarhang*, camels coming!" Negadar burst into the house as we were eating dinner. The kids jumped up and ran out the door.

"Aunt Lil, go get your camera. The camels are here." Jim commanded and we started out the door. All year long nomadic tribes collected camel dung for fertilizer to sell to the merchants in Tehran. Just before *No Ruz* camel drivers would pile the sacks onto the backs of the camels and come to the city. Some thought this was the secret of the famous Persian gardens. After unloading their wares, they would seek out the homes where the crazy Americans lived who would allow their children to ride the camels.

Out in the *kuchee* was a caravan of five adult camels and one baby.

The adult camels had heavy blankets under their saddles. These were decorated with large yarn balls in shades of reds, blues, greens and purples at the edge of the blankets and around the camel's ears. The baby was unadorned. Negadar told Jim that Akbar, the driver, wanted to know if the children could ride the camels. Jim walked over, putting his hand out, "*Salam alekam, hale shoma chetor-e?*" (Hello, how are you?) Akbar was very tall, over six feet, dressed in ballooning white pants, a full, long-sleeved white shirt and a colorful vest woven in a geometric pattern. His white turban wound around his head and ended with a long tassel that flowed down his left shoulder. His black boots came up to his knees. He had piercing black eyes, heavy eyebrows knitted together and an impressive hooked nose over his massive moustache. He smiled at Jim, showing straight, beautiful teeth. He returned Jim's greeting, and negoiations started about the amount to be paid for the rides. The kids were impatiently waiting to get on the camels and, after the deal was struck, the driver got one of the camels down so Jimbo could get on. As soon as the camel could feel Jimbo on his back, he rose, first going forward as the hind legs stood and then rearing backward as the front legs rose. Fortunately, Jimbo held on tight to the saddle horn during this rocking motion. Jim held onto Pat and Peg, cautioning them to hang on tight as they mounted their respective camels. All were safely on when I realized Aunt Lil was not with us. I looked around just as she emerged from the front door. She had changed her clothes and had on a pantsuit. And was it a pantsuit! It was electric blue with enormous orange hybiscus flowers on a silken fabric that clung to her ample shape. Then it dawned on me; she didn't realize I had been joking when I suggested that she should ride a camel. Jim and I wouldn't have thought of riding those filthy animals. "I'm ready to ride a camel!" she said excitedly as she handed her movie camera to Jim and the still camera to me. "Take lots of pictures, please."

Akbar brought his biggest camel over and forced it down to allow Aunt Lil to mount it. Confidently, Aunt Lil approached the camel, swung her right leg up onto the saddle and stopped. She was stuck doing the splits; her legs were too short, the camel too tall. Jim and I were laughting so hard; I was doubled over, unable to take any pictures. A long moment went by with everyone looking at Aunt Lil, laughing but not helping. Suddenly, Akbar came to the rescue;

he rushed over and, with a big push on her rump, Lil vaulted onto the back of the camel, almost going completely over the other side on her head. She managed to hold on as the camel, feeling her on his back, stood up and started following the other camels. Aunt Lil was draped on her stomach over the saddle, her head and arms were on one side, her legs were on the other. She was hysterically laughing, and I was afraid she would fall off. She managed to right herself and was grinning broadly as her camel fell into line with the other camels. The caravan went down to the end of the *kuchee*, circled around and came back toward our house. Aunt Lil was sitting tall with a pleased look on her face, enjoying another accomplishment for this majestic lady.

No Ruz, the Iranian New Year, is celebrated on the first day of Spring (the vernal equinox), which generally falls on the 21st or 22nd of March. The tradition of *No Ruz* began with the reign of Cyrus the Great in the fifth century B.C., when the Persians followed the teachings of the prophet Zoroaster and his sun worshippers, and has survived for 2500 years. This is a very happy holiday that lasts for two weeks and has many aspects of our Easter, Holloween, Thanksgiving and Christmas observances. Prior to the celebrations, houses must be cleaned thoroughly and the Persian carpets are sent out to Rey, an ancient village south of Tehran, to be washed in the natural hot springs. If the family is too poor to send the carpets to Rey, they put the carpets face down in the streets for cars to run over them. To their way of thinking, at least the dirt would be knocked out of the fibers, and it saved a lot of labor-intensive rug beating.

It is imparitive to have new clothes for the beginning of the new year, and so it is required that servants be paid double their wages for that month. The women spend hours making *nune shekari,* (sugar cookies), *baklava,* and *badam choragi* (almond cookies). Two weeks prior to *No Ruz,* lentil seeds are planted in a water-filled, shallow bowl. When the seeds sprout, a thick green cake is formed. Several days before the celebration, children dress in costume and go to various relatives, banging loudly on a begging bowl to collect money and other gifts. Beggers take advantage of this custom and go to the houses of *farangi* (foreigners), playing discordant music, loud drums and performing an obscene version of the belly dance until the occupants give them money to go away.

The Wednesday before the vernal equinox , known as *Charshanbeh Suri*, Negadar and some of the other gardeners set small bonfires in the middle of the *kuche* for everyone in the neighborhood to leap over while chanting, "May your red radiance come to me. May my yellow tiredness go to you." This is a purification rite meant to replace sickness with wellness. We all jumped over the required seven times, including Aunt Lil.

It is traditional at this time for Persians to return to the villages where the family originated, and the roads are filled with traffic. Relatives begin arriving, bearing bouquets of yellow daffodils and red tulips. Whole lambs are grilled on spits above a roaring fire, chickens are fried, various *khoreshes* (sauces) made from vegetables and fruits are prepared to go over the *chello* (cooked rice). In the house, a special *No Ruz* table is set with *haft sin* (seven offerings) of items that begin with the letter S in Farsi; *sumac, samanoo* (grain), *sib* (apple), *sir* (garlic) *serke* (vinegar), *sabzi* (greens), *sangin* (rue). There is a mirror to deflect evil; two candles to represent light and dark; a bowl of goldfish to portray life. The goldfish are sold in small bowls, and the family gathers around the table watching the goldfish. The radio is on and the exact second of the vernal equinox is announced and the goldfish changes directions. (Of course, he changes directions every second because the bowl is so small!) These celebrations go on for two weeks, and on the thirteenth day (*Sizdah*) everyone is supposed to leave the house at sunup and have a picnic next to a stream. The green cakes of lentils are thrown into the water, and with it are supposed to go all the anger and bad feelings family members have felt toward each other during the past year. It is considered bad luck to return home before sunset.

Negadar only wanted to go to his family for the last week of *No Ruz*, so we gave him an extra month's pay, filled his knapsack with frozen pigeons, rice, *panir, mast* (yogurt), eggs and Peggy's chocolate chip cookies. Off he went to visit his wife and five-year-old son, Ali, for that week. His family lived in south Tehran, and during the rest of the year he would go every third weekend for three days. We always filled his knapsack before he left. Sometimes his wife and boy would make the journey to our house for a day or two. Jimbo and Pat always found some of their toys to give to Ali, and we kept the little guy in shirts, pants and heavy winter coats that Pat outgrew.

It was time for Aunt Lil to go with the Women's Club to Moscow, and Jim drove her to the Officers Club to meet with the rest of the group. She was as excited as a little kid and promised to make notes so she could tell us all about the trip when she returned.

When it was time for the Women's Club group to fly back to Tehran, the whole family went to the airport to get Aunt Lil. We were in the waiting rooom when the group arrived, and it was not hard to spot our aunt. She had on the biggest, reddest fox fur hat we had ever seen. As she approached us, she took the hat off and put it on my head. "Here, Shirley, this a present from Russia for you since you could not go on the trip."

The next afternoon Jim and I were listening to Aunt Lil tell us about all the things she had done and seen in Russia when the front door flew open and Jimbo raced in screaming, "The wild dogs are chasing Pat." Jim leaped up, ran to the *umbar* for his shotgun and was out the door. I followed as fast as I could, and as I rounded the wall on the west of our house I saw Jim had grabbed Patrick up from the ground where he had fallen. Pat ran to me, and we quickly returned to the house while Jim continued going after the dogs. We ran upstairs to our bedroom to watch for Jim and saw him well to the south of our house, stalking the wild dogs. "Jimbo, what in the world happened?" I demanded.

"Pat and I were out with our BB guns when we came upon the dogs. We started shooting at them, and one of them turned on us. We started running for home, and I heard Pat cry out and saw that he had fallen, so I came running in the house for Dad."

Pat excitedly said, "When I tripped over the log, I decided to stay still, hoping the dogs wouldn't see me. I knew Jimbo could run real fast and that Dad would rescue me." Just then we heard Jim fire his shotgun and saw the biggest dog go down. Four more shots and all the dogs were dead. We ran back downstairs to welcome our Hero. As Jim came in he told Negadar, "Go bury those dogs." Negadar dutifully got the shovel and left.

As we went into the living room, we saw that Aunt Lil was having another attack just like the one she had in Virginia when Bandit fell off the wall. This time, we knew what to do and quickly got her into bed and gave her the medicine she kept for these attacks.

"Jim, why is it that everytime Aunt Lil comes for a visit we have some kind of an incident with dogs! I bet she thinks twice before ever coming to visit us again!"

We went upstairs to watch for Negadar. He was out in the middle of the field digging graves for the dogs. When he returned an hour later he lamented, "*Sags kheyli borzorg!*" (Dogs very big)

The next day Elias showed up with some carpets to show Aunt Lil. When she saw a blue and beige Kashan, she said, "Oh, I like this one a lot." Jim and Elias sat down cross-legged on either side of the carpet and commenced the usual pleasantries that preceeded all dealings in Iran. I poured tea for all and sat with Aunt Lil on the couch to watch the show. When the first cup of tea was finished, Aunt Lil asked Elias how much he wanted for the carpet.

"Not yet, Aunt Lil. Elias needs more tea," Jim said as I quickly refilled both tea cups.

When Elias had finished his tea, he told Aunt Lil the price, and she immediately reached for her handbag. "Not so fast, Aunt Lil," Jim said and, turning to Elias said, "That is much too much, you must give us a better price."

"No, Col. Estarkey, this is a good price."

"Elias, you know you can give us a better price."

"Oh, Col. Estarkey, you are too hard. I must think about this," Elias was saying as I was pouring him more tea.

Jim said, "Elias, this carpet is worth much less than you are asking."

Frowning, Elias responded, "This is the amount I will settle for." He wrote the amount on a piece of paper and handed it to Aunt Lil. She immediately reached into her purse, and again Jim stopped her. "Let me see that." He looked at the amount and then wrote down what he thought the carpet was worth. He handed the paper to Elias, who sighed and shaking his head said, "If you can come up to this amount, we can agree." Elias wrote down another amount.

Jim took the paper and wrote another amount.

Elias looked at it and shrugged. "Okay, you win. I will sell the carpet for this amount, but my brother will not be happy."

Since there was no way for Elias to cash a check from the United

States, Jim said, "Mrs. Starkey will bring the amount over tomorrow after we get a check cashed."

"That is a good idea, as I have another carpet I'm sure Madame Estarkey will like," Elias said with a grin.

"Thanks a lot," Jim groaned.

Aunt Lil was invited to join another Women's Club trip, this time for a week spent in Isfahan, Shiraz and Persepolis. This was a chance for Lil to see a lot of the country, and we encouraged her to take advantage of the opportunity. As usual, she didn't wait to be asked twice. She came back very enthusiastic about the history of Persia and was especially impressed with the beautiful city of Isfahan. She had only three days left on her visit, so we took her to the basement of the Bank Melli to view the Crown Jewels. We walked into a large, dark room manned by guards standing every three feet wearing dark blue uniforms with gold designs on the sleeves, lapels and shoulders. There were glass displays containing several crowns worn by the Shah and the Empress Farah; mannikins wearing the gowns of Farah and the uniforms of the Shah; incredible rings, necklaces, earrings, and bracelets in every precious and semi-precious stone available. In the middle of room, behind rope partitions, was an enormous globe of the world. Each continent was inlaid in a different precious stone: Africa was in rubies, South America was in emeralds, etc., while the Equator was in diamonds. There were pirate chests filled with pearls cascading over the side; medival armour studded with semi-precious stones; in the center of the room was the Peacock Throne, the symbol of the Persian monarchy. Covered in jewels, it was breath-taking. We were told that this display was only a fraction of the wealth of the Iranian government and was the backing of the rial. The Crown Jewels of Great Britain that are on display at the Tower of London can't hold a candle to what we saw in Iran.

In 1964 we had visited Pasargadae, where a British archeologist, Richard Campbell, was excavating the palace of Cyrus the Great. We later learned that he had discovered a cache of jewels hidden in a clay pot at the foot of a tall column on the site. We remembered the column because there was a stork's nest on it that was so big it was flowing over the side. Later, at a cocktail party, Jim introduced me to Captain Lopez who wanted to become an archeologist after he left the army and had spent many weekends helping Campbell at the dig. One of the items Campbell discovered in the clay pot was a pair of earrings that had a large diamond at the earlobe, three very thin strips of curling gold hanging down and, at the end of each strip, was a small diamond. Lopez said that Campbell brought the earrings over to Lopez' house before turning them over to the Iranian authorities. Lopez discribed them to us as being so delicate that you couldn't hold them without causing them to tremble. As we toured the Crown Jewels, Jim came to a special display of these earrings with the descriptions of where they were found. "Shirl, come here. Here are the earrings Lopez told us about." I ran over just as Jim decided to knock on the glass to see if he could make the earrings tremble. Suddenly, we were surrounded by guards, and we were told to back away. Jim explained to the head guard what he was trying to do, and the guard was polite but firm in telling us not to touch any of the displays.

Two days later we took Aunt Lil to the airport for her flight back to the States. She was overcome with all the thrills she had experienced during her visit and kept saying, "No one is going to believe me when I tell them about all the things that I have seen and done here."

"I know the feeling, Aunt Lil. My friends all looked at me as if they thought I had lost my mind when I tried to tell them about the things that go on in this country when we returned before. There is nothing like living in Iran for excitement," I said. Little did I know how much more excitement we were in for in the coming months.

Chapter 19

In Washington a bomb exploded in the Senate wing of the Capitol in protest to the Vietnam War. President Nixon pledged to withdraw 100,000 from Viet Nam by December. In Communist China, the U.S. table tennis team arrived and three newsmen are allowed to enter the country; President Nixon eased trade embargos of non-strategic exports. 10,000 anti-Vietnam protestors disrupted the capitol for several hours as they battled the police and littered the streets with garbage. Angkor Wat, Cambodia's magnificent 12th century temple was damaged during a fight between the Viet Cong and Cambodians.

The baby was due the end of April, and I was getting big, clumsy and uncomfortable. The veins in my legs hurt all the time in spite of the heavy elastic stockings I put on before getting out of bed every morning. I had to rest several times during the day with my legs elevated.

Jim and I decided we should talk about the name for the baby and we should include the children in the decision, so I bought a baby-naming book at the Embassy co-op. I read out loud some names and told what each name meant. Naming a boy became easy after the kids found out that Richard meant 'a rich king.' "If it's a boy can we name him Richard so he will be a rich king?" Jimbo asked.

"Yes, yes, let's name him Richard," Pat chimed in.

"Well," said Peggy, "we're going to have another girl, not a boy."

"In that case we had better find a girl's name." said Jim. Girl's names were a lot more difficult. I liked Samantha and Victoria; both suggestions being greeted with a big Ugh. Several other names were thrown around, and there was always someone to veto each suggestion. Finally, we gave up, deciding to try again at a later date.

I received a letter from Betsy Whitehold, a friend from Fort Leavenworth. Betsy was always the one to call if you wanted information on anyone and, true to form, her letter was full of gossip about many of the people we knew at Leavenworth. The news that hit me the hardest was the fact that the colonel who took Jim's place as the Army attaché in El Salvador had been ambushed on a jungle road outside San Salvador and murdered. I wondered if the lady in front of me in line at the Ft. Leavenworth bookstore, who turned around so suddenly when she heard me say Jim's orders were for El Salvador, was the colonel's widow.

Bev Wilcox called me to see if I wanted to join the Women's Club in a Good Samaritan effort. The Women's Club had received permission to go to the local orphanage and help the children in any way they could. It was an all day excursion and I had to decline because I picked up Peggy from kindergarten at noon. The next day Bev came to our house for tea. When she described the conditions of the orphanage, I was glad I hadn't gone. The dormitory the kids lived in was filthy; the children looked as if they hadn't had a bath in months. They were all tied to their beds and no matter how old they were, they were in diapers - and those were only changed twice a day. The first thing the Americans did was to untie the children and exercise their limbs. Bev said it was the saddest thing she had ever seen; the children didn't know how to smile. "Shirley, I kept working with one little girl, singing and moving her arms and legs and trying so hard to get some response from her, but she was like a zombie. I had nightmares all last night from that experience. Some of the women plan to go back, but I'm not sure I have the stomach for it."

"How can any country treat their children like that?" I asked.

"We were told that these children were from prostitutes, and the Muslim religion does not believe in prostitution, so these children do not exist. How logical is that?"

Shaking my head, I said, "Yesterday when I went to Peg's school I passed some boys who were torturing some pups in the jube. Apparently, life in any form is not honored here as it is in Western societies. I wanted to stop and yell at those kids, but there was a long line of traffic behind me so I didn't have a chance."

Bev shook her head, "The Muslim Religion is supposed to be peaceful but it doesn't seem to be very kind."

There was a big shindig at the Officers Club in honor of several VIP's from the Pentagon. I stuffed myself into my best maternity dress, very unenthusiastic about going to a party. It was getting close to my due date and, all the way over to the Club, the baby was practicing trampoline jumping. While Jim was busy talking to some general, I waddled up to the bar to get a glass of water. A very nice colonel said to me, "Well, my dear, how are we feeling?"

First of all, I'm not your dear and that's a dumb question, "we" feel like Hell, I thought. Controlling myself, I politely said, "Well, I'm doing quite well, thank you."

"What would you like to have, a boy or a girl?"

Looking right at him, I evenly said, "I don't believe I am having a boy or a girl. I believe I am carrying a kangaroo." The colonel looked startled, not knowing if I were kidding. He decided not to find out and, with a weak smile, he said, "I wish you good luck," and rushed away.

Oh well, so much for impressing the visiting brass. I should have stayed home, I thought.

Jim told me that General Saleh, the head of the Iranian Transportation Corps, had said, "Col. Estarkey, when your wife has her baby, please let me know. It is our custom to visit the new mother in the hospital."

Being in a very anti-social mood I grumbled, "Don't you dare!"

Two weeks later, when I went for my doctor's appointment, I was still in the same, if not bigger, shape. Dr. Kazami assured me the time was getting close, but that didn't relieve my depression. This was replaced with shock the next morning when we learned

that three American teenagers had been killed as they were coming out of a movie theater in Tajrish, the most northern suburb of
Tehran. A drunk taxi driver had been driving erratically north on
Pahlavi Avenue and, at a major intersection, the cab jumped the
curb and ran directly toward the exit to the movie theater. The
three American teenagers were laughing about the movie they had
just seen as the taxi plowed into them. Colonel Howard, from the
Army section of ARMISH-MAAG, had gone to a store for some
Cokes when he saw the crowd and stopped to see if he could be of
assistance. As he pushed his way through the throng, much to his
horror, he saw his son lying on the ground. He desperately tried to
apply artificial respiration, but his son was already dead. One of the
boys was George Jacoby, the son of a diplomat at our Embassy, and
the third was Charlie Wilson, who lived across the street from us.
Charlie's dad was a civilian who worked for the Oil Consortium.
Everyone in the American community knew one or more of the
families of these boys, and the whole American community went
into mourning. A memorial service was planned for the three victims at the Community Church the following Thursday. I barely
knew our neighbor Charlie's mom, Amy Lou. We had visited a
few times, and I liked her heavy Oklahoma accent, but we didn't
have much in common; never the less, I felt obligated to attend the
service to show support for all three families. I was parking the car
in the church lot when I saw Dr. Morrow. I waved to him as I got
out, and he came rushing over to me with a distressed look on his
face. I started to say something about how tragic this was when he
hugged me hard and cried, "Shirley, do you realize that today is the
anniversary of our Bobby's death?" Tears were streaming down his
face as he added, "You and Jim are the only ones in all of Iran who
would know what I am talking about." I was shaken to the core,
and I thought my legs would buckle.

"Dr. Morrow, where is Mrs. Morrow?" I managed to say.

"She's at home. She never goes out on this anniversary."

"Don't you think you should be home with her?"

"Well, I knew these boys, and I thought I should come. Do you
think it would be okay if I just go home?"

"Yes, I do. Mrs. Morrow needs you more, and there are so many
people here, no one will notice. I'll sign your name if there is a book

to sign." He thanked me and left.

I was upset, but I went inside anyway and signed all three books for both the Morrow and Starkey families, then I went home.

The next morning my neighbor Amy Lou came over, crying. "Shirley, if your baby is a boy, will you please name him after Charlie?"

I lost my breath: my throat was dry and I could barely speak. Gulping a couple of times and never answering her request, I finally was able to say, "Oh, Amy Lou, I am so sorry about Charlie. What are your plans now?"

"The American ambassador told my husband, Jack, that he was temporarily assigning Jack to the Embassy so we can legally take Charlie out of the country, along with the other two boys. Since we are civilians, otherwise, we would have had to stay in country and go through inquests and a lot of red tape. Other civilian families who have had a member die here have been kept in Iran for many months and had to pay a lot of *baksheesh* (bribes) to just about everyone. We're lucky, we're leaving tomorrow to take Charlie back to Oklahoma for burial in our family's plot."

I gave her a big hug and wished her well. "You will name your boy after Charlie, won't you?" she insisted.

Shrugging my shoulders, I lied. "Dr. Kazami tells me I'm having a girl."

"Oh, I didn't realize they could tell if it's a boy or a girl."

Lying further, I said, "Oh, there are so many new advancements these days."

She left, and I sank down on the steps of the stairs and started crying. The tears would not stop. *What was that woman thinking, asking me to name my baby after her son? What kind of a bad omen would that be?* I thought. After going through half a box of Kleenex, I finally stopped crying. I called Dr. Kazami's office and demanded that his nurse give him the phone. "Dr. Kazami, when am I going to have this baby? It's two weeks overdue," I shouted hysterically.

"Mrs. Starkey, come to the hospital tomorrow morning. We'll induce labor."

After breakfast, the boys got on the school bus, Jim and I dropped Peggy off at her kindergarten and went to Tehran General Hospital, the most modern, state-of-the-art hospital in Iran. Jim kissed me goodbye, assured me everything would be fine (*easy for him to say*) and went to his office until it was time to get Peggy at noon. He had an important meeting that morning about the upcoming war games the American advisors were planning for the Iranian generals. The Shah was wary of Saddam Hussein, suspecting the Iraqi dictator wanted full control of the oil-rich entrance to the Persian Gulf. He knew Saddam would use any excuse he could to invade Iran. Jim had offered to cancel the meeting but I told him that was unnecessary as Dr. Kazami had said it would probably take several hours for my labor to start.

The nurse prepared me and, after donning the prerequisite itsey-bitsey hospital gown, I was wheeled into the labor room. It was a large room with several beds close together, separated by curtains. As far as I could tell, I was the only patient in the room. The nurse gave me a shot to induce labor, hooked me up to various machines, pulled the curtain around me and left me to read my Helen McInnes mystery. After a couple of hours, my labor pains started, very slowly at first. Every time a pain started I would dutifully start the proper breathing and singing of *Mairsey Doats*. I was in the middle of one of these pains when I heard a commotion as someone entered the room. Soon some screaming ensued on the other side of the curtain, followed by rapid Farsi. Someone was climbing into the next bed, more screams, then some smooching sounds, followed by soft-spoken Farsi words of endearment. Just then my nurse came in to check on me. I asked her what was going on. She told me the girl next to me was having her first baby and, since she was only fifteen years old, her mother was with her, trying to help. The mother's idea of helping was to hold her daughter, kiss her and then tell her how beautiful she was. Up to that time I had had a fairly easy time, but then my labor pains started getting sharper and closer together while next to me the screams were getting louder and more frequent. This clamor went on for a couple of hours. My nurse was with me and was coaching my breathing and singing *Mairzey Doats* right along with me. Jane Kazami had done a great job of training her maternity nurses. Finally it was determined that I was dilated enough, and with great relief I was wheeled out of that bedlam. As we progressed down the hall the young girl's screams followed us. If I had not been dealing with my own discomfort, I would have felt more sympathy for her.

It did not take long after Dr. Kazami arrived for him to tell me to push, and I did push, just as hard as I could. Within minutes, Richard Carmichael Starkey made his appearance into this world. It turned out that he arrived butt first and this pretty much has been a harbinger of his life! He was smaller than his brothers, weighing in at 7 lbs 6 oz., was 20 inches long and had light brown hair. The nurse cleaned him up and Rick was put into my arms. He was all rosy and so cute! I thanked God, and wondered how I could ever have considered not having this precious baby.

After the delivery, I was taken into a large, private room on the south side of the building. The walls were painted yellow and the trim was white with crisp white and yellow checkered curtains at the windows. It had a definite un-Iranian look which I attributed to Jane Kazami's input. Outdoors the plane trees waved in the breeze, and I could see the gardeners trimming the grass around the flower beds. The atmosphere was very cheerful and soothing. Jim came in and we smiled at each other. "Well, here we have another boy. Did you get to see him?"

"Oh, yes, I checked to make sure he had all of the required appendages."

"What do the kids think of him?" I asked.

"Peg's a little disappointed that she doesn't have a little sister to dress up. I told her she could dress Rick as long as she didn't put dresses on him. The boys are very excited to have a little brother and want to know when you are going to bring him home."

"I'm ready to come home just as soon as the doctor will let me." I yawned.

"By the way, you get double congratulations, Babe."

"Why?"

"Yesterday I entered two of your oil paintings in the Art Show at the Officers Club - you won First Prize for the painting you did of sunflowers blowing in the wind. You have a blue ribbon to go with our new son!"

"Oh, Jim, that's amazing! I totaly forgot about that art show. How did you remember it?"

"Actually, I didn't. Yesterday when I took Peggy home from kindergartner I got a phone call from Beverly asking where your paintings were. I chose the one of the mullah and the sunflower one."

"Thank you, hon. This has been a blue ribbon day, hasn't it?"

"It sure has. I left the kids in the car, so I'd better get them home and let you sleep." He kissed me and left.

I quickly fell asleep. It was late afternoon when I awakened. The nurse came in and asked me, "How many people do you expect for dinner?"

"I'm sorry, what did you say?" I asked, frowning in confusion.

"How many people will be here for dinner?" she repeated.

"Just me, and I'm ready to eat anytime."

The nurse looked at me sympathetically and said, "I'll bring your dinner in very soon," and she left the room. *What a strange thing to say,* I thought.

After eating, I decided to take a walk to find out when the nurse would bring Rick to me so I could feed him. Down the hall, I heard a lot of commotion coming from a room. I looked in and saw several men sitting on a carpet and eating from the platter in the center of the circle. The radio was blaring out a soccer match and the men were cheering and laughing in between eating and smoking smelly cigars. Beyond them was a woman in the bed, trying to sleep and next to her was a *badjii* in a dirty dress holding a baby. The room was crowded with baskets of flowers. *This must be what General Saleh was talking about when he said it is our custom to visit the new mother,* I thought. My nurse, Ashraf, was coming down the hall carrying Rick. We returned to my room and I asked Ashraf about the people in the other room. She told me the girl was the fifteen year-old who had been next to me in the labor room, and she had a very difficult birth. Her baby weighed over ten pounds and, to make matters worse, she had a girl and her forty-two year old husband was furious. All his friends came to cheer him up, but her mother and father didn't come, as they were ashamed that their daughter did not have a male. The party in that room went on far into the night, and I had to close the door so I could get some sleep. I could still hear the commotion; it was like being in all-night cocktail party. There was a sign at the entrance to the hospital stating the visiting hours but, just like traffic rules, these rules were meant to be ignored.

Every time Rick was brought to me, he looked like a mummy, with only his head visible. The hospital did not use American-style cloth diapers, but instead used a length of cloth eight inches by five feet. Rick was wrapped several times between his legs and then his legs were wrapped together and his arms were enclosed straight down his sides, making him look like a old-fashioned wooden cloths pin. The end of the cloth was tucked in at the neck area. Jim arrived just as I was unwrapping our bundle of joy. As Rick's arms were released, he started flailing them, and the same thing happened when his legs were uncovered. The 'diaper' was soaking wet and Rick's bottom was beet red with a bad case of diaper rash. Jim was horrified at Rick's condition and quickly left the room. When he returned, I asked where he had gone. "I found the head nurse and told her that Rick's diaper was soaking wet and asked her when he had been changed. She told me they change the diaper in the morning and in the evening. I told her that was not enough and that she needs to see to it that my son has his diaper changed every time he dirties or wets it. You let me know if they don't do it."

After Jim left Ashraf, came in. "Oh, Missus Estarkey, American men are so wonderful. They really care about their children. Iranian men, they don't care at all. If they have a *pesar* (boy) they go around so proud." At that, Ashraf stuck her thumbs in her armpits and wriggled her fingers as she strutted around the room like a rooster. "But, if they have a *dukhtar* (daughter) Iranian men are so sad, as if the world would end." She changed from the rooster to a bent-over old lady, dragging around the room. I was in hysterics, laughing at this talented comedian. Soon Ashraf was laughing uproariously and the two of us made so much noise the head nurse came in. In rapid Farsi the head nurse questioned Ashraf, who answered something I couldn't follow. More Farsi and with a frown, the head nurse left. Ashraf put her hand over her mouth to stop a giggle, shrugged her shoulders and winked at me.

When Dr. Kazemi came by, he announced that I could go home the next day. I couldn't wait to give Jim the good news. Dr. Reed, the head of the American Hospital, stopped in to congratulate me on my successful birth. I thanked him for using the word 'abortion' when talking to me. "Dr. Reed, if you hadn't used that word and made me feel so guilty, I would not have had such a beautiful boy and, by the way, we named him Richard." Dr. Reed looked surprised and then embarrassed and quickly left. That's when I remembered that Richard was his first name and, since I had made such a big deal of thanking him, perhaps he thought we had named Rick after him.

That evening, my room was invaded by some of the men from the young girl's room. They felt sorry for me because I was so alone. We did have a nice conversation, and they were very happy for me because I had a boy. When they learned I had three boys, I was told to be sure and congratulate my husband on his success. I was also assured that it was all right to have a girl, since I had done my duty and produced three boys. If they thought I was the one who 'done my duty' why did they want my husband congratulated?

Jim and the kids came to get Rick and me, bringing in an enormous purple hydrangea plant. The three children stared at their new brother as if he were from Mars. Each one took turns holding Rick's tiny hands, spreading the fingers and marveling at his microscopic fingernails. Rick was dressed in a blue jump suit and wrapped in a white receiving blanket. The children wanted me to take off the little booties so they could look at his toes. Finally, Jim said, "Let's go home. You can examine Rick all you want there."

As we drove in the compound, a grinning Negadar opened the car door and kept saying *"Khali khob, Madame"*. (very good) I was holding Rick on my lap, and I opened his receiving blanket for Negadar's inspection. *"Khali khob pesar,"* he exclaimed, clapping his hands and bowing to Jim. *"Sarhang, Sarhang, khali khob."* This male oriented society was really beginning to irritate me.

We sat in the living room and let the kids examine their little brother. "He's so tiny." "Look at his dark blue eyes." "When is he going to smile?" "How soon until he learns to walk?" The comments and questions flew around the room. When Rick messed his diapers, the kids held their noses and scattered. New little brother had lost his charm. I carried Rick upstairs, changed his diaper, fed him and put him to bed. As I came downstairs, I saw that Negadar had the hydrangea plant in the back yard, and I walked outside to show him where I wanted it planted. "Let's put it here." I said, pointing to the ground. He shook his head and said, *"Neest, Madam, khali bad"* (No, Madam, very bad). He moved the plant *four inches* to the right of where I had indicated and declared, *"Enjas, khali khob"* (Here, very good) I looked at him, nodded okay and walked into the house, defeated - once again realizing I was not in charge of this house!

Jim and I had decided not to move the boys into one room, as they were enjoying having some privacy, so we put Rick's crib in our room. It was the first time any of our children had shared our room but, since the room was thirty feet by twenty feet, it was plenty big enough and would work until we left Iran. With Rick's arrival, we needed to find a *badjii* and I had heard about an Embassy family, the Smithsons, who were leaving and wanted to find a place for their *badjii* to work. I drove over to their house and was introduced to Saffron, where I was surprised to learn she spoke a little English. I liked her immediately. She stood about five feet three inches tall, was built square like a refrigerator, and had heavy, thick, strong hands with short fingers. Her feet looked like the 50's cartoon character Alley Oop, almost as wide as long. She had bright, inquisitive brown eyes that were constantly moving and noticing everything. Her shiny black hair was cut short, unusual for an Iranian. The most eye-catching feature of hers was an enormous smile. It reminded me of a slice of watermelon, and her hearty laugh was contagious. Saffron had on a colorful full skirt over black, loose-fitting rayon pants and a beige cardigan sweater over her white blouse. She looked very clean, as if she cared about her appearance. Mrs. Smithson told me about Saffron's salary, and I agreed to the amount. Saffron asked if she could see our house, and when I agreed, she donned her chador and got into the car. In the close confines of the car, I noticed she did not have the usual body odor that is common to people whose custom is to visit the community bathhouse only once a week. When we arrived home, Negadar opened the car door and seemed pleased when I introduced Saffron to him. The two of them had an extensive discussion in Farsi. I caught enough of the conversation to know she was questioning Negadar about our family. Negadar, taking charge, first showed her the Persian toilet and then proudly took her to the laundry room; she was obviously pleased about the modern appliances. He then led her into the side door of the kitchen and opened the refrigerator and freezer for her inspection.

"Thank you, Negadar, I'll show Saffron the rest of the house," I said, taking control of the situation. We walked throughout the downstairs and, climbing upstairs, we went into the master bedroom where Peggy was keeping an eye on her little brother while I was gone. Peg had just passed her sixth birthday and, with her usual confidence, had assured me she was capable of watching Rick for the short time I was gone to interview Saffron. To Peggy's surprise, Saffron hugged her and told her she was so pretty. When Saffron saw Rick, she squealed with delight and promptly picked him up. It was easy to see she loved children. We continued the inspection of each of the other bedrooms, and as we came downstairs she met Pat and Jimbo, who eyed her with a mixture of curiosity and suspicion. After another long Farsi conversation with Negadar, apparently we passed, and she agreed to come to work for us. I drove her back to Smithson house and made arrangements for Saffron to come to work the following Saturday.

I returned home and got out the Sears Roebuck catalogue to order two sets of uniforms for Saffron. Saffron would go to her home every night on the bus and return in the morning, and I didn't want her handling Rick while wearing her own clothes. With two uniforms, one would always be clean.

Patrick started having problems with chronic sinus infections in September and by November he had suffered some hearing loss in both ears. The Iranian doctor suspected his adenoids might be the cause and said they probably should be removed. When I took Patrick to the American doctor at our clinic, he was unsure that was the problem and suggested that I would have to take him to Germany that summer to see a specialist. Saffron would be invaluable to our family if I had to leave.

Much to my relief, Saffron arrived on Saturday just as she said she would. With Iranians, you never knew when they would show up. I remembered that Saffron did not say *Enshallah* after she told me when she would arrive. (One never knew what Allah had in store for us.) When she came in, the first thing she did was wash her hands, another good sign. She immediately started loading the dishwasher the correct way. After she had cleaned up the kitchen, I showed her how to use the washing machine, the dryer and the vacuum cleaner. She was very quick to catch on to everything. She knew how to soak the vegetables and made many wonderful Iranian dishes for us. She and Negadar became good friends, and I would frequently hear them conversing and laughing together. Though it was not in the agreement, Saffron shared her noon meal with Negadar, which we provided. I talked to her about her background and

I learned that she was not Iranian. She said her mother was Turkish and her father was a Russian Cossack soldier. She had been married at fourteen to an Iranian and had two sons, but when her husband got tired of her, he divorced her so he could marry a much younger woman. She was thrown out of the house and was not allowed to see her sons. I asked her why her husband just didn't take a second wife as the Moslem religion allows. "He not have money," she answered. The Koran allows for a man to have as many as four wives, but he must have enough money to treat all wives the same.

Rick's playpen was set up downstairs in the hallway next to the big stove. I hung some blankets over the sides to keep out any drafts. He was put in there after his afternoon nap so he would get used to the noise of the kids, the snoring of Bandit and the general chaos of the house. Everyone who went by Rick, including Negadar and Saffron, would talk to him or tickle his tummy. It didn't take long for Rick to start recognizing voices and responding. When the kids arrived home from school, the first thing they did was check on their little brother. He was constantly the center of attention. He was not allowed to cry for even an instant or Saffron, Negadar, the kids or even Bandit would look at me as if to say, 'Do Something.'

Once a month, the Army section of ARMISH-MAAG had dinner party at the Officers Club, where the men and spouses mingle, awards were given out and gossip was exchanged. At the party in June, we were to be honored for having a new baby. We had cocktails and, after sitting down before the meal, General Patton started making announcements and giving out awards. His *aid'd camp*, John Higgins, stood by his side and handed him a silver baby cup. Looking down at the cup the general said, "I have here a baby cup that says Richard Carmichael 10 May" A long pause ensued as the general tilted his head and frowned; then he turned to John and said, "Who in the Hell is Carmichael?"

Keeping a straight face, John said, "Sir, that's Col. Starkey's son. Carmichael is the middle name."

General Patton started laughing and turning to the audience, loudly said, "Starkey, get up here and accept this cup. So you named your son Richard Carmichael Starkey. Very impressive!" Later he apologized and said he was unaware that it was customary for only the first and middle name to be engraved on a baby's cup. "I thought I had someone in the command named Carmichael who I didn't know about," he said.

Jim brought home the package from Sears Roebuck that contained Saffron's uniforms. The next morning, when Saffron arrived, I showed them to her and told her I wanted her to wear them when she was at our home. She took one of the uniforms, inspected it, wrinkled her nose and declared, "This bad, very bad. I no wear this."

"Yes," I insisted, "You must take off your clothes and wear this when you take care of Rick."

"I no wear this!"

I was alarmed at Saffron's attitude, which had been very amiable until now, and I got angry. "Go into your bathroom, take off your clothes and put on this clean uniform!" I commanded.

"I not do," Saffron replied stubbornly with pursed lips.

"Yes, you do, if you want to work here," I slowly and firmly said. I could feel my face getting red.

"I must work here," Saffron insisted.

"What do you mean, you must work here?" I answered, raising my voice.

"I must work here. No one else can take care of Monsieur Rrrick," she announced.

"What do you mean, no one else can take care of Monsieur Rick. I can take care of my own baby, and if you don't want to wear this uniform you can LEAVE."

I was shouting at the top of my lungs and I could feel the veins on my neck sticking out. I was trembling all over as I glanced at Saffron and was surprised at the look on her face. She had a half-smile as she gazed at me, and then she turned and slowly walked down the stairs. I went into the bathroom to put cold water on my face and try to calm down. I few minutes later, I walked into Peggy's room and looked out the window at the front compound, wondering if I would see Saffron leave. Much to my surprise, there was Saffron with the blue uniform on over all her own clothes talking and laughing with Negadar. She won, because she did not take off her own clothes, and I won, because she had on a clean uniform. From then on we never had a cross word.

Chapter 20

In July, after getting recommendations from two Iranian ear specialists who claimed that Patrick would have to have his tonsils and adenoids out, the American doctor at our small clinic made arrangements for Pat and me to go to Germany. Patrick would see a specialist at the American Army hospital at Landstule, Germany for his tonsil-adenoid problems and would also get an eye examination. Armed with the necessary paperwork, doctor appointments and wish lists from all the family, Pat and I climbed on a Pan-Am flight bound for Frankfurt. Ever since our dust-up over uniforms, Saffron had been a model *badjii*. I felt secure in leaving the children in her care, even though school was out and the kids were home all day. She took excellent care of Monsieur Rick, (as she called him), and Peggy liked to help her with Rick and in the kitchen. Under the watchful eye of Negadar and Saffron, Jimbo could not get into too much trouble. Jim planned on leaving the office early in time to get Jimbo to baseball and Peggy to her ballet classes.

The flight to Frankfurt was uneventful, and when we arrived at the international air port we were able to get a train to Rein-Main Air Force Base. The train tracks were high over the landscape, and from there Pat and I got a good look at the tiny plots of land next to the highway that were filled with vegetable gardens and fruit trees. We could see people industriously working in the soil. Most of the plots had a shed for tools, camping chairs and tables for the picnics.

"What are those people doing down there?" Pat asked.

"Planting gardens, I guess, but the spaces are so small it doesn't seem to be very efficient," I remarked.

We took a cab to the visiting Officer' quarters and checked into a room that had twin beds. I was hesitant about the arrangement when I discovered we had to share a bath with three other rooms - and all three were occupied by men. I had a friend who was living in Frankfurt, and I called her. Karen immediately invited Pat and me to stay with them, and I accepted with relief. I had first met Karen and Bert Hays in Honolulu when both Bert and Jim were on R & R from Viet Nam. Jim and I spent a lot of time with them drinking Blue Hawaiians at the Monkey Bar at Pearl Harbor. After Viet Nam, both Jim and Bert had been stationed at Ft. Eustis, where Karen and I got to know each other very well. Karen was German, a tall, willowy blonde with sky-blue eyes, the perfect Aryan that Hitler admired. She told me that during World War II she would shake her fist at the American bombers who were decimating Frankfurt. After the war, she became a successful model at a large firm. She met Bert and, after an extensive courtship, they were married and soon thereafter Bert was assigned back to the States. At Karen's insistence, Bert had been trying for twelve years to get orders to go back to Germany and, when he was successful, Jim and I had been invited to their farewell party at their home in Williamsburg, Virginia. Karen and I had corresponded regularly after that, and now I was excited to see them again. Karen picked Pat and me up in a red convertible and, before going to their quarters, gave us a tour of Frankfurt, proudly indicating a giant billboard on one of the high-rise buildings. There was beautiful Karen, all four stories high, advertising some company. She said she was trying to get her modeling career back on track. "It looks to me as if you're doing very well," I said.

The Hays' quarters were one of many look-alike red brick buildings arranged in seven rows with ten buildings in each row. (I wondered how you could tell one place from the other in a dark night, especially if you had imbibed too much.) Karen had placed a dried fruit wreath on the front door of their quarters in an effort to make the entrance different. The inside of the home was beautifully decorated in Danish Modern furniture, displaying another of Karen's talents. Their daughter Laura was at camp, and I was given her room. Their son Joey's room had twin beds, and Karen said Patrick would sleep there. Joey was at a friend's house, and Karen went to the phone to call him home. A few minutes later, when Joey walked in, Karen introduced them. The two seven-year olds eyed each other for a moment, then Joey invited Patrick to play a board game and they went into Joey's bedroom. Karen and I sat in the living room talking. I was surprised that Karen smoked so many cigarettes and when Bert arrived home a little after five o'clock, he immediately started smoking, too. He was over six feet tall, thin and lithe, with sandy hair and crinkly brown eyes. "How is Jim?" he asked, seeming pleased at unexpected guests, and the three of us sat for several minutes while he questioned me about Jim's job, what it as like to live in Iran and what were we doing here in Frankfurt. I told him about Patrick's appointment the next day and he offered to take us to Army Hospital in Landstule. "Can you get away from work so easily?" I asked.

"At the moment things are very quiet, so I don't think it will be a problem" he said. He went into their bedroom and changed out of his uniform. Standing in the doorway, he said to the boys, "Joey, you and Pat come outside and practice shagging balls. We better hurry, as it will be dark in half an hour." Turning to me he said, "I'm the coach of Joey's baseball team and he needs help in fielding flies."

"That's great, Pat can use some practice, too, since he's missing a couple of games and practices while we are here." Joey handed Pat an extra glove and the three left for the park. As the three left, I noticed that Bert and Joey looked like Pete and repeat, Joey being a smaller version of Bert. Karen and I got busy in the kitchen, fixing dinner and catching up on the news of mutual friends. When the boys came in and washed up ,we ate, watched some TV and then went to bed.

The next day we were up early and after breakfast Bert, Pat and I left for Landstule. Karen had a hair and makeup appointment before going to a modeling job, so she did not join us. As we left the city, seeing the green fields and trees of Germany was a treat after the barren brown tones of Iran. The town of Landstule is high on the hills north of Frankfurt and, as we wended our way up and around, we could look back at the pollution surrounding the city. Bert told us that right after the war the commanding officer of the Landstule

Hospital noticed that a shepherd brought his flock of sheep to graze on the grass around the hospital, keeping it neatly trimmed. The generous American didn't think it was fair for the man to mow the grass and not get paid so he started paying the shepherd to graze his flocks on the hospital grounds! "Good Heavens, no wonder the world takes advantage of us," I exclaimed. "I once asked an Iranian what he thought of Americans, and he said he thought Americans were very nice, but not very smart. I asked him why, and he said "because you give your money away."

Bert shook his head disgustedly, "And we pay for it with our high taxes."

Landstule Hospital is in a huge compound with many buildings. After saluting LTC Hays, the MP's at the gate requested to know our destination. "We need to go to the Ear, Nose and Throat clinic," I said. The MP got a map and drew a circle around the area we were looking for and pointed out which way to go. When we arrived, we found the clinic overflowing with patients, but we didn't have to wait long, as we were given first priority since we had come from Iran. The young pediatrician was efficient, checking Pat carefully. He swabbed Pat's throat and ordered some blood and urine tests and told us to call the next day for the results. From there we went to the Eye clinic and were told to come back after lunch. We had a lunch of bratwurst and fries, under an umbrella, on the veranda looking toward the mountains. What a beautiful setting. "The German people live for the few months of sunshine," Bert remarked. "You see them basking on their balconies, trying to get a tan any time the sun shines."

"Pat and I noticed some small gardens that we could see from the train. What is that all about?"

"Before the war, most Germans were farmers and, after the war, when people came to the cities to work and started living in high rises, the government decided to lease small plots to the people to grow their own vegetables to help relieve food shortages. Remember, it has only been a few years since the German economy has started to improve and that food has become plentiful. It took a long time for rationing to be over. These plots have had an additional psychological effect on the people. They are so much happier digging in the soil and basking in the sun. The funny thing is, most of the apartment dwellers don't know their neighbors at their apartment complex, but they know their fellow gardeners. They work on their plots, socialize with each other and trade produce."

"That is a good idea. The Germans have always been known to be industrious and hard workers," I commented.

"You can say that again. It hasn't been easy keeping up with that little *fraulein* I married," Bert said, smiling. Looking at his watch, he said, "We'd better get over to the Eye Clinic."

Once again we were given priority over the rest of the people waiting to see the Ophthalmologist. Pat was given a thorough eye test, and I was told his eyes had changed. He needed a new prescription and it would take three days to get his new glasses. When I told Bert that, I said, "Maybe Pat and I should get a hotel room."

"Absolutely not. You will stay with us as long as it takes," he commanded me.

"Aye, aye, Sir," I said saluting, thinking how alike all Army officers were. "If you think it will be all right with Karen, we would love to stay with you."

The next morning Joey invited Pat to go swimming. I said it was okay, assuming the pool was on Post and gave Pat some spending money. I called the hospital clinic and was very happy to learn that Pat did not need to have his tonsils or adenoids out. There was nothing wrong with them that a prescription of decongest wouldn't cure. The Iranian doctors who had wanted to operate just wanted Uncle Sam's money. I was told I could pick up the prescription at the pharmacy at the hospital.

Karen and I decided to go shopping at the PX for school clothes. I was amazed at the size of the PX; it was the biggest one I had ever seen and was stocked with almost anything anyone needed. I bought jeans, underwear, socks for the boys and dresses and tights for Peggy; shoes and jackets for all three. I stocked up on books and painting supplies for me and some military items that Jim had requested. I had to buy a duffle bag, as our two suitcases wouldn't handle all the items I had purchased. Over a lunch of Caesar's salad, Karen and I lingered for an hour. She started complaining about the problems she was having with Bert and saying what a mistake it had been to get married just when her career was taking off. And the worst part was having two babies, which absolutely ruined her breasts. I was amazed at the attitude and couldn't imagine how anyone could be so negative about her family. All the time she was talking, I was thinking about how much I missed the rest of my family. I told Karen about how close I came to aborting Rick, and she looked at me as if I had two heads. "Why didn't you? Do you realize you're going to be stuck for the next twenty years?" she exclaimed.

What does she mean, stuck? This gal has a screw loose, I thought. I felt sorry for her; it was obvious she was very unhappy. Changing the subject, I said, "Could we go to the Commissary so I can by some spices, spaghetti and noodles that are hard to come by in Iran?"

We spent another hour in the commissary and arrived home about three o'clock. I got busy taking off tags and repacking the clothes and other stuff I had bought. When four thirty arrived, I asked Karen, "Shouldn't the boys be home by now?"

"No, they have a long way to go swimming, and Joey usually isn't home until about five."

"A long way to go?" I repeated. "Isn't the swimming pool nearby?"

"No, there isn't a pool here on Post. The public pool is on other side of Frankfurt."

"WHAT did you say?"

"I said the pool is on the other side of Frankfurt."

"How did the kids get there? Did some parent take them?"

"No, they caught the train," Karen calmly said.

"By themselves? My God, they are only seven years old! They can't take a train by themselves!"

"Well, they did, and besides that, Shirley, you should cut the umbilical cord. Pat needs to grow up sometime."

I was speechless.

Karen must be crazy to think it is okay for two seven year-olds to go clear across a major city like Frankfurt by themselves. She really doesn't care about anyone but herself, I thought. I wanted to say that out loud, but felt constrained since we were her guests. Just then Bert arrived home from work. He could tell I was upset and asked why. Karen said, "Shirley is upset because the boys aren't back from swimming yet."

"Where did the boys go swimming?" Bert asked.

Karen gave him the name of the pool, and Bert was as incredulous as I was. "You let the boys go over there by themselves? You always take Joey, don't you?" he asked.

"No, he and his friends have been going by themselves this year. They know how to get on the trains."

Bert was livid, and they started fighting. I don't think there was much communication between them, except maybe yelling. I walked out of the kitchen and went outside. I could hear the accusations they were hurling at each other, so I walked to the corner to watch for Pat. Much to my relief, I saw him two blocks away, running toward the housing area. I was standing under a lamppost, as it was getting dark. When Pat saw me, the panicked look left his face and he rushed into my arms. "Where is Joey?" I asked.

"He's hiding from me. Mom, I was so scared. We went clear across the city on the train. Joey wouldn't even buy tickets. He jumped over the stile, and I didn't know how to buy tickets, so I did too. When we got to the pool, the water was black, and Dad told me never to swim in dirty water. I wouldn't get in the pool, so Joey got mad. He swam for awhile and then we changed clothes. He was still mad, so he started running away, trying to ditch me. I ran as fast as I could, trying to keep up. I just barely caught the train, and it was a good thing because I didn't know which train to catch and where to get off. As soon as we got off, Joey ran away and hid someplace, and I never found him, so I started walking back the way I remembered all the houses were. I'm so glad you were waiting at the corner for me."

We hugged for a minute, and I said, "It's okay, honey, you're safe now. You were very smart to remember the route to these houses. I'm not sure I could. Let's go tell Col. and Mrs. Hays that I found you."

We started back to the house just as Bert came out. He was relieved to see Pat and asked where Joey was. Pat told him the truth; that Joey had ditched him. Bert was furious, his face was red and the veins on his neck were sticking out. "Wait until I get my hands on that kid," he muttered. "Let's go on into the house."

Karen seemed strangely calm after the blowup between Bert and herself. Soon Joey arrived, and Bert grabbed him by his ear marching him into the bedroom. We could hear Bert threatening Joey with his belt and Joey trying to explain. I told Pat to get washed up for dinner, and I went into the kitchen to help Karen. Several minutes later Bert came in with Joey. "Where is Pat?"

"He's in the bathroom, washing up" I answered.

"Joey has something to say to Pat." I called Pat, and the two boys glared at each other. "Joey," prompted Bert, "what do you have to say to Pat?"

"Pat, I'm sorry I tried to ditch you, but I was mad because you wouldn't go swimming with me."

Now it was my turn to prompt Pat. "Pat, tell Joey why you wouldn't go swimming."

"My Dad told me never to go swimming in a dirty pool, and the water was black at that pool."

Bert started laughing. "Pat, the water looked black because the bottom of the pool is painted black. The pool is very safe. The water is clean."

We all looked at each other and started laughing. Joey said, "Pat, you're pretty sharp. I tried real hard to ditch you, but you were too smart."

"Okay, boys, shake hands and let's forget about this. Mom, what's for dinner?" Bert asked. The boys shook hands and smiled at each other. Peace reigned again for awhile.

The next day Karen took Pat, Joey and me downtown to shop. We went into several department stores and different boutiques. The boys spotted a pet store and dragged us in. We looked at the puppies, kittens, gerbils, mice, guinea pigs, birds, snakes and, to my surprise, baby tortoises, just like the desert tortoises we had in Tucson. "Mom, can we take some baby tortoises back to Iran?" Pat asked. They were very small, no bigger than a silver dollar.

"Pat, that's a good idea. We can get four, one for each of you kids." Pat carefully chose four tortoises, I paid for them, and the saleslady placed them in a cardboard box. As we left the store, I was thinking about how to get them past Iranian customs. Karen had a sturdy basket for magazines, and I decided I wanted one also. "Karen, where did you get that basket you have in the living room? I'd like to get one to carry these tortoises in." Karen took us to the basket store and I made a purchase. Then Joey said, "Mom, can we go to the store where you can get all those funny tricks?"

"Yes, we'll go there now. Maybe Pat will want to get some jokes to take home."

The store was full of costumes, masks, trinkets and all manner of jokes. Pat decided to buy a plastic form that looked like dog potty. "First I'll trick Jimbo and Peggy with it and, then we can trick Negadar and Saffron." He pulled out his wallet and bought it with his allowance.

That night we all went to a Polish restaurant with sawdust on the floor and wooden picnic tables in long rows. The place could seat several hundred patrons and, on the stage, a large group of rotund musicians were playing polkas. Big, bosomy women dressed in dirndl skirts, white blouses, fancy embroidered vests and snow-white aprons were serving huge steins of beer and plates of steaming pork hocks. Clouds of cigarette smoke filled the air, and it was so noisy you could hardly hear yourself think. I was sitting next Karen and across from Bert, Pat and Joey. Karen and Bert were smoking a cigarette, as usual, and Bert offered me one to be polite. I had never smoked, although when I started college at the University of Arizona, a group of us from Tucson High sat on the floor at Maricopa Hall trying to learn to smoke. This was a sign of sophistication, we thought. After all, didn't everybody in the movies smoke? And we all wanted to look like Lauren Bacall. I was told to inhale, so I complied, taking a deep breath. The smoke went down, searing my lungs, and I thought I would die on the spot. I had never felt such pain, and I thought to myself, *This is the stupidest thing I have ever done.* I got up and walked home, vowing never to inhale again. That didn't stop me from occasionally pretending to smoke when everyone around me was smoking. I would take a cigarette if I were playing Bridge or at a cocktail party and wanted to look 'sophisticated.' So, when Bert offered the cigarette, I took it. I put it to my lips, Bert held a match to it and I puffed. Just then I noticed my son glaring at me. Patrick had a round face, a blond crew cut and thick glasses that made his blue eyes enormous. His eyes were like laser beams boring into me. I pretended to ignore him as I held my cigarette dramatically between my fingers. Suddenly, Pat got up, walked around the table, took the cigarette out of my fingers and angrily crumpled it into an ashtray. Looking directly at my surprised eyes, he said in a slow, menacing voice, "My Dad told me to take care of you." I gasped in shock and felt my face get red. I was mortified as I watched Pat marching back to his seat. Bert and Karen had amazed looks on their faces, and

I have never in my life felt so ashamed. I have also never accepted another cigarette!

In the morning, Pat and I caught the shuttle to Landstule to get his glasses and decongestant prescription. I called Pan Am and made arrangements to fly back to Iran the next day. I called Jim and told him the good news. He told me that everybody was doing well and that Saffron had been especially good. Pat and I went back to the PX and got a skirt and blouse (not a uniform) for Saffron and two long-sleeved shirts for Negadar, as special gifts. When we got to Bert and Karen's quarters Joey showed Pat a gerbil he was taking care of for his friend who had left on vacation.

Karen and I went in the kitchen to start dinner. She was excited because she had received a phone call about a casting call for a movie that was going to be made in Frankfurt. She was laughing when she said, "Shirley, maybe I'll become a great movie star and you can say you knew me when." I sincerely wished her well and hoped she would be successful.

After dinner, Bert, Karen and I were watching a movie on TV while Pat and Joey were in the bathroom. Pat came out and whispered to me, "Mom, Joey is trying to drown the gerbil." I looked at Bert and said, "You better check on Joey in the bathroom." Bert went in and the yelling started. I could hear Joey saying, "I was just trying to see if the gerbil could swim!" The gerbil was rescued, dried off and Joey was banished to his bedroom. When Bert returned he said to Pat, "Pat, thank you for letting me know what Joey was doing. You're a fine young man." Pat was pleased with the compliment and sat next to me until it was time to go to bed. He went into Joey's room and soon came into my room. "Mom, can I sleep with you? Joey said he's going to kill me for telling on him."

"Yes, honey, you sure can. And remember what Col. Hays said. You did the right thing. Can you imagine how disappointed Joey's friend would be if he came home and found his gerbil dead. Don't worry. We'll be up early in the morning to catch the plane back to Tehran."

With a devilish look on his face, Patrick said, "I can't wait to play that trick on Jimbo and Peggy and won't they be happy to have the tortoises! How are we going to carry them?"

"I've got a scarf that I'll cover them with and I'll put newspaper in the bottom of the basket. I'm sure they will be okay."

Our flight was scheduled to leave at 6:00 am and we left the house before Joey and Karen were awake. Bert drove us to the airport and, as we said goodbye, Bert said, "Shirley, you and Jim are great parents, and I can't tell you how impressed I am with Pat. I would like to know that boy when he grows up. He'll make a fine adult, thanks to you and Jim. Be sure and give my best to that guy you married." I thanked him profusely, and he hugged Pat and me.

Arriving at Mehrabad Airport, I handed the tortoise basket to Patrick. We walked up to the customs agent and while I was showing our passports, Patrick casually walked with the basket out to where Jim, Jimbo and Peggy were waiting. Everyone was excited to have the four tortoises, and we got a happy reunion when we got home. The first thing I did was to run up the stairs to see Rick. He was sleeping peacefully, clean and sweet-smelling. Jim was right; Saffron had done a very good job.

Years later when we were stationed in Stuttgart, Germany, we heard that Joey, just an eighth grade student, had been arrested for dealing drugs. The Germans insisted he leave the country. Bert retired to the state of Washington and took Joey and Laura with him. Karen refused to leave Germany.

A message arrived from Mostafa Byat, the Iranian friend from our first tour, and we invited him to dinner. Mostafa's family was one of the Thousand Families of Iran who, until the Shah's White Revolution, had owned, along with the Shia clergy called the *Ulama*, almost all of the country of Iran. The families had become very wealthy from the labor of the serfs who populated the farms and villages. Mostafa had been sent to Europe and then to the United States at an early age for schooling. He graduated with an Engineering degree from the University of Arizona in 1962, the year Jim was assigned to Iran the first time. My mother was the manager of the University's Park Avenue Bookstore at the time, where she met Mostafa. She gave him Jim's address, and he looked us up when he returned to Tehran. We saw him frequently during our first two-year tour and witnessed his metamorphous from sounding like an American to becoming

Iranian. He was prepared to become a gentleman of leisure while managing his extensive income from his family's holdings when we first visited with him and then the Shah came out with his White Revolution, giving the land deeds to the serfs. Mostafa complained to us that although he had a degree in Engineering, he could not get a job in Iran. "Iran does not have a General Motors," he said. The last time we had seen him, we had been invited to a party at his house. All the young Iranians there were openly complaining about the Shah and particularly about his twin sister, Ashraf, who was building mansions in Tehran and the Caspian. They must have felt comfortable with us, because to talk against the Shah could bring problems from SAVAK, the Shah's secret service, but they didn't seem to care. By the time we left in 1964 Mostafa was working for the Iranian government stamping passports. The year before, when we arrived in Iran, Jim had tried to get in touch with him and had learned that he was with the Iranian Embassy in Belgium.

Friday, he arrived bearing flowers for me and candy for the children. We introduced our growing family to him. "Mostafa, are you married?" I asked.

"No, not yet. My mother is dealing with a marriage broker to find a suitable mate for me now that I am back in Iran. Things work very differently here than in the States. Seeing your children makes me want to get married soon, so I can have as fine a family as yours."

The kids grinned at the compliment, and then asked Jim if they could go upstairs to watch cartoons. Permission granted, they scampered up the stairs.

Jim served us drinks, and we settled in the living room. Mostafa had aged a lot in the last eight years and looked very distinguished with a neat, salt-and-pepper beard. "Mostafa, you look like a diplomat," I exclaimed.

"Well, Shirley, that is my hope. I have been recalled to help with organizing the guest list for the Shah's big celebration honoring the 2500 years of the Persian monarchy founded by Cyrus the Great."

"That sounds like a big promotion for you," Jim said. "Tell us about the plans."

"The theme is to be the Cyrus Cylinder, the first human rights document to embrace Freedom of Religion. The main activities will take place at Persepolis, where they are building a tent city. I understand the French are designing it and trying to copy the famous 1520 Field of the Cloth of Gold where Henry VIII of England met with Francis I of France. All the heads of state and monarchs will be invited, and my job is to place everyone according to protocol."

Jim frowned, "Mostafa, that sounds like a major headache! How do you decide between a Premier and a King?"

"Monarchs always come first, but you are right, it is a headache. I'll either be a hero, or you may never hear from me again!" He nervously laughed.

Jim and Mostafa talked about the bombs that had been going off all over Iran in an effort to disrupt the preparations for the celebrations. This was the first I had heard about it and I demanded, "Jim, you never told me about any bombs."

"No, I didn't want you to be upset, but there has been a lot of bombing down around Ferdowsi Street."

Mostafa broke in. "Yes, we're trying to keep it quiet so as not to alarm all the dignitaries coming for the celebration." Just then Saffron announced that our dinner was served, and we spent the rest of the evening listening to Mostafa gossip about all the important heads of states that would be arriving in Iran in October. When he left, we wished him well in this assignment. Jim later commented that that was one job that he would never want.

Some friends of ours were invited to an Iranian wedding and described it in great detail. It was very traditional, with the groom sitting on a throne surrounded by his buddies, all eating, laughing and drinking wine. Across the room sat the bride on a similar throne, under a canopy, surrounded by her attendants. One of the attendants stood behind the bride rubbing large cakes of sugar together. The grains fell upon the canopy to insure a sweet marriage. Everyone was talking and laughing at once, completely ignoring the mullah who was reading aloud from the Koran. The male guests were dressed in black suits and the female guests had on black chadors. The bride wore a traditional Parisian white wedding dress with the side seams slit all the way to the waist, showing off white satin, hip-hugger hot pants! The bride's attendants were attired in various pastel-colored hot pants but without the benefit of a long overskirt. It was a perfect example of the schizophrenic lifestyle that is modern Iran.

Caddy-corner from our house was the two houses built by the Shah's Court Minister, Mr. Alem, for his two daughters. One daughter was married to an Iranian, who disliked the Shah. The other daughter was married to an effeminate Englishmen named John, who was happy to be a court hanger-on. That family was part of the entourage who went on vacation with the Shah. Their nanny, Bridget, a Scot, would frequently come to our house for tea. She was a fountain of information and gossip about the royal family. She informed me of which of the Shah's brothers was the unofficial pimp of the court, who was an alcoholic, who was feuding with whom and which family member was on Princess Ashraf's hate-list.

Jim took leave so we could take the kids to the Caspian for a brief vacation before school began. We loaded the car and got an early start and, as we drove up into the mountain leaving the congestion of Tehran, the sky was clearer and Mt. Damavand was visible. "Look, there is our disappearing mountain," Jimbo exclaimed. We all admired the 'ice cream cone mountain,' pink as strawberry in the early morning light. The steep drive over the Elburz Mountains was scary with sharp hairpin turns on single lanes at the edge of cliffs. Several times, we met trucks coming toward us. We stopped and hugged our position, praying we wouldn't be knocked over the brink. The landscape looked like a movie about the moon with bleak, grey slate rocks that nothing would grow on. We breathed a sigh of relief as we arrived at the summit, stopping at a wide, level lookout to stretch our legs. We walked to the edge to look back at where we had been, and we could see hundreds of miles south to the brown haze that covered Tehran. We inhaled the fresh, cool mountain air as Jim led the kids in exercises. Then he ordered the kids to run to a fence and back as fast as they could. I held Rick so he could watch the action. At three months, he was very observant and was starting to smile. Panting after several runs, our youngsters were laughing as they demanded lunch. I passed out the sandwiches, which were wolfed down as I fed Rick. After a diaper change and bathroom stop, everyone piled back into the station wagon. We started down the backside of the Elburz Mountains and instantly the scenery changed dramatically. A canopy of arching tree branches threw dappled shadows on the road; flowering bushes covered the ground and water bubbled over a rocky path. As we rounded a curve, we came to a group of houses built on stilts. It was as if we had been transported by a magic carpet to Southeast Asia. The Caspian side of the Elburz gets so much rain that rice and tea are grown there in abundance. Wild pigs roam undisturbed by the Muslim population and are only in danger when Christian hunters prey upon them. In the distance the blue Caspian gleamed in the afternoon sun.

We entered a wide valley and could see the peasants working in the rice fields. Further on I pointed out the Assassins Fortress to the children. The story we heard the first time we were in Iran was that on a wide plateau high in the mountain, in the year 1162 AD, Hasan-e-Sabbah, the first Lord of Alamut, built enchanting gardens filled with fruit trees and flowering shrubs. Called the Old Man of the Mountain, he built palaces inhabited by beautiful women dressed exotically and skilled in singing and dancing provocativly. The old man claimed to be a prophet with the power to decide who could enter Paradise. He looked for young men between the ages of twelve and twenty who were skilled in martial arts. He would feed each boy hashish until he was in a coma and then would transport him to the gardens. When the boy awoke, beautiful women were surrounding him, offering exotic food and wines. After a week of living in this Paradise, the youth was once again drugged and taken away. He was granted an audience with the Old Man, who told him that if he did as he was told and defended his lord, he would return to Paradise. The Old Man created a cult of young recruits that he controlled by giving them hashish. He trained them to become killers and would send them to all parts of the world to murder the enemies of whoever paid the highest price. The recruits were known as "hashishiyyin." The term evolved into the word 'assassin'. As I gave my school teacher lecture, I noticed the boys suddenly became fascinated when I came to the word 'killing'. This produced speculation as to how the people were killed, with Jimbo suggesting a long saber and Pat dryly stating it was probably with a gun.

We turned onto the cluttered road to Chalus, and Jim had to watch for the water buffalo that wandered aimlessly across the road. Young boys used sticks to try to direct the buffalo, to no avail. Women, in full, bright-hued skirts swaying around their bare feet, walked along the side of the road with large baskets on their head, carrying everything one could imagine. One woman had a 20 liter can of kerosene in her basket. Many of the women also had a baby wrapped in a shawl that was tied to the mother's back. A two-wheeled cart full of grain was pulled by a lone donkey and guided by a small boy.

As we entered the village, the scene became more chaotic; it was market day, and the Turkoman tribes had come to bargain. The Turkoman is a nomadic tribe that has wandered through Afghanistan, Russia, Iran, Turkey and Iraq for centuries. Modern country boundaries mean nothing to them; even the Russians have given up trying to contain them.

We found the cabin that had been assigned to us, and the kids immediately got on their bathing suits. They ran outside to jump in the sea but soon returned. "Mom, this isn't a sandy beach. It's full of small rocks that hurt!" they wailed. After putting on tennis shoes, they hit the beach and dived into the ultramarine water, only to come running out again because the sea was frigid, much too cold to enjoy. The rest of the week was spent walking along the beach, going into town to bargain for fresh produce, bread, eggs, and trinkets. I bought some Turkoman jewelry from an ancient woman whose face was covered with dark blue tattoos. She was selling the necklaces because she had no other means of buying food. She told me her husband had abandoned her for a younger woman. I didn't bargain with her; I paid what she asked of me, and afterwards I slipped her extra money. Her toothless smile warmed my heart.

We spent the mornings of our vacation walking along the beach, collecting any seashells we could find and enjoying looking at the beautiful blue sea. We found two large glass floats and speculated that they had come from a 'dreaded' Russian boat. In the afternoon we went into town to bargain with the Turkoman tribesmen who were selling carpets. On the fourth day we packed up and drove back to Tehran, a little sunburned but happy.

Chapter 21

It was time to start school and while the boys were excited to see new friends, Peggy was jumping up and down in anticipation of going into first grade. She couldn't wait to ride the rickety school bus that stopped at the corner. Her teacher was Mrs. Hunt, the wife of a naval captain and a good friend of mine. When the magic day arrived, confident Peggy went off to wait for the bus as if she had been doing it all of her life. That afternoon, I got a full report on the behavior of her brothers, something I could do without.

Monsieur Rick was four months old and spent most of the day lying in his playpen that was set up in the entrance hall over the large Kashan carpet that Elias, the carpet dealer, had left. Bandit became his guard dog, lying as close to the playpen as he could. Rick held court there for his many admirers; Jimbo and Patrick would tickle him and make cooing noises at him, Peggy loved to dress him and became proficient in changing his diaper; Negadar and Saffron talked endlessly to him in Farsi. Everyone who went passed would stop and to say something and he would honor them with a big grin. He followed all the action with his alert blue eyes. He was a remarkably easy baby. For a kid who had crashed the party, he turned out to be the life of it!

Jim received a message from the Red Cross that Margaret, his mom, had been in a car accident, and he was called home. He caught Air Force planes to Germany, New Jersey and on to Davis-Monthan Air Force base in Tucson. When he arrived, he learned that his mom had been very drunk, got in her car to go to the grocery store, ran a stop sign and got hit by a motorcycle. She was hit just behind the driver's side, causing the man riding a motorcycle to fly over the vehicle, breaking his leg. The side of the car was crushed in, almost to the other side, and was a total wreck. Knowing that his mom's condition was not likely to improve, he signed her into a nursing home where alcohol would be unavailable. He found another place for Mrs. Powder, put the furniture in storage and turned the house over to a rental agency. He moved the Funbuggy over to my folk's back yard, shopped for all of us and flew back to Tehran.

The big celebration of 2500 years of Iran's monarchy, that our friend Mostafa had been working on for almost two years, finally took place in October 1971. After SAVAK, the Shah's secret police, learned of several plans to bomb Persepolis while all the world's dignitaries were there, the militants were rounded up and put in jail. Everything came to a standstill; school was out, offices were closed and, since Jim was in Tucson on emergency leave because of his mother's car accident, the kids and I hunkered down at the house. Most of the celebration took place in Pasargadae, the site of the Cyrus the Great palace and at Persepolis, where an elaborate tent city was built. A new airport had been built in Shiraz and a new highway ran from there to Persepolis; 3200 schools had been constructed all over Iran, two luxury hotels and a stadium seating 100,000 were built in Tehran. The Shah inaugurated the Shahyad Tower in Tehran to commemorate the event, and it would soon hold the Museum of Persian History. Heads of State and high officials from all over the world came; 25 kings, grand dukes, sultans and emirs; 26 presidents and prime ministers; Emperor Halie Selassie of Ethiopia was the ranking dignitary; President Nixon sent Spiro Agnew; Prince Phillip and Princess Anne filled in for Queen Elizabeth, as security was suspect. Orson Welles was quoted: "This was no party of the year; it was the celebration of 25 centuries." One wag snidely quipped: "You weren't anyone if you weren't invited and you weren't anyone if you went!" There was much criticism from Iranians, because everything in the celebration came from France and the West; the food, the decorations, the tents etc.; only the caviar was Persian. From the site of Ali's tomb in Najaf, Iraq, Ruhollah Khomeini roared his disapproval, saying that anyone who organized or participated in these events was a traitor to Islam and the Iranian nation. Immediately the *ulama* (Shia hierarchy) decided that, rather than just trying to reintroduce Islam *sharia* law into the Iranian legal system, they would go for the total destruction of the Shah.

In November, the British were withdrawing their forces from the Persian Gulf and giving the United Arab Emirates their independence. The British navy also abandoned the small islands in the Persian Gulf that they had occupied since the 1800's, when it was imperative to stop the piracy that was rampant at that time. Six weeks after the celebration in Persepolis, the Shah, with the support of the United States under the Nixon Doctrine, occupied the strategic islands of Abu Musa and Greater and Lesser Tunbs. This happened the day before the UAE's independence. The next day Iraq severed diplomatic relations with Iran, claiming Iran was becoming expansionist. The tone was jittery, as the Shah expected Saddam Hussein to attack. In the meetings in the War Room, Jim, along with other American advisors, would assist the Iranian generals in planning for an attack from Iraq. To the frustration of the Americans, the Iranian generals were very reluctant to commit themselves to any one strategy, as they were aware that if the Shah disapproved of any plan, the advocating general would not be at the next meeting.

The Nixon Doctrine, pushed by Henry Kissinger, made the Shah a partner in the American global strategy of creating a deterrent to Russia. Iran was buying helicopters from an Italian diplomat named Count Agousta. The count was a real wheeler-dealer, who was importing parts from Boeing Aircraft, assembling Chinook helicopters in Italy and reselling them to Iran. Jim convinced the Iranians to buy directly from Boeing, thereby saving money for Iran and making more money for the United States.

Periodically we would hear of bombings and incidents of uprisings against the Shah, which were promptly put down, and there would be demonstrations in south Tehran. Tension escalated when some members of the Mujahidin ambushed and assassinated General Farsian, the prosecutor of the Tehran military tribunal. This happened on Dowlat Street, close to where I took our clothes to the *Barf* Cleaners, just a mile from our house.

The assignment division of the Pentagon called Jim and told

him that the Iranian government had requested Jim to extend his tour for one more year. Jim and I talked about it; I was willing, but he thought it was a bad idea - and things were becoming more dangerous. I knew about some of the bombings, but Jim was in a position to know more than he could say, and I readily agreed with his decision. When he informed the man at the Pentagon of his decision, Jim was told he had a choice of staying in Iran or going back to Viet Nam, where the fighting was still intense. Jim chose Viet Nam, telling the astonished man back in Washington DC that the safety of his family was more important to him.

The holidays were coming up and Jim decided we should have a party, since we had not done any major entertaining due to my pregnancy. So many people had given baby gifts to Rick and we wanted to show our appreciation. We sat down to make a list and after putting down the names of our close friends, those we were obligated to, and those we should invite, we had the astounding number of 100 names. Not to worry, we decided we would make it an Open House where the people could come and go within a three hour period. I wrote out the invitations for the tenth of December with the time listed as being from 1800 to 2100 hours. I made arrangements with the Officers Club to cook a twenty pound turkey, a thirteen pound ham and beef tenderloin in a burgundy sauce. Saffron made Persian rice, a vegetable plate with dips and four cheese rolls while I made chili con queso. We had twenty pounds of shrimp from the Gulf with sauce for dipping. The buffet table was truly a groaning board, with not an inch of space to spare. Jim made our infamous Bride's Bowl punch. This innocuous refreshment is made with pineapple juice, lemon juice, sugar water, soda water and rum. Jim garnished the punch with floating strawberries. It is such a light, refreshing drink people tend to think it is lemonade. I made a different 'without' punch that contained no alcohol. I had made arrangements a month early for Hassan, a waiter from the club, to tend to the drinks. Half an hour before the party, Hassan had not arrived. Jim called the club and was told that someone had neglected to put Hassan's name on the want list and he was visiting his mother in Hamadan. Jim demanded that another waiter be sent, but there was none available.

I went in the kitchen to enlist Saffron, but she adamantly refused. "NO, Madam, no, Madam I no talk people, I in kitchen." Negadar was needed out in the kuchee to guard the cars. Jim went outside and discovered Jimbo, Pat and Peggy standing in a receiving line, shaking the hands of the early arrivals. "Come inside, kids, we need your help. Jimbo, you stay at this punch bowl and serve the cups. Pat, you are to be at the other punchbowl, serving, and Peggy, your job is to collect dirty cups that people have put down, take them to Saffron to wash and bring back the clean ones," Jim ordered.

"Yes, Sir" Jimbo answered, and it was echoed by Pat and Peggy. Like good little Army brats, the kids took their places as the house filled with people. It seemed that everyone arrived exactly on time and didn't leave until the end. There was no such thing as coming and going, this bunch came and stayed. Fortunately, ten couples had sent regrets, so we only had 80 people in the house. Saffron made sure Peggy was kept busy bringing in more food and cups, and emptying ashtrays. A lady (I wasn't too fond of, especially after I was told of her remark) was overheard saying that wasn't it clever of Jim Starkey to save money by putting his children to work. One colonel, a strict Baptist, was told the 'without' punch was red - so he chose the one with the floating strawberries. One of my more catty friends whispered to me, "He drank one cup of that and never knew he could feel so good!"

It was a joyous group of people and, at one point, I found Jimbo wrestling on the floor with Johnny Hubble. General Williamson, the head of ARMISH-MAAG, was very reluctant to leave at 9:00, but Mrs. W. insisted. In the military, it is customary for no one to leave a party until after the Commanding General leaves. Soon after that the house was empty of our guests. I heaved a sigh of relief as I viewed the empty platters on the buffet table.

"Babe, this was a big success. I think everyone had a good time," Jim remarked.

"Well, we couldn't have done it without the children. Weren't they remarkable?" I answered.

"Yes, they were - and so were Saffron and Negadar. We couldn't have done it without them, either." Jim called them into the hallway and thanked them profusely. "Have some dinner before you start cleaning up," he ordered. The next day I fielded many phone calls thanking us and many added, "It was the best party we've been to in Iran".

Tehran got hit hard with cold weather during Christmas. We had several inches of snow, the airports were closed down and driving was almost nonexistence. All the neighbors' kids were out in the *kuchee* making snowmen and having snowball fights. One of our neighbors was the ambassador from Columbia, where snow is never seen. His boy, Carlos, was having a wonderful time. The children were a mixture of diplomat kids and gardener kids; it didn't seem to matter - everyone was having fun. Saffron made some cocoa, and I handed out cups of it to all.

During January the cold continued; it was the worst winter in thirty years. The snow stayed on the ground and the temperatures rose over 32 degrees only three or four times during the month. Tehran was in the grip of a flu epidemic, and I sent Negadar home with a warm jacket and Levis' for his son. The school closed an extra day each week because so many children were absent. We avoided the flu but, two weeks after school resumed, Peggy came home with a light, lady-like case of chicken pox. The following week Patrick and Rick became sick, and soon both of them had the worst case of chicken pox I had ever seen. Pat was covered from head to toe in an ugly red rash. He had sores inside his throat, tongue, his eyelids and even on the bottom of his feet. I took him to the doctor when Benadryl didn't seem to be helping and was told that Pat had an extra bad case that would take a longer time to heal. The doctor gave him a shot and sent us home. When the doctor was informed of Rick's bad case he was amazed that eight month-old Rick would get the pox; he was supposed to be carrying my immunity. Rick was beet-red with the rash, but it didn't seem to bother him so much, as he always had a big smile for me. Both were on Benadryl for a week, which kept them comfortable and sleeping most of the time.

It was late in February when Jim, Smoke Stover and Col. Ravanpay, an Iranian who worked with Stover, planned a trip to the Caspian area to hunt ducks and wild pigs. When Patrick came home with a perfect report card, Jim decided to reward him by taking him on this hunting trip. Jimbo had hunted many times with Jim, but this was a first for Pat, who immediately helped Jim get all the gear ready. Pat proudly showed me the hunting knife Jim had given him to carry. When Smoke heard that Pat was going, he decided to take his thirteen year-old son, Bill. I packed a big lunch of sandwiches, potato chips, fruit and hot cocoa and bade them farewell. There was still a lot of snow on the ground, but the roads were clear as they headed west to Resht. They were in Smoke's station wagon, which made it up the steep grades of the Elburz Mountain to a clearing where the road ended. It was already dark when they parked the car in an area right off the main highway. There they met some villagers, who guided them, and they started walking on a narrow path. They stomped through the eight inches of snow that covered the path while on either side the snow was piled up six feet high.

Patrick, carrying a heavy load, struggled valiantly until he slipped and fell backwards, unable to move. "Dad, dad," he cried, "Help me!" Jim pulled Patrick upright and brushed the snow from Pat's clothes.

On they trudged for another two hours. They finally arrived, wet and cold, at a small, stone hut, used for years as a hunting lodge. The low, con-caved roof was laden with several feet of snow. There was only a narrow opening, covered by a heavy, faded woolen blanket that failed to keep out the cold. The tiny, windowless room was bare except for a stack of blankets and thick mats in the far corner. The walls and ceiling were black with the soot of past fires. The only light came from the glowing, charcoal-filled *khorsi* in the center of the hard, dirt floor. Patrick immediately sat in front of it, trying to get warm.

Suddenly, into the room burst three Kurdish guides. All were well over six feet tall, wearing high turbans and thick soled boots that made them even taller. The dark, swarthy faces, heavy eyebrows, hooked noses, moustaches, and coal black eyes were menacing. They wore dun-colored, heavy, long coats over their baggy, black pants. Tucked into their belts were jeweled daggers and over their shoulders were ancient rifles. Overwhelmed, Patrick shrunk back in fear, looking to his father for help. Ravanpay and the guides were shouting greetings, slapping each other on the back and carrying on a simultaneous conversation in Farsi. Soon the Kurds turned to look at the staring Americans and, when the introductions were made, the broad smiles on the faces of the Kurds changed their whole demeanor. Mohammad, the tallest guide, paid special attention to Pat, as he seemed to sense Pat's initial fear. All the Kurds were pleased to see Pat and Bill included in this adventure, especially when they learned it was the first hunting experience for both.

One of the men left and soon returned with a huge platter of rice covered in a beef sauce and placed it over the *khorsi*. The hungry group devoured the meal, during which Ravenpay and the guides talked hunting strategy. Afterwards blankets and mats were placed side-by-side around the fire, filling the room. There was barely enough room for everyone to lie down, and soon everyone was asleep. The next day the hunters were up early for some tea and *nune* and then out into the elements. Pat was a real trouper, having no problem keeping up with Jim. "Pat, would you like to shoot the shotgun?" Jim asked.

Smiling, Pat eagerly nodded. Jim patiently showed him how to hold the shotgun and how to line up the sight. "Now, Pat, line up the front and the back sights to find your target. Make sure the stock is firmly against your shoulder, and remember to squeeze the trigger, don't yank it."

Pat aimed at a sea bird and pulled the trigger. A loud explosion and the unexpected kick from the discharge knocked him to the ground. He lay there stunned as all the men laughed and yelled. "You got him, you got him." Pat felt himself rising and turning; he looked into the snow-white teeth of the grinning face of Mohammad. "*Bala, bala, kucheeloo*" (up, up, little one), he said. He brushed the snow from Pat's clothes and pointed out his kill. The very dead bird lay on the ground, and a sudden feeling of remorse washed over Pat. He didn't know whether to be pleased that he was successful or sad that the bird was not.

They trekked most of the day looking for prey. They didn't see a duck or a wild pig all day until about three in the afternoon, when Ravanpay shot a pig. Being Muslim, he would not touch it, so Jim and Smoke gutted and skinned it. They left it outside during the night and early the next morning, as they said goodbye Mohammad solemnly shook Pat's hand and said *Khaili khob, kuchek mard*" (very good , little man).

As the hunting party started back to the station wagon, Ravenpay said, "Mohammad is the headman of the Kurds in the Caspian area.

Pat, you made a friend of a very important man." They walked the long way back to the station wagon, only to discover it wouldn't start. Fortunately, they were able to flag down a passing truck and got a jumpstart. It was 11:30 at night when Jim and Pat returned, tired, hungry and dirty. I made some scrambled eggs and toast while they regaled me with their adventures and, after eating, they both hustled upstairs to a shower and bed. Quizzing Pat the next day, he was very proud that he had gone, but I got the distinct feeling he was sure the trip was his 'reward' for making good grades.

Monday morning I received a phone call from Marian Hunt, Peg's teacher. "Shirley, I have bad news." My heart dropped, until she went on quickly. "Peggy wet her pants in the classroom. She's waiting in the room right now, and I have the other children outside. I don't believe they noticed her dilemma."

"I'll be right over with clean clothes," I said. I dashed upstairs, grabbing clean panties and white tights and another skirt, just in case. Arriving in the classroom, I saw Peggy calmly coloring a picture. Smiling, I said, "Come on, honey, let's go into the bathroom." She put her hand in mine as we walked. I didn't say anything to her, afraid she would get upset. I got her cleaned up, changed and watched as she happily joined her friends in the playground.

After school I said, "Peggy, why didn't you ask to be excused?" She looked at me intently and determinedly said, "I did, but Mrs. Hunt told me I should have gone at recess, but I was thirsty and there was a long line at the drinking fountain and I didn't have time to go to the bathroom before recess was over, so I raised my hand after we got back into the classroom. Mrs. Hunt wouldn't excuse me and I didn't think that was right, because I never ask if I don't need to, like some of the kids, so I stood up and wet all over the floor. I just showed her," she breathlessly informed me.

Shocked at the audacity of this little girl, I could only say lamely, "I'm sure she'll let you go next time you ask."

Jimbo was crazy about his little brother and would get him out of the playpen and encourage him to crawl. The first time Rick made a movement forward, Jimbo yelled out, "He's crawling!" and the whole family gathered around to watch. Rick tried again to scoot on his tummy but was laughing so hard he fell on his face. It wasn't very long before Rick was crawling everywhere, and soon he learned to pull himself up. His little fingers would hold on to the mesh of the playpen, and he would stand there grinning at everyone. One day while looking through the Sears catalogue I came upon a picture of a backpack made for carrying a child. It was the first time I had seen anything like that, and I immediately ordered it, knowing it would come in handy whenever we traveled.

We were scheduled to leave Iran in June, so we decided take the children to Isfahan, Shiraz and Persepolis, since there had been a lull in bombings during the unusually cold winter. Jim requested a week's leave time in March, just before *No Ruz*. Early Thursday morning, in a blinding rainstorm, we loaded up the station wagon, put Rick's playpen in the back and waved good-bye to Negadar and Saffron. It took us more than two hours to negotiate the heavy traffic of Tehran, made twice as bad by the weather. With great relief we left the capital and headed straight south toward Qom. As the weather cleared, we could see in the distance the golden dome of the shrine of Fatima, built to honor the sister of the Eighth Iman. We did not plan to stop in Qom, as it was a hotbed of radical Islam and the place where Ruhollah Khomeini commenced his fight against the Shah. We stopped briefly at a roadside gas station beyond Qom and then continued on the desolate route. The children started to get restless, so I asked them what they had learned in school about Isfahan. The American school had a program called Iran Cultural Studies for two hours a week. Each class was geared toward the level of understanding of the children. Jim and I were amazed to hear Jimbo tells us the things he had learned in school about the history of Iran. His sixth grade teacher, Mr. Wright, had fascinated the class with stories of various Shahs, Genghis Khan, Tamerlane and Alexander the Great. Patrick and Peggy chimed in with some other facts they had learned. We were very impressed.

The broad expanse of the Dast-t-Kavir, the great salt desert, came into view on our left. Jim regaled the children with his experience during our first tour when he had to cross the desert to find a downed airplane. We hit a patch of bumpy road where repairs were being made. I looked back to see how Rick was handling the abrupt, erratic movements of the car. Laughing hysterically, he was hanging onto the mesh of the playpen like a monkey, swinging back and forth. He seemed to have the ability to find amusement in everything.

We started up a steep hill which ended in small village filled with mean, colorless adobe huts. We could see the men working the fields with ancient plows, some pulled by donkeys and others pulled by the peasant harnessed to the plow. It was a scene that hadn't changed since Biblical times. Off to the west, the massive Zagros Mountains, its heights covered in snow, dominated the view. Soon we saw the black tents of the Baktiari tribes and knew we were close to Isfahan. We entered a plain filled with green fields with massive trees lining the roadway. It was obvious that this part of Iran received more rainfall. Traffic got heavier, and Jim demanded to know how we were to get to our hotel. I attempted to read the map Jim had given me and, much to my surprise, I was able to get us to our destination. After checking into the Intercontinental Hotel, we had a wonderful dinner of Chelo Kabab, the country's most famous dish of rice and spicy ground lamb. Showers and bedtime followed.

The next morning, after breakfast, Jim hired an English speaking guide to take us around Isfahan. It was a clear, beautiful day and, with Rick in the backpack on Jim's back, we were eager to see the sights. Our guide, Mahmood, took us to the side entrance of the Maidan-e-Shah, a rectangle square that is twice the size of Red Square in Moscow, and seven times the size of the Piazza San Marcos in Venice. As the full import of the space in this square seizes you, it is impossible not to gasp. The Maidan was planned and built in the 17th Century by Shah Abbas I. At the southern end is the Royal Mosque, the largest and most spectacular building, with blue tiled dome and minarets. Facing it, a quarter of a mile away on the north, is the Grand Bazaar. To the west is the Ali Qapu, a two storied palace, and opposite that is the jewel-like Sheikh Lutfullah Mosque. In the middle of the square, in 1384, Tamerlane's soldiers played soccer with the severed heads of the captured Persians, while Tamerlane watched from the porch of the Ali Qapu. We had been unimpressed with the Ali Qapu palace the first time we had seen it ten years before. At that time the insides were plain, white-washed walls, although the music room was impressive with its cutout designs that made the room acoustically perfect. This time, upon entering the palace, we were amazed to find the walls were covered in delicate mosaic designs. Our guide explained that the Empress Farah had ordered all the plaster removed to reveal the mosaics painted centuries earlier. We walked out onto the porch to view the entire Maiden-e-Shah. Children were playing in the fountain in the center of the square; various vendors were providing ice cream, fruit drinks, roasted corn and kebabs to the hungry throng. Men were sitting on benches playing with their worry beads while elderly matrons watched the children and gossiped. The whole area was teeming with colorful people from all walks of life.

We walked through the throng of humanity over to the bazaar. This bazaar was different from the one in Tehran, which came about in a higgledy-piggledy manner as Tehran grew in importance. The Isfahan Bazaar, designed by Shah Abbas I, is an architecturally beautiful building with a massive wooden door at the entrance and organized areas of commerce. The domed vaults have circular openings to allow light to enter, as well as rain. Entering the bazaar, one is overwhelmed with the fragrance of herbs and fruits, saffron and other spices, as well as pomegranate peel used in dyes for yarns. We passed through dimly-lit shops, ignoring the pleas from the vendors to "come see my goods." Outside, in a courtyard, we passed enormous vats of dyes and crisscrossed racks of newly dyed wools hanging in the sun. Mahmood took us to see the blind camel walking in circles, pulling the stone that was grinding spices. We wondered if it was the same bedraggled camel Jim and I had seen ten years before.

As we walked along the square watching the various artisans work, Jimbo noticed a man pounding a design onto a tin-washed copper platter. "Mom, look, he's doing our family." I looked down and there, engraved on the platter, were our three big children, me, and Jim with Rick on his back. Never mind that Rick looked like a monkey clinging to his father - we had to buy the platter. The guide took us out to the Shaking Minarets. Jimbo immediately climbed up on one minaret and started shaking it, which forced the other minaret to shake. As I nervously watched, Pat and Peggy soon followed, repeating the shaking.

After returning to the city center, we paid the guide and continued on to a special copper dealer to order gifts our various family members desired. Some of the items would take a couple of days to finish, and Jim made arrangements to pick them up after we had visited Shiraz and Persepolis.

The next morning, we headed south over the Zaindeh River to Shiraz, passing mile after mile of desolate, white salt flats glistening in the sunshine. In the middle of the incessant desert, we soon came upon increasing numbers of black wool tents and camel herds of the Qashqais tribal people. It was too soon for them to start their semi-annual migration up to the cool heights of the Zagros Mountains. The Qashqais are a free-spirited people who have resisted the Shah's attempts to change their nomadic ways. The women are unveiled and dressed in vivid, full skirts and multi-colored blouses adorned with ribbons and lace. Their black, wavy long hair swung from beneath colorful head scarves as they tended the herds of goats.

We passed the entrance to Persepolis, which Jim suggested we visit after seeing Shiraz. We checked into the hotel in Shiraz that had been built specifically for the 2500 year birthday party and were stunned at its opulence. Huge red Persian carpets covered the marble floors, enormous pots of palm trees and flowers turned the lobby into a garden. We learned that the French designer of the hotel purposely wanted the lobby to look like the Tulliaries Gardens in Paris. Our room was massive, with a sitting area of couches that made into beds for the children and an alcove-bedroom for Jim and me. We unloaded our gear and then went to the nearby park so the children could play and get rid of their pent-up energy. Our dinner was served at eight o'clock and well worth it. We had *khoreshe holu,* chicken served with a spicy peach sauce over the rice, and for dessert, *baklava.* By the time our meal was over, we were stuffed and ready to go to bed.

The bazaar is the life of every Iranian city or village. It can be a massive building or a simple open-air space, but is always where you go to get the feeling of the area. So, the next morning we headed for the Shiraz bazaar. It was packed with various animals and humanity. As we entered the bazaar, Jim, with Rick on his back, strode into the crowd, dodging donkeys, sheep, Qashqais tribesmen, herdsmen and men hawking their wares. Patrick and Peggy followed behind Jim, with Jimbo and me bringing up the rear. Suddenly, Jimbo and I were separated from the rest of the family when a herder drove his goats in front of me. I stood still, telling Jimbo to stand quietly and not to look into the goat's eyes. I didn't want us to be butted like our car had been!

We had to run to catch up with the rest of the family and as Jim whipped through the crowd, we saw the people stop to stare at this crazy American with a baby on his back. As they nudged each other, they saw the two white-blond kids following. Pointing and chattering, most of the people made way for us to pass. In a country where one never saw a man so much as hold a child's hand, it was a freakish thing to behold a man carrying a child! And then to be followed by two blond children was another amazing event.

After a visit to the tombs of Hafez and Saadi, Iran's most famous poets, we headed forty miles northeast to Persepolis. As we paid the entrance fee, a handsome Iranian man dressed in a black suit, white shirt and green necktie, approached us and said in perfect English, "Sir, are you interested in a guide? I am Ahmad and I am at your service." He looked as if he should be in a courtroom arguing a case, not here in the middle of a desert wasteland guiding tourists. Being impressed, Jim readily agreed to his price. As we started through the main gate, Jim introduced us to Ahmad and then asked, "Ahmad, you speak perfect English. Where did you go to school?"

"I have a Master's Degree from Stanford in the United States. Here in Iran my family owned many villages and farms for centuries - until the Shah gave all our property away. My father is very ill, and I only came back to Iran to care for him. When he dies, I shall take my mother and return to the States, where I will complete working on my doctorate. In the meantime I pass the time guiding visitors here at Persepolis."

"Can't you get a job teaching in a university or some other occupation?"

"I'm afraid not. In order to take a job teaching I would have to say that I will stay in Iran forever, and I can't make that promise. My father's health is such that the doctors have said he probably won't last another six months."

He was an excellent guide and paid particular attention to the children, making his descriptions of the carvings and buildings easy for them to understand. Ahmad showed the children the steps leading up to the Gate of Xerxes that were wide enough for chariots with four horses to climb. Flanking the gate were a pair of statues of a bull and a winged man. We walked up the *Apandana*, or great

Audience Hall, noting the perfectly preserved carvings showing the important men of the kingdom nonchalantly gossiping as they made their way to attend the King's New Year reception. On the eastern staircase we studied the carvings depicting the diplomats of the various conquered territories bringing *No Ruz* (New Year) gifts. Ahmad showed us the name Stanley carved in black marble that was left in 1871 by Stanley on his way to find Dr. Livingston in Africa. Stanley had taken a pretty wide eastern detour in his efforts to find Livingston.

After walking all around the site of the ancient ruins for more than an hour, we headed up to where the Shah had placed his tent city set up for the 2500 anniversary party. Ahmad made this comment, "I was chosen to accompany Prince Reza during the ceremony. Prince Reza is the same age as your son Jimbo but has his own automobile." He laughed. "I had the 'honor' of sitting next to him as he drove his car all over the area."

Jimbo perked up. "Was he a good driver?"

"Yes, he was a good driver, and I came to like the Prince very much. I'm not too fond of his father for what he did to our family's fortune, but I did like his son."

As we drove away from Persepolis, I reflected on the logic of the Shah's government sending bright students to schools and universities in the West but demanding that after graduation, the students return to Iran, where there was nothing for them to do. Just as Mostafa Byat had told us, "Iran has no General Motors. What am I supposed to do with my engineering degree?" No wonder so many educated Iranians decided to move permanently to Europe or the United States.

After an early breakfast, we headed back to Isfahan to pick up the gifts we had ordered. It was still early in the day, so we decided to drive back to Tehran. It was very late when we arrived home and awoke the surprised Negadar. The next morning, we gave Saffron and Negadar a *No Ruz* bonus, filled two gunny sacks full of meat, rice, *panir,* and eggs and sent them home to their families for a week.

Chapter 22

I was leading an exercise class at the Officers Club, and one of the attendees was Mary Fleit. Mary's husband, Bob was an engineer working with the Oil Consortium. They were from Oklahoma but had spent most of Bob's career living overseas. When they first married, they were sent to Australia and, having little money, Mary spent a lot of time gathering furniture and household items at flea markets and at the Salvation Army. Her house was amazing with interesting items from everywhere. She showed me a beautiful black vase with ornate gold designs that she had bought at a junk shop in New Zealand. That same year, at Thanksgiving, she used the vase as part of a dramatic centerpiece for the table. One of the guests at the feast was a New Zealander, who queried Mary on the origins of the vase. Mary told him and he smiled strangely, proceeding to tell Mary that the vase was a funeral urn. Mary was horrified. She remembered that when she was cleaning the vase some grey dust fell out of it. Everyone at the meal said a prayer for the soul of the person whose remains were flushed down the toilet. Mary and I had to laugh at her story. She had a quirky sense of humor that I loved. After class one day she said, "Shirley, the American Women's Club is organizing a trip to Afghanistan. Would you like to go with me?"

"Would I? Are you kidding? Of course I would, but I'll have to check with Jim. I'll let you know." I couldn't wait for Jim to get home, I was so excited at the prospect of an adventure. Jim's immediate answer was, "Why not? Saffron is here and takes good care of the kids. Yes, I think you should go." I signed up for the trip that was leaving the end of March.

Johnny and Sarah Hubble came over for dinner that night and, when they came in, I could tell from their faces that something was very wrong. Johnny always had something funny to say to the kids, but he wasn't amusing this night. Jim made us a drink and, as we settled in the living room, Johnny proceeded to tell us that their middle son, Duncan, who was in his plebe year at West Point, had decided to quit. Johnny was devastated; it had meant so much to him that Duncan had been accepted at the military academy, which was no easy feat. Sarah proceeded to blame Duncan's girlfriend, who apparently hated anything having to do with the military and was influenced by the anti-war zealots. We read in the Paris addition of the Herald-Tribune about the continuing rioting and demonstrations against the Viet Nam War by the long-haired hippies. "What is Duncan going to do now?" I asked.

"We're sending him a ticket to Tehran, and I guess we'll decide that when he gets here," Johnny answered.

There was a group of twenty who signed up to go to Afghanistan, and when we met later in the month to discuss the trip, I was pleased to learn that the Hubble's had signed up Duncan. He was a strapping, six foot tall, happy-go-lucky, nineteen year old with sandy hair and freckles. He had the same goofy sense of humor as his dad, which immediately endeared him to me. He never called me Shirley; I was always Lady Starkey. At the meeting, one of the other advisors, a Col. Davis, approached me and introduced me to his mother, who was visiting from Washington DC. Mrs. Davis was a large, big-bosomed woman whose body was a rectangle from her shoulders to her hips, all held up by long, skinny legs. She wore her grey hair in an outmoded beehive; her arched, plucked eyebrows and beady eyes gave her face a perpetual suspicious look, and her thick lips were smeared with a bright red lipstick. She immediately launched into a soliloquy on the backward customs of the Middle East. Col. Davis faded away, leaving me to cope with Mommy dearest. She was very impressed with her status in life and kept referring to "my son, the Colonel," as if there were only one colonel in the whole world. She kept dropping the names of famous people in Washington, as if she knew them personally.

I bet she's going to be a problem on this trip, I thought as I hid my thoughts with a sickly smile. *I'm sure Col. Davis will be glad for her to be out of his hair.* I excused myself when I saw Mary Fleit enter the room and walked away, determined to avoid Mrs. Davis as much as I could.

When the day of departure arrived, Jim drove Duncan, Mary and me to Mehrabad Airport. We flew to Mashhad, a major city in northeastern Iran, the site of the magnificent mosque that housed the Imam Reza Shrine. The eighth imam, Reza, is the only Shia imam buried in Iran and every year, at the end of *Ramazan,* pilgrims of the Shia branch come to pray.

There was a bus waiting at the airport to take us to the shrine. Our group was given special permission to visit the mosque, but only if the females wore a chador and kept our hair and mouth covered. We had been warned ahead of time to wear black shoes and clothes for this visit. Hanging on hooks at the entrance to the mosque were black chadors for the females, and we were free to use these. I covered myself up the way Saffron had showed me and followed our group, keeping my head lowered as I admired the intricate tiles on the floor of the open courtyard. Men sat hunched over in the shade of the walls, fingering their worry beads as they surveyed the crowds of humanity. Passing a group of men I heard one of them disgustingly remark, *"Amrikan"* (American) as he spat on the ground. I wondered how they knew that we were American - until I turned around and noticed Mrs. Davis. She was striding purposely along, barely holding her chador at her chin. The chador was flying behind her like Superman's cape, and she was wearing hot pink pants and matching tennis shoes. So much for respecting another country's culture! Mrs. Davis gave new meaning to the term Ugly American.

While we could not go near the tomb of Imam Reza, we were permitted to visit the craft shop where the detailed designs were painted on the tiles. We got to watch as the artisans meticulously worked with brushes made with only five sable hairs. These brushes allowed the painters to get the tiny flowers, leaves and tendrils perfect. In another part of the factory, men were gluing the tiles together that would be used to repair the myriad of tiles on the domes of all the buildings in the compound. My request to buy one of the tiles was denied, as the extra tiles were shipped to other mosques in Iran in need of repair. Our bus returned us to the airport, and we caught a flight to Kabul, Afghanistan.

As we deplaned we saw a sign on the airport terminal that read: THIS AIRPORT TERMINAL WAS BUILT WITH FUNDS FROM UNITED STATES OF AMERICA AID TO AFGHANI-STAN and there was a picture of the flags of the United States and Afghanistan crossing each other. I later learned that while the United States built an airport terminal for the people of Afghanistan, the Russians built a four-lane highway from the border to Afghanistan all the way south to the border of Pakistan. After the Shah of Iran fell, Russia invaded Afghanistan - using this road.

Our hotel was the Intercontinental Kabul, located on a steep hill high above the city. After we got checked in, Mary and I were excited to see the view from our balcony was of the fabled, snow-covered Hindu Kush Mountains. We had a tasty evening meal of something mysterious and turned in.

Early the next morning, we left for a forty-five minute ride in a plane barely large enough to carry the twenty members of our group and our guide, Abdul. Our destination was the Bamyan Valley, located on the ancient Silk Road, the camel caravan route that has linked China to western Asia and Europe for 2000 years. We landed on a smooth dirt runway and were met by a middle-aged man smiling and bowing to each of us. He was our bus driver, Javer, and the tips we would leave him would feed his family for a month. The bus was very old, and the sides were painted with scenes of mountains, flowers and portraits of the Prophet Mohammad. Though the roads were dusty, the bus was immaculate on the outside and, more importantly, the inside. Abdul told us that the driver had polished the bus in anticipation of our visit.

Javer drove us through the verdant valley where wheat and potatoes were grown. Women, wearing scarves and long jackets, were hoeing in the fields; young children smiled, waved and sometimes chased our bus through the clouds of dust. We went through a village of dun-colored mud and stone huts with laundry hanging from the bushes. Men in turbans, ballooning pants, and colorful vests over white blouses stared at us from the shops and tea houses. One man yelled at Javer, who grinned importantly as he waved out the open window. At one tea house I saw a huge brass samovar three feet tall and wished I could get off the bus and bargain for it. I didn't know how I would get it home, but wouldn't it be worth the try?

The decrepit bus groaned up a hill and came to a grinding stop. We got out into the balmy, spring air and breathed deeply; the sky was a deep ultramarine blue with streaks of mare's tails dancing high in the atmosphere. We stretched our legs as we walked to the edge of the bluff that overlooked a vast valley. In the far distance, at the foot of the beige earth mass, was a truck that looked like a tiny toy. As our eyes moved up the side of the mountain range, we gasped in unison. Deep in the Hindu Kush Mountains, carved into the wall of massive rock stood two gigantic Buddhas. The largest one, known as the Great Buddha, stood 180 feet tall; it was carved around 550 A.D. and was the largest Buddha in the world. The Buddha's dress, a Greek tunic, was a style believed to have been introduced by Alexander the Great. The smaller Buddha was built in 507 A.D. and was only 121 ft. tall. All around the Buddha's were abandoned caves carved into the side of the Bamyan cliffs that had housed the monks of the monastery. In the interior of the caves, long-ago monks had painted scenes of monks working, tending gardens and praying, and these paintings are believed to be the oldest oil paintings in the world.

When the Taliban took over in Afghanistan, a movement arose to destroy the Buddhas. In 1999, despite a decree from Mullah Mohammed Omar to preserve the Buddhas, radical clerics banned all forms of imagery in a strict interpretation of Islamic Law and ordered them destroyed. A meeting of ambassadors from 54 member states of the Organization of Islamic Conference tried to stop the destruction, to no avail. Both Buddhas were dynamited out of existence in March of 2001.

Late in the day we flew back to Kabul, and the next morning we had an orientation bus tour. It was a dismal city with few paved streets; the poverty was evident everywhere we looked. It is the capital of the country and yet it looked like a huge, meandering village of low-slung stone buildings. Large plane trees shaded book stalls, flower shops, falconry shops, and fruit stands of oranges, pears and pomegranates. Men sat on carpet-covered wooden platforms smoking tobacco in hookahs. A mule-drawn gharry full of goods piled high was driven by an angry man who was trying to avoid a flock of geese being herded by a small, barefoot boy. The streets were full of old buses belching fumes as they groaned along carrying men inside and outside, hanging on the roof and the sides of the vehicle. Trucks, carrying merchandise of all natures, were moving scenes of advertisements, cartoons and landscapes; every inch of space was utilized in some kind of a painting. Pieces of tin and small bells were strung between the pictures, making the buses glitter and clang as they moved through the traffic. There was a lot of artistic talent being utilized on the beat-up transporters.

The clamorous sounds were ear-piercing - the rumble of bullock carts, braying of donkeys, screech of brakes from the gaudy buses, screaming of taxi-drivers and the calls from the shopkeepers. Stray, emaciated dogs roamed among the crowds of people who were strolling aimlessly in the middle of the road as our bus driver honked incessantly, in an effort to get them to move over. Ghostly shapes in various colors of blue, saffron, purple, chartreuse, and scarlet shopped at the green grocer. These are the *chadri*-clad women of Afghanistan. The *chadri* (sometimes referred to as a *burqa*) is one piece of many meters of silk or rayon that covers the entire body from the top of the head down the back to the feet. The front of the *chadri* only comes to the hip-line to allow the woman to use her hands to carry items. Underneath the *chadri,* the women were wearing black ballooning trousers, black stockings and sandals. The eye opening is a grill of the same fabric that allows the woman to see. The top of the cap is decorated in embroidery, and the fabric is pleated all the way to the ground. According to *Hadith,* (the collected traditions of the life of Mohammad), men and women are required to dress modestly in public. Although the *burqa* is not mentioned in the Quran, tradition varies from country to country; the more radical the clerics are, the more covered the women are.

We started down one street, and suddenly, the driver braked and started backing up around the corner. Coming down the street we had just entered, was a gang of men in lines stretching from one side of the street to the other and several lines deep, and all were carrying signs and placards written in Farsi. Our guide, Abdul, explained that it was a Communist demonstration, and we wanted no part of it. The bus turned around and we headed in the opposite direction. We drove into the older section of the city and were shown various government buildings and the palace of King Zahir Shah, the present ruler; everything was in disrepair. We went through an older section of mansions protected from our view by high walls. Then our driver took us to the commercial zone of Kabul - to the Big Bazaar and to the smaller Green Door Bazaar, which was fairly close to our hotel. He told us this was the best place to shop. Mary and I looked at each other and smiled. Now this was information we could use.

After lunch, Mary and I walked outside of the hotel where men had cyclos for rent. The cyclo is a cross between a bicycle and a small carriage. The front wheel, the handlebars and the seat of the bike is there, and behind the seat is a couch meant for two, covered on the top and sides and resting on two large wheels. It is similar to a rickshaw but, rather than a man pulling the carriage, the man is riding a bicycle. Asking the price of a trip to the Green Door Bazaar, we were told it cost the equivalent of 10 cents each to go down the hill, but to come back up the steep hill to the hotel, the price was double. As was expected, we got into the first cyclo in line, in spite of the fact that our driver looked ancient, emaciated and likely to have a heart attack at any moment. He couldn't have weighed more than 100 pounds; his yellow skin was tightly drawn across Mongolian features, emphasizing his slanted eyes; he had a beard about two inches wide at the bottom of his chin and it hairs must have been growing for all of his adult life, as the grey hairs were more than two feet long. He was wearing blue plastic flip-flops, black pants with wide legs, a clean, white shirt, and a green beanie covered his bald head. He pushed off and suddenly we were racing down the bumpy, dirt road holding on for dear life. Our driver's beard was flapping back, almost hitting my face as we careened around a curve, avoiding a flock of sheep. The road became steeper, and we kept going faster and faster. No roller-coaster could be scarier. My eyes were stinging from the wind, my knuckles were white from tightly clinching the bar in front of me, and I stopped breathing. At the bottom of the hill, we hit a bump that almost sent us flying. Suddenly, we were on a level paved street, and our driver turned to give us a yellow-toothed grin. From then on we moved at a snail's pace as the weight of the load caught up to his skinny legs. Finally, he pulled up at the entrance to the Green Door Bazaar and hopped out to give us a hand in getting out of the carriage. We thanked him profusely for not killing us as we gave him his fare. Not understanding English, he grinned and bowed to us.

We walked through the bright green portal of the open air bazaar. This looked just like a swap meet one would see back in the States, with vendors setting up their wares on tables inside individual tents, and like items set together in sections. We wandered through the dusty paths looking at everything. The first section we came to was for brass and copper. I bought the boys some brass soldiers; two for each of them, including Rick, even though he was too young to play with them. I stopped to look at some pots when I became aware that I was right next to a *chadri*-clad woman. It was unnerving to be next to this oval of humanity where the only protrusion in the silhouette was the nose. I wanted to talk to her; I wanted to see her face; it was upsetting to think that crazy laws made her cover up completely. Suddenly, I wanted to avoid her as if she had an awful disease. I hurried away sensing twin emotions: being very sad and feeling very guilty.

I stopped at the fabric section and spotted a table of embroidered vests. I chose a couple of small ones for Peggy and one for myself. One of Peggy's was a long vest of beige, felt-like material embroidered in gold thread; the other was a short red velvet vest embroidered in black flowers; mine was a hip-length purple vest with white and black flowers. I also bought several wide cloth belts in different colors covered with fancy embroidery of birds, flowers and leaves. The next table was full of dolls dressed exactly like the woman I had stood next to. Peggy had a collection of dolls from every country we visited, so I chose a doll that was about 12 inches tall with the feet nailed to a block of wood so the doll could stand upright. It was dressed in a green *chadri* and black pants. When I took the *chadri* off, I was surprised to see that the face of the doll was really ugly. I giggled, wondering if the women of Afghanistan were really that ugly and maybe that was why they stayed covered. At the next table, an artistic display of many *chadris* in green, yellow, cobalt blue, dark blue, turquoise, and purple shimmered in the sunlight. Off in a corner the black *chadris* were heaped in disarray, as if the proprietor wanted no part of them. I had to know what it was like to wear one, so I bargained for a purple one. This provoked the surrounding vendors to stand around watching. The woman at the kiosk laughed at the *Amerikan* wanting to buy a *chadri* and showed me how to put it on. The world around me was seen through tunnel-vision in a misty purple haze, but it was amazingly comforting to know I could see out but no one could see in. It made me feel like a small child playing hide and seek. I could stick my tongue out at an obnoxious vendor and he would be unaware of my actions. Mary was slowly walking along two kiosks away, carefully examining the merchandise on her quest for a Russian or Greek icon. As she approached me, I stepped directly in front of her and said softly, "Boo," She jumped back with a wide-eyed startled look on her face. I burst out laughing and Mary relaxed in relief and joined me in laughing, as did the vendors, who had been watching in fascination. I was sure we would be the talk of the whole bazaar before teatime. As I removed my *chadri* Mary was already bargaining for a bright chartreuse one. "Won't we have fun at Halloween?" she exclaimed.

Mary was anxious to look at carpets, so we kept walking until we came to the carpet section. While Mary bargained for a small tribal carpet, I decided to buy three *kelims* to use as bedspreads for the boy's beds. The *kelims* are heavy woven fabric that the nomadic tribes use as wall hangings and floor coverings in their tents. I figured the *kelims* would be tough enough for our rambunctious kids. Both Mary and I could use our Farsi in our bargaining and for the next forty minutes we haggled like pros. When we finally completed our buying we realized our purchases were very heavy and we decided to return to the hotel. We didn't want to witness some poor cyclo guy trying to get up that steep hill so we chose to ride in a taxi.

The next day, we were given the choice of visiting museums or going shopping and, of course, Mary and I decided to shop. Mary had her heart set on finding an original icon of the Greek Ortho-dox or Russian Orthodox religions, so we went back to the Green Door Bazaar. This time Mary carried a large canvas tote bag that reminded me of the magical bag Felix the Cat had carried in the cartoons. It turned out to be a magical bag, as it was full of all kinds of junk that Mary had brought from her house. We looked in vain at all the stalls near the entrance that carried small items of every nature that didn't belong in any of the other sections. Finally we came to a large tent where a tall, boney, dark-skinned man beckoned us to enter, assuring us he had wares we couldn't resist. He had an enormous black moustache and thick eyebrows, an engaging smile, and he spoke near-perfect English. His tent contained a variety of artifacts and we walked around looking at everything. I knew it was important to act casual and uninterested when viewing any item that one might be interested in buying. When I saw an old sword made by the Wilkinson Sword Company of London, I felt sure it had belonged to some British officer during the time of the Raj, when this part of the world was part of the British Empire. I had to buy it for Jim. I felt light-headed and breathless as I appeared to casually examine it. It had a leather sheath in fairly good condition; its' silver hilt or handle was embossed with a crown over the initials G R T and flowery designs were etched along the length of the blade.

I needn't have worried about acting casual as the shopkeeper was not paying a bit of attention to me. I looked across the room to where Mary was bargaining for a funny-looking burp gun, but she wasn't talking about money. Instead, she had pulled out an egg timer from her tote bag. The owner played with it for a minute, and then shook his head and wrinkled up his nose, "Madam, I will take this, but it is not enough. What else do you have to offer?" Mary peeked into the tote bag and rummaged around, looking for something else. The owner moved very close and tried to see what was inside the bag. Mary moved away, turning her back to him. I made my move, as I loudly asked the price of the sword. The owner frowned at me and quoted a price. I countered with a much lower price as the owner returned to trying to see what Mary was doing. With an irritated look, and to my surprise, the owner agreed to my price. I quickly pulled out my money and handed it to him. He stuffed it into his vest pocket, wrapped the sword in a piece of cloth and, handing it to me quickly, returned to dealing with Mary. I was smiling in satisfaction at my purchase as I watched in admiration the best bargainer I had ever witnessed. Mary played that owner like a violin, starting to pull something out of the tote bag, then changing her mind, closing the bag and frowning at something in the distance as if she were thinking hard. This went on for several minutes. The owner was getting agitated, dying of curiosity as he moved closer to Mary and Mary coyly moved away. Finally, Mary pulled out a portable radio. Small portable radios were a scarce commodity in 1972 Afghanistan. The owner's eyes lit up as Mary turned the radio on, and tinny, discordant music blared out. He was smiling like a kid at Christmas and told Mary that the burp gun was hers. Mary thanked him sweetly, rose up and said, "Shirley, let's get out of here," and started walking rapidly toward the door. I stopped to look at another item, and Mary loudly said, "Shirley, let's get out of here NOW."

She was out the door and quickly turned a corner where the shop keeper would not be able to see her. I ran to catch up and suddenly she sprinted as she shouted, "Run, Shirley, run," as she headed toward the gate.

I caught up with her at the taxi stand. "What's the matter?" I demanded as Mary climbed into a cab. Motioning me to get in, she said, "That radio only works for about fifteen minutes, and we can never come back to this bazaar again." I was shocked at first - and then irritated with her for pulling this stunt; she hadn't given that owner any money, only left him with an egg timer and a radio that didn't work. I didn't have much to say on the way back to the hotel.

I was excited about my purchase, and it must have shown, because when I went to the desk to get my key, the deskman asked what I had bought. I unwrapped the sword and the man's eyes widened. "Madame, where did you get this?"

"I got it at the bazaar. Why?"

"Madame, you must let me take this to the Ministry of Antiquities to see if it has value. How much did you pay for this?"

I ignored his question and shook my head saying, "Never mind. If you think I shouldn't take it out of the country I'll take it back to the shop and get my money back." I turned and took the elevator upstairs. I met Duncan in the hallway. "Dunc, come back to my room. I have something to show you."

I put the sword on the bed and took the cloth off. Duncan whistled in admiration. "Lady Starkey, this is really neat," he said as he inspected it. I told him the whole story and said, "I knew if I gave this to the guy at the desk, I would never see it again - so I told him I would take it back. I feel sure he would sell it to someone else. I'm not taking it back. I bought this for Jim. Do you think I'll have trouble getting it back to Iran?"

"You might. Let's figure out what we can do. I brought two empty duffle bags that we could tie together to carry the sword in."

"Well, I just brought the kids some *kelims* to be used as bed-spreads. We can wrap the *kelims* around the sword."

"Good idea. I'll go get the duffle bags." When he returned a few minutes later, I had the sword on top of the *kelims,* and we carefully rolled the kelims up as tightly as we could. We put the two duffle bags together and tied them with a clothesline rope Duncan had brought. He must have been a Boy Scout, because he certainly was prepared. He did a beautiful job of tying the bags and even made a handle with the rope to make it easy to lift. It was so well tied even a curious maid would not think of messing with it. He earned his rope tying badge that day.

The next morning the group was going on an excursion to eastern Afghanistan, but Mary talked me into going with her to the Big Bazaar. I didn't think much about it, as I had visited the Big Bazaar in Tehran, Isfahan and Shiraz many times. As always, I dressed very modestly in a beige safari pantsuit. We took a cab to the entrance and entered the high arching gates. It was early, and not many people were around. I spotted an interesting, old carved-stone oil lamp and paid the equivalent of 25 cents for it. Further on, I came to raised carpet-covered platform where three men were drinking tea and smoking the hookah. In front of them was a terra cotta water urn with no handle, just a spout. It wasn't large, maybe it held one liter, but the proportions were what caught my eye.

I would like to use that in a still life, I thought. *I wonder if they would sell it to me?* Feeling very brazen, I said in my best Farsi, while indicating in sign language, "*Salaam allecam*, Monsieur. Would you consider selling me the water jug?" The three men looked at each other startled, and then back to me and back to each other. Much Farsi ensued, and finally one of them agreed to sell me the jug for the equivalent of $1.00. There were smiles all around as the money was handed over and the jug was given to me. I knew the men thought they had made a killing, but I knew I had. That is the definition of a perfect deal.

Mary was nowhere to be seen, so I continued my walk down the same aisle. Suddenly, a small boy grabbed my hand. I looked down into his grubby face, and he haltingly said in English, pointing to the oil lamp I was carrying, "How much you buy?" Then I saw another oil lamp in his hand so I answered "25 cents." He pushed his oil lamp toward me and said, "You buy this 25 cents." "Okay," I agreed and handed him the money. When I took the second lamp I wondered if it had been such a smart idea. This lamp was coal black, very rustic, ugly and extremely heavy. Now I had two lamps and a pot to carry and the three of them weighed a lot. I put them into my canvas bag; at least I could shift from one hand to the other as numbness set in. I came to a junction and spotted Mary looking at a leather pouch and talking to a man who was minding the shop. Gleaming in the window was a beautiful rifle encased in silver filigree, and I asked the price. The man could not tell me; I would have to talk to the owner. "When will he return?" I asked. Shrugging his shoulders he answered, "*Farda, enshallah*" (tomorrow, if Allah wills it). Disappointed that I could not buy this beautiful rifle for Jim, I asked if he knew where I could buy some lapis lazuli, the blue stones found in Afghanistan and Columbia. He directed me to another shop that was near a second entrance to the bazaar. That shopkeeper had a very meager supply of lapis, and I asked him why. He told me that as part of some agreement Afghanistan had with the Soviet Union, Afghanistan must give the Russians first choice of all the lapis mined in the country. I realized then that this country was really under the thumb of the big northern bear. After buying a few pieces, we left the bazaar.

We walked a few blocks from the bazaar entrance, looking for a cab, when we saw a sign in English 'Antique Store.' "Mary, let's go in and see what these oil lamps are worth," I suggested. She agreed, and inside we met a European-looking gentleman. He wouldn't say what the lamps were worth but he told me the black ugly one I had bought was very, very old while the first one (and my favorite) was "made yesterday."

When we entered the hotel I was met by an angry Duncan. "Lady Starkey, where have you been? You were not on the trip with us. Where did you go?"

"Mary and I went to the Big Bazaar," I calmly told him.

"Are you out of your mind? Don't you know that is dangerous? Women should never go down there; that is for men only. Not only that, but knifings are common there. You should not have gone there."

He made me feel like a naughty little girl being lectured to by my father. I meekly said, "Come to think of it, we didn't see any other women there, but we were treated with great courtesy. How do you know women are not supposed to go there?"

"I've been talking to a lot of people, and that's what they say. Col. Starkey would be angry if he knew what you just did. From now on, I'm keeping you in my sight," he declared with great authority.

The next day we boarded a plane for Herat, a major city near the Iranian border. And true to his word, Duncan stayed with me and helped to carry my bags.

Luck was with me, as I was assigned a window seat. As we flew westward over the Bamiyan Valley, I could see the green valleys, the beige plains and the soaring, snow-capped mountains piercing the sky. Afghanistan is a tough, rugged country, and so are the people who inhabit it.

Herat is in the heart of an agricultural belt. As the plane circled low prior to landing, I could see miles of orchards of pistachio, pomegranates and walnut trees, fields of wheat, potatoes and grapes, but everything looked very dusty. As we deplaned and got into the bus, our new guide gave us a running lecture on the city's history, as well as its current economic status. He told us that the whole area had been in the throes of a major drought for the past three years. He mentioned to us that the landlords, saving money, had kicked out the tenants, and the city was teeming with beggars of all sizes. The bus took us into the city but stopped several blocks from our hotel, as the streets were too narrow for large vehicles. "As you walk to the hotel notice the beauty of our architecture, parks, and flowers," our guide said, and then added, "Do not give any beggar anything, or the other beggars will try to take your pocketbooks."

The minute we left the bus, we were enveloped in a sea of children blocking our path. They were sad, dirty urchins in tattered clothes who grabbed at us, as we tried to walk along the sidewalk, crying out piteously for money or food. I kept my eyes straight ahead, but a small hand suddenly grabbed my hand. I instinctively looked down into the face of a child not more than four years old. Her brown eyes wept, pus was running down the side of her face; her hair was matted and tiny insects were moving on the top of her head. I yanked my hand from hers and ran to catch up to our guide, who was swiftly leading us down the street. Yah, I was really going to enjoy the architecture of this beautiful city!

Our hotel was an old Victorian building but inside it was very modern. I ran to the restroom and washed my hands three times. I shuddered and couldn't get the vision of that poor child out of my mind. I thought of my own children with their clear, inquisitive eyes and smooth, clean skin, and a wave of homesickness washed over me. I took several deep breaths getting myself under control. *We'll be back in Tehran the day after tomorrow*, I thought, *and, in the meantime, I'll survive this.*

Our guide assigned our rooms and told us that dinner would be served in two hours. We caught the elevator and found that our room was large and airy with a balcony hanging over a garden and swimming pool. Mary wanted to go shopping, but I declined. "No thank you, I'm not facing that horde of kids out there. I'll just stay here and read my book."

Mary returned after a hour. "I should have stayed in with you as I didn't get close to the shopping district. Those beggars were all over me. I've never seen anything like it."

After dinner we had a lengthy lecture on the history of Afghanistan. Like Iran, Afghanistan has been invaded in past centuries by Mongols, Turks, Persians, Moslem Arabs, Alexander the Great, Timur and Genghis Khan.

Breakfast was served at seven and at eight we were on our way to the bus. The sidewalks were vacant except for some sleeping bodies lying in doorways. We toured the city, passing the decaying remains of the citadel built by Alexander the Great. The Masjet-e-jam Mosque, or the Blue Mosque, as it is known, is one of Islam's most beautiful, with is majestic minarets reaching toward Heaven. It's amazing to me that from ancient times, the common man has toiled on for years in the name of all religions and have built these amazing structures that are still standing today.

We stopped at a tea house for an elaborate meal of *chelo kabab*, the lamb and rice dish we enjoy in Iran. Herat is only 100 kilometers from the Iranian border, so it was normal for the food to be similar. After lunch, we departed for the Musalla Complex, a large area that contained a mosque with a collection of minarets and a *madreseh*, an

Islamic school. The bus parked on a hillside, in the shade of massive plane and cypress trees. Our dear Mrs. Davis stated loudly that she intended to stay on the bus, which didn't surprise anyone, as she had declined to get out of the bus anyplace we went. She hadn't even seen the Great Buddha from her throne in the first seat on the bus, where she always established herself. I hadn't witnessed her experience walking through the urchins on our way to the hotel, but Duncan told me she had actually hit some of the children. No one wanted to be around this obnoxious person who complained constantly about the food and the lodgings and would yell demands at our guides. We were always relieved when she decided to stay on the bus.

The ground was covered in fallen leaves so thick it was hard to walk on them. We trudged down the hill and through the residue for many minutes until we got to a stone path. From then on, our journey was easier, and we could enjoy the balmy weather and, from the sounds high up in the trees, all kinds of birds were welcoming spring. Our guide took us to the *madreseh* to visit a classroom, but when we got to the school we found that the Mullah, who was teaching a class of seven year-old boys, had decided the weather was so nice he would have his class outside. The class of twelve little boys was sitting quietly in a circle around their sleeping teacher. We tiptoed past the 'classroom' and, as I got near, I put my finger to my lips in a shush gesture and smiled. All the little boys grinned at me and echoed my pantomime. I couldn't imagine twelve American seven year-olds staying quiet for even three minutes, but that Mullah had a real hold on those kids.

The mosque has been described as 'the most beautiful example of color and architecture ever devised by man to the glory of God' but, like so much of Afghanistan, it was crumbling in neglect. The tiles on the main building and the minarets were an iridescent turquoise that sparkled in the sunlight, but there were whole areas where the tiles had fallen off, leaving a muddy color. By this time we had attracted a crowd of children, mostly little girls, who were not allowed to go to school. The children followed us back to where the bus was parked, but it was not time to leave, so I decided to climb the hill to sketch the minarets. A polite boy of twelve followed me, offering some pieces of the fallen blue tiles. No one else was near as I sat on an almost flat rock and began my sketch. The boy, uninvited, sat next to me on the rock, watching my every move. He had a big smile and I noticed that, unlike the other children, he was very clean. His dark pants and white shirt, while well-worn, were spotless. I could tell he had a mother who took pride in her boy. To his delight, I started talking to him in my limited Farsi. His name was Ali, and he told me that he was the oldest in his family and that he had three younger sisters. I told him I had three boys and one girl. He seriously said it was good to have so many boys. He had finished his schooling and would soon start to help in his father's bakery and mentioned that he also liked to draw. I couldn't resist; I gave him my sketchbook and pencil and told him to hide it from the other children, as I did not have any more to give them. He lifted up his long shirt, revealing pants that were held up by a man's leather belt many sizes too big. He stuffed the art supplies between his stomach and his pants and dropped his shirt down, covering our secret. I thanked him for the pieces of tile he had given me, and he was grinning happily as we started back to the bus.

Suddenly, we heard a commotion and saw a group of children next to the bus fighting, screaming and rolling on the ground. A flash of orange appeared periodically among the chaos. The bus driver and Duncan waded into the fray to get the children to stop. One little girl was bleeding profusely about her nose and mouth. The guide yelled a harsh command, and all the kids dispersed. Then he turned to our dear Mrs. Davis and in low, threatening tones said, "Didn't I tell you not to give anything to the beggars? You see what happened? You gave that orange to the little girl, and the rest of the children almost killed her for it. Don't you *ever* do that again!" For the first time Mrs. Davis was chagrined and didn't say another word. I said goodbye to Ali and wished him well as I climbed onto the bus.

Our last night in Afghanistan was spent in the hotel dining room, where we were treated to a belly dance. We had just finished our dinner when the lights dimmed and a spotlight shown on a curtained doorway to the right of our table. The music started and a woman slid out onto the dance floor. She was brightly made up with kohl painted around her eyes, green eye shadow, red lips and too-much rouge. Long black hair cascaded from under an elaborate, jewel-incrusted headdress. Huge gold loops were attached to her earlobes. She had a bra top of gold and green sequins; her skirt, with a wide belt of similar sequins, sat low on her hips and from it cascaded diaphanous green fabric that reached the ground. She was barefoot and around her ankles was a circle of bells; she wore large rings on her fingers, and she was playing the castanets and undulating her hips in rhythm to the music. She was a talented dancer but, being fifty pounds overweight, with her stomach hanging over the broad belt, the dance did not seem as sexy as the ones seen in Cecil B. DeMille's movies. She came close to our table, fixing her eyes on Duncan, flirting outrageously. Duncan was beet-red and looked as if he wanted to run and hide. Suddenly, the dancer was on top of our table, moving faster and faster to the crescendo of the music. The room was very warm; the dancer was perspiring heavily from her exertions and flinging sweat all over us. When the music finally stopped and the dancer stepped off our table, we were all relieved. Our guide informed us we should tip her and reluctantly we did, glad to see her leave.

Our wakeup call was for five a.m. for our bus drive to the border and on to Mashhad to catch the plane back to Tehran. As we came close to the border, we could see many people sitting in front of a building with their belongings all around them. Our guide explained that this was the checkpoint where we would relinquish our visas and our luggage would be searched. My heart fell into my stomach, which was churning wildly.

Oh my Gawd, I thought, *I'll be put in jail when they find the sword.* I almost never sweat, but now I was sweating profusely. I looked at Duncan and saw his eyes wide with concern. "Stay cool, Lady Starkey, we'll get through this," he calmly said. Our bus stopped and our guide told us to claim our luggage and go to the left entrance of the building. I grabbed my suitcase and small makeup case, while Duncan hefted his backpack and carried my duffle bag. We stood in line as an official of the Afghan government checked our passports and retrieved our visas. As my turn came, I was beginning to hyperventilate, so scared I could hardly move. "Your passport, Madame," the official said. I handed him my dull green diplomatic passport; he looked at it and politely said, "You have a diplomatic immunity, Madame. You may take your luggage back to the bus. It will not be searched." I wanted to hug the man, but I felt Duncan's finger pushing into my back so I quickly left. Duncan also had a diplomatic passport, as we were both a dependent of an official of the United States Government. We almost skipped back to the bus, we were so relieved. When everyone was on board, we drove only to the edge of the border, where we left our guide and bus, stepped over the line and entered a very modern Iranian bus. It drove us the 200 yards to the Iranian checkpoint where the same thing was repeated. It took two hours to cross the border between Afghanistan and Iran and, as we left the checkpoint, our Iranian driver took off at eighty miles an hour. What a difference in comfort; now we had air conditioning, clean, soft chairs and clean, wide windows.

At the airport, we checked everything except my makeup case and, as usual, Duncan insisted on carrying it. A stern-looking, heavy-set woman herded us into an area and immediately motioned for the men to go right and the women to go left. As I entered a room, I was led by another no-nonsense, hairy female into a cubby where she told me to take my slacks and shirt off and proceeded to check everything on my body. I had never been frisked like that. Her hands were everywhere, and I didn't know what was in store for me. Suddenly, she was finished, told me to put my clothes back on and left to grab another victim. I went into the bathroom area and put myself together again.

When I emerged, I was met by an irate Duncan. "Lady Starkey, don't you ever put me in this kind of a position again. You're my friend, but friendship only goes so far," he sputtered.

"What are you talking about?" I demanded.

Duncan proceeded to tell me that his investigator, a big, tough-looking Iranian had checked out Duncan and then opened my makeup case. When he saw all the jars of cold cream, powder, mascara and lipstick, he started looking Duncan up and down with great interest. After poking his fingers all around the insides of the jars, carefully looking at the lipstick and mascara, he started smiling sweetly at Duncan. "The guy was a queer. I couldn't wait to get out of there. I thought he was going to proposition me" he declared indignantly. I was bent over, laughing hysterically. It was a wonderful way to end this very disturbing day.

Chapter 23

The whole family was at the airport to greet me; I was so glad to get home and show off my purchases. Jim liked the sword, but Jimbo and Pat were not impressed with their new 'bedspreads.' Pat, in his usual direct way said, "Mom, it stinks." Jimbo chimed in with, "Yea, it smells just like a camel. I don't want that on my bed." Pat nodded in agreement, and so the kelims were exiled to the umbar downstairs. The boys were pleased with their brass soldiers and the Afghani coins I saved for them. Peg was delighted with her vests and the doll, and we all laughed when she removed the chadri from the doll, and we saw the ugly face. I tried on the purple chadri and even though he had seen me put it on, Rick started crying. Saffron had fixed us a dinner of morg polo (chicken and rice). While we ate, I described my adventures. The children listened in wide-eyed surprise and could not imagine kids fighting over an orange.

After getting the children to bed, Jim calmly said, "We had a little incident while you were gone."

"What happened?"

"We have a new driver named Karim, and when he came to pick me up last Monday that dog that belongs across the street that the gardener is always beating, was in front of our house, had the driver cornered and was growling furiously. Negadar had tried to get the dog away, but he wouldn't move. When I tried to get him to leave, he turned on me with a menacing growl, so I got my shotgun and killed him. I told Negadar to bury the dog, and Karim and I got into the car, picked up Canfield and Smoke and went to work, not thinking much about it. Yesterday I was informed that the dog I killed belonged to the Shah's Attorney General. I have an appointment with the Attorney General tomorrow to explain what happened."

What are you going to say?"

"I'm going to tell him the truth about how that gardener constantly beats the dog and that I felt Karim and Negadar were in danger."

When Jim came home that evening he told me the Attorney General was very nice and, after the prerequisite two cups of tea, Jim relayed to him what had happened. "The General agreed that I had done the right thing, and I promised him I would get him another dog."

The next day Jim came home with a huge red dog. He looked like a Labrador retriever with thick, coarse, dark red fur but, at ninety pounds, he was much bigger than any retriever I had ever seen, He had the same happy attitude that Lab's are known for and had belonged to a family that was returning to the States. "Jim, this is a wonderful dog. We can't let that awful gardener have him. What if he beats him? Besides, I'd like to keep him."

"Absolutely not. Babe, we'll be leaving in a few months and besides, I promised the Attorney General, and I can't go back on my word." Jim told Negadar to take Big Red over to the gardener.

It was quiet at the gardener's for a couple of days, and then one afternoon Negadar told me he heard the gardener beating Big Red. I sent Negadar to tell the gardener we would take the dog back if he didn't stop beating him. As Negadar left our compound, he saw that Big Red had escaped and the gardener was trying to catch him. The nasty little man was carrying a big stick, holding it up high while yelling obscenities in Farsi. While Negadar stood by the gate to let him in, in case Big Red came by, I ran up to Jimbo's room and out onto the roof to watch the action. Jimbo, Pat and Peg followed me and we watched as Big Red would lope a ways; look back at his tormentor and wait. Just as the gardener almost got to Big Red, Big Red loped further away and the dance was repeated.

We watched for an hour as Big Red led the gardener on a merry chase, with the gardener getting angrier and angrier. He would pick up a rock and hurl it at Big Red, who dodged it like a pro. It was obvious the dog was smarter than that bandy-legged, little monster gardener. I swear I could see Big Red smile; he was certainly getting even in his own special way. It was getting late, and the sun was almost setting when the gardener finally gave up and returned to his compound. Big Red took off down the street away from our house. As he disappeared around the corner, the kids and I came downstairs, disappointed that Big Red was gone. I helped the children with their homework as I started dinner. The front door opened and Negadar, with a big grin on his face, was standing there next the triumphant Big Red. We were all excited and showered the dog with hugs and pats; even Bandit welcomed him. I gave him a big dish of Bandit's dog food, which he wolfed down. I suspected he hadn't had very much to eat, if anything, at the gardeners.

Jim arrived home and after being regaled with the events of the afternoon, the kids all starting asking him if we could keep Big Red. "We can't keep Big Red. We're due to leave shortly, and it would cost a fortune to ship him home. Besides, we don't even know how old he is or anything about him. He can stay here until I can find him a good home." That night Big Red slept with Negadar, and I imagined they snored in concert. I marveled at how different Negadar was, with his love of dogs, from most Iranians.

The next afternoon Jim was followed home by a Jeep driven by Sergeant O'Malley, who worked in Jim's office. The back of the Jeep was full of three little boys aged four through nine, O'Malley's children. They piled into our compound and immediately attacked Big Red, who greeted them with slobbering licks.

Jim introduced us and said, "Sgt. O'Malley has agreed to take Big Red home with him. He needs a dog to guard his compound." We were all disappointed that we could not keep Big Red, but we were glad to see him go to a good American home. O'Malley lived downtown near the American Embassy in a very crowded section, and Mrs. O'Malley had wanted a dog for protection.

The next day Jim came home laughing when he told us about Big Red's first night at his new home. "Big Red was left in the compound while the O'Malley's were eating dinner. Afterwards, the kids went out to play with him, and he was gone. They scoured the neighborhood and couldn't find him. The kids were hysterical, and

O'Malley and his wife had a hard time settling the kids down and getting them to bed. At ten o'clock, when O'Malley and his wife went to bed, there in the middle of the king-sized bed was their dog. Because the doors here in Iran have handles rather than knobs, Big Red had opened the door with his teeth and made himself comfortable on the bed."

Every evening, when Jim came home, the kids asked about the latest Big Red stories. Big Red was terrorizing the whole neighborhood, as he loved to walk on the walls between each compound. Mrs. O'Malley felt very safe as the Farsi grapevine let everyone know about the borzorg sag (big dog) that lived at the O'Malley home.

Driving in Tehran was getting worse daily. One Friday Jim had suggested we go to the Officer's Club for an early dinner. The children, including Rick, were all dressed up and excited. As we drove down the two-lane Saltanabad Road, a small car loaded with Iranians tried to pass us on the right. Jim saw this in the rear view mirror and slowly edged to the right. The Iranians persisted, and Jim guided the car even farther to the right. As the Iranians moved more to the right, suddenly their two right-side tires fell into the jube - and they were stuck. Our kids thought that was the funniest thing they had ever seen. After two years of witnessing chaotic, bumper-car driving, it was fun to get even.

For some reason, many Iranian drivers would pass on the left to make a right hand turn in front of you or pass on the right to make a left-hand turn in front of you. Along with not obeying stop signs and gathering five in a row at a light where only two lanes existed, it made driving in Tehran hazardous to your health.

Carol Ebert called to say their car was in the shop. "Shirley, are you doing anything today? I need to get to the Post Office at Gulf District. Could you give me a ride?"

"Sure, I'll be glad to. I'll pick you up at ten o'clock." Carol was one of my favorite people. She was a petite little gal with four children who had just learned that one more was on the way. Brown-eyed, with dark, naturally curly hair and a winning smile, she was fun to be with. We saw the Eberts frequently, and their daughter Janie was Peggy's best friend.

I picked Carol up and we chatted as we drove toward Gulf District. There is a steep hill just before coming to Gulf District, and we had started down the hill when a car full of Iranian men pulled up on our left side, gunned their car and passed me, turning right directly in front of me in order to turn into a street on our right. I got angry; I could have braked and avoided a collision, but for some unknown reason, I didn't. I let our big station wagon plow right into the back of the puny Pekan car, making a big dent in the trunk. I stopped the car, put on the emergency brake and, as I leaped out of the car, I yelled to Carol, "Go get Mr. Malek, the attorney." Carol got out of the car and left on foot to get the attorney who had handled my problem when I ran over the boy's shoe. I ran to the driver's side of the Pekan and, as the driver got out, I put my hand out, palm up, and demanded loudly, "You wrecked my car. You must pay me!"

Four young men were in the car, and the driver stepped out with a shocked look on his face, as I repeated my demand. This was not supposed to be happening. A woman did not make demands of a man - especially an American woman who is rich, the driver's expression told me. I kept repeating what I said as the driver remained speechless. Just then Carol returned with Mr. Malek, who looked at me and said, in a resigned voice, "Ohhhhh, Mrs. Starkey, it's you again." I told him what happened, and we both inspected the front of our car, which had a small dent and a broken headlight. Mr. G. said, "Please leave, Mrs. Starkey. I will take care of this." So Carol and I went on our way. When I got home I called Jim and reported what happened. "For God sake, Shirley, why didn't you stop?"

"I was mad. These jerks are always turning in front of me like that, and I've just had enough."

Two days later Jim received a call from the owner of the Pekan, who demanded that Jim bring our car down to this man's business near the Big Bazaar in south Tehran, so the damage could be seen. Jim does not take demands from strangers and firmly replied "No, if you want to see my car, I will give you my address."

The owner abruptly ended the conversation.

The next day the Pekan's owner had his insurance man call Jim to say that we should take our Ford to the Ford dealership to be repaired. When I took the car into the shop, I showed the mechanic all the dents accrued during our two years of driving in Iran, including the dent on the side of the car put there by the big goat. (Jim was fond of saying that by the time I had driven the big Ford station wagon for two years it was two feet shorter than when we first brought it to Iran). It took three days for the job to be finished, and when Jim picked up our car it looked like new. The Ford people had done a wonderful job. We planned to sell the station wagon, and the word went out on the Farsi grapevine.

It was the beginning of May, and we got ready to sell all our American furniture and appliances before we left Tehran in June. Throughout the past two years, Elias Shaoolian, the Jewish carpet dealer, had brought a constant supply of carpets to our house for our perusal. He knew we loved Persian carpets and would buy a houseful. He never expected money, knowing that at the end of our tour we would sell all our American goods and end up with too many rials to take out of the country. That is when he would get paid. Almost all the carpet dealers trusted the honest Americans, but they never trusted any other nationality; not the Danes, Germans, French - and especially not the English. I never understood that, but I suppose they had good reasons.

We planned to sell our washer, dryer, dishwasher, stove, re-frigerator, freezer and all the furniture from the bedrooms, living room, dining room and Rick's high chair, play pen, and crib - in other words, everything we had brought over with the exception of the swimming pool filter which Jim had promised to Col. Atlassi. The children were excited to sell their toys, games and clothes, and we included them in our plans on how to organize a Big Bazaar in our home.

Elias brought over a 10 ft. x 13 ft. Kashan carpet with a beige background and a medallion in the center of ultramarine blue with tendrils swirling around flowers in shades of blue, crimson and light jade. The design was copied from the mosaics uncovered in the Ali Qapu Palace in Esfahan. It had graced our living room floor for several months, and I followed the negotiations between Elias and Jim with great interest. I was determined to have that carpet. By May they were still miles apart in price. One day Elias came by with another exquisite tribal carpet in reds and blue. He knew our tastes, and he wanted to send us back to the States with a house full of Persian art that he had sold us. I was definitely on his team in this effort. I could tell Jim was taken with this newest carpet but was purposely ignoring it.

After sitting opposite each other on the floor and drinking two cups of tea, Jim started the conversation. "Okay, Elias, have you decided to become reasonable on the price of this carpet?" indicating the Kashan carpet they were sitting on.

"Colonel Estarkey, you are a very difficult man to deal with. I believe you are more of a Jew than I am."

"Elias, you know this carpet is not worth what you are asking. If I were to pay this much I would be taking the milk from my children. You're trying to take the blood from my arm." He dramatically hit the inside of his left arm. This made Elias laugh. After taking another sip of his tea, he frowned in a serious manner and said, "Colonel Estarkey, I must have this much for the carpet or I will lose."

The negotiations went on for many minutes, and Saffron filled the tea cups two more times. Negadar found a reason to be in the house, and he and Saffron were hovering in the background watching intently. Finally, Jim said, "If you will not be reasonable, you can take the carpet away." He stood up abruptly. With a startled look on his face, Elias rose up. His face turned scarlet and he started to roll up the carpet. I was shocked at this turn of events and, as Elias put the carpet under his arm and started toward the door, I burst into tears. Everyone turned and looked at me in amazement as I sobbed. Elias dropped the carpet, turned to Jim and said resignedly, "Coronel Estarkey, I cannot disappoint Mrs. Estarkey. This carpet is yours, but you must pay me a good price for these other carpets" He swept his hand around the room, indicating all the other carpets he had left in our house, and turned, without saying another word, and walked out the door.

Now it was my turn to be shocked. I looked at Jim, "Does that mean he will accept our price?"

"I believe it does. By the way, that was an Academy Award winning stunt you just pulled," Jim told me with admiration in his voice.

"I wasn't pulling any stunt," I protested. "I was afraid I would never see this carpet again."

I was so happy that we were getting that carpet. Jim can be very difficult where money is concerned. It seems to me that some people are born with a certain attitude. Jim was born with what I call a 'money attitude.' Jim's father once told me that about the time

Jim was five, he gave Jim money to treat his aunts and uncles to ice cream cones. They all piled into Uncle Ralph's car and drove to the Bucky O'Neil Square in the center of Prescott, Arizona. Everyone ordered their ice cream cones and, when it came time to pay, Jim refused to part with the money. The aunts and uncles thought that was so cute, they let the little brat get away with it and paid for their own ice cream! All his life Jim as been watchful about money, but not frugal. When he buys something, he buys the best; he just doesn't waste it on ice cream.

Speaking loudly as he entered the house, Jim shouted, "Shirl, you're going to get to meet the President of the United States!"

"Are you being assigned to President Nixon?" I excitedly replied.

"No, he is coming here. He and Kissinger are in Moscow on a State Visit right now and are coming here for three days on their way back to Washington. We drew straws in the office, and you and I will be in the official farewell party, as will the Canfields and Stovers."

The next day the word was out, and the excitement was conspicuous. Street sweepers were everywhere with their short handled brooms; shopkeepers were washing the windows of their shops and everywhere pictures of Nixon appeared beside the required one of the Shah. Two days before the president arrived, Smoke Stover reported that his phone was out of commission. He tried to get the phone company to come out and fix the problem but was told there would be a two weeks wait. When the big day arrived, we watched on the television as the Shah met the President's plane, and President Nixon and the Shah reviewed the honor guard while the Iranian Army band played. Iranian and American flags were everywhere as the entourage made their way to the Gulistan Palace. During the next two days, we kept getting reports of bombs going off all over the city. At the last minute, the schedule was changed and a bomb exploded at the Tomb of Reza Shah just one hour before President Nixon placed a wreath. Several black ARMISH-MAAG cars were bombed, but fortunately no casualties were reported.

We awoke early the morning of the third day of President Nixon's visit, as Jim and I were scheduled to be on the farewell committee. I stayed in my bathrobe as I made breakfast. The children were surprised to see their father eating with us, as he usually had left for work before they had their breakfast. While we ate, we explained that we would be saying goodbye to the President of the United States and it was a great honor.

"What are you going to say to the President?" was Patrick's question.

Jim laughed and said, "I will probably say 'Pleased to meet you, Sir.'"

"Aren't you going to tell him we voted for him? If you said that, maybe you'd get a better assignment and wouldn't have to go to Viet Nam," I giggled at the silliness of that statement. I looked at my watch, "Oh, my gosh, kids. Get your teeth brushed. The bus should be here in ten minutes."

I started making their lunches as they scooted upstairs. Soon all three were clamoring downstairs, grabbing their lunches as they headed out the front gate. Saffron was just arriving, and they yelled hello to her as they raced for the beat-up yellow bus waiting at the corner.

"Salaam alekam, Madam," Saffron greeted me. I smiled as I told her what was happening today. "We get to meet the president and Mrs. Nixon," I reported.

"Oh, Madam, khaili khob." Saffron, displaying her 1000 watt smile, was as pleased as if she were getting this honor. I started up the stairs, nervous with excitement, anxious to get dressed in my new turquoise blue dress. Jim had just finished shining his shoes and was starting on polishing his brass belt buckle when the phone rang. I picked it up and through a lot of static I could barely hear Smoke Stover. With no greeting he shouted, "Let me talk to Jim."

Jim listened for a minute and said, "Oh my God, Smoke, what is the number where I can reach you?" He motioned for me to write down a number as he repeated what Smoke was saying.

He hung up and started dialing the number for the Duty Officer. He identified himself and then said, "I have just received a call from Col. Stover. A bomb has exploded in front of his house, and it appears that General Price's car has been damaged." There was a long moment of silence, and then Jim said, "Of course I will wait." He stood there holding the phone, his squinting eyes staring into space. I had learned a long time ago to keep quiet when Jim had that expression on his face. A few moments later he said, "Yes, Sir,

I'll notify Stover and Canfield of the change."

He hung up, called Smoke and said, "I've notified headquarters. They are sending an ambulance and we have been told to meet at Gulf District ASAP instead of the Officer's Club. We'll see you and Donna there." He called Herb Canfield and said, "Instead of meeting at the Officer's Club, we're to go to Gulf District and a bus will take us to the airport. I just got a phone call from Smoke, and he said he was eating breakfast when he heard a loud explosion in front of his house. He climbed the wall and saw that General Price's car was on its side, and there is a huge crater in the street. Smoke's phone isn't working, so he went over the back wall and called me from the grocery store on the corner. Maybe we'll know more by the time we get to Gulf District."

He hung up and turned to me, "Babe, I'm not sure what is happening, but it looks like the rebels are targeting officers. We'll have to be very careful and keep a close eye on the children. Write a note to Jimbo and tell him to stay in the house with Negadar and Saffron and tell him not to let Pat or Peggy go outside either."

I quickly finished dressing and went downstairs to tell Saffron what was happening. A cloud of distress filled her face as she called out to Negadar in Farsi. He came into the kitchen as Saffron turned on the radio to see if she could find any more news. I sat down at the dining room table to compose a letter to Jimbo.

I wrote and underlined: Jimbo, whatever you do, do not leave the compound and make sure Pat and Peggy stay in also. Stay upstairs in the television room with Negadar and Saffron. You must obey me and do exactly as I say. I signed it Mom and Dad. I told Saffron to prepare spaghetti and salad for the children, Negadar and herself, as I wasn't sure what time we would be home.

Jim was very quiet as we drove to Gulf District. Finally he said, "This country is getting very dangerous for Americans. I'm glad I'm going back to Viet Nam rather than staying here another year. I just hope these idiots don't get an idea to bomb the American school; if they want to get headlines around the world that would really do it."

I gasped at the thought, feeling myself closing in. I couldn't speak; I was trembling too much. When we arrived at Gulf District, Jim had to show his ID to an MP before the gates were opened. This was the first time I had ever seen the gates closed; always before the gates were wide open.

Smoke and Donna Stover arrived at Gulf District a few minutes after we did. Smoke strode toward us and said to Jim, "I talked to General Price's aid de camp, Capt. Rogers. He said the general is leaving Iran next week, and they were going to a farewell review at the Iranian Air Force Base. Rogers is unhurt, but the driver and the General have severe injuries. They were being transported to the hospital as we left. Apparently, a bomb was planted in the street the day my phone went out. The aid thinks he saw a man run down the street just as the explosion went off, so it must have been a hand-held device. He said there were two badjii's walking in the road and the general's driver swerved the car to the left in order to avoid them. That undoubtedly saved the lives of everyone in the general's car. It didn't help the badjii's at all as they were right on the spot where the bomb was planted. They were blown to smithereens. I saw a leg hanging from the tree in front of the house next door to the generals. Our new veterinarian, Major Thomas, just moved in there last week."

"What a lovely reception he has received," Jim drily commented. Everyone kept coming up to Jim and Smoke, and the story was repeated over and over again. I started feeling faint, so I moved over in a corner and sat on a chair, quietly praying that our children would be safe. Donna soon joined me, and we sat in quiet camaraderie. The wait was endless as many phone calls were received and made, in order to coordinate everything. Soon Jim came over and sat down next to me, saying in a soothing voice, "Babe, our kids are going to be all right. Just stop worrying, besides, those rebels wouldn't want any American kids. If they got them, they would send them right back!"

His effort at levity did not help my mood. Donna disgustingly said, "I can't wait to get out of this blinking country. Smoke is talking about retiring in two years after Bill starts college. We want to live in a quiet community someplace in Florida and forget we ever heard of Iran."

"For the most part, I have enjoyed our tour here but this certainly puts a different light on our life in this country," I agreed.

After more than an hour, a bus arrived and some MP's came in. "Sorry folks, I've been ordered to frisk everyone to make sure there are no guns or other weapons on you." This was unbelievable! A room full of American officers has to be frisked? The ladies' handbags were thoroughly searched, as well as all cameras and cases. Finally, we were allowed on the bus. Jim and I took a seat at the very back of the bus, so we had a view of the whole bus plus the back and side windows. Then we waited another forty minutes while the bus idled, as the air conditioning kept us cool. An MP came on board and said something to the driver. The driver nodded his assent and started the bus. We moved through the Gulf District gates which were immediately locked behind us. The driver turned the bus north, although Mehrabad Airport was in the south. We drove up into the foothills of the Elburz Mountains before we turned west on a single lane paved road. I was surprised to see a sign for Qasvin, which I knew was sixty miles southwest of Tehran.

We came to a crossroad and the driver turned south. The land was flat and barren with nothing to see but the pale mountains far to the west. We were in a desolate area with no sign of habitation of any kind. My head was on a swivel as I continually looked up front toward the driver, through the window to the road we were on; to each side through the windows and then to the back window. I saw a tiny speck on the road behind us, and I stared at it until I could make out a man on a motorcycle. Quickly I commanded, "Jim, look behind us. Do you think that man might have a grenade?" Jim watched intently for a minute and then turned around saying, "I don't think so, Babe, quit worrying. Everything is going to be all right."

"That is easier said than done," I replied as I continued to keep an eye on the cycle. It was going much faster than our bus and soon overtook us. The cyclist sped past us, and I breathed a sigh of relief as he disappeared into the distance.

We entered an industrial area for several miles with car repair shops, factories, cement plants and vacant lots filled with rusting metal and garbage dumps. Pitiful dogs lay about scratching their fleas, and we saw more than one man squatting next to the road to pee. We turned onto a dirt road that led to the back of Mehrabad Airport. A plane took off directly over us, and we could feel the wash of the downdraft as dust curled around us. The bus pulled into a back gate of the airport, and two Iranians got on to check our purses and camera cases. They made the ladies hold out our arms and looked to see if we had any unusual bulges, but did not frisk us as they did the men. They were very respectful but efficient, and soon told the driver to continue taking us to our meeting point.

We drove through two more checkpoints, where the driver was frisked and asked to show his credentials. The bus pulled up next to a tent and we were told to deplane. We got off and walked into the tent where we assumed we would have a reception with the president, but that was not to be. We were led through the tent onto the tarmac and told to stand in a square that was cordoned off. To the east of us we could see Air Force One, the President's airplane. Again we waited, standing first on one foot and then the other. No one seemed to know what was going on, and the Iranians weren't telling us. Jim and I stood quietly together, listening to the gossip that was going on around us. "What's the news on General Sullivan's condition?" "Do you think he is still alive?" "How many bombs have gone off since the President arrived?" The questions swirled around us.

All of the sudden someone exclaimed, "Here comes the President!" We looked toward a low, metal building fifty yards to the west of us and saw President Nixon, accompanied by two aides and Mrs. Nixon, walking toward us. Jim and I moved to the ropes as Jim got his camera out. More people, at least thirty, were slowly walking out of the building forming a parade led by our President. As the President got closer, I said to Jim, "He looks pretty fat." Jim laughed and said, "He's wearing a flak jacket under his clothes." I looked carefully at the president's wide triangular body, thinking he looked like the comic "The Little King" I read as a kid. The President was almost to us when we noted that Henry Kissinger, also looking very fat from the flak jacket under his suit, was bringing up the rear of the parade, staying as far away from Mr. Nixon as possible. We waited patiently, thinking the President would stop to shake our hands, but it didn't happen. Nixon and his entourage breezed right passed us. Someone called out, "Hello, Mr. President." The President barely raised his eyes to the greeter. Mrs. Nixon walked by, surprising me at how pretty she was. Her pictures did not do her justice.

The entourage continued toward Air Force One, where the Shah, the Empress and many Iranians in military uniforms waited to say goodbye to the most powerful man in the world. A band struck up martial music as the President shook hands with the Shah. We watched from afar as Jim whispered to me the names of the men standing next to the Shah. "The man to the left is the Army's Chief of Staff, General Khosradad. He's the one I had a meeting with last week. A very intelligent man." Several minutes later President Nixon went up the steps, and at the door he turned to give his trademark wave. All the others followed and disappeared into Air Force One. The door closed, the engines started and the plane taxied down the runway.

Suddenly behind us we heard the sound of a helicopter's rotary blades starting up. It was the Shah's helicopter, ready to take him back to Niavaran Palace. We turned back to where the Shah was and saw that he, his wife and many men in dark suits were walking toward us. We froze in place, not knowing what to do. The air was thick with uncertainty; our general was lying in the hospital some-where in Tehran and might or might not be dead; the Shah of Iran was headed right toward us and no one knew the protocol for such a situation As the party came closer, the men in suits eyed us with suspicion - and we returned the look with apprehension. We were in the middle of a viscous cloud of raw emotions that one could cut with a knife. In front of us, wearing a military uniform loaded with medals, was the man whose picture was in banks, in offices, green grocer shops, carpet shops, fabric stores and diary shops. Everywhere in this land his eyes stared and watched. I had expected a giant, but the Shah was just an ordinary man, shorter in stature than I had thought. Bushy brows lay over his piercing black eyes, a large Semitic hooked nose reached down to a thin, wide mouth; his white hair was brushed straight back under his military visored hat. His face reminded me of an American Bald Eagle. The Shah's entourage was right in front of us when suddenly, a big, tall American Air Force colonel stuck out his huge paw and, in a broad Texan accent roared, "Howdy, Shah."

Shockwaves rolled around as the Shah's eyes widened, and on his face it was easy to read his thoughts. Do I shake this guy's hand or do I have my guards arrest him? The men in suits started toward Colonel Ryan as the Shah made his decision. He grabbed Ryan's hand, smiling, and said, "How do you do, Colonel." This was the signal for the rest of the Shah's party, and we were quickly engulfed with well wishes from all of them.

The Empress Farah, dressed in a beige silk suit with a matching

451

pillbox hat, lightly grasped both of my hands in her fingers. They felt as soft as a bird's feathers. "How do you like Iran, my dear?" she said in perfect English. I was breathless with admiration for this beautiful woman in front of me, and I barely managed to say, "Iran is a most interesting and exciting place. I like it very much." She smiled graciously and moved on with the rest of the group. The Shah appeared to be having a good time shaking everyone's hand and encouraging all his guards to do the same. For several minutes everyone was milling around and greeting each other and, suddenly, it ended as fast as it had started as the Shah left for the helicopter with his group following him. We all looked at each other in amazement, not sure we had really witnessed the whole thing.

Someone told us to get back on the bus, which we did, returning to Gulf District a different, out-of-way route. It was dark by the time we got home to find the children, Negadar and Saffron all upstairs in the TV area watching Gunsmoke. The kids were excited to tell us they had watched President Nixon leave the country but were disappointed that they didn't see us. Then we related that we had spoken to the Shahenshah and the Empress; Saffron and Negadar were speechless with admiration.

Chapter 25

Everything went into high gear as we prepared to leave Iran. A wealthy man, Mr. Rezvane, called Jim and said he was interested in buying our station wagon. Jim named his price, and Mr. Rezvane was willing to pay the asking price with no haggling. Jim insisted we be allowed to keep the car until he could check out a Jeep for our transportation. Mr. R. agreed but then said, "Coronel Eestarkey, I would like to get the station wagon checked by the authorities. May I send my men over to your house at your convenience to pick it up?"

"What kind of a checkup?" Jim asked.

"We must take it to the tax authorities and they will tell us how much tax will be charged. We would like to take off some of the chrome so the car does not look so nice, so we will not be charged so much money." It was a typical Iranian gesture that we were used to after four years in the country. It was also one of the reasons Mr. Rezvane had a lot of money. Jim agreed, and the next Thursday five scruffy men showed up at our door. Jim pulled the car out of the compound and parked it on the dirt road in front of our house. Like ants, the five men swarmed all over the vehicle with tools and started taking off all the chrome, the side mirrors, the hubcaps, the rear view mirror, the license plate holder, the Ford insignia, the spare tire, and anything that identified the car as being the high-end station wagon that we had purchased four years earlier. When they were finished, they brought all the items they had removed into our compound and asked if they could leave them there while they took the car to be appraised. Jim agreed, and all five piled into the wagon and took off in a cloud of dust. The whole family watched in dumb fascination at the transformation of our car. "That is the junkiest-looking car I have ever seen!" I remarked.

"That's the purpose of this. Mr. Rezvane is a smart man. He's hired these seedy-looking guys to take the car to the tax authorities, knowing they will be charged very little because they are so poor. Rezvane will pay them well for their work."

"If they don't return, I guess we could take all this junk back to the States and sell it at a swap meet." Jimbo said, seriously.

We all laughed and Jim assured him, "Don't worry, Jimbo, they'll be back"

Four hours later, they were back with the station wagon. With the same efficiency, they put everything back where it belonged and, once again, we had a new-looking, dent-free station wagon.

Jim had an office at the Iranian Transportation School and one day he was walking on the grounds with his interpreter, Ali. "See that man over there?" Ali said, pointing to a heavy-set, frowning man in an ill-fitting brown suit. "He is Russian. I will introduce him to you." The Russian also had an interpreter with him, and soon the conversation was four-way from English to Farsi to Russian and back to Farsi to English. It made for a very disjointed conversation, which was basically the 'how-are-you,' 'isn't-this-beautiful-weather' type of a discussion. Soon everyone said goodbye and went about their business. Four days later, Jim received an order to appear in the G2 Intelligence Office of Colonel Hawkins. He was asked if he had spoken to a Russian. He answered 'Yes.' "What did you talk about?" Jim gave Hawkins a summary of the conversation. "Why didn't you write up a report of the encounter?"

Jim answered, "I didn't think it was of any consequence. There was nothing of importance said." Hawkins asked him several more questions and had Jim repeat several times exactly what he remembered about the encounter. Finally Jim was excused with the admonishment, "From now on, any time you are in a conversation with a Russian, write a report and state exactly what was said." Jim agreed.

Iran was swiftly changing from the backward country we had

first encountered in 1962. The Shah had made remarkable progress in the past twelve years, dragging the country (with the help of our dollars) from the 16th Century into the 20th Century. All the major cities had good potable water, dependable electricity; schools for both boys and girls had opened in many of the villages (much to the dismay of the local mullah), the Army had a battalion of female parachutists and new roads and skyscrapers were being built at a rapid pace. Women were enjoying equality with men in every field. In 1962, 90% of the cattle in Iran had tuberculosis; now it was almost totally eradicated. Health clinics offering immunizations were available for everyone.

On the downside, the Shah brought in many scholars from universities around the world to assist in the government. Many of these were radical professors from the University of California at Berkley, who managed to stir up the students against the Shah. Ruhollah Khomeini, whom the Shah had evicted in 1964, had moved to Karbala, Iraq and was fomenting against the Sunni sect and Saddam Hussein. Finally, having enough, Saddam kicked the troublemaker out of Iraq, and Khomeini took his entourage to Paris. From there he launched a tirade against the Shah via tape recorders. The tapes were sent back to Tehran and played during the Friday services in the mosques of Iran. A group known as the Mujahidin, formed back in the 60's to overthrow the Shah, became stronger and more militant. Their weapon of choice was a bomb, which they had been utilizing with mixed success for many years. When President Nixon visited Iran, it was the Mujahidin's who planted the bomb that exploded in front of Smoke's house, breaking General Price's leg. They planted bombs in dozens of sites, including the Iran-American Society, United States Information Office, the Pepsi Cola plant, and the offices of General Motors and Shell Oil.

The time to leave was rapidly approaching, and we planned to sell everything American, including all our appliances, furniture, toys clothes, shoes and my paintings. The umbar became a bazaar as Saffron and I set up lines to hang the clothes, racks for our shoes and displays of kitchenware and toys. I gave Negadar and Saffron first choice of anything they wanted, charging a minimum five rial (7 cents) for anything they wanted. I had learned the hard way during our first tour that if you gave an Iranian something and he was not allowed to give you something in return, he would 'lose face' and hold you in contempt. No one, no matter how poor, likes to feel like a charity case. When I gave Nagadar a warm coat for his son during the flu epidemic he accepted it because it was for someone else, so he was not offended. Saffron was so disgusted that her large, very wide feet would not fit in Jim's shoes. "Maybe I work for black man," she said with a laugh. "I have black man feet."

The Farsi grapevine worked like a charm, and soon we were inundated with wealthy Iranians, dealers and common people coming to view our goods. Anything sold from the umbar could leave our house immediately, but the big items had to stay in the house until we were ready to move out. The first things to be sold were all the kitchen appliances. Everyone paid the full amount and they were told that all items could be picked up the last week in May. The Iranians knew we could be trusted not to renege on the deal because "all Americans tell the truth."

Elias kept tabs on how our sales were progressing and increased his visits, bringing new carpets to our home once a week, knowing full well we would return to the States with many of them. After looking at dozens of carpets, Jim and I had decided on the carpets we would purchase and Jim decreed, "No more carpets." One evening Elias, (undoubtedly looking for some money) arrived while I was watching the kids play soccer in the kuchee. Jim was involved in negotiating with a doctor who wanted our living room and dining room furniture. "I'm sorry, Elias, Jim can't talk to you right now because he is busy selling our furniture." Elias shook his head in wonderment. "Coronel Eestarkey, he will not lose," he muttered as he left.

When we first arrived in Iran, we had learned we could order furniture from China. Jim had bought a carved teakwood Chinese chest when he was in Hong Kong on R & R from Viet Nam, and I loved it. From a catalogue we ordered two more chests and a large desk. We requested a secret drawer be put in the desk. In April, the furniture arrived, and we were stunned at the beauty of the carvings on the teakwood. Soldiers on horseback wielding spears marched across the front and top of the chests; each panel of the desk displayed domestic scenes, all intricately carved in the dark wood. We carefully inspected the upper right-hand front of the desk, looking for the secret drawer. We compared the drawing of our desk the Chinese company had sent, saw where the secret drawer was supposed to be and still could not find it. The inscrutable Chinese managed to hide the drawer from us and, to this day, we still have never found it.

On our first tour in Iran when our friends, the Hessons, were in Pakistan, they went to India with American money hidden in a tampax container and bought a carved screen for us. This time, when Dr. Morrow was going to India, we asked him to buy us another screen, which he did. By selling all our American goods, we were going back to the States with only carpets, samovars, tons of copper items, chests, screens and one very large desk. What a strange house we would have!

As an advisor in Transportation and Aviation, Jim (and family) had been sent over to Iran by the U.S. government. By agreement, all of us would be sent back to the States on the Shah's dime. His idea of travel was very different from the frugal American idea. Jim was presented with six first-class tickets back to Tucson, plus 300 pounds excess baggage for each of us! The dollar amount was staggering! Even sixteen-month old Rick had a first-class ticket and a 300 pound allowance. Jim immediately took the tickets to the Pan Am office and exchanged them for vouchers allowing us to use them any way we wanted, as long as they were used up within a year. Then he was told that he was one of three advisors who were invited to visit Moscow and Leningrad, Russia for three and two days respectively, as guests of the Russian government. We couldn't believe our good fortune. Finally, after trying twice during our last Tehran tour to see Russia and missing the trip Aunt Lil took because I was pregnant, I was going to Russia. I was so excited, and we started planning to go back to the States by way of Moscow, Leningrad; Helsinki; Copenhagen; and Lisbon. Jim took our passports to the Russian Embassy to apply for visas and was told to check back in two weeks for them.

Since we would be taking more than two weeks to get home, Jim thought we should airmail Bandit back to Tucson. I wrote to our nephew Billy Condit, who was a student at the University of Arizona, asking him to pick up Bandit at the airport. He was happy to oblige. Jim bought a wire travel cage for Bandit and then rigged up a place for the children's four baby tortoises. He took one of my metal loaf pans and wired it to the top of the cage. The vet, Major Thomas, checked Bandit and the tortoises and gave us the necessary papers to get the animals into the United States. We put the pets on a Pan Am around-the-world flight to Los Angeles and on to Tucson. They arrived in less than twenty-four hours in perfect shape. Billy was at the airport to get them and took them to my folk's house, where he turned the turtles loose in the big back yard. Dad was delighted to have Bandit to take care of since Spookie, the dog my dad inherited when Jim and I got married, had died at age sixteen two years before.

Johnny and Sarah Hubble gave us a wonderful going-away party. Sarah had decorated the table lavishly with a Persian table cloth, candles in brass holders and a profusion of flowers. As usual, she outdid herself in the food preparation. Sarah is one of the best cooks I have ever known. The day of the party, Sunday afternoon, turned out to be unusually cool, with puffy, white clouds. The house and patio were filled with our friends, drinking, laughing and sharing stories of our life in Iran.

Moving week was a turmoil of activity; the living and dining furniture went first and, as the moving company started the preliminary packing, workmen arrived to take apart our washer, dryer, stove, and dishwasher for the new owners. Jim was at home supervising, so I left to buy some eggs and cheese for Negadar and Saffron at the store on Saltanatabad.

"Babe, go to Elias' shop and tell him we'll come by after the movers leave to pay him," Jim said. He didn't have to ask me twice, as I loved Elias' shop.

"Salaam alekam, Elias." I said as I entered his shop. That's when I noticed the backing of a rolled-up blue carpet. "Elias, may I see that carpet?" Elias pulled down the most exquisite blue Kashan I had ever seen.

"Mrs. Eestarkey, you have excellent taste. Look at the quality of this masterpiece. See the warp? It is of silk. The weft is of the finest wool taken only from the throat of the young lambs. Notice the beautiful medallion in the center. The design is the same as the carpet in the Shah's Audience Chamber." He went on and on with his sales pitch, but it didn't matter. I had to have this carpet, but first I had to get past Jim's edict of "No more carpets."

"Elias, we will come to your shop as soon as the movers leave the house to pay you for our carpets. Let's show this carpet to Col. Starkey." Elias grinned in agreement and I left the shop. All the way home, I planned my strategy. As I entered the house I said to Jim, "You won't believe the carpet I just saw." With a stern look on his face Jim intoned, "I said no more carpets."

"Well, I was thinking about that and realized with you going to Viet Nam, you won't be around for Christmas, my birthday, our anniversary, Valentine's Day or Mother's day. If you bought this carpet for me, you wouldn't have to worry about gifts for all those holidays," I said slyly. Jim glared at me and turned to answer a question from one of the men packing our crystal.

As soon as the packers left, we jumped into the borrowed Jeep and drove to Elias's shop. As we entered, I didn't see the carpet anywhere. I was panicked at the thought that someone had already bought it. Jim said, "Okay, Elias, how much are you going to overcharge me today?"

Elias pulled out a copy of the agreement he and Jim had signed and said, "This is our agreement, and you are getting the best deal of anyone in Iran." Jim laughed and counted out the money owed to Elias.

Then I casually said, "Elias, where is that carpet you showed me today?" With true showmanship, Elias brought out the rolled up carpet and, with a flourish, unrolled it. I heard Jim's intake of breath. He reached for it and felt the softness of the pile, turned it over and counted the stitches. He studied it for several minutes while I held my breath. Finally he asked, "How much?"

Elias named a price, and Jim counted out half that amount and put it on the counter, saying, "I will pay this much for it."

Elias looked at the money for the longest time and finally said, "Coronal Eestarkey, my brother will kill me for this, but you have been a good customer and a fine negotiator. You may have it." He picked up the money, shook Jim's hand, bowed to me and said, "Have a safe trip home." I was so ecstatic I hugged Jim before getting into the Jeep and said, "Thank you, thank you!"

Jim grumbled, "I probably could have gotten it for less."

I laughed.

When we returned to our house I placed our newly-acquired,

gorgeous Kashan in one of the carved chests. I didn't want the packers to see it, as I was afraid it would 'disappear' while being packed. The next day we supervised our goods being placed in Connex containers and sealed shut. After the movers left, we walked all around our empty house checking for stray items and mentally saying goodbye to the place that held such happy memories. Negadar was waiting patiently in the front compound and Jim handed him an envelope of money. He looked sad as the children lined up and shook his hand; even little Rick mimicked his brothers and sister and put out his hand. It was an emotional moment for me when I said goodbye, realizing how much we had depended on Negadar for the past two years. He was always available when needed, even though I resented him for making me feel as if I was not in charge of the house. As we drove away he stood at the open gate watching us, while the kids waved at him. "Negadar is finally going to have some peace and quiet," Jim commented. "I bet he is going to miss all the commotion."

We checked into the Intercontinental Hotel where we would be staying for the next week while Jim cleared all the paperwork. Saffron arrived the next morning to take care of the children while I went to a farewell luncheon at the Officers Club. She was going to work for our friends, Carol and Bob Ebert. Carol was expecting their fifth child and Saffron was excited to have another baby to spoil. Two days before we were scheduled to depart for Moscow, Jim went to the Russian Embassy to pick up our passports and visas. He was astounded to learn that our visas were denied. He asked several Russians "Why?" and the only answer he got was "*Nyat*" (no). He tried in vain to learn why we had been denied visiting Russia when the two other officers and families were given visas. We never did learn the reason for the denial.

Jim came back to the hotel with the disappointing news that a trip to Russia was denied us. We quickly had to make changes in our itinerary and decided we would go to Athens, Zurich, and on to Copenhagen, Amsterdam and Portugal. The Eberts picked us up early the morning of our flight and took us to the airport. They sat with us until it was time to get on the plane. We took a final look back as we entered the plane and once more we said goodbye to Iran. The Elburz Mountains were a soft pink in the morning light and swiftly disappeared as we headed toward Greece.

With the children settled in, I breathed a sigh of relief and mentally reviewed the last two years. I smiled, remembering the various driving incidents; (especially running over the pink plastic shoe) the ups and downs of dealing with Negadar and Saffron; the shooting dogs' incidents; Aunt Lil's visit and all the wonderful friends we had made. The scary times would never be forgotten, but they faded in significance compared to all the good memories. I silently wished the best for Iran and its peoples and knew it would always have a place in my heart.

Like a book, life in the military is divided into chapters, delineating where the family is living, if the head of the house is with you and what child is born where. I look across the aisle to where Jim is sitting with Jimbo and Patrick, watching them as they played a card game. Sitting next to me is our fourteen month-old Rick being entertained by his watchful sister, Peggy. As this chapter ends, we look forward to introducing Rick to his native land. I settle back in my seat, contented and turn the page to the next chapter.

Chapter 26

As the plane banked over the Mediterranean Sea entering Athens airspace we could look down at the tiny ships below us. Peggy was showing this to Rick, his eyes wide open in surprise. He was thoroughly enjoying this new adventure. At the airport Jim immediately led the way to the concierge to request accommodations and soon we were on our way to the center of Athens. It was mid-day and the traffic was heavy but orderly. We arrived at a small hotel, inspected our rooms, dumped our suitcases and left to find a restaurant. After our meal we returned to the hotel for a quiet afternoon. We stopped to ask the concierge for ideas for activities. She recommended Piraeus, the port south of Athens. She provided directions to the bus.

The next day after a meager breakfast we walked the three blocks to the bus depot. The air was very humid and warm; it was going to be a hot day. After many negotiations we were directed to a very old decrepit bus. When we got on we discovered it was already full of workers and there was no place to sit down. The only air circulation was provided by narrow windows next to the roof. All of us were standing at the front of the bus facing the riders. Rick was in Jim's back-pack and this caused many comments. Sitting in the seat in front of Jim, were an elderly couple arguing. The lady emphatically was trying to get the man to give Jim his seat since he had a baby on his back. Using hand signals Jim thanked the lady but refused, much to the delight of the man. I was standing next to Jim and was holding on to Peggy, as the bus weaved through the traffic. Two rows back were two teen-age boys making goo-goo eyes at Peggy. Peg maintained a haughty look as one of the boys patted the space between his legs and motioned for her to join him. Suddenly Peg gave him the snottiest camel kiss I have ever seen. The shock on the kid's face was priceless.

The port of Piraeus is huge with vessels of every size from small, one-man boats to enormous ocean-going ships. As we embarked from the bus we were engulfed with hundreds of voices yelling, calling, swearing, and shrieking. The crowds were milling about, each man engrossed in an important endeavor. Several men spotted the American tourists and brought their wares for us to peruse. Jim kept us moving along rapidly on our way to the docks to watch the ships come and go. Jimbo was fascinated with the various fish being caught. Everyone was very friendly wanting to show us their catch. We spent an hour meandering until Rick declared he was hungry. It took us another hour to find a restaurant with outdoor seating. The waiter, speaking broken English told us a large catch of octopus had just arrived at the restaurant, so Jim ordered some.

"Oh! Yuck" said Pat. "I don't want to eat octopus!"

"You're not going to," said Jim. "We are dining on calamari!" Just then the waiter placed a large platter full of calamari, sliced lemons and a loaf of crunchy bread on the table along with six small plates. Jim filled the plates for the older kids then squeezed lemon on the calamari and handed them to our suspicious kids. We watched as each hesitated, taking a very small bite. Suddenly in unison they said, "This is good!" I gave a piece of calamari to Rick and got the same reaction. We ended up ordering two more platters as the kids were eating so much. Calamari straight from the ocean is indeed manna from heaven. Nothing is better.

The next day we hired a guide to show us the sights. He mentioned that in the evening there would be an outdoor show at the Acropolis so we bought tickets to it. Our guide came in the late afternoon to take us. Our seats were high on the hill so we had a lovely view of the sapphire Mediterranean Sea with the clouds above in pinks, lavenders, and corals. The colors kept intermingling and changing until darkness came. Suddenly martial music blasted, search

lights came on and soldiers marched in. The story being told was of
the Greeks trying to defend the Acropolis from the invading Persian
army. Of course the Greeks won, never mind History!

On the way home I mentioned to the children, "Remember
when we were at Persepolis and our guide explained how Alexander
the Great destroyed Persepolis in retaliation for the Persians sacking
the Acropolis? That is the story you just saw except in real life the
Persians won." The sleepy kids barely nodded.

The next afternoon we were at the airport on our way to Amsterdam. At Schiphol Airport we were guided to a B & B in the
residential district of Amsterdam. The houses along the street were
all connected and were several stories high. We were met at the
door by an apple-cheeked, smiling matron, who welcomed us to
her home. Inside the immaculate house we were surprised at how
narrow the room was. Madame von Hoff told us we would have
the rooms on the second and third floor. Jim and the boys started
to carry our luggage up. The stairs were so narrow Jim had to walk
sideways as his shoulders were too broad. We decided that Jim, Peg,
Rick and I would take the larger first room with Jimbo and Pat on
the third floor. After a stern warning from father, the boys went to
their rooms to get ready for bed.

The next morning as we descended the stairs Madame told us
our breakfast was in the basement. As we walked in the room we
were amazed to see a groaning board of every kind of cheese, bread,
fruit, juices as well as ham and different sausages. The man of the
house kept us in coffee and the children in cocoa. After the niggardly
rolls, butter and jam of Greece we were delighted. The Dutch know
how to eat!

The von Hoff's were very helpful in explaining their bus system
and giving directions on getting downtown. At the bus stop Jim
directed Jimbo and Pat to get on the bus first and find seats for the
rest of the family. As we drove along I was amazed at the number
of bicyclists; it seemed as if there were more bicycles than automobiles. Canals were everywhere and the streets were immaculate. We
got off the bus at the Rijksmuseum to view, among other works;
Rembrandt's painting of the Night Watch. We were allowed to
spend many minutes viewing this remarkable painting up close.

We wandered around the city, went to the Ann Frank home which was not open, had lunch and took a bus to a village that was set up in the manner of the 18th century. Everyone was dressed in period costumes, wearing wooden shoes and hawking all manner of souvenirs. Tulips, windmills and canals completed the feeling of living in the past. We had an early dinner of typical Dutch fare and gratefully returned to our B & B.

Madame von Hoff told us about the current flower show and explained how lucky we were to be able to see it as it only occurred once every ten years. We caught the bus to an area outside of Amsterdam and were blown away at the extent of the show. It was acres and acres of every flower imaginable, some organized by color and type, others in creative arrangements. It seemed we walked for miles engulfed in every hue. We came to a lift, much like the ones at a ski resort that would take us over a six-lane highway to more flowers. Pat and Jimbo got on the first car and I directed Peggy to get on the next car with me. Just as I started to get in Jim asked me to help him get Rick off his back. As I turned to do that Peg's car took off. Jim, Rick and I got on the next one. As I saw how high up we were, how busy the highway was my first thought was "Please don't let the boys start wrestling." There was a net beneath the lift to prevent anything falling from hitting the cars on the highway. When we got to the other side the first thing Peggy said to me was "I didn't know if I was supposed to jump on the net!"

The next day we were on an airplane headed for Copenhagen. Upon landing we were directed to a small pension in a residential district. The setting was not as picturesque as Holland but there was a grocery store on the ground floor. I had brought several jars of baby food to supplement Rick's diet which were almost gone. When I announced that I was going to the store the kids asked me to get some milk. At the store I had fun looking at labels trying to figure out what the baby food jars contained. I picked up several packages of snacks and two quarts of milk. Back in our hotel the kids all wanted a glass of milk as they had not had any since leaving Iran. Apparently Europeans don't give their children milk like Americans do.

I poured out the milk and as they drank suddenly they all gagged.

"Mom, what is this?" Jimbo hollered.

Jim grabbed Jimbo's glass, tasted it and laughed, "Butch, you bought butter milk!" I took the unopened bottle of milk back to the store and explained to the clerk what had happened. She was very nice and after laughing at my problem got me two bottles of regular milk. I visited with her for a bit, asking questions about what sights she would recommend. "Of course, you must go to Tivoli Gardens, visit the Little Mermaid statue, watch the Changing of the Guards at the King's palace," she declared. "Oh, there is so much to see in Copenhagen you will have to stay many weeks!"

Tivoli Gardens was the favorite of the children since the theme was about Hans Christian Andersen and his stories. After seeing the Changing of the Guards at Amalienborg Palace, viewing the Little Mermaid Jim suggested we go to Sweden.

We caught the hydrofoil for the fast trip to Malmo. On the way over we were sitting next to two couples from the United States. One of the women looked askance at us and said in a haughty tone, "We left our children back home."

I answered in a superior tone, "We love our children too much to be away from them. Besides, traveling is a special learning situation." That ended our conversation!

Later Jim remarked, "Butch, you really told that gal off. I was proud of you." Everywhere we went in Europe we were met with suspicious looks from all when they saw our four children. Many times at a restaurant we would be approached by someone who would complement us on how well behaved our children were. Our kids are very well behaved in all situations as Pat remarked, "We know what to expect if we don't."

The next leg of our trip took us to Lisbon, Portugal. Jim was interested in seeing a Portuguese-style of bullfighting, where the bull is not killed. After checking into our hotel Jim bought tickets for the following evening. We spent the next morning browsing the area around the hotel, buying souvenirs, and having lunch. We returned to the hotel to take a nap in preparation for the bull fight.

Arriving at the arena at 9:00 pm, we were swept up in the excitement of the music, the crowds of fancy dressed people, the impressive amounts of flowers being hawked; the whole atmosphere put us in sensory overload. We settled into our seats as a horseman, dressed in an 18th century costume entered the ring. He is called a cavaleiro and he fights the bull from horseback. His purpose is to stab three or four bandeirilhas (small javelins) in the back of the bull. The cavaleiro works the horse much as the Spanish matador uses his cape. The horse is forced to dance to and fro; to entice the bull ever closer in order to allow the cavaleiro to stab the bull. When the bull is weakened and his head is down the forcados enter. The forcados are a group of eight men who challenge to bull directly without any protection or weapon. The front man, wearing a long red cap with a green pompom on the end, provokes the bull into a charge to perform a pega de cara (face catch). When the bull charges, the front man leaps onto the bull's head, wraps his arms under the chin and holds on for dear life. The other forcados each grab the bull in assigned places while the last guy grabs hold of the tail and the bull runs madly around trying to dislodge his assailants. It was funny to watch. When the bull tires he is led off the field to the ovation of the spectators. The bull is not killed and after a good performance he is released to pasture for breeding. After three fights we were all exhausted and ready to go to the hotel.

After brunch the next morning Jim suggested we have a picnic. That sounded like a great idea as restaurant food was growing tiresome. At the grocery store we purchased three different kinds of canned of sardines, four kinds of cheese and a large loaf of crunchy bread, wine and bottled water. We caught a bus and headed out into the country side. We chose an area by the sea that had many trees. As we settled down to have our picnic we were surprised to find a tractor with a grass mower in the back heading towards us. The man driving it was scowling at us. We jumped up, gathered our picnic and moved to another area. No sooner had we settled down when the tractor appeared again. The driver hunched over the steering wheel, was very determined to get us out of his way; obviously we were interrupting his important work. So we moved again and again he came after us. Finally Jim led us back to the place where we had started that was neatly mowed. "That guy is some piece of work", I muttered.

"He's only doing his job", was Jim's reply. We ate our lunch in peace while keeping an eye out for our antagonist. We saw him return the tractor to a shed, close and lock the door. As he started to walk away Jim suggested I take a picture of him as a remembrance. I ran toward him, camera in hand and gestured that I would like to take his picture. Suddenly this nasty-looking grouch turned toward me and posed with a million watt smile!

The next morning we boarded a plane for the long flight back to the States. We were all so ready to get home. Arriving at JFK we were told our flight to Tucson was delayed. Rick was hungry so I opened the last Danish surprise baby food. Rick took one spoonful uttered a "Yuk" and promptly spit it in his hand. We all laughed and Jim said, "OK, Rick. It's time you had some real American food." He left and soon returned with a huge hotdog. Rick ate every bite; he was officially an American kid.

Chapter 27

Stepping off the plane in Tucson we were hit with the heavenly smell of warm, dry air. My Dad met us and we introduced our latest off-spring to him. On the way home he regaled us on the latest news that we had missed while traveling. Mom had snacks ready for us when we arrived and wanted to hear all about our travels. We were so happy to see Bandit and the kids scoured the backyard looking for the baby tortoises where out cousin Billy had left them but they were never found. After visiting for awhile Jim got antsy and enlisted the help of Jimbo and Pat in getting the Funbuggy out of the backyard. Our first task was to find a place to live while Jim was in Viet Nam. It didn't take us long to find a four bedroom house in Rolling Hills Country Club. It sounds more elaborate than it was; I guess if there is a golf course and club in the housing development it can be called a country club. It is very close to Davis Monthan Air Force Base so most of our neighbors were retired, active-duty military or waiting wives, the term used when husbands are on unaccompanied tours. Several of the women were married to husbands who were POW's in the Hanoi Hilton camp.

Since we knew we would sell all our furniture in Iran we had ordered furniture from a North Carolina catalogue. As soon as we had an address we notified that company as well as the military and soon we were inundated with moving vans. We registered the children in school; Pat and Peggy were in the elementary school but unfortunately, Jimbo's junior high school was on split-shift and he didn't go to school until noon and getting home at six o'clock. It is a lot of fun bombing a teen-ager out of bed by ten o'clock in order to do homework that he hadn't done the night before.

Jim's mother Margaret was in a nursing home where Jim had placed her after having to take emergency leave from Iran. He had taken Rick with him when he visited her and reported that his mom was her usual charming self, swearing at him for placing her in the nursing home.

With the house in good order it was time for Jim to go to Viet Nam. On the way to the airport he told me to look for some land to buy. "We will want to build a home here when I retire," he stated. Did that get me excited! Every time we were home on leave Jim and I would look at land. I was always ready to buy but Jim was very reluctant to commit so much money.

The day after Jim left I overheard Jimbo telling Peggy and Pat about the lake nearby that was full of golf balls. I was busy with something else and didn't pay much attention to the conversation. After dinner we watched The Waltons and The Carol Burnett Show and went to bed. I was sound asleep when Jimbo came in and told me they were going to the lake to get some golf balls. I was struggling to wake up and suddenly, the full import of what Jimbo had said caused me to be wide awake. I ran to the front door but the kids were gone. I realized I didn't know where the lake was. I put on a robe and ran across the street to a house where I had seen a couple about my age. Pounding on the front door I heard a man say, "What do you want?"

A woman's voice said, "Don't say anything."

Trying to sound calm I said, "My name is Shirley Starkey and I live across the street. My kids have gone to the lake and I don't know where it is. Can you help me?"

The woman said, "Don't answer her."

That surprised me and I said, "If you can just tell me where the lake is, I'd be eternally grateful." The man gave me directions, and thanking him, I jumped in the car and drove to the lake. I saw my three darlings sitting on the bank trying to figure out how to get the golf balls from the bottom of the lake. I hugged them in great relief and brought them home.

The next day I was watering the plants in front of the house when my neighbor came over. "Hi," he said, "My name is George Wilson. I was the one who gave you directions to the lake last night." I introduced myself again and thanked him for his help. We visited for several minutes and he commented that he had been fascinated with all the moving vans that came and went at our house. I explained my situation and we laughed about it.

Just then a crippled woman came out of his house and demanded, "George, come home right now." I recognized the voice from last night. George looked embarrassed and said goodbye.

A couple of days later I called a realtor who specialized in land sales and explained what I wanted. "I just got a listing on some land near the Saguaro National Monument. When would you like to see it?" Stan asked.

I was thrilled, "How about this afternoon as soon as I get my son off to school?" I replied. He said he would pick me up at 1:00. Stan arrived on time and Rick and I climbed into his jeep. We headed east toward the Rincon Mountains as Stan explained that he had two listings for four acres next to each other. As we arrived we realized the land was directly across the road from the Monument. The rolling hills were full of saguaros, mesquite and palo verde trees, and every cactus variety the Sonoran desert is known for. We tramped the eight acres looking for the perfect spot for a house. We found three or four that were high with views of the Catalina Mountains to the north and the Santa Rita Mountains to the south. I could not decide which four acre plot had the best views so I said to Stan, "I will buy both plots but you must tell the seller I want a better price."

He was shocked. "Mrs. Starkey, I have never had a women bargain before but let me talk to the seller." Two days later Stan reported that my price had been met and we had the land. I couldn't wait to write to Jim as I knew he would be so proud of me. I described the land, the vegetation, my bargaining; I even drew a picture of the area. Letters to Viet Nam took almost ten days so I had to wait to get my kudos from Jim.

I invited my mother-in-law to lunch on Saturday so she could see the children. Rick and I drove to the nursing home and when Margaret entered the car Rick turned to her and angrily said, "What did you do with my Dad?"

471

Margaret was shocked and cried, "I didn't do anything to your Dad." Rick continued to glare at her all the way home. Apparently the argument and swearing that Rick had witnessed caused him to blame his grandmother on his father leaving. I was amazed at his statement as that was the first full sentence Rick had ever uttered.

The ringing phone awakened me at four am. Before I could get the phone to my ear I heard Jim's voice, 'WHAT IN THE HELL ARE YOU DOING?"

"I beg your pardon. Who is this?" I innocently asked.

"YOU KNOW DAMN GOOD AND WELL WHO THIS IS! Whatever gave you the idea to buy eight acres of land?" he was starting to calm down.

"You did, that was the last thing you told me before you got on the plane."

Exasperated he replied, "Butch, I told you to look for some land, not to buy it."

"Oh Jim, this is the most gorgeous land. I was afraid it would be sold to someone else if I didn't buy it." I went on and on describing it in detail and then I added, "Besides I bargained for it, you would have been proud of me."

"Yeah, I'm sure I would have been. I just hope you haven't put us in the poor house." He didn't even say goodbye before he hung up.

Chapter 28

It is autumn 1972 and our country is gearing up for a presidential race. President Nixon is running for his second term. A small article in the paper mentions that five burglars are caught in Watergate offices; the Democrats name Sen. George McGovern and Sargent Shriver to the ticket; B52's stage biggest raid on North Viet Nam and at the Munich Olympics Arabs massacre eleven Israelis. In Paris the peace talks between our nation and Viet Nam seem to be stalled.

One Saturday Jimbo walked in the house with a black Labrador retriever pup. The pup was very hungry so we gave him some of Bandit's food. Jimbo told me where the pup had been, "Mom, he was in this big vacant lot where there was a lot of cholla cactus. I was afraid he was going to get stuck. Can we keep him, please?"

"No, Jimbo, I'm sure his owners are looking for him. We'll advertise and if no one claims him we will consider keeping him." We waited three weeks and no one claimed him so Jimbo wanted to name him Moreover. "Where did that name come from?" I asked.

"From a TV show we watched the other night." all the kids responded.

Jimbo was anxious to learn to play golf so I enrolled him in lessons on Saturdays. Patrick joined Cub Scouts while Peggy started gymnastics. I began to notice the kid's reluctance to go to Sunday school at St. Mark's Presbyterian Church where Jim and I were married. As they got in the car one Sunday after church Pat announced that he would not go back to that Sunday school. "Why not? What happened?"

Before Pat could answer, Peggy said, "Is Dad really killing babies in Viet Nam?"

"WHAT?" I asked.

Jimbo said, "That's what they are saying in Sunday school but I don't believe it."

"Of course your father is not killing babies and neither are the other Americans over there. Unfortunately there are a lot of people who want us out of Viet Nam and will do or say anything to accomplish that. We will ignore them and you do not have to go back to Sunday school." I was furious and had Jim not warned me to keep quiet about where he was, due to the crazies in Tucson, I would have marched into the church and given the devil to Reverend Sholin. From then on, most Sunday we would pack a picnic lunch and visit our land. It was so peaceful! I would spread our old Army blanket in a sandy wash, the kids would get busy building forts for their plastic soldiers while Rick would play in the sand.

Before Jim left he gave his mother permission to move into an apartment attached to the nursing home where she could have some independence but still have meals provided. When Margaret was not drinking she was a very capable person. One day after Pat and Peg came home from school we got in the car to do some errands. After we finished we stopped by Margaret's. While Margaret was talking about her new neighbors I noticed Pat squirming in the chair. After we left Pat said, "Mom, Grandma has a bottle under the cushion where I was sitting."

Oh, no, I thought, *not again.* I turned the car around and returned to Margaret's apartment. As I entered I went straight to the chair where Pat had been sitting, pulled the cushion up and discovered a bottle of vodka. Without saying a word I took it to the sink and emptied it. Returning to the living room I stated in a very angry voice, "Grandma, if you do this again you will have to go back into the nursing home. You promised Jim you would not drink anymore and that is the only reason he let you move in here." Margaret was surprised, as I rarely talked to her like that. In a calmer voice I said,

"Remember you told Jim you would go to AA meetings. When is the next one? I will take you there." Two days later I drove Margaret to an AA all day meeting. When I went to pick her up she told me she wanted to stay for the potluck and evening meal. She called me later to tell me she had a ride home. I was relieved I didn't have to go get her. The next morning she called and invited the children and me to a picnic at Randolph Park the following Saturday.

"It is for all the family members of the AA people and I want to show off my grandchildren so please say you'll come." I agreed and told her I would make a big batch of potato salad to contribute. The kids were excited and I promised them we would also go to the zoo. At the picnic Margaret introduced me to several people among them a man about my age named Charlie. He hung around Margaret the whole time making small talk. I thought it strange that he would be attracted to her and vice versa but nothing surprised me about Margaret.

That evening Charlie called me, "Shirley, I was wondering if you would go to the movies with me tomorrow night?"

"Charlie, you know I am married…What made you think I would go out with you?"

"Margaret told me you would and that I should ask you." Furious, I hung up the phone and dialed Margaret's number.

"What the hell were you doing telling Charlie I would go out with him?" I shouted.

Butter wouldn't melt in her mouth when she innocently replied, "I just thought you might." I slammed the phone down. I was furious. I knew Margaret was unhappy when Jim announced that he had asked me to marry him. In fact, Grandpa had told me that Margaret and Aunt Agnes had cried over the phone every night for three days. Was she hoping I would be unfaithful to Jim?

Every night after the children went to bed I would sit down and write a letter to Jim. The kids provided much of the news and sometimes the letter would be several pages long. I felt it was important to keep Jim apprised of his family's happenings. I neglected to write about the drawbacks in regards to Margaret as he didn't need to worry about something he couldn't do anything about.

Chapter 29

Arabs massacre 11 Israeli Olympians in Munich. Nixon and Gromyko sign a limited arms treaty and in November Nixon won his second term by a landslide. B-52's set a one-day bombing raid on North Viet Nam.

September 1972

A letter arrived from Jim stating that Col. Jersey's wife had visited him in Viet Nam. An idea came to me, "If Claudia Jersey can go to Viet Nam, so can I." I sat down and wrote to Jim asking him what he thought about me going to Viet Nam. After all we still had all those tickets from the Shah that would expire after a year. It took two weeks for me to get word from Jim that he loved the idea. I called Pan American Airlines and was told that only military, government or reporters with Diplomatic Passports were allowed to go to Viet Nam. Disappointed I reported this to Jim. Another two weeks went by until Jim's letter told me to send the tickets to him and he would buy my ticket in Saigon. I quickly mailed them off and started making plans.

I told my Mom of my plans and she told me about a lady who would stay with the children. Mrs. Sawyer was a short, slightly over-weight lady with grey hair worn in a bun at the back of her head. She had a friendly smile, told me how much she loved children and would love the job. I explained our crazy schedule, we discussed the meals she was willing to make, and I assured her that my Army brats are geared to eat anything put in front of them. She had a shocked look on her face when I said that! After much discussion about pay and mad money for buying milk and other items that came up we agreed that Mrs. Sawyer would take care of the kids. That left telling the children what my plan was. The older ones were very unhappy at the idea of an unknown woman taking care of them; they were much too old. I assured them that she was hired to take care of Rick and to cook for them. I emphasized that I knew each of them were capable of taking care of themselves and I expected them to help Mrs. Sawyer in every way they could. They solemnly promised that they would and I promised to bring them something special from Viet Nam.

The next morning as I was watering the plants in front of the house my neighbor, George came over. Excitedly, I told him of my plans. He looked at me with a silly grin and said, "You're kidding, right?"

"No I'm not." He frowned and turned away shaking his head.

When the expected day arrived Dad took me to the airport and regaled me with his opinion that I had lost my mind. Undeterred, I smiled and kissed him goodbye. The airplane was packed going to Hawaii but after that there were only seven people on the plane so I was able to stretch out and sleep. I arrived in Saigon a little after 9 am and got a big hug from Jim. He took me to his quarters which were at Circle 34 at Ton Son Nut airport. He had a large apartment with a bedroom and sitting room. Since his apartment was on the first floor facing the street, Jim had his airplane maintenance men put steel panels across the front of the building to prevent someone from lobbing a grenade into the window. It gave the apartment the feel of an intimate, darkened bar.

He showed me a flak jacket and helmet and sternly announced, "I have to get back to work. If I call you and tell you to put on the helmet and jacket you are to go into the bathroom and stay there. Do not leave the bathroom. It is the farthest from the windows and the safest place." With a quick peck on my cheek he left me.

Well, that was pretty romantic, I thought as I started unpacking. I got out my Christmas cards and started writing to friends. An hour later the phone rang and I heard a gruff voice say, "Do you remember what I told you? Do it. Right now!"

"Yes, sir" I replied to the dead phone. I put on the very heavy flak jacket and helmet and gathered up my cards. Sitting on the toilet I continued writing my "you will never guess where I am" notes. Year's later friends would tell me that was the most interesting Christmas card they had ever received.

I had been in there more than an hour listening to loud booms and writing when the phone started ringing. I wasn't sure what I was supposed to do. The ringing was incessant so I finally left the bathroom to answer it. A harsh voice said, "I told you not to leave the bathroom."

"What was I supposed to do?"

Laughing, Jim said, "Butch, a major who works for me was scheduled to fly out this morning for Australia to get married. He is afraid he will miss his connecting flight and he is driving me crazy, so I've told him to go to the mess hall. Will you meet him there and talk to him and keep his mind off what's happening?"

"What is happening?"

"We're getting rocket fire onto the airport."

"Do I have to wear the helmet and jacket?"

"No, the mess hall is in the interior of the building. Just turn left when you leave the room and continue to the end of the hall. Turn right and you're at the mess hall."

I got to the mess hall just as a very jumpy Major entered from the opposite doorway. We introduced ourselves, got coffee and sitting down I asked him to tell me about his fiancé. He started talking about his amazing bride and all I did was listen. Forty minutes later Jim came in and announced that it was all over. The Major leapt to his feet and ran out the door.

"Come on, Butch. Let's go see the damage."

We jumped into a jeep and drove all over the landing strip counting the number of large holes in the pavement. We had lunch in the mess hall and Jim escorted me back to his quarters and left to return to work. Suddenly I couldn't keep my eyes open. I laid down on the bed and fell asleep.

Jim woke me at 5:00 when he returned from work. There was a tiny, wrinkled Vietnamese lady in the room. "Butch, this is Mama-san. She is my housekeeper. Mama-san, this is my wife Madame Starkey." At the introduction Mama-san gave me big, betel-stained, almost toothless grin. Grabbing both my hands and bowing up and down she said a long statement in Vietnamese.

"What is she saying?"

"She thinks you are a movie star."

"She does not. You're making that up. You don't speak Vietnamese."

Laughing, Jim said, "I have no idea what she said but obviously she approves of you." Mama-san picked up Jim's laundry and shoes and bowing, left the room. "She's great. She shines my shoes, does my laundry and cleans the rooms."

"Can I take her back with me? That's a souvenir I would like!"

That night we went to a French restaurant in downtown Saigon for the most amazing dinner I had ever eaten. Sipping the last of our wine Jim told me we had been invited the next night to a party at a home rented by the pilots of Air America. "Air America is part of the CIA. The pilots are mostly ex-military and have an important position here in Viet Nam. I did a favor for them and they are returning the favor. They're going to fly us down to Vung Tau the day after tomorrow."

"What is Vung Tau?"

"It's a beautiful beach on the South China Sea. I'm more than ready for some R & R so I'm taking a few days off. The beach is the purest white sand I have ever seen. By the way, my secretary Susie Q, wants to take you to a beauty shop tomorrow for the works."

"Is Susie Q. her real name?"

"Not exactly but it's close to her Vietnamese name. She's engaged to a captain in my office. I don't know when they will get married as its pretty complicated getting Uncle Sam's permission. I've written my recommendation so now everyone is just waiting. She speaks perfect English, you'll like her."

The next morning after breakfast I went with Jim to his office. He was in charge of all the Army aircraft in Viet Nam and had dozens of people working for him. He introduced me to Susie, a petite, beautiful girl with a sparkling smile that could light up any room. She studied language at the University and spoke flawless English. I learned later that she also spoke, French, Spanish and some German as well as the various dialects of the Vietnamese.

Susie and I left for a girl's day of beauty. And what a day it was! We had facials, massages, manicures, pedicures, shampoos and sets. I felt like a new woman when we left. Susie hailed a pedicab to give me a tour of the city. Pedicabs are bicycles that have a carriage on top of the back wheel and are driven by a man working the pedals. Its hard work as the carriage holds two people.

The wide streets were lined in enormous trees that helped cool the city. Since Viet Nam was part of the French colonial occupation from the 19th century until 1954, the French built all the major buildings, which is why the architecture reminded me of Paris. We drove by the American embassy, a stately white building with many columns across the front. It looked like a copy of Monticello, Thomas Jefferson's home. We drove though residential areas filled with beautiful homes and returned to the main thoroughfare. The traffic was minimal with only military vehicles and pedicabs but the sidewalks were full of people walking.

"I really like the dress of the women in this country." I remarked, indicating several ladies walking together. Each had on a long, close fitting tunic with a high neckline, long sleeves and was slit to the waist at both sides. Under that they were wearing long flowing pants in white or black. The tunics were of various bright colors; yellow, apple green, cobalt and pink.

"Those are called ao dai. Would you like to get one?"

"Yes, I would."

"I will tell our driver to take us to the shop where you can order one." Speaking in rapid Vietnamese to the driver Susie had us on the way to the dressmaking shop where we were met by a middle-aged woman who hugged Susie. "Shirley, this is my Aunt Shoshi. She'll take good care of you."

Aunt Shoshi took out her measuring tape and quickly entwined my waist, bust and hips. Then she measured the length from my shoulder to the floor and smiling asked me to choose the fabric I wanted. I decide I would get two tunics and one pair of white pants. I chose a plain yellow fabric and a turquoise fabric with gold thread embroidery. As I was thanking Aunt Shoshi she grabbed my two hands and started bowing as Mama-san had. I found myself mimicking her and the two of us were bobbing up and down like geese during mating season! Susie started laughing and told me I was learning how to express my thanks in Vietnamese.

That evening Jim and I arrived at a palatial home situated in the middle of an enormous garden. It was the home of the head of the Air America crew. Music was blaring and several couples were dancing. After the introductions we were served drinks and sat with a group who were debating about the Paris Peace talks. Ideas were flying around but I noticed Jim was listening intently, never saying a word.

It was after eight and I was getting hungry. Finely when dinner was announced we lined up for an authentic Mongolian hotpot meal. As instructed by Jim I piled my plate with many uncooked vegetables, beef, pork, chicken and shrimp and when my turn came, this huge, beefy Chinese man flipped the contents onto a red hot grill and everything sizzled together. The cook added sauces to the finished product, pushed it on my plate and waved me away. At the table bowls of rice and additional condiments were available as well as beer and wine. The food was exceptional! I can't believe I'm in a war zone. The party broke up soon after eating as everyone had to work the next day.

Chapter 30

Early in the morning we boarded an Air America plane for Vung Tau. As we took off and gained altitude the pilot banked the plane turning south. Jim said, "Butch, do you see the jungle down there? See the dirt road going through the jungle? That is not a road. That is where Agent Orange has been dropped."

I couldn't believe my eyes. That dirt road went as far as I could see from the airplane. Agent Orange had totally destroyed all vegetation down to the dirt. "Why was it done? What was it supposed to accomplish?"

"Damned if I know."

Vung Tau beach was everything Jim had described. We checked into one of the trailers the military had for R and R (Rest and Recuperation). I was pleased to see that the trailer was fully furnished with linens and cooking utensils as well as many books and the latest magazines. We changed to our bathing suits and taking a blanket and towels headed for the beach. Just being able to talk to Jim and have him answer without having to wait two weeks was such a treat. I was able to convince Jim that my purchase of the eight acres was a good deal and he quit grumbling about it. After an hour we decided we had enough sun for the day.

"We best get out of the sun before we look like lobsters. We should go to the small store for some sandwich makings. We'll go out for dinner tonight but we must be back in the trailer before dark"

"Why?"

"Because Vung Tau belongs to the Americans by day but the Viet Cong take it over by night."

I laughed, "What kind of a war is this?"

"I'll admit it; it is a pretty crazy situation but it is what it is!"

We walked into the village to go to the store. We passed a hotel and Jim said, "Remember the last time I was here and I told you about Captain Carmona who worked for me? He was the one always drunk who I sent down here as he wasn't fit to fly. That's the hotel where he and the whore fell off the third floor balcony while making love and both ended up with broken backs. The Army is better off without guys like that."

We wandered around the village, shopped in the mini-PX for groceries, decided on the restaurant for that evening and headed back to the trailer. I opened a cabinet that I hadn't noticed before and found that it was full of dozens of VHS tapes of all the latest movies. I made sandwiches while Jim chose a movie for us to watch while eating our lunch. We spent the next two days doing pretty much the same things.

The last afternoon we were there we went to the Black Rock restaurant situated on the top of a (you guessed it) big, black hill overlooking the ocean. We enjoyed an early meal of lobster complete with martinis, wine and wonderful unusual vegetables. As we started to leave, a Korean colonel rose from his seat, started screaming incoherently and brandishing a pistol. Jim ushered me quickly out of the restaurant and as we walked down the beach we could hear gunshots. We never found out what the problem was. The next morning, when the Air America pilot came for us Jim told him about the incident. He shook his head and muttered, "This country is insane!"

Monday morning Jim went to work and Susie Q and I went shopping. Our first stop was to Aunt Shoshi's shop to pick up my purchases. The shop was filled with bolts of beautiful fabrics of every hue with many having delicate embroidery on them. I chose four different colors of four meters each. I planned to give one to Mom and one to Aunt Lil, the others for me.

We went to the big open market in the center of Saigon. The displays of fruits, vegetables, clothing, and souvenirs were lined up on both sides of the open space, which was filled with teeming humanity; mothers with babies riding in shawls on their backs, bare bottom toddlers running wild, old men sitting on benches observing the action, an organ grinder with his monkey performing for a crowd of children and people haggling over the price of the goods. It was total bedlam! Much of the produce was unknown to me but Susie told me what each was called and how it was cooked. She bought a very ugly piece of fruit asking the vendor to cut it open. I tasted it expecting to not like it but, to my surprise it was wonderful! After buying souvenirs for the kids and a cute covered basket for me we left. "I'm going to use this for a sewing basket," I announced.

"That's a cricket basket. People catch crickets in it to use for fishing bait," she informed me.

"Well, it's going to make a perfect sewing basket."

Our next stop was a shop laden with beautiful wooden carvings, a special love of mine. The first thing I noticed was a very large solid wood carving of Buddha. I really wanted that but I couldn't begin to lift it. Wandering around I chose several items and while I was paying for them Susie left to find transportation back to Ton Son Nut airport. Due to all my purchases Susie hired two pedicabs, one for each of us. Susie's driver was a skinny, little man with crinkly eyes, while my driver looked like Genghis Khan. He was enormous with bulging muscles and a sour look. The two were in a rapid conversation and suddenly without any warning we were off. I grabbed the sides to keep upright as this was the fastest I had ever been in a pedicab. We came to a V in the road and Susie's driver took the left road while Genghis took the right while speeding even more. There were no buildings along this road only thick jungle. I was petrified, hanging on for dear life *Oh, my God. I'm being kidnapped. Jim will kill me if I get taken by the Viet Cong* was my incoherent thought. We flew down that road like a bat out of Hell in what seemed like forever, when suddenly we were at the gates of Ton Son Nut airport where the laughing Susie and the other driver were waiting. Genghis Khan reluctantly handed money to Skinny. He had lost the race to an older man!

The morning of my departure we were sound asleep when suddenly we awaken by a loud explosion. The next thing I knew I was flying across the room landing on the cold slate floor. Before I could look up I was hit by a heavy flak jacket, followed by a helmet.

"Put these on, NOW!"

As I slowly got up to do as I was told, I saw the funniest sight! My hero was in a flak jacket, helmet and carrying a funny-looking gun in shooting position, wearing only his blue briefs. As he ran out the door to save the world I went into the bathroom and waited for further instructions. He soon returned and announced that the Viet Cong had infiltrated the ammo dump across the river and was setting it on fire. Since there was no immediate danger we got dressed, ate breakfast and came back to the room so I could finish packing. It was eleven o'clock before my flight was able to take off. I said a tearful goodbye to Jim and after getting instructions to give the kids a hug from him I boarded the plane. As we took off the captain banked the plane so everyone could see the ammo dump with explosions going off. I prayed our plane wouldn't catch one of the missles!

The flight was filled to capacity with returning military. There was much happy talk about the relief of finally leaving Viet Nam. To my surprise Col. Donald Hudson, our sponsor from our first tour in Iran, was on the plane. That's life in the military…you keep running into former friends in the most unusual places. We spent several minutes catching up on our experiences in the intervening years. I regaled him with stories of our recent tour in Iran as he shook his head.

"I think Coleen would have divorced me if I had returning orders to Iran." From his comments I deduced Coleen was still unhappy with military life and Don mentioned that he was thinking of retiring. I don't think her attitude will change no matter where she is!

Due to the departure delay in Saigon I missed my connection in Hawaii and was given a hotel room and a chit for breakfast the next morning. After the long trip and time changes I fell into bed gratefully. I awoke at 5:00 and couldn't get back to sleep, so I got dressed. I went downstairs to locate the breakfast area. It was closed. I wandered through the room looking for someone to tell me when the restaurant would be open when I heard someone talking in the next room. I walked into a darkened kitchen and saw on a young girl deep in conversation with a rotund man in a white apron. Suddenly the girl turned to me with a shocked look on her face, "I know who you are!" she exclaimed.

"You do? And who am I?"

Proudly she said, "You are Jacqueline Kennedy Onassis."

"What?"

Putting her finger to her lips she announced, "Your secret is safe with me."

I solemnly said, "Thank you." And turned and left the room shaking my head, Boy, that gal is either blind or has had too much to drink. Never the less I was pleased. I hurried back to my room to write a letter to Jim. I knew he would laugh about it.

When my plane finally arrived in Tucson it was early afternoon. My dad met me and all the way home I was told, in no uncertain terms, how selfish I was to leave my very bad children and how awful they were. What a welcome home.

Rick was taking his nap and Jimbo was at school when I arrived. Mrs. Sawyer was a nervous wreck. She didn't have a lot to say to me but wanted her money in cash. I didn't have enough so I pulled out my checkbook. "Oh, I don't want a check. I'm afraid I will lose my Social Security if I accept it."

"If you come back tomorrow I will have cash for you."

"Oh no, never mind. Just give me a check." She said breathlessly. When I gave it to her she jumped up and without another word left the house.

I kissed my sleeping Rick, unpacked my suitcase and changed clothes. I was sorting mail when Pat came through the door. When he saw me he shouted "Mom" and rushed into my arms almost knocking me down. As he hugged me I noticed Peggy had come in. She was standing with her hands on her hips, looking at me with ice blue squinting eyes and pursed lips.

"Hi, Peg."

"Why did you leave us with that woman who wouldn't even let me pour my own milk?" Each word dripped with anger.

I grabbed her to me and while holding both Pat and Peggy I said, "I'm very sorry. I really thought Mrs. Sawyer would be good to you. It won't happen again."

Pat piled more guilt on me when he said, "Mom, she was terrible. Rick was the only one she was nice to. Please don't ever do that again!"

"I promise. Now tell me about school. How are you doing?"

The kids didn't really want to talk about school. They kept coming back to how bad their life was with Mrs. Sawyer. When Jimbo arrived it all started again. While I was gone, Pat and Jim had pooled their allowance, gone to the pet store and each bought a gerbil. Unfortunately, they forgot to feed them. By the time I arrived home one of the gerbils had eaten the other. The smell in their room was indescribable.

The next day George came over when he saw me watering. "So, you went to Viet Nam, huh?" he said in a teasing manner.

"Yes I did." I started telling him all about it when he interrupted me.

"You mean you really did go to Viet Nam?"

"Yes, that's what I've been telling you"

"I I I didn't believe you," he stammered. He proceeded to ask questions until his wife noticed he was missing and yelled for him to come home.

Chapter 31

The last and longest Apollo moon visit ends. President Harry S. Truman dies. The last issue of Life magazine was published. After two weeks of heavy bombing raids on North Viet Nam Nixon orders the end of the American air offensive and agrees to resume peace talks in Paris.

December 1972

Rumors were flying that the Peace talks would be fruitful. Everyone's hopes were up. Peggy announced that one of her friends in her class had not seen his father in six years and couldn't remember what he looked like.

One cold Saturday morning Rick was bugging his big brothers and after much chasing, laughing and yelling they caught up with him and hung him up on the round doorknob by his underwear. It was the ultimate wedgy. I heard screaming and dashed in to find Rick struggling, his arms and legs waving in the air, while the boys were laughing hysterically. I released Rick who then started chasing the boys all over the house. Peggy got involved and the melee continued into the afternoon. The kids were having fun so I left them alone until I finally had enough. I tried to get their attention but they couldn't be stopped. I had a headache so I finally went in my bedroom, locked the door, took an aspirin and lay down. The noise continued until

Pat said, "Where's Mom?" It got quiet. Jimbo knocked on my door and said, "Mom, are you alright?" I didn't answer.

The kids were softly talking among themselves. Pat knocked on the door, "Mom, are you okay?" No answer.

I heard Jimbo tell Peggy to ask me. She knocked on the door and said, "Mom, please talk to me." No answer.

I heard more whispering and then the front door opened. Someone left the house. Soon the front door opened and I heard a soft knock and my next door neighbor softly said, "Shirley, may I come in?" I opened the door and let Miriam in. "Are you okay?"

"Yes, I'm fine. I was so upset with my kids I was afraid I would kill them, so I came in here to calm down." I know I sounded near hysteria.

"Well, you're coming home with me. I'll have Jack fix you a martini you can relax." She grabbed my hand and led me into the living room. The kids all had scared looks on their faces when Miriam commanded, "You kids sit down, watch TV and behave yourselves. I'm taking your mother to my house."

Miriam's husband Jack was a retired Air Force colonel and he made me one of the best martinis I have ever had, in fact I had two. I stayed for two hours visiting with them and was feeling no pain when I returned home. The kids were engrossed in watching The Waltons on television. When they saw me all had anxious looks as if expecting me to punish them. I gathered them in my arms hugged them and told them I loved them. All is well!

I received a letter from Carol Ebert in Tehran. She told me three American colonels had been walking outside the Iranian Army Headquarters when two men on motorcycles drove by, shot and killed them. One of advisors was Jim's replacement. "I guess Jim was lucky he chose Viet Nam over Iran", she wrote.

It was early December and time to gear up for Christmas. Mom called me to say that my niece, Susie was planning on getting married on the 27th of December. Susie was born Christmas day on my 19th birthday.

"Why would she pick that day to get married when her birthday is on Christmas?"

"That's not the only thing," Mom said laughing. "Her fiancée's birthday is the 26th of December. They will be doing a lot of celebrating all at once for the rest of their marriage. But he's in the military and that is the only time he can get off. Honey, I'm so sorry to tell you that Dad and I will be driving to Houston for the wedding so we won't be able to spend Christmas with you."

I was very disappointed but didn't want Mom to know it so I said, "Well, since it's the first grandchild to get married I guess I can forgive you."

When Aunt Lil heard that Mom and Dad would not celebrate Christmas with the children and me she decided to first come to Tucson for Christmas and fly to Houston on the 26th. I was so pleased and planned a big celebration with my brother Bill's family and Aunt Lil. We had a feast and Billy put up a piñata for the kids to hit.

Chapter 32

In January the United States agreed to a truce in Vietnam. On the 27th all fighting is to cease, at least on paper. Lyndon Baines Johnson, our 35th president suffers a heart attack. Ironically, he dies just as the war that chased him from the White House is ending. On Valentine's Day the first of the POWs is released.

January 1973

The phone was ringing incessantly. I staggered out of bed noticing 2:15 on the clock. Answering I heard a happy voice, "Butch, I just got my orders for Germany. We'll be at Patch Barracks in Stuttgart."

"Wow, that's wonderful." I'm wide awake now. "When will you come home?"

"I don't know, probably when the last of the POW's are released. The last to come to Vietnam will be the last to leave. But whenever it is I'll take some leave before going to Germany and you and the kids can come when school is over. It will take awhile to get quarters anyway. I can't talk anymore right now but I'll write more tonight." He hung up.

There was a PTA meeting at Pat and Peg's school and the room that had the most parents attend would get an award. As I was signing in for both Pat and Peggy's rooms I was aware of the buzz about the release of the POW's. Many waiting wives were living in our area and were attending the meeting. A woman approached me with an eager look on her face. "Is your husband attending the meeting?"

"No, he's not. He's in Viet Nam."

Excited she said, "Oh is he a POW?"

"No, he's stationed in Saigon."

She looked disappointed and turning her back on me she walked away. Oh, well, I guess I'm not a celebrity!

On March 29th the last of the POW's were released. In Saigon there were twenty planes ready to take all the remaining military personnel back to the States. During the last two months as more military left Saigon Jim's responsibilities became greater. He even ended up being the officer in charge of the mess hall and bar. The bar was decorated with all the flags of the 50 states so Jim told his men to take their state's flag. He brought home the flag of Arizona. While at the bar Jim decreed that the drinks were five cents each, so they managed to toast the president, each other, the world, the universe and anything else they could think of so that when they boarded the planes they were feeling no pain. The Viet Cong were at the planes and counted off everyone who was leaving. Jim's plane was number seventeen to take off.

He arrived in Tucson on Saturday afternoon. We gave him a hearty welcome at the airport and when we arrived home we discovered that the neighbors had put up a huge WELCOME HOME sign.

Again the moving vans came and went from our home much to the interest of our neighbor George. When Jim's goods arrived from Vietnam I was pleased to see the giant wooden Buddha I had described to Jim. He also bought six ceramic elephants of blue, green and white. Our house was taking on a Middle East/Far East look and I hadn't even had a chance to shop in Europe yet!

Jim took a liking to Moreover and told Jimbo that we could take her to Germany. Bandit was getting very old so we decided to leave him with Mom and Dad.

Jim's orders were for the United States Headquarters of Europe and the Middle East located near Stuttgart and he left two weeks later. The kids were finishing up their school work while I was busy deciding what furniture we could take to Germany and what would go into storage. Life in the military seems to be all about moving vans! Moreover got a clean bill of health from the vet and I received an official looking paper attesting to that. The vet gave me some pills to give to the dog before putting her on the plane and strongly suggested that I not feed her for a day before we left. I bought the largest kennel I could find as Moreover was now full grown. I sent half of our furniture to a storage facility, sent the rest of our goods on to Stuttgart, got our suitcases packed and moved to my folk's house. Jimbo and Pat helped me put the Funbuggy in Dad's back-yard the way Jim had done before. The next morning Mom drove us to the airport.

Chapter 33

Watergate hearings in Washington DC are in full swing. John Dean pleads the 5th amendment and later accuses Nixon and aids H.R. Haldeman and John D. Ehrlichman of taking part in the Watergate cover-up. Secretariat wins the Triple Crown.

June 1973

While we were waiting for our plane Ricky needed to get his diaper changed. When I returned Mom was talking to a couple who had a boy with them about Jimbo's age.

"Shirley, this is Mr. and Mrs. Gooden and their son, Frankie. Frankie is going to Germany to spend the summer with his sister and her husband, who's stationed there. I told the Gooden's that you would take Frankie with you and make sure he got to Frankfurt."

I was speechless.

Mrs. Gooden said, "I hope this is not too much trouble for you. Your mother was so kind to offer your assistance."

"Oh no" I stammered, "It won't be any trouble at all. Does he change planes in New York?"

"Yes. Then he'll get a different plane to Frankfurt. That is the part I was worried about."

"That's fine. I'll make sure he gets on the right plane." Thanks, Mom. I only have four of my own kids plus a large dog to get to Germany. I

494

really need a fifth kid to watch over!

The non-stop flight to Kennedy Airport was uneventful as Jimbo and Pat sat with Frankie, who turned out to be a nice young man. When we arrived I discovered we had to take a bus to the other side of the airport where the overseas flights originated. But first we had to get Moreover. We went to the baggage area and waited for our dog. All the bags arrived as well as extra containers, but no Moreover. I was told to go downstairs to the office of the Baggage Control. The secretary was eating her lunch and told me she would let her boss know I was there. She continued eating. I noticed the name McMillan on the door. My time was limited and I decided the only recourse was to invade. I said, "Come on, kids. Follow me." I marched into McMillan's office with my five charges following. Pat immediately started checking a strange lamp, turning it over to see how it worked. The others were milling around and I didn't stop them. McMillan rose up from his sandwich, a shocked look on his face. "Young man, don't touch that lamp!" he commanded.

Interrupting him I said, "Mr. McMillan, we can't find our dog and we've got to get a plane to Germany in one hour." We actually had a four hour wait but I didn't think exaggeration would hurt.

"Follow me," McMillan said as he sped out the door and over his shoulder said to his secretary, "Call Jasper and find out where the dog is." Turning to me he asked what breed was our dog. "Tell him it's a black Lab," he yelled over his shoulder. He led us to the far end of the area and told us to wait while he went into another office and conferred with Jasper. Jasper grabbed the phone, talked a few minutes and turned to the McMillan. I don't know what was said but McMillan emerged and walking very fast led us to an elevator. He told us to wait there and our dog would be coming down. He sped away back to his office, glad to get rid of us.

We waited several nervous minutes until the elevator opened and there was Moreover's kennel. We were so glad to see her but when we opened the door to let her out she had a very sheepish look on her face. That's when we discovered that she had had an accident all over the kennel. Never have I seen and smelled such a terrible mess. Apparently the pills and fasting had not worked. We got her out and started cleaning her up. Fortunately I had a box of Wipees for Rick and, half a box later, she was clean. The kennel had an extra perforated insert that was piled with lumps of feces. I took it out, told the kids to wait while I went to the ladies room to clean it up. Holding the insert as far away from me as possible, I went up the escalator and entered the ladies bathroom. It was full of women waiting in line. Remarkably, the line parted and I made my way up to the sink. I was busy washing the insert and using a bobby pin to poke all the holes when I looked up and realized I was the only one left in the bathroom. I had cleared everyone out! As I finished I suddenly thought, *Good grief, I have left my kids alone in New York, in the crime-ridden capital of the world. I hope they haven't been kidnapped!* Entering the escalator I looked down and beheld a scene right out of a Norman Rockwell painting. Five children guarded by a big black Lab, surrounded by luggage, patiently sitting on a bench. Pat had the briefcase full of our important papers, Jimbo had Moreover's leash and Peggy had her arm protectively around Rick while Frankie played with his yo-yo.

I took the kennel apart, put the top up-side down on the bottom and filled it with our carry-on luggage. "Jim, you and Frankie carry the kennel, Pat, you lead the way with Moreover. When we get to the bus don't say anything, get on quickly and go to the back and sit down. If there is a problem with the dog I will deal with it."

The bus driver was standing at the door of the bus and as we approached Pat started to say something to him. I immediately stuck my fingernail into Pat's back, hissing, "Get on the bus. Now!" We all piled in and no one said a word about the dog.

Our first priority upon arriving at the international wing of JFK airport was to check Moreover in. We found a bench near the check-in, unloaded the kennel, put it back together, and left Pat, Peggy, Rick and Frankie. Jimbo carried the empty kennel, while I took Moreover's leash. An attendant checked Moreover's paperwork, stamped it and told us to put the dog in her kennel. I scratched Moreover's head and told her we would see her in Germany and off she went on the moving belt.

Hurrying back to the bench I realized there was not much time to get Frankie to his plane. The gate was the farthest from ours (isn't that always the way?). "Come on, Frankie, we don't have much time." I started running past sixteen gates with Frankie following and we made it to his gate just as the passengers were boarding. I had written our address on a piece of paper so that Frankie's folks could send me a thank-you card if they wished. I handed it to Frankie who grabbed it and without a backward glance or comment he ran to get boarded. I got the strangest feeling that he thought he had been placed with a slightly insane lady. I never got a thank-you.

Returning to my charges I led them to a restaurant where we ordered Cokes. When our flight was announced we made our way to our gate. "Mom, there's Moreover!" Jimbo yelled. We could see our plane and going up the moving ramp along with luggage was our dog.

We were making our way through security when suddenly screeching alarm bells went off. Jimbo and Pat were ordered to unload their pockets and out came steel balls the size of baseballs. I was completely unnerved and shaking badly. The boys thought it was a big joke until they were told they could not keep the steelies. I took several deep breaths to calm myself and led the way to our seats. As I sat down I heaved a sigh of relief and said to Peggy, "Finally we're on our way. The next stop is your father!"

Just then an attendant said to me, "Mrs. Starkey, I believe this is yours." She handed me my briefcase that was full of all our important papers; insurance, stock certificates, checkbooks, bank statements, birth certificates, in other words, our life. After all the drama of this trip I had dropped it when the alarms went off!

The rest of the flight was uneventful. The kids were impressed with the meals and the many movies at their disposal. "I'm going to watch movies all night long," Pat announced but he soon fell asleep as we all did.

We lost a whole day and it was early evening when we arrived in Germany. I had the paperwork in my hand as we entered Passport Control. Rick spied his father and yelling, "Daddy," ran toward him. I looked up at the tall heavy-set German official, expecting a reprimand, but instead he said in a deep guttural accent, "Es goot, go to fadder." The other three took off and almost knocked their dad down as they piled on. The control officer gave me a big grin as he stamped our passports, "Velcome to Chermany," he intoned.

It was a wonderful reunion and we took turns hugging each other and laughing in happiness. We gathered up our ten suitcases and Moreover, (who was squeaky clean, fortunately) and piled into the Volva station wagon Jim had purchased.

Our quarters were on the top floor of a three –story building which had three stairwells serving two families on each floor. Our one building had eighteen families. There were five rows of these buildings with six buildings in each row. Every apartment seemed to have at least three kids so the rough total would be 1620 kids just at our housing area. Wow!

Jim had stocked the refrigerator, ordered a meal from the Officer's Club and had all the beds made up ready for us. He had arranged for beds from the excess furniture the military has. It was past midnight by the time we finished eating. Jim told Jimbo to take Moreover outside before going to bed. A few minutes later we heard the high-pitched barking Moreover used when chasing a cat. We opened the window and could see Moreover racing down the area between all the buildings trying to catch the cat. Jimbo was running after her as fast as he could. We heard angry male voices yelling obscenities echoing back and forth between the buildings. I started laughing hysterically, "Well, Jim, I guess we've introduced ourselves to Germany!"

The next day was Friday and Jim left early for work. The kids were sleeping late which gave me the chance to unpack my things and get them organized. Our apartment had four bedrooms so Peggy and Rick each had their own room while Jim and Pat shared. Ricky was the first to wake up and he 'helped' me unpack his things. He was anxious to get his toys. I awakened the others and by the time Jim showed up for lunch we were completely unpacked. He announced that our furniture from Tucson would arrive the next morning. So once again we're getting rid of the extra beds, placing our own furniture and carpets, hanging pictures and organizing the kitchen. After finishing that, we have a new home.

The boys quickly got involved with the hordes of other kids playing kick ball or baseball in the large spaces between buildings. Peggy spent a lot of time playing with Rick as he was too little to go downstairs. When it was time to call the boys in for dinner Jim would stick his head out the window and emit a unique, sheer whistle that could be heard three blocks away. The boys never failed to come running.

We were living at Patch Barracks in Stuttgart-Venagain which was the headquarters of all of the European and Middle Eastern Theaters. Consequently there were more generals or admirals stationed there than there were lieutenants or captains. It was a small village with lots of gossipers. Many of the generals were the sons of famous World War II generals. When General George S. Patton the 3rd arrived, the rumor was that he was unhappy that a large tree outside his window blocked the sunshine. So he proceeded to cut it down and make firewood in preparation for winter. The Forestmeister arrived and informed the general that while the United States rented the area it did not include the trees. So he confiscated the wood and fined the general a lot of money. Gen. Patton had his father's temper and was furious. I heard this story while getting my hair done. I laughed and, only joking, said, "Did you hear that it turned out that Gen. Patton's father had run over the Forestmeister's father with his tank?" My German hairdresser was alarmed and said, "No, I hadn't heard that!" The next week when I went to the hairdresser's she told me the same story I had told her the week before. The amazing thing was that she had actually believed that ridiculous tale and was passing it around! I decided then that I would be very careful of what I said and to whom. Sometimes my sense of humor gets me in hot water.

Summer in Germany is beautiful with lots of sunshine and outdoor activities. One of the favorites is the Volksmarches. Volksmarching is a form of non-competitive fitness walking that developed in Germany in the early 1960s. Participates typically walk 5 kilometers (3.1 mile), ten kilometers (6.2 miles) or 20 kilometers (12 miles). These take place on a pre-determined outdoor trail or path with the aid of posted signs or markings. The Volksmarching associations offered incentive awards to those who completed the march. In addition to a certificate, a medal is available for a small price. Our family embraced this custom with gusto. Early Saturday morning we would drive to a village and register. We would be given maps of the march with instructions to keep Moreover on her leash. The well-marked trail wended through the woods with frequent stops where first aid, drinks, garbage cans and benches were available. Germans are fastidious about keeping the forests clean and are not afraid to call someone out who drops as much as a gum wrapper. At the end of the five kilometer markings would be a picnic area with trucks selling bratwurst, sauerkraut and hamburgers. An Oomph band would be playing polkas with some energetic couples dancing. It was festive and up-lifting, as well as tiring.

One evening we were having a dinner party when there was a knock on the door. A man wanted to know if Col. Starkey was available. I got Jim and Major Forrest introduced himself. "Sir, my boy is having trouble. Apparently your sons gave him and several other boys something, and my son has been on the toilet all afternoon. I just want to know what they gave him." I ran into the boy's room, "Your father needs to see you right now!" Jim ushered the boys into the hallway and closed the door, not wanting our guests to be disturbed.

"What did you give the kids on the playground?" Jim demanded.

Pat and Jimbo looked at each other and finally Pat, looking solemn said, "We went to the PX and bought some laxative chewing gum and shared it." Jimbo was grinning like a Cheshire cat.

"Wipe that grin off your face, young man. And, you two apologize to Major Forrest." Jim said in his sternest voice. The boys shook the Major's hand and offered their apologizes. The Major accepted and Jim sent the boys to their room. After they left Jim and Major Forrest had a good laugh.

"Well I'm glad to know it wasn't something worse. Billy could use a good cleaning out," the Major said as he shook Jim's hand.

Chapter 34

The Senate Watergate hearings continue, U.S. puts Skylab into orbit, Henry Kissinger becomes Secretary of State and Vice President Spiro Agnew resigns over income tax evasion charges. Nixon nominates Gerald Ford to be the Vice President.

Fall 1973

It was time to register for school and all three would be going to school at a nearby village of Boblingen. Peggy was in third grade, Pat in fifth grade and Jimbo in seventh. I discovered that the Officers' Wives Club hired an artist to teach oil painting once a week so I signed up for it. There was a nursery on the top floor of a wooden barrack and I took Rick over there to check it out. It was run by a tall, handsome black woman who was married to a Sgt Major. Mrs. Washington was efficient and business-like when dealing with adults and loving and funny when dealing with children. I liked her immediately. I filled out the essential paperwork and Rick was enrolled. The first time I took him there he cried and clung to me, not wanting me to leave him. Mrs. Washington came over and helped pry him loose. She took him into the gated area where other children were playing while Rick kept screaming.

"Mrs. Starkey, go. He'll be alright," she commanded. I left with a massive guilt feeling. I had abandoned my child! I was upset most of the morning, hardly paying attention to the instructor. When I picked Rick up he was happy to see me and appeared to be fine. After I paid the attendant she handed Rick a lollypop. He was subdued on the way home.

The following Thursday I was invited to a luncheon and I planned to take Rick to the nursery. When we arrived he again started screaming, not wanting to stay. He had his arms and legs wrapped around me like an octopus and again, Mrs. Washington came to my rescue, tearing my child away from me. When I got in the car I realized I had forgotten to give Rick's lunch to the attendant. As I walked up the stairs to the nursery I was dreading facing my bawling child. Entering the nursery I saw Rick with another boy racing trucks and laughing about something. I was surprised that he wasn't crying. Mrs. W. saw the look on my face and smiling, told me he stopped crying the minute I left. "Mrs. Starkey, he's putting you on. He has the most fun of any of the children here. He is very sociable. Don't worry about him he is doing just fine." I left, at first relieved and then, the more I thought about it, the madder I got. That little monster, I'm going to wring his neck! When I picked him up I stopped the attendant from giving him a lollypop. Rick was very upset, "Mama, I want a lollypop."

Calmly I answered him, "I'm sorry, Ricky, only the Good children get a lollypop. Only the Good children that don't cry when going to the nursery get a lollypop." When we got in the car Rick was quiet for the longest time and finally in a small voice he said, "Mama, if I don't cry next time can I get a lollypop?"

"Of course you can." And he was never a problem after that.

The art class was held in a cold basement of an abandoned building on the edge of the woods. The art instructor, Herr Schmidt, was a thin, pasty-face man with a prominent hooked nose. He was demanding but very helpful at critiques. He insisted that we sketch the still life on drawing paper and get his approval before drawing it on a canvas. He would not allow any artificial light and we had to rely on the light from the two small windows that were six feet off the floor. This was a challenge during the gloomy, rainy days of winter. My class had between six and ten students on any given day. Joanne Patton, the general's wife was one of them. She was a quiet, lovely lady. There were three other general's wives who came sporadically.

I noticed that when those ladies were talking, no matter what the subject was, Herr Schmidt was very alert to the conversation. I'm sure he reported what he heard to someone.

The second year we graduated from still life to portraits. Herr Schmidt brought in his 99 year old friend who had been an organ grinder, entertaining the crowds in the marketplatz of Stuttgart. That is, he did until his monkey died. Herr Schmidt asked us to hire him to pose for us as he had no income. We were so glad to get a live model we accepted happily.

Herr Meyer was tiny, about five feet tall, with a bald head and a luxurious beard. He had twinkly blue eyes that expressed a sense of humor. Herr Schmidt posed him on a chair with his face facing the light. He never moved a muscle and seemed to be in a trance. He had so many wrinkles on his face we had to count which ones we were working on.We would be busy working on our paintings when suddenly; someone would notice that Herr Meyer's fingers were turning blue. One of us would rush to him and start messaging his hands while others would get him some hot coffee. Then he would get up, walk around the room looking at his portraits critically. When he came to mine he shook his head, frowning and said, "Nein, nein," and indicated that I had painted his beard too long. I looked again and realized he was correct. I immediately painted the coat up to cover some of his beard and the next time he came around he looked at my painting and with an approving smile, said, "Es goot, es goot!" I had just received the Seal of Approval.

Herr Schmidt told us about a man named Maroger, who was a restorer at the Louvre in Paris. He knew that many of the great artists died young, probably as a result of dealing with the chemicals used in oil paints. He also knew that they left behind a myriad of paintings. He wondered how they could have been so prolific when it took so long for the paint to dry. Did they work on many paintings at one time? Did they hire many apprentices to complete what the artist had started? Or did they use a quick-drying additive to the paint? He decided to investigate so he started taking tiny bits of the paint from the canvases and analyzing them. He came up with a recipe that allowed one layer of paint to be added on top of another layer without smearing. This was the additive Herr Schmidt sold to us and it worked beautifully. He gave us the recipe and one day my friend Marilyn asked me if I wanted to help her make some of this additive. I was game and we made arrangements to cook it in the studio on a Saturday. We had a Bunsen burner, an old pot, a wooden spoon, a candy thermometer and the ingredients. We put the recipe together, stirred it over the heat and carefully watched the temperature rise. When it reached the exact degree we took it off the burner and let it cool. We poured the concoction into baby food jars. We had a supply of fourteen jars each. The next art day we told Herr Schmidt what we had done. He was horrified. That's when he told us that if the temperature had gone five degrees higher it would have exploded and blown the building apart! Wouldn't that have been a scandal if we had blown up the Headquarters of the European and Middle Eastern Command! God watches over fools.

Fall arrived, the weather turned cooler and football was in the air. Our family went to the football game between Patch Barracks and a team from the Frankfurt area. It was a close, exciting game when suddenly an authoritative voice boomed over the intercom saying 'all those with a (certain) designation report at once.' Jim, along with many of the audience got up. "Don't wait up for me, Butch. I don't know how long I'll be gone" he said and left.

The next day the Stars and Stripes newspaper reported that the Egyptians and Syrians had launched a surprise attack against Israel in the middle of Yom Kippur, the most religious Jewish holiday. Israeli jets knocked out nine bridges along the Suez Canal. Israeli soldiers pushed the Syrians and Egyptians back to the 1967 ceasefire line and continued driving toward Damascus. Secretary of State Kissinger flew to Moscow for talks while the United Nations called for a cease fire. Israeli Premier Golda Meir rejected a truce saying the enemy hadn't been "beaten enough". After more negotiations she changed her mind and a cease fire went into effect on the 22nd of October. Jim was gone for three days. When the kids asked him where he had been he told them he had been jumping on a giant trampoline!

In retaliation for the United States support of Israel the four Persian Gulf States joined the other Middle East oil producing countries in embargoing all oil shipments to the United States. They vowed to cut productions and sales until the Israeli's gave back the land captured in the 1967 war. Soon the embargo affected industrialized countries and third-world countries worldwide. A ban on Sunday gasoline sales and other restrictions on oil use were imposed. Germany declared that Sundays would be a non-driving day except for emergency vehicles. Our family walked to the overlook of the autobahn and it looked like something out of a fantasy movie. There was not a car in sight on the lonely highway. In December we received a lot of snow and when it came time to buy a Christmas tree we walked to the commissary after a storm had dumped 12 inches of snow on the ground. Jimbo and Pat took turns pulling a sled with Rick on it. After much scrutiny the tree was chosen and Jim tied it to the sled. Rick got to ride on top of the tree, much to his delight. I felt like we were living an old-fashioned Christmas.

Chapter 35

Jim's boss, Col. Langford was an avid skier and had started a Sitz Marker club. The patch for the club was of a skier on his back with his skis high in the air. Col. L. convinced Jim that our kids should take advantage of the snows and learn to ski. Jim, remembering how the children had enjoyed their brief excursion in skiing in Iran readily agreed. A sale of new and used ski clothes and equipment was held at the Officer's Club and we were able to completely outfit all three older kids. We even found a tiny pair of skis for Rick.

Col. Langford recommended a small ski run very close to Patch Barracks and we headed for it the next Saturday. It was a crisp, sunny day with the smell of pine over-powering. We were directed to an area with a rope tow for learners. Jim hired a teenager instructor and after an hour our very athletic kids were on their own; they just needed practice. The worst part for them was learning how to handle the rope tow. For an hour we watched as they struggled and finally Jim bought tickets for the ski lift. Jimbo was the first on the lift and, unbeknownst to me, Moreover was watching intently. As Jimbo rode up the mountain Moreover jerked out of her leash and started after him, barking excitedly. It was exhilarating to see a black dog against the white snow racing as hard as she could go. Jimbo grabbed her when he got off the lift and, to our surprise, was able to ski down the mountain with her, without a problem. I retrieved a very wet, smelly dog and Rick, Moreover and I headed for the restaurant. Germans welcome dogs anywhere as long as they are well behaved. We took a window seat and Moreover settled underneath us next to the heat vent. Rick and I drank hot chocolate while watching the skiers from the window. An hour later the rest of the family joined us for lunch, all talking at once about their experiences. "Butch that looked like so much fun you and I are going to get skis," Jim announced.

The next weekend we returned and this time Jim and I were the students. Jim had skiing conquered in no time at all while I struggled on that damn rope tow. I never could get the skis going in the same direction while holding onto the rope. After four or five tries I gave up and hired an instructor to go up on the lift with me and talk me down the mountain. That's when I learned how to ski.

Every weekend we spent one day on the slopes and soon we were all pretty good skiers. Jim started helping Rick with his skis but not with much success. Jimbo excelled quickly and joined the high school ski club. The ski club went to France during the winter break.

The junior high members of the Sitz Marker club were going on ski trip to Zell am See, Austria at the same time and Jim was asked to be a chaperone. When he found out that all of us could go for nothing he agreed. Excitedly we prepared for the trip. At the orientation meeting we met Major and Mrs. Pringle and Captain Jenkins who were also chaperones. During the conversation we learned that Capt. Jenkins was a good skier and the Pringles were intermediate skiers. There was no doubt that Jim and I were beginners! We also learned that half of the 22 kids going on the trip were offspring of Generals with World War II famous names. We would soon learn that they gave the term Army Brat new meaning!

Our bus to Austria left at seven in the evening and after much confusion in loading all the gear we were on our way. Inside the bus was bedlam until 9:30 when everything got quiet. We slept the whole way and arrived at six in the morning. The club had rented a small hotel with room and board and we were served a healthy breakfast before leaving for the slopes. The bus took us there and would return at 4:00 pm for us. Lunch was on our own. The ski area was immense and I wondered how we would be able to keep track of our charges. At Capt Jenkins suggestion it was decided that Jim and I would patrol the lower level, the Pringles would be in charge of the middle runs and Capt. Jenkins would basically cover the whole mountain. We counted heads frequently…it wouldn't do to lose one of these 'special' kids. The first day went very well and everyone skied all day. Back at the hotel the kids ate their dinner and everybody went straight to bed. The dormitory rooms for the girls and boys were furnished with bunk beds and at the end of the rooms were bathroom facilities.

The second day went pretty much the same as the first. But in the middle of the night one of the girls came to our room crying, saying that the girls were telling ghost stories and she was scared. I was fast asleep and was unaware of the problem. Jim took the girl back to the dorm room and asked to hear the ghost story. After it was repeated Jim changed the story into a comedy and had everyone laughing. He came back to our room and all was quiet after that.

The third day the kids were beginning to get tired of skiing and Jim and I had to chase them out of the restaurant. We would find them eating French fries as well as using the fries to write in ketchup on the table.

It turned out that Capt. Jenkins was an excellent skier and covered the whole mountain many times during the day. He came to us and asked if he could take Rick on a ski run. "Jim, he's only three years old!" I protested.

"He's almost four and he'll be fine. Capt Jenkins will take good care of him." Jim assured me. I held my breath as I watched them go on the gondolier up to the top of the mountain. Later Jenkins told us that he stood Rick between his legs and instructed him to wrap his arms around his legs. They pushed off and skied all the way down to the bottom. Ricky was ecstatic, laughing and telling us that he wanted to do it again. A skier was born!

We were having lunch in the restaurant where I overheard a conversation at the next table. Someone was saying that Peggy was coming down the World Cup run. It took me a minute to realize that there was only one Peggy in our group. "Did you say Peggy is coming down the World Cup run?" I asked. "Did you mean my daughter?"

"Yes, Capt. Jenkins is leading several down the cup and Peggy insisted on going."

"My God, Jim, she's only seven. She'll kill herself." I yelled as I headed for the door. We ran to were the run ended and looked up the mountain. We could barely make out a tiny figure in blue with long, blonde pigtails cascading down the front of her jacket. There was no mistake, it was Peggy. Breathlessly, we watched her all the way down the mountain. There was a creek with a narrow bridge that she had to navigate to get to where we were waiting. *She'll ever make it, I just know it*, I thought.

Jim is shouting, "Come on, Peg, you can make it." She crouched down and pushing on her ski poles she came right into her father's arms with the biggest triumphant smile I have ever seen.

On the way back to the hotel our four couldn't stop talking about their day. After five days of skiing everybody was ready to go home.

Chapter 36

Living in foreign countries requires learning typical traits. For instance, in Iran I always insisted on carefully examining any produce I bought at the local green grocer, making sure it was perfect, as I had to soak it in Cholox water. Iranians were known to foist off bad produce on unsuspecting customers. When we arrived in Germany the first time I went to the green grocer I picked up a juicy, red tomato for inspection. Immediately the owner slapped me hard on my hand. My hand stung for several minutes as did my face from embarrassment. I learned my lesson; in Germany all produce for sale is perfect.

Germans are very clean. You never see a piece of paper on the side of the road. In the morning the hausfraus sweep the walks energetically. If a man were to drop a cigarette butt on the ground three Germans would call him out. The streets are immaculate. After the war the Germans solved the problem of what to do with the bombed buildings. All the debris was piled up to form a mountain. Then the Germans filed it in with massive amounts of dirt and planted trees and greenery. The road from Patch Barracks to Stuttgart went over the winding large man-made mountain. At the top were a fire lookout and a revolving restaurant that served the best German chocolate cake I've ever tasted.

We also learned that all Germans were against Hitler and there were no concentration camps! Germans, in general, are innovative, energetic, smart, honest, and aggressive. Nowhere was the latter truer than on the ski slopes. In the 1970's the skis had a lever in the back of the skis that had to be poked with ski poles to release the boot from the skis. On the slopes it was very common for Germans, in line for the ski lift, to keep inching their way forward to get ahead of others in line. My boys figured out a way to stop them without starting a problem. As the culprits were visiting with each other and pushing ahead, my boys would use their ski poles to pop the bindings. When they started moving their boots came out of the skis. They had to step out of line in order to put their skis back on. My boys got on the lift laughing.

Little did I realize when we brought Moreover to Germany we had a built-in babysitter? While the older kids were at school Ricky was left to entertain himself. I would be cleaning up the kitchen or vacuuming and Moreover would nudge my thigh. That was my signal to look for Ricky. Invariably, I would find him playing in the toilet or up on the window sills looking out. Since we lived in the third story I didn't think that was a good idea.

Early one Sunday morning when Jim was on a trip I was awakened suddenly. I put on my red corduroy bathroom and checked the kid's rooms. The older ones were sound asleep but Ricky's room was empty. Walking into the kitchen I saw Moreover standing in the doorway. Ricky was on the counter with a container of cocoa open and was pouring the contents on Moreover's back. Moreover, standing like a statue, was looking at me with pleading eyes. I set Rick down and turned to the dog. I gently led her to the front door, careful that nothing spilled from her coat. I opened the door and she was out like a flash, racing down the three flights of stairs. I ran after her intending to get her at the entrance. Unfortunately, someone opened the front door just as Moreover got there. Outside she continued running, with me right behind her. I could hear Ricky laughing as he followed us. Moreover ran down the hill straight into the General's quarters. If anyone had been looking it must have been a sight; a large, black dog running, a crazy lady in a red housecoat chasing and a three year old laughing hysterically. I finally corralled her at the end of the area and started home. I had to pass all of the housing but since it was six o'clock in the morning, fortunately, no one was around.

One day I started downstairs with some laundry and noticed the door to the vacant apartment across the hall was open. There was a tall, blonde man in an air force uniform looking around the living room. I said "Hi, are you moving in here?"

"Yes," he replied. "My family is coming from Michigan this week"

"I'm sorry but you are not allowed to move in here unless you have a three year old," I joked.

He laughed, "As a matter of fact I have a daughter who is three."

Delighted, I introduced myself and we visited for awhile. The McHales had two older children in school and three year old Jennifer. Finally, Ricky would have someone to play with. Jennifer was a cute little brunette and for Ricky it was love at first sight. Her mother, Betty and I got along well and soon, when we were both home, we would leave our front doors open so the little ones could run back and forth.

One Saturday evening while Jim and I were getting ready to go to a party my sister Alice called from Tucson. "Shirley, Mom is in the hospital and just had exploratory surgery. It is confirmed that she has colon cancer and they will operate again tomorrow to get it all." I let out a scream and Jim grabbed the phone. He finished the conversation with Alice as I was seized with the most terrible pain in my abdomen. I doubled over and couldn't move. I was paralyzed. Jim picked me up and carried me to our bed. He got the heating pad and placed it on my stomach. Gradually, I was able to straighten my legs. He held me for a long time and assured me that Mom would be alright. I stayed in bed and fell asleep until the morning. Alice called the next evening to report that the doctors said the operation went well and they were able to remove the whole tumor. Alice said that Mom was resting comfortably and she would stay with the folks until Mom was able to drive. I said a prayer of thanks.

Part of Jim's job was briefing the heads of state and the high ranking military of our allies. This meant lots of travel to Brussels, Milan, Venice, London, Paris, Bonn and Amsterdam. He would come home and regale me with all the wonderful exotic foods he was enjoying. Since I was on the hamburger and hotdog circuit his comments did not please me. I was not amused.

On these trips he rarely wore his uniform, opting instead to wear an expensive suit. One day he was catching the train to Bonn, the capital of Germany. He entered a nicely furnished, deserted car and settled in to work on some papers. A porter came in to ask Jim if he wanted breakfast. Jim declined but asked for coffee. This was delivered to him in a silver urn with cream, sugar and cookies. He had a pleasant three hour ride with a porter always nearby to take care of any requests he might have. As he left the train three porters bade him "Good day, sir. I hope you enjoyed the ride." He was very impressed and vowed to take the train more often. He later learned that he had been riding in the transportation president's private car and was mistaken for the boss.

Chapter 37

I received a letter from Mom stating that she had recovered completely from her surgery and she and Dad would come to Germany in May. I was very pleased but surprised, because when I got the letter from Jim in Viet Nam that our next station was Germany, I had told my folks they had to visit us. Grumpy Dad had growled, "I have no use for the Huns. They've been causing trouble my whole life. My brother-in-law was gassed in the First World War and then we got Hitler. Thanks but no thanks."

I quickly penned a letter to Mom telling her how happy we were that they would be visiting. I asked her what had changed Dad's mind. She replied that he told her before her surgery, that if she survived he would take her to see me.

On a beautiful, clear May morning we piled into the Volva station wagon and drove to Frankfurt to welcome Mom and Dad. The Lufthansa plane was two hours late and when we finally saw Mom and Dad, true to form, Dad was fuming. The first words out of his mouth were, "The Goddamn Germans don't have any drinking water on the plane. All they could offer me was beer.

"Daddy, that's the first time I ever heard you complain about too much beer." I was trying to make a joke. Dad would have none of it and continued his rant.

Jim said, "Come on, Ed. I'll get you some water." He ushered us into the nearest airport restaurant and told the maitre'd that we needed water, quickly. The maitre'd shook his head and said, "Ah! Another American. You Americans drink too much water."

After Dad had quenched his thirst he became human. On the drive back to Stuttgart Jim mentioned that he had just returned from Venice and wondered if Mom and Dad would like to go there. They were both excited at the prospect. We gave them two days to recover from jet lag. The kids were still in school but assured us that they were capable of taking care of themselves. Peggy had been helping me in the kitchen since Iran so I knew that problem was solved. Jim set them down and exacted a promise from them to behave and do their homework. Very early the next morning we left. Dad sat in the front seat while Mama, Rick and I were in the back. All the way down to Venice my Dad entertained us with history lessons. Dad was an avid reader and should have been a teacher. We got lectures on the Second World War, on Hannibal crossing the Alps and, as we entered the valley in northern Italy, we could see several different bunkers. Dad was able to identify them by what war they were used in. That valley has a very active history.

Jim had made reservations for us at the Hotel Bonvecchiati in the center of Venice. It was a beautiful hotel with a lovely garden restaurant. We checked in, went to our rooms and freshened up. We met my folks downstairs, ready to find a restaurant. I noticed Mother was giggling and Daddy had a funny look on his face. Mom told me later that Dad had never seen a bidet before. He bent down to figure it out, turned on the faucet and got a face full of water.

Early the next morning after eating our breakfast in the garden we set out to explore. Venice is amazing with its winding narrow walkways next to the canals. We came to St. Marks Square and Ricky let out a squeal and proceeded to chase the pigeons. We wandered around enjoying people watching and ended up at St. Marks Basilica. What an amazing building. The uneven floors were bothering Dad so we left. Mom wanted to go to the top of the tower but Dad elected to sit on a bench. The rest of us climbed the stairs for the breath-taking views. Ricky was more impressed that he could look down and see his grandfather sitting on the bench. When we returned Dad suggested we get a pizza. We were all in favor of that and chose a restaurant next to the square. The waiter suggested we order the pizza with everything. When it came we were surprised to see a fried egg in the center of the pie. It looked like a bloody eye!

We spent the next two days seeing the sights in and around Venice and then headed for home. We found the house and kids in good shape. Jim went back to work and I became a tour guide. We'd get the kids off to school and then my folks, Ricky and I would take off. We would drive to the small villages looking at everything. Mom loved the flowers and antiques while Dad was interested in the butcher shops. One day we stopped at a restaurant for lunch. We were the only patrons. The restaurant was circular with upholstered cushions going around the whole circle while tables were in front. Dad and Mom sat in the chairs while Ricky and I were on the cushions. After finishing lunch, for some reason, Ricky decided to run on the cushions all the way around the room, laughing. Angrily, I got up and chased him. When I caught him I marched him into the ladies room. I pulled down his pants to swat him when I notice an immense pair of shoes next to him. I slowly looked up to see a very large German woman, hands on her hips and a scowl on her face. It scared me to death! I quickly pulled up his pants and left going straight out to the car. Mom and Dad were laughing when they joined me.

After a week Dad announced that they wanted to go to Italy and Greece. He made the arrangements and I took them to the airport. At a party, a week later, a friend asked if the folks had left. No, I said they are traveling in Italy and Greece. She was amazed. She said her folks had sat on the couch for three weeks just waiting to be entertained. Two weeks later I received a phone call from Dad telling me that they would be in Stuttgart the next evening. Jim and I drove to the airport to pick them up. We noticed an ambulance met the plane. It came right up to the airport and discharged my Mom. She had broken her leg! While they were in Athens Daddy's legs were giving him problems so he didn't want to walk up to the Acropolis but insisted that Mom go up and tell him about it. She was standing on uneven ground when a group of rambunctious boys ran past her. One of them nudged into her and down she went. It turned out that the hospital, doctors and hotel management went out of their way to assist Mom. Her leg was put in a cast, she was given crutches and everywhere they went they got the royal treatment. When we got home Jim had to carry Mom up the stairs to our apartment. They only stayed another two days deciding to tour England on the way home. "Are you sure you want to continue with your travel plans? I asked.

"Of course," answered Dad. "We've never had it so good with Mom's disability. We get treated like royalty. I think every time we travel one of us should be in a wheelchair!"

Chapter 38

The Supreme Court in an 8 to 0 decision ruled that President Nixon must turn over the tapes from his office. By a 27 to 11 vote the House Judiciary committee recommends impeachment. It is the first time in American history since the 1860's when President Andrew Johnson was tried for impeachment. President Nixon chooses to resign rather than put the country through a trial. Our vice president, Gerald Ford is sworn in as president. He chooses Nelson Rockefeller, the former governor of New York as his vice president. One of his first actions is to grant a full and unconditional pardon to Richard Nixon. He said "This act will spare the nation additional grief in this American tragedy."

July 1974

The first Sunday in the month the Officers Club sponsored a bazaar where shop owners were allowed to show their wares. One Sunday I went to see what was for sale. A clock merchant had an interesting and beautiful blind man's clock. It was called that because it chimes the hour and, at fifteen minutes after the hour it chimes the hour and one different chime indicates fifteen minutes after. At the half hour the hour is repeated and two chimes are added. At forty-five minutes after, three chimes are added. I really wanted to buy it but hesitated since it was not cheap. I couldn't wait to tell Jim about it. "Are you crazy? We don't want a clock like that. Do you realize that at twelve o'clock it would be chiming for an hour? Can you imagine that in the middle of the night? If you want a clock we can get one but not that one."

The next Saturday we drove to Ulm to a clock shop that had been recommended to Jim. We found a lovely wall clock and bought it. I asked the owner, Herr Hauptmann if he ever got a grandfather clock. He told me his brother was behind the Iron Curtain looking for clocks right now and would be back in ten days. (After the war when the Soviet Union became our enemy, Winston Churchill coined the term Iron Curtain to indicate the line between the West and the Soviet–held territories. The owner's brother was in what is now the Czech Republic.) There was not supposed to be any commerce between the two factions but, if you greased the right palms, anything was possible.

Jim was on a three day trip when Jimbo came to me complaining about being bullied. I told him what I thought his father would say. "Don't put up with that. Ask him to stop and if you have to, punch him."

The next day I got a phone call from the school principal telling me that Jimbo and another boy got in a fight. I immediately went to the school and, as I walked in the hallway, I saw blood on the stairs. Jimbo was in the principal's office looking sheepish. Brian, the other boy was not around. "Mom, I did what you told me to do. I hit him right in the nose and he got a terrible nosebleed." The principal came out of his office and after Jimbo promised not get into anymore fights we were free to go.

"Mr. Henderson, I just want you to know that Jimbo was being bullied." He was not interested in hearing that and dismissed us. Later that evening there was a knock on our door. Brian and his parents came in and immediately Brian apologized to Jimbo. The boys shook hands and Jimbo told Brian he was sorry he had hit him so hard. Brian's nose was swollen and was bandaged. It was an awkward moment but Brian's parents were very gracious and his father said he would have told Brian the same thing I told Jimbo. I wished Jim had been home to deal with it. At school the word got around and Jimbo was never bullied again.

Ten days after our visit to Ulm Jim went to work and the kids left for school. I called Herr Hauptmann and inquired if his brother had found a grandfather clock. "Yes, he brought one in last night." I told him I would come down to see it today. "Madam, it is not ready. There is much work to be done to it."

"That's okay; I just want to see it." I got Ricky ready and we took off on a cold, miserable, foggy day. There was not much traffic on the autobahn. An hour later as we entered a mountainous area the road had many deep dips in it. In good weather it wasn't noticeable but on this day every time we entered a dip it was so foggy I couldn't see the road. *I should turn back, this is getting worse*, I thought. There was no place to turn around so I kept going. The fog lifted just as I got to the clock shop.

The grandfather clock was made of oak in a plain design and was magnificent. Herr Hauptmann told me the price and said he could have it ready for me in two weeks. He would come to Patch Barracks and set it up. I said I would have to consult with my husband. "Mrs. Starkey, I will take a picture of it with my Polaroid camera for you to show him." He posed Ricky next to the clock so Jim could tell how tall it is.

Ricky and I stopped at a restaurant for lunch and when we left the rain had stopped and the sun was shining. All the way back I planned my strategy on how I could convince Jim to buy the clock.

When I showed him the picture I could tell he was impressed. We drove to Ulm the next weekend. Jim inspected the clock, asked many questions and pulled out his checkbook.

Two weeks later Herr Hauptmann called to say he could bring me the clock the next day. He carried the clock up the three flights of stairs with no problem. While he was adjusting the clock he told Rick the story of the clock. "Mr. Ricky" he said in his deep, guttural German accent, "this clock was in the home of a family of sheep."

"A sheep's family owned a clock?" Rick said incredulously.

"Yah, yah. Don't interrupt me, young man." He continued. "The mama sheep had to go to the grocery store and told her lambs not to open the door to anyone, especially the big, bad wolf. As soon as mama left the big, bad, wolf forced his way into the house. He started gobbling up the lambs." I looked at Rick he was enthralled.

Herr Hauptmann went on. "One lucky lamb jump into the well of this clock and kept very quiet. The wolf ate all of the other lambs and staggered out of the house. He could barely walk he was so full. He started yawning, lay down in the grass and fell asleep. When mama came home the little lamb jumped out of the clock and told her what happened. Mama got her scissors and cut a big hole in the wolf's stomach and let all her babies out. Then she got a big stone, put it in the wolf's stomach and sewed it up. When the wolf woke up he couldn't move and the forestmiester took him to jail."

Rick was sitting there his eyes big as saucers. "Tell me again." He demanded.

"No, no, little man. I must go back to my shop. But you can remember the story and tell your brothers and sister."

Chapter 39

Jim announced that we should take a trip to Munich to see Dachau. "You think we should take the kids to see a death camp?" doubt was in my voice.

"Yes, I think they should see what the war was all about. If people don't see it it could happen again."

"Yes, but it's pretty gory for kids, don't you think?"

"Well let's ask them."

At dinner that night Jim asked the kids if the subject of the concentration camps came up in school. Jimbo answered, "Yes we've been studying World War Two and the camps have been mentioned."

"Would you like to see one?"

"Yes, I would", said Jimbo.

Pat was skeptical. "What's concentration camp?"asked Peggy. I looked at Jim, smiling. *Now you've started something*, I thought. But as usual, Jim was up to the task and gave a good accounting of the facts that Peggy could understand. They were on board with the trip. On the next Saturday, a crisp June day, we drove to Munich. We stopped at a restaurant for lunch and asked the waitress directions to Dachau. She frowned and said in a gruff voice, "There is no Dachau. You Americans made it up." She turned and walked away.

"Well, there goes her tip." Jim remarked. We stopped at the gas station, the question was repeated and Jim got directions.

Dachau was the first of many camps built in 1933 by the Nazi's to house political prisoners. Later it held Jews, gypsies, homosexuals, and other undesirables. It was a work camp where prisoners, under horrible conditions, labored to help the Nazi's war machine. They were fed very little and worked very hard. An estimated 188,000 prisoners were kept there with over 32,000 of them were killed or died of disease or starvation. The Americans liberated it in 1945. At least 4,000 Soviet prisoners of war were murdered by the Dachau commandant guard at the SS shooting range from 1942 to 1944.

When we reached Dachau we entered a gate with the words ARBEIT MACHT FREI (Work Makes One Free). The compound's surrounded by a high wall with look-out towers. The main square was used for counting prisoners and inflicting punishments. A hospital was used for medical experiments. There was a large room next to a kitchen. Several rooms had displays of items from the prisoners such as suitcases, shoes, teeth, and hair. Another had manikins of people with deformities. Two barracks had been rebuilt and stocked with uniforms. The crematorium was in working order. There were 32 concrete foundations that hadn't been destroyed. As we were leaving Jim looked around and remarked, "Do you realize workers could be brought in to rebuild this place. The barracks are there for the living quarters and there's a dining room and kitchen. This place could be back in operation in two weeks." A cold shiver ran down my back.

A letter was waiting for us from Aunt Lillian who announced that she would come to Stuttgart in late August. The whole family cheered. Aunt Lil has been taking all kinds of trips with expensive travel agencies but, this time, she was flying direct to Stuttgart. "You two should take a trip somewhere by train so Aunt Lil can see how the common folk travel." Jim suggested.

"That's a good idea. I'd like to go to Paris."

The day arrived and our gang was so excited to see Aunt Lil. When she saw us she ran to us smiling, and hugged us all in her usual enthusiastic manner. She was full of news about all the members of the family, the different places she had been to and the people she met on her latest flight. I took her shopping for vegetables, to the hair dressers, to the factory that produces wooden Christmas ornaments and to an Officer's Wives luncheon. She loved it all and managed to be the center of attention wherever we went. My friends couldn't believe she was so interesting and interested in everything. They couldn't get over the fact that at the very old age of seventy-six she was traveling by herself.

When Jim suggested to Lil that she and I should take a train to Paris she jumped at the idea. "You'll get to see how Europeans travel, Aunt Lil. You'll enjoy it." She agreed with him and he had his secretary order the tickets. On the day we were ready to go Aunt Lil appeared in her traveling outfit. It was a bold red plaid pantsuit that matched the red plaid of her suitcase! The suitcase had wheels, the first we had seen.

The train station in Stuttgart is a Gothic architectural wonder. We hugged and kissed the kids and Jim goodbye and made our way to the train. Lil and I entered an unoccupied cabin with long couches on either side. We sat opposite each other by the window. Just as the train started to move the door opened and a stubby little man came in. He had an immense moustache stained yellow, rosy cheeks, clear blue eyes and a happy smile. Tipping his hat he bowed to Aunt Lil and murmured, "Bon jour, Madame." He sat on my side of the couch and plopped a large haversack next to him. He said something to us in French and I said, pointing to Lil and myself, "American" and shrugged my shoulders. He didn't try to converse with us until later, when he pulled out a long sausage and offered it to Lil. She declined but he insisted. He pulled out a knife, cut a piece off and shoved it to her. She pulled back, shook her head no and frowned. The little man looked so unhappy I indicated that I would take it. He handed it to me and I put it in my mouth. It was delicious though very garlicky. I told Aunt Lil she was wise to not take the sausage as her delicate stomach would have rebelled. I opened our lunch and shared a turkey sandwich with our friend. When we arrived in Paris our friend insisted on helping Aunt Lil off the train. When the porter handed us our luggage Aunt Lil took off like a bolt of lightning, pulling her suitcase behind her. As I ran to keep up I noticed the shocked looks on the crowd as they beheld my short, rotund Aunt, wearing a red plaid pant suit and dragging a matching suitcase!

The next three days were filled with touring the Louvre, the Eiffel tower, Notre Dame Cathedral, the Paris fashion houses and the Musee d'Orsay. After we visited the Sacre-Coeur we ate lunch at the Moulin Rouge and went to the flea market. Two very tall, dark African men approached me with wooden carvings for sale. Since I know no French we conducted our business in pantomime. I asked the price and one of the men wrote the price on his hand. I looked shocked and gave him a camel's kiss and wrote a much lesser amount on his hand. He laughed at first and then frowned and business-like counter-offered. I shook my head no, no and wrote my next offer. Again he and his buddy disagreed. I pointed to a smaller carving and indicated I would pay their price if they would include that carving. Both of them laughed and shook my hand in agreement. As one was wrapping up my purchase the other one said something in some language and it was obvious to me they were talking about my bargaining. Perhaps I was the first white person who bargained with them. Aunt Lil was amazed to watch the interaction and I was happy to practice my hard-earned talent in dealing with third world business practices.

On the way home we talked about our purchases. Aunt Lil had bought three beautiful plates from the House of Dior, intending to give one to my Aunt Olive, one to my mom and one for herself. When she returned to Boulder City Aunt Olive convinced Lil that she should have two of the plates for herself and Uncle Casey. Mama never got her plate.

Chapter 40

Jim received a telegram from the Red Cross that he was needed in Tucson to help his mother. He caught an Air Force plane to Washington and on to Davis Monthan Air Force base in Tucson. Ten days later he was back with bad news. His mother had been caught shop-lifting a bottle of Popov vodka and had been jailed as she could not make bail.

The kids were in bed and we were sitting on the couch drinking a Scotch. Jim was very depressed. "Butch, we're the only family she has. There is no one in Tucson to help her and she definitely needs help."

"What are you saying?"

"I'm saying I think it is time we returned to Tucson and take care of my mother."

"You want to retire? But, Jim, you love the Army and what will you do in Tucson?"

"You're right, I do love the Army and I've given 24 years to it. I have no idea what I will do in Tucson."

"We don't need to decide anything tonight. Let's put it in our Scarlett basket."

"In our what?"

"In our Scarlett basket. My mom always said that when she had to make a decision and didn't want to. You remember in Gone With the Wind Scarlet O'Hara would always say, "I'll think about it tomorrow." Well, that was what my mom was referring to."

Jim gave me a scathing look and said disgustingly, "That's the dumbest thing I have ever heard."

On April 30, 1975 Saigon surrenders to the Viet Cong. We sat glued to the television watching the scene of hundreds of Vietnamese trying to climb to the helicopter pad on the roof of the American Embassy, hoping to get a ride to safety. Helicopter after helicopter picked up evacuees and flew them to an aircraft carrier. As soon as all were off the copter it was pushed into the ocean to make room for more people. We sat there stunned at what we were witnessing. I have never seen Jim so distraught. He had spent two years helping the people of Viet Nam keep their independence and now it was all over. How many thousands of Americans had been killed? In his last assignment there he was responsible for all the Army aircraft in the country and now he was seeing them being pushed off into the ocean. "Why couldn't I have just one of those helicopters?" he muttered.

The children had two weeks off for spring vacation so Jim put in the necessary papers that allowed us to drive to West Berlin through East Germany. We left on a beautiful sunny day for the drive to the area where West Germany and East Germany met. The children and I had to go into a small building with our papers. Jim, wearing his uniform sat in the car. The kids were dressed in new outfits and carried small American flags. The East Germans who processed me and the children were stern and very important. Jim stared straight ahead ignoring them. We got back in the car and as we entered the East German territory we drove through several check points all manned by the Vopos, the East German secret police. We were motioned on and when I turned to check on the kids all four of them were smiling and waving their American flags at the glum and taciturn group. I was so proud of them.

The road we took was through beautiful forests. Much to my disappointment we did not drive through any villages. There were several large billboards in English touting the wonderful life East Germans were experiencing. I took many pictures of these. When we arrived at Berlin we found a large, busy bustling city. We checked into a small bed and breakfast hotel and quickly found a gasthaus where we devoured a refreshing lunch.

When we had finished the kids wanted to see was the Berlin wall. We drove to the site where steps and a viewing stand had been built next to the wall. When we climbed to the top the sight made me gasp. There was nothing but dirt for several football fields deep clear up to the apartment buildings where all the windows were boarded up. There were signs in German warning of buried explosives. We could view a lot of East Berlin from where we stood. There was much evidence of bombed out buildings all over. On the highest point in East Berlin a Catholic church used to stand. It was not destroyed during the war but the Russians tore it down to build a tall TV tower. At the top of the tower was a perfect sphere that reflected the light in the form of a cross. The Russians tried to cover it up but to no avail. The West Berliners referred to it as the Pope's Revenge.

A museum across from the viewing stand told the stories of the many people who had tried to cross over to West Berlin. Those who were successful had been ingenious in their methods. Sadly, many were not successful.

The next morning we went to Check Point Charlie to cross over to East Berlin. We entered a bus on the western side and after crossing the border we drove several blocks to a parking lot. The children and I were told to exit the bus, to stand in a line while our papers were examined. Jim and the other American military stayed on the bus. When all was in order we were given a map and told to only go where we were directed and no other place. It turned out we were directed to a large beautiful park filled with gorgeous flowers. It also had enormous statutes of Stalin, Lenin, Mother Russia and various other famous Russian writers and composers. We walked the entire route as suggested, all the while being stared at by the East German people who sat huddled together on the benches along the way. We retraced our steps and returned to the bus. As the bus got to Check Point Charlie again the children and I had to disembark along with the other civilians. We stood in a line while the bus was searched inside and out. The guards took a long-handled mirror and moved it under the bus to detect anyone hiding there. It took about thirty minutes before the East Germans were satisfied that no unauthorized person was trying to get to West Berlin. Finally we were allowed back on the bus and disembarked on the West Berlin side. So much for seeing communist Germany!

The rest of the trip we spent enjoying the sights, restaurants and museums of West Berlin. We viewed the original painting of the Man with the Golden Helmet. I was impressed that the impasto on the helmet was almost three inches deep. There was a sign next to the painting stating that it was believed that Rembrandt had not painted it. It is now claimed to be painted by Anonymous.

After five days we left West Berlin and were again followed the whole way through East Germany by the Vopos. I took many pictures during our trip of the wall, the trip to East Berlin, West Berlin and the signs along the route and the Vopos following us. When we were back at Patch Barracks I took the film canisters to the PX to be developed. The PX sent the films to a local shop in Stuttgart for development. After two weeks of waiting I finally got a message that the films had been lost. What are the chances of all of my ten rolls of film being lost?

Jim's retirement papers came through, the kids were out of school and it was time to depart the Army. Again the packers arrived and for two days the house was a mess of strangers getting our treasures ready for shipment back to Tucson. We were feted with many farewell parties from all the wonderful friends we had met. The boys were excited to get back home where their dad had assured them that they could go hunting with him. Peggy, on the other hand was upset to leave her friends. She made very fast friends wherever she went. I expect it was because she was the only girl in the family and craved female companionship.

We cleared our quarters and two days before we were scheduled to leave, Jim was the subject of a retirement ceremony. The children and I watched as Jim, dressed in his uniform for the last time, marched in a parade. He was given a citation and General Hayden made a speech about how invaluable Jim had been to him. The pomp and circumstance, the music, the marching, the citation, the speech was all wonderful but a great sadness swept over me as I realized this was the end of our military career. Yes, I said our career because I was every bit a part of it all, whether I was with Jim or back in Tucson while he was in Korea or Viet Nam. I miss military life to this day.

Glossary of Persian Words

ashgal	garbage
bacheh	baby
badjii	maid
bakhshesh	gift,tip,bribe
barf	snow
bali	yes
barenj	uncooked rice
befarmaid	welcome
buro	go
chador	covering for Moslem women
chelo kabab	Iranian national dish of rice & lamb
enjas	here
enshallah'	if Allah wills it
farda	tomorrow
farci	Iranian language
gusht-e-khog	pork
holu	peaches
jube	ditch
khali	good
khodah fez	goodbye
khoreshe	sauce
khub	very
kojas	where
kuchee	alley or small street
leemu	lemon
madreseh	school
manzel	house
muezzin	man who calls the faithful to prayer

morgh	chicken
nami-danam	I don't know
NoRuz	Iranian New Year
nune	bread
padar	father
panir	cheese
polo	cooked rice
poshti	big cushions
qanats	ancient water system
raftan	go
rial	Iranian currancy
sag	dog
salaam	greetings
taarof	flowery speech
tesbih	worry beads
toman	ten rials
ulama	Shia clergy
umbar	storage
wadi	wet sand
yavash	slow down

Strength at Home

By Ben Stein

(This is a letter I wrote to the newsletter of an Army unit called The Strykers, stationed in Iraq out of Ft. Lewis, Wash. The editor asked me what I would say to make the wives feel appreciated while their husbands are in Iraq. This is what I wrote to one soldier's wife.)

Dear Karen,

I have a great life. I have a wife I adore, a son who is a lazy teenager but I adore him, too. We live in a house with two dogs and four cats. We live in peace. We can worship as we please. We can say what we want. We can walk the streets in safety. We can vote. We can work wherever we want and buy whatever we want. When we sleep, we sleep in peace. When we wake up, it is to the sounds of birds.

All of this, every bit of it, is thanks to your husband, his brave fellow soldiers, and to the wives who keep the home fires burning while the soldiers are away protecting my family and 140 million other families. They protect Republicans and Democrats, Christians, Jews, Muslims and atheists. They protect white, black, yellow, brown and everyone in between. They protect gays and straights, rich and poor.

And none of it could happen without the Army wives, Marine wives, Navy wives, Air Force wives—or husbands—who go to sleep tired and lonely, wake up tired and lonely, and go through the day with a smile on their faces. They feed the kids, put up with the teenagers' surliness, the bills that never stop piling up, the desperate hours when the plumbing breaks and there is no husband to fix it, and the even more desperate hours after the kids have gone to bed, the dishes have been done, the bills have been paid, and the wives realize that they will be sleeping alone—again, for the 300th night in a row.

The wives keep up the fight even when they have to move every couple of years, even when their checks are late, even when they have to make a whole new set of friends every time they move.

And they keep up the fight to keep the family whole even when they feel a lump of dread every time they turn on the news, every time they switch on the computer, every time the phone rings and every time—worst of all—the doorbell rings. Every one of those events—which might mean a baseball score or a weather forecast or a FedEx man to me and my wife—might mean the news that the man they love, the man they have married for better or worse, for richer and for poorer, in sickness and in health, is now parted from them forever.

These women will never be on the cover of People. They will never be on the tabloid shows on TV about movie stars. But they are the power and the strength that keep America going. Without them, we are nothing at all. With them, we can do everything.

They are the glue that holds the nation together, stronger than politicians, stronger than talking heads, stronger than al Qaeda.

They deserve all the honor and love a nation can give. They have my prayers, and my wife's, every morning and every night.

Love, and I do mean Love, Ben.

Mr. Stein, a television personality and writer, is co-author with Phil DeMuth of "Can America Survive," forthcoming from Hay House.

Wall Street Journal
Aug. 18, 2004